AMERICAN SECRET PROJECTS

FIGHTERS & INTERCEPTORS 1945-1978

*To the many designers and
engineers who created these
fantastic shapes*

**American Secret Projects –
Fighters & Interceptors 1945-1978**
© Anthony Leonard Buttler, 2007

ISBN (10) 1 85780 264 0
ISBN (13) 978 1 85780 264 1

First published in 2007 by
Midland Publishing
4 Watling Drive, Hinckley, LE10 3EY, England
Tel: 01455 254 490 Fax: 01455 254 495

Midland Publishing is an imprint of
Ian Allan Publishing Ltd.

Worldwide distribution (except North America):
Midland Counties Publications
4 Watling Drive, Hinckley, LE10 3EY, England
Tel: 01455 233 747 Fax: 01455 233 737
E-mail: midlandbooks@compuserve.com
www.midlandcountiessuperstore.com

North America trade distribution by:
Specialty Press Publishers & Wholesalers Inc.
39966 Grand Avenue
North Branch, MN 55056, USA
Tel: 651 277 1400 Fax: 651 277 1203
Toll free telephone: 800 895 4585
www.specialtypress.com

All rights reserved. No part of this publication
may be reproduced, stored in a retrieval system,
transmitted in any form or by any means,
electronic, mechanical or photo-copied, recorded
or otherwise, without the written permission of
the copyright owners.

Design and concept
© 2007 Midland Publishing and
Stephen Thompson Associates
Layout by Russell Strong

Printed by Ian Allan Printing Limited
Riverdene Business Park, Molesey Road,
Hersham, Surrey, KT12 4RG, England.

Visit the Ian Allan Publishing website at:
www.ianallanpublishing.com

Photograph on half-title page:
**Model of a proposal from 1953 for the Northrop
N-126 long range interceptor project.** George Cox

Photograph on title page:
Model of the North American WS.300A project.
Jim Keeshen

AMERICAN SECRET PROJECTS

FIGHTERS & INTERCEPTORS 1945-1978

TONY BUTTLER

MIDLAND
An imprint of
Ian Allan Publishing

Contents

	Introduction	5
	Acknowledgements	6
Chapter One	**The First Air Force Jets**	7
Chapter Two	**The First Navy Jets**	29
Chapter Three	**The First 'Centuries'**	49
Chapter Four	**Later 'Centuries' and Other Concepts**	68
Chapter Five	**The Quest for a Long-Range Interceptor**	89
Chapter Six	**Naval Progress**	113
Chapter Seven	**Vertical Take-Off**	136
Chapter Eight	**Boat Fighters**	155
Chapter Nine	**Into the 1960s**	161
Chapter Ten	**Lightweight Fighters**	185
Chapter Eleven	**In Conclusion**	209
	American Secret Fighter & Interceptor Colour Chronology	210
	Glossary	224
Appendix One	**American Fighter Projects Summary**	225
Appendix Two	**Fighter Specifications**	237
	Bibliography and Source Notes	238
	Index	239

Introduction

Model of the North American NA-323. George Cox

Over the course of aviation history the United States has produced many outstanding fighters. The P-51 Mustang, the F-86 Sabre, the F-4 Phantom II, the F-14 Tomcat, and today's F-35 Lightning II, are all examples of aircraft at the very forefront of contemporary fighter design. But the history of fighter design isn't solely charted by the successful outcomes. For every aircraft that achieved success, others never got beyond the prototype stage. For those that flew, others were scrapped before completion. And for those that were built, dozens never got beyond the drawing board. These were not all failures in design terms, in fact in many cases far from it. Some fell victim to circumstances, whether changed requirements, political pressures or lack of funding; others were intermediate steps en route to successful fighters, and some simply explored ideas whose time had not yet come. An understanding of the history of fighter design therefore requires an appreciation of the many proposals that never saw the light of day.

This book looks at the American fighter projects that were proposed during the period following the Second World War though to the late 1970s. It was arguably the most exciting era in terms of fighter development: a period during which the jet engine took over from the propeller, wings took on entirely new shapes, the 'sound barrier' was breached and maximum speeds tripled. It was an era in which aeronautical engineering became much more complex but when the computer had yet to come to the designer's assistance. This meant much more of a 'try it and see' attitude to new ideas. Therefore, when an air arm required a new fighter, several design teams could prepare proposals that were very different from one another.

Of course design is a continuous process. Many of the projects of this period originated in earlier thinking and many of the designs of subsequent years were founded during this time. But the advent of the jet engine at the start, and the onset of stealth technology at the end, makes it a reasonably logical period for study in a topic whose total span is far too great for any one volume.

Having already written on British and Soviet projects of this era, I approached this current book with both excitement and trepidation. I was aware of the enormous amount of fighter design work that had taken place in the USA but was concerned about how much information still existed and how much any one person could uncover. My task was made possible – and extremely enjoyable – by the help and generosity of many people. I had the great fortune to spend time in the archives at

American Secret Projects: Fighters & Interceptors

Grumman and Vought, the Cradle of Aviation Museum, the San Diego Aerospace Museum and the National Aerospace Museum. I had the privilege of meeting many archivists, historians, engineers and industry experts. In addition I also received considerable assistance from a number of individuals who over the years have assembled collections of the original models that the aircraft companies used to illustrate their ideas: in many instances saving and restoring such models for posterity. I hope the long list of credits does justice to all of these individuals and to the tremendous amount of help I was given.

My aim was not to assemble a random list of projects but rather to put the various design proposals into context, explaining where they fitted within the overall history of fighter design, and particularly how they related to the progressively advancing requirements of the US Air Force and the US Navy. I have therefore concentrated on the designs that I felt to be most significant. Inevitably much of the information – highly secret when it was originally produced and hence shut away from public scrutiny – has been lost over the years, but I am sure that much still remains to be discovered, buried in archives, personal collections or simply people's memories. The book therefore makes no claims to be exhaustive. A number of gaps remain and I would welcome any further information that any reader might have. Indeed, I have included a number of photographs of models where it is uncertain exactly which projects are represented. The fact that a professionally constructed model was made (usually in the aircraft company's own model shop) is testimony that the design reached an advanced stage of consideration. If any reader can identify these projects, I would be extremely grateful.

For unbuilt designs the descriptions in the text are complemented by tables with estimated data. For comparison purposes these include equivalent figures for most of the jet fighter designs that were actually flown. In many cases the 'real' data comes from *The American Fighter* by Angelucci and Bowers, a magnificent book that has to be a prime reference for this category of aircraft. The data given for unbuilt projects is usually the manufacturer's estimates.

The research, planning and writing of this book has dominated my life for about six years. Putting it together has been a fascinating and immensely enjoyable journey, and I hope those reading it are not disappointed. In summary I would welcome any information, via the publisher, that will help to complete the picture that I have assembled: a picture that I hope reflects the enormous ingenuity and achievements of the US aerospace industry. In the meantime, it is hoped that a companion volume covering bombers and attack aircraft for the same period will follow. Given my experience researching this book it is a task that I look forward to with great enthusiasm.

Tony Buttler MA, AMRaeS, AMIM
Bretforton, August 2007

Acknowledgements

My sincere thanks goes to the following for their help in researching this book. I apologise if I have left anyone out: Gerald H Balzer (Northrop); Bob Bradley and the staff of the San Diego Aerospace Museum; John S Brooks (McDonnell); Joe Cherrie; Peter Clukey (Lockheed Martin); William E Elmore (McDonnell); John Farley; Larry Feliu, Lynn McDonald, Bob Tallman and the staff of the Northrop Grumman History Center (Bethpage); Dan Hagedorn and the staff of the National Air and Space Museum; James F Hart (Northrop Grumman Intellectual Property); Roy Hawkins; Eric Hehs (Lockheed Martin); Mike Hirschberg; Dennis R Jenkins; Mary Kane (Boeing Image Licensing); Craig Kaston; Jim Keeshen; Yvonne Kinkaid (Bolling Library); Mike Lavelle; Neil Lewis; Denny Lombard (Lockheed); Scott Lowther; Mike Lombardi (Boeing Historical Archives 'Boeing'); Mike Machat; Pat McGinnis (Boeing Historical Archives 'Douglas'); Paul Martell-Mead; Larry Merritt (Boeing Historical Archives 'McDonnell'); Evan L Mayerle; Thomas Mueller; Ken Neubeck; Lon O Nordeen (Boeing, St Louis); Steve Pace; Terry Panopalis; Dan Pattarini and Leon Kaplan (EDO); Alain J Pelletier; Stan Piet (Glenn L Martin Aviation Museum); Erasmo Pinero (Lockheed Martin); Jim Pratt; Edward Rankin (General Dynamics); Clive Richards (UK Ministry of Defence Air Historical Branch); Jesse J Santamaria (Vought); Gary Schurr; William J Simone; James P Stevenson; Joshua Stoff, Barbara Cavanagh, Robert Muller and the staff of the Cradle of Aviation Museum library; Mike Stroud; Tommy Thomason; Pierre Trichet; Jim Upton (Lockheed); John D Weber (Wright-Patterson AFB).

Extra special thanks go to the following: John Aldaz; Dick Atkins (Vought Archive); Tony Chong; Chris Gibson; John Hall; Larry McLaughlin; Jay Miller; Jonathan Rigutto; Chad Slattery and Allyson Vought for their substantial help, at times well beyond the call of duty. Thanks to Midland Publishing and Ian Allan, Tim O'Brien for the cover painting and Russ Strong for the design. Finally, I must make special mention of my great friend George Cox who edited a lot of the text and contributed so much more to the completed work.

Tony Buttler MA, AMRaeS, AMIM
Bretforton, August 2007

Chapter One

The First Air Force Jets

America's first jet fighter, the Bell XP-59A Airacomet made its maiden flight in October 1942. It was not a success but the small production run provided useful experience in the operation of jet aircraft. The US Army Air Force's first production jet fighter was the highly successful Lockheed P-80 Shooting Star, which flew in October 1943. It entered service in 1945 just before the end of the war in Europe, though too late to see combat. Other early jet fighters aimed at the USAAF included the Convair XP-81 with a mixed turboprop/jet powerplant and the Bell XP-83 heavy jet fighter, both of which flew in 1945. Neither design progressed beyond the prototype stage but they were followed by two very successful designs: the Republic P-84 Thunderjet and North American F-86 Sabre. The Thunderjet made its appearance in February 1946 and went on to be built in substantial numbers. It was also the start of a whole family of successful Republic fighters.

The F-86 was an even more advanced aircraft, introducing swept wings for the first time: indeed it was a major milestone in US fighter development. The F-86 was built in great numbers, proved highly successful in the first jet-on-jet air warfare in Korea, and served in the air forces of many counties around the world. In one step it put the USA, which had lagged behind the British and Germans in the early development of jet aircraft, into the very forefront of fighter design: a position it would retain thereafter. However, these companies were not alone in producing fighter proposals built around the potential that the new jet engine offered. Such was the nature of the new and fast-evolving technology of jet fighter design that virtually all of the established aircraft manufacturers were engaged in producing new projects long before the war finished.

One thing that these aircraft all have in common is that they appear to have been cre-

Lovely air-to-air photograph of the XF-92A, now fitted with an extended rear fuselage to accommodate an afterburning powerplant. This modification gave a better balance to the aircraft's appearance.

ated without direct competition from other manufacturers. Each was an independent initiative: a not uncommon event in the early days of jet fighter design when aircraft manufacturers worldwide were moving into the relative unknown. Since they were initiated before the end of the Second World War, their history falls outside the scope of this book. However, they are mentioned to show how America started its jet fighter development programs and they set up the story for what follows. Only in mid-1945 did the USAAF launch design competitions between companies for new jet fighters meeting specific needs and performance criteria. Three different types of aircraft responding to such requirements form the primary subject of this

American Secret Projects: Fighters & Interceptors

The North American F-86 Sabre set the standard for the jet fighter designs that were to follow from American manufacturers. This picture shows an F-86F.

Model of the two-seat Republic AP-85 development of the Thunderstreak.

This twin-engined F-84F development had its power units mounted on top of the wings.
Cradle of Aviation Museum

first chapter. However, studies were also made around this time to extend and develop those types already mentioned, so it is appropriate to begin with a brief review of some of that work.

Before doing so, a couple of important points need to be noted. Firstly, in 1947 the United States Army ceded control of the country's air force to a new independent service. The former USAAF became the United States Air Force (USAF). Secondly, in June 1948 the long-used designation letter 'P' for pursuit was switched to 'F' for fighter, more accurately reflecting the role that the new types had to perform. As such the P-80, P-84 and P-86 were re-designated F-80, F-84 and F-86 respectively. In this chapter, reference will be made to the appropriate 'P' or 'F' designations depending on the date concerned.

Republic F-84F and other F-84 Developments

The most important development of the original straight wing F-84 Thunderflash was the F-84F swept-wing variant first flown on 3rd June 1950. It was known initially as the YF-96A, but thanks to budget politics and other reasons it was soon redesignated as the XF-84F Thunderstreak. The first production machine flew on 22nd November 1952. Over 2,700 more followed plus another 700 RF-84F Thunderflash photoreconnaissance variants fitted with a solid nose and wing root intakes. The F-84s, along with the Navy's Cougar and Panther fighters, remain the only aircraft to have gone into service in both straight and swept-wing versions of the same basic aeroplane.

However, two further swept-wing developments have been traced, neither of which was built. Republic's AP-85 project was a two-seat version of the F-84F with an extended nose for the extra crewmember and a rounded tip to its fin. The other was a quite different twin-engine version of the F-84F with its powerplants housed in overwing nacelles. This design also had a solid nose to house a small radar but in most other respects its fuselage and flying surfaces were clearly F-84F vintage.

A straight-wing Republic F-84E kitted out for ground attack operations with two 500lb (227kg) bombs and 5in (12.7cm) unguided rocket projectiles.

The Republic F-84F Thunderstreak displays its swept wings in a photograph thought to have been taken in 1954.

The First Air Force Jets

Lockheed F-94 Starfire

Bringing the first generation of post-war designs to fruition took a great deal of effort and it was quickly realized that a stopgap was needed. This became more critical after the Berlin blockade of 1948 signalled a deterioration in relations with the Soviet Union, and was made worse by the fact that the only available 'all-weather interceptors' were actually piston-engined. The planned Northrop F-89 was some time away from entering service, so anything that could be thrown into the front line of defence more quickly would be a big help – in fact by January 1948 the need for a new fighter with all-weather capability was approaching a near-desperate situation. The obvious solution was to turn to the Lockheed F-80, which was already in service as a day fighter. The resulting substantial redesign produced the F-94 Starfire, an interim interceptor which made its maiden flight on 16th April 1949. The first production machines joined the USAF right at the end of 1949, within a year of their being ordered. Over 850 were built and served throughout the 1950s before being replaced by the F-101B, F-102 and F-106 – not a bad result for a stopgap design! It was one of the few straight-wing fighters capable of being dived supersonically.

North American F-86D Sabre

The original F-86 and all of its variants were essentially daytime fighter-bombers but the basic design was also developed to fill two other roles that required a high level of modification. One was the YF-93, to which we will return; the other was the F-86D that, apart from sharing the same wing and general layout, was pretty much an all-new aircraft. The prototype YF-86D first flew (under the original designation YF-95A) on 22nd December 1949 and orders for this mark and further developments stretched beyond 3,800. Unlike the Starfire this was a single-seater, the second crewmember being made unnecessary by electronics that were highly advanced for their time. Again it was the slippage in the F-89 program that prompted the move to develop and introduce a design based on an earlier airplane.

The Lockheed F-94 Starfire was a substantial redesign of the original F-80 Shooting Star. This picture shows an F-94C prototype, a much improved version. Only the two prototypes were built, the first of these flying on 18th January 1950, and the initial designation for the 'C' was YF-97A.

1/8. A North American F-86D 'Dogship' Sabre fires a salvo of 18 lb (8.2kg) Mighty Mouse air-to-air rockets from their lower fuselage housing.

American Secret Projects: Fighters & Interceptors

A New All-Weather Fighter

With the end of World War Two, which had seen rapid advances in military technology, one might have expected to see the pace of aircraft development slow down. This was not to be the case. The war had shown the devastating effect of airpower and suspicion of the expansionist aims of the Soviet bloc maintained the pressure for ever more effective air defence.

Despite the arrival of the jet-powered fighter before the war's end it was clear that the design of new fighters and the technology that went into them would change dramatically in the next few years. Those types currently in service would become obsolete very quickly and by the spring of 1945 the Army Air Force's planners had identified three potential types of new fighter that would be needed in the near future. All of them would be jet or rocket powered and work began on preparing draft requirements. One was a rocket-powered interceptor, the second a large penetration fighter and the third an all-weather fighter. The all-weather type had to be able to seek out and destroy enemy aircraft and ground targets and give air cover to ground troops whatever the weather conditions. This requirement was heavily influenced by the experience of the then-recent Battle of the Bulge in Europe. During the final winter of the War this attack by German ground forces could not be countered by the use of the heavily superior Allied tactical air power due to the poor weather conditions. A prime consideration was to prevent such a situation happening again.

In late August 1945 the basic requirements for what became MX808 were circulated to industry. However, a revision with more specific requirements was completed in November and issued on the 23rd of that month as 'Military Characteristics for an All-Weather Fighter'. The specified performance limits at full weight were a minimum top speed of 550mph (885km/h) at sea level and 525mph (845km/h) at 35,000ft (10,668m) plus the capability of reaching 35,000ft within twelve minutes. The radius of action at the type's best operational altitude had to be 1,000 miles (1,609km). Armament should include six 0.5in (12.7mm) or 0.6in (15.2mm) machine guns or 20mm cannon plus an internally housed battery of air-to-air or air-to-ground rocket projectiles, and there had to be the facility to carry bombs of up to 1,000 lb (454kg) for ground-attack operations. These were highly demanding requirements for their time but several companies responded. The proposals were presented in October 1945 and the main ones are described below. There were also designs from Bell and Goodyear but, to date, no drawings or details have been traced for these contenders. One was jet powered but the other may have been propeller driven, which in fact had been the preferred power unit in the very early stages of the Army Air Force studies.

Convair (Vultee) All-Weather Fighter

The Consolidated proposal came from its Fort Worth Texas facility, the Vultee Division having looked at the requirement only briefly. It was based on a very advanced forward-swept wing bomber design, which was itself to be ordered as the XA-44 (and redesignated XB-53 in 1948). Few details are available, but the fighter had moderate forward sweep, a bicycle undercarriage and four wing root-mounted engines that were, most unusually, placed one above the other. There was also a very large vertical fin. This was a heavy aircraft with an estimated gross weight of 52,000 lb (23,587kg) and it would need thirteen and a half minutes to get to 35,000ft (10,668m) rather than the specified twelve minutes. Convair expected to deal with this performance shortfall by fitting afterburning to the engines or booster rockets to the airframe but, according to the manufacturer's estimates, there would be no other shortfalls against the specified limits.

Douglas All-Weather Fighter

The Douglas design was based on the company's project that had recently been proposed in response to the US Navy's night fighter requirement, and that was eventually put into production as the F3D-1 Skynight (discussed in Chapter Two).

Curtiss-Wright XP-87

The Curtiss-Wright two-seat project resulted from the abandonment of a ground-attack aircraft called the XA-43 that had been planned before the end of the war. However, shortly after the XA-43 project had been started, new information regarding the proposed powerplant revealed that this aircraft would be incapable of meeting its required range. Work was therefore stopped and the remaining unexpended funds were diverted to the new XP-87. The fighter was built under the original XA-43 contract: this, in the past, has given rise to the erroneous opinion that the XP-87 was the XA-43 with a new designation. In fact the two types were entirely dissimilar in size, equipment and mission. The XP-87 project became active in December 1945 after an agreement was reached between Curtiss-Wright and Air Material Command to build one prototype; a second prototype was approved on 31st January 1946. The Curtiss all-weather fighter proposals were thus based on an already established program, covered by MX745. In its early form the XP-87 was intended to carry a remotely controlled defensive tail turret mounting two guns, but a switch to limiting the aircraft to night and all-weather operations allowed this installation to be dropped.

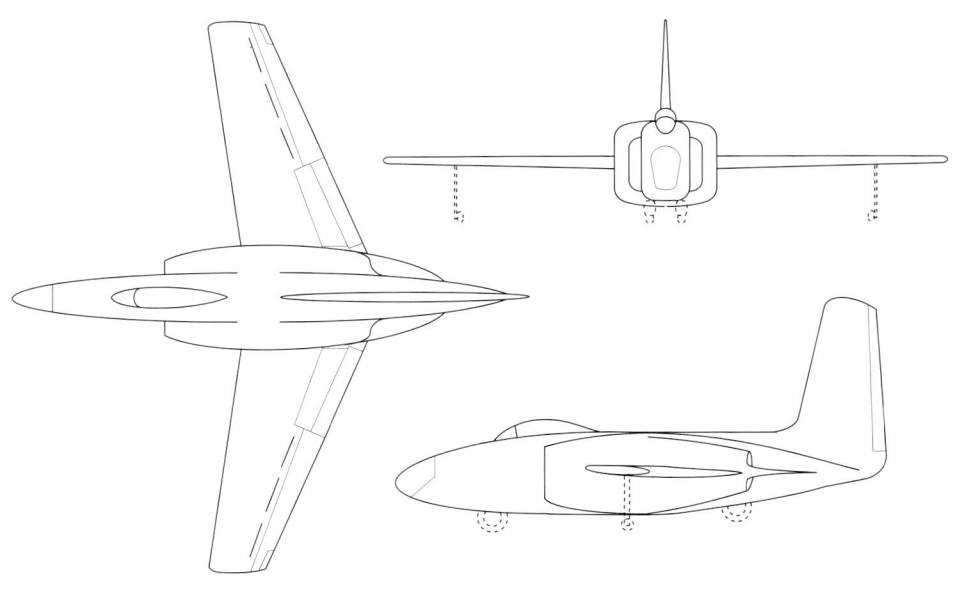

Drawing of what is thought to be Convair's forward-sweep All Weather Fighter proposal (10.45). Chris Gibson

The First Air Force Jets

Northrop N-24

No less than four swept mid-wing designs were submitted by Northrop on 29th November, comprising two basic layouts each with two alternative powerplants. The principal difference between the two versions was that one was conventional with full-span flaps and spoiler-type ailerons plus split flaps to act as dive brakes, while the other utilized Northrop's extensive experience in flying wings in that it had no horizontal tailplane (or stabilizer). Northrop had undertaken a great deal of work on tailless designs, with the series of aircraft leading up to the XB-35 bomber and the XP-79 flying wing fighter prototype. The 'flying wing' N-24s had partial-span flaps while trailing edge elevons used up the remaining space. Adding the tail to the alternative design called for a slightly longer fuselage, which was otherwise quite similar in each layout. Magnesium skinning was to be used in the fighter's construction.

The engine combinations were either two General Electric/Allison TG-180s (which later became the J35) in the lower fuselage or three less powerful axial-flow Westinghouse 24C units (later the J34), with two in the lower fuselage and the third beneath them in a protruding nacelle. An armament of four 20mm cannon was housed in the nose and there was a rearward-firing 20mm for tail defence. A turret had been planned but there was insufficient space to allow this to be fitted. Instead the forward-firing weapons could be rotated, the point of rotation being near the muzzles to allow an elliptical cone of fire to plus or minus 15°; the rear gun also had 13° of freedom in the horizontal plane and 15° in the vertical. There were external hardpoints for drop tanks or 1,000lb (454kg) bombs. The N-24 Designs A and C designs had the TG-180s, B and D the 24Cs, while A and B had the tailplane and C and D were tailless.

The official evaluation and assessment of these projects listed the designs in order of merit as follows – Northrop N-24 'Design A', Goodyear, Curtiss-Wright, Douglas, Northrop N-24 'Design B', Bell, Northrop N-24 'Design C', Northrop N-24 'Design D' and Consolidated. Although Goodyear was second it possessed no "individually outstanding features" while Curtiss-Wright's project had already been ordered. N-24 'A' was favoured because it used the TG-180 power unit at a time when production difficulties were beginning to appear for the Westinghouse engine. (Westinghouse was to experience substantial production problems with its engines over the next few years which badly hampered several US Navy designs as described in Chapter Two.) In addition N-24 'A' was one of the lightest proposals, had an acceptable wing loading and a good all-round performance, although improvements in the take-off and climb were thought desirable. Overall the design's stability was expected to be satisfactory, but thorough testing was deemed to be necessary in the directional and lateral areas.

Northrop N-24 'Design B' had the three 24C power units which were expected to give poor stability and control characteristics; in particular the directional problem that might be evident in Design 'A' would be exacerbated in this design. There were also weaknesses in 'B's climb and range but the overall performance was expected to be okay; the spin recovery situation, however, was not acceptable. 'Design C' and 'D' were not popular in that the tailless format offered poor longitudinal stability and control while the pilot sat well behind the leading edge of the wing which severely reduced his view out of the cockpit. Their performance was fine overall apart from the take-off and climb, and the spin recovery was expected to be "marginal". In the end both 'C' and 'D' plus Consolidated's offering were eliminated because they "exhibited one or several basic deficiencies in

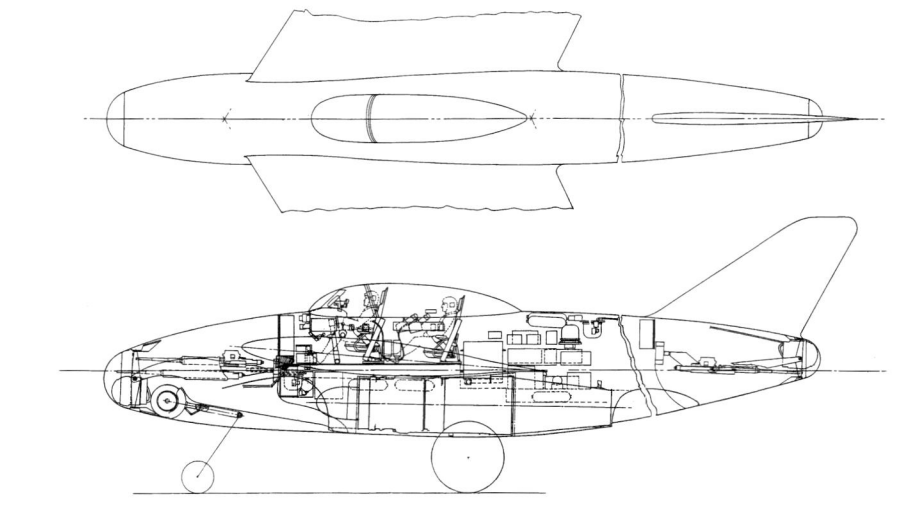

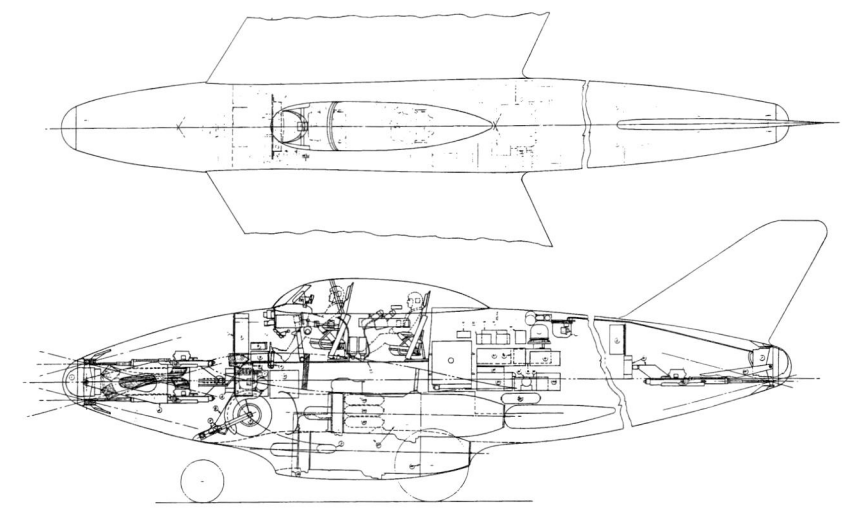

Fuselage arrangement for the Northrop N-24 'A' and 'C' projects, powered by two TG-180 power units (29.11.45). Gerald Balzer

Fuselage arrangement for the Northrop N-24 'B' and 'D' projects, powered by three 24C power units. Note the different nose cannon installation to the other pair of designs. Each engine on these four projects had its own intake and jet pipe (29.11.45). Gerald Balzer

The Curtiss XP-87 prototype, photographed before it received the designation XF-87. Terry Panopalis

design". Recommendations were placed for ordering two prototypes of Northrop's N-24 'Design A' and it was stated that the designs from Goodyear and Curtiss did not "warrant consideration" ahead of the N-24 'A'. However, some further evaluation was undertaken before any final decisions were made.

Curtiss-Wright XP-87 Blackhawk

Returning to the Curtiss XP-87, after the November 1947 specification had been released a further set of requirements for the Curtiss heavy fighter had been requested which called for the type to be able to operate at night as well as in poor weather. Army Air Force planners soon realized that in good daylight weather conditions the all-weather fighter would be unable to compete with daytime air superiority fighters, so 'all-weather' was redefined as night and inclement weather. In addition, it had earlier been established that prior commitments at Westinghouse would preclude the use of the prototype's XJ34 units in production aeroplanes so, during a design conference held on 29th May 1946, Curtiss presented four alternative engine combinations for assessment. A twin Allison J33 arrangement appeared to be the most attractive and a new version of the fighter was therefore planned which would have its four Westinghouse engines replaced by two J33-29s with afterburners (although no definite decisions were reached and Curtiss was instructed to proceed with the mock-up based on four XJ34s). This new variant was called the XP-87A and was to have been the production type, but it was never flown and the contract was terminated.

Meanwhile the prototype's construction progressed at a slower rate than had been expected by the contractor, and when completed in September 1947 it was six months late. In August 1946 Curtiss submitted a request to the Aeronautical Board to call the type 'Bat' but it was rejected because that name was being used by a guided missile, so instead Curtiss offered 'Blackhawk'. The XP-87 (soon to be XF-87) made its maiden flight on 5th March 1948 but flight testing soon revealed some aerodynamic deficiencies including a lack of manoeuvrability. In addition the critical Mach number for the tail assembly was lower than that calculated for the entire aircraft, which created buffeting at higher Mach numbers: a flaw that Curtiss was never able to cure completely before the program was closed. An order for production F-87A Blackhawks was also terminated. The

second XF-87 prototype, the last Curtiss fighter of all, was also never completed, despite plans to modify it as the XRF-87C photo reconnaissance variant with a wing incorporating another 140ft^2 (13.0m^2) of area. This machine was accepted in an unfinished condition and used as a source of spare parts. The Curtiss F-87 program was primarily abandoned because of the superiority demonstrated by the XF-89.

Northrop XF-89 Scorpion

A letter contract was issued to Northrop on 3rd May 1946 for two prototypes, designated XP-89 and powered by two TG-180-D1 engines, plus a full-size mock-up. However, as the process of detail design progressed through 1946 it became clear that, in terms of the aerodynamics and the efficiency of carrying weapon loads, a straight-wing layout would be more suitable for this type of air-

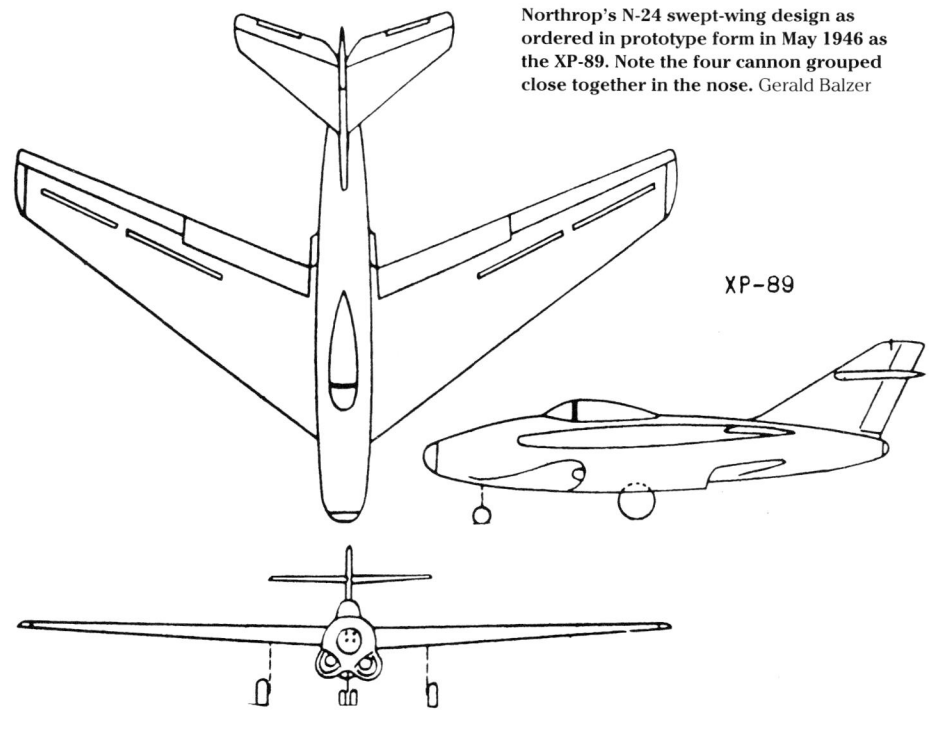

Northrop's N-24 swept-wing design as ordered in prototype form in May 1946 as the XP-89. Note the four cannon grouped close together in the nose. Gerald Balzer

The First Air Force Jets

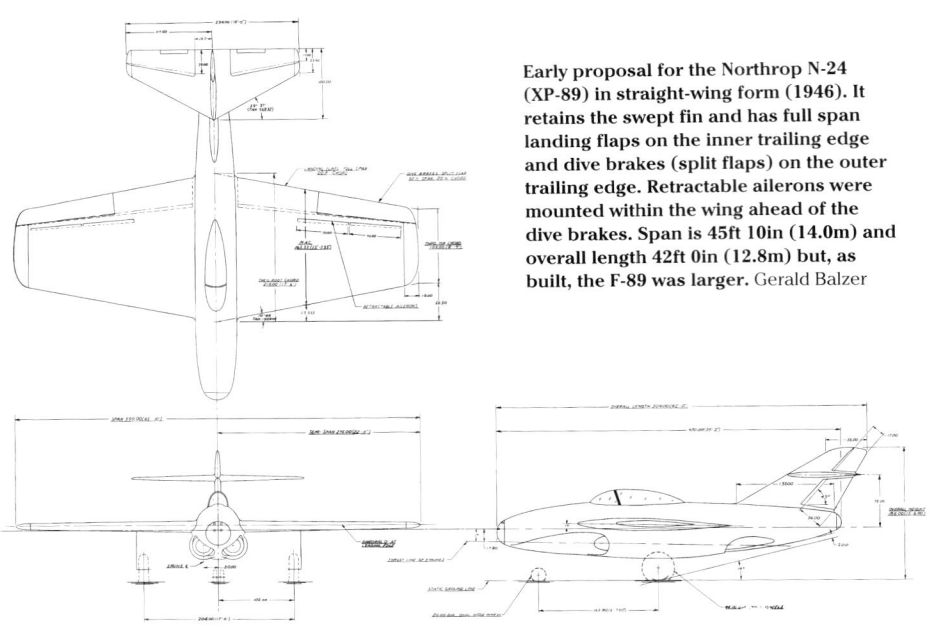

Early proposal for the Northrop N-24 (XP-89) in straight-wing form (1946). It retains the swept fin and has full span landing flaps on the inner trailing edge and dive brakes (split flaps) on the outer trailing edge. Retractable ailerons were mounted within the wing ahead of the dive brakes. Span is 45ft 10in (14.0m) and overall length 42ft 0in (12.8m) but, as built, the F-89 was larger. Gerald Balzer

craft. A great deal of research was undertaken by the Wright Field Aircraft Laboratory to assess the type's high speed performance with differing levels of wing sweep. The full-size mock-up (with swept wing) was officially inspected on 25th September 1946 but received a lot of criticism from Air Material Command. When re-inspected on 17th December many of the faults had been corrected but, most important of all, the XP-89 now had a thin straight wing; in addition the tail gun was also deleted during the fall of 1946.

Certain elements within official circles wanted the Northrop project cancelled but decisions were made in its favour and the program went ahead. As built the (redesignated) XF-89 used an aluminium rather than magnesium structure and carried four (later six) fixed 20mm guns instead of the original 'rotating turret'. The first prototype XF-89 made its first flight on 16th August 1948 and the type entered service as the Scorpion, although production machines were to differ substantially from the first aircraft. Although large, straight-winged and looking somewhat cumbersome and less advanced than some of its contemporise, the aircraft proved very effective in its role. Scorpions served with the USAF in several versions until 1961 and then with the Air National Guard right through to the end of the 1960s, a remarkable achievement for an early post-World War Two design.

In early October 1948 a conference was held to assess in detail the XF-89's capabilities (including performance, operational aspects, maintenance, etc) against the XF-87 and naval Douglas XF3D 'Skynight', plus a paper proposal for a modified version of the Lockheed L-153/XF-90 (described below). The examination looked closely at the flight test data which showed that, collectively, none of the types were completely satisfactory but the XF-89 would be the best solution. Performance-wise the XF-89 was the fastest at Mach 0.85 (or 0.80 with tip tanks) followed by the XF-87 at Mach 0.78 and the XF3D at 0.75. None of them showed a good time to height capability but it was thought that higher thrust engines would help cure this deficiency in the XF-89 (in due course later versions of the F-89 did get more powerful J35 engines with afterburning).

The current production schedules also brought the need to study interim alternatives and it was here that the Lockheed F-94, at this time still described as a modified TF-80 Shooting Star trainer, became an active element of the overall program. But a need for a 'definitive' more advanced all-weather fighter was also recognized. This led to the Convair F-102 and F-106 covered in Chapters Three and Four. Very soon afterwards it was agreed that work should stop on Curtiss' XF-87 and that its production contract should be cancelled, by then the type was considered too large to operate as an interceptor. Further consideration of the Douglas XF3D-1 for the USAF all-weather requirement would also come to an end and consequently the F-89 would be ordered into quantity production. In addition these meetings also decided that the order for the YF-93A development of the F-86 Sabre described shortly would be reduced to just two machines.

View showing the fifth production Northrop F-89A Scorpion which was used for trials. The fin serial number above the horizontal tail and a nose instrumentation boom have been removed from the print for security purposes.

A New Penetration Fighter

The second competitive requirement was for a new 'Penetration Fighter'. The principal requirement for this new type was a long range to allow it to escort bombers over enemy territory, but within a minimum size/weight limit and with good steep angle dive performance (a sustained steep dive was considered to be very important). This all-purpose jet fighter, designed to go deep into enemy territory, called for a bigger and heavier airframe than was usual for fighters. It was to be a single-seater and would carry six 0.5in (12.7mm) or four 0.6in (15.2mm) machine guns or four 20mm cannon. Two engines were specified, housed very close to the fuselage centreline to ensure that the aircraft's single-engine handling would not be problematic, and the flying surfaces had to be swept. The performance limits included a maximum speed of at least 600mph (965km/h), the ability to get to 35,000ft (10,668m) within ten minutes, a ceiling of 40,000ft (12,192m) and a combat radius of 900 miles (1,448km). Some of these values were soon increased – in particular the ceiling was raised to 50,000ft (15,240m) and the time to this height now had to be five minutes. The document (which after the competition became MX811) was released to industry on 28th August 1945. All the major players responded as did two private organizations, 'John Abbeman' and 'Management and Research'. There were also submissions from Curtiss-Wright and Goodyear about which little is currently known. The resulting aircraft would have been operated by Strategic Air Command.

Convair (Vultee) Penetration Fighter

The Convair project had a configuration that was similar to the night fighter design that Convair had already proposed to the Navy (discussed in Chapter Two). There were two differences. One was that the wings were swept back at 35° with the intention of achieving a higher critical Mach number. The other was that, the Army Air Force project was to have two jet engines, apparently in pods, whereas the Navy design had three. The design study was submitted to Wright Field in late October or early November 1945.

Lockheed L-153

Lockheed used the project number L-153 to cover a host of different design configurations. In fact a total of over sixty were studied before the layout that became the XF-90 was finally selected. Most of the delta-winged options came under the L-167 designation (discussed below) leaving the L-153 to cover just about everything else – swept wings (forward or back), variable geometry wings, W-shaped wings, twin booms, V-tails, and with up to three engines mounted everywhere from on top of the fuselage to the tips of the wings. They would make a book in their own right! It is impossible to cover all of these projects here, so one or two layouts have been selected to illustrate the range of options considered. Some L-153 drawings actually no longer exist, and many of those that do appear to have been quick assessments without too much detail.

L-153 studies were under way during September 1945 and 'Phase 1' was based on developments of the P-80 Shooting Star, two of the three suggested layouts having swept wings which formed part of a long investigation into the feasibility of using a wing swept at 45°. However, the P-80 outgrowth ideas were abandoned and there were problems with the second set of studies embracing W-wings. To quote Bill Slayton in *Aerospace Projects Review*, 'It was soon found that the desired high speed drag properties of these wings could only be achieved if a high degree of boundary layer control could be retained at the intersection of the swept portions of the wing. The L-153-6 with its engines at this intersection appeared to be the only feasible arrangement.' (L-153-6 actually had its engines in underwing pods mounted at the intersection.)

'Phase 3', also started in September 1945, looked at various all-new designs with swept

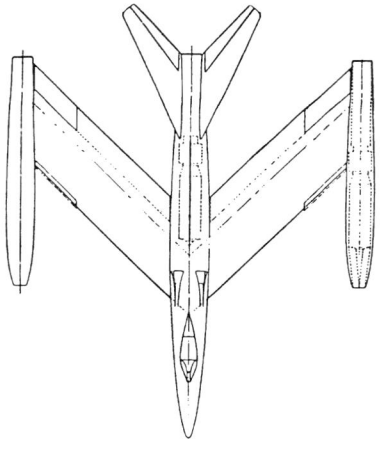
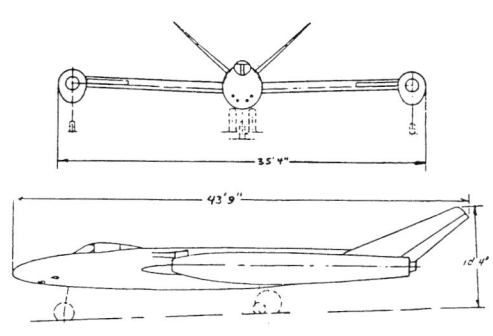

Lockheed's L-153-13 swept wing design with tip-mounted engine nacelles (approx. late 1946). Note the ear intakes behind the cockpit, the bicycle undercarriage, V-tail and four nose guns. This aircraft had a span of 35ft 4in (10.8m), overall length 43ft 9in (13.2m) and wing area 300ft² (27.9m²).
Scott Lowther archive

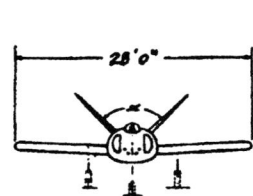
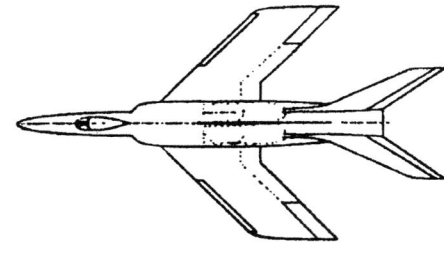
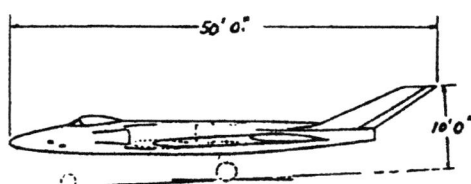

Lockheed L-153-14 swept wing design with a V-tail set at 36° dihedral (9.45). Again there are four cannon in the lower nose and small intakes in the fuselage just above the wing roots. Span here is 31ft 6in (9.6m) and length 42ft 0in (12.8m). Scott Lowther archive

The First Air Force Jets

Cut-away drawing of Lockheed's L-153-14 which shows well just how tightly packed with equipment and fuel a jet fighter can be. The image is dated 20th September 1945. Alain Pelletier

wings. Some of these revealed features found later on the XF-90 prototypes. Two projects (one of which, the L-153-13, is shown) had engines mounted on the wingtips in large nacelles. This would surely have given severe asymmetric control problems in the event of an engine failure. By April 1946 swept wings seemed to offer the best solution if the aspect ratio could be reduced sufficiently to prevent flutter-related problems. When powered by Lockheed's own L-1000 jet engine, the estimated performance for some swept-wing proposals suggested maximum speeds above 650mph (1,046km/h) both at sea level and above 35,000ft (10,668m), together with an outstanding rate of climb. These figures considerably exceeded the specification requirements. However, throughout Lockheed's L-153 studies swept wings presented the problem of undesirable low-speed flight characteristics and so, in an attempt to prevent this, the final set of designs looked at variable geometry wings.

The intention was to have 45° of sweep for flight at high speeds, but for low speed flight, take-off and landing the outer portion of the wing would be moved forward to present either a straight wing or just a few degrees of leading edge sweep. During the 1960s this concept would become common on military aircraft, but in the late 1940s it presented a considerable advance. Indeed given the difficulties of structural complexity and coping with the aerodynamics of shifting centres of lift it was arguably too advanced for the time. Lockheed's results indicated that the mechanical variable-sweep mechanism would be complex, it would add around 400lb (181kg) to the weight and there would be less space available for the main undercarriage and fuel (it was preferable to house all of the fuel internally since carrying underwing tanks at all wing angles would be problematical). Also there were likely to be drag problems at high speeds around the fillet covering the sweep panel roots and, finally, two engines would have to be used to meet the requirements. An official presentation on the swing-wing L-153 was made to Wright Field personnel during mid-November 1946, but consideration of this configuration was halted on 1st December. Now Lockheed's effort was switched to delta wing studies under the L-167 designation.

Lockheed L-167

At the start of its penetration fighter studies Lockheed had thought that delta wings would be undesirable because of anticipated problems in obtaining adequate control during flight at low speeds. In addition it was perceived that assistance would be required to achieve a recovery in a dive, to which the eventual answer was to place an auxiliary trim surface control high on the vertical tail. The worry had been that wing pitching moment could not be controlled in the dive at high transonic Mach numbers, but the new surface would be placed far enough away from the wing to prevent it being affected by changes in the wing characteristics at high speeds. Estimates suggested that pitching control would now be satisfactory up to Mach 1.3, and consequently design work went ahead.

On 12th September 1946 'Kelly' Johnson, Lockheed's famous designer, gave the go-ahead for a delta wing study powered by two engines and wind tunnel testing of the basic design got going in January 1947. In the event three layouts were drawn under the L-167 designation and the L-167-2 offered some promising figures. Calculations suggested that this aircraft would be capable of a rate of climb at sea level of 11,200ft/min (3,414m/min), an absolute ceiling of 45,700ft (13,929m) and a combat radius of 900 miles (1,448km). Internal fuel totalled 1,400gal (6,366lit) and the 9,800lb (43.6kN) thrust Lockheed (Mensaco) L-1000 engine was again a possible alternative that offered slightly improved performance figures.

It is not the intention of this book to include any and every available drawing of unbuilt fighter projects. However, since the Lockheed L-167 studies embraced just three delta wing designs, it is interesting to put all of them in together to illustrate the type of variables that were considered when undertaking research into a new project. (The L-153 studies were made towards the same penetration fighter requirement.) L-167-1 has tip fins and no horizontal tail (in fact it has a blended body with almost no fuselage), L-167-2 introduces the high horizontal tail surface while L-167-3 has a more conventional fuselage. All were to be powered by two 24C engines with afterburning mounted side-by-side in the body and had three guns mounted in each outer wing. L-167-1's span was 30ft 10in (9.4m), length 39ft 10in (12.1m) and wing area 476ft² (44.3m²).
Scott Lowther archive

McDonnell Model 36

There were three initial designs from McDonnell: Models 36A, 36B and 36C. The first was a development of the straight-wing XF2H-1 Banshee naval fighter discussed in Chapter Two. Apart from the intakes it had 30° of leading edge sweep but a straight trailing edge, a thickness/chord ratio of 6.5% and two engines mounted in the wing roots with individual intakes and a bifurcated jet pipe; four 20mm guns were mounted in a line across the lower nose. McDonnell's engineers described this as a 'conservative delta' but, despite having numerous advantages, the project was stopped because there were doubts regarding the quality of the airflow over the wing roots at the required higher speeds. Model 36B was quite similar with the same leading-edge sweep and straight trailing edge, but the two engines were now moved out to wingtip nacelles with a consequent reduction in span. The wing itself was moved from its earlier mid-fuselage position to a low setting and, overall, the project offered many advantages in terms of simplicity and ease of maintenance. However, an engine failure at low speeds would give a severe yawing moment that could not be compensated by a fin of moderate size, while the airflow around the engine nacelle and wing intersection could also give problems. Finally, it was realized that having weight in three separate bodies so far apart, connected by a thin wing, presented the possibility of severe aero-elastic problems.

Both of these initial projects were quickly dropped with neither being offered to the Army Air Force, so the more promising Model 36C was officially submitted on 13th October 1945. The 36C was a handsome, more balanced and modern-looking design with a

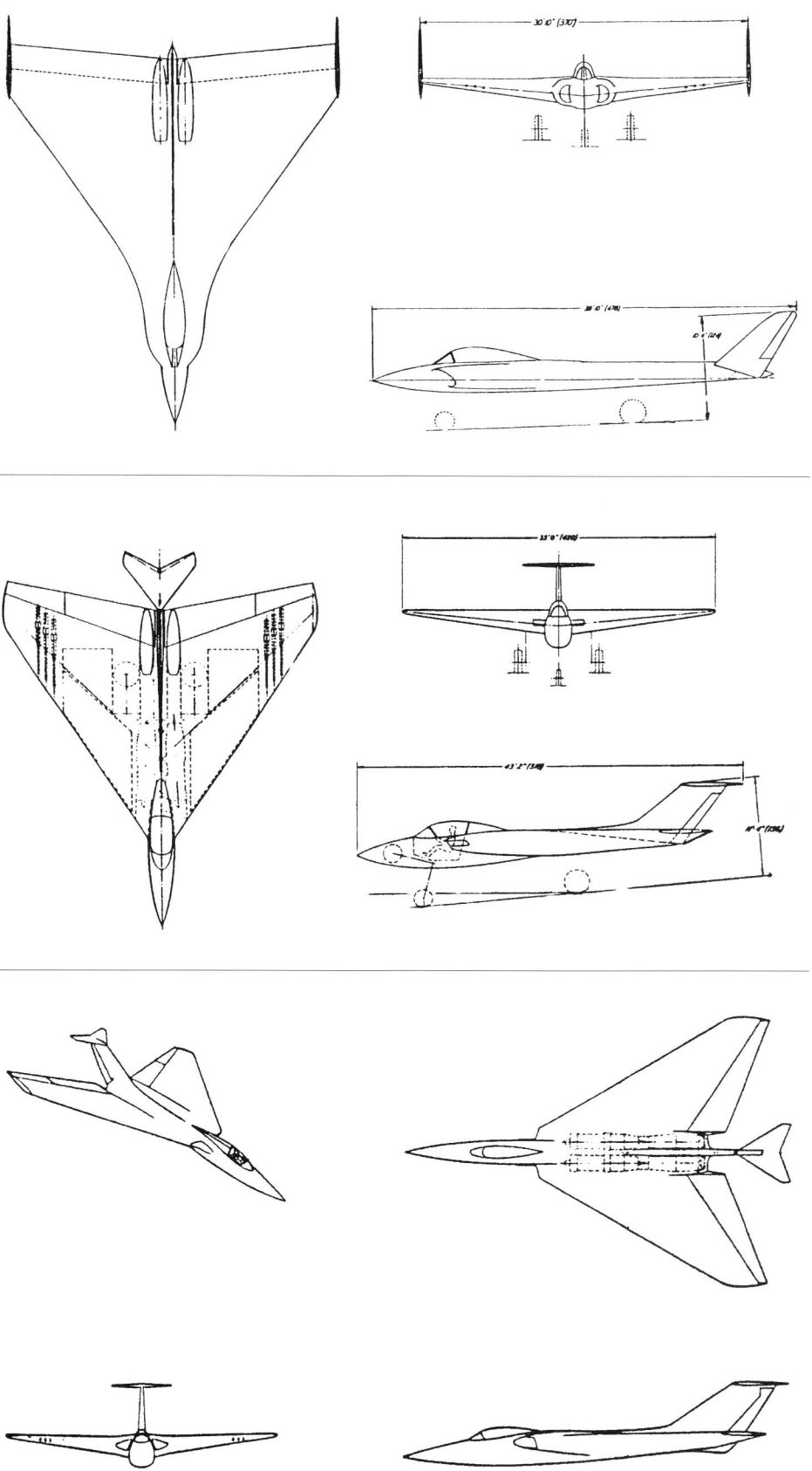

The First Air Force Jets

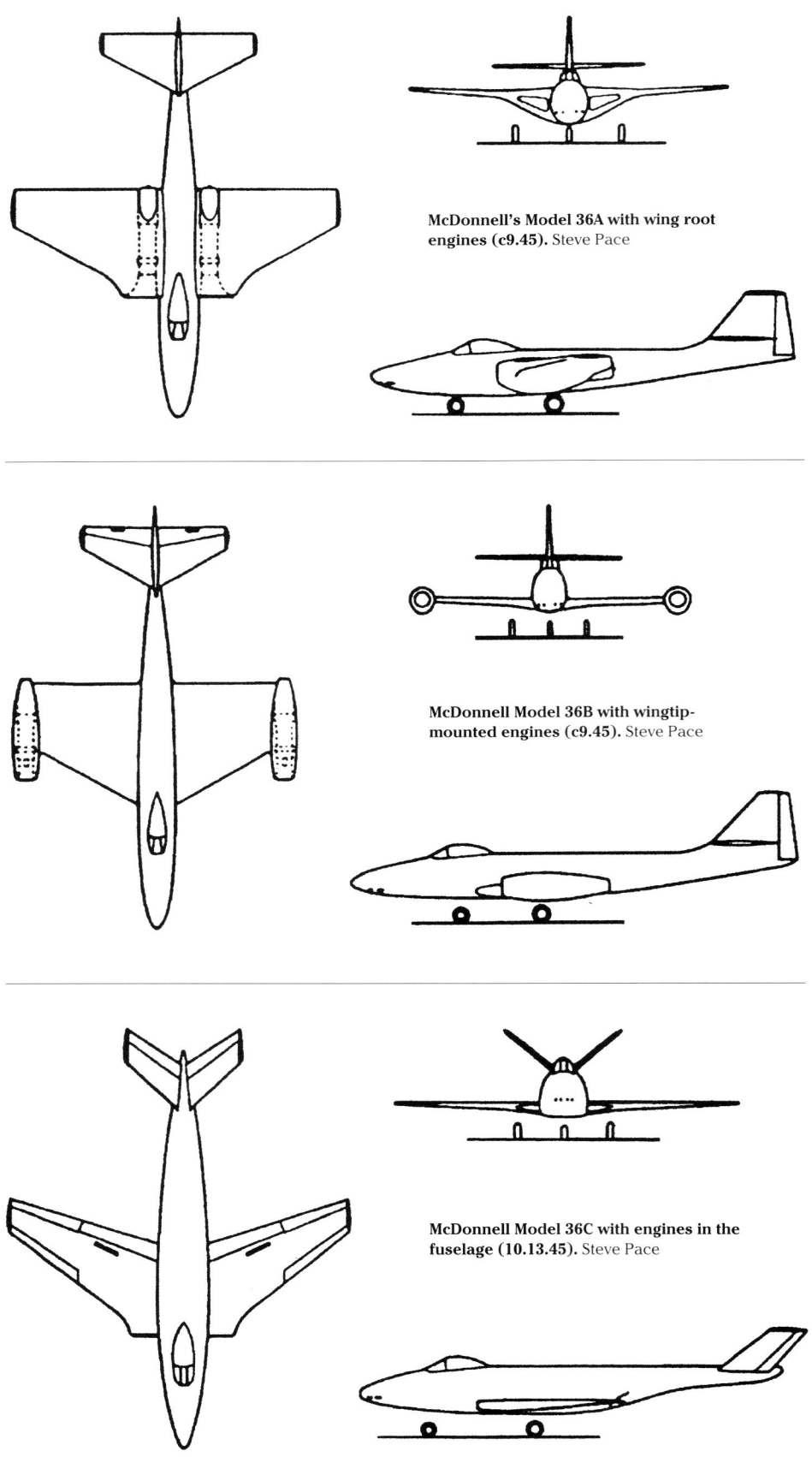

McDonnell's Model 36A with wing root engines (c9.45). Steve Pace

McDonnell Model 36B with wingtip-mounted engines (c9.45). Steve Pace

McDonnell Model 36C with engines in the fuselage (10.13.45). Steve Pace

fully swept wing set at 39° on the leading edge (except around the intakes where the leading edge was straight), a swept V-tail and four cannon across the lower nose. It was a big aircraft with an internal fuel volume of 1,434gal (6,520lit). The engines, two Westinghouse 24C-4 (J34-WE-13) units, were placed in the wing root position with the jet pipes exhausting beneath the fuselage a little behind the wing trailing edge. Two developments of the 24C/J34 with higher thrust ratings were expected from Westinghouse and these were eventually adopted for several naval fighter projects (they became the J40 and J46 respectively), so McDonnell arranged the Model 36C to be able to receive any of these units. In due course the Model 36 designation was used substantially to cover follow-on developments of the original 36C design, leading eventually to the 36W, which became the F-101 Voodoo covered in Chapter Three.

Northrop XP-79Z

On 1st November 1945 Northrop proposed a combined project, developed from its unsuccessful XP-79 prototype, that was designed to meet the penetration and the interceptor fighter requirements together. The XP-79 had crashed on 12th September 1945 and discussions were held with Air Technical Service Command to assess the changes that would be required from the original design. The resulting tailless project was influenced directly by these discussions and featured a thin wing swept 40° 42' at the leading edge (more than had been employed on the XP-79), a Westinghouse 24C turbojet for the penetration type and a rocket motor for the interceptor in an underfuselage nacelle (in essentially the same airframe), and a small fin and rudder. Split flaps for landing plus dive brakes were mounted on the inner wing trailing edge, while the outer portion had elevons.

Like the XP-79, this new development had a prone pilot, and he had a large clear forward canopy to see out of with an entrance hatch behind. The idea of a prone pilot had obvious appeal in terms of reducing required frontal area. It was also thought to have advantages in terms of improving the body's resistance to manoeuvring forces but the associated physiological problems were not to be understood for another decade.

The XP-79's landing gear would comprise two main wheels, one housed in each inner wing section, plus a small wheel on each wingtip. Four 0.5in (12.7mm) machine guns were mounted in the leading edge wing roots and the aircraft's structure would be largely

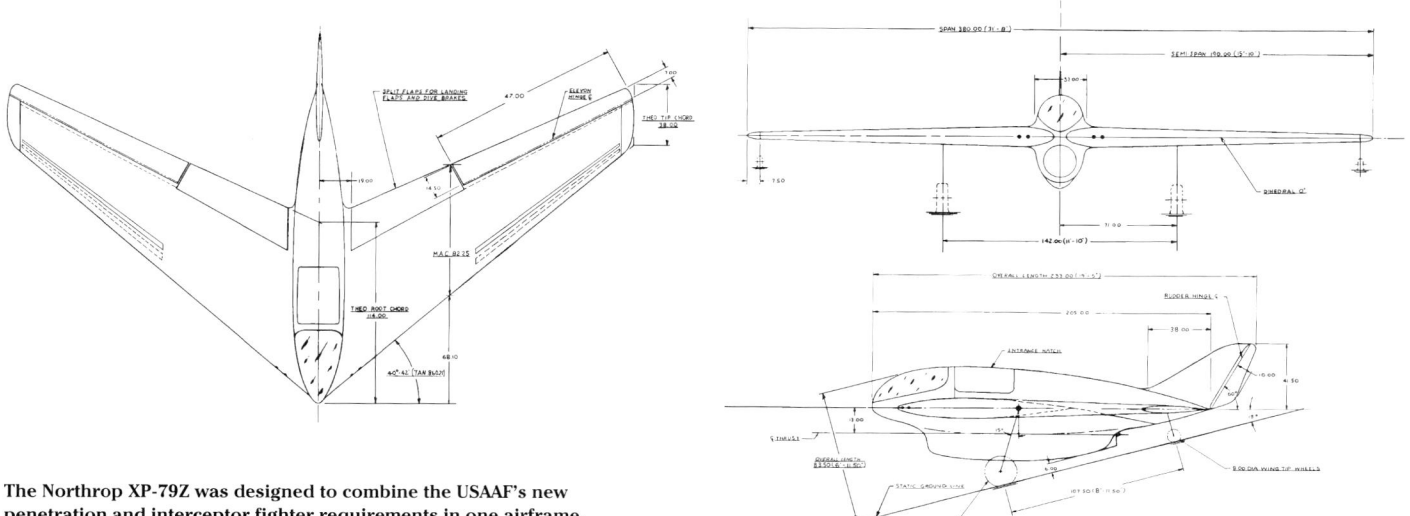

The Northrop XP-79Z was designed to combine the USAAF's new penetration and interceptor fighter requirements in one airframe, although with different powerplants (1.11.45). Gerald Balzer

75S aluminium alloy. At a gross weight of 6,555 lb (2,973kg) for the penetration aircraft, this seems to have been a very small design with which to do the job, although the estimated range was 2,000 miles (3,218km) with the 24C (but just 163 miles [262km] with the rocket). The XP-79Z was described as a configuration study and appears to have been dropped soon after work began on the N-24 all-weather fighter.

Convair's records show that on 15th February 1946 the company was informed that it was a winner in the penetration fighter competition and that a Phase I study contract for a development program, covering extensive wind tunnel model research, engineering data plus a full-scale mock-up, would shortly be under negotiation. McDonnell was declared the runner-up but that fact that Convair would also win the interceptor requirement (below) soon counted against the company. The Deputy Assistant Chief for the Air Staff at the Pentagon, General Thomas S Power, overturned the decision made by Wright Field stating that only one contract was allowed per manufacturer to ensure that business would be spread across the industry more evenly. Consequently, on 12th June, Convair's contract to build its penetration fighter was cancelled and it was to be Lockheed and McDonnell who would build prototypes but, as the Lockheed story illustrates, big changes had still to be made. In part this was because the Specification requirements themselves were still being amended and updated.

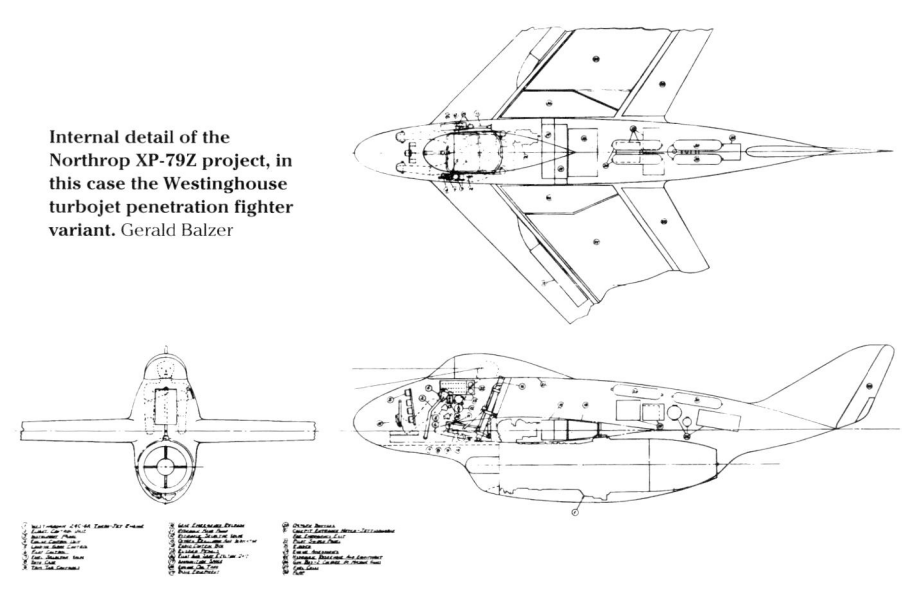

Internal detail of the Northrop XP-79Z project, in this case the Westinghouse turbojet penetration fighter variant. Gerald Balzer

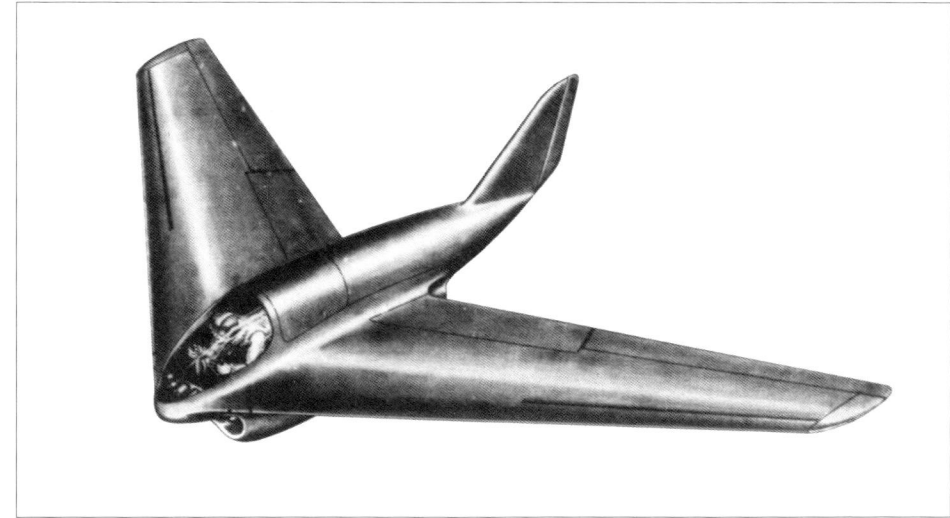

Artist's impression of the Northrop XP-79Z. Gerald Balzer

The First Air Force Jets

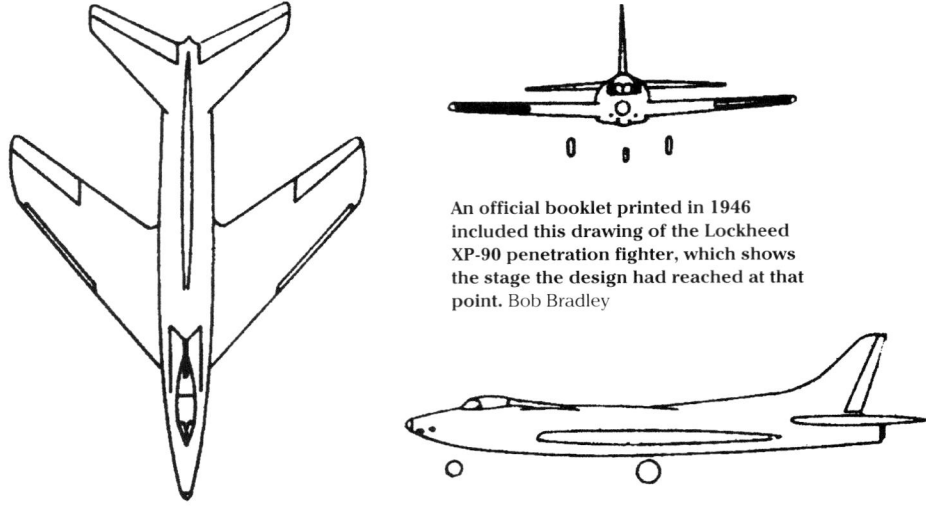

An official booklet printed in 1946 included this drawing of the Lockheed XP-90 penetration fighter, which shows the stage the design had reached at that point. Bob Bradley

Lockheed XF-90

By early April 1946 the Army Air Force was calling the L-153 the XP-90, and Lockheed labelled it the Model 90 when a Phase I study contract was placed in June 1946. An initial disclosure of the delta L-167 to officials at Wright Field in November 1946 brought considerable interest and by early December it looked as if the conventional L-153 would be dropped for an 'XP-90 Delta'. This was confirmed by a letter from Wright Field on 3rd February 1947 and work on an 'XP-90 Delta' mock-up began later that month.

The objective was a normal gross weight of 21,000 lb (9,526kg) and overload 25,000 lb (11,340kg) but when wind tunnel results completed by the California Institute of Technology at Pasadena were assessed in early April it was realized that there would be problems with the delta. There was evidence of rolling instability at high angles of attack, and 'Kelly' Johnson also noted that the fuselage was 'much too small', yet the design gave considerable drag. By mid-May it was most apparent that the delta was too heavy, it gave too much drag and would be difficult to trim at high lift. Despite further testing to try and find a cure, by July it was clear to Johnson that a conventional fixed swept-wing design would be superior. On 14th July the assessors and officials at Wright Field were informed of the problems, but fortunately they were very supportive of a swept-wing XP-90/Model 90 and the work progressed well. The completed mock-up was inspected by Army Air Force officials in early December and the manufacture of the prototypes began. The fighter was covered by MX812.

Nevertheless, there were still many changes to be made and these delayed the maiden flight considerably, the first XF-90 prototype finally getting into the air on 3rd June 1949. However, Lockheed had been informed on the previous 1st February that any plans to produce the F-90 in numbers were to go on hold until the type had been evaluated against the XF-88 and XF-93. In fact, as explained shortly, Lockheed's penetration fighter would never enter production and the two prototypes principally served as trial aircraft for new technology. An elegant aircraft, the XF-90 looked the part, but it was far too heavy for the powerplants available at the time. However, much was learnt from its development and, in a slight dive, it was possible to take the XF-90 through Mach 1.0. The fighter carried six 20mm cannon in its nose and was also flown with a 1,000 lb

The first Lockheed XF-90 prototype seen without wingtip tanks.

Lockheed engineers inspect a model of the XP-90 (XF-90) Delta. Alain Pelletier

The first McDonnell XF-88 prototype photographed on the occasion of its rollout on 11th August 1948. The XF-88 was a particularly handsome aircraft.

The first North American YF-93A prototype pictured before its first flight. In due course the design of the side intakes was much modified.

(454kg) bomb under each wing. After the XF-90 had lost out in competition with the XF-88 (discussed below), further L-153 studies were made for an escort fighter plus ground attack and reconnaissance variants. There were also studies for single-engined versions fitted with an Allison J33 or General Electric J47. None of these came to anything.

McDonnell XF-88 'Voodoo'

As built, the XF-88 dispensed with the V-tail and sported a more conventional style of tail configuration. The 'V' had been chosen because it was predicted that compressibility effects would create problems and it was thought that a reduced number of tail intersections would make things simpler. It was also considered to be cheaper from a manufacturing point of view and that it would incur little or no weight and low-speed drag penalty. However, further tunnel testing indicated that the V-tail would give insufficient longitudinal stability when close to the stall and would have adverse rolling moments. Similar tests showed that a conventional horizontal/vertical tail arrangement was actually pretty free of aerodynamic problems and so this was adopted. In addition, the XF-88 received swept air intakes to increase the critical speed of the lips and also had six 20mm cannon, three on each side of the nose.

The first XF-88 prototype made its maiden flight on 20th October 1948 but without afterburning, which meant that the machine was underpowered. Nevertheless, like the XF-90, McDonnell's aircraft could go supersonic in a dive. In due course the fighter did receive afterburners (thus becoming the XF-88A) while in 1953 a nose-mounted Allison XT38-A-5 turboprop was tested on the first prototype, making it the XF-88B. There were plans to procure a run of F-88 Voodoos but in December 1948 development work on the production variant was suspended by the Engineering Division of Air Material Command. A two-seat F-88 proposal was also made in 1948 as an all-weather fighter but this was rejected in favour of the projects described earlier. Although not built in production numbers the XF-88s demonstrated excellent flight characteristics and provided their designers with a great deal of knowledge for the future. It laid the foundation for a far more capable fighter: the F-101 Voodoo.

North American YF-93A and NA-166

So many lines of research were under way during this period that it will not be a surprise to find that a third prototype contender appeared for the penetration fighter requirement, the North American Aviation NA-157 – despite the fact that North American had not been one of the original competitors. This single-seat radar-equipped development of the F-86 day fighter was powered by one Pratt & Whitney J-48-PW-6, which was the British Rolls-Royce Tay centrifugal engine built under licence. Two prototypes were ordered and the design was at first designated P-86C but, because of the substantial alterations with a solid nose and side intakes, it soon became the P-93A. A production order for 118 fighters was also placed and in June 1948 these became F-93As. However, this order was cancelled in February 1949, in part because the design actually departed considerably from the F-86, and the two prototype YF-93s, the first of which flew on 25th January 1950, were to be the only examples built. In addition, North American also designed the NA-166, which was a proposed two-seat version of the YF-93 that would serve as an all-weather (night) fighter. One example was ordered in 1949 but it was cancelled before completion.

The placing of any production orders for the three types of penetration fighter built in prototype form was put on hold pending a fly-off competition between them, and this was finally held between 30th June and 8th July 1950. By then however, the whole penetration fighter program was about to be abandoned because, with the growing threat of nuclear delivery by Soviet Union bombers, priority had switched to developing a dedicated interceptor. Thus the fly-off results were largely academic. Nonetheless on 15th August 1950 McDonnell's XF-88A was declared the winner, with Lockheed second and North American third. In truth none was thought to possess enough range to complete the original mission and they represented

The First Air Force Jets

little improvement in overall combat performance over the F-84E and the F-86. Nevertheless, all of these manufacturers would in due course be kept busy with new fighters, although McDonnell's F-101 was the only new type to be developed out of the rejected designs.

There were a number of external factors that also influenced the decision-making process around the penetration fighter. Budget restrictions during the late 1940s and the advent of the Korean War in 1950 made it necessary to improve existing types rather than introduce a new design. In addition, part of President Truman's restriction of funds imposed in May 1948 included a policy of using up stored reserves of World War Two aircraft before asking for money to buy new types! Those funds that were available in the restricted 1950 budget were to go largely into the huge Convair B-36 bomber, a type that the F-88 had not been designed to escort. By the end of the Korean War the F-88 represented an outmoded concept.

This original North American display model is called the 'Two-Place All-Weather Fighter Version of the F-93' and is almost certainly the company's NA-166 project, for which a single prototype was ordered but not built. It has a longer nose plus a larger canopy and extra seat; structurally there are many similarities to the single-seater. Calculated from the model's dimensions, this fighter's span would have been 47ft (14.3m) and length 54ft (16.5m). Jonathan Rigutto/photo © 2005 Chad Slattery

Chance Vought V-367

Before we leave the subject of penetration fighters there is another proposal that deserves mention. In 1949 Chance Vought offered a design for the USAF based on its Cutlass naval fighter (Chapter Two) but powered by a single Westinghouse XJ-40-WE-10 rather than the Cutlass's two J-34 units. The estimated top speed at 45,000ft (13,716m) was 614mph (988km); and with 1,490gal (6,775lit) of internal fuel aboard, and another 1,000gal (4,547lit) in two large external tanks, the estimated radii of action were 660nm (1,222km) and 1,000nm (1,852km). There was also the potential to store four Hughes air-to-air missiles beneath the wings. The Cutlass was a boldly innovative design based on German wartime research. However, although it saw brief service with the US Navy (after a substantial re-design), it was not a great success. It is not surprising that the USAF found a penetration fighter derivative unattractive.

The Chance Vought V-367 penetration fighter designed for the USAF, which essentially was a single-engined version of the company's Cutlass naval fighter. This drawing is dated 3rd July 1950 but the first proposals had been made over a year earlier. Dick Atkins, Vought Archive

A New Interceptor

The third design competition was intended to find a new short-range interceptor to be operated by Air Defence Command, a brand new organization given the task of dealing with incoming high-speed enemy bombers approaching at high altitude. This type of aircraft was seen as the last line of defence with the interceptor operating close to its base. It needed to be a high-speed, high-performance, high-altitude aircraft. The requirements were demanding with a top speed at sea level of 600mph (965km/h), rising to 700mph (1,126km/h) at 50,000ft (15,240m) – in other words, supersonic at altitude. That height had to be reached in just four minutes but the endurance requirements comprised five minutes at full power, twenty-five minutes at 50,000ft while flying at around 80% maximum speed, plus another five minutes cruise to get back home. The armament was four 0.5in (12.7mm) machine guns while the powerplant was expected to be rocket motors only (20mm cannon came into the picture soon afterwards). The document was issued to industry in August 1945 and, besides the main manufacturers' responses described below, the private organization 'Management and Research' was again one of the teams to submit proposals. To date no details have been found for either the Douglas or the North American interceptor proposals.

Bell

During this period Bell's studies into fighter design included 'weaponised' versions of its straight-winged rocket-powered X-1 research machine, which in October 1947 had been the first aircraft in the world to break the sound barrier. Not surprisingly therefore Bell's submission for the interceptor requirement was rocket powered but it had a 45° delta wing. Had it gone ahead it would have benefited considerably from the experience already acquired from the X-1 program.

Convair (Vultee) Interceptor

Convair felt that swept wings would help produce an aircraft that could meet the performance requirements and the resulting project had 35° of sweep plus a V-tail. The 'ducted rocket' powerplant, an augmented rocket propulsion system, had air passing through the aircraft that was then heated by the rocket motors before being mixed with additional fuel and ignited. As a result additional power was available in a form similar to a ramjet that, with the rocket motors mounted in the augmenting duct, gave a total thrust of 3,700lb (16.4kN). The rockets supplied thrust of their own and served as the igniters for the 'ramjet' part of the powerplant, but there were another four 1,200lb (5.3kN) booster rocket motors fixed around the rear fuselage, which were needed to get the aircraft flying at a high enough speed to allow the 'ramjet' to be brought into use. Finally there was a small conventional Westinghouse J-30 jet engine placed in the aft end of the fuselage centrebody that would be used to provide power (and an electrical and hydraulic supply) for the return part of the mission.

The interceptor had a bicycle undercarriage together with jettisonable take-off gear and there was also the possibility that external fuel tanks could be carried. Convair felt that the production prospects for this type of aircraft were good and probably better than those for the penetration fighter. The company also thought that this type could serve for as long as fifteen years before new tech-

Artist's impression of the Convair swept wing interceptor. San Diego Aerospace Museum

This view of Convair's interceptor shows good detail of the rocket motor installation.
San Diego Aerospace Museum

The First Air Force Jets

Side view of the Convair swept wing interceptor (11.45). San Diego Aerospace Museum

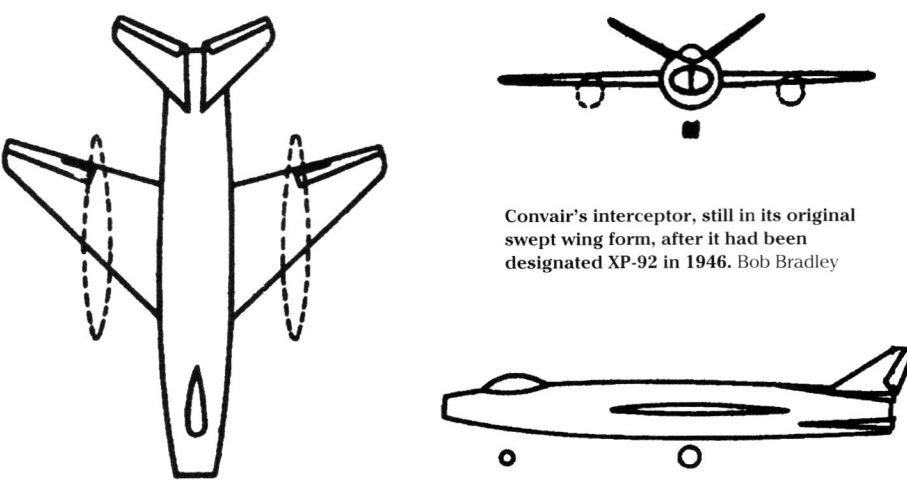

Convair's interceptor, still in its original swept wing form, after it had been designated XP-92 in 1946. Bob Bradley

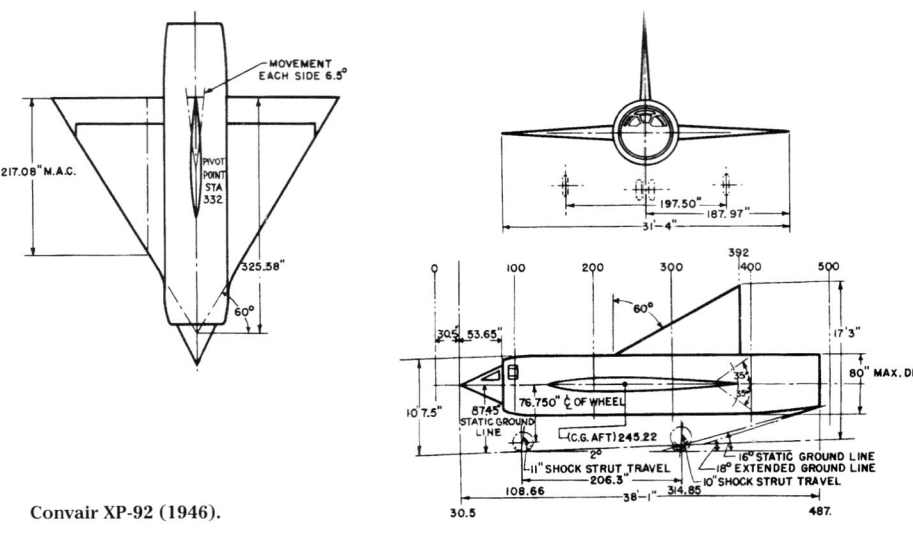

Convair XP-92 (1946).

nology allowed the development of suitable surface-to-air missiles as the final line of defence.

Northrop XP-79Z

The competing Northrop design was described under the penetration fighter section and was essentially the same aircraft but powered by a rocket motor rather than the Westinghouse jet. The type of rocket motor was not clarified on the drawings but the interceptor's gross weight was much higher than for the jet-powered version.

Republic AP-31

The Republic project featured a combined rocket/jet engine installation plus a variable-incidence wing (that is, an adjustable wing angle of attack) and inversely tapered wings. The initial powerplant proposal was one 5,200 lb (23.1kN) General Electric TG-180 (J47) jet plus a Curtiss-Wright XLR27-CW-1 four-chamber rocket motor placed above and below the jet, giving a maximum thrust of 8,400 lb (37.3kN) (2,100 lb [9.3kN] per chamber). Stressed skin construction was to be employed along with a cantilever wing.

Convair XP-92 Dart

Following an evaluation by Headquarters Air Material Command, Convair was named as the winner of the interceptor competition on 12th April 1946 and its project was officially designated XP-92, with MX813 being assigned to the overall requirement. A Phase I contract for tunnel testing, detail engineering and a full-size mock-up followed on 2nd May, the XP-92 being the only type requested to continue development from the interceptor competitors. Development work began soon afterwards but wind tunnel testing gave some unsatisfactory results; in particular poor lateral control was indicated together with tip stalling at an angle of attack of just 5°. Examination of various research reports, especially from Michael Gluhareff (who had emigrated to America from Russia) plus Alexander Lippisch's wartime research in Germany, suggested that the delta wing offered the best solution and several forms were subsequently assessed with leading edge sweep angles between 45° and 70°. The results were good and the XP-92 was therefore completely redesigned. The switch to a delta wing began Convair's long and very successful association with this planform.

The new XP-92 looked less attractive to the eye than the original swept wing proposal. It

Model of the Convair XP-92.

The Convair XF-92A research aircraft seen in its original form with a non-afterburning engine.

Model showing an early configuration of Republic's AP-31 project fitted with two large external tanks on the wingtips.
Cradle of Aviation Museum

Drawing showing the Republic AP-31 project as it stood on 19th November 1946, after the prototypes had been ordered. At this stage the span was 31ft 4in (9.55m), length 49ft 9in (15.2m) and wing area 320ft^2 (29.8m^2).

had a relatively short 80in (2.03m) diameter metal tube as its fuselage with a mid-position 60° delta wing and an all-moving half-delta vertical fin, the new fuselage being necessary to supply the volume of air needed by the propulsion system. A large conical centre-body 'spike' was placed in the nose to house the prone pilot, set at 50° for best efficiency, with the air entering around this to feed a Westinghouse 24C jet. The ducted rocket part of the powerplant was made up with sixteen 50lb (0.22kN) thrust rocket motors that were mounted internally inside an air duct. In addition another four externally mounted 2,500lb (11.1kN) turborocket engines were available to serve as boosters, but these were later replaced by three 4,000lb (17.8kN) units when the smaller type was dropped from the Air Force's engine development program. When Curtiss foresaw delays with the 4,000lb rocket's development, these boosters were

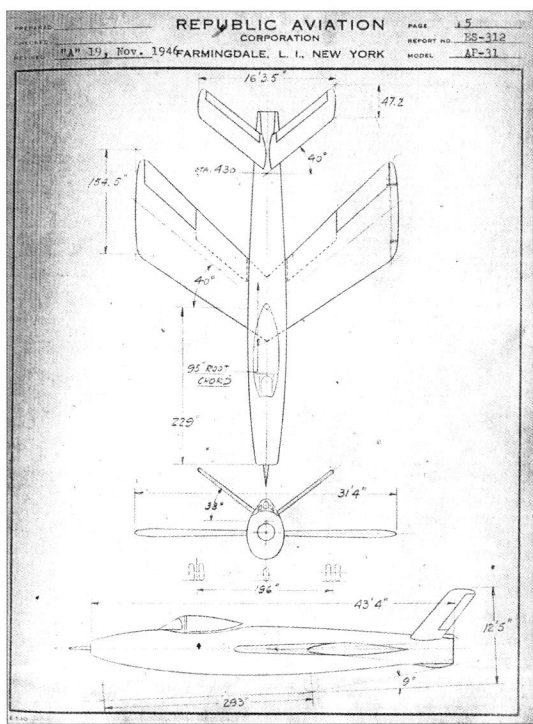

The First Air Force Jets

25

changed again to RMI 6,000 lb (26.7kN) rockets. The 24C was also taken out when it became clear that the XP-92 might be able to reach speeds and altitudes at which this jet would be unable to function properly, and the main powerplant was much altered during the design process. The 24C was replaced by a midget racing car engine to supply hydraulic and electric power.

XP-92's all-metal wing would use multi-spars and spanwise stiffeners beneath heavy sheet skins. The fuselage was also all-metal and the rear section of the latter formed the ramjet tailpipe. Maximum thickness/chord ratio was 6.5% and the wing had full-span elevons. Take-off would be made using a cart that stayed on the ground but there was a tricycle undercarriage for landing (with minimal fuel on board). Early in the program it was planned to have an underfuselage fuel tank but in due course this was replaced by two massive underwing drop tanks. A total of 7,200 lb (3,266kg) of fuel would be carried internally plus another 8,792 lb (3,988kg) of rocket propellant externally, the latter to be used in the early stages of a sortie. In an emergency the whole of the forward fuselage was detachable, which was then decelerated by a parachute to allow the pilot to escape. Pilot access was by a hinged centre panel on the top of the spike centrebody and the armament, four 20mm cannon, was also housed in the spike, two to each side of the cockpit.

XP-92 was to serve as a point defence interceptor and, with its complex powerplant, was pretty well tied to its home base. It was estimated to be capable of a top speed of Mach 1.75 at 50,000ft (15,240m) and take just 3.8 minutes to get to that height from a static start; service ceiling would be 60,000ft (18,288m). Two prototypes were ordered and Wright Field gave its approval to the new program in November 1946. A full-scale flying model was also to be built to test the aerodynamics and this would be powered by an Allison J33 turbojet.

Then in August 1947 the Aircraft and Weapons Board decided that no interceptor fighter would be procured and that, for research purposes, only the experimental properties of the aircraft would be examined. When the XP-92 mock-up was inspected in April 1948 the first machine was expected to be finished in early 1949. However, in August 1948 the program was terminated, in part because of development and financial problems with the powerplant. XP-92 was technically a very complex aircraft and one report acknowledged that it was a 'manned recoverable ramjet missile'. In December 1948 the National Advisory Committee for Aeronautics (NACA) stated that it did not consider the design to be a representative supersonic configuration because the diameter of its fuselage was large compared to the wingspan. Previously, during the mock-up examination, representatives of the Flight Test Division at HQ Air Material Command had also noted 'the airplane in its present configuration is highly impractical for any use other than a research aircraft'.

Convair XF-92A Dart

Work however, did continue on the conventionally powered full-scale flying model that was known in-house as the Model 7002, then Model 115 and finally as Model 1 in Convair's new numbering system. It was officially designated XP-92, thus taking the now vacant number, but this was changed to XF-92A in mid-1949. In today's world this research aircraft would have been given an X-Plane designation. The prototype was first proposed by Convair in September 1946 at the same time as the change was made to a delta wing on the interceptor, and it was ordered in November. It had the J33 engine used by the Lockheed F-80 Shooting Star plus many other 'off-the-shelf' parts from other aircraft, including the undercarriage and ejection seat. Construction work began at the Vultee Division at Downey but this facility was closed in 1947 and the part-complete airframe was then moved to San Diego, which brought a substantial delay.

The XF-92A made its maiden flight on 9th June 1948 (in fact a two-mile [3-km] 'hop' at Muroc) and then its official first flight was completed on 18th September. It was the world's first delta wing jet aircraft and, although underpowered, proved to be a successful technology demonstrator. Later an afterburning version of the engine was fitted which required a rather longer tail pipe. The XF-92A continued to be used for research flights until October 1953, paving the way for the Convair fighters that followed, but once the XF-92 interceptor had been abandoned, no further consideration was given to developing a service aircraft out of the research machine. Late in 1951, when Convair and the Air Force were negotiating for the building of the F-102 (Chapter Three), some consideration was given to rebuilding the XF-92A as a flying prototype for the new interceptor. It was decided that re-building and redesigning the XF-92A for this purpose would not be economically sound because of the many changes that would be required.

Republic XF-91 Thunderceptor

Although Convair's design was the winner of the interceptor competition, Republic's project was also ordered as an experimental type and covered by MX809. An initial contract was placed for two prototypes in March 1946, the aircraft being designated XP-91 (later XF-91) and subsequently named Thunderceptor. One proposed configuration had two large wing tanks on the inverse-taper wing and also a V-tail. However, a conventional tailplane was in place for the XF-91's first flight on 9th May 1949, but the butterfly V-tail was flight tested later in the program and one prototype also received a nose radome with the intake placed underneath. The original Curtiss-Wright rocket motor was cancelled and on the XP-91 it was replaced by a less powerful Reaction Motors XLR11-RM-9 giving 1,500 lb (6.7kN) of thrust per chamber (6,000 lb

The first Republic XF-91 seen on a test flight over Southern California.

Artist's impression of the Republic F-91A. It features a solid nose and fuselage-mounted NACA-style air intakes, there is a V-tail plus built-in rocket motors. Another model of this project shows a conventional fin and horizontal tail (as per the XF-91 at initial roll-out) and near identical intakes but placed further back level with the cockpit. Cradle of Aviation Museum

[26.7kN] in total). Flight testing showed that the unusual wing worked very well and did indeed reduce wingtip stalling.

There were plans to build an F-91A interceptor with a radar in the nose. A mock-up of the XF-91A shows an F-86D-style nose with a radome above and an intake beneath it. However, production machines were apparently to have a solid nose and side intakes. The type was seen as an interim interceptor to fill the gap prior to the arrival of Convair's F-102 program (Chapter Three), but the project was halted in October 1951 after the full-size mock-up had been inspected. After a decision was taken to speed up the F-102's arrival the F-91A was cancelled, although the two XF-91s were kept flying to serve as high-speed armament test vehicles. Given its plethora of new features – variable incidence wing, inverse taper, mixed powerplant – the XF-91 was a remarkably successful 'technology demonstrator' (as we would call it nowadays).

Other Projects and Developments

Boeing Model 449

Of all of the manufacturers who received the three principal documents for new fighter types, Boeing was the only one to decline to submit official proposals. The company claimed at the time that it had 'no particular interest in developing fighter aircraft' but, in mid-1945 it did draw a private interceptor proposal called the Model 449. This had a nose intake feeding two Westinghouse 24C engines placed side-by-side in the rear fuselage, four guns in the nose, a high swept wing and a V-tail. No orders were placed. There was also a forward-swept wing version.

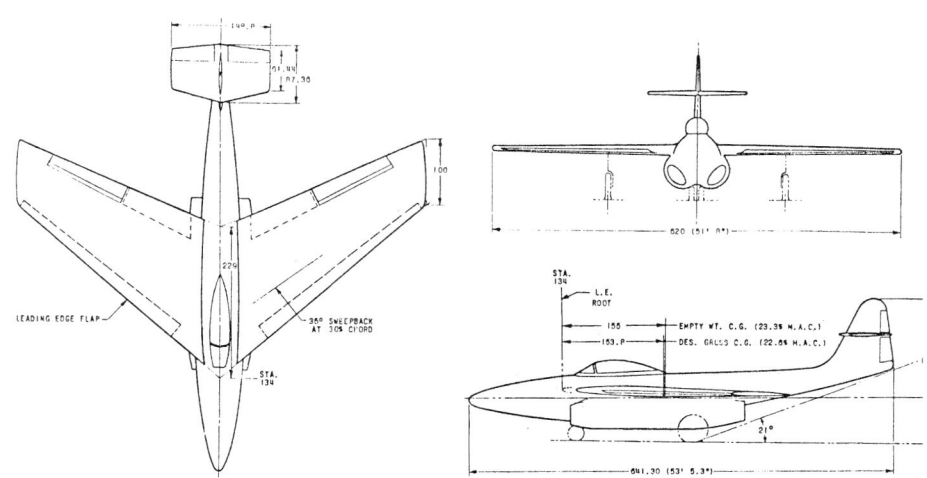

Northrop 'F-89 Swept Wing Fighter' (30.9.49). Gerald Balzer

The First Air Force Jets

Northrop Swept Wing 'Super' Scorpion

Another proposed Scorpion development saw a return to the swept wing (some sources have called the type 'Super Scorpion'). The single seat 'F-89 Swept Wing Fighter' was presented in a company brochure as an all-weather interceptor on 30th September 1949 and showed an F-89 fuselage fitted with a wing swept 35° at 30% chord. This had 'Krueger'-type leading edge flaps, inner trailing edge split flaps and combined outer wing ailerons/speed brakes. While the tail showed little change from the standard aircraft the horizontal tail was clipped substantially to a span of 12ft 6in (3.8m), reducing area by 25%. 'Useful load' was given as 10,522 lb (4,773kg) and the fighter could carry 1,350gal (6,138lit) of fuel internally plus another 1,200gal (5,456lit) externally in jettisonable tanks mounted on struts beneath the wing. A second crewman could be included if required and six 20mm cannon in the nose formed the primary armament, but alternative removable noses would be available with thirty-six 2.75in (7.0cm) rocket projectiles, or photo-reconnaissance cameras. Estimated sea level rate of climb without the afterburner operating was 13,700ft/min (4,176m/min), with afterburner 35,100ft/min (10,698m/min), time to 50,000ft (15,240m) 9.1 minutes, combat range with maximum fuel 2,650 miles (4,264km) and service ceiling 66,460ft (20,257m).

Early USAF Fighter Designs in Perspective

The pressures to produce the first jet fighters for the US forces resulted in three highly successful designs, the F-80 and the later F-84 family and the outstanding F-86. Pushing beyond these into the next generation proved a major challenge. In retrospect it is a challenge that the available technology – particularly with regard to engine development – wasn't really capable of meeting. Nevertheless the competitive tendering process produced a wealth of innovative design thinking and this work, and the research that accompanied it, laid the foundation for the future success of the US fighter industry.

Post-War USAF Jet Fighters – Estimated Data

Project	Span ft in (m)	Length ft in (m)	Gross Wing Area ft² (m²)	Gross Weight lb (kg)	Engine lb (kN)	Max Speed / Height mph (km/h) / ft (m)	Armament
All-Weather Fighters							
Curtiss-Wright XF-87 Blackhawk (flown)	60 0 (18.3)	65 6 (20.0)	600 (55.8)	49,687 (22,538)	4 x Westinghouse J34-7 3,200 (14.2)	583 (938) at S/L	4 x 20mm cannon. Also bombs up to 1,000 lb (454kg) weight on wingtips
Northrop XF-89 Scorpion (prototype – flown)	52 0 (15.8)	50 6 (15.4)	606 (56.4)	43,910 (19,918)	2 x Allison J35-A-9 4,000 (17.8)	566 (911) at S/L, 527 (848) at 35,000 (10,668)	4 x 20mm cannon. (16 x 0.5in [12.7mm]) RP on early production)
Penetration Fighters							
Lockheed L-167-2 (Typical Figures)	35 0 (10.7)	43 2 (13.2)	586 (54.5)	27,000 (12,247)	2 x Westinghouse 24-C 7,000 (31.1) ab	727 (1,170) at S/L, 672 (1,081) at 35,000 (10,668)	6 guns
Northrop XP-79Z	31 8 (9.7)	19 5 (5.9)	200 (18.6)	6,555 (2,973)	1 x Westinghouse 24-C (J34) 3,200 (14.2)	630 (1,014) at S/L, 570 (917) at 45,000 (13,716)	4 x 0.5in (12.7mm) machine guns
Lockheed XF-90A (flown – second prototype)	39 11.5 (12.2)	56 2.5 (17.1)	350 (32.6)	29,427 (13,348)	2 x Westinghouse 24-C (XJ34-WE-15) 3,600 (16.0), 4,200 (18.7) ab	668 (1,075) at 1,000 (305)	6 x 20mm cannon
McDonnell XF-88 (flown)	39 8 (12.1)	54 1.5 (16.5)	350 (32.6)	18,500 (8,392)	2 x Westinghouse 24-C (XJ34-WE-15) 3,600 (16.0), 4,200 (18.7) ab (XF-88A)	641 (1,031) at S/L (XF-88A)	6 x 20mm cannon. 2 x 1,000 lb (454kg) bombs or 8 x 0.5in (12.7mm) rockets
North American YF-93 (flown)	38 11 (11.9)	44 1 (13.4)	306 (28.5)	21,610 (9,802)	1 x P&W J48-P-6 6,000 (26.7), 8,750 (38.9) ab	708 (1,139) at S/L, 622 (1,001) at 35,000 (10,668)	6 x 20mm cannon 2 x 1,000 lb (454kg) bombs or 8 x 0.5in (12.7mm) rockets
Vought V-367	38 9 (11.8)	46 7.5 (14.2)	520.7 (48.4)	32,914 (14,930)	1 x Westinghouse XJ40-WE-10 9,500 (42.2), 12,350 (54.9) ab	700 (1,126) at S/L, 623 (1,002) at 35,000 (10,668)	4 x 20mm cannon or 2 x 20mm plus air-to-air rockets
Interceptor Fighters							
Northrop XP-79Z	31 8 (9.7)	19 5 (5.9)	200 (18.6)	10,000 (4,536)	1 x Rocket Motor ?	650 (1,046) at S/L, 695 (1,118) at 45,000 (13,716)	4 x 0.5in (12.7mm) machine guns
Convair XP-92 Delta (as ordered)	31 4 (9.5)	38 1 (11.6)	425 (39.5)	29,534 (13,397) w/o t/off cart	See Text	1,165 (1,874) at 50,000 (15,240)	4 x 20mm cannon
Convair XF-92A Dart (flown)	31 3 (9.5)	42 5 (12.9)	425 (39.5)	14,398 (6,531)	1 x Allison J33-A-29 5,200 (23.1), 7,500 (33.3) ab	718 (1,155) at S/L, 655 (1,054) at 35,000 (10,668)	None fitted (4 x 20mm cannon considered)
Republic XF-91 (flown)	31 4 (9.55)	43 4 (13.2)	320 (29.8)	19,825 (8,993)	1 x Gen Elec J47-GE-3 5,200 (23.1) + 4 x Reaction Motors XLR11-RM-9 rockets 1,500 (6.7)	1,126 (1,812) at height	4 x 20mm cannon (not fitted) 4 guns
Boeing Model 449	30 0 (9.1)	39 5 (12.0)	?	8,660 (3,928)	2 x Westinghouse 24-C 3,200 (14.2)	?	
Northrop Swept Wing Scorpion	51 8 (15.7)	53 5 (16.3)	710 (66.0)	39,114 (17,742)	2 x Allison 450-E1 10,000 (44.4), 15,000 (66.7) ab	731 (1,175) at S/L	6 x 20mm cannon, 36 x 2.75in (7.0cm) rockets

Chapter Two

The First Navy Jets

This Douglas F4D-1 Skyray was photographed flying from USS Forrestal on 11th October 1958 whilst serving with VF-102. It carries Sidewinders and drop tanks.

While the Air Force was developing and acquiring its first jet fighters the US Navy was making its own entry into the jet era, albeit somewhat more cautiously. As already described, the Army Air Force had acquired its first jet aircraft in something of a random manner, before adopting a more systematic approach and introducing competitions for specific new types of fighter. Much the same happened with the Navy. It initially acquired rapidly produced jet aircraft that added to experience rather than operational capability but, by 1945/46, the Navy's views on what it needed had become clearer. The Service issued three new specifications for fighter types – a day fighter, a carrier-based night fighter and a long-range escort fighter – to be followed in 1947 by another requirement for a carrier-based interceptor. All of this was intended to upgrade the Service's airborne capability. Any review of the Navy's entry into the jet age therefore needs to look at both the early – in many ways, stopgap – designs and the response to the various open competitions.

The US Navy became aware as early as 1943 that it must have jet-powered aircraft in its inventory and that it needed to move quickly if it was not to be left behind. Consequently in August of that year it ordered the prototype of a conventional straight-wing fighter from McDonnell, the FD-1 Phantom The first example made its maiden flight on 26th January 1945. In some ways this was a surprising choice of supplier: McDonnell was a new manufacturer as far as the Navy was concerned and indeed had only built one other fighter, the piston XP-67, for the USAAF. However, the design proved to be reasonably successful and when one hundred production machines were ordered in March 1945, it became necessary to allocate a new designation letter specifically for McDonnell to prevent the 'D' clashing with designs from Douglas. The letter allocated was 'H' and in 1947 the XFD-1 and production FD-1s became the XFH-1 and FH-1 respectively.

Less surprisingly perhaps, the Navy also quickly turned to a more established fighter manufacturer for a new aircraft: North American Aviation. However, whilst the Air Force was to order an advanced swept-wing fighter from the company – the outstanding F-86 – the Navy opted initially for a more conservative approach. It ordered the tubby, straight-winged FJ-1 Fury. In fact the first F-86 design also had a straight wing, but the Air Force had that replaced before the first flight. Subsequently the Navy would go on to order a version of the F-86 heavily adapted for carrier use. The FJ-2 Fury was very similar in appear-

American Secret Projects: Fighters & Interceptors

The straight-winged North American FJ-1 Fury.

An example of the ultimate North American Fury, an FJ-4.

Both of McDonnell's first two jet fighters are shown in this picture. An FD-1 Phantom sits behind the second XF2D-1 Banshee prototype 99859. These aircraft were soon redesignated FH-1 and XF2H-1.

ance to the F-86, but further developments followed. The final version, the FJ-4 had a taller fin and much deeper fuselage and was a very capable, highly adapted carrier-borne aircraft. In all, over a thousand Furies were built and they served right through the 1950s.

Hedging its bets, the Navy also opted for a third early design: the Chance Vought F6U Pirate. This was first flown on 2nd October 1946 but it proved to have a disappointing performance, and by the time the first of thirty production machines finally appeared in 1949 the type was already out of date.

Although the Navy appreciated the need to keep up to date with jet fighters, it was also somewhat sceptical in its approach because it anticipated some unique problems associated with operating jet aircraft from carriers. One would undoubtedly have been the much slower response of early jet engines to throttle changes. As a result several fighter projects were also pursued that used a combination of both propeller and jet powerplants. This continued for several years after the war, resulting in aircraft like the Ryan FR-1 Fireball.

Given the novelty of jet propulsion, the unproven reliability of jet engines and the higher operating speeds of the aircraft – even more so once you bent the wings back – the Navy's early caution was not necessarily unreasonable. It was echoed across the Atlantic by the Royal Navy, which was also slow to embrace high-performance jets. However, the competitive bids for the next generation of Naval fighters would result in some much more adventurous proposals, but before moving onto the Navy's new fighter design competitions there is one more private venture fighter which can be considered almost as a true post-war type. There is also a single design from Grumman on which work had begun before the end of the war.

McDonnell F2D-1/F2H-1 Banshee

Although the FD-1 Phantom had proved a disappointment, McDonnell was clear how it could be improved. Prototypes of a follow-on fighter were ordered in March 1945 just a couple of weeks after the FD-1 production contract had been placed. Still straight-winged, the XF2D-1 (which quickly became XF2H-1) was to be a much heavier 'big brother' to the Phantom. A much more capable machine, it had more powerful engines and greater all-round performance, and had cannons instead of machine guns. The first prototype flew on 11th January 1947 and substantial production orders followed, with later marks receiving a radar, which added an all-weather role to the type's capability. As the F2H Banshee, versions of McDonnell's second Navy jet fighter served in the front line until 1959 and with second-line units right up to the mid-1960s. In 1962 the Banshee was redesignated F-2 in a new Tri-Service set of numbering sequences introduced in an attempt to simplify the overall system.

Grumman Design 71

In November 1944 Grumman completed a design for a small single-seat, jet-engined, carrier-based, high performance fighter. Design 71, or G-71, had a full cantilever mid-position wing with no wing-fold facility, dive recovery flaps on the underside of each wing, and ailerons and slotted flaps. All of the flying surfaces were to be built in aluminium alloy, as was the fuselage, and there was a tricycle undercarriage with the main units set outside the intakes and retracting outwards (the main gear was also used as an airbrake). Power would come from a Westinghouse 24C unit rated at 3,000 lb (13.3kN) thrust with air supplied by intakes in the wing roots angled into the fuselage. Four 20mm cannon were mounted across the nose and an alternative installation of six 0.5in (12.7mm) machine guns was also available.

Normal internal fuel load was 350gal (1,591lit) giving a gross weight of 8,794lb (3,989kg), although a maximum overload with 610gal (2,773lit) of internal fuel was also quoted for a top weight of 10,426 lb (4,729kg). Two fuel tanks were available, both situated behind the cockpit, but there was no capacity for carrying external fuel. At the 'normal' weight the G-71's rate of climb at sea level was 4,930ft/min (1,503m/min), and 2,225ft/min (678m/min) at 20,000ft (6,096m), and the estimated time to get to 20,000ft was 5.9 minutes. Service ceiling would be 40,000ft (12,192m), combat radius 348 miles (560km) and maximum range (at 30,000ft [9,144m] altitude) 1,461 miles (2,351km). In retrospect the G-71 sounded promising, and the reason why it was rejected is not clear.

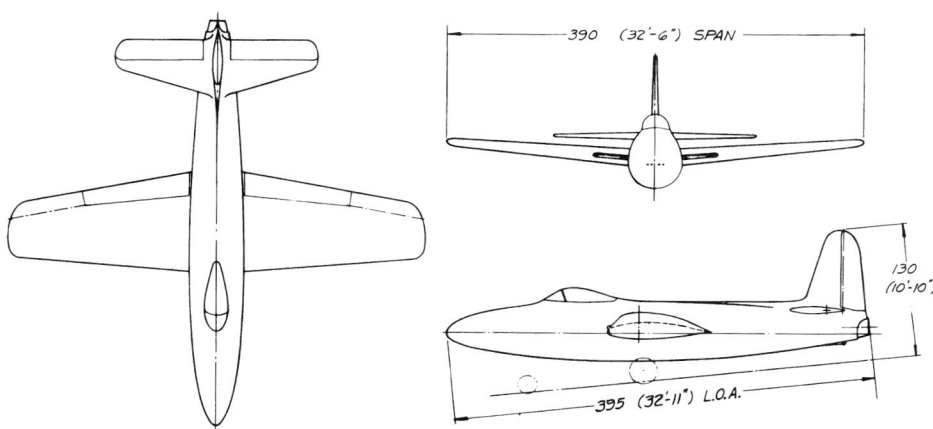

The Grumman G-71 project (11.44). Grumman Corporation / Grumman History Centre

Two views showing a model of the very neat little Grumman G-71 jet fighter. Grumman Corporation / Grumman History Centre

The First Navy Jets

A New Carrier-Based Night Fighter

The memoirs of George A Spangenberg – who was deeply involved in the specification and evaluation of Naval Designs over many years – report that, during the War, the Navy 'had no design competitions, but rather initiated new aircraft by direct negotiation with both our major and minor producers. With the war's outcome no longer in doubt, we returned to our normal method of aircraft acquisition'. The first fighter competition – the first in fact since a 1941 contest was won by the Grumman F7F Tigercat – was for a night fighter primarily for use aboard aircraft carriers. It called for a top speed of at least 500mph (805km/h) and the ability to intercept an enemy aircraft, even in poor weather conditions or at night, a minimum of 125 miles (201km) away at an altitude of 40,000ft (12,192m); a secondary mission was to be the destruction of ground and waterborne targets at night. For storage on carriers the maximum folded span had to be 46ft (14.0m) and the manufacturers were left to choose their powerplant. The document was released to industry in August 1945 and the major responses are described below. Curtiss and Kaiser-Fleetwings also offered projects but no information is available for these designs.

Convair (Vultee) Night Fighter

The Convair (Vultee) proposal was a straight-winged aircraft powered by three jet engines. It had a wing area of 380ft² (35.3m²) and a gross weight of 25,000 lb (11,340kg). The estimated maximum speed was 561mph (902km/h). It is understood that engines would have been mounted in wing pods, so it seems likely that the third unit would have been placed in the fuselage.

Douglas D-561

The Douglas D-561 was a twin-engined straight-wing project with two Westinghouse 24C power units mounted on the fuselage sides beneath the wing roots.

Grumman G-75

This Grumman twin-engine design was, in its appearance, a jet-powered development of the Tigercat. It was to have a mid-position full cantilever wing with overhead folding, built entirely in aluminium alloy (folded span was 30ft 0in [9.1m]). The ailerons on the outer wing had internal sealed pressure balances while the inner wing's slotted flaps had a pre-selected position control. Dive recovery flaps were provided on the undersurface of each wing. The rudder was also designed to act as a speed-reducing device. It could be split in a similar way to a double split flap, the maximum angle between the two 'flaps' being 120°. The drag device would also continue to act as a rudder and the sides of the fuselage below the horizontal tail could also open up in a fashion similar to the rudder. The combination of these drag devices was calculated to give a maximum deceleration of 0.4G. Operated by the pilot's brake pedals when the landing gear was retracted, the degree of deceleration was fully controllable, just like wheel brakes.

Both tail and fin were all-metal, and so was the fuselage which was flush jointed and flush riveted. However, the extreme nose and tail of the fuselage, in the vicinity of the radar antenna, would be constructed in a plastic material. The radar would be housed in the nose and the two crew were seated side-by-side just behind. Outboard of the fuselage and slung beneath each wing was a nacelle containing two Westinghouse 24C engines, with the main landing gear of the tricycle undercarriage in between them. The inboard 24C-4 'main powerplant' engines in each nacelle were identical to the outboard 24C-6 'booster' engines, except for some accessory drives. Two 20mm cannon were located below the jet units on each nacelle to either side of the main gear, while the nosewheel was placed beneath the cockpit with a much longer leg than the main wheels to give a nose-high attitude on the ground.

G-75's rate of climb at a combat weight of 22,944lb (10,407kg) (with 860gal [3,910lit] of fuel aboard) was estimated to be 11,400ft/min (3,475m/min) at sea level and 4,170ft/min (1,271m/min) at 30,000ft (9,144m), and the time taken to reach that height would have been about 4.2 minutes. Maximum fuel load was 1,530gal (6,957lit), housed in three fuselage tanks behind the cockpit, which offered a combat radius of 447 miles (719km) and a maximum range at 30,000ft of 2,000 miles (3,218km). The aircraft's endurance was expected to be 6.14 hours with this load and there was no provision for external droppable tanks.

The designs from Grumman and Douglas were selected as the best and orders were placed in April 1946 for prototypes of what were to be the XF9F-1N and XF3D-1 respectively. During the design process Grumman's G-75 was altered in several ways whilst still retaining the basic layout, and ended up with a revised span of 55ft 6in (16.9m), length 50ft 5in (15.4m) and wing area 569ft² (52.9m²). To the Service assessors, Grumman's choice of a four-engine powerplant was a surprise when compared to the other proposals. Quoting from George Spangenberg's archives discussing the contrasting approaches from Douglas and Grumman, 'the very different design solutions were due to the definition of the combat portion of the design mission for the airplane. Historically, all previous problems had required maximum thrust/power to be used but in this competition, the combat position was specified to be at 400mph (644km), well below the maximum speed of the Grumman design. This came about due to the project officer's insistence that any higher speed could not be used tactically at night with the radar then available and guns as

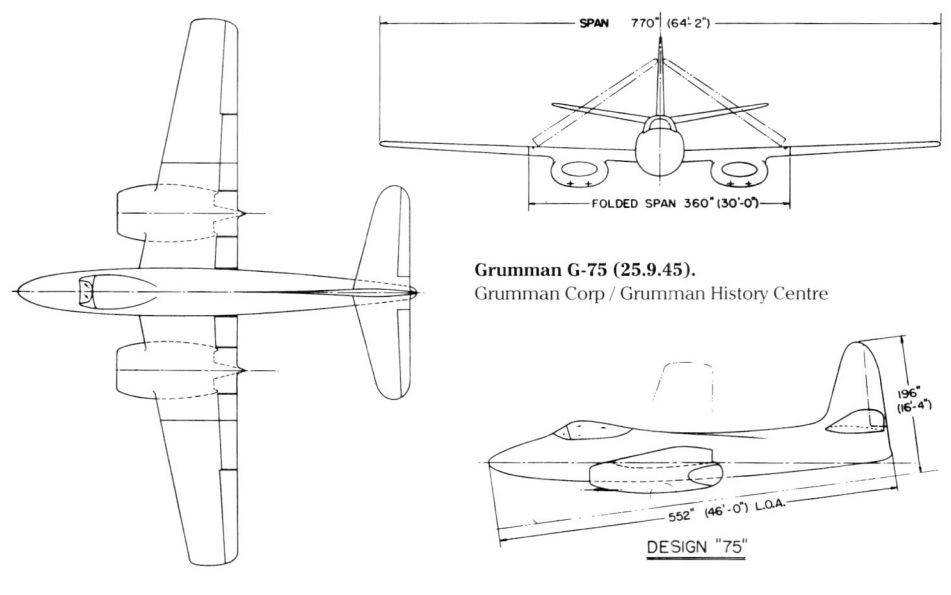

Grumman G-75 (25.9.45).
Grumman Corp / Grumman History Centre

Artist's impression of the Grumman G-75 which shows nicely the split intakes on each nacelle, giving an individual air supply to each of the fighter's four engines. Note also two 20mm cannon mounted in the bottom of each nacelle. Grumman Corporation / Grumman History Centre

armament. If full power was used for combat the Grumman design was woefully short-legged.'

It was during the early fall of 1946 that it was realized that Grumman's night fighter would possess insufficient performance and so during September the contract was changed to cover a new single-seat single-engined fighter bomber from the same manufacturer, designated XF9F-2. The XF9F-1 was cancelled on 9th October but Douglas's night fighter was taken through into production.

Douglas F3D Skynight

To avoid confusion with McDonnell's F2D Banshee, Douglas's night fighter was designated F3D-1 and the first of three XF3D-1 prototypes made its maiden flight on 23rd March 1948. The first production aircraft flew in February 1950 and the type served in the Korean War and through much of the 1950s. Some examples were still in service at the start of the Vietnam conflict and from April 1965 they operated in that arena as electronic countermeasures platforms (having by then been redesignated F-10). Over the years published sources have called the F3D both Skyknight and Skynight, but an original Douglas photo shows the word Skynight and so the author has assumed that to be the correct spelling. This aircraft was primarily flown by Marine Corps units.

Grumman G-79 and F9F-2 Panther

Grumman's straight wing G-79 studies were undertaken against a new requirement for a naval fighter offering a combat performance which would be superior to current experimental naval fighters, but with good takeoff and low speed handling qualities. Designs 'A' and 'B' both had a composite powerplant. The former had a British Rolls-Royce Derwent VI jet in the fuselage tail plus a Pratt & Whitney R2800-E piston at the front, giving an appearance similar to the Ryan FR-1 Fireball mentioned earlier, or Grumman's own F8U Bearcat piston fighter but with a longer fuselage and air intakes either side of the cockpit. Design 'B' was very similar except that there

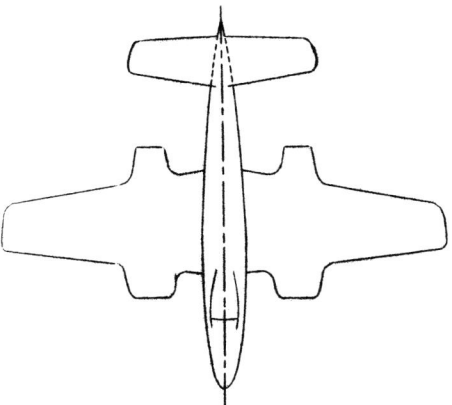
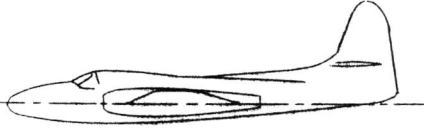

This sketch, found in the Grumman archives and labelled XF9F-1N, suggests that the aircraft would have been a little different from the original proposal had it been built. Such changes are of course typical for any new aircraft design and the biggest modification here appears to be larger engine nacelles stretching beyond a wing trailing edge which itself is no longer straight. Grumman Corporation / Grumman History Centre

Douglas F3D-2M Skynight prototype 127038. Sixteen Skynights were modified to this standard fitted with wing pylons to carry Sparrow missiles.

The First Navy Jets

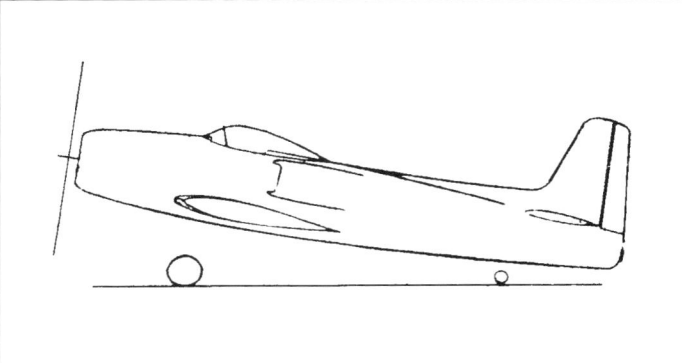
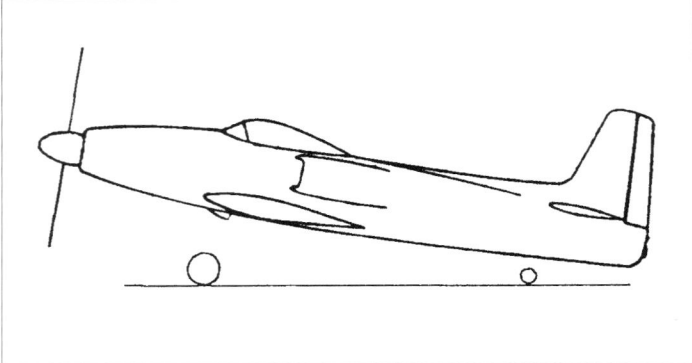

Top left: **Side view for the Grumman G-79 Design 'A' (3.46).** Grumman Corp / Grumman History Centre

Top right: **Side view for the Grumman G-79 Design 'B' (3.46).** Grumman Corp / Grumman History Centre

The straight-wing Grumman F9F Panther was the company's first jet fighter to fly. This shot shows a production F9F-2 flown by Grumman test pilot 'Corky' Meyer. Grumman Corporation / Grumman History Centre

The F9F-6 Cougar introduced swept wings and this F9F-8 variant is seen carrying four early Sidewinder air-to-air missiles plus two drop tanks.

was a nose extension to take a General Electric TG-100 turboprop rather than the piston unit. The third concept, Design 'C', was quite different because this featured two Derwent VIs in wing nacelles and a mid-fin horizontal tail; as such it looked remarkably like the British Gloster Meteor which had first flown in March 1943. Finally Design 'D' looked at a smaller aircraft powered by a single Rolls-Royce Nene jet. The estimated sea level rates of climb for these designs, with such contrasting powerplants, makes interesting reading – respectively 'A' to 'D' 7,950ft/min (2,423m/min), 9,170ft/min (2,795m/min), 10,320ft/min (3,146m/min) and 10,550ft/min (3,216m/min).

In truth both 'A' and 'B' were already obsolete concepts, the swift development of new powerplants and aerodynamics having left such configurations behind. But Grumman was very keen to proceed with Design 'C' and pushed its case strongly, the theory of having twin-engine safety on a naval type being one important argument. Grumman was less keen to develop the single-Nene Design 'D'. Despite the fact that this was one of the best and most powerful engines around at the time, it was thought that engine availability might be a problem. However, once Pratt & Whitney acquired a licence to build the Nene as the J42, the Navy selected Design 'D' for prototype testing. When it flew on 24th

November 1947 the first XF9F-2 looked little different from the original proposal (a slightly longer nose plus a larger tail pipe were the principal changes), but the third prototype was designated XF9F-3 to acknowledge the fact that it was powered by an Allison J33-A-8. Production runs followed, the new fighter bomber being named Panther, and when examples went to war over Korea in 1950 it became the Navy's first jet to go into combat.

Douglas D-601/F3D-3 'swept wing Skynight' (6.12.49).

Grumman G-93 and F9F-6 Cougar

Notwithstanding all these developments, Grumman's role in this part of the story had another interesting dimension. Very soon after the Panther prototypes had been ordered the Bureau of Aeronautics asked the manufacturer to consider a version of the aircraft fitted with either a swept or delta wing. Despite at this point having worked on swept surfaces for about a year, Grumman's response was cautious. The company felt that its research was not sufficiently advanced for a full proposal to be made. It was not until December 1950 that a swept wing Panther was finally submitted. Three prototypes were ordered during the following March to be powered by Pratt & Whitney J48 engines. This program appears to have been separate from any other naval fighter design competition and the development process was hastened by the Korean War, the type being seen as something of a stopgap to provide the Navy with a swept wing fighter capable of matching the Soviet Mikoyan MiG-15. The first machine flew on 20th September 1951 and the new aircraft was ordered into production as the F9F-6 Cougar. It was built in numbers and stayed in service long enough to be redesignated F-9 in 1962.

Douglas D-601

The idea of putting swept wings onto an already proven design was an obvious way of moving forward and the Panther was not the only Navy night fighter to be proposed for modification in this way. In late 1949 Douglas proposed fitting swept surfaces to its Skynight. The resulting D-601 had a fuselage which externally differed relatively little from the original, but the wings, tail and fin were all now swept and two Westinghouse J46-WE-4 power units had replaced the J34s. Span with wings folded was 32ft 9in (10.0m) and the internal fuel load was 7,230lb (3,280kg); another 1,800lb (816kg) could be carried in external tanks which pushed the maximum weight up to 28,885lb (13,102kg). Four cannon

Model of the Douglas D-601/F3D-3.
Allyson Vought

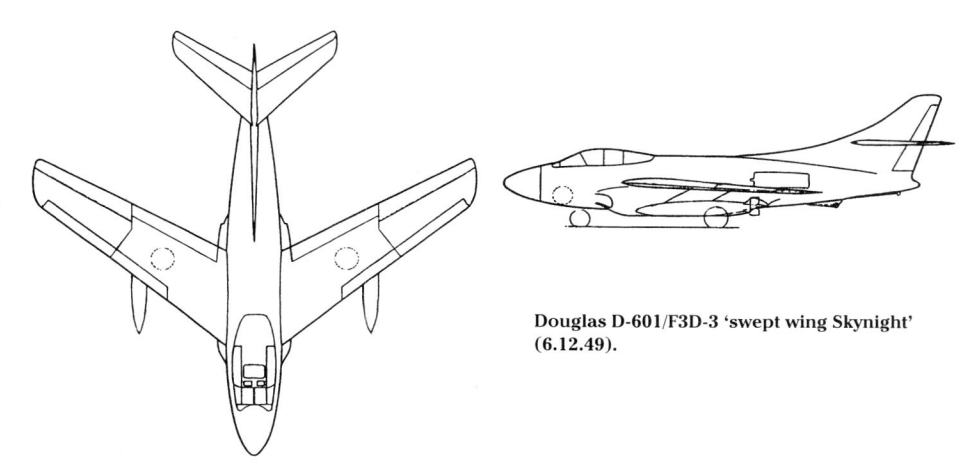

The First Navy Jets

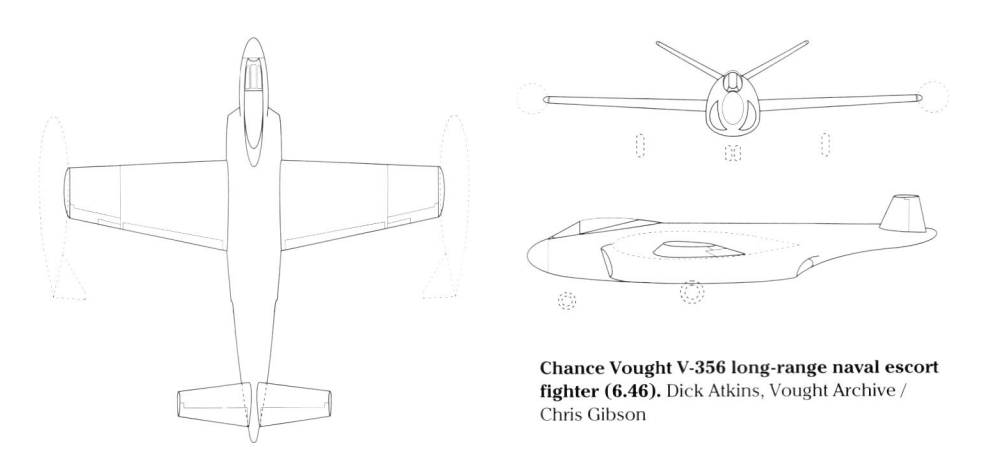

Chance Vought V-356 long-range naval escort fighter (6.46). Dick Atkins, Vought Archive / Chris Gibson

were housed in a recess under the nose. On normal internal fuel, at a weight of 25,550 lb (11,589kg), the D-601 had an estimated sea level rate of climb of 4,670ft/min (1,423m/min), it would take 9.6 minutes to reach 30,000ft (9,144m) and had a service ceiling of 43,300ft (13,198m). At the gross weight of 26,735 lb (12,127kg) with full internal fuel these figures became 4,430ft/min (1,350m/min), 10.3 minutes and 42,400ft (12,924m). An order for production aircraft, called F3D-3s, was placed in 1951 but was cancelled in February 1952: the main problem being the lack of power from the engines.

A New Carrier-Based Long-Range Escort Fighter

Another competition was held for a new carrier-based long-range escort fighter. Sadly it has proved difficult to uncover much information about this program. It appears that work began in the second half of 1946 and Convair and Vought, for certain, prepared designs. However, no hardware was produced and the specification was revised in 1947/1948. As such it was issued as OS-112 and rather more response from industry was then forthcoming. Taking the 1946 work first, no information has been traced for Convair's multi-engine 'VF' escort fighter project, but some drawings are available for Vought's proposals under its Model V-356 project.

Model of the Chance Vought V-356 fighter by John Hall.

36   American Secret Projects: Fighters & Interceptors

Chance Vought V-356

The Chance Vought project encompassed both a fighter aircraft and an attack type, the latter an entirely different layout being a turboprop-powered development of the same manufacturer's Cutlass described shortly. The fighter was a rather more conventional-looking straight-wing design although, like many early jet fighter projects, it had a V-tail. It was to be powered by the then new British AJ-65 engine being offered by Rolls-Royce (AJ-65 standing for axial jet 6,500lb [28.9kN] thrust), which after a troubled period of development successfully entered service as the Avon. The two engines were fed by individual intakes on the sides of the lower fuselage and the exhaust came though a jet pipe in the lower fuselage halfway between the wings and tail. Internal fuel totalled around 3,500gal (15,914lit) and there was the option to carry another 1,600gal (7,275lit) in two large tip tanks. The drawing gives no details of the size of the V-356's gun armament or where it would have been mounted, but the aircraft was to have had a tricycle undercarriage with twin wheels on the nose leg.

Four manufacturers appear to have shown interest in the 1948 OS-112 requirement for a new long-range naval fighter. This requested a top speed of 535mph (861km/h) at 40,000ft (12,192m), a sea level rate of climb of 5,800ft/min (1,768m/min) and a combat radius of 1,200nm (2,224km). None of the designs discussed below reached the hardware stage and in due course the concept of the long-range escort fighter was to disappear in a similar way to the Air Force's penetration fighter. This was in part due to the changing threat posed by the latest developments in Soviet Union aircraft design.

Boeing Model 482

Boeing's Model 482 was a big design with a wing swept 20° on the leading edge and a folded span of 36ft (11.0m). It had a crew of four, upper and lower search radars in fuselage pods and a tracking radar on the top of the fin. Two 20mm cannon were housed in a forward turret and two more in a tail turret. The powerplant was two Allison XT40 turboprop engines each driving 14ft (4.3m) diameter contra-rotating propellers with eight blades on each nacelle. A bicycle undercarriage was to be used, supported by outriggers in the engine nacelles, the forward twin wheel main gears being placed beneath the cockpit and the rear set roughly halfway between the wing and tailplane. At 41,350lb (18,756kg) weight the limiting dive speed was given as 510mph (821km/h), maximum speed at 40,000ft (12,192m) was 506mph (814km/h) and sea level rate of climb 6,300ft/min (1,920m/min); at the aircraft's gross weight the equivalent rate of climb was 5,450ft/min (1,661m/min). Range was 1,940 miles (3,121km), service ceiling in excess of 45,000ft (13,716m) and maximum internal fuel 1,995gal (9,071lit). Comments in an official document show that the Model 482 did not meet the specification requirements with regard to either speed at altitude or range.

Chance Vought V-363 and Douglas D-585

No information has been traced for the relevant Chance Vought or Douglas projects, although they are known to have been under study in January and April 1948 respectively.

Lockheed L-180

The Lockheed L-180 project number covered five designs, although the L-180-5 carrier-based bomber was presented as an addendum to the brochure for a type that, under most operational conditions, would not be expected to need any fighter escort. The layout, which was designed directly against OS-112, was the L-180-2 and this had a crew of four and shared much in common with Boeing's proposal. There was 20° of sweep on the leading edge and power again came from twin turboprops, this time with 13ft (4.0m) diameter contra-rotating eight-blade propellers. Nose and tail turrets each housed two 20mm cannon, but this aircraft did have a tricycle undercarriage with twin wheels on the nose gear. The wings could fold rearwards with the hinge point just outboard of the engine nacelles and it had very small tip ailerons with spoilers inboard; folded span was 33ft 0in (10.1m). Two large fuselage tanks behind the cockpit housed 777gal (3,533lit) and 877gal (3,988lit) of fuel respectively and the upper and lower radars were fitted between these and the rear fuselage.

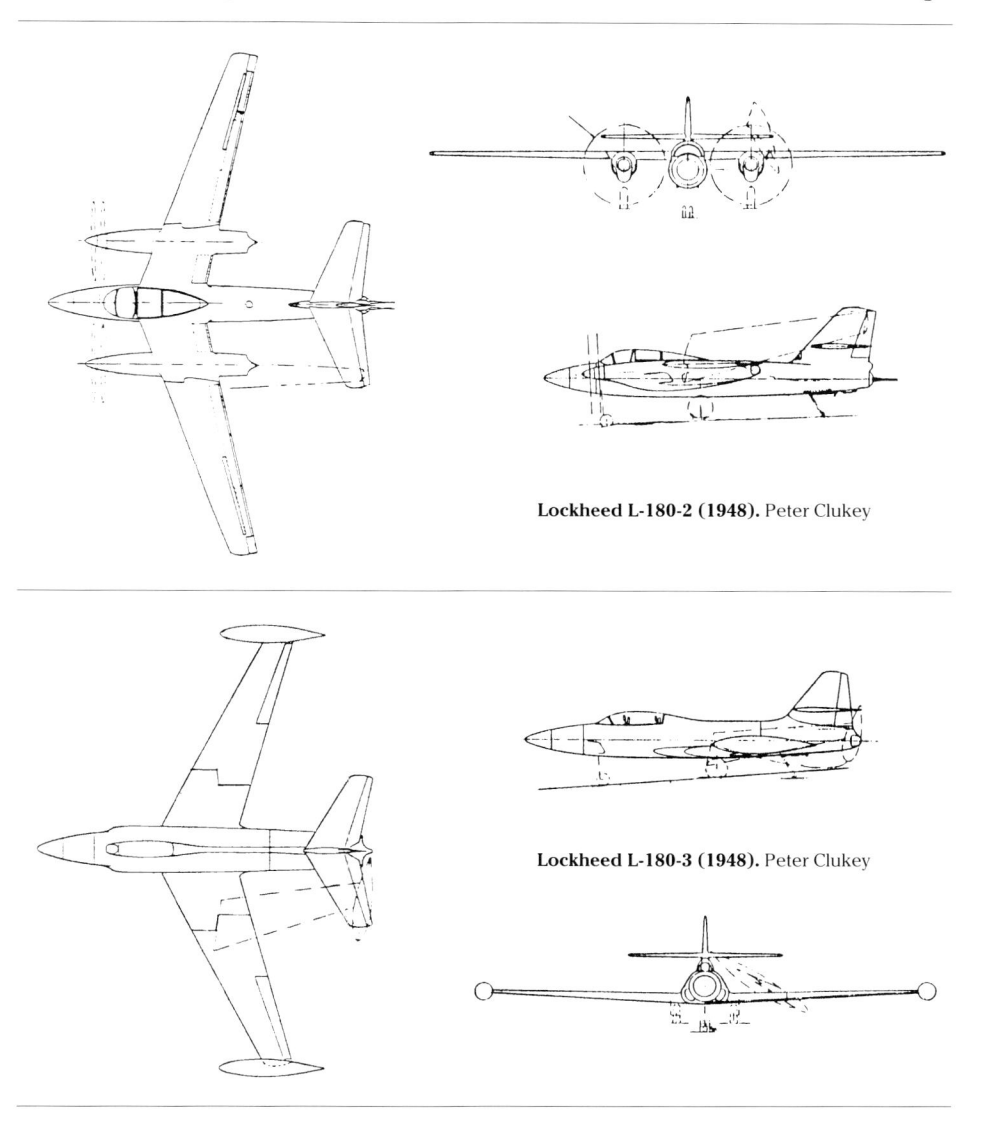

Lockheed L-180-2 (1948). Peter Clukey

Lockheed L-180-3 (1948). Peter Clukey

The First Navy Jets

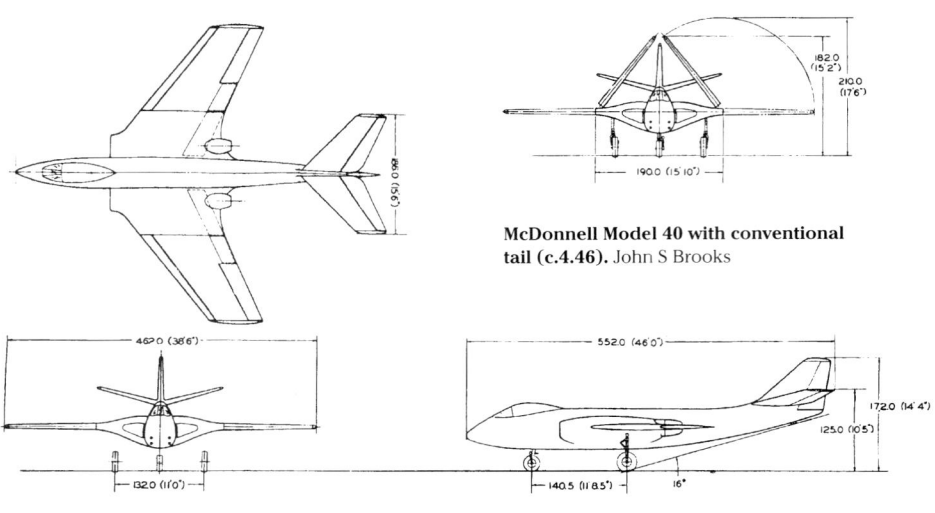

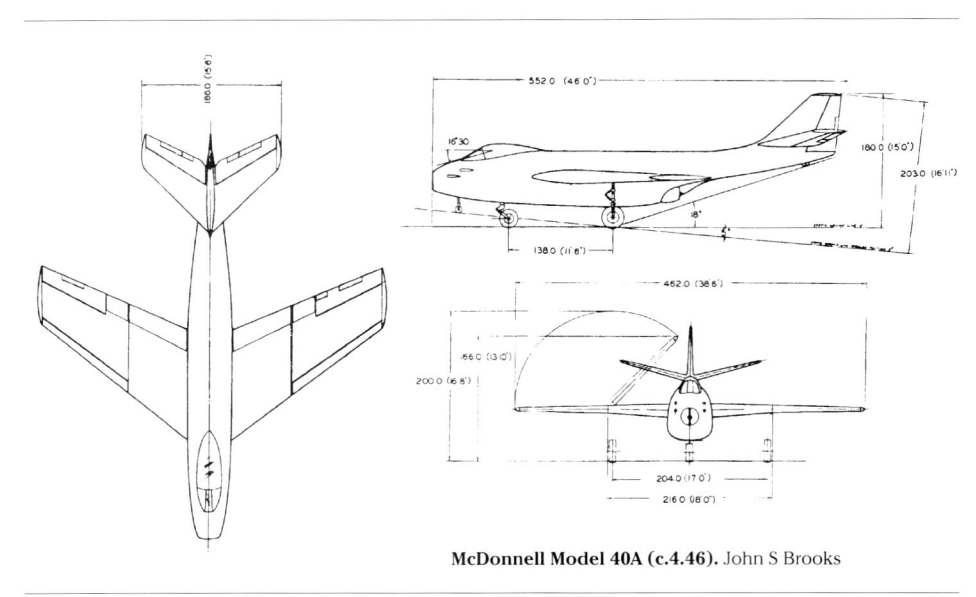

Martin Model 235 (c4.46). Stan Piet, GLMMAM

Lockheed concluded, as one suspects did other manufacturers, that the L-180-2 idea was just too large and too heavy for operations aboard all but the largest carriers, but a smaller, lighter and faster jet fighter might satisfy the requirements and mission. As an alternative Lockheed included two further proposals called the L-180-3 and L-180-4. The former was a compromise two-seat design of lower weight but offering less range. In appearance it was similar to an F-80 Shooting Star but had a longer more pointed nose, much longer wings swept 25° on the leading edge (with tip tanks) and a nose turret. Power came from two Westinghouse 24C-10 jets with afterburners and the L-180-3's span was 69ft 4in (21.1m), length 63ft 4in (19.3m) and wing area 600ft^2 (55.8m^2). Internal fuel totalled 1,900gal (8,639lit) and another 600gal (2,728lit) could be carried externally. The L-180-4 was an even more simplified effort which, essentially, was the XF-90 described in Chapter One but with more wing and tail area.

A New Carrier-Based Day Fighter

The competition for a new carrier-based day fighter was described by George Spangenberg as 'the Navy's first real fighter design competition after the war'. This was indeed quite a big contest. The term 'real fighter' is assumed to have meant a type capable of air combat and dogfighting and the new aircraft had to be capable of reaching a top speed of at least 600mph (965km/h) and altitudes around 40,000ft (12,192m); it would also be a single-seater. In general the proposals came in two sizes powered either by Westinghouse J34 (24C) engines or General Electric/Allison J35s (TG-180): small and large engines respectively. The requirement generated twelve submissions, all of which had to be delivered by April 1946. No details could be uncovered for the Curtiss-Wright and North American designs but the other submissions were as follows.

Douglas D-565

The Douglas D-565 was a three-engine project completed in late March 1946.

Martin Model 235

It is uncertain if the Model 235 was Martin's submission to the fighter competition, but it is the only entry in that company's project list that fits the description and timescale. This relatively small design had a long, slim body

McDonnell Model 40 with conventional tail (c.4.46). John S Brooks

McDonnell Model 40A (c.4.46). John S Brooks

with power being provided by two engines, one in a pod beneath the lower forward fuselage and the second in the rear fuselage. The latter appears to receive its air supply from a slim intake on the back of the fuselage. Both wings and tail were swept and two cannon were mounted on each side of the lower forward fuselage.

McDonnell Models 40 and 40A

This set of McDonnell designs were all powered by two Westinghouse 24C engines and clearly related to the Phantom and Banshee family. The most obvious advance was that they had swept flying surfaces. Leading and trailing edge flaps were fitted to the wing as high lift devices, the wing itself being swept 35° on the ¼ chord line. Model 40 had the engines mounted in the wing roots while Model 40A had them inside a wider fuselage. The former's four 20mm cannon were mounted in the lower nose while the 40A saw the guns moved to a higher position to avoid the nose intake. There was a tricycle undercarriage and also a version of Model 40 fitted with a V-tail, all three projects having the same span, length and wing area. The 'conventional' Model 40 had three fuel tanks, containing 290gal (1,319lit), 350gal (1,591lit) and 340gal (1,546lit) respectively. These filled almost the entire middle fuselage while the 40A had to have the two engines underneath these tanks.

Chance Vought V-346

A series of four layouts was covered by Vought's V-346 designation, design work having begun in 1945. The dimensions for these designs are uncertain but all were to be powered by Westinghouse J34s. The first, the V-346A, was a tailless twin-fin design, the decision to leave off the horizontal tail prompted by the need to deal with problems of compressibility that were expected at the high speeds flown by the aircraft (Mach 0.9+). The power units were housed side-by-side in the rear fuselage with the fins placed on the rear of the inner wing trailing edge. The lack of elevators was countered by having 'ailevators' on the outer wings, which would perform the jobs of both the ailerons and elevators, while slats mounted on the wing leading edge gave the assistance at slow speeds that would normally be provided by flaps.

The V-346B was a much more conventional-looking creation, still with two engines fuselage-mounted side-by-side but now with a swept wing and a horizontal tail (placed in the mid-fin position). It also reverted to more conventional flying surfaces. V-346C was the

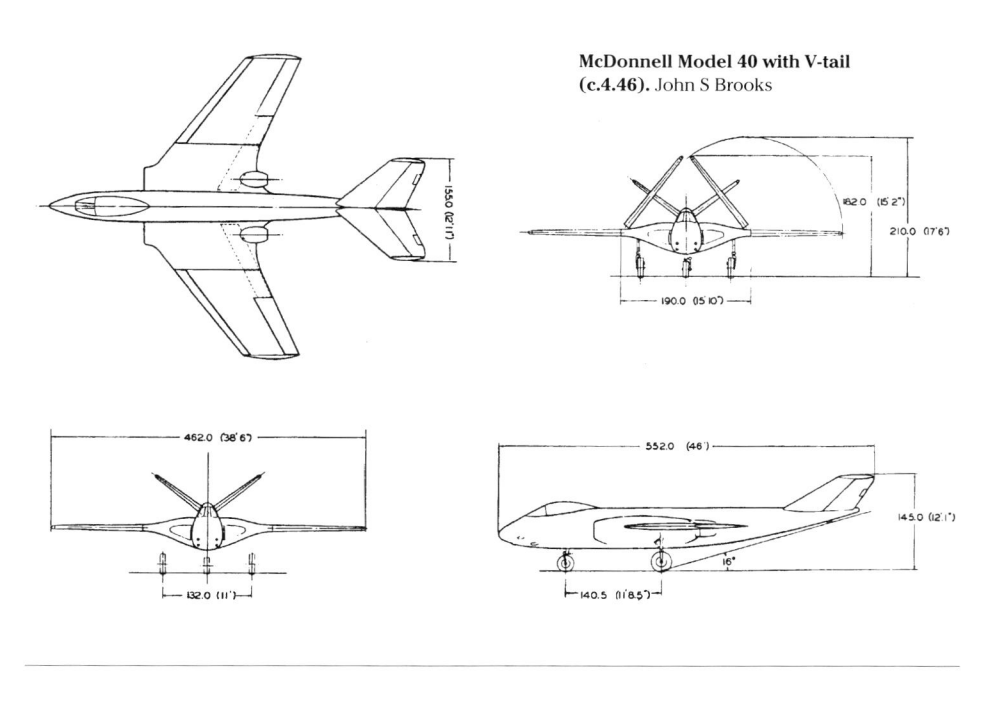

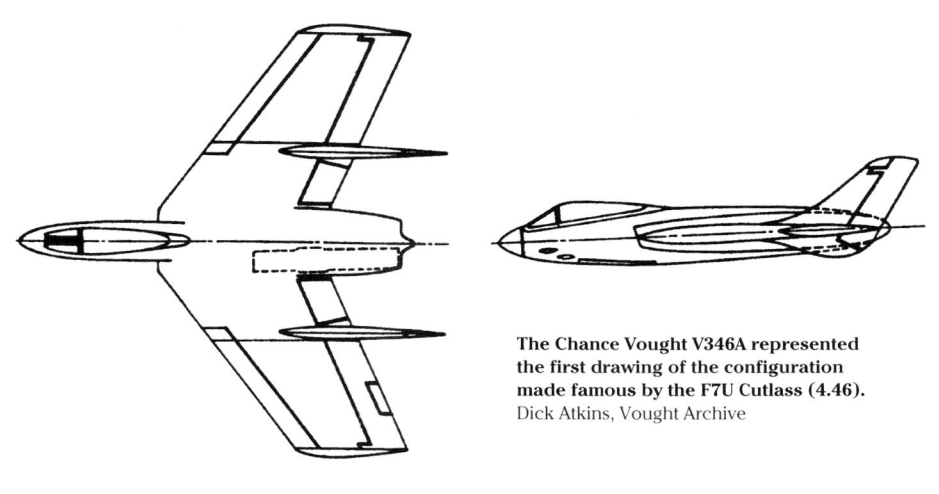

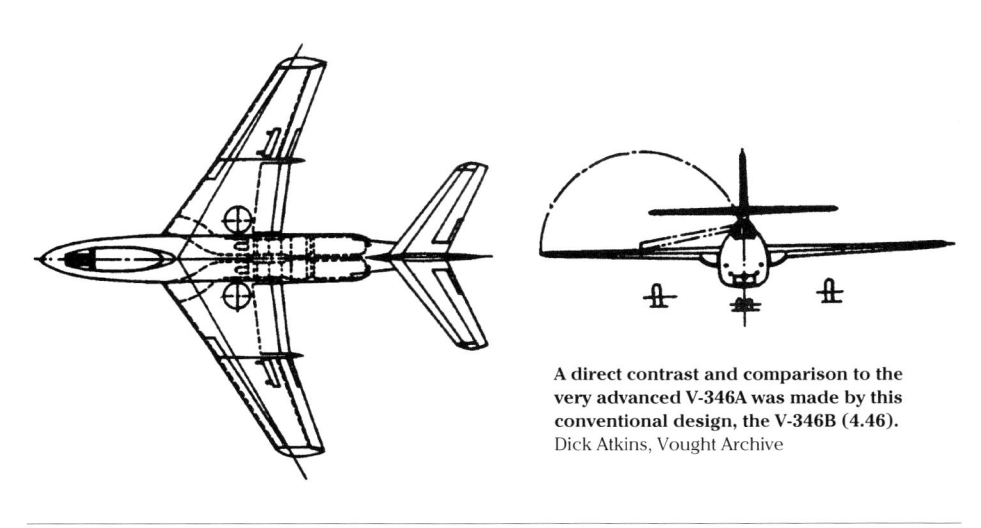

McDonnell Model 40 with V-tail (c.4.46). John S Brooks

The Chance Vought V346A represented the first drawing of the configuration made famous by the F7U Cutlass (4.46). Dick Atkins, Vought Archive

A direct contrast and comparison to the very advanced V-346A was made by this conventional design, the V-346B (4.46). Dick Atkins, Vought Archive

The First Navy Jets

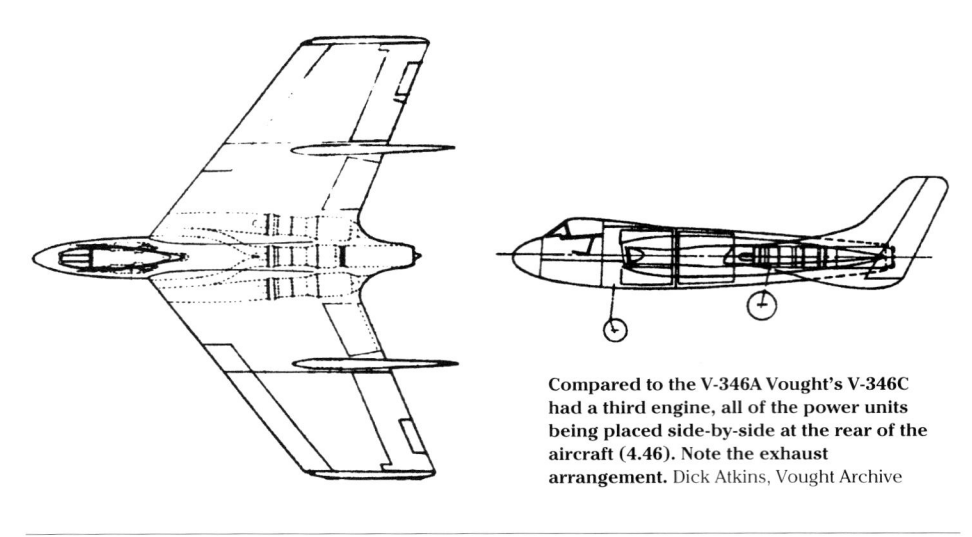

Compared to the V-346A Vought's V-346C had a third engine, all of the power units being placed side-by-side at the rear of the aircraft (4.46). Note the exhaust arrangement. Dick Atkins, Vought Archive

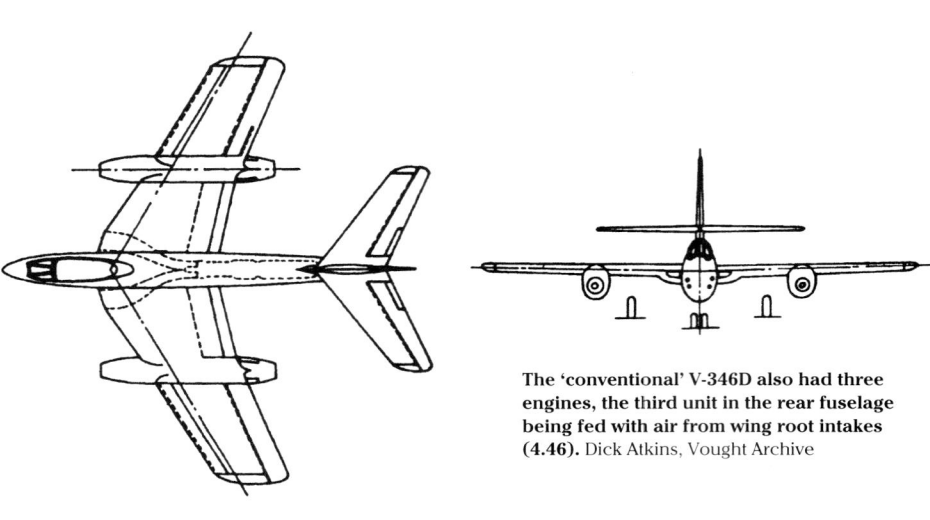

The 'conventional' V-346D also had three engines, the third unit in the rear fuselage being fed with air from wing root intakes (4.46). Dick Atkins, Vought Archive

original 'A' configuration but with a third J34 in the centre fuselage, which moved the original engines out into the wing roots where they exhausted through the trailing edge adjacent to the fuselage. The extra engine increased the performance but also pushed up the weight. V-346D reverted to the normal 'swept wing and tail' format but had two J34s in underwing nacelles plus a third in the rear fuselage with its own jet pipe. V-346A's gross weight was 14,300lb (6,486kg) and its predicted performance included a maximum speed of 714mph (1,149km/h) and a rate of climb of 6,500ft/min (1,981m/min). The equivalent figures for V-346B were 15,700lb (7,122kg), 697mph (1,121km/h) and 5,800ft/min (1,768m/min), for V-346C 17,500lb (7,938kg), 754mph (1,213km/h) and 9,700ft/min (2,957m/min), and for the V-346D 20,950lb (9,503kg), 702mph (1,130km/h) and 7,000ft/min (2,134m/min). Later there was a proposal to re-engine the V-346 with a single J42 (Nene) centrifugal engine.

Boeing Model 454

It is understood that Boeing did not make an official submission to this competition, but company records show that during late 1945 two naval fighter designs were being considered, albeit briefly, which match the dates of the requirement. Model 454 had a wing that was highly swept for its time (42° on the leading edge) and used a tricycle undercarriage. Two 20mm cannon were mounted in the nose and there was also a battery of unguided rockets. Two Westinghouse 24C engines were mounted beneath the rear fuselage and served by a combined tail jet pipe, although some artwork shows an alternative configuration with the powerplant attached in a 'pod' beneath the fuselage level with the wing. Span was 37ft 0in (11.3m), length 38ft 6in (11.7m) and gross weight 14,525lb (6,589kg).

Boeing Model 459

In contrast to the Model 454, but still very advanced for the time, the Model 459 used a large swept 'delta' wing with a sweep angle of 49° at the leading edge. There was no horizontal tail but a lovely curved fin was drawn and two Westinghouse 24Cs were housed in the rear fuselage. These were fed by wing root intakes and again shared a common jet pipe. The cockpit was small and the pilot sat with his legs stretched out ahead of him. No clear details of armament are available though it appears that a battery of unguided rockets was available beneath the fuselage. Span was 39ft 6in (12.0m), length 29ft 7in (9.0m), gross wing area 500ft^2 (46.5m^2) and gross weight 15,606lb (7,079kg). A total of 912gal (4,147lit) of internal fuel was to be carried.

Chance Vought F7U Cutlass

The choice was narrowed down to the Vought V-346A, B or C plus Douglas's D-565. On 25th June 1946 the V-346A was declared the winner because, according to George Spangenberg, 'it offered by far the best performance of all of the proposals'. Three prototypes were ordered as the XF7U-1 Cutlass and the first took to the air on 29th September 1948. Production F7Us followed but they suffered numerous problems (often associated with a lack of power) and the type did not enter service. In due course the J34's were replaced in the F7U-3 variant by the more powerful J46-WE-8 and many other changes were introduced, particularly to the fuselage and including a larger canopy. The first of this variant flew in December 1951 while the near-identical F7U-3M introduced the ability to carry four Sparrow air-to-air missiles. These variants did serve with a number of squadrons but the Cutlass's front line service was relatively short and came to an end in 1958.

Chance Vought's fighter did achieve some landmarks however. It was the first tailless design from the United States to reach production status and it was also the Navy's first swept wing jet. It also changed the Navy's reputation within the industry for acquiring only conventional aircraft. In fact during the early post-war years the impression was that the Service's experts would never approve a tailless design. But they did. Unfortunately turning it into an all-weather fighter by adding the Sparrow missile system pushed the weight up by a considerable margin, thus making it a more aircraft difficult to handle.

Jesse Santamaria worked as an engineer at Vought for fifty-four years, which included periods as Chief Engineer, Chief of Propulsion Design and Chief of Advanced Systems, so no-one is better qualified to comment on the Cutlass's radical design. He points out that

One of the Vought XF7U-1 Cutlass prototypes, 122474, photographed at Patuxent Naval Air Station on 29th September 1948.

An early production example of the much modified Vought F7U-3 Cutlass showing the considerable alterations from the original aircraft, especially the larger cockpit. Dick Atkins, Vought Archive

The First Navy Jets

when the new fighter requirement was received by Vought a team of about twelve people looked at all of the possible configurations, with or without tails. No single design would be perfect but the Cutlass arrangement was found to be the lightest that could do the job. Stability was expected to be a problem but this layout offered better overall qualities than an aircraft designed with a tail. The later F7U-3 had to be developed because of problems with the earlier version's engines and the fact that visibility for landing on the original F7U-1 was found to be poor – hence the new high cockpit. The original F7U-1 was a quite beautiful aircraft.

The Cutlass was one of the boldest of the early post-war designs, and one might commend both the spirit of the Navy and the work of Convair in getting such a radical aircraft as far as carrierborne service. Sadly, their efforts were not rewarded with a highly successful operational career.

A New Carrier-Based Interceptor

Swift advances in aerodynamics and technology generated frequent new competitions for future service aircraft in the late 1940s. One of these, laid down in 1947, was for a new interceptor to defend the fleet. General specification SD-24-F was completed on 2nd April of that year and described a single-seat short-range fighter with a high performance that was required to get off the carrier's deck and climb to height very quickly, and then intercept incoming bombers. The contender from Douglas however, actually began its life during 1946 and won a Navy contract that was, in part, a research project.

Douglas D-571

One of the windfalls of the defeat of Germany was that the Allied Forces were able to plunder the results of the enemy's aeronautical research, including information on swept and delta wings. One American manufacturer to send a team to Germany to collect documents and data was Douglas and the result was the adoption of a 'delta-type' wing in a design that was essentially a flying wing. The layout offered low transonic drag-rise coupled with structural strength and simplicity and also offered more space for fuel, thus reducing the problem of the high rate of fuel consumption – and consequent limited range – suffered by early jet engines. In late December 1946 the studies were brought together into a more concrete proposal. In its earliest form the design had no fuselage as such, the pilot being seated very close to the nose with the wing swept a full 50°. Four 20mm cannon were housed in the nose and power came from two Westinghouse 24Cs. Wing area was 700ft^2 (65.1m^2) and gross weight 15,000lb (6,804kg).

Douglas received a contract to build two prototypes of its D-571 naval all-weather interceptor, now designated XF4D-1, on 17th June 1947. However the design process, particularly the results of wind tunnel testing, brought changes. In due course the D-571 acquired a forward fuselage ahead of the wing and when work reached the D-571-4 of March 1948 there had also been an engine change. Now the aircraft was to be powered by a single XJ40, a new and much more powerful unit from Westinghouse that promised great performance. D-571-4's wing area was 676ft^2 (62.m^2) and gross weight 15,700lb (7,122kg), but the eventual Skyray prototypes would receive a smaller wing.

In the meantime the full interceptor fighter requirement became known as OS-113. This document required the interceptor to be capable of reaching 50,000ft (15,240m) in just six minutes. The aircraft also had to be capable of controlled diving flight at supersonic speeds at both medium and high altitudes while top speed in level flight had to be Mach 0.95 at 50,000ft (around 630mph [1,014km/h]) and Mach 0.905 at sea level (690mph [1,110km/h]). After OS-113 was issued with a Request for Proposals in May 1948, it is understood that a total of eleven projects were submitted by six manufacturers (including the D-571 which does not appear to have been offered with an additional rocket motor). However, not all of these could be identified today.

Grumman G-86

Grumman's submission had a highly swept high-position wing and a conventional tailplane and fin. The wing was equipped with a drooped leading edge and Fowler flaps. It was also adjustable in incidence for landing, improving the pilot's view for the approach. Speed brakes were provided at the rear of the fuselage and the controls were standard ailerons and elevators. An XJ40 jet was mounted in the rear fuselage and fed by side intakes while a Curtiss Wright rocket motor and all of its fuel, consisting of 186gal (846lit) of liquid oxygen and 242gal (1,100lit) of water-alcohol, was housed in a removable fairing running along the bottom of the fuselage. The rocket was to be used for climb or 'flash performance' and was inclined downwards 16.5° so that its thrust line passed through the aircraft's centre of gravity. There was a narrow-track tricycle undercarriage and the 2.75in (7.0cm) diameter fin-stabilized rocket launchers were mounted in small mid-wing nacelles; there would be no gun. Folded span was 23ft 8in (7.2m) and wing sweep angle 42.5°, and total jet fuel (all internal) was 374gal (1,701lit) in wing tanks and another 226gal (1,028lit) in fuselage tanks. G-86's structure would employ conventional metal construction for maximum smoothness.

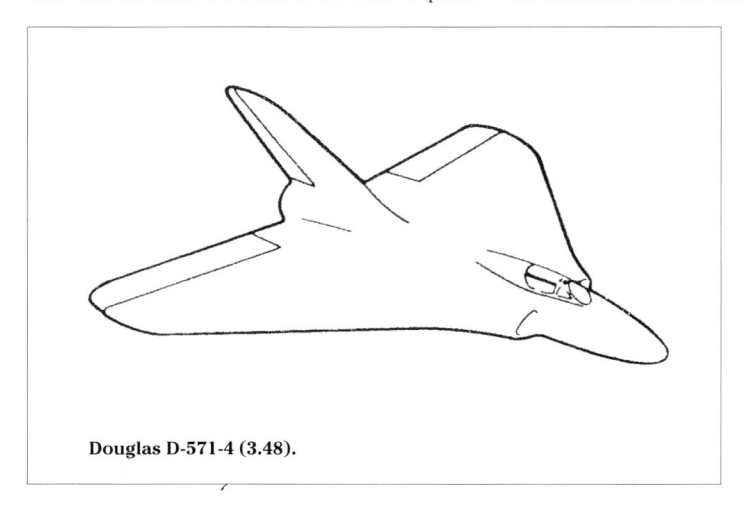

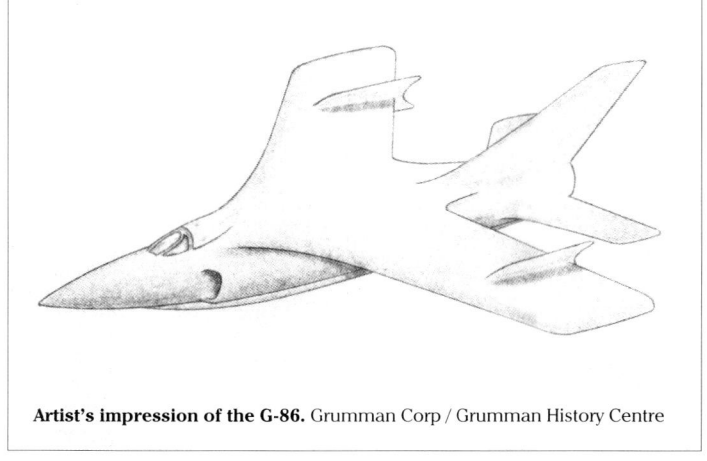

Douglas D-571-4 (3.48).

Artist's impression of the G-86. Grumman Corp / Grumman History Centre

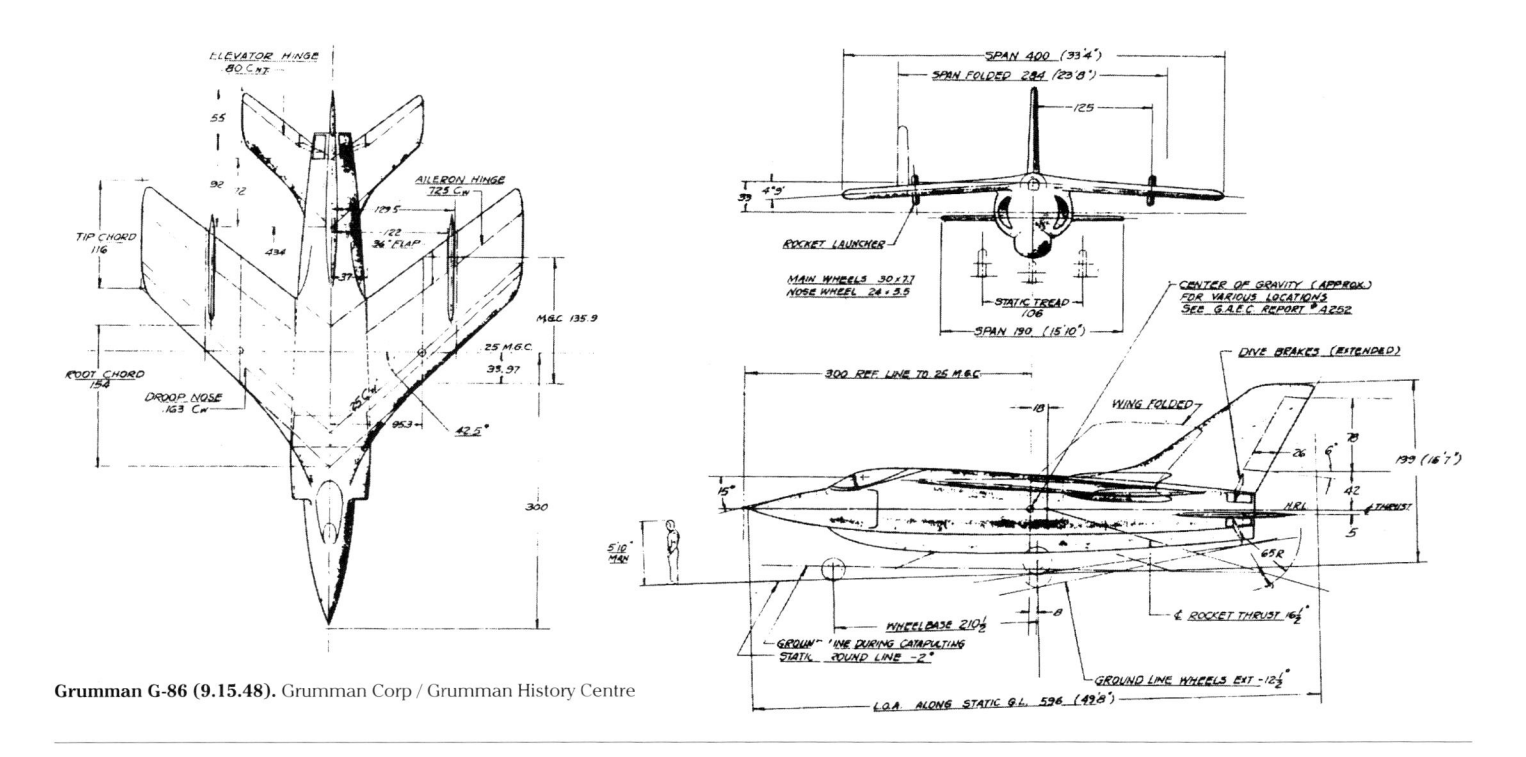

Grumman G-86 (9.15.48). Grumman Corp / Grumman History Centre

Grumman stated that the G-86's performance characteristics were outstanding when compared to the specification, the combination of a single XJ40 jet plus a 5,000 lb (22.2kN) rocket giving a time from sea level to 50,000ft (15,240m) of just two minutes (not including take-off and acceleration), or 2.5 minutes if some rocket fuel was retained for combat. At a weight of 21,758 lb (9,869kg) the maximum sea level rate of climb was 32,000ft/min (9,754m/min), and 16,900ft/min (5,151m/min) at 50,000ft with weight reduced to 17,754 lb (8,053kg) after expending some fuel. Top speed at that altitude would be Mach 1.5, or Mach 0.95 on just turbojet power alone, and the sea level rate of climb on just jet power with afterburner was 22,900ft/min (6,980m/min). Service ceiling on jet power only was 52,000ft (15,850m).

Lockheed L-183

As usual Lockheed studied a variety of designs to meet OS-113 but the definitive aircraft was to be the L-183-6. This used a single turbojet but also incorporated a variable geometry wing to give the best possible performance at both low and high speeds. L-183-6 had a low wing, side intakes ahead of the wing roots and a tricycle undercarriage. The variable sweep mechanism was housed within the fuselage (hence the whole of the wing moved) and the outer portion could be folded; folded span was 25ft 4in (7.7m). Sea level rate of climb was 16,300ft/min (4,968m/min) and the estimated time to 50,000ft (15,240m) 5.94 minutes. Lockheed stated that the L-183 would meet or better all of the specification requirements.

McDonnell Model 58

The McDonnell 58 was a swept wing proposal using a single XJ40 power unit with side intakes and a tricycle undercarriage. The jet exhausted beneath the tail unit in an arrangement similar to McDonnell's twin engine XF-88. None of the original estimated performance data is currently available but the Model 58 was armed solely with internally mounted rocket projectiles.

McDonnell Model 60

McDonnell's Model 60 was a 60° delta wing version of the Model 58. A close examination of its forward fuselage against the eventual XF3H-1 prototypes shows them to be very similar. A single XJ-40 was employed and the Model 60 would have a simple structure using conventional materials and methods of fabrication. No auxiliary lift devices would be needed and McDonnell reported how tunnel testing had confirmed that the delta would give stable and easily controllable flight at transonic speeds and the highest critical diving speeds. In addition, eliminating the

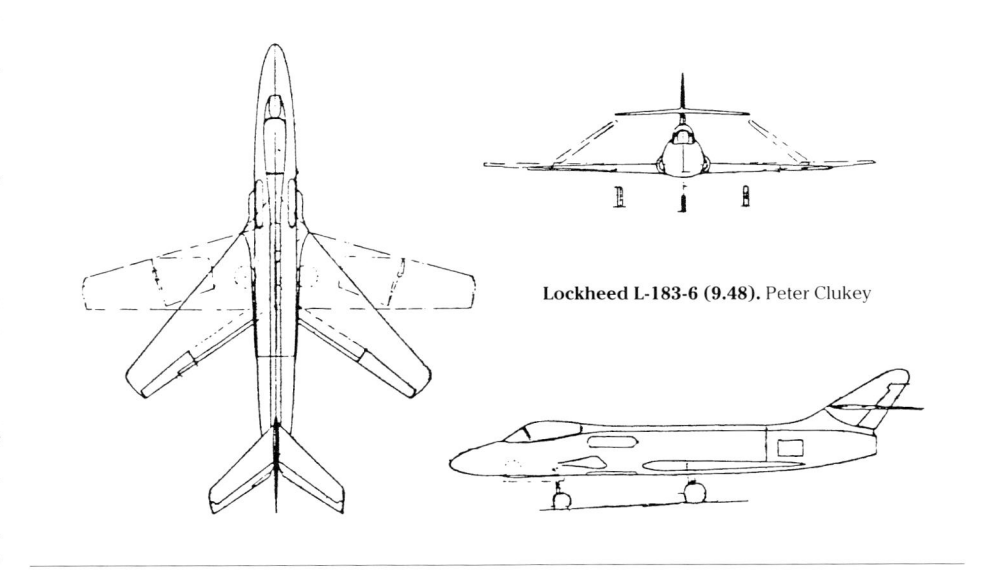

Lockheed L-183-6 (9.48). Peter Clukey

The First Navy Jets

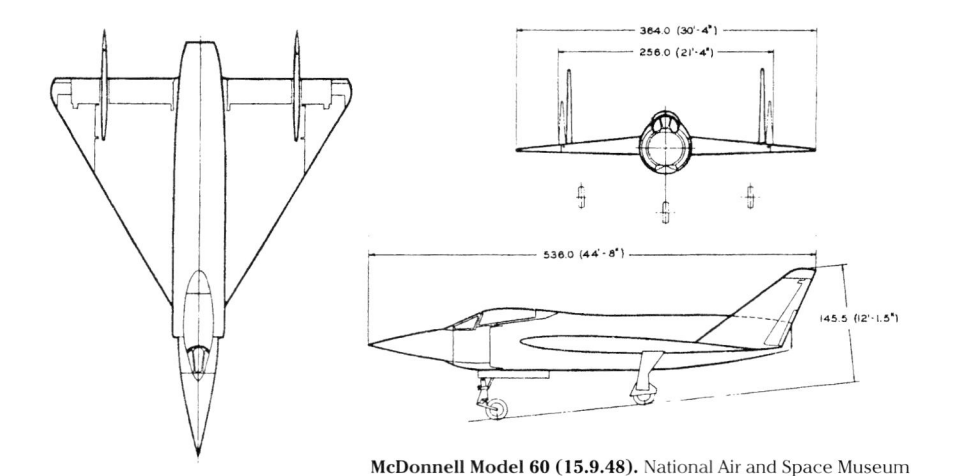

McDonnell Model 60 (15.9.48). National Air and Space Museum

horizontal tail and locating the twin vertical tails on the wing permitted satisfactory low speed stability. The control system consisted of two manually operated rudders and differentially operated elevons. A tricycle undercarriage was fitted (the nose gear could retract independently to allow the fighter to 'kneel' for on-deck stowage) and the wingtips could fold to give a folded span of 21ft 4in (6.5m). The fin-stabilized rockets appear to have been housed beneath the lower nose and again there was no gun. Total internal fuel was 264gal (1,200lit) in fuselage tanks and another 462gal (2,101lit) in four wing tanks.

This manufacturer also declared that the project's estimated performance exceeded all of the stipulated requirements and that the Model 60 would be capable of controlled flight in excess of Mach 1.5. Time to 50,000ft (15,240m) was just 5.0 minutes, sea level rate of climb 30,450ft/min (9,281m/min) but at 50,000ft just 1,150ft/min (351m/min). Despite its large increase in tactical performance McDonnell noted that the Model 60's low stalling speed, of 104mph (167km/h) with power on, was no greater than current jet carrier aircraft.

Left: **Model of the McDonnell Model 60 by John Hall.**

Below left: **Model of the Republic NP-48 project (c9.48)** Cradle of Aviation Museum

Below right: **This view of the NP-48 reveals the position of the air intake – directly beneath the cockpit. The inverse taper wings are well shown.** Cradle of Aviation Museum

American Secret Projects: Fighters & Interceptors

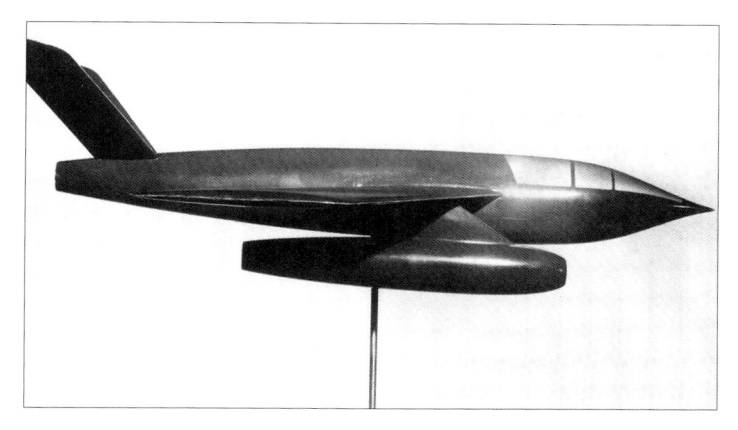

Above left and right: **Model of the Republic NP-49 project 'Version A' (c9.48)**
Cradle of Aviation Museum

Right and below: **Model of the Republic NP-49 project 'Version B' (c9.48)**
Cradle of Aviation Museum

Republic NP-48

Another attractive design, Republic's swept mid-wing NP-48 proposal clearly made use of its manufacturer's design experience with the AP-31/XF-91, complete with inversely tapered mid-position wings and a V-tail. The model photos show a sleek, slim fuselage and suggest that a single jet engine would have been used (with the air intake placed underneath the cockpit). A small rocket motor appears to have been mounted beneath the jetpipe.

Republic NP-49

Republic also had a sister design to the NP-48 utilizing a similar wing and tail arrangement but with a much different powerplant arrangement. Two different versions of the NP-49 have been found in model form and both appear to have jet engines in underwing nacelles and possibly a rocket motor in the fuselage. The models give little away in terms of detail, but 'Version B' appears to show air intakes on either side of each nacelle.

For the decision to select a winner, made at the end of 1948, we need to visit the George Spangenberg website again. He notes 'the official decision probably says that McDonnell won the competition and we just continued the [Douglas] F4D program. In fact the F4D Skyray was by far the better airplane. I didn't think we should have bought the McDonnell airplane myself but we did and then it was touted as a great idea to have competitive programs going anyway.' Prototypes were thus ordered for McDonnell's Model 58 as the Demon to go alongside Douglas's contract. However, both types were to be seriously delayed and affected by development problems with Westinghouse's new engine. The J40 was intended for both Skyray and Demon, and also Douglas's A3D Skywarrior carrier bomber, but in the end it proved too difficult to develop fully and was finally abandoned. In due course the two fighters were successfully re-engined with Pratt & Whitney's J57 and Allison's J71 respectively, but both were late entering service and were fitted with guns to serve in other roles. The Skyray and Demon represented the end of the subsonic fighter era for the US Navy.

Douglas F4D Skyray

The XF4D-1 was first flown on 23rd January 1951. Although given a delta wing the tips were rounded off and this did much to ensure that the exotic-looking interceptor received the official name Skyray. With the J40-WE-8, a potentially very impressive interceptor had been created but problems with the intended engine meant that production machines received the J57-P-2 offering 9,700 lb (43.1kN) thrust dry and 13,500 lb (60.0kN) in afterburner, which gave an excellent thrust-to-weight ratio. Skyray flew with the new engine for the first time on 5th June 1954.

The J57 was actually started by the Air Force as a bomber engine but Pratt & Whitney fitted it with an afterburner, which turned it into a very fine fighter engine as well. Up to this time Air Force and Navy policy was to develop their own engines with the Air Force receiving odd numbers (J57) while the Navy allocated even numbers (J40). Nevertheless, although it was an Air Force engine, the Navy considered the J57 to be the best around. In due course 420 production Skyrays were completed and the type stayed in frontline service well into the 1960s. Its service career was relatively modest but it did achieve a number of speed and climb records. The aircraft's design began before the first generation of air-to-air missiles had made their

The First Navy Jets

One of the McDonnell XF3H-1 Demon prototypes seen at the manufacturer's St Louis factory in August 1951.

A lovely photograph of a McDonnell Demon. In fact serial 133549 shown here served as the prototype of the F3H-2N version. Terry Panopalis

appearance but, in due course, Skyray was able to carry four AIM-9 Sidewinder missiles. In 1962, when the fighter was redesignated F-6A, it was already being moved into second-line and reserve units.

McDonnell F3H Demon

Two prototype Model 58 fighters, designated XF3H-1, were covered by a Letter of Intent issued on 3rd January 1949 and the full-size mock-up was inspected in mid-July. The first machine, powered by an XJ40 giving 6,500 lb (28.9kN) thrust dry or 9,200 lb (40.9kN) with afterburner, made its first flight on 7th August 1951 and fifty-eight production F3H-1s were manufactured with an improved version of the Westinghouse engine installed. These were a failure but the introduction of the more powerful and more reliable Allison J71, as the F3H-2, salvaged the program and allowed another 459 aircraft to be completed. The first entered service in 1956 and the type stayed in the front line until 1964. The Demon eventually served as an all-weather fighter, or as a fighter-bomber depending on the variant, and late marks carried four AIM-7 Sparrow or four AIM-9 Sidewinder air-to-air missiles. Demon proved to be the Navy's first true all-weather missile fighter and in 1962 the type was redesignated F-3.

A First Attempt at Variable Geometry

There remains one further subsonic naval fighter type to discuss. In mid-1951 Bell Aircraft flew the first of two small variable geometry swing-wing research aircraft called the X-5. The interest in variable geometry (VG) wings grew throughout the post-war years, the concept of having the wings in different positions to ensure good flight characteristics at both ends of the speed range seemingly quite straightforward. However, there were acute mechanical problems – in particular the hinge point had to be at or near the wing root, which is also the position where the structural loads and bending moment are at their most severe. In addition, keeping the movements of the centre of pressure and centre of gravity balanced when changing the wing sweep angle at transonic speeds was difficult and it is no coincidence that the first viable VG combat aircraft did not make their debuts until much later in the 1960s. In the early 1950s the company that examined VG in the greatest depth was Grumman.

Grumman G-83 and XF10F-1 Jaguar

Sometimes, as already noted with Republic's XF-91, a design breaks new ground, paving the way for future aircraft without itself being successful. Such was the case with Grumman's Jaguar. It has already been seen how Grumman had fitted swept wings to its F9F Panther fighter to turn it into the Cougar, and how that development program was delayed until the designers were ready. In fact, on 3rd September 1947 Grumman actually submitted a proposal for an all-new swept wing jet fighter design to the Bureau of Aeronautics called Design 83 (work had been ongoing on the project since the previous November). The G-83 had a slim fuselage, a mid-position wing and a T-tail, four 20mm in the lower nose plus wing root intakes; and it impressed

American Secret Projects: Fighters & Interceptors

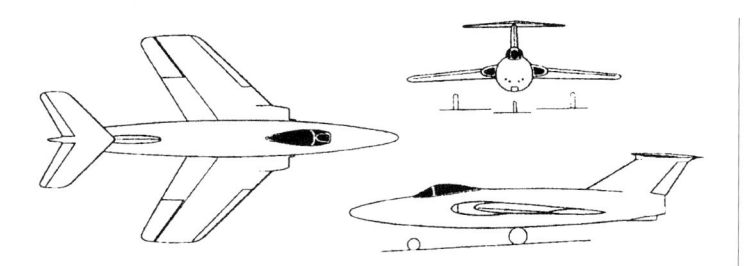

Grumman G-83 as accepted by the Bureau of Aeronautics in March 1948. Grumman Corporation / Grumman History Centre

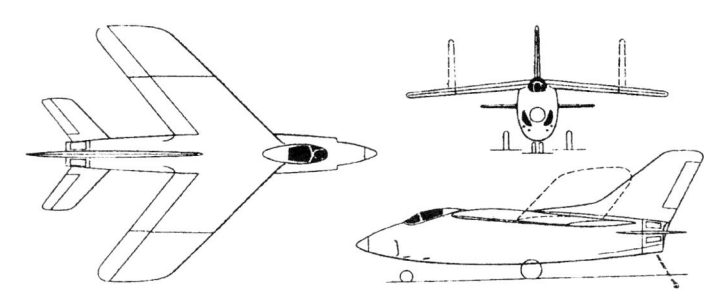

Grumman G-83 as redesigned in November 1948. Grumman Corporation / Grumman History Centre

the Bureau sufficiently for it to issue a Letter of Intent on 7th April 1948. Estimated rate of climb was 11,650ft/min (3,551m/min), operating range 468nm (867km) on the maximum internal fuel load of 5,460lb (2,477kg), and endurance 4.05 hours when carrying 7,260lb (3,293kg) of fuel in the overload condition. In January 1948 the designation XF10F-1 was allocated to two prototypes with first their flights planned for August and October 1949. Initially G-83 had been considered as a modified F9F Panther, but extra changes forced the new designation to be introduced.

During March tunnel tests revealed poor characteristics at both high and low speeds and revisions to the design began. The Pratt & Whitney J42 (Nene) in the original layout was replaced by the same manufacturer's J48 and in this form the rate of climb was increased to 14,750ft/min (4,496m/min) and top speed 731mph (1,177km/h), but operating range and endurance were down to 295nm (547km) and 3.22 hours respectively. The specification covering the XF10F-1 was completed in May 1948 and then, during the fall, the Navy requested a range of 600nm (1,112kg). This necessitated a further substantial redesign (completed in November and shown in the drawing) that brought with it a gross weight of 26,283lb (11,922kg) and a wing area of 450ft² (41.85m²) to compensate. Now the fighter had a much deeper fuselage and a high-position wing, wing folding, a low tailplane and intakes around the lower forward fuselage with the four guns underneath. The wing was now of the variable incidence type to improve the approach attitude and give a better view for the pilot. G-83 also had a Westinghouse XJ40 engine plus afterburner and a larger radar dish, up from 30in (76.2cm) to 35in (88.9cm), to give better sensitivity. As such it carried 9,000lb (4,082kg) of fuel for an endurance of 4.2 hours (4.9 hours with overload) and it met the range requirement: in fact, 750nm (1,390km) was possible with overload fuel. Maximum rate of climb was 17,500ft/min (5,334m/min).

The mock-up was officially reviewed in late April 1949, with the gross weight now at 26,991lb (12,243kg), but it was soon evident that further changes made by the Navy to the requirements would add even more weight. In response, on 7th July Grumman formally proposed fitting the fighter with a variable geometry wing that would increase the rate of climb and the range while reducing the stalling speed, and this was accepted; there was also a return to the T-tail. After another redesign, work went ahead on the prototypes and production orders for a total of 112 F10Fs were placed in 1950 and 1951. The first machine made its first flight on 19th May 1952 but the powerplant, the notorious XJ40, gave problems and the aircraft was also heavy for carrier operations. Only the first prototype ever flew and the production machines were eventually cancelled. Nevertheless, the Jaguar became the first jet fighter to be designed as a production VG aircraft and, although never entering service, the experience gained from operating the prototype proved extremely valuable for the American VG programs that followed in the 1960s – as we will discuss later.

The Navy Completes its Entry into the Jet Era

Although slightly cautious at the outset, it can be seen that the US Navy went on to initiate a great deal of innovative design thinking amongst the various aircraft manufacturers. Indeed it took two remarkably radical designs – the tail-less Cutlass and bat-winged Skyray – right through into carrierborne service. Given the greater demands of carrierborne operations, it is perhaps not surprising that none of these designs matched the success of the Air Force's F-86, nor proved the basis for a future family of fighters. They did, however, move the Navy firmly into the jet era. Moreover, the experience was to pave the way for some really outstanding fighter designs in the future.

The only Grumman XF10F-1 Jaguar to fly was prototype 124435, which is seen here undergoing taxi tests at Bethpage in May 1952 prior to its first flight. Grumman Corp / Grumman History Centre

The First Navy Jets

Post-War USN Jet Fighters – Estimated Data

Project	Span ft in (m)	Length ft in (m)	Gross Wing Area ft² (m²)	Gross Weight lb (kg)	Engine lb (kN)	Max Speed / Height mph (km/h) / ft (m)	Armament
Grumman G-71	32 6 (9.9)	32 11 (10.0)	207 (19.3)	8,794 (3,989)	1 x Westinghouse 24-C 3,000 (13.3)	533 (858) at S/L, 535 (861) up to 10,000 (3,048)	4 x 20mm cannon
All-Weather Fighters							
Grumman G-75	64 2 (19.6)	46 0 (14.0)	553 (51.4)	26,964 (12,231)	4 x Westinghouse 24-C 3,000 (13.3)	608 (978) at S/L, 546 (879) at 30,000 (9,144)	4 x 20mm cannon
Douglas XF3D-1 Skynight (flown)	50 0 (15.2)	45 5 (13.8)	400 (37.2)	18,668 (8,468)	2 x Westinghouse J34-WE-24 3,000 (13.3)	510 (821) at S/L, 543 (874) at 11,000 (3,353)	4 x 20mm cannon. Up to 4,000 lb (1,814kg) bombs
Grumman G-79A	40 8 (12.4)	37 7 (11.5)	322 (29.9)	14,500 (6,577)	1 x P&W R2800 piston + 1 x RR Derwent VI jet c3,500 (15.6)	548 (882) at 15,000 (4,572)	4 x 20mm cannon
Grumman G-79B	39 10 (12.1)	39 6 (12.0)	311 (28.9)	14,000 (6,350)	1 x GE TG-100 turboprop + 1 x RR Derwent VI jet c3,500 (15.6)	557 (896) at 15,000 (4,572)	4 x 20mm cannon
Grumman G-79C	42 5 (12.9)	40 0 (12.2)	362 (33.7)	16,300 (7,394)	2 x RR Derwent VI c3,500 (15.6)	598 (962) at S/L	4 x 20mm cannon
Grumman G-79D	37 0 (11.3)	38 0 (11.6)	276 (25.7)	12,400 (5,625)	1 x RR Nene 5,000 (22.2)	598 (962) at S/L	4 x 20mm cannon
Grumman XF9F-2 Panther (flown)	35 3 (10.7)	37 3 (11.4)	250 (23.3)	16,450 (7,462)	1 x RR Nene J42-P-6 5,000 (22.2)	550 (885) at 22,000 (6,706)	4 x 20mm cannon. Up to 2,000 lb (907kg) bombs
Grumman F9F-6 Cougar (flown)	34 6 (10.5)	41 5 (12.6)	300 (27.9)	18,450 (8,369)	1 x P&W J48-P-8 6,250 (27.7), 7,250 (32.2) ab	654 (1,052) at S/L, 591 (951) at 35,000 (10,668)	4 x 20mm cannon. Up to 2,000 lb (907kg) bombs
Douglas F3D-3 (swept wing)	51 0 (15.5)	50 0 (15.2)	442 (41.1)	26,735 (12,127)	2 x Westinghouse J46-WE-4 4,080 (18.1)	529 (851) at 14,000 (4,267)	4 x 20mm cannon
Long-Range Escort Fighters							
Chance Vought V-356	42 9 (13.0) 49 0 (14.9) w tanks	46 0 (14.0)	355 (33.0)	25,666 (11,642)	2 x Rolls-Royce AJ-65 6,500 (28.9)	?	?
Boeing Model 482	68 0 (20.7)	55 2.5 (16.8)	720 (67.0)	46,000 (20,866)	2 x Allison 500 (XT40-A-6) turboprop 5,100shp (3,803kW)	530 (853) at 30,000 (9,144) at 41,360 lb (18,761kg) weight	4 x 20mm cannon
Lockheed L-180-2	81 6 (24.8)	55 0 (16.8)	?	?	2 x Allison 500 (XT40-A-6) turboprop 5,100shp (3,803kW)	?	4 x 20mm cannon
Day Fighters and Interceptors							
McDonnell Model 40	38 6 (11.7)	46 0 (14.0)	385 (35.8)	?	2 x Westinghouse 24-C 3,000 (13.3)	High subsonic	4 x 20mm cannon
McDonnell Model 40A	38 6 (11.7)	46 0 (14.0)	385 (35.8)	?	2 x Westinghouse 24-C 3,000 (13.3)	High subsonic	4 x 20mm cannon
McDonnell Model 40	38 6 (11.7)	46 0 (14.0)	385 (35.8)	?	2 x Westinghouse 24-C 3,000 (13.3)	High subsonic	4 x 20mm cannon
Chance Vought F7U-1 Cutlass (flown)	38 8 (11.8)	40 11 (12.5)	496 (46.1)	20,038 (9,089)	2 x Westinghouse J34-WE-32 3,020 (13.4), 4,900 (21.8) ab	693 (1,115) at S/L, 626 (1,007) at 35,000 (10,668)	4 x 20mm cannon
Douglas F4D-1 Skyray (flown)	33 5 (10.2)	45 4 (13.8)	557 (51.8)	25,000 (11,340)	1 x P&W J57-P-8 10,200 (45.3), 16,000 (71.1) ab	722 (1,162) at S/L, 695 (1,118) at 36,000 (10,973)	4 x 20mm cannon or 76 rocket projectiles or 4 Sidewinder AAM
Grumman G-86	33 4 (10.2)	49 8 (15.1)	375 (34.9)	22,311 (10,120)	1 x Westinghouse XJ40-WE-8 7,310 (32.5), 10,900 (48.4) ab + 1 x Curtiss Wright rocket 5,000 (22.2)	745 (1,199) M0.975 at S/L, 996 (1,603) M1.5 at 50,000 (15,240)	24 x 2.75in (7.0cm) RPs
Lockheed L-183-6	38 9 (11.8) fwd 30 4 (9.2) swept	47 3 (14.4)	?	?	1 x turbojet	759 (1,221) M0.99 at S/L, 649 (1,044) M0.98 at 50,000 (15,240)	2.75in (7.0cm) RPs
McDonnell Model 60	30 4 (9.2)	44 11 (13.7)	440 (40.9)	17,182 (7,794)	1 x Westinghouse XJ40-WE-8 7,310 (32.5), 10,900 (48.4) ab	762 (1,226) M1.00 at S/L, 654 (1,052) M0.99 at 50,000 (15,240)	24 x 2.75in (7.0cm) rocket projectiles
McDonnell F3H-2N Demon (flown)	35 4 (10.8)	59 0 (18.0)	519 (48.3)	29,020 (13,163)	1 x Allison J71-A-2 9,500 (42.2), 14,250 (63.3) ab	727 (1,170) at S/L	4 x 20mm cannon + 4 x AAM
Grumman G-83 (3.48)	32 4 (9.85)	49 6 (15.1)	360 (33.5)	18,729 (8,495)	1 x P&W J42 Nene 5,000 (22.2)	686 (1,104)	4 x 20mm cannon
Grumman G-83 (11.48 – XF10F)	36 8 (11.2)	48 8 (14.8)	450 (41.9)	26,283 (11,922)	1 x Westinghouse XJ40 7,310 (32.5), 10,900 (48.4) ab	736 (1,184)	4 x 20mm cannon
Grumman XF10F-1 Jaguar (flown)	50 7 (15.4) fwd 36 8 (11.2) swept	55 7 (16.9)	467 (43.4) fwd 450 (41.9) swept	31,255 (14,177)	1 x Westinghouse XJ40-WE-8 7,400 (32.9), 10,900 (48.4) ab	710 (1,142) at S/L, 632 (1,017) at 35,000 (10,668)	4 x 20mm cannon + 2 x 2,000 lb (907kg) bombs or various RPs

Chapter Three

The First 'Centuries'

Model of an unknown North American fighter project which appears to fit the requirements of the '1954 Interceptor'.

On 14th October 1947 a straight-winged American rocket-powered research machine, the Bell X-1, became the world's first aircraft to exceed the speed of sound. It was a major milestone in aviation history. The X-1 introduced a long line of successful research aircraft that were to push back the frontiers of aeronautical development in many areas. Both the X-1 and the follow-on swept wing Bell X-2 were specifically designed to examine the problems of high speed flight; so too was the Navy-sponsored Douglas D-558-I Skystreak and later D-558-II Skyrocket. Progress was dramatic! The Skyrocket reached Mach 2, and the X-2 eventually reached Mach 3. As has often happened in aviation history, once a boundary has been broken, new combat aircraft soon arrive on the scene exploiting the newly acquired knowledge. That was certainly the case here – the achievements of the X-1 were quickly followed by the first proposals for supersonic fighters, starting with the North American Aviation F-100 Super Sabre. The latter's designation was fortuitous, giving a name to a whole series of supersonic aircraft – the 'Century' fighters.

Certain earlier types like the North American F-86 could go supersonic in a dive, but the ability to go supersonic on the level was seen as the key requirement for the future: indeed within less than a decade the target would rise to Mach 2. The technological challenges were daunting. Flying beyond Mach 1 was more than just a matter of pushing a subsonic airframe a little harder: the whole science of aerodynamics took on a new dimension as airflows became compressible and temperatures and pressures changed instantly across shock waves. As well as creating a new source of drag, those shock waves also posed control problems: for example causing pitching moments that conventional elevators couldn't overcome. A further problem that had to be tackled was the increasing speed range over which the aircraft was required to operate. A wing optimised for flight at high supersonic speeds had just the opposite characteristics to those required for take-off and landing.

The solutions required some fundamental re-thinking about fighter design. Progressively the introduction of new wing shapes, 'all-flying tails', variable geometry air inlets and a host of other features – backed by more powerful engines – all helped to overcome the obstacles. The formulation of the 'Area Rule' by Richard T Whitcomb in early 1952 was an important breakthrough. Whitcomb demonstrated that in the transonic region drag could be minimised if the total cross-sectional area plotted over the total length of the aircraft was merged into a smooth curve. This resulted in the curves, bumps and occasional 'coke bottle' shapes that were to become a feature of supersonic designs. It was also the breakthrough that saved the troubled Convair F-102 program described shortly, an aircraft that stubbornly refused to go supersonic until the necessary bulges and 'waisting' were added. However all of these developments, along with the more advanced guided weapons and avionics that also had to be carried, came at a price. They pushed up the complexity of the new aircraft, and with it the weight and the cost. These issues were to have as much a bearing on

American Secret Projects: Fighters & Interceptors

which designs proved successful as did the aircraft's estimated performance.

A principal factor driving the demand for such advanced designs was America's defence policy. During the greater part of the 1950s President Eisenhower relied heavily on a programme of 'deterrence' and 'massive retaliation'. This resulted in the development of fighters tailored for specific missions and operating environments. At this time, the ability to carry out a long-range nuclear attack (with either missiles or bombers) or to defend the USA against waves of Soviet bombers coming over the Pole, dominated military thinking. The development of nuclear weapons and the bombers and missiles to carry them took priority in military spending. The capability of fighters to manoeuvre and dogfight got left behind in the quest for ever higher speeds, ceilings and ranges.

For the purpose of this book the 'Century' series is defined as the F-100 through F-108. The series embraced many forms of wing shape, different powerplants and weapon combinations. The competing designs that were turned down brought with them even greater variety and three chapters will be devoted to these remarkable aircraft and their competitions. This first effort looks at the F-100 to F-103, four very different aircraft with very different backgrounds.

North American's Supersonic Sabre

The phenomenal success of the F-86 Sabre, both from an aerodynamic and a sales point of view, meant that North American Aviation was naturally very keen to find a supersonic successor. The resulting project began its life as a development of the F-86 and eventually came to fruition as the F-100; it was inevitably named the Super Sabre. But the design didn't get there in one jump.

Beautifully finished model of the North American 'Advanced F-86 Day Fighter' project, the initial form of the company's 'Sabre 45' proposal (1949/1.51). Jonathan Rigutto / photo © 2005 Chad Slattery

Planview showing the new 45°-sweep wing on the 'Advanced F-86' and its slightly longer fuselage. This model, in 1/30th scale, has a span of 14.6in (37cm) and a length of 18.1in (46cm), giving equivalent full-size figures of span 36ft 5in (11.1m) and length 45ft 3in (13.8m).

The quality of North American project models is shown to advantage in this view of the company's 'Advanced F-86 Day Fighter'. Note the position of the airbrakes, very similar to the F-86. Jonathan Rigutto / photo © 2005 Chad Slattery

50 American Secret Projects: Fighters & Interceptors

Model of the North American 'Sabre 45 Air Superiority Fighter' project. It is understood that this is how the design looked in August 1951.
Jonathan Rigutto / photo © 2005 Chad Slattery

Planview of the Sabre 45 Air Superiority version. Although pretty similar to the 'Advanced F-86', this design has a full-length fuselage spine and a horizontal tail of greater area. Span is unchanged but this 1/30th scale model was only 17.7in (45cm) long, giving a full-size length of 44ft 3in (13.5m).

The position of the airbrakes is not indicated on the model of the Air Superiority Sabre 45.
Jonathan Rigutto / photo © 2005 Chad Slattery

North American Sabre 45

The first studies for an advanced variant of the F-86 began in 1949 as the 'Sabre 45', the designation coming from the fighter's 45°-sweep wing, which replaced the 35° wing employed on the F-86. This was a company-sponsored program and North American's engineers selected the 45° angle as being sufficient to achieve Mach 1.0. It is understood that when detailed drawings were completed in September the powerplant was an unspecified engine giving 9,000 lb (40.0kN) of thrust dry and 12,000 lb (53.3kN) in full afterburner. In January 1951 work had progressed sufficiently for North American to make an unsolicited proposal that was favourably received, the project being described as the 'Advanced F-86 Day Fighter'. Apart from the increased sweep on the wings, tail and fin, it had a longer and somewhat sleeker-looking fuselage, but the design's relationship to its ancestor was very evident and it shared many common features. The Sabre 45 was a single-seat, single-engine aircraft with a nose intake, leading edge slats and trailing edge flaps on the wing, and an all-moving horizontal tail.

In August 1951 a General Operational Requirement was raised to cover the project, now upgraded to an air superiority fighter, with service entry preferably in 1955 and not later than 1957. As such the type was re-titled 'Sabre 45 Air Superiority Fighter' and it showed some refinements from the earlier proposal. During October the Air Force Council pressed for the development of a further revised Sabre 45. However, to obtain an in-service aircraft quickly, it also agreed to authorise production before a first flight had been made. This was in spite of the risks that would be involved with subsequent modifications. In due course it was found that, to achieve supersonic performance, a new specially designed fuselage would be required which was substantially different from the early Sabre

The First 'Centuries'

45 layouts. On 30th November the Sabre 45 was officially designated F-100 and two YF-100 prototypes were ordered on 3rd January 1952. North American called its fighter the NA-180 and it was to be covered by MX1894.

North American F-100 Super Sabre

The full-size Sabre 45 mock-up was inspected in early November 1951 and resulted in a number of modifications being specified, many of which had been completed when a second mock-up review took place on 21st March 1952. The results were satisfactory and in the following August bulk orders were placed for production machines. The first YF-100A prototype (re-designated to reflect the various design changes) made its maiden flight on 25th May 1953. Not surprisingly for such a new aircraft, flight testing revealed numerous problems which led to substantial delays. Not least was a serious weakness in directional stability that required modifications to the vertical fin. Once the problems had been sorted out the F-100 Super Sabre, the world's first supersonic aircraft to enter production, went on to become a great success. Interestingly, much of that success came in the role of ground attack aircraft, for which its supersonic capability was not that relevant.

Opposite page:

The North American YF-100A prototype trails its drag chute at the end of a test flight.

This unidentified single-seat development of the F-100 Super Sabre may have been North American Aviation's proposal to the interceptor competition won by the McDonnell F-101B. When this image was made the fin and tail required some repair. John Aldaz

This page:

Right and below: **The 'Super Sabre Development' model has a span of 7.75in (19.7cm) and a length of 13.5in (34.3cm).** John Aldaz

Bottom: **A production North American F-100A Super Sabre is prepared for another sortie.**

The First 'Centuries'

McDonnell F-101 Series

In Chapter One we left McDonnell's XF-88A penetration fighter as the best of its breed after a fly-off competition, but having failed to gain any production orders. One deficiency exhibited by the XF-88A was 'equipmentitis' – the accumulation of extra equipment and weapons on an already weighty airframe that made the fighter just too heavy. McDonnell had designed the proposed F-88 production machine around the Westinghouse J46 engine, and then in December 1951 it advocated the Allison J71. However, in order to ensure that the type would be supersonic, on 15th January 1952 the Wright Air Development Center recommended using Pratt & Whitney's J57 in any future developments that might enter production. This was accepted and McDonnell recalculated its figures, the resulting design becoming the F-101 Voodoo.

Although the Korean War was to kill off the concept of the heavy penetration escort fighter, in January 1951 Strategic Air Command requested such a type to escort its long-range B-36s. It presented some minimum performance limits for what was considered to be an interim aircraft for the 1952/1953 timescale. These were covered by General Operational Requirement GOR-101 (and Weapon System WS-105) and most of the proposals made in May 1951 were versions of aircraft already flying (all of them covered in Chapter One). They included variants of Lockheed's F-90 and F-94, Republic's F-84F and F-91 and North American's F-93 plus a development of Northrop's F-89. There was also a version of Republic's F-84F with a turboprop engine (which as the XF-84H was ordered in 1952 and flown in July 1955), along with a development of McDonnell's F-88 with the same basic configuration but having a longer fuselage.

McDonnell F-101A Voodoo

McDonnell's F-88 variant was selected as the winner. The new type was designated F-101A and orders for pre-production machines were placed in May 1953, but by September 1954 SAC realized that this large single-seat fighter might still not carry enough fuel to escort its bombers all the way to their targets and so cancellation was a distinct possibility. However, at this point Tactical Air Command thought that the F-101A airframe might make a good nuclear strike fighter-bomber (or strategic fighter). This idea was accepted and the F-101A was given some different avionics to allow it to perform its new task with TAC. The first F-101A made its maiden flight on 29th September 1954 and the first squadron was equipped with the type in 1957.

Northrop Interim Escort Fighter

Northrop's offering was a development of its F-89 Scorpion called the F-89E. This single-seater was based on the F-89D production airframe but was designed to have more power, speed and range and also had improved aerodynamics to give less drag. A new thinner 64ft (19.5m) span 700ft^2 (65.1m^2) area wing was fitted together with two 9,100 lb (40.4kN) thrust General Electric J47-GE-21 engines, whilst the weapons (fifty-four rocket projectiles) were to be carried (along with fuel and the main wheels) in two pods under the inner wings. Despite having a weight of 56,900 lb (25,810kg), this aircraft was expected to achieve Mach 1.0 in a dive, 687mph (1,105km/h) Mach 0.91 at sea level and 590mph (949km/h) Mach 0.90 at 40,000ft (12,192m), and to reach that height in just seven minutes.

The F-101A was not to be the end of the Voodoo development story. It was followed by the strengthened F-101C plus reconnaissance versions of both 'A' and 'C', and also the F-101B, which was a different animal. As described later, in 1949 the USAF laid down its requirements for an interceptor that would eventually be won by Convair's F-102 design. However, the latter project suffered substantial development problems and entered service much later than expected while Convair's follow-on F-106 (Chapter Four) did not arrive as quickly as planned either. In addition, the overall urgency for a new interceptor was heightened substantially once the Soviet Union had exploded its first thermonuclear device in August 1953, less than a year after America had detonated its first. Finally, Air Defense Command (ADC) stressed the argument that having two new interceptors would provide greater security pending the arrival of the F-106.

ADC was impressed by the F-101 and in October 1952 put forward the idea that this airframe could also serve as an interceptor. USAF Headquarters initially turned the idea down but in April 1953 ADC tried again when it suggested that an F-101 interceptor could operate on the perimeters of American home territory where ground-based radars were inadequate. As a result, later in the year the Air Force Council requested that industry be invited to enter a competition to find an interceptor that would fill the gap between the F-89 and F-106, and complement the F-102. A two-seat F-101, an interceptor variant of the F-100 and an advanced F-89 were the three proposals submitted.

The McDonnell F-101 Voodoo was an immensely impressive aircraft. This shot shows a single-seat F-101A fighter-bomber.

North American Interceptor

North American's Model 211 project (Chapter Four) was begun during this period and is understood to have been the company's offering against the new requirement – it was seen as a potential back-up to Convair's F-102. A manufacturer's display model of a radar-equipped Super Sabre development has been discovered, but its precise identity is currently unknown. This design has relatively large side intakes that sit low on the fuselage just behind the cockpit beneath the wing; it also has an all-moving horizontal tailplane and a single engine with afterburner and it carries a single large-calibre underside cannon set slightly offset to port from the centre-line. The NA-211 itself forms part of a separate story leading to the F-107 and so is discussed again in Chapter Four.

Northrop N-81/F-89F all-weather interceptor project (11.51). Gerald Balzer

Northrop N-81, N-82 and F-89X

The N-81 all-weather interceptor project was actually started in 1951 and presented a quite substantial development of the standard F-89 Scorpion, all part of Northrop's considerable efforts to upgrade the aircraft. It was known as the 'Advanced F-89' and the biggest new feature was a large mid-position centre wing nacelle on each side that housed four 320gal (1,455lit) fuel tanks, the main undercarriage wheel and, in its nose, a battery of fifty-two 2.75in (7.0cm) air-to-air folding fin rocket projectiles. A fuel tank in the rearward part of the fuselage nose ahead of the cockpit housed another 282gal (1,282lit) and three more behind the rear crew's seat contained 300gal (1,364lit), 336gal (1,528lit) and 282gal (1,282lit) respectively. Electronic equipment was housed in the nose and rear fuselage.

Power came from two General Electric XJ73-GE-5 engines and the aircraft's enlarged fuselage, with the spine deepened and faired into the fin, employed semi-monocoque, all-metal, stressed-skin construction throughout. The slightly swept wing was also built in aluminium alloy stressed-skin and incorporated wingtip ailerons (known as 'rototips'), split trailing-edge flaps, hinged leading-edge flaps, and a split-type aileron-speed brake combination in the outboard section. The complete horizontal tail surface (or 'rotovator'), moved to a lower position, was movable whereas the vertical tail surface was of the conventional stationary fin and movable rudder type. The aircraft carried two crew and was equipped with an all-weather interception radar. Its

Model of the Northrop YF-89F all-weather fighter at July 1952. Note the different nacelle arrangement to the original F-89F layout. George Cox

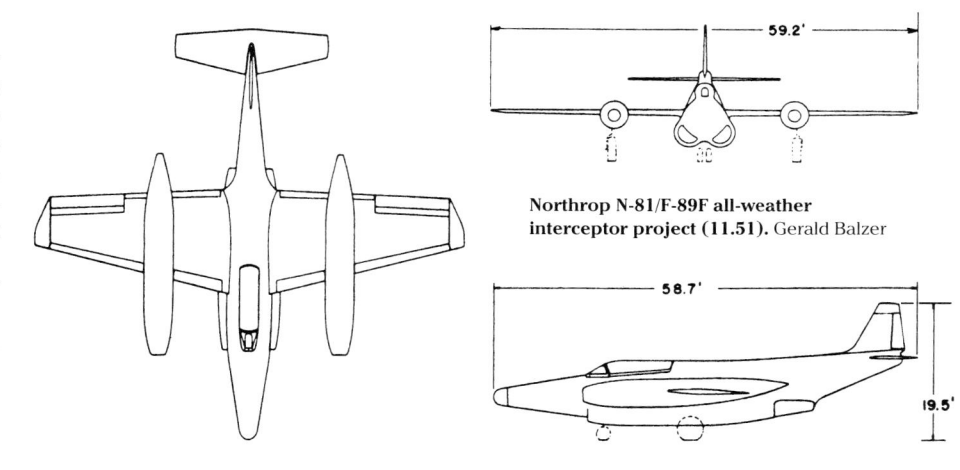

The First 'Centuries'

basic armament comprised 104 rocket projectiles, but there were a number of other options including 30mm cannon in the nose (four) or nacelle (four in each), or T-110 rocket guns (two in the nose or four in each nacelle) or Hughes Falcon air-to-air missiles (four in each nacelle).

As the F-89F the aircraft's performance was expected to be much improved over the older Scorpion. At gross weight the estimated rate of climb at sea level was 20,100ft/min (6,126m/min), time to 30,000ft (9,144m) 4.8 minutes and service ceiling 47,400ft (14,448m). The interception altitude was given as 50,000ft (15,240m) and the service ceiling at a combat weight of 44,124lb (20,015kg) was 53,000ft (16,154m). Most of the performance data was actually based on more power being made available from the XJ73s, namely 9,034lb (40.15kN) dry and 13,050lb (58.0kN) in full afterburner.

During 1952 the F-89F underwent detail design and reached the full-size mock-up stage (inspected on 26 May), and by July the planned YF-89F pre-series aircraft (designated the N-82) was showing some subtle differences, principally in having its nacelles moved to underneath the wing. This project was one of several to appear as a by-product

The two-seat all-weather interceptor version of the Voodoo was called the F-101B. This is the prototype 56-232, which was actually designated NF-101B to acknowledge its permanent test status and first flew on 27th March 1957.

of President Truman's reduced national defence budget introduced at the end of the 1940s. More money was generally available to designs described as improvements of current aircraft rather than all-new types with new designations, so the designers tried to keep even near 'all-new' types like the F-89F within the confines of modifications to ensure that sufficient funding could be obtained. The F-89F was eventually cancelled in August 1952, principally because its weight continued to increase. However, Northrop's 1953/1954 proposal against McDonnell and North American in the back-up interceptor competition is described in official literature as 'an Advanced F-89', so it is possible that a version of the F-89F was still seen as the solution.

There was also the F-89X which was a two-seat interceptor proposed in mid-1954 (or February 1952 according to another source) and powered by 7,800lb (34.7kN) thrust Wright J65-W-6 engines (10,200lb [45.3kN] with afterburner). This design was indeed considered as an interim type pending the arrival of the '1954 Interceptor' but, apart from the new powerplant, it showed few other changes to the airframe. An improved rate of climb was expected with an increase in speed to Mach 0.83 at 50,000ft (15,240m) and ceiling to over 56,000ft (17,069m), but the design was rejected in November 1954 because essentially it would be an all-new aircraft.

McDonnell F-101B Voodoo

In June 1954 the ADC announced that the F-101 interceptor would best meet its requirements and a go-ahead was given for its development on 25th February 1955 under WS-217A. The powerplant was to be two advanced Pratt & Whitney J57 engines, the aircraft would be a two-seater and heavier than the A-model. The first flight of the first F-101B took place on 27th March 1957, nearly a year later than initially estimated. In all 480 were built but they stayed in frontline service only until the early 1970s. It is understood that the F-101B was one of several projects earmarked to receive the F-109 designation, but in the event that number was never used.

The '1954 Interceptor'

Describing the F-101B program in full has taken this part of the story a little out of order because, in terms of timescale, the start of the Convair F-102 interceptor pre-dates the F-101B. In 1948 and 1949 the crisis generated by the Soviet Union's blockade of Berlin, plus the deterioration in relations between the countries that went with it, crystallized sharply the need for an effective interceptor to defend the US homeland. By 1951 Northrop's F-89 and Lockheed's F-94 were in service, but a much more advanced airframe was needed to match the ever improving capability of Soviet bombers. In addition better weapons were required to help deal with the threat. The result was the opening of a competition in 1949 for a '1954 Interceptor', the date signifying the planned year of the type's entry into service.

The resulting aircraft was to become one of the first examples of a weapon system where the airframe was designed around the equipment to be carried, rather than having the weapons and systems tacked on after its design was under way. The ever-increasing complexity of airborne weapons and avionics no longer allowed their development to continue as isolated programs. Instead such items and their carrier would be developed together so that the whole programme would cover the sum total of the airframe, the equipment and weapons, and their backup and maintenance equipment. The avionics, a Hughes-designed electronic fire control system that had itself won a 1950 competition against a large number of other electronics companies, was to be covered by MX1179 and the aircraft by MX1554; later the winning F-102 program was covered by Weapon System WS-201A. As such the specially designed '1954 Interceptor' was intended to surpass the estimated speed and altitude performance expected from Soviet intercontinental bombers at that time.

The requirements for this new interceptor, which would be a single-seater and armed with air-to-air missiles, were assessed from January 1949 onwards and formed into MX1554 in 1950. The airframe was to be structurally capable of withstanding a speed in excess of Mach 1 at heights above 50,000ft (15,240m) and a request for proposals was made on 18th June 1950. A total of nine projects had been submitted when bidding closed in January 1951.

Chance Vought V-371
Work on the Chance Vought V-371 design, which was extraordinarily advanced-looking for its time, began in late September 1950. It showed a very long slim fuselage, a short thin wing, engines mounted in slim 32ft 5in (9.9m)-long wing nacelles, a delta tail placed relatively low on a triangular-shaped fin, and a bicycle undercarriage with outriggers. Both fin and tail were swept 55° on the leading edge while the inner wing was swept about 18.5°. The small nosewheel was positioned a short distance behind the cockpit while the twin-wheel main gear was housed in the fuselage level with the centre of the wing. Each outrigger was placed in an engine nacelle that also

Chance Vought V-371 interceptor project (22.1.51). Dick Atkins, Vought Archive / Chris Gibson

Two views of a model of the Vought V-371 by John Hall.

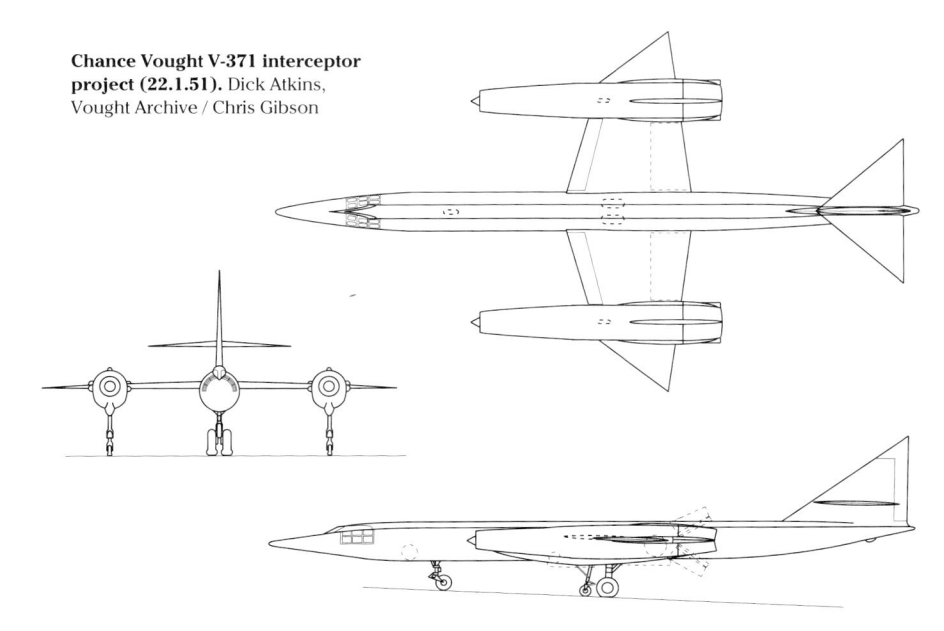

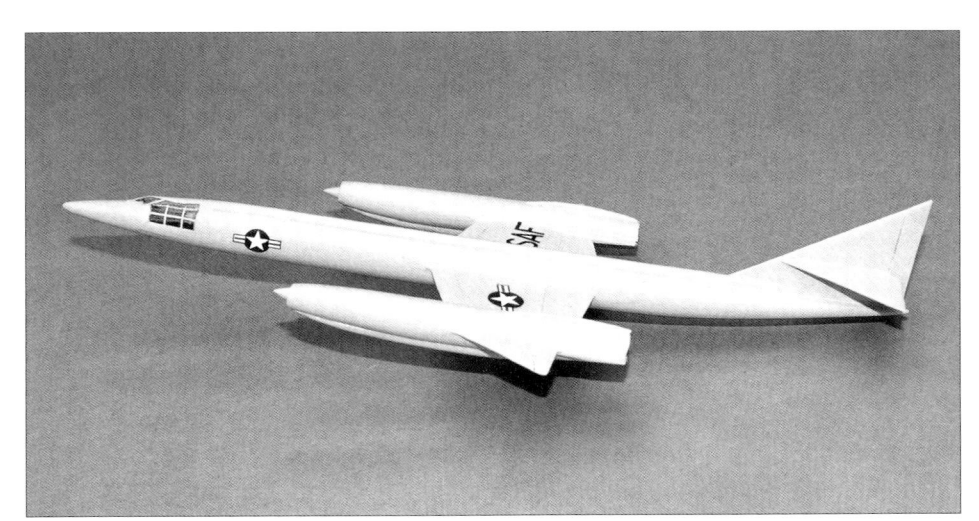

The First 'Centuries'

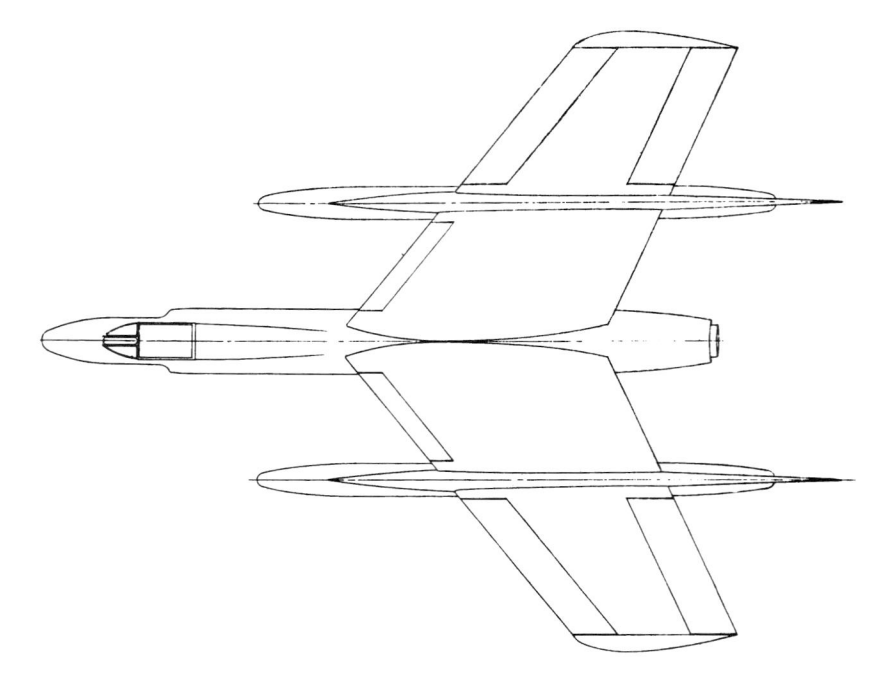

had, above and below its tail end, a set of speed brakes. Each inner wing carried leading edge droop flaps and trailing edge flaps while the small portion of wing fitted outside each nacelle formed an all-moving aileron with 15° of deflection both up and down; in addition the horizontal tail was an all-moving surface – all very advanced thinking.

Weapon details are unknown but it seems likely that any missiles (almost certainly Hughes Falcon among them) would have been carried in a fuselage bay and no gun is marked on the drawing. This document gives a weight for 'useful load', which will include the pilot and his equipment along with the weapons, as 10,778 lb (4,889kg), while a total of 5,900 lb (2,676kg) of fuel was to be carried. There was an alternative V-371B project powered by Wright XJ67-W-1 engines and also a V-371X that had Pratt & Whitney XJ57-P-1 powerplants; their respective gross weights were 47,870 lb (21,714kg) and 47,330 lb (21,469kg).

Convair Interceptor Project

Just the one proposal was made by Convair, utilizing the company's experience in delta wings gained from the XF-92A. However, a solid nose was introduced to house a radar with air intakes placed at the sides of the single seat cockpit. The wing trailing edge carried combined ailerons and elevators (elevons). It seems that the powerplant for this aircraft, at least for the prototypes, was to have been a single Westinghouse J40 that offered an estimated maximum speed of Mach 1.88 and a ceiling of 56,500ft (17,221m); in the event however, both prototypes and production aircraft were destined to be powered by a Pratt & Whitney J57. Convair's interceptor proposal had a span of about 40ft 6in (12.3m) and a length of 52ft 6in (16.0m) and weapons were to be carried in an internal bay.

Vought's single-seat V-373 project was a long-range fighter and research project started very soon after the '1954 Interceptor' competition. It represents possibly the last development of the old Cutlass arrangement and this is the only known drawing. The reason for including it here is to compare it with the very different V-371, both designs reflecting Vought's current ideas for supersonic fighters. Powered by one Pratt & Whitney J57 engine with afterburner, V-373's span was 44ft (13.4m) and length 54ft 11in (16.7m) (13.2.51). Dick Atkins, Vought Archive

These two views of an original Convair model from 1951, in need of some restoration, show the company's initial proposal to the '1954 Interceptor' requirement (1.51). The model's span is 15.25in (38.7cm) and length 19.7in (50cm). John Aldaz

American Secret Projects: Fighters & Interceptors

Douglas Model 1245

This attractive single-seat design from Douglas had side intakes feeding a single, reheated Wright YJ67-W-1 engine, a swept wing with leading edge slats, large trailing edge flaps and smaller ailerons, an all-moving tailplane with 5° of dihedral, and a fixed fin with a rudder. The Model 1245's empennage was placed well out of the way above the large jetpipe and there was a tricycle undercarriage with the main legs folding into the fuselage side. To allow the pilot to get aboard his seat would be dropped down in front of the nosewheel – after taking his position he would then raise the seat back into its cockpit. Fuel was housed in six fuselage tanks, in a line from behind the cockpit to level with the jet pipe, and a dive brake was placed in the bottom of the fuselage roughly midway between the nose and main gears. A big difference to the other MX1554 contenders was the lack of an internal weapons bay, the missiles (which on the model are unidentified) being carried under the wing. Ed Heinemann, chief engineer at Douglas, was a strong advocate for keeping down weight and so carrying the weapons like this may have resulted in a lighter aircraft. There were five underwing hardpoints per side, the innermost pylons taking drop tanks leaving the outer pairs for missiles. No gun was carried.

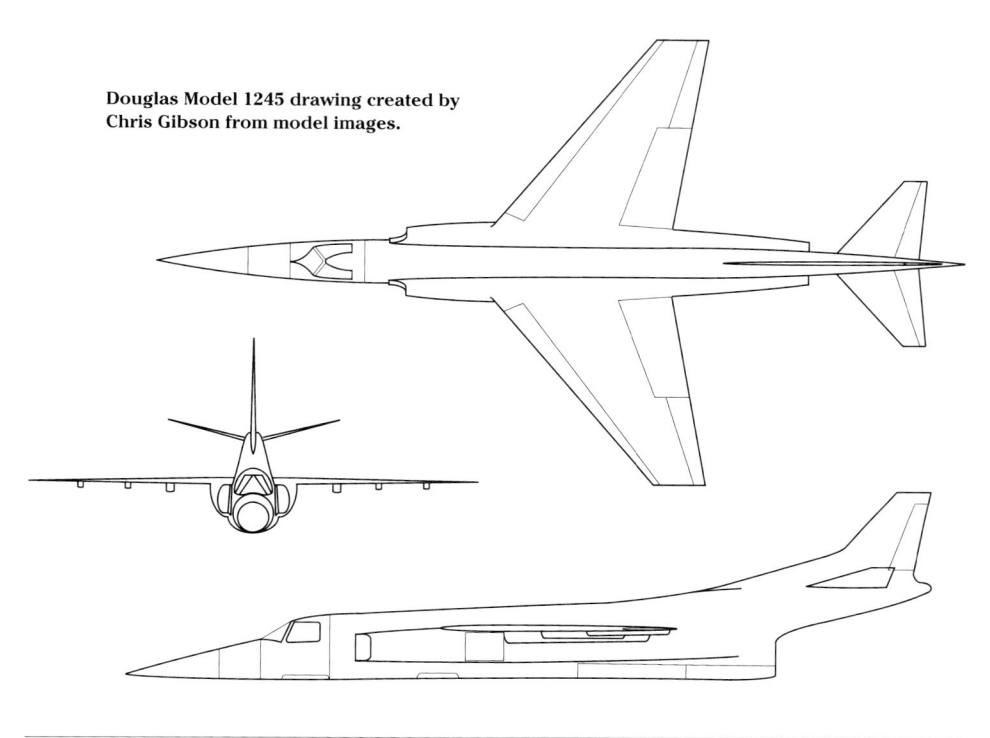

Douglas Model 1245 drawing created by Chris Gibson from model images.

Three views of a model of the Douglas 1245 to MX1554. This is a large model with a span of 22.8in (58cm) and a length of 39.8in (101cm). John Aldaz

The First 'Centuries'

Lockheed L-205 (1.51). Peter Clukey

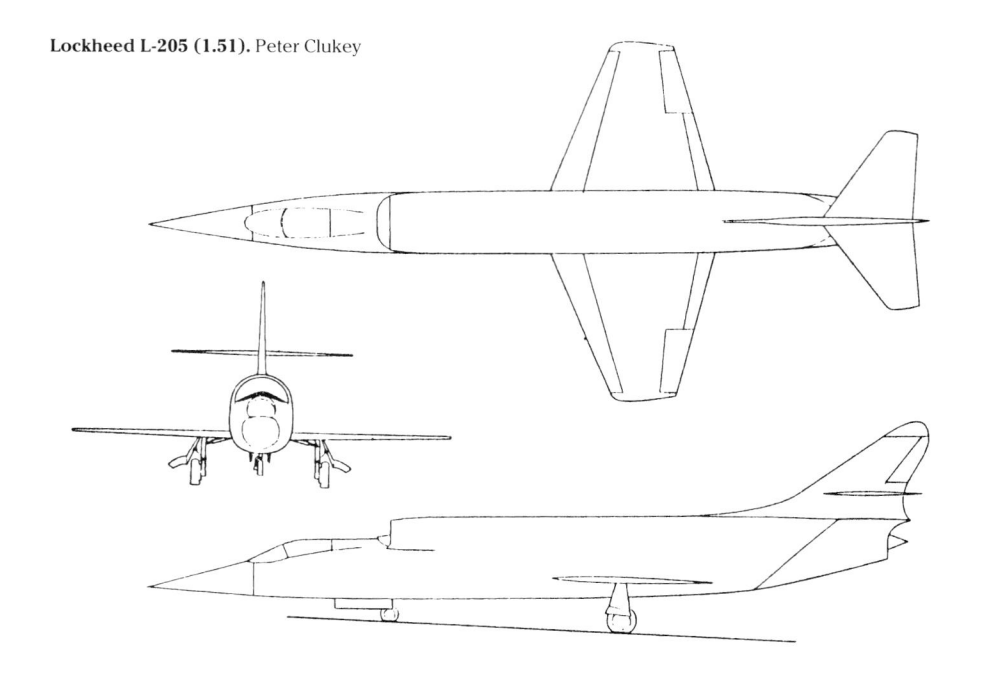

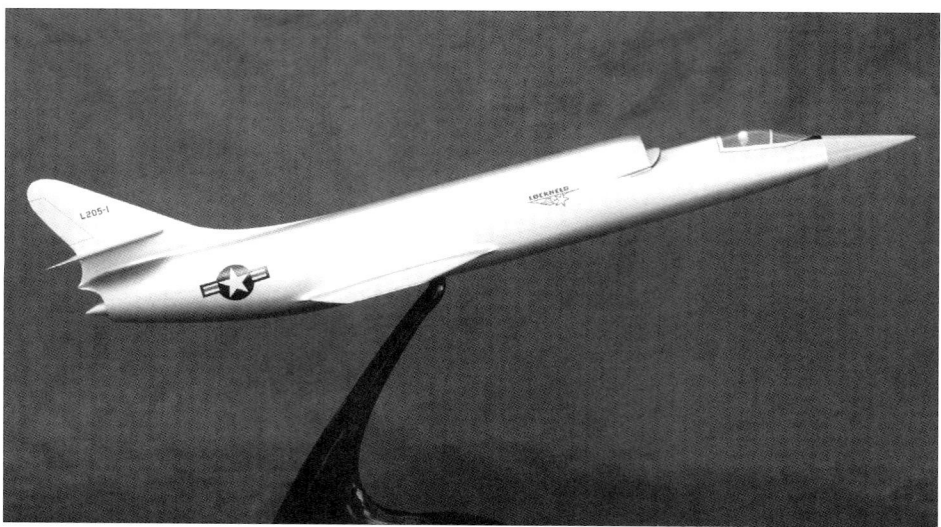

Lockheed L-205

Lockheed was the fourth manufacturer to make only one submission, which in appearance had much in common with the company's later F-104 Starfighter discussed in the next chapter. This project preceded the F-104 studies by a year or two but some of Lockheed's theories for small thin straight wings had clearly been established by the time the USAF requested its new interceptor. L-205 had a delta tail, a dorsal air intake just behind the cockpit, a low-position wing and a tricycle undercarriage. Six Hughes Falcon air-to-air missiles were housed in a mid-lower fuselage bay and twenty 2.75in (7.0cm) folding-fin rockets were placed on the sides of the bay. Estimated performance figures for the L-205 included time to 40,000ft (12,192m) 1.6 minutes, combat ceiling 63,000ft (19,202m) and maximum range 1,530 nautical miles (2,834km).

North American Interceptor Projects

North American submitted two designs but it hasn't proved possible to uncover their details. However, it seems fair to assume that at least one of the designs would have been based on the contemporary Sabre 45 project leading to the F-100 Super Sabre. The accompanying picture of a manufacturer's display model is of an unknown design but it almost certainly comes from North American. It also fits the size and style that might be expected from that company to fulfil the interceptor requirement. It is a single seater and has a single-engine high delta wing layout with a low tail position and a chin intake. No gun or external weapons are visible.

Northrop N-65

As a later chapter will show, during the 1950s Northrop became heavily involved in the design of interceptors and in fact its N-65 project is listed as a '1954 Interceptor'. However, it is known that Northrop did not complete a submission to the interceptor competition because no references are made to the company in official documents.

Republic AP-44 and AP-57

Three projects were submitted to the competition by Republic, one of which led to the XF-103 discussed below. In October 1947, while the XF-91 program was under way, Republic privately and in some depth began looking at high Mach number interceptors for the Air Force. The result was a brochure submission to the Service made in early 1948 that

Model of the Lockheed L-205. Jim Keeshen

American Secret Projects: Fighters & Interceptors

Model of an unknown North American fighter project. This beautiful design appears to fit the requirements of the '1954 Interceptor' and the model has a span of 12.7in (32.3cm) and length 21.3in (54cm). At 1/32nd scale this corresponds to a span of 33ft 10in (10.3m) and length 56ft 8in (17.3m). Jonathan Rigutto / photo © 2005 Chad Slattery

contained four interceptor projects, differing mainly in their powerplant. One, the AP-44A, was described as a Mach 3 all-weather high altitude defence fighter to be powered by a turbo-ramjet dual-mode powerplant (a combination of a turbojet and a ramjet which used a common air intake and exhaust). When the pilot wanted to take the aircraft to its highest speeds the afterburner part of the turbojet would be used as the ramjet, the air supplied to it bypassing the compressor and turbine. This facility would extend the aircraft's maximum possible speed beyond the Mach 2 limit of the turbojet.

At the time there was considerable interest in ramjets as the means of achieving very high speeds. The fundamental limitation of turbojets was well recognised: namely the fact that turbojets cannot handle supersonic airflow and incoming air has therefore to be reduced to subsonic speed before reaching the compressor (the reason for the variety of shock-cones and intake spikes that were subsequently to appear in air-intakes). The problem this brings, aside from complexity of intake design, is the big rise in temperature that it produces. On the other hand, ramjets work very efficiently at high speeds but need to be propelled a long way up the speed scale before they work at all. Mixed powerplants therefore seemed a logical answer. However, in practice exotic forms of propulsion, like ramjets and rockets, were to find very little application in manned aircraft over the coming years, the turbojet would reign supreme for the next half century – but this was far from clear back in the early 1950s.

Of the other three Republic designs, one used a single turbojet with a large afterburner that automatically restricted the top speed to Mach 2; another used an afterburning turbojet plus a big throttleable rocket motor; and the last had a large turbojet only, which was not fitted with an afterburner. The latter was considered to offer long range but problems were envisaged with the size and weight of the power unit. Despite the highly advanced

North American fighter. Chris Gibson

Model of an unknown Republic fighter project with intakes on the sides of the fuselage and the designer's now characteristic inverse taper wings. It appears to have a rocket motor mounted above the jetpipe, which makes it possible that this design formed part of the company's MX1554 proposals. Cradle of Aviation Museum

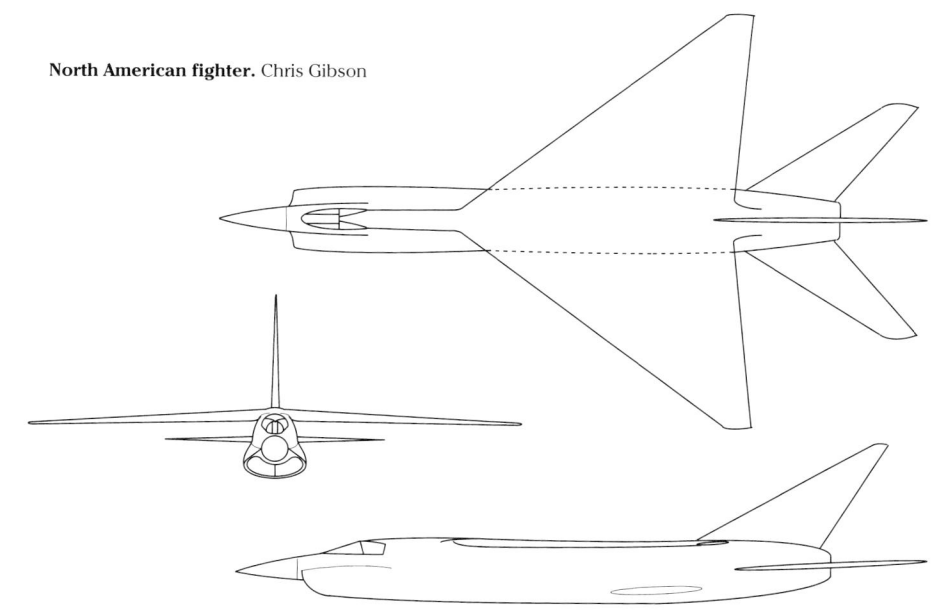

The First 'Centuries'

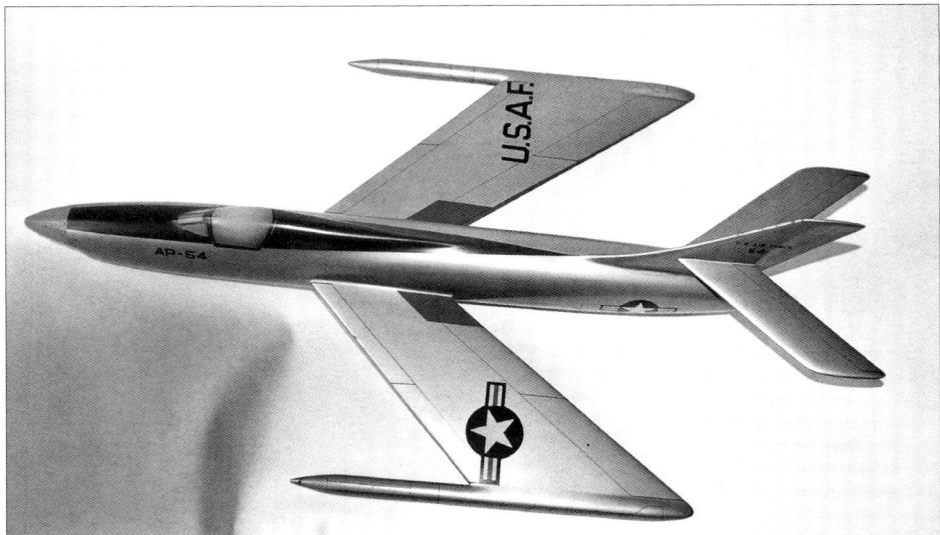

It is also possible that Republic's AP-54 all-weather interceptor project shown here in model form may also have been part of the company's '1954 Interceptor' studies. The inverse taper wings have long slender pods at the tips; there is a medium-size radome with a chin intake; a single seat and a single power unit (and possibly a small rocket motor beneath the jet). Model span is 13.0in (33.0cm) and length 21.75in (55.25cm), giving real dimensions of 34ft 8in (10.6m) span and 58ft (17.7m) length.

nature of its engine, Republic considered the AP-44A to be the most promising of the four ideas. However, the USAF took no action and the company had to continue its turbo-ramjet studies privately, which culminated with the submissions to the '1954 Interceptor' requirement.

The reason why Republic submitted three designs to satisfy MX1554 was that the company felt this would give the opportunity to move in any direction the Air Force wanted to take. The AP-57, the latest stage of the turbo-ramjet studies, filled one of the company's solutions; while in-house the second design was described as the 'XF-91B'. Developed from the original XF-91, the XF-91B would use a Westinghouse fire control system that was based on the Hughes MX1179 system and it had a retractable rocket pack in the lower forward fuselage housing a battery of 2.75in (7.0cm) projectiles. In addition, supplementary power for high-altitude performance would be supplied by a large Aerojet rocket motor fitted inside a special Teflex filled and coated cell, the engine using nitric acid as its oxidant. Lastly there was a conventional Mach 2 aircraft, powered by an afterburning turbojet, which Republic presented with less emphasis, considering it from a technical point of view to be the least satisfactory approach. However, with this final concept the design team had covered itself against those officials within the Air Force who were strictly against having rocket motors, and also others who might consider the dual turbo-ramjet powerplant just too bold a step.

Three winning designs were named on 2nd July 1951, from Convair, Lockheed and the turbo-ramjet proposal from Republic, and all were requested to proceed at least up to the full-size mock-up stage, a process known as Phase 1 development. However, the Air Force quickly realised that funding three such programs would be costly and so the Lockheed interceptor was cancelled in its entirety well before the end of the year. A full go-ahead was eventually given to both Convair and Republic, although the latter was redesignated as a research project at the same time as the Lockheed was dropped.

American Secret Projects: Fighters & Interceptors

Lockheed Model 99

After the award of the Phase 1 development contract, Lockheed replaced the L-205 Temporary Designation Number with Basic Model Number 99, signifying that detail design of the aircraft had begun. As noted, a full-scale mock-up was planned as part of the Phase 1 program but the Model 99 was soon scrapped. It is understood that problems with increasing weight and consequent reductions in performance may also have contributed to the decision, and the Model 99 was rated the lowest of the three designs anyway. Lockheed's research and development was switched to a new day superiority fighter concept that would come to fruition as the F-104 Starfighter.

Convair F-102 Delta Dagger

Convair was in truth the clear winner of the competition, the excessively advanced nature of Republic's design ensuring that it would take a lot longer to develop than Convair's interceptor. When the Air Force agreed to accelerate Convair's new interceptor program on 24th November 1951 the decision spelt the end of the Republic XF-91A project, which had been seen as an interim interceptor. Ten pre-production aircraft, designated YF-102s, were ordered the following month and the first of these flew on 24th October 1953. However it exhibited disappointingly poor performance, top speed being limited by drag rise to Mach 0.98 and ceiling to just 48,000ft (14,630m). Wind tunnel testing was by then predicting that the YF-102 would not achieve its original performance estimates, the designers having failed to allow for the considerable drag generated by the aircraft's bulky rear fuselage.

The aerodynamic problems suffered by the first prototypes and Convair's efforts to deal with them have been well documented, but in essence the aircraft would not go supersonic. In due course the airframe was redesigned using Whitcomb's 'area rule' that allowed aircraft designers to greatly reduce transonic drag. The YF-102 was given a new fuselage that was slimmer in the region of the

Three photographs revealing the development process of Convair's interceptor. The first image shows the model of Convair's original submission to the '1954 Interceptor' competition. The second is a YF-102 model with its larger body while the third shows the slimmed area rule fuselage and the sleeker appearance overall of the F-102A. All of these models were made by the manufacturer at the time the versions were first designed and the F-102A indicates subtle differences from the real thing. John Aldaz

The First 'Centuries'

This is the second prototype Convair YF-102, the aircraft having made its maiden flight on 11th January 1954.

The YF-102's aerodynamic problems were solved by a major redesign, the new type being designated YF-102A. This is the first prototype pictured in 1955 and it shows the extent of the alterations. When the production F-102A Delta Dagger entered service its wing shape was a new feature for Air Force fighters.

wing to compensate for the extra cross-sectional area introduced by the latter (the 'coke-bottle' configuration), the idea being to keep any increase in area along an airframe within a smooth curve when plotted on a graph. The new fuselage was also longer and there were numerous other changes and in its new form the aircraft was designated YF-102A. It took to the air for the first time on 20th December 1954 and achieved – to everyone's undoubted relief – Mach 1.22 and an altitude of 53,000ft (16,154m).

However, along with the fighter's aerodynamic problems the MX1179 system also suffered from slow progress and this brought an official recommendation to produce an 'interim' F-102. This would be powered by an 'interim' Pratt & Whitney J57 engine and have a less capable 'interim' fire control system, while the 'ultimate' aircraft would get the Wright J67 which had been earmarked for production MX1554 machines. As such the 'interim' interceptor duly entered service as the F-102A Delta Dagger, while the 'ultimate' F-102B was eventually redesignated F-106. The F-102A entered service in 1956, 875 were built and they served in the front line for most of the 1960s, and with Air National Guard units until 1978.

American Secret Projects: Fighters & Interceptors

Republic AP-57/XF-103
The story of Republic's winning selection is thoroughly covered in *Valkyrie: North American's Mach 3 Superbomber* by Dennis R Jenkins and Tony R Landis. It would be wasteful to repeat it here so the aircraft is described relatively briefly. After receiving its Phase 1 development contract the Republic AP-57 or XF-103 (as it was officially designated) appeared on the USAF's books as Weapon System WS-204A. At this stage the aircraft had a conventional canopy over its cockpit but, after a full-size metal mock-up was inspected on 2nd March 1953, a flush cockpit was introduced with the pilot seeing out by means of a periscope. It was felt that the Plexiglas canopy would suffer from kinetic heating at high speeds while the protruding shape would add drag (it was at this point that the development contract was also extended). The aerothermal heating problem was caused by the friction of air against airframe, something that the veteran American commentator Walter Cronkite called the 'heat barrier' or 'thermal thicket', and it would be a factor in the design of many of the fighters covered by this book.

Since the fighter was designed to operate at Mach 3+ and at heights of up to 80,000ft (24,384m) it was automatically going to push the boundaries of current technology further ahead. Thus the various lines of development for the XF-103 included state-of-the-art research into titanium fabrication, high-temperature hydraulics and downward escape capsules for the pilot. Titanium was a metal then new to aircraft manufacture and the XF-103 was to be constructed entirely from it. In the XF-103's forward fuselage six Falcon missiles and two batches of eighteen 2.75in (7.0cm) 'Mighty Mouse' folding fin aerial rockets (FFAR) were housed in retractable bays.

All of this was on top of the dual-cycle propulsion system. The turbojet engine was to be a Wright XJ67-W-1 (licence-built British

Drawing showing the Republic AP-57 as at 10th September 1951, not long after it had been selected as one of the three winners in the '1954 Interceptor' contest. It has a few more 'rounded edges' than the later XF-103, but from the layout point of view everything is pretty well there. Span is 35ft 8.5in (10.9m), length 73ft 7in (22.4m) and wing area 401ft² (37.3m²). Scott Lowther archive

This model of the Republic AP-57 shows what the aircraft looked like during 1951. Cradle of Aviation Museum

Model of the Republic XF-103 as ordered, with its original cockpit canopy. Jonathan Rigutto / photo © 2005 Chad Slattery

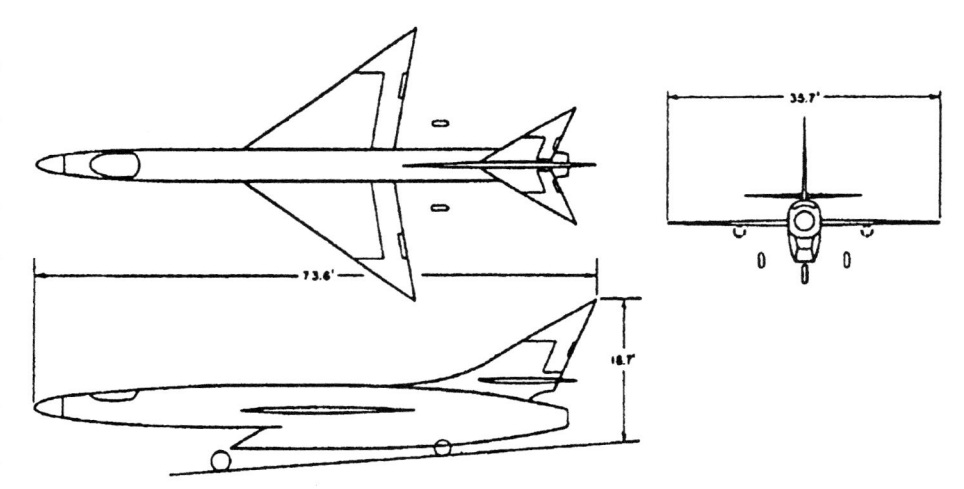

The First 'Centuries'

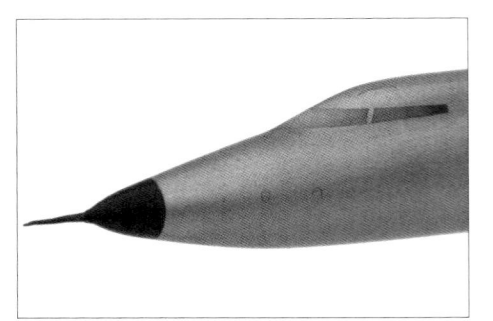

Close-up of the nose on the first XF-103.
Jonathan Rigutto / photo © 2005 Chad Slattery

The later XF-103 showing its weapon arrangement. Two Falcon missiles are seen extended from the armament bays on 'zero rail' launchers (a further Falcon was housed on each side of the fuselage). Behind the Falcons is an extended pack of eighteen 2.75in (7.0cm) folding-fin rockets.
Jonathan Rigutto / photo © 2005 Chad Slattery

Planview of the Republic XF-103 with its weapons deployed. Larry McLaughlin

Olympus) while the separate Wright 'afterburner' or ramjet was designated XRJ55-W-1. The latter could be operated as an afterburner when the J67's exhaust was directed into it, but if the turbojet were shut down the XRJ55 would operate as a ramjet. The complete powerplant was fed by a huge scoop intake placed beneath the fuselage and level with the wing root leading edge, and the ramjet would usually only operate at speeds above Mach 2.25.

Operating as a turbojet with afterburner the maximum available thrust was about 19,500 lb (86.7kN), and as a ramjet apparently 18,800 lb (83.6kN) when flying at 55,000ft (16,764m), the switchover taking just ten seconds. By 1957, when the surviving prototype had been modified for research, the turbojet was expected to give 13,950 lb (62.0kN) of thrust dry for thirty minutes and 22,100 lb (98.2kN) in afterburner for five minutes; the ramjet was expected to give 37,400 lb (166.2kN) thrust above Mach 2.24 and 35,000ft (10,668m). Some astonishing performance figures were expected from the XF-103, including a sea level rate of climb as an interceptor of 38,200ft/min (11,643m/min) or 35,900ft/min (10,942m/min) with the original canopy in place; time to 60,000ft (18,288m) 7.1 minutes or 9.0 minutes; and a combat ceiling of 73,000ft (22,250m) or 70,500ft (21,488m) with the original canopy. Calculations made in 1957 suggested that the maximum possible speed would be around Mach 3.7: a staggering figure and one that was not to be achieved by any aircraft (other than an air-launched rocket) over the next half century.

To help keep the project moving, and because the XF-103 seemed to hold so much promise, the Air Force allocated some scarce research and development money. In June 1954 Republic finally received a contract for three aircraft, but progress throughout was slow, there were numerous setbacks and in early 1957 the order was cut to just one airframe and two flight engines. Then on 21st August 1957 the XF-103 program was cancelled in its entirety, the pace of development being so slow that there was no longer any justification for spending further money. The Air Force's announcement cited budgetary aspects plus the expected availability of alternative vehicles in the future to provide similar test data. Also, the introduction of the Long Range Interceptor, Experimental (LRI-X), as discussed in Chapter Five, moved the emphasis away from the XF-103. At the time of its cancellation the XF-103 was thought to be around a year away from its maiden flight.

American Secret Projects: Fighters & Interceptors

Parallel Developments in Weaponry and Engines

Numerous references have already been to air-to-air missiles (AAMs), at that time a new type of weapon for carriage by the F-102 and other fighter aircraft both for the Air Force and Navy. Such weapons were tailored to the greater levels of performance made available by jet-powered fighters and they introduced new methods of attack. For example offensive missions by fighter-launched guided weapons against bombers, at longer ranges than previously, could nullify the latter's conventional defensive armament or its evasive action. In addition missiles homing on to a target would provide much greater tactical freedom to the fighter during and immediately after an attack. The Hughes MX1179 system was actually required to 'direct' some type of air-to-air guided missile and the only suitable weapon proved to be the Hughes MX-904 Falcon, America's first successful AAM, which had several other designations (including XF-98 and GAR-1) before becoming AIM-4 (Air Interception Missile 4). Falcon incorporated a semi-active target seeker and depended on radar 'illumination' of the target by the interceptor. It required a direct hit for detonation and had a range of 5 miles (8km), and a speed of about Mach 3 at launch down to Mach 1.2 when hitting the target.

Two other missiles to make their appearance during this period were the less complex AIM-9 Sidewinder (initially designated GAR-8 by the USAF), and the AIM-7 Sparrow. Sidewinder was a small missile fitted with an infra-red proximity fuse that was designed by the Naval Weapons Center at China Lake and commercially produced by Philco. It was intended to home in on heat sources emanating from its target and the first successful firing was made in September 1953; upgraded versions of this immensely successful weapon still serve to this day. Raytheon's larger Sparrow was begun in the late 1940s as a beam-riding weapon but was subsequently modified to operate with semi-active radar homing. New versions were being produced in the 1970s and Sparrow was carried by or nominated for many of the fighters and fighter projects described in later chapters.

Developments in weaponry were matched by new engines. During the Second World War the mighty Curtiss-Wright Corporation produced a vast number of piston engines but it was slow to take on the jet. As a result it acquired licences to produce the British Armstrong Siddeley Sapphire (as the J65) and the more powerful Bristol Olympus (J67). The former was a success, finding a number of fighter and bombers to use it, but the J67 found no successful application – although as Concorde's powerplant it was to clock up more supersonic hours than any other engine. Eventually Curtiss-Wright lost its eminent position in the aero-engine world. Much more successful was Pratt & Whitney, whose JT3 (J57) was first designed in 1948/1949 and got aboard many of the fighters in this book (plus Boeing's B-52 Stratofortress bomber and 707 airliner, and Douglas's DC-8 airliner, all hugely successful aircraft). Pratt followed it with an enlarged version called the J75, which was designed for Mach 2 fighters and powered the F-105 and F-106 (next chapter). However, a supersonic engine rival was also forthcoming from General Electric in the form of the J79 that got aboard the F-104 Starfighter and F-4 Phantom, two of the biggest selling American fighters. From this point Pratt & Whitney and General Electric were to lead the manufacture of jet engines in America.

The USAF Goes Supersonic

Although some of the more ambitious designs failed to make it through to flight status, the first Century fighters moved US fighter design – and USAF fighter operations – successfully into the supersonic era. Would some of the more exotic designs have been successful? Subsequent experience indicates that this is unlikely. The first Century fighters – the F-100, F-101, and F-102 – were quite big enough steps in their own right.

'Century Series' Fighter Studies – Estimated Data

Project	Span ft in (m)	Length ft in (m)	Gross Wing Area ft² (m²)	Gross Weight lb (kg)	Engine lb (kN)	Max Speed / Height mph (km/h) / ft (m)	Armament
NAA YF-100A Super Sabre (flown)	36 7 (11.2)	47 1 (14.3)	385 (35.8)	24,789 (11,244)	1 x P&W XJ57-P-7 9,500 (42.2)	660 (1,062) at 43,350 (13,213)	4 x 20mm cannon
McDonnell F-101A Voodoo (flown)	39 8 (12.1)	67 5 (20.5)	368 (34.2)	48,120 (21,827)	2 x P&W J57-P-13 10,200 (45.3), 15,000 (66.7) ab	1,009 (1,623) at 35,000 (10,668)	4 x 20mm cannon
Northrop N-81 'Advanced F-89'	59 2.5 (18.0)	58 8.5 (17.9)	650.7 (60.5)	47,674 (21,625) (with rockets)	2 x GE XJ73-GE-5 8,765 (39.0), 12,660 (56.3) ab	714 (1,149) at S/L	See text
McDonnell F-101B Voodoo (flown)	39 8 (12.1)	67 5 (20.5)	368 (34.2)	45,664 (20,713)	2 x P&W J57-P-55 11,990 (53.3), 16,900 (75.1) ab	1,134 (1,825) at 35,000 (10,668)	2 x AIR-2A Genie AAM, 2 x AIM-4C Falcon AAM
'1954 Interceptors'							
Chance Vought V-371	41 4 (12.6)	86 0 (26.2)	480 (44.6)	48,500 (21,997)	2 x P&W J57-P-5 with ab	In excess of Mach 1	Falcon AAMs & RPs
Douglas Model 1245	37 6 (11.4)	66 1 (20.1)	400 (37.2)	26,800 (12,156)	1 x Wright YJ67-W-1 11,800 (52.4), 19,700 (87.6)	High supersonic	6 x AAM, RP details unknown
Lockheed L-205	30 4 (9.2) (w/o tip tanks)	63 9 (19.4)	300 (27.9)	32,125 (14,572)	1 x GE XJ53-GE-X10 15,000 (66.7) ab	1,253 (2,016) at 35,000 (10,668)	6 x Falcon AAM, 20 x 2.75in (7.0cm) RPs
Convair YF-102 (flown)	37 0 (11.3)	52 6 (16.0)	661 (61.5)	26,404 (11,977)	1 x P&W J57-P-11 9,200 (40.9), 14,800 (65.8) ab	Mach 0.98 at altitude (Mach 1+ in a dive)	6 x Falcon AAM, 24 x 2.75in (7.0cm) RPs
Convair F-102A Delta Dagger (flown)	38 1.5 (11.6)	68 4.5 (20.8)	695 (64.6)	28,150 (12,769)	1 x P&W J57-P-23 10,200 (45.3), 16,000 (71.1) ab	825 (1,327) Mach 1.23 at 36,000 (10,973)	6 x Falcon AAM, 24 x 2.75in (7.0cm) RPs
Republic XF-103 (1957 as research aircraft)	35 10 (10.9)	81 11 (24.7)	401 (37.3)	38,200 (17,328) (40,000 [18,144] air defence role)	1 x Wright turbo-ramjet See text	1,980 (3,186) Mach 3 above 47,500 (14,478)	6 x Falcon AAM, 36 x 2.75in (7.0cm) RPs (as interceptor)

The First 'Centuries'

Chapter Four

Later 'Centuries' and Other Concepts

A model of the North American WS.300A project. Jim Keeshen

Overall the Century Series competitions resulted in some remarkable aircraft designs, not only involving different configurations but embodying quite different design philosophies. Whereas the F-101, F-102 and F-103 continued the trend towards ever larger and more complex interceptors, the next in the series took a totally different line. The F-104 offered a much lighter and in many ways simpler approach. The F-105, however, returned to the format of large and heavy aircraft and the F-106, dubbed by its manufacturer as the 'ultimate interceptor', was a highly sophisticated machine. Four of the six Century designs to enter service were evolved from earlier aircraft, albeit with much higher performance, while two were radical new designs. With the addition of a naval aircraft (the McDonnell F-4 Phantom), these machines were to provide the backbone of USAF fighter capability for the next three decades. The Century fighters therefore represented an enormously important period in the development of US fighter design. This Chapter looks at the concepts that led up to, competed with, or represented possible developments of the F-104, F-105 and F-106.

Lockheed's Starfighter

The background to the F-104 has been told many times. Following the air combat experienced by American pilots during the Korean War there was a call for a pure fighter that was light, simple and ideal for dogfighting. Such a type had been pretty well ignored by the Air Force for some time. By November 1952 Lockheed was fully aware that the Air Force was seeking a new air superiority fighter. Korean experience had shown that it should be capable of operating from forward airfields and have the ability to gain height quickly and be able to fight at high altitudes. In fact the Air Force felt the solution would be a relatively heavy delta-wing aircraft but Lockheed saw that a lighter straight-wing design could be both better and cheaper. The result would still be a relatively advanced and complex machine – as Lockheed's chief engineer Clarence 'Kelly' Johnson observed 'you simply don't fly at 40,000ft at those kinds of speeds just by throwing a saddle over the thing and riding it' – but the designers believed that the ongoing trend towards ever larger, more complex and more expensive fighters could be brought to a halt. The studies leading to the F-104 were extensive and involved much research.

As a result in November 1952 Lockheed made an unsolicited proposal to the Air Force for a straight-wing design, the L-246. Seeing the potential of this new line of thinking, a General Operational Requirement was raised very quickly for a lightweight air superiority fighter to replace Tactical Air Command

(TAC) F-100 Super Sabres from 1957 onwards, a move which brought the rest of industry on board in a design competition after the new document had been released on 12th December. The aircraft's top speed had to be at least Mach 1.3 at 35,000ft (10,668m) with a radius of action of at least 350nm (648km). It must be able to take off from 3,500ft (1,067m) runways, carry the 'equivalent firepower' of two 30mm cannon (another possible armament option being infra-red guided missiles), and be able to make four two-second firing passes per mission. The Air Force also specified an optical sight, with radar ranging regarded as 'optional' and no search radar required. However, the resulting F-104 was so fast that a visual search and acquisition of an airborne target was extremely difficult; by the time its pilot had found and assessed his target it was too late to do anything about it! Consequently a much better fire control system had to be developed, which was called the MA-10.

In January 1953 additional bids were assessed from North American and Republic and it is believed that Northrop also responded. MX1853 was issued to cover the new type, describing it as a Lightweight Day Fighter, and the summary below covers the known project design work undertaken by all four teams on lightweight fighters. Other sources suggest that there might have been more than one competition. For example, the British magazine *Flight* reported in its issue of 6th August 1954 that 'with a view to future procurement the USAF will evaluate four new lightweight fighter proposals next month. They are the Lockheed XF-104, Northrop Fang, North American Guppy and a Republic project'. By that stage the XF-104 was already flying. Before we examine any of these projects however, mention must be made of the role played by an earlier experimental design from another manufacturer.

Douglas X-3 Stiletto

The projects leading to the F-104 were, in part, a continuation of the fighter research started by Lockheed with the XF-90, described earlier in this book. However, it also benefited from the data generated by an experimental aircraft built by Douglas, the X-3 Stiletto. This had a very long slim fuselage and short stubby thin wings; it was powered by two Westinghouse J34-WE-17 engines and flew for the first time on 15th October 1952. Designed for high-speed research, it proved to be something of a failure. The prime reason was a lack of sufficient power; the early engines simply didn't match the airframe's potential – a problem with many early jet aircraft. Moreover, the X-3's narrow fuselage prevented the installation of larger engines. However, the aircraft did supply information on the relationship between aerodynamics and load distributions and also pioneered the employment of titanium in airframe design, several parts being made in this new and difficult material. To help with the design of the new fighter, and ensure that it gained as much as possible from the money that had been spent on the X-3, the Air Force ordered Douglas to supply Lockheed some Stiletto material.

Lockheed L-227

The first series of potential layouts for Lockheed's new fighter came under the Temporary Design Designation L-227, work having started back in March 1952. The illustrations give an idea of the different directions that the design team explored. One common feature of the designs shown is that they were all powered by a single engine. Two of the initial possibilities, both somewhat Russian in appearance, were the L-227-0-6 with a nose intake and sliding centrebody, and the rather

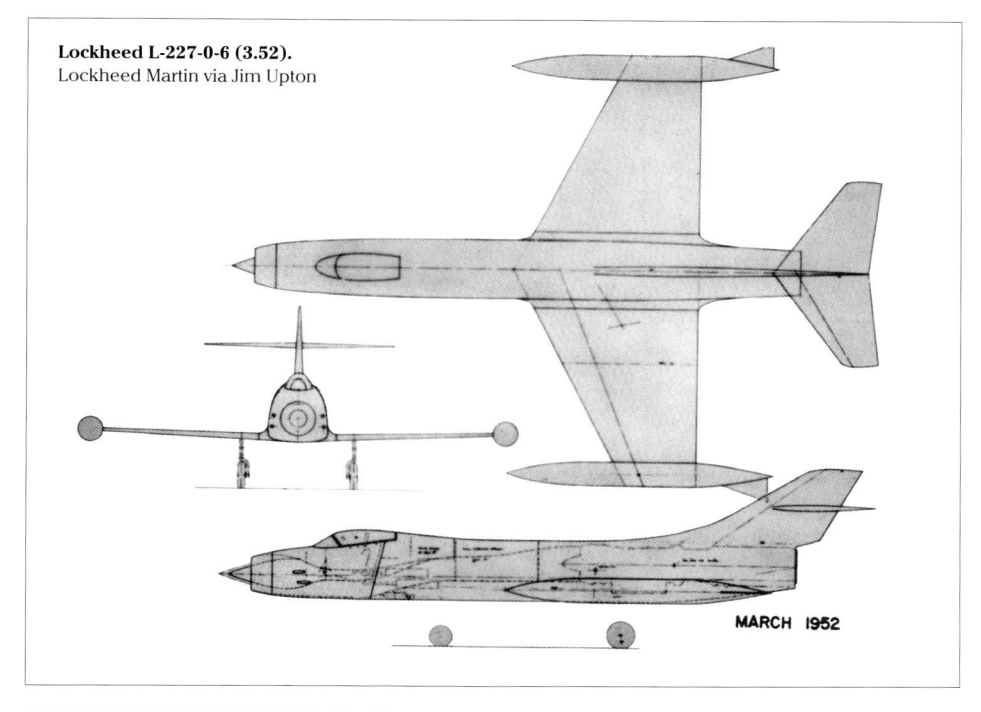

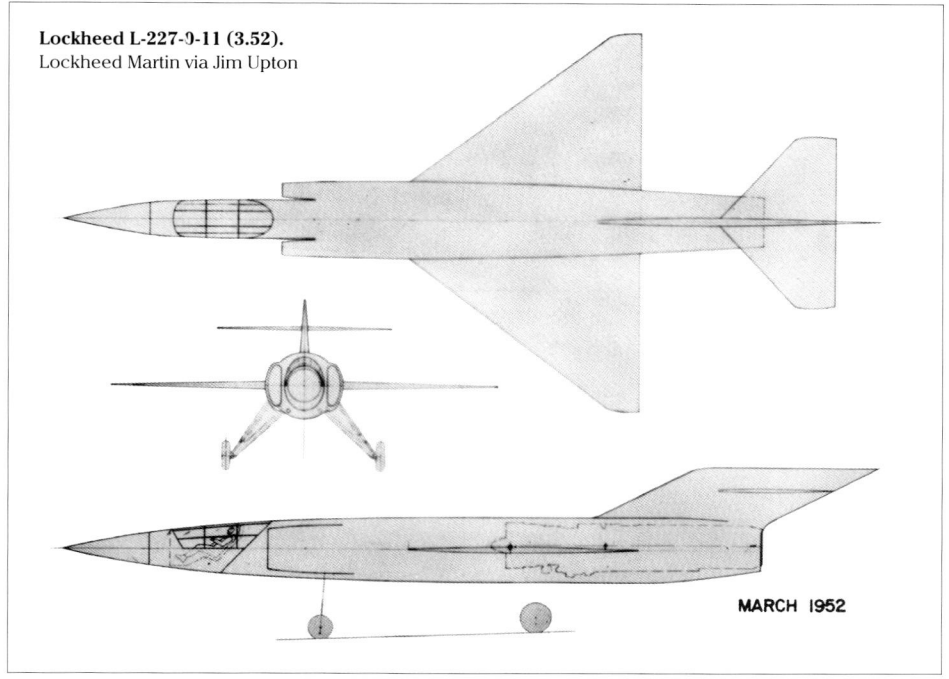

Lockheed L-227-0-6 (3.52).
Lockheed Martin via Jim Upton

Lockheed L-227-9-11 (3.52).
Lockheed Martin via Jim Upton

Later 'Centuries' and Other Concepts

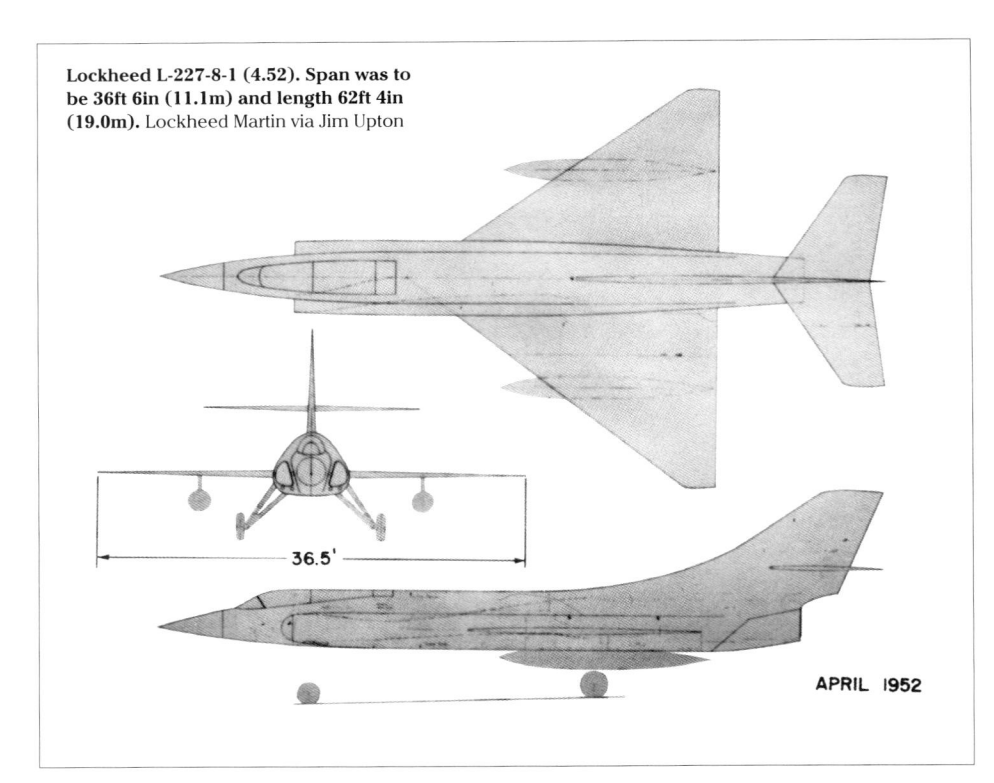

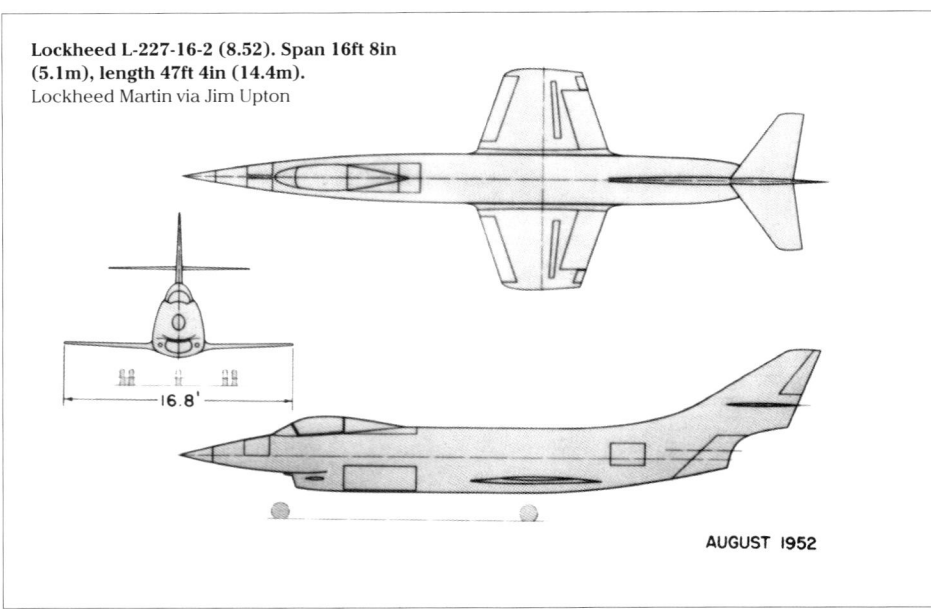

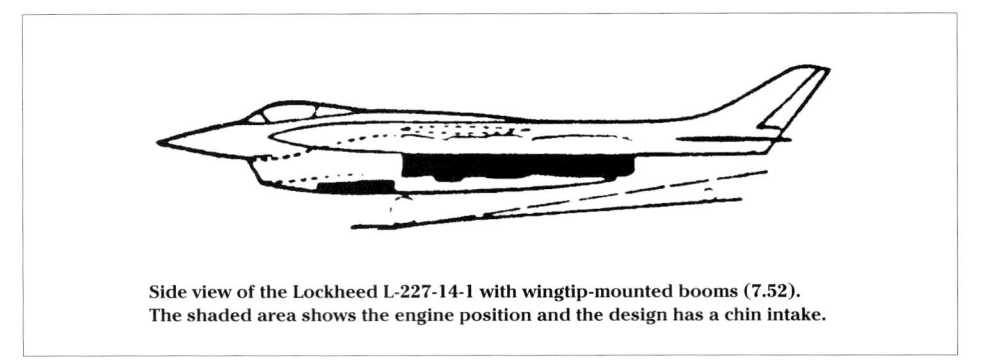

Lockheed L-227-8-1 (4.52). Span was to be 36ft 6in (11.1m) and length 62ft 4in (19.0m). Lockheed Martin via Jim Upton

Lockheed L-227-16-2 (8.52). Span 16ft 8in (5.1m), length 47ft 4in (14.4m). Lockheed Martin via Jim Upton

Side view of the Lockheed L-227-14-1 with wingtip-mounted booms (7.52). The shaded area shows the engine position and the design has a chin intake.

less conventional-looking L-227-0-11. L-227-0-6 had a low wing, tricycle undercarriage and two cannon in the nose either side of the inlet while L-227-0-11 had a pure delta wing, a flush cockpit, side intakes and an unusually long but stubby fin. Tunnel testing on 0-11 showed that the mid-position wing offered less drag when flying supersonically, but the delta itself was later found to give more drag than a simple straight wing, while the flush cockpit was also considered to be too limiting in terms of visibility.

By April the L-227-8-1 had advanced the delta arrangement into a beautiful design that featured side intakes, two cannon beneath each intake and underwing fuel tanks. However the performance requirements meant that this aircraft would weigh over 30,000 lb (13,608kg). It would have carried 1,640gal (7,457lit) of fuel internally plus 250gal (1,136lit) in each underwing tank. Model L-227-13-1 of August 1952 went to even greater extremes, with a weight in the region of 50,000lb (22,680kg), while the L-227-14-1 (July) had wingtip-mounted booms. In an attempt to reverse the weight growth the L-227-16-2 was drawn in August 1952 and this came out at just 8,000lb (3,629kg) and featured an amazing short unswept wing of 3.6% thickness/chord ratio. In fact its symmetrical-section, low-aspect-ratio, ultra-thin wing would become standard for many subsequent projects in this research. L-227-16-2's tricycle undercarriage featured twin main wheels identical in size to the nosewheel and there were just two guns mounted at the sides of the chin intake. The series also included a small rocket-propelled design of 15ft 8in (4.8m) span drawn in August. This possessed some similarities to the Bell X-1 research aircraft, but it suffered – as did all rocket-based proposals – from inadequate range.

Finally there was the L-227-20-1 of October 1952 that from the side looked rather like the L-227-8-1, but with the latter's delta being replaced by the favoured new short tapered wing; the design overall showing many signs of the forthcoming F-104. In slightly revised formed, and now called the L-227-1, this did become the definitive aircraft from the study. As a 'pre-F-104' it led directly to the L-246 below and then the F-104. L-227-1 carried 1,530gal (6,957lit) of fuel and there were external tanks on the wingtips containing another 240gal (1,091lit) in each, plus a further tank underneath the fuselage. Four cannon were housed in pairs around the lower fuselage beneath the intakes and a there was tricycle undercarriage. L-227-1 offered an outstanding performance with a combat ceiling of 52,600ft (16,032m), sea level rate of climb 47,000ft/min (14,326m/min) and combat radius of 350nm (648km).

Lockheed L-246

The long run of Lockheed's parametric studies culminated in work completed under the designation L-246. The L-246-1-1 of December 1952 was almost there, although the eventual F-104 had different intakes and a horizontal tail raised to the top of the fin to eliminate inertia coupling, plus minor changes to the wing. Also Lockheed was still not happy with the 'V' windshield, feeling that a flat screen would be better for gun sighting. Span was 22ft 1in (6.7m) and length 45ft 9in (13.9m) and the project had an estimated top speed of Mach 1.91 (Mach 2.0+ would be possible with an uprated engine), combat ceiling 54,200ft (16,520ft), sea level rate of climb 52,700ft/min (16,063m/min) and combat radius 375nm (695km). In December a briefing on the L-246 was made to the Air Force at Wright-Patterson Air Force Base by Kelly Johnson and several of his team. It was well received. Three designs in all were presented, including the L-246-3 and delta wing L-246-2, but it was the L-246-1 that was eventually procured.

North American NA-212

This NA-212 project, developed from the F-100 Super Sabre forms a big part of the background to the F-107 and so is fully described in the relevant later section of this book. Published sources have stated that this was North American's submission against the L-246 but the earliest dates given for the competition and for the start of the NA-212 do not match up. Consequently there are doubts regarding the identity of North American's submission to the requirement.

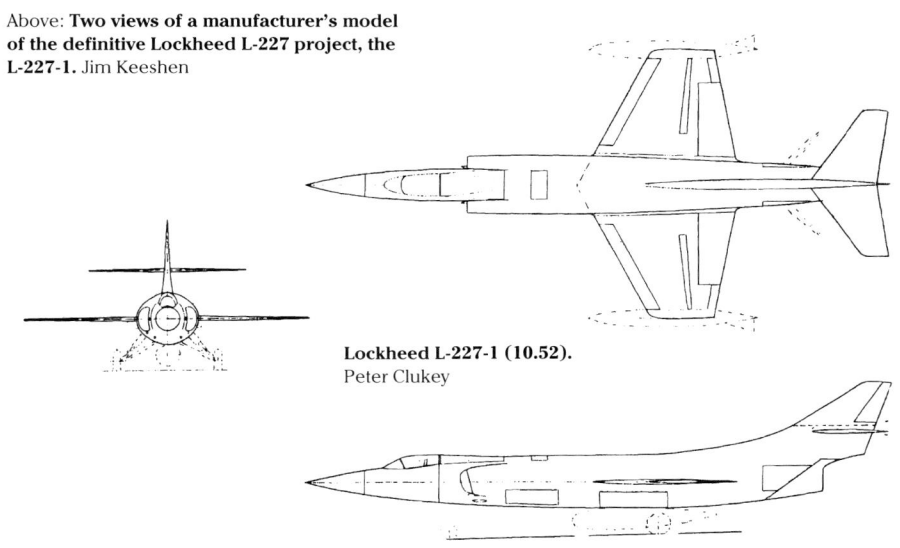

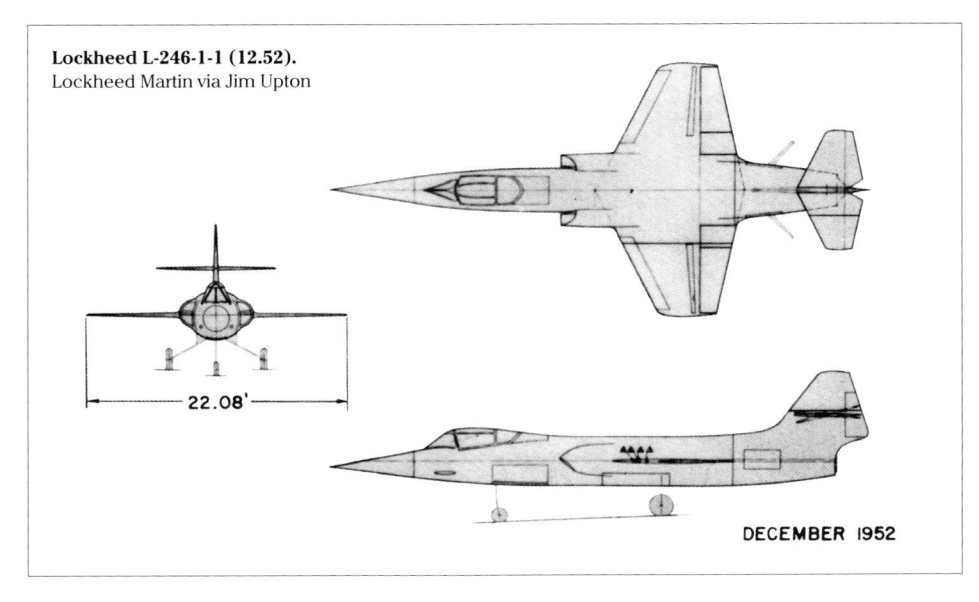

Above: **Two views of a manufacturer's model of the definitive Lockheed L-227 project, the L-227-1.** Jim Keeshen

Lockheed L-227-1 (10.52). Peter Clukey

Lockheed L-246-1-1 (12.52). Lockheed Martin via Jim Upton

Later 'Centuries' and Other Concepts

Republic AP-55

Again published sources have indicated that Republic's AP-55 was submitted to the competition. In fact work on the AP-55 was under way some time earlier, certainly by April 1950, but it may be that the official proposal was a later version. Three variants of this single-seat light fighter/interceptor project have been traced, all of them in model form. Little data is available but the configurations of these projects suggest that they would all have been capable of subsonic or low supersonic performance. Each showed a highly swept wing, twin tail booms and an inverse V-tailplane – the main variations came in the region of the cockpit canopy, air intake and jet pipe arrangements. The fact that several versions of the AP-55 were produced as models indicates that Republic examined this concept in some depth.

This first model of the Republic AP-55 is perhaps the most attractive in terms of appearance and balance. It shows neat side fuselage NACA-style air intakes, a high position wing and a short jetpipe. The model has a span of 11.0in (28.0cm) and length 18.2in (46.2cm) that, at 1/32nd scale, gives a real span of 29ft 4in (8.9m) and length 48ft 6in (14.8m).

Underside view of AP-55 model 'Number One', revealing details of its short fuselage/engine 'pod' and air intake. The lines drawn on the model indicate a tricycle undercarriage with the nosewheel just ahead of the intakes and main wheels in the forward thicker section of the tail booms level with the wing trailing edge. There is no indication on any AP-55 model of armament, but cannon should have been carried.

Opposite page:

Top: **The second AP-55 design was a longer and larger aircraft with relatively large high position side intakes, and a much longer fuselage. This model also shows a flush canopy and its span is 12.75in (32.4cm) and length 23.8in (60.5cm) – real dimensions would have been about 34ft 0in (10.4m) and 63ft 6in (19.3m).** Cradle of Aviation Museum

Centre left: **Another view of the second AP-55, after the model had been repainted.**

Centre and bottom right: **Republic's third AP-55 is something of a cross between the first two with a raised canopy, high side intakes and a relatively long fuselage. In fact this is the longest of the three designs, with a model length of 25.0in (63.5cm) while having the lowest span of 10.3in (26.2cm). The model is another made in 1/32nd scale, giving a real span of 27ft 6in (8.4m) and length 66ft 8in (20.3m). The date of the original photo is 4.1.50.** Cradle of Aviation Museum; Larry McLaughlin, respectively

Bottom left: **This rear view of the third AP-55 model suggests that the single engine intended for the fighter would have been quite substantial.**
Larry McLaughlin

Later 'Centuries' and Other Concepts 73

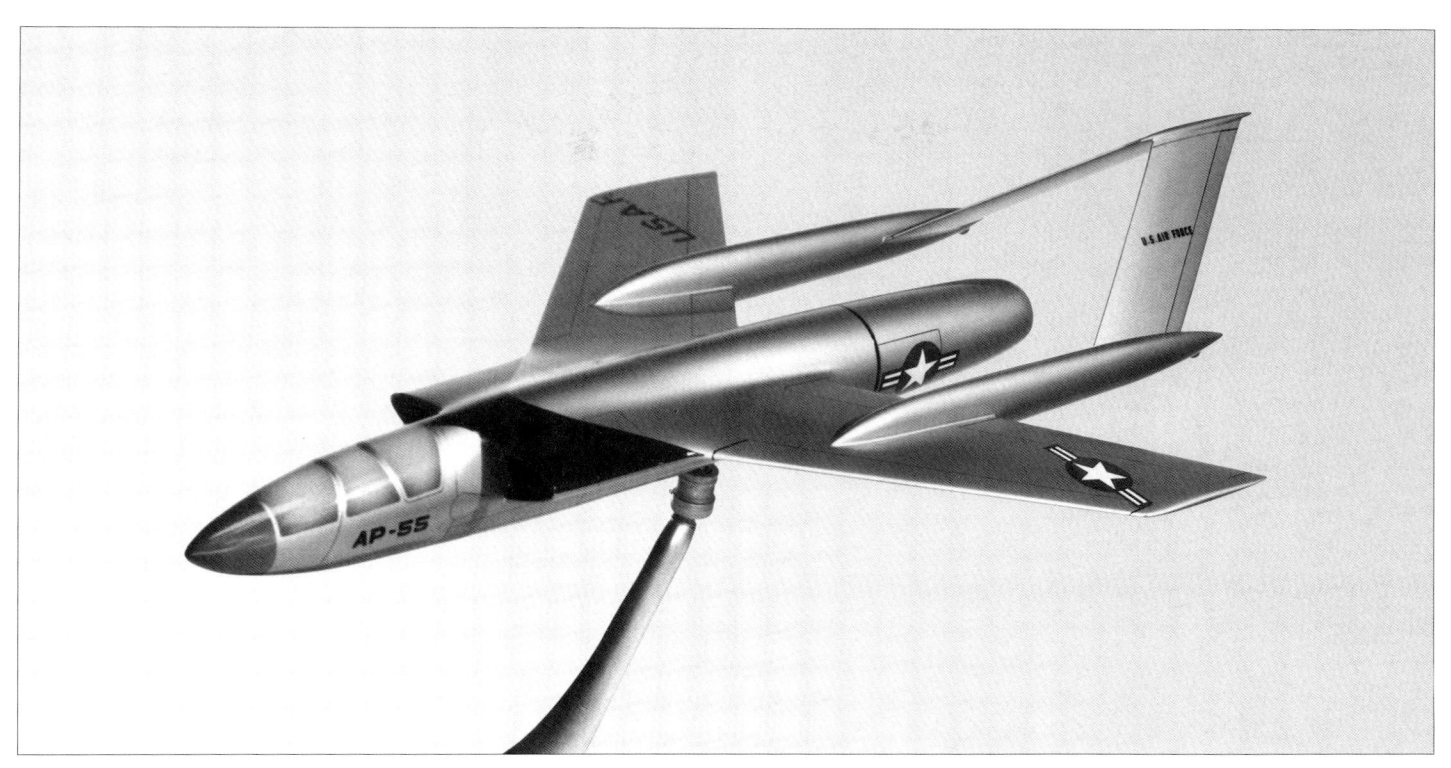

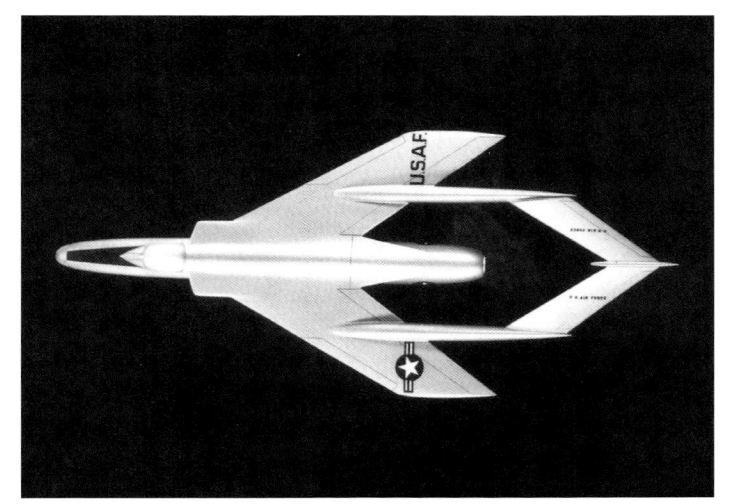

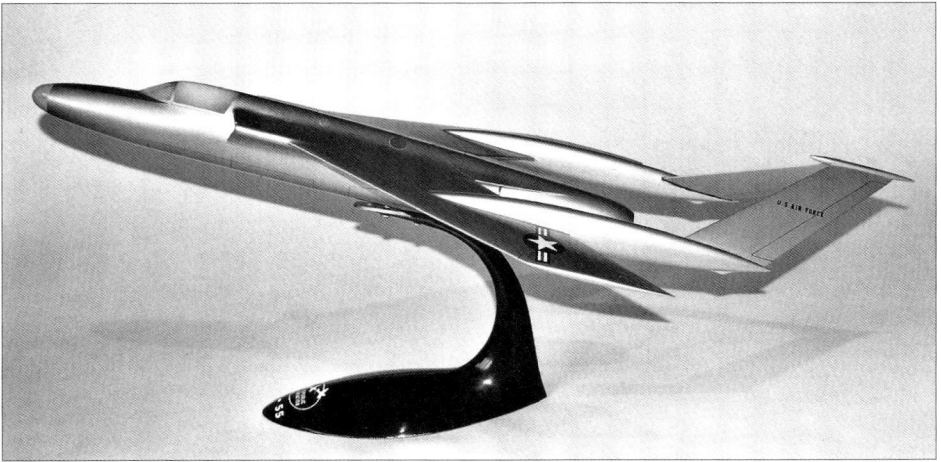

Northrop N-102 Fang in its original form with conventional tail unit and all-moving horizontal surfaces (12.52).

Northrop N-102 Fang with V-tail (mid-1950s).
Northrop Grumman Corp, Tony Chong collection

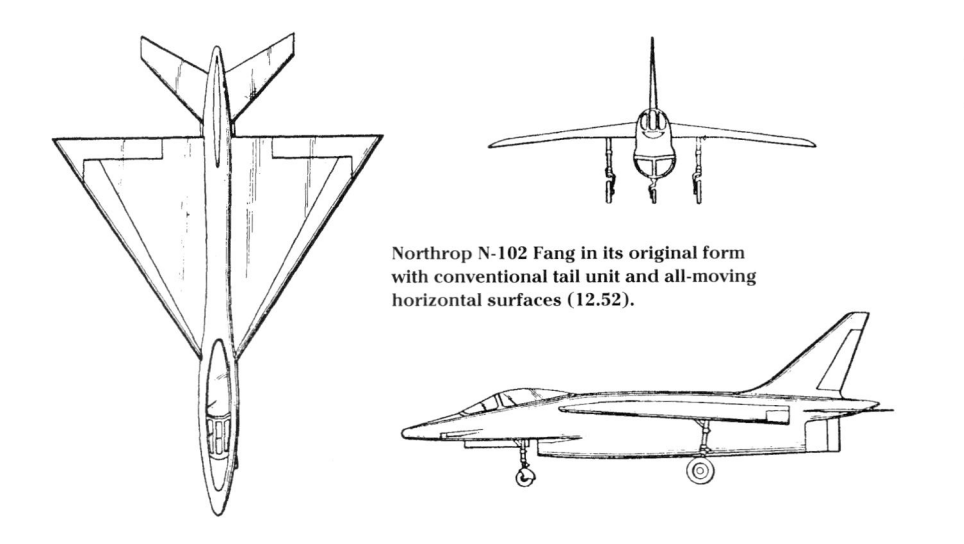

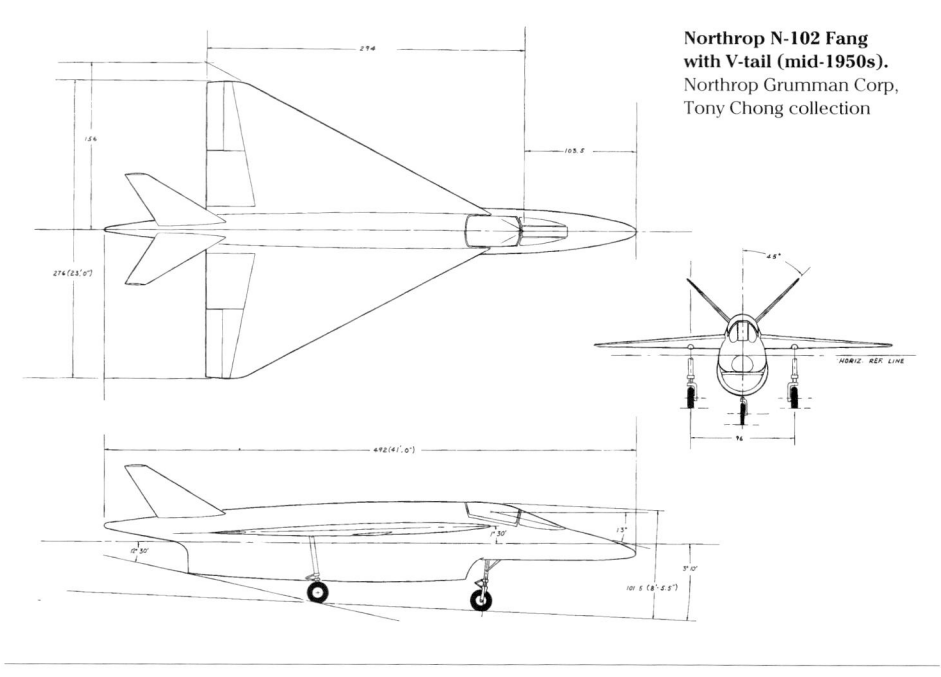

Northrop N-102 Fang

The date of Northrop's lightweight N-102 project certainly ties it closely to the competition for a lightweight day fighter. Known as the Fang, work on this project was inaugurated in December 1952. It was designed by Edgar Schmued, Northrop's Vice President of Engineering, with Welko E Gasich leading the preliminary design team. The project was kept a closely guarded secret. An important factor in the N-102's creation was its potential for overseas sales to European and South East Asian air arms, offering a design that was small and compact with easy access for maintenance. In addition, thanks to a low gross weight and high installed thrust, the Fang would be capable of high supersonic performance and altitudes up to 59,300ft (18,075m).

The fighter presented quite an unusual appearance with a large thin delta wing of 4.0% thickness/chord ratio, an under-fuselage intake and tricycle undercarriage. It was to be manufactured in aluminium alloy using stressed-skin, corrugation-stiffened wing panels plus multiple spars and ribs. Initially the Fang featured a swept fin and an all-flying horizontal tailplane, but one of the final proposals introduced a V-tail. There was a single 20mm cannon in the port side lower nose but alternative weapons for internal carriage included two 20mm or 30mm cannon, four 0.5in (12.7mm) machine guns or launchers for several sizes of rocket projectiles, including one for a 38mm rocket. There were also six underwing pylons to carry Sidewinder or Sparrow air-to-air missiles, Ding Dong missiles, napalm tanks, rockets or external fuel tanks. N-102 was designed to take five different engine installations, with conversion from one to another made easy by the power unit being suspended from the lower fuselage primary structure rather than being integrated into it, but a single General Electric J79 with afterburner was the favoured powerplant. Fang's final estimated ceiling with this power unit and the V-tail tail was around 67,000ft (20,422m).

In the end one of the Fang's weaknesses was the fact that it was a small fighter filled with a single powerful engine, which limited the airframe's potential growth. In 1953 Northrop built a full-size engineering mock-up in wood and metal (with the vertical fin) as a private venture but, despite considerable efforts to gain support to construct a prototype, that was to be the limit of the design's progress. The project was finally abandoned

Centre: **Full-scale mock-up of the N-102 Fang.**
Terry Panopalis

in 1956 although the mock-up was used at Northrop's Hawthorne plant to test new engineering ideas through the mid-1950s, before passing to the company's Aeronautical Institute for student training. Overall however, the experience Northrop acquired working on such designs served the company well when it moved on to other light fighter projects like the N-156 which we will come to later.

Lockheed Model 83 and F-104 Starfighter
Despite the presence of a design competition the situation favoured Lockheed from the start. Principally this was the reward for the company's prolonged research but it also reflected an Air Force wish not to have North American and Republic monopolize the supply of new fighter aircraft, the companies having had large production runs with their F-86 and F-84 respectively. Consequently, in January 1953 an endorsement was given to Lockheed's L-246 proposal and a contract was placed in March for two XF-104 prototypes to be powered by licence-built British J65 engines giving 8,000 lb (35.6kN) thrust dry and 11,500 lb (51.1kN) with afterburner. Production aircraft would receive the new higher thrust General Electric J79 giving 14,000 lb (62.2kN) in afterburner and the hardware was to be produced under Weapon System WS-303A. The L-246's high tail made the vertical fin very effective – excessively so in that during rolling turns it behaved almost like a wing. As a result the prototypes were given negative dihedral on their 3.36% thick wing to neutralize this feature.

The first prototype flew on 28th February 1954 and, from a development point of view, the F-104 Starfighter was brought to flight status with relatively few problems when compared to others in the Century series; however, the subsequent test program did suffer considerable difficulties. The first flight was surrounded by much secrecy and it was some time before the outside world was given sight of the aircraft. As can be imagined, its dramatic appearance caused quite a stir.

The Starfighter proved to be the first USAF combat aircraft to be capable of achieving a speed in excess of Mach 2. Orders were slow to arrive but eventually a total of 722 were planned for the Air Force, although this figure was drastically cut back in December 1958 and only 294 were actually procured. However, after Lockheed had subsequently turned the basic aircraft into a much more capable (and complex) multi-mission aircraft, it

Model of the V-tail Northrop N-102 Fang.
All Northrop Grumman Corp, photo Tony Chong

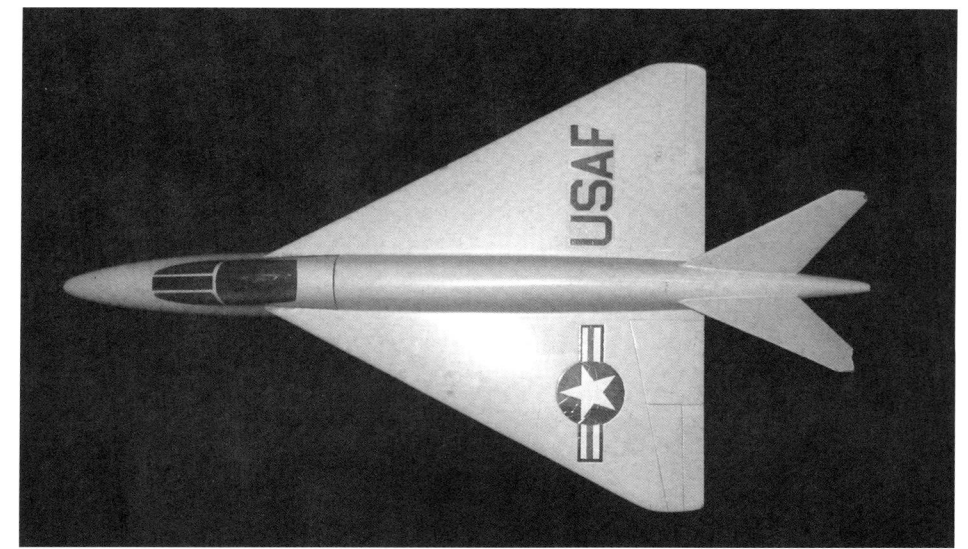

Later 'Centuries' and Other Concepts

The first prototype Lockheed XF-104, described as a single-seat tactical fighter, is seen carrying wingtip tanks during an early test flight.

achieved substantial sales to a number of overseas air arms, particularly in Europe, and these aircraft served their owners for many years. Italy, for example, retired its last Starfighters in 2006 – over half-a-century after the prototype first flew. If anyone had looked at Kelly Johnson's highly secret drawings of his lightweight interceptor for the USAF in the early 1950s and told him that what he had actually designed was an ideal European ground attack aircraft for the latter part of the century, one can only imagine his response!

Republic's Fighter Bomber

Parts of the background to the Republic F-105 story remain unclear, but it appears that MX1764 may have been a kick-off point. It is known that North American and Republic undertook some studies for a new 'All Weather Fighter-Bomber' to MX1764. Then Weapon System WS-300A was raised for a new fighter-bomber but no details are available concerning a competition, apart from the designs so far tracked down, and the F-105 itself was developed as a private venture. However, an impressive North American design was produced to WS-300A, and possibly the Vought V-382 was a response as well, so it seems sensible to group these projects together. The resulting Republic F-105 was covered by WS-306A while a later rival, the North American F-107, was dealt with by WS-306B.

Republic AP-63 and F-105

By all accounts the very smooth streamlined fighter design, the AP-63, was a development of the manufacturer's RF-84F Thunderflash, a reconnaissance version of the swept wing F-84F Thunderstreak. However, the AP-63 also possibly represents the last outgrowth of the XF-91 series, though all trace of the latter's inverse taper wing had now gone. Developed privately by Republic from 1951 onwards, the manufacturer actually studied many configurations for a Mach 1.5 successor to the F-84F, all of them under the AP-63 designation. The resulting single-seat, single-engine aircraft was intended to serve in a nuclear role (but it would also have an air-to-air capability)

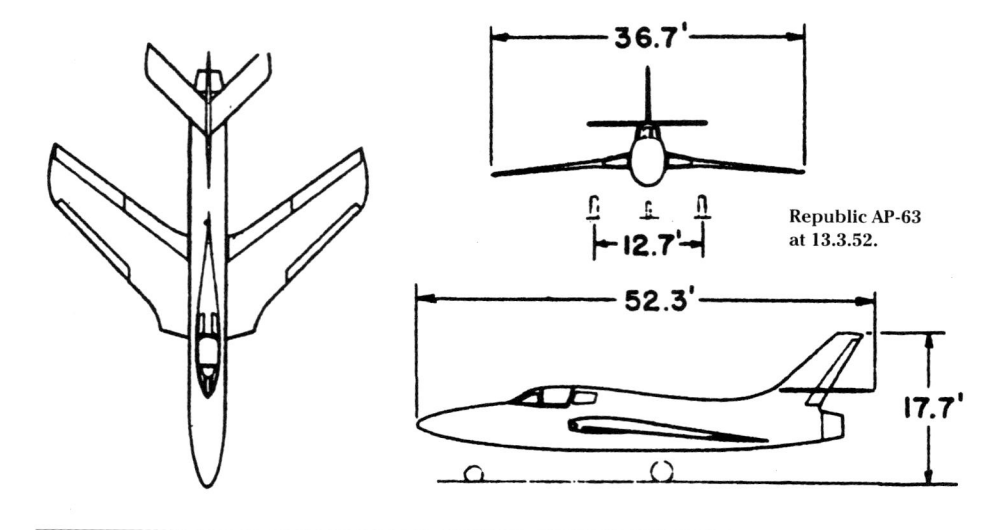

Republic AP-63 at 13.3.52.

and from the start it was designed to carry a 'special' nuclear store in an internal lower fuselage bomb bay. However, a subsequent change in strategy meant that the aircraft would also become a ground attack fighter. The project therefore became known as the AP-63-FBX (Fighter Bomber Experimental).

An official proposal for the AP-63 was made in April 1952. Its internal bomb bay could hold a single nuclear weapon or two 1,000 lb (454kg) iron bombs, while more 1,000 lb bombs could be carried on underwing pylons. Four T-130 0.6in (1.52cm) machine guns were housed in the nose. The aircraft was to be powered by an Allison J71-A-7 engine in the rear fuselage giving 14,500 lb (64.4kN) of thrust with afterburner and the wing root intakes had no 'sweep'. There were leading edge flaps, trailing edge Fowler flaps on the inner wing and, rather than the usual ailerons, there were moving outer wing surfaces called 'spoilerons'. Other photographs of the model show two batches of eight rocket projectiles carried under each wing, while 1,910gal (8,685lit) of fuel could be taken aboard in a set of fuselage tanks plus another 600gal (2,728lit) in an external tank.

In May the project got the go-ahead as the F-105 but at the time no general operational requirement was issued to cover it (the eventual document, GOR-49, did not appear until December 1954). A contract for manufacture was placed in September and a full-size mock-up was inspected in October 1953, but by that time a string of changes had been made to the initial layout. As built, the F-105 retained the AP-63's basic configuration and shape, but proved to be an altogether larger and beefier aircraft. The fuselage was much longer while a further change introduced the distinctive forward swept air inlets. At this stage the first aircraft was scheduled for delivery in the spring of 1955 but delays to the program brought various reductions and reinstatements in orders. An influence was the ending of the Korean War in 1953, which lessened the urgency to acquire the new type.

The first YF-105A, now named Thunderchief, made its first flight on 22nd October 1955, a Pratt & Whitney J57 engine having replaced the J71, but only two examples of this version were to be built because the succeeding airframes were redesigned to incorporate area ruling and also Pratt & Whitney's J75 engine. As such the second version became the F-105B and the first YF-105B flew on 26th May 1956. However, the first

Model of the Republic AP-63, which was originally chosen as the design to be built as the F-105.
Larry McLaughlin

Later 'Centuries' and Other Concepts

production delivery did not arrive until August 1958, three years later than planned. The delays actually tempted the Air Force to abandon the F-105 and order the North American F-107 instead, but in the event this option was never taken up. In due course over eight hundred F-105s were delivered and they racked up an impressive service record, particularly during the war in Vietnam. The F-105 proved to be an excellent tactical bomber but its size ensured that it had a hard time when operating as a pure fighter – it was never designed for manoeuvring in air combat.

Chance Vought V-382

Very little information is available for the single-seat fighter-bomber project from Chance Vought called the V-382, but the artwork suggests another attractive design. It shows a

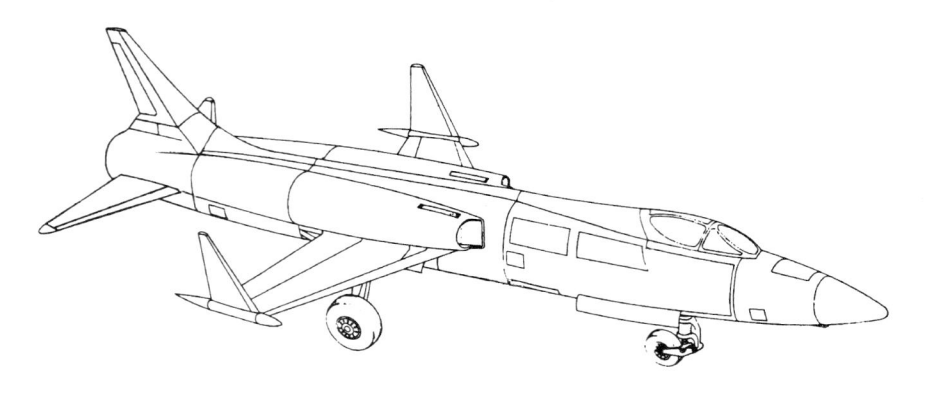

Republic F-105 Thunderchief heavy fighter-bomber photographed on 5th October 1963 near Singapore, en route to Vietnam, by a British de Havilland Sea Vixen carrier fighter of No 893 Squadron. The Vixens provided flight refuelling and the picture was taken using the flight reconnaissance camera mounted under one Sea Vixen's port wing. Sir Mark Thomson

The Republic F-105C was a projected two-seat version of the Thunderchief for advanced training. This view shows the full-size mock-up but no example was built. Cradle of Aviation Museum

Sketch showing Chance Vought's V-382 fighter-bomber project (19.11.52). Dick Atkins, Vought Archive

American Secret Projects: Fighters & Interceptors

long slim fuselage with split air intakes above the wing roots supplying a single engine, a tricycle undercarriage, full-length leading edge slats and trailing edge flaps, and unusual finlets on the wingtips to complement the rather small central fin. A gun appears to be protruding underneath the nose.

North American WS-300A Fighter-Bomber
The North American WS-300A shows features more in keeping with a later time period, and appears to have much in common with the Soviet Union's Mikoyan MiG-25 rather than the F-105. It was to be powered by two large afterburning turbojets mounted side-by-side in the rear fuselage and fed by large box intakes. The latter pre-date many designs from the 1960s and on top of the ducting are sets of supplementary doors. The design has clipped delta wings, a low-position, all-moving tailplane, twin vertical fins and twin ventral fins, the latter presumably folding away for landing. It was a single-seater and, on the starboard side at least, there was a cannon mounted in the bottom of the fuselage directly beneath the cockpit; there also appears to be an internal weapons bay. The North American project list notes the NA-237 of 12th June 1955 as a study for a 'Fighter-Bomber System' for the Air Force. This was undertaken by the company's Los Angeles facility and designated 'FBX', so it is possible that this model represents the NA-237, WS-300A having been used as a target specification.

No 3-view drawing is available for the immensely impressive North American WS.300A project. Therefore, for modelling purposes, a selection of photographs of this beautiful model have been included taken at different angles. Jim Keeshen

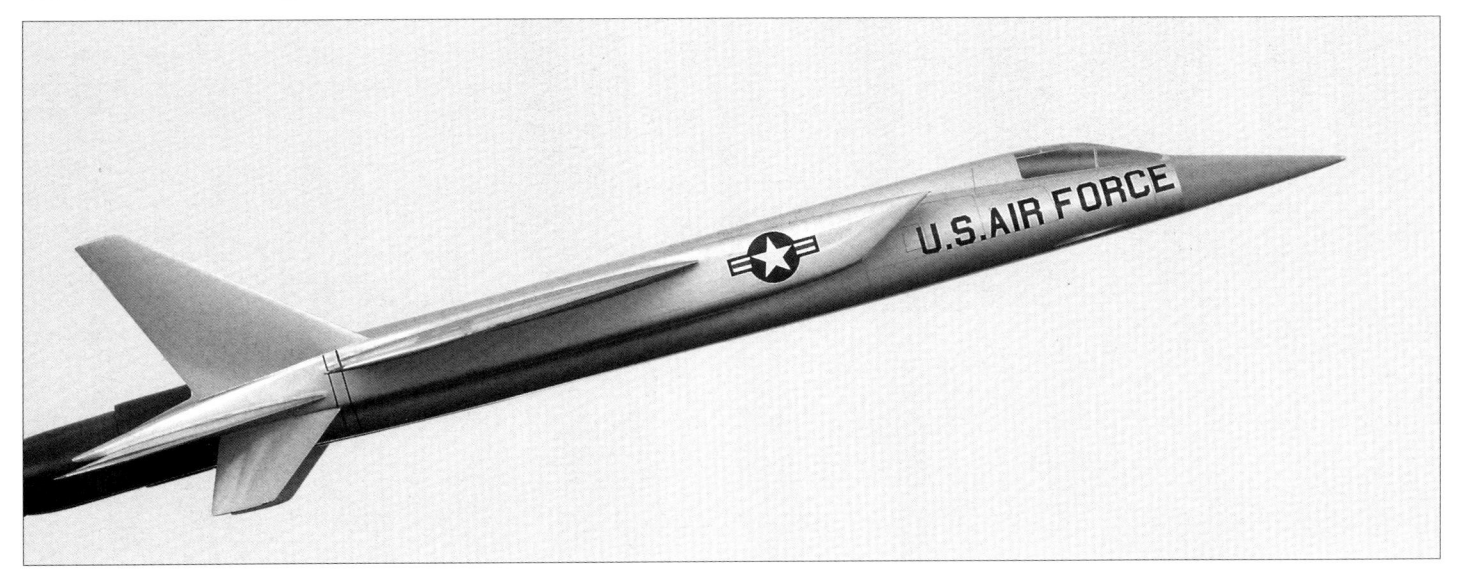

Later 'Centuries' and Other Concepts

Convair F-102 development powered by two General Electric J79 engines (24.11.54). This design's span was to be 38ft 1.5in (11.6m) and length 59ft 5.3in (18.1m). San Diego Aerospace Museum

Convair's two-seat, carrier-based attack-fighter version of its Model 8 (F-102) as proposed to the US Navy (3.1.55). Span is 39ft 10.5in (12.2m), length 62ft 2in (18.9m) and wing area 705ft² (65.6m²). Note the wing-fold facility. San Diego Aerospace Museum

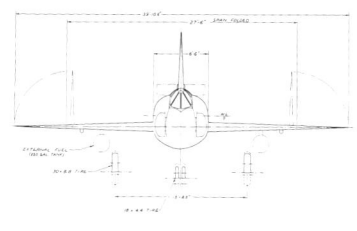

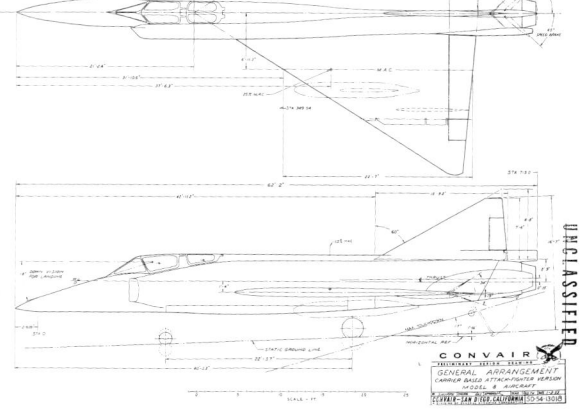

Convair F-106 Delta Dart – The 'Ultimate Interceptor'

The section in the previous chapter describing the Convair F-102 Delta Dagger noted how the F-102A eventually became an 'interim' interceptor while the F-102B/F-106 was to be the 'ultimate' interceptor. As such the latter was no longer referred to as the '1954 Interceptor' in a move that signified a later entry into service (there was no design competition). The two aircraft were originally intended to use the same airframe although the F-102B would have a Wright J67 engine and of course the highly sophisticated avionics from Hughes developed to MX1179. However, numerous problems were experienced in getting the F-102A into service, especially with the airframe aerodynamics, and these pushed the F-102B part of the program rather into the background. The development schedule for the MX1179 equipment also slipped badly and by August 1953 Wright's J67 program was nearly a year late. In fact approval to replace the J67 with the Pratt & Whitney J75 was given in early 1955.

In the event far more 'interim' F-102As were procured than had initially been planned, but the first F-102Bs were ordered in November 1955. On 17th June 1956 the 'ultimate' interceptor's designation was altered to F-106 to reflect the changes made, and also that more were on the way. In fact the resulting aircraft showed some external changes to the F-102, the most obvious being a new

The ultimate Convair delta wing fighter was the F-106 Delta Dart all-weather interceptor. This image shows a production F-106A.

American Secret Projects: Fighters & Interceptors

nose, a different intake position moved further back to the wing leading edge and a revised tailpipe area; aerodynamically the airframe was much cleaner. Weapon System WS-201B was raised to cover the more capable aircraft, which was named Delta Dart, and no guns were carried, only missiles in a weapons bay. The first YF-106A flew on 28th September 1956 and 277 F-106As were built together with another 63 two-seat advanced trainer F-106Bs – it had been expected that far more would be procured. These first entered service in 1959 and lasted a long time (in the mid-1980s a substantial number were still serving with Air National Guard units). The F-106 Delta Dart proved to be the last dedicated interceptor to be put into service by the USAF but, as Chapter Five shows, at the time this was still unknown and considerable efforts would be made to produce an even more capable successor.

Convair F-106C, F-106-30 and Other Variants

There were also several attempts to develop other versions of Convair's delta interceptors. For example one project, dated 21st December 1956, looked at installing a British Rolls-Royce R.Co.11R Conway engine into an F-106A airframe, which gave an estimated take-off weight of 33,743 lb (15,306kg) against the standard aircraft's 33,370 lb (15,137kg). However, one of the earliest proposals was actually a development of the F-102, since the F-106 designation had still to be applied.

On 24th November 1954 Convair completed a preliminary study for an F-102 interceptor powered by two General Electric J79s installed in the fuselage, a version with pod-mounted power units having been rejected because that arrangement gave more drag. Fuel had been added in the aft wing bay and outboard of the wheel well, which provided a greater internal fuel capacity than the basic F-102 wing: 1,500gal (6,820lit) versus 1,050gal (4,774lit). Despite the aircraft having two engines this extra fuel would ensure a 375nm (695km) radius of action without the need for fuselage or external wing tanks. Preliminary estimates suggested a combat ceiling with a rate of climb of 500ft/min (152m/min) of about 52,500ft (16,002m) and other visible changes included large 'ear' air intakes plus twin wheels on the nose gear.

A development that actually reached the hardware stage was the F-106C, which represented a standard F-106 fitted with a longer nose to house a 40in (101.6cm)-diameter radar dish. Two YF-106C 'prototypes' were built although only the one flew with these changes, making its initial flight in 1958. During 1957 the Air Force anticipated buying at least 350 F-106Cs but the program was cancelled in 1958. However, a Convair drawing from November 1957 shows an earlier study for an F-106C with two seats and a longer fuselage, large shock cone spikes in the intakes and twin wheels on all three undercarriage legs. The mid-fuselage weapon bay had been retained while the powerplant was a Pratt & Whitney JT4B-22 engine. This aircraft's span would have been 38ft 3.5in (11.7m), length 73ft 3in (22.3m), wing area 695ft² (64.6m²) and gross weight 42,140 lb (19,115kg).

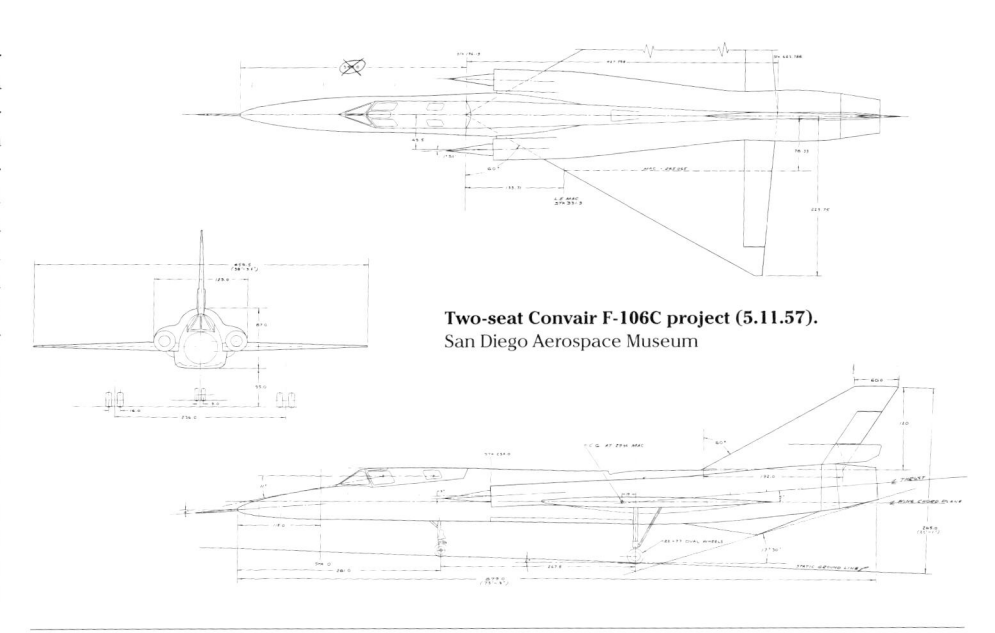

Two-seat Convair F-106C project (5.11.57).
San Diego Aerospace Museum

The search for more capable F-106 developments continued with the F-106-30, a study into single- and twin-engine variants of the original interceptor. Both types were two-seaters, the single-engine variety having a longer nose, long, slim intakes with shock cones and canard foreplanes. The power unit was a Pratt & Whitney J58-JT11-5A, an immensely powerful engine in the 30,000 lb (133.3kN) thrust class, versions of which were used in the phenomenal Lockheed Mach 3 YF-12A interceptor (Chapter Five) and SR-71 strategic reconnaissance aircraft. The single-engine F-106-30 would also carry two GAR-9 air-to-air missiles and have an estimated gross weight of 47,900 lb (21,727kg).

The twin engine F-106-30 was proposed either in late 1957 or early 1958 but supplementary data was still being added in March 1958. Apart from the underwing pod engine layout, the biggest difference in the twin-engine type was the use of two General Electric J93 (X-279E) units in lieu of the single J58. The J93 was another powerful engine that was earmarked for the North American F-108 (Chapter Five), but in the event it was only ever to fly in the same manufacturer's XB-70 Valkyrie Mach 3 bomber prototypes. Apart from the powerplant, Convair declared that the twin-engine version had a fire control system (a Hughes 5082 pulse Doppler unit), armament, weapon system effectiveness and time schedule that were comparable to the single-engine -30. In fact, if a go-ahead could be given on 1st January 1958, the brochure stated that a first flight would be made around 1st November 1960.

In general the performance characteristics of the F-106-30 with two J93s did not differ appreciably from the single-engine aircraft; however, there were sizeable gains in acceleration and climb. For example, the time to accelerate from Mach 0.95 to Mach 2.5 was 1.8 minutes, and the time to climb to 50,000ft (15,240m) from brake release was 3.8 minutes. The J93-powered aircraft would have an aluminium alloy airframe that brought with it a design limit speed of Mach 2.5. The engines were mounted in very slim underwing nacelles with internal compression inlets and a total of 17,200 lb (7,802kg) of fuel could be carried internally: 15,000 lb (6,804kg) in the wing and 2,200 lb (998kg) in the fuselage) plus another 6,500 lb (2,948kg) externally. There were two crew (pilot and radio operator/navigator). The estimated level flight ceiling when flying at just below Mach 1 was 54,000ft (16,459m), rising to 76,500ft (23,317m) at Mach 2.5, but altitudes in excess of 85,000ft (25,908m) were thought possible in a zoom climb.

The F-106-30 appears to have been the culmination of the 1950s studies for more advanced F-106s. Earlier however, on 1st May

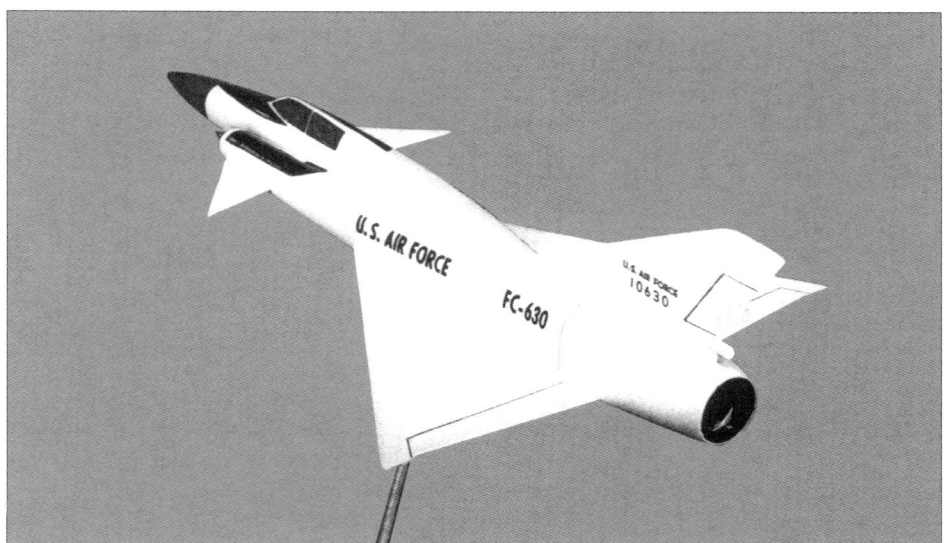

Model of the single-engine Convair F-106-30 (c3.58). San Diego Aerospace Museum

1957, Convair had proposed an 'Advanced F-106' with a canard foreplane, this time to the US Navy. Previously versions of both the F-102 and F-106 had been offered to the Navy but were not taken up. For example an adapted F-102 two-seat attack-fighter was suggested in early January 1955 powered by a 21,500 lb (95.6kN) J67 engine (13,200 lb [58.7kN] dry), which was expected to achieve Mach 2.0. Convair suggested that the delta wing would require carrier approach speeds only slightly in excess of conventional transonic swept wing aircraft, while also offering high supersonic speeds. The 1957 'Advanced F-106' used a 26,500 lb (117.8kN) thrust version of Pratt & Whitney's J75 engine for a gross weight of 47,473 lb (21,534kg). The only differences from a land-based 'Advanced F-106' were long stroke landing gear struts and the arrester hook – there would be no changes in equipment and the aircraft was expected to achieve a maximum Mach 2.5 at height. In the event this and other projected versions of the Delta Dart would never serve aboard a carrier.

In fact further efforts to improve the F-106 were made well into the 1960s and included, in 1962, a proposed long-range interceptor. Brief mention must also be made of the F-106X, a project examined in some detail in 1968. This was to be a much-upgraded F-106 with a new and larger radar and radome plus more advanced up-to-date avionics and air-to-air missiles having a 'look-down, shoot-down' capability. The missiles would have included the AIM-54 Phoenix. The program was approved by the Defense Department to be included in Fiscal Year 1969 budget requests as a substitute for the Lockheed F-12, but the F-106X was never ordered.

The 'Ultimate Sabre'

In August 1953 North American began work on developments of the F-100 Super Sabre. One resulting project was an interceptor called the NA-211 and the second a fighter-bomber development called the NA-212. Prototype orders were placed for the latter and then in December 1954 some further requirements were produced by the Air Force that forced North American to introduce considerable alterations to the airframe; with these came a change in designation to F-107. The story behind the F-107 is rather complex and many parts still provide something of a mystery; in addition numerous published

Convair F-106-30 with two General Electric J93 engines (c1.58). San Diego Aerospace Museum

Sketch of the twin-engine Convair F-106-30. San Diego Aerospace Museum

accounts give contradictory information. The following has been compiled using available original documents or trustworthy secondary source material, plus the author's judgment.

North American NA-211

The originating date for the NA-211, an F-100 interceptor development from North American's Columbus Division, is 7th October 1953. Several published sources have stated that one of the two models described shortly under the NA-212 designation (with the radar in the nose) was actually the NA-211 interceptor, but the identities given on the original North American display models suggest otherwise. Project engineer for the NA-211, sometimes known as the F-100B interceptor, was Harold Dale and the type was expected to be capable of Mach 2. Dale was also project engineer on the fighter-bomber that, to begin with, shared the same wing, rear fuselage and powerplant as the interceptor. As noted in the previous chapter, this interceptor project may have been a submission in the competition won by the McDonnell F-101B (the dates certainly match), but the F-100 interceptor's development ended after the aerodynamic problems suffered by the Super Sabre itself had begun to surface.

North American NA-212 and F-107A

The first known configuration for the NA-212/F-107 fighter-bomber concept shows a design that is clearly based on the F-100, with a nose intake and a very similar wing and horizontal tail. However, although many sources have called the original fighter-bomber project the F-100B, this model (a North American original) is actually labelled F-100C (the real F-100C was a fighter-bomber version of the basic Super Sabre). An evaluation of the NA-212 was presented to Air Research and Development Command Headquarters on 2nd October and resulted in a recommendation to place an order. In May 1954 the project was authorized by Air

Drawing showing what is believed to be the initial configuration for the North American NA-212/F-100B (10.53). Its span is 36ft 7in (11.2m) and length 52ft 5in (16.0m), but in due course this arrangement was to be drastically revised. The project has four cannon around the lower fuselage and an F-100A-shape wing, an all-moving horizontal tail and a fixed vertical tail complete with rudder. Steve Pace

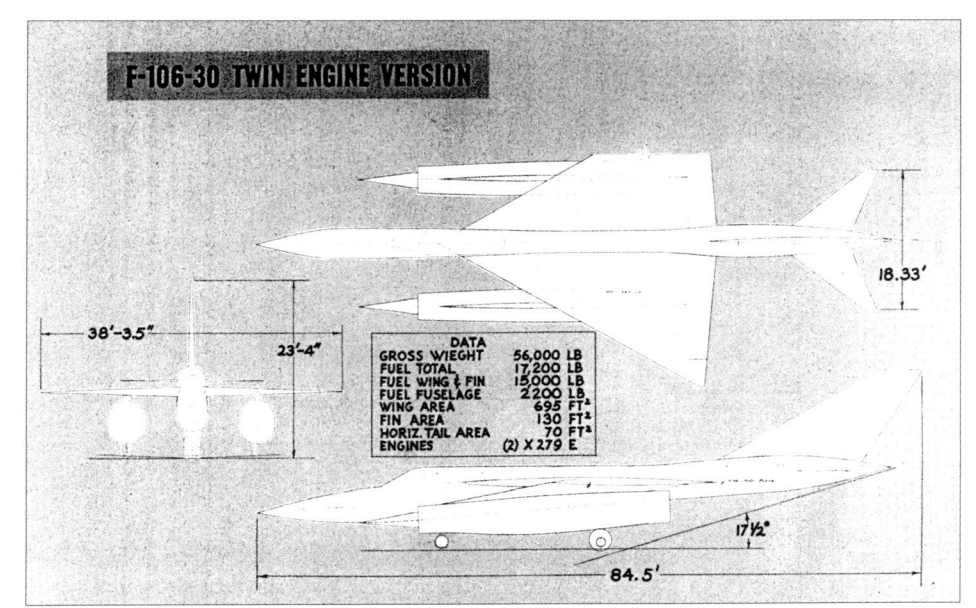

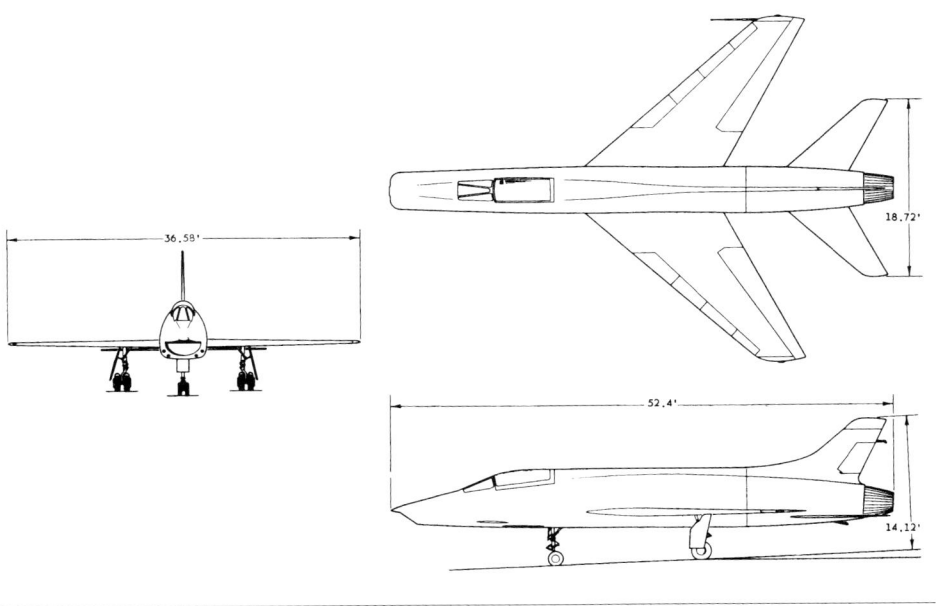

Later 'Centuries' and Other Concepts

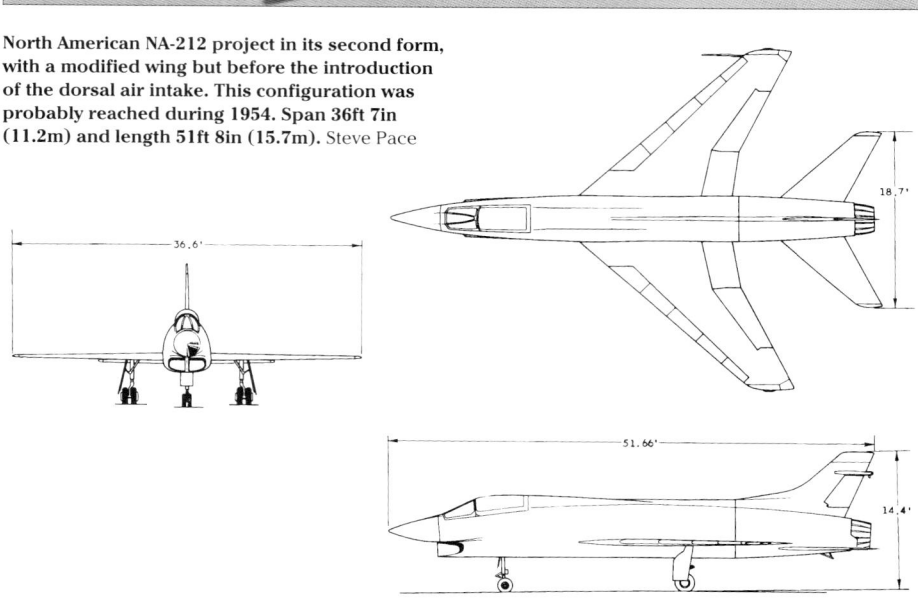

Model of the early North American NA-212 with 'duckbill' nose intake. John Aldaz

Force Headquarters under Weapon System WS-306B and a contract followed soon afterwards, which covered a mock-up and long-lead materials.

North American documents state that, at 1st June 1954, the aircraft was expected to be powered by a J57 engine fitted with an afterburner. This power unit was the same as used in production F-100A Super Sabres but it was to be fed by a variable intake and would also have a convergent-divergent nozzle. Fuel was housed in both the forward and rear sections of the fuselage, which employed a semi-monocoque structure built of aluminium alloy at the front and mostly titanium around the engine (the latter alloy offered better high temperature properties in the heat generated by the power unit). Wing sweep angle was 45° and four 20mm cannon were mounted in the fuselage, while two underwing hardpoints could take various sizes of bombs up to 2,000 lb (907kg) in weight or pods containing either eighteen or thirty-six 2.75in (7.0cm) unguided rockets.

A meeting held on 24th June declared that this new type was now a different aircraft to the F-100A. There were plans to build thirty-three of them as F-100Bs and a full-size mock-up was formally inspected on 7th September 1954. On 16th December GOR.68 was raised to cover the design and it also expanded the aircraft's role to embrace air superiority day and night fighter duties together with the fighter-bomber task. The project was now officially designated F-107A but North American was in the process of making substantial changes to the configuration to try and improve the estimated performance and also introduce semi-submerged centreline stores. A decision had been made to carry a nuclear store semi-recessed beneath the fuselage, but the nose intake created shock waves which affected the ballistics of this under-fuselage weapon and created problems. Consequently, the intake was switched to the rather unusual dorsal position, which in due course was made more familiar by the F-107 prototypes.

North American NA-212 project in its second form, with a modified wing but before the introduction of the dorsal air intake. This configuration was probably reached during 1954. Span 36ft 7in (11.2m) and length 51ft 8in (15.7m). Steve Pace

Opposite page:

Top and centre: **North American-made display model of the NA-212/F-100B project shown here carrying two drop tanks. No guns can be seen on this model.** Jonathan Rigutto / photo © 2005 Chad Slattery

Bottom: **Artwork showing the NA-212/F-100B.** Terry Panopalis

American Secret Projects: Fighters & Interceptors

Later 'Centuries' and Other Concepts

The second North American F-107A prototype.
John Aldaz

In July 1955 it was agreed to cut F-107 procurement to nine aircraft plus one static test airframe, and then in June 1956 the total was further reduced to three. The first of these made its maiden flight on 10th September 1956 and all of them flew well, achieving Mach 2 on occasion. Some published sources have called the prototypes YF-107As but they always had F-107A painted on the body; the aircraft did not receive a name. As built the F-107 embraced several features that were very advanced for the period, including an all-moving vertical fin plus a variable-geometry air inlet fitted with a wedge and a two-position ramp for optimum operation. Apart from the nuclear store the F-107 could also carry 1,000 lb (454kg) bombs beneath the inner wing pylons and all four wing pylons could take napalm bombs, rocket projectiles or drop tanks.

Such was the promise held by the F-107 that in mid-1956 the Air Force considered dropping Republic's troubled F-105 program and replacing it with North American's aircraft, since the latter demonstrated superior speed and manoeuvrability over the F-105 in its prototype form. However, according to official documents the F-107 showed limited options for expanding its mission range and, even if its development and production went smoothly, it would still not be available to the Air Force ahead of the F-105. The competition brought a detailed analysis of the two aircraft's respective merits and performance capabilities, and some severe disagreements within the Air Staff as to which aircraft was the best and thus should be produced. However, in February 1957 the F-107 program was halted and GOR.68 was cancelled on 22nd March.

Speaking to former engineers it appears that the F-107 struggled to acquire enough funding, in part because the F-105 was developed to its own specification while the F-107 was not. In fact, to help, some money had to be taken from Air Material Command procurement support funds, this finance having previously been earmarked for machine tools and the like. At this time the current worldwide situation demanded that Tactical Air Command had to get into the 'nuclear' business with an aircraft that could carry nuclear weapons and the F-105 benefited here in having a weapons bay, which the F-107 did not possess. Eventually the F-107A prototypes were used by NASA for supersonic research and astonishingly, considering the company's record over the previous fifteen years, they proved to be the last new fighters to be built for the USAF by North American's Inglewood plant.

Other Projects

Up to now this book has concentrated on what one might term the principal lines of development in fighter and interceptor design, almost all of which were cultured by requirements from the Air Force or Navy. There were however, some other private venture studies, plus one or two official requirements, which appear not to have been around for very long or which fall outside the main lines of research. Those known to the author are reviewed below.

Strategic Fighter
A review of the MX-series of code numbers for new aircraft and equipment shows that in 1953 MX2140 was issued to cover some design studies for a new strategic fighter. It lists designs from Chance Vought (believed to be the V-386 of April 1953), Convair, Lockheed, North American and Northrop (the N-132), but no further information has been traced in official or published records to either the designs or requirements. Therefore, it would appear that MX2140 was a relatively short-lived document. McDonnell's Model 94 of March 1953 is also listed as a strategic fighter and most likely will have been produced against MX2140. Since it is known that the Model 94 resulted in the

Model 36AE series, this particular design must have been based on the F-101 Voodoo.

Northrop Export Day Fighter

In July and August 1955 some company-sponsored preliminary design studies were made by Northrop for three military aircraft types for export – a day-fighter, an interceptor and a trainer. These were designed to meet the performance requirements of the European theatre of operation, and to utilize engines, weapons, fire control and other system components that were available to friendly European nations. These designs did not receive a number in Northrop's project series.

The day fighter was basically a redesign of the N-102 Fang discussed earlier, retaining its chin intake but incorporating wing pod armament plus a British Armstrong Siddeley Sapphire engine giving 12,000lb (53.3kN) of thrust. A total of 756gal (3,437lit) of fuel was carried in the middle of the fuselage, a range and search radar was housed in the nose and the wings were swept 46° 30' at the leading edge and had a thickness/chord ratio of 3.5%. The day fighter's estimated combat ceiling was 52,500ft (16,002m), combat radius 300nm (556km) and sea level rate of climb 30,800ft/min (9,388m/min). The armament pods on the wings could each hold two 30mm cannon or forty-six 75mm folding-fin rockets, while a wide selection of external weapon and weapon/fuel combinations were possible using the four wing-mounted pylons; the tricycle undercarriage main wheels were also housed in the wing pods. There was provision to install a 21,500lb (95.6kN) Bristol Olympus in the future, which offered a maximum speed of Mach 2.09 at 50,000ft (15,240m). This day fighter could be converted to a two-place supersonic trainer by interchanging the nose section forward of the fuel bulkhead.

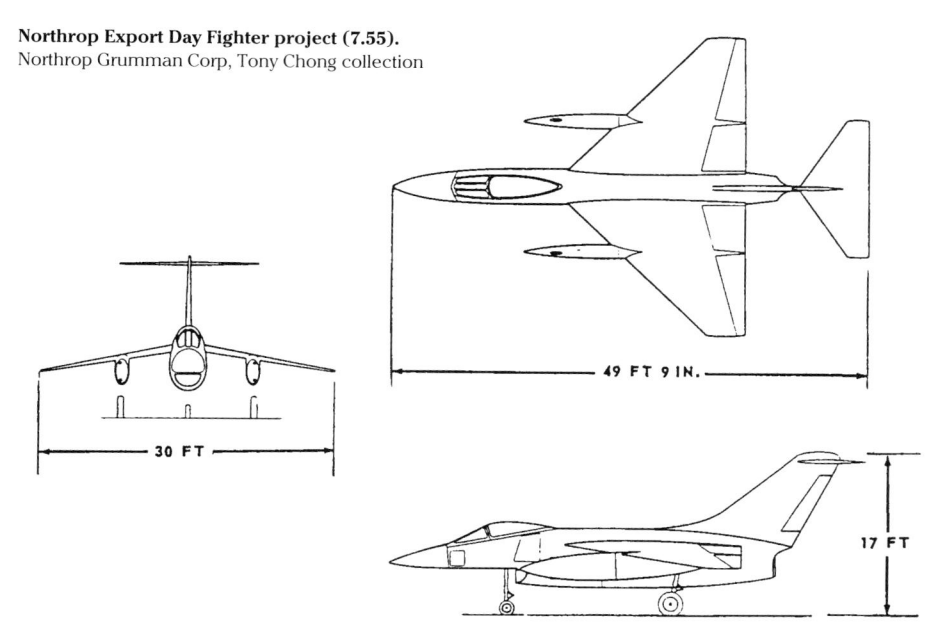

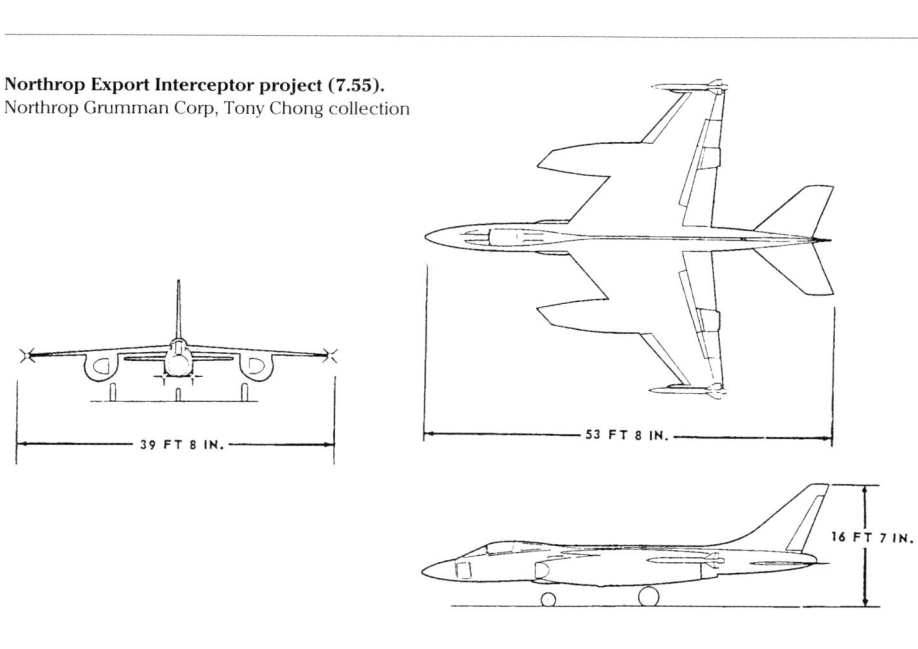

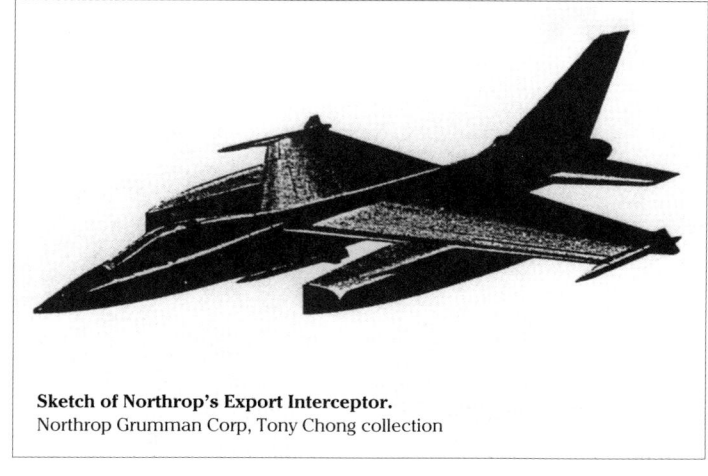

Northrop Export Day Fighter project (7.55).
Northrop Grumman Corp, Tony Chong collection

Northrop Export Interceptor project (7.55).
Northrop Grumman Corp, Tony Chong collection

Sketch of the Northrop Export Day Fighter.
Northrop Grumman Corp, Tony Chong collection

Sketch of Northrop's Export Interceptor.
Northrop Grumman Corp, Tony Chong collection

Later 'Centuries' and Other Concepts

Northrop Export Interceptor

The 'Northrop Export Interceptor' design was similar to an earlier Northrop project for a Navy attack-bomber. It showed a tandem two-seat layout equipped for all-weather operations and the basic powerplant consisted of two 12,000lb (53.3kN) Armstrong Siddeley Sapphires, although the airframe was designed to accommodate higher 15,000lb (66.7kN) thrust Sapphires or 17,500lb (77.8kN) Rolls-Royce Avons. The wing had 35° of sweep at quarter chord and a thickness/chord ratio of 4.0%, and 1,470gal (6,684lit) of fuel could be housed internally in large fuselage tanks. Combat ceiling would be 56,000ft (17,069m), combat radius 300nm (556km) and sea level rate of climb 41,900ft/min (12,771m/min). There was a search and track radar in the nose coupled with an automatic lead computing sight. The basic armament was four air-to-air missiles equivalent to the Sparrow II, two carried beneath the fuselage and one on each wingtip. The tip weapons could be switched for disposable wingtip pods holding sixty-two 2in (5.1cm) folding-fin rockets, or pods containing a combination of rockets and missiles. Northrop noted that it would be possible to adapt the interceptor to undertake escort fighter, night intruder or ground support duties by adding various weapons carried on four underwing pylons.

Century Summary

The above then represents what can currently be gleaned about the development of the Century fighters and the design thinking that accompanied them. They reflected an intensive period of research and design thinking, as fighter aircraft moved from the subsonic or transonic era into the regime of supersonic flight. The outcome of the competing approaches – often based on politics and prevailing military thinking as much as design merits – was to have an enduring influence on airpower for the rest of the century.

'Century Series' Fighter Studies – Estimated Data

Project	Span ft in (m)	Length ft in (m)	Gross Wing Area ft² (m²)	Gross Weight lb (kg)	Engine lb (kN)	Max Speed / Height mph (km/h) / ft (m)	Armament
F-104 Background							
Lockheed L-227-8-1	11.1	54 11 (16.7)	525 (48.8)	33,895 (15,375) (max take-off)	1 x Wright YJ67-W-1	Supersonic	4 x cannon
Lockheed L-227-1	30 0 (9.1)	62 2 (18.9)	360 (33.5)	31,850 (14,447) (max take-off)	1 x Wright YJ67-W-1	1,274 (2,048) Mach 1.92	4 x cannon
Northrop N-102 Fang (Dec 1952)	30 6 (9.3)	45 10 (14.0)	366 (34.0)	18,760 (8,510)	1 x GE J79 9,290 (41.3), 14,350 (63.8) ab	Mach 2	1 x 20mm cannon, various combinations of bombs and rockets
Northrop N-102 Fang (V-tail)	23 0 (7.0)	41 0 (12.5)	314 (29.2)	?	1 x GE J79	Mach 2	See text
Lockheed F-104A Starfighter (flown)	21 9 (6.6)	54 8 (16.7)	196.1 (18.2)	22,614 (10,258)	1 x GE J-79-GE-3A 9,600 (42.7), 14,800 (65.8) ab	1,037 (1,669) at 50,000 (15,240)	1 x 20mm cannon, 2 x AIM-9B Sidewinder AAM
F-105 Background							
Republic AP-63 (at 12.52)	36 8.5 (11.2)	52 3.5 (15.9)	366 (34.0)	27,550 (12,497) (combat weight)	1 x Allison J71-A-7 14,500 (64.4) ab	921 (1,482) at 35,000 (10,668)	4 x 0.6in (1.52cm) machine guns, 1 x nuclear or 6 x 1,000lb (454kg) bombs, 32 RPs
Republic F-105B Thunderchief (flown)	34 11 (10.6)	63 1 (19.2)	385 (35.8)	34,870 (15,817) (combat weight)	1 x P&W J75-P-3 17,200 (76.4), 23,500 (104.4) ab	864 (1,390) at S/L, 1,376 (2,214) at 36,000 (10,973)	1 x 20mm cannon, rocket projectiles, missiles, or up to 8,000lb (3,629kg) bombs
F-106 and Developments							
Convair F-106A (flown)	38 3.5 (11.7)	70 9 (21.6)	631.3 (58.7)	33,370 (15,137)	1 x P&W J75-P-17 17,200 (76.4), 24,500 (108.9) ab	1,525 (2,454) at 40,000 (12,192)	1 x AIM-2A Genie AAM, 4 x AIM-7F Sparrow AAM
Twin-Engine F-102	38 1.5 (11.6)	59 5 (18.1)	?	37,050 (16,806)	2 x GE J79 14,350 (63.8) ab	cMach 2	Not given but probably similar to F-102
Convair F-106-30 (twin-engine)	38 3.5 (11.7)	84 6 (25.8)	695 (64.6)	56,000 (25,402)	2 x GE J93 (X-279-E) c22,500 (100.0) ab	Mach 2.5 at 43,000 (13,106)	2 x GAR-9 AAM
F-107 Background							
North American F-100B (at 1.6.54)	36 7 (11.2)	54 3.5 (16.6)	367 (34.1)	29,749 (13,494)	1 x P&W J57 10,950 (48.7), 17,200 (76.4) ab	Mach 1.7 at height	4 x 20mm cannon, up to 72 x 2.75in (7cm) RP, 2 bombs of sizes up to 2,000lb (907kg)
North American F-107 (flown)	36 7 (11.2)	61 10 (18.8)	395 (36.7)	39,755 (18,033)	1 x P&W J75-P-11 17,200 (76.4), 24,500 (108.9) ab	890 (1,432) at S/L, 1,295 (2,084) at 36,000 (10,973)	4 x 20mm cannon, 2 x 1,000lb (454kg) bombs, various RPs or one thermonuclear store
Northrop Export Fighters							
Northrop Export Day Fighter	30 0 (9.1)	49 9 (15.2)	366 (34.0)	19,270 (8,741)	1 x Arm Sidd Sapphire 12,000 (53.3) ab	Mach 1.34 at 35,000 (10,668)	4 x 30mm cannon or 46 x 75mm RP. Various underwing loads.
Northrop Export Interceptor	39 8 (12.1)	53 8 (16.4)	525 (48.8)	33,881 (15,368)	2 x Arm Sidd Sapphire 12,000 (53.3) ab	Mach 1.84 at 35,000 (10,668)	See text

Chapter Five

The Quest for a Long-Range Interceptor

Manufacturer's model of the Northrop N-144.
Northrop Grumman Corp, photo Tony Chong

Despite the F-106 being labelled the 'Ultimate Interceptor', expected improvements in the capability of future Soviet bombers ensured that America's fighter design teams continued to strive for ever more advanced interceptors. The thinking was not unreasonable; now that much further information has come to light, it is clear that the Soviets were indeed working on some very advanced bomber concepts. Evidence for this can be seen in another Midland book *Soviet Secret Projects – Bombers since 1945*, by Tony Buttler and Yefim Gordon published in 2004.

The results of this pressure to counteract high-speed, high-flying bombers as far out as possible from their nuclear targets produced some of the most extraordinary 'fighter' designs ever proposed. The USA was not alone in this thinking. In 1955 the United Kingdom issued a requirement for a high-altitude all-weather Mach 2 interception system. The latter was won by a design from Fairey Aviation in the form of a huge two-seat delta wing fighter – known in-house as the 'Fairey Delta III', indicating its origins in the company's earlier, highly successful Delta II research aircraft. The Soviet Union itself shared similar concerns. Indeed there the research went further with a series of heavy interceptor projects reaching prototype status, the biggest being Lavochkin's 'Aircraft 250' (nicknamed Anaconda) and Tupolev's 'Aircraft 128'. The latter entered service as the Tu-28 (NATO codename *Fiddler*) with a gross weight in the region of 95,000 lb (43,092kg). Avro Canada's CF-105 Arrow, which entered prototype testing in 1958, was another large and very impressive long-range interceptor. An enormously capable aircraft, it was cancelled in 1959 amid much controversy. In America the planned solution was known as the Long Range Interceptor or LRI. The resulting program never reached fruition but it came close to putting a hugely impressive aircraft into USAF service.

Long-Range Interceptor

The immediately preceding USAF standard interceptors the already described Convair F-102 and F-106 were very successful in their own right but were designed for point defence within the heart of the country's integrated ground air defence network. McDonnell's F-101B could do battle farther out from the target areas, but not that much farther. In fact the need for a longer-range interceptor

American Secret Projects: Fighters & Interceptors   89

Boeing's Model 712 long-range interceptor (6.54).
Chris Gibson

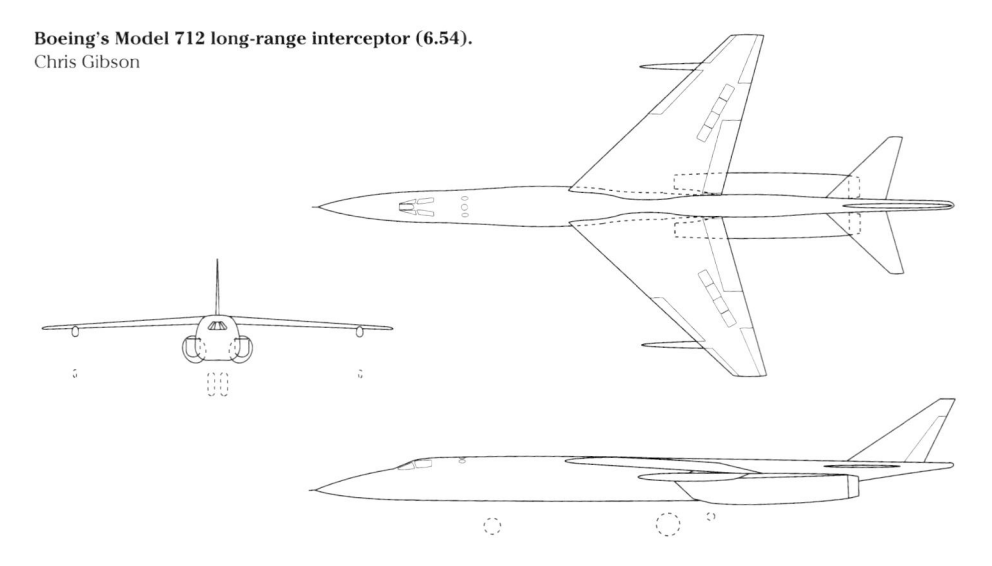

had been acknowledged many years earlier. In February 1952 the commander of Northeast Air Command, Maj Gen L P Whitten, opened formal discussions for the possible development of a very long range, high-speed, high-armament-capacity interceptor. His ideas were based on a belief that the interceptors then in existence, or even in the planning stage, could not fully exploit the extended airborne and ground radar network being assembled within his command.

The ground control Whitten was talking about was SAGE, for Semi-Automatic Ground Environment. This was to be an integrated system of radar, surface-to-air missiles and interceptor fighters, linked together by digital computers and long-distance communication systems. It was designed to protect fully the airspace over America and Canada from attack. SAGE was a massive undertaking in every sense: size, technology and complexity and work on it really got moving in October 1952. Whitten declared that the warning time available from the network should be used to launch long-range interceptors that would be capable of attacking oncoming bombers well before they could threaten the key industrial targets of either Canada or the United States. What followed was years of discussion, decision making and decision reversal, before the resulting finalised design, the F-108, was cancelled in 1959.

Whitten did not however, define the exact character of the new aircraft and it was left to Maj Gen F H Smith Jr, vice-commander of Air Defense Command (ADC), to lay down a possible specification. Smith's estimated figures were put together in April 1953 and called for an aircraft having a combat ceiling of 60,000ft (18,288m) and a combat radius of action of between 700nm (1,297km) and 1,000nm (1,852km). Two engines were favoured for enhanced reliability and the aircraft's speed would be between Mach 1.4 and 1.9 at 35,000ft (10,668m). No formal program was authorized by the Pentagon at this stage but Air Defense Command continued to push for the type's acceptance, the discussions lasting through much of 1953. One outcome of this situation was the elimination of an open competition (at least for the time being), but two existing proposals were analysed. The first was McDonnell's plan to build a two-place version of its F-101 Voodoo (which, it is understood, was not the same project that eventually became the F-101B interim interceptor discussed in Chapter Three), the other was known as the 'Delta Scorpion' – which we will come to shortly.

Model of the Boeing 712 by John Hall.

American Secret Projects: Fighters & Interceptors

The official evaluation reported that McDonnell 'did not have a valid proposal'. This seems surprising as it apparently met the speed and altitude requirements (if not range) and, being a derivative design, could be available before the Delta Scorpion. Northrop's offering came close to meeting the performance requirements and could achieve the desired operational radius. However, the manufacturer's timescale estimates for a first flight twenty-one months after a contract had been signed, with the first production aircraft following four months later, were thought to be optimistic; a figure of twenty-eight to thirty-two months for the production machine being assessed as more likely. Neither McDonnell's F-101 variant nor the N-126 was finally accepted, despite Northrop making great efforts to sell its paper aircraft. Air Defense Command apparently supported the N-126 but USAF Headquarters was not convinced.

In December 1953 the Air Council at last took steps to establish some clear military characteristics for the LRI. A decision was also made to hold an industry competition and the winning design was to be 'operationally available' by mid-1958. In late December the Pentagon began to yield to the pressure exerted by ADC, and by Northeast Air Command and Alaskan Air Command, and a requirement for an LRI was published by the end of April 1954. This two-seat twin-engine all-weather weapon system was to be capable of operating up to at least 1,000nm (1,852km) outside the ground electronic network, but it was also to have some capacity for point defence. The radar had to be able to search to a distance of 100nm (185km) and the weapons would comprise 'a type of guided missile which can be launched at a great distance to keep the interceptor out of enemy defensive fire or warhead damage area'. Their warheads were to be atomic, although a secondary conventional armament was also stated, and an advanced fire control system was to be installed together with the 'best possible' communication and navigation system. The minimum weapon load to accomplish the required task was stated as three unguided atomic warhead rockets and forty-eight 2.75in (7.0cm) rockets, or eight GAR-1A (Falcon) air-to-air missiles with the same load of rockets.

The interceptor had to be airborne two minutes after scramble (while on 24-hour alert status) and was to be capable of 'at least three separate kills of manoeuvring and non-manoeuvring aircraft flying individually or in formation'. It would have a combat ceiling at a rate of climb of 500ft/min (152m/min) of at least 60,000ft (18,288m); a level flight maximum speed at 40,000ft (12,192m) of Mach 1.7 or greater; and a radius of action of at least 1,000nm (1,852km). In addition, at 40,000ft the aircraft had to be able to accelerate from Mach 0.9 to 1.7 within three minutes. The first flight of a prototype with the design engine had to occur thirty months after the program had been officially established, the start date being 1st January 1955. These hugely demanding requirements were embraced within the designation Weapon System WS-202A.

Prospective firms were to be invited to bid by 10th May with the evaluation of the submissions beginning not later than mid-July, although it was acknowledged that the fire control system could not be developed within the same time schedule as the airframe. In fact some projects were not submitted until August and several manufacturers appear to have continued their studies long after that. Seven proposals were submitted that fully responded to the published specification, along with twelve further proposals that reflected suggested modifications to the specification. All the known submissions are described below, although which category they fall into is not always clear.

Boeing Model 712
A slim high-wing design with a tapered swept wing and all-moving tail, Boeing's Model 712 used two Wright J67-W-1 engines mounted in nacelles that were placed adjacent to the rear fuselage. The middle fuselage was area ruled to accommodate this feature. The wing's thickness/chord ratio was 5.0% at the root and 3.5% at the tip, leading edge sweep angle 45° 50', and there were leading and trailing edge flaps and relatively small ailerons. A bicycle undercarriage was employed with the outrigger wheels housed in small narrow nacelles fitted to the wing leading edge just inboard of the tips; the main gear had twin wheels. The fuselage weapons bay held the specified load of eight Falcon air-to-air missiles and forty-eight 2.75in (7.0cm) rocket projectiles, and the second crewman appears to have been given very little in the way of windows. Combat gross weight was given as 56,700 lb (25,719kg) but the available paperwork gives no details on the 712's maximum speed, although it would clearly have been highly supersonic.

Douglas Model 1355
Described as a conventional aircraft of all-metal design, the two-seat Model 1355 had a thin high-position sweptback wing and a fuselage contoured to provide low drag at transonic and supersonic speeds; the all-moving horizontal tail was placed low down. Single slotted all metal wing flaps were employed, the wingtips were squared off to form tip ailerons and a hydraulically operated irreversible system was provided for each primary flight control. A combined all-weather search and fire control system and a self-contained Doppler navigation system were incorporated. The powerplant was again two Wright J67-W-1s with afterburners, installed in wing pylon-mounted nacelles stretching well ahead of the leading edge, and reverse thrust units were located on the aft end of each engine.

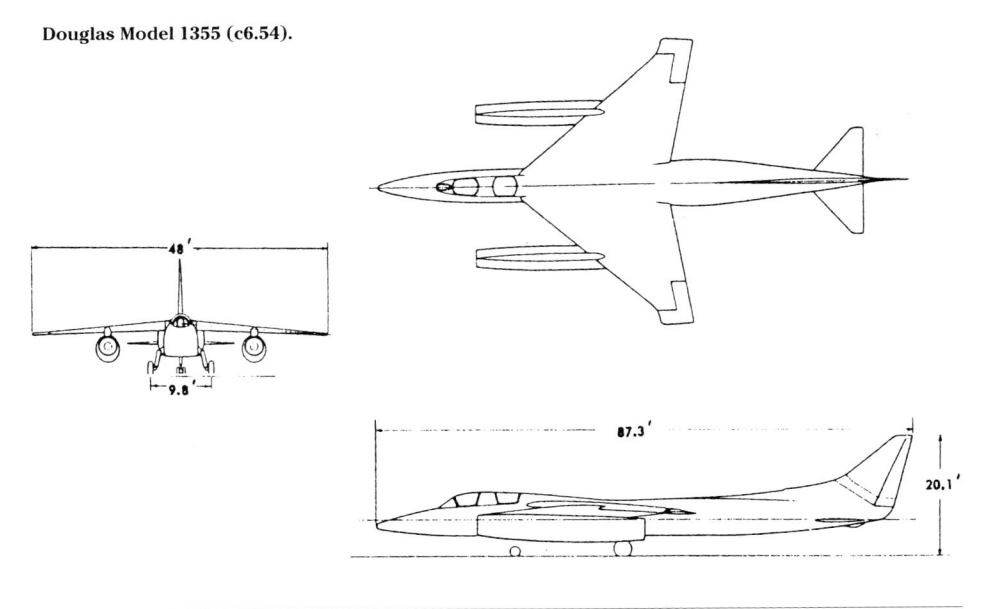

Douglas Model 1355 (c6.54).

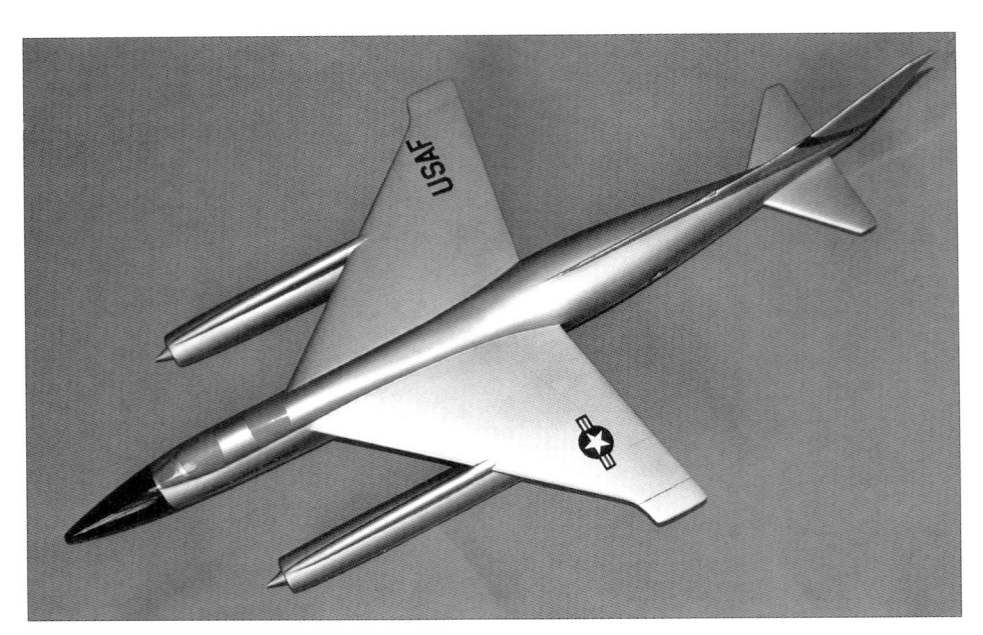

The armament load was contained in three individual missile bays in the fuselage that incorporated hydraulically actuated retractable launchers. A total of 3,846gal (17,487lit) of internal fuel was carried in two wing tanks plus two more in the fuselage, one forward and one aft of the centre of gravity. The forward weapon bay, housing the rockets, was placed beneath the first of these fuel tanks just behind the rear (radar operator's) seat, while the eight Falcons went in two more bays underneath the aft tank just behind the line of the main undercarriage. A tricycle undercarriage was fitted with a twin nosewheel and single main wheels and the 1355's combat weight was 56,200 lb (25,492kg).

Lockheed CL-288

Although a much bigger aircraft, Lockheed's CL-288's family likeness to the F-104 was very obvious. In fact it was an F-104 substantially scaled up, the CL-288's wing construction, empennage, landing gear design, downward aircrew ejection seat and other parts were to be used 'cold' direct from the F-104 or with only minor modifications. One change was the introduction of wing nacelles to house the engines (with nose shock cones), rather than putting them inside the fuselage. There were leading and trailing edge flaps, the tail was all-moving, speed brakes were placed on the sides of the rear fuselage and, again, a weapons bay was employed. The design was submitted in June 1954 but work on the project lasted several months. CL-288's combat ceiling was expected to be 60,800ft (18,532m) and combat radius 1,000nm (1,852km).

American Secret Projects: Fighters & Interceptors

Opposite page:

Model of the 1355 long-range interceptor.
George Cox

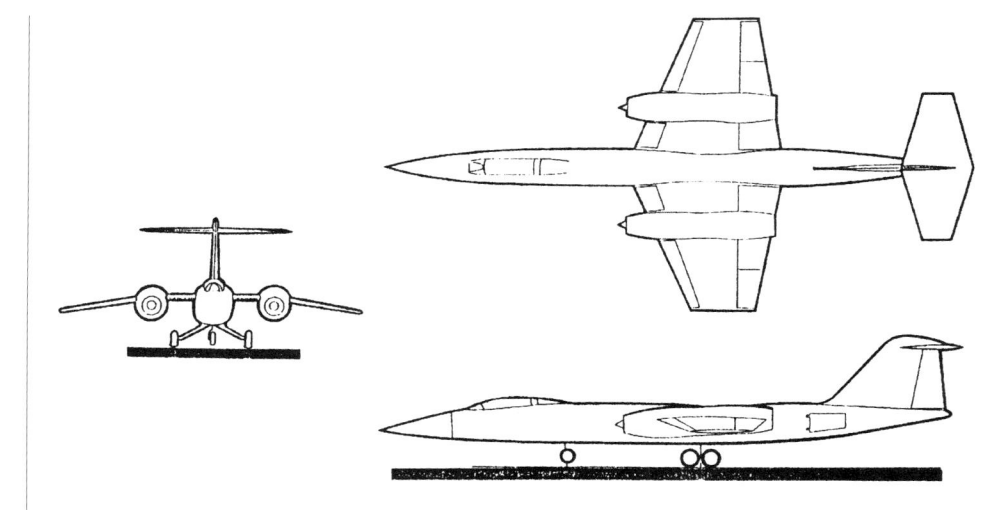

This page:

Right: **Lockheed CL-288-1 (5.54).** Peter Clukey

Below: **Model of the Lockheed CL-288-1.**
John Aldaz

The Quest for a Long-Range Interceptor

McDonnell Model 110A (14.7.54).
National Air and Space Museum

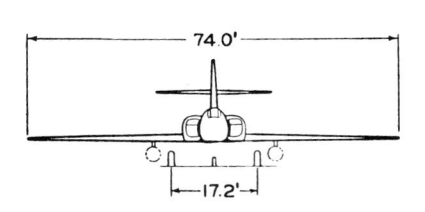

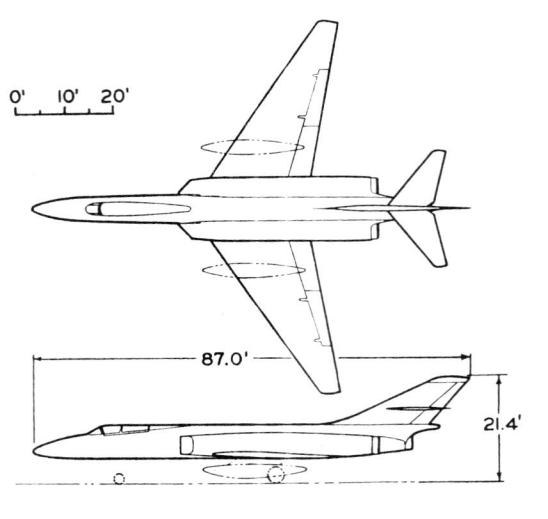

Martin Models 302, 308 and 314

Martin's records list the Models 302, 308 and 314 as long-range interceptor projects, but there are no drawings surviving in the Martin archive for any of them. Models 308 and 314 are listed as alternatives to the initial Model 302 but again no details and data exist, except that one of them at least was expected to achieve a top speed of Mach 1.92.

McDonnell Model 109

The 'A' version of the McDonnell Model 109 was dated 17th June 1954 and was similar to the manufacturer's F-101A Voodoo. This two-seater had the apparently standard two J67-W-1 powerplant but it carried six Falcons or three of McDonnell's own Model 103E missiles. Length was 89ft 9.5in (27.4m) and wing area 600ft^2 (55.8m^2). The Model 109B (number assigned 18th August 1954) was the same as the 109A except that it was longer at 96ft 6in (29.4m) and had a larger wing.

McDonnell Model 110

The McDonnell Model 110 designation also covered two versions, Models 110A and B. The 110A, dated 14th July 1954, was clearly an outgrowth of the company's F-101 Voodoo and, being a two-place high-performance long-range interceptor, had been designed with the objective of obtaining maximum high altitude performance, both in the subsonic and supersonic regimes. The need for ready access for quick servicing and rearming was another key element. Power came from three J67-W-1 units, although there was provision for an alternative powerplant of three Pratt & Whitney J75-P-1 jets. The

Model of the McDonnell 110A by John Hall.

94 American Secret Projects: Fighters & Interceptors

engines were placed approximately side-by-side in the rear fuselage, but with the middle unit slightly higher and further back.

Model 110A incorporated a swept-back wing with a cambered leading edge and it had trailing edge flaps, hydraulic power-operated irreversible flight controls, an all-moveable stabilizer, speed brakes, provision for in-flight refuelling (using the Probe-Drogue method) and single-point refuelling. The basic armament was located in a long single bay in the lower centre fuselage level with the intakes and forward wing, and a combination of Falcon missiles and 2.75in (7.0cm) rockets was carried on two tandem racks that extended from this bay for firing. An alternative armament would provide three unguided atomic warhead (UAW) rockets combined with the 2.75in rockets on a single rack carried and extended from the same bay. The 110A would have 3,147gal. (14,309lit) of fuel in six fuselage and three wing tanks, plus another 1,000gal. (4,547lit) in two underwing external tanks. Its fire control system was expected to achieve the 100nm (185km) requirement.

The 110A's estimated performance for its basic area intercept mission, with no external tanks aboard, included a sea level rate of climb in afterburner of 56,200ft/min (17,130m/min) and a combat ceiling of 61,900ft (18,867m). Combat weight was 60,638lb (27,505kg) and combat radius 683nm (1,265km) but these figures were increased to 63,395lb (28,756kg) and 1,000nm (1,852km) when the drop tanks were aboard. In the point intercept role the combat weight became 55,811lb (25,316kg), combat ceiling 63,400ft (19,324ft) and sea level rate of climb 61,020ft/min (18,599m/min). The 110A's best service ceiling, at a 100ft/min (30.5m/min) climb rate, was 66,100ft (20,147m).

Design work on the Model 110B was started during mid-August 1954. The aircraft shared the same armament and fire control system as the 110A, but the powerplant was cut back to just two J67s while the length was reduced to 79ft (24.1m) and the wing area to 819ft² (76.2m²).

McDonnell Model 111A
This project appears to have been started in October 1954, after the end of the competition, but it completes McDonnell's studies into this type of aircraft. Model 111A received the same weapons and fire control as the 110A but was powered by just two J67s (two Pratt & Whitney J75-P-1 were an alternative). In general appearance the 111A was very similar to the 110A with wing plan and undercarriage roughly the same, but the fuselage was

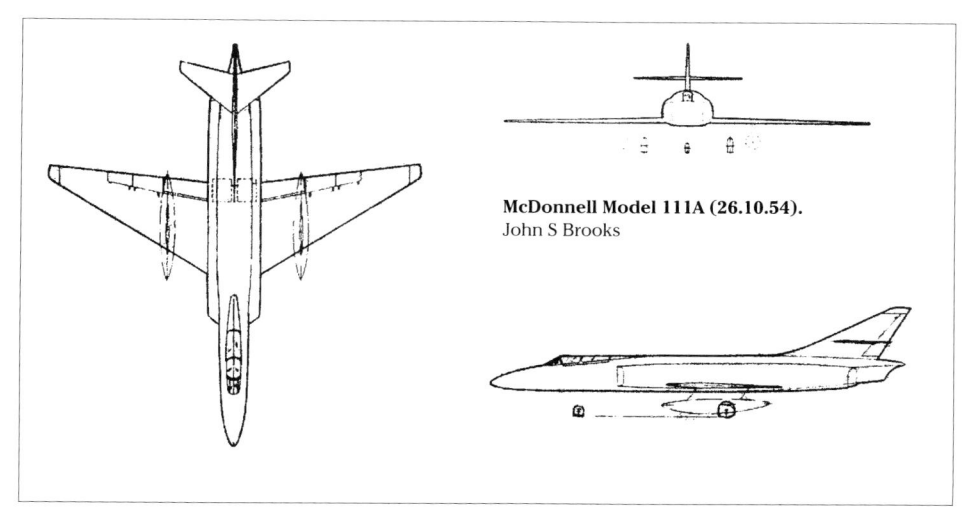

McDonnell Model 111A (26.10.54).
John S Brooks

slimmer and the intakes smaller due to the need to supply less air to the two power units. The wing, swept 27° at the ¼ chord line, was also smaller and trailing edge flaps were employed with boundary layer control to give high lift. Maximum internal fuel was 2,212gal (10,058lit) and, like the 110A, another 1,000gal (4,547lit) could be carried in two underwing tanks to give the 1,000nm (1,852km) area intercept radius. Combat weight was 52,065lb (23,617kg), estimated combat ceiling 59,070ft (18,005m) and at this weight the sea level rate of climb was 40,200ft/min (12,253m/min) with time to 35,000ft (10,668m) altitude just over 1.3 minutes.

Identical to the 110A, there was a tricycle undercarriage with a single wheel on each leg and, as usual, two crew – pilot and radar-navigator. The armament load was unchanged, again carried internally and extended for firing from the underside of the fuselage. No accurate details had been made available for the Unguided Atomic Warheads and so McDonnell had assumed the following – weight 800lb (363kg), length 180in (457cm) and diameter 15in (38.1cm). Although these McDonnell LRI studies were similar, the switch to two engines meant that the Model 111A could not quite reach the specified 60,000ft (18,288m) cruise altitude. Overall producing an aircraft that could do Mach 2 at 60,000ft proved to be difficult, which is why McDonnell chose three J67s on the 110A – at the time the J67 was the biggest engine available.

North American WS-202A
No project number was allocated to North American's initial proposals to the LRI requirements, but this submission was perhaps the most advanced of any put forward. The proposed interceptor was quite spectacular: with a large area delta canard, very long slim fuselage, box intakes feeding two side-by-side engines (presumably J67s), a cropped delta wing, and twin upper and lower fins. The two crew were seated in tandem and there was a large volume available in the middle of the fuselage to house the weapons, fuel and electronics.

Northrop N-126 Delta Scorpion
Northrop's design effort towards a long-range interceptor opened with the N-126, work on which began in February 1953. The first proposal was completed in May and showed a modified version of the subsonic F-89D Scorpion fitted with a new delta wing (hence the name which was carried through to later N-126 studies) plus two Wright YJ67 engines. It carried eight Falcon semi-active radar-homing air-to-air missiles as its primary armament, together with seventy-four 2.75in (7.0cm) pod-mounted unguided rocket projectiles and 15,400lb (6,985kg) of fuel. This project's estimated take-off weight was 50,000lb (22,680kg) and it was expected to operate at around 46,000ft (14,021m). However, this design was rejected because of insufficient performance and Northrop moved on to another delta project with a much longer fuselage.

In fact more than fifty configurations were assessed before the designers settled on this layout and, following the consideration given to the Delta Scorpion prior to the start of the full LRI competition, in August 1954 it was dusted down and re-submitted to WS-202A. Although continuing with the name 'Scorpion', this was now a totally different aircraft to its predecessor. It had a long slim fuselage, a big 45° delta wing of thickness/chord ratio 4.5%, powerplant in underwing nacelles and a low-position horizontal tail. The wing trailing edge had an arrangement made up of a

The Quest for a Long-Range Interceptor

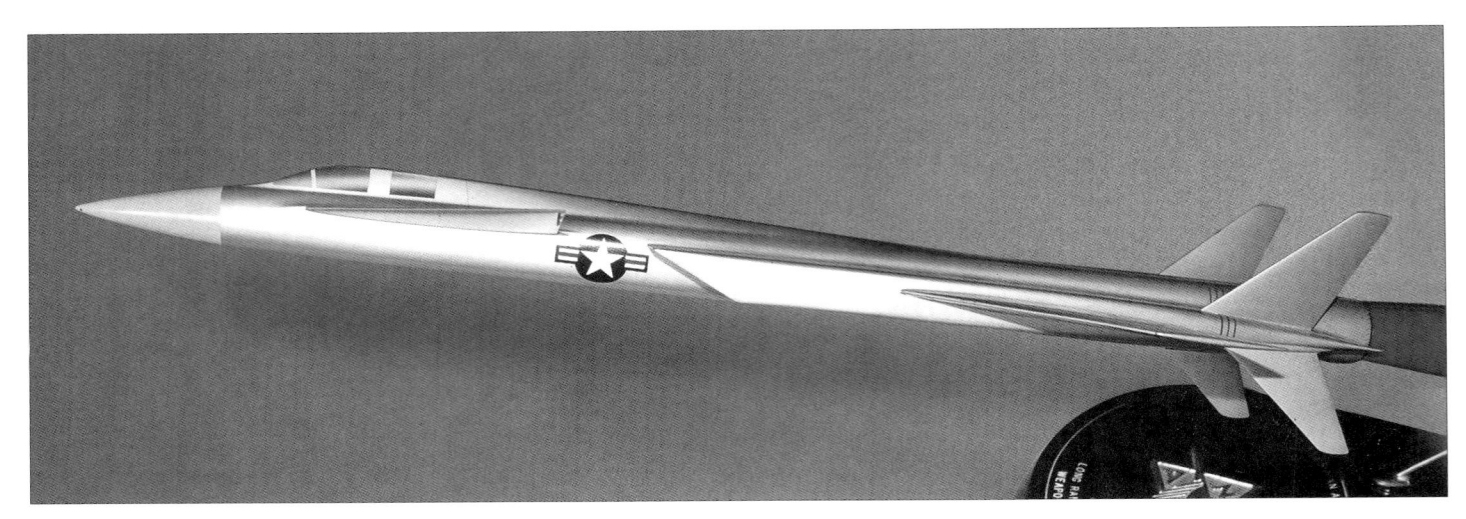

This page:

Model of North American's proposal to Weapon System 202A. The model's span is 8.3in (21.1cm) and length 18.0in (45.8cm). George Cox

Opposite page:

This original manufacturer's wood model of the Northrop N-126 is a little damaged, but it gives every indication of what an impressive beast the aircraft would have been had it been constructed. Northrop Grumman Corp, photo Tony Chong

American Secret Projects: Fighters & Interceptors

split speed brake on the outer wing, an aileron in the middle and then inboard a surface that was described as an 'altitude flap'. The favoured engine was the Wright J67-W-1, but the less powerful Allison J71-A-11 was a possible substitute. There was a bicycle undercarriage, with twin wheels on both central units plus outriggers fitted between the engine nacelles and wingtips.

One of the few items to be carried through from the Scorpion, in fact the F-89H variant, was the Hughes E-9A fire control system coupled with a 40in (102cm)-diameter long-range search radar offering 100nm (185km) range. A 20ft (6.1m) long internal weapon bay could carry eight Falcon missiles and two packs of twenty-four 2.75in (7.0cm) folding-fin rocket projectiles in retractable packages, but the Falcons could be replaced by four Ding Dong nuclear rockets, six Sidewinder or two Sparrow air-to-air missiles. Various combinations of weapons were also possible loaded on the four external pylons and space was available for a 1,640lb (744kg) bomb. The fuel load was 4,844gal (22,025lit), with 31,470lb (14,275kg) in one massive and two smaller wing tanks plus two large fuselage tanks while another 1,600gal (7,275lit) could be held in two external tanks on the wing pylons.

On internal fuel only the N-126 was estimated to show an operating range of 800nm (1,482km) and, besides fulfilling the LRI requirements, it was expected to be capable of intercepting enemy bombers twenty-seven minutes after the initial order to scramble, at a distance of 360nm (667km), in a mission that embodied a supersonic cruise out at Mach 1.6. The aircraft's combat weight was 59,280lb (26,889kg) for area interception and 49,700lb (22,544kg) for point interception, combat ceiling in the area role 56,200ft

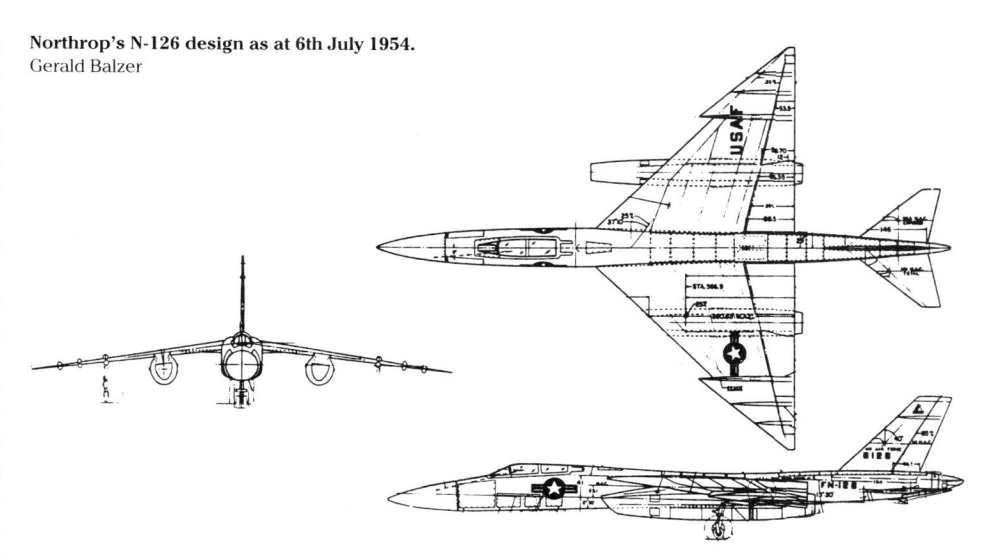

Northrop's N-126 design as at 6th July 1954.
Gerald Balzer

The Quest for a Long-Range Interceptor

Northrop N-144 (26.7.54). Gerald Balzer

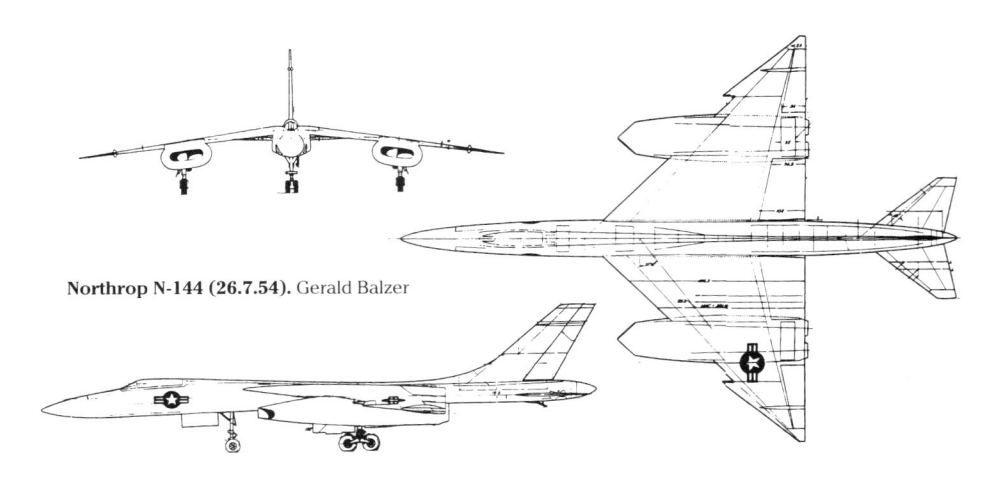

(17,130m) and the point role 59,600ft (18,166m), sea level rates of climb 35,100ft/min (10,698m/min) and 41,100ft/min (12,527m/min) respectively and, in its lighter condition, the machine would take 2.45 minutes to reach 40,000ft (12,192m). N-126's service ceiling was 60,380ft (18,404m) and combat radius 1,010nm (1,871km). In July 1954 Northrop estimated that the aircraft's first flight would take place in June 1957.

Northrop N-144

The four-engined delta wing N-144 of July 1954 was the proposal that Northrop had designed explicitly to meet the requirement. The brochure declared that it offered outstanding airborne performance complemented by a fast turn-around capability and, due to its size, there was great scope for alternative roles. N-144 was essentially a scaled-up N-126 and had much in common with the earlier project, including the E-9A control system and 40in (102cm) scanner and the bicycle undercarriage, here with a four-wheel main gear. The delta wing arrangement on these projects offered a low weight for such a large aeroplane coupled with minimum drag, plus plenty of interior space for weapons, fuel and equipment. Wing leading edge sweep angle was again 45° and thickness/chord ratio 4.5%.

N-144's combat weight was 91,600lb (41,550kg) and a total of 6,910gal (31,419lit) or 44,940lb (20,385kg) of fuel was to be carried; as a result great portions of the fuselage and wing were taken up by the fuel tanks. In the area interception role the fighter's combat ceiling was 60,000ft (18,288m) and combat radius 1,010nm (1,871km); in the point intercept role the ceiling became 63,000ft (19,202m) and the aircraft would take 1.9 minutes to reach 40,000ft (12,192m). Alternative weapons for the rear fuselage internal bay, along with the standard forty-eight 2.75in (7.0cm) rockets, were twelve Falcon or six Ding Dong missiles, two 'special stores', 452 2.75in rockets or 782 2in (5.1cm) rockets, while another large combination of weapons including bombs could be carried on four external wing pylons. The N-144 was truly a monster interceptor, and it was bigger than many bombers.

The N-126 and N-144 (and N-149 below) shared the same basic layout with engines mounted in underwing pods and the armament in the fuselage. This arrangement gave scope for fitting more powerful engines with

Manufacturer's model of the Northrop N-144.
Northrop Grumman Corp, photo Tony Chong

American Secret Projects: Fighters & Interceptors

a relatively simple intake design that avoided fuselage boundary layer problems; it was also safer in the event of fire. A low wing loading was selected which gave a higher cruise altitude and allowed take-offs and landings to be made without using complex flap and slot arrangements. The additional horizontal tail, in each case an all-moving 'flying' surface, gave increased stability and better handling and, being placed below the level of the wing, it avoided pitch-up at high centres of lift and low speeds. The low-speed characteristics were also enhanced by large ailerons and leading edge extensions on the wings, while to cut drag and weight trailing edge flaps had been rejected. However, the wing did have a constant per cent chord flap that would be retracted when the aircraft was flying supersonically. Surprisingly, area ruling was not applied, but Northrop noted that the advantages at high speeds offered by this feature were offset by the lack of any benefit at low speeds, while no area rule also gave a simpler layout. During this period Northrop's studies into long-range interceptors were substantial and the designers concluded that such an aircraft, through additional power and other modifications, would during its life see improvements in top speed and ceiling by around 14% together with a similar reduction in take-off weight.

Northrop N-149

The N-149 was also completed in July 1954 and was proposed in order to complete a full study of the entire weight spectrum possible with an LRI type of aeroplane. This project was offered as the aircraft of least weight that could still perform the long-range intercept mission, utilising external fuel to accomplish the task. These factors were reflected by weights and fuel volumes that were rather less than those estimated for the N-144, although the N-149 used the same aerodynamics with the same leading edge sweep and thickness/chord ratio as the bigger aircraft but with the wing scaled down. It also used the same fire control system and radar scanner. Combat weight was 43,400 lb (19,686 kg) and the internal fuel totalled 2,050 gal (9,321 lit), or 13,310 lb (6,074 kg), housed in one massive tank spread across the inner wings and upper fuselage plus another in the fuselage just behind the cockpit and one more just ahead of the rear

Northrop N-149 (26.7.54).
Gerald Balzer

This fifty-year-old manufacturer's wood model of the Northrop N-149 also shows some damage, both to the fin and horizontal tail. Two external fuel tanks are visible between the fuselage and engine nacelles. Northrop Grumman Corp, photo Tony Chong

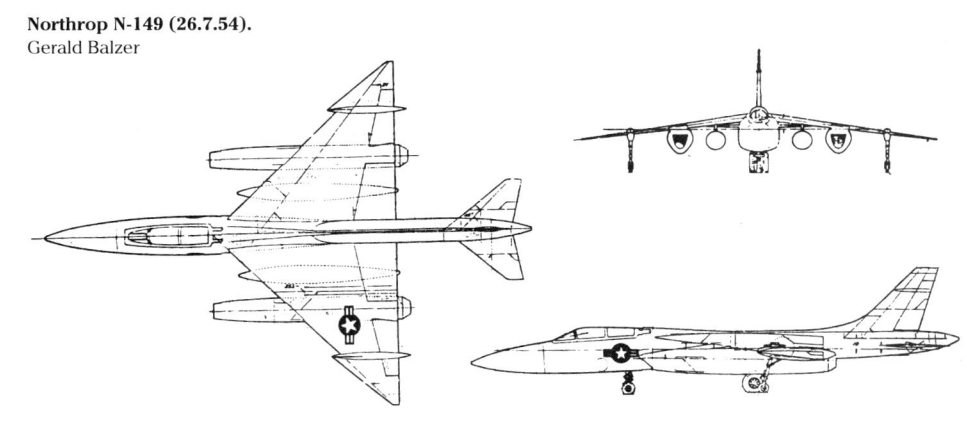

The Quest for a Long-Range Interceptor

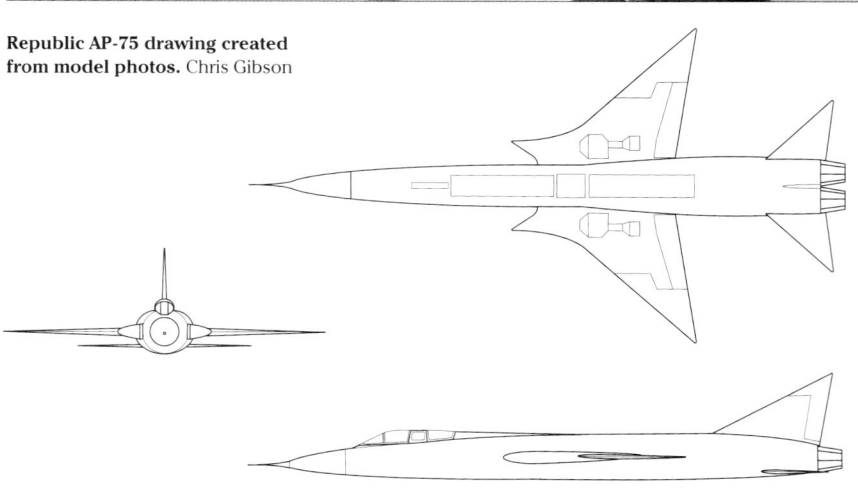

Republic AP-75. This model has a span of 15.3in (38.9cm) and length 27.25in (69.2cm), which at 1/32nd scale gives a real span of 40ft 9in (12.4m) and length 72ft 8in (22.1m). AP-75 was revealed to the public in an article published in 'Aviation Week' for 12th May 1958 that described a recent Open House at Republic's factory. Other models on display included the F-103, AP-54, AP-55 and AP-63 (all described elsewhere), and the NP-52 anti-submarine aircraft. Larry McLaughlin

View giving rear fuselage detail for Republic's AP-75 long-range interceptor proposal (c5.54). Larry McLaughlin

Republic AP-75 drawing created from model photos. Chris Gibson

fuselage. The external fuel comprised 1,200gal (5,456lit) or 7,800lb (3,538kg) in two tanks.

Combat ceiling for the point intercept mission was 55,700ft (16,977m), and for area interception 52,800ft (16,093m). For the latter role the combat radius was 770nm (1,426km) while at the lighter weight for point interception the N-149 was expected to take 3.1 minutes to reach 40,000ft (12,192m). On the N-149 the alternative internal weapon loads included one 'special store', one Sparrow II fully active seeking air-to-air missile or four Sidewinder infrared missiles, another 105 2.75in (7.0cm) rockets (on top of the forty-eight in the basic armament) or 270 2in (5.1cm) rockets. There were four underwing hardpoints for external weapon carriage but two of these were also used to carry the 600gal (2,728lit) fuel tanks. Both legs of the bicycle undercarriage had two wheels.

Northrop stated that the N-149 could be ready for its maiden flight in the summer of 1957. However, after a full power take-off and

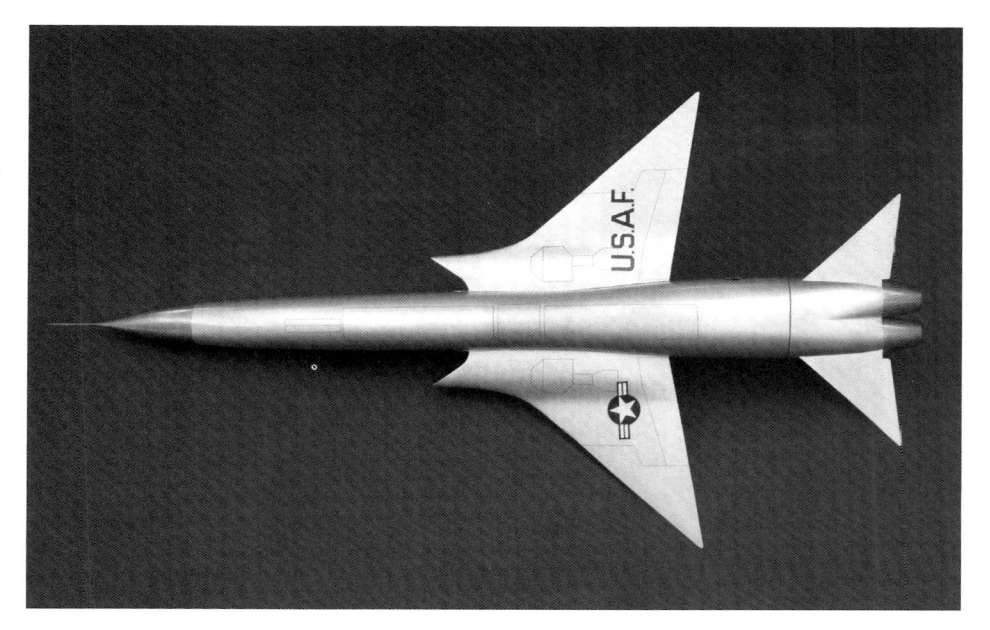

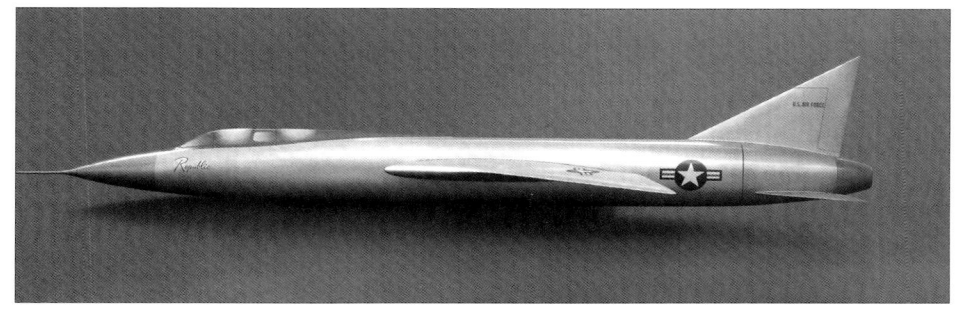

Two views of a second manufacturer's model of the AP-75, showing clearly the area ruling given to the rear fuselage. John Aldaz

climb to 50,000ft (15,240m), the machine offered a loiter time at 35,000ft (10,668m) of just twenty minutes plus five minutes combat at full power, points that proved to be a factor in the N-149's eventual rejection.

Republic AP-75

In appearance the Republic AP-75 represented a cross between Republic's XF-103 and F-105 discussed in earlier chapters, from an aesthetic point of view taking on board the best aspects of both. AP-75 was a sleek handsome design that encompassed a long, slim area-ruled fuselage, twin engines side-by-side in the rear fuselage served by Republic's trademark Ferri air intake scoops in the wing roots, thin delta wings and an all-moving low delta tail. The model suggests that the wings had inboard flaps and all-moving wingtips, the latter presumably performing the role of ailerons. Two crew were seated in tandem, the AP-75 had a tricycle undercarriage and, like other LRIs, its weapons were to be housed in an internal bay.

Chance Vought V-391

The official document from which much of the F-108 story has been gleaned (*The Controversial Long Range Interceptor*, written to form part of a report called *The Development of Airborne Armament, 1910-1961*) does not mention Chance Vought submitting a design, but the company's project index lists the V-391 as a long-range interceptor. Its date, 24th May 1954, ties in with the competition, but no papers covering the V-391 have survived in the Vought archive.

Grumman G-107

This manufacturer undertook studies into a conceptual long-range interceptor, but then decided to withhold its bid. During May and June 1954 Grumman's team evolved a design that, according to a company document and based on a preliminary performance analysis, exceeded or equalled the general requirements. The airframe had a large 45° sweep mid-position wing, mid-position tailplane and twin Wright J67 engines with afterburners placed one above the other in the rear fuselage; these were fed by side intakes. There was a long slim boom fitted into the middle of the leading edge of the wing and it appears that the two crew sat side-by-side. The choice of a 45° angle was determined mainly by the acceleration requirement from Mach 0.9 to 1.7, which for the G-107 was estimated to be just 1.8 minutes. G-107's combat weight was 49,500 lb (22,453kg) and the design offered a top speed at 40,000ft (12,192m) of Mach 1.26 in cold afterburner and Mach 2.14 with the afterburner lit. Radius of action was approximately 1,000nm (1,852km) and the ceiling in afterburner was 60,800ft (18,532m) when flying subsonically and 63,600ft (19,385m) when supersonic. Maximum sea level rate of climb in afterburner was about 48,500ft/min (14,783m/min).

Grumman's preliminary estimates for maximum speed and ceiling strongly indicated that the latter would be a governing design requirement, particularly if the maximum ceiling was required at subsonic speeds (it had been assumed that a subsonic ceiling was desirable). Because of the very low dynamic pressure corresponding to a high subsonic speed at 60,000ft (18,288m), it was immediately apparent that the wing loading must be kept sufficiently low to prevent buffeting (with the attendant increase in drag) at the ceiling. The value that had been achieved here was 50 lb/ft^2 (244kg/m^2). Grumman concluded that, from the aerodynamic viewpoint, the aircraft appeared to be quite feasible and the specification could be adequately satisfied. However, the studies also indicated that the size of this aircraft was out of the field for which Grumman had facilities to handle, and consequently the company decided not to submit a proposal to the competition.

Of the seven 'specification' proposals, Wright Field's evaluators rated Northrop first, Lockheed second and Douglas third, with Martin, Boeing, McDonnell and Republic following in that order. Material Command (basing its ratings on ease of maintenance, production estimates and costings) favoured Lockheed, Douglas and then Boeing for the highest ratings, followed by Republic, Northrop, Martin and McDonnell. None of the seven fully met the performance requirements. The four-engine Northrop N-144 came closest with a combat ceiling of 58,500ft (17,831m), a radius of 1,015nm (1,880km) and a top speed of Mach 1.76 (these were the assessor's estimates, the figures given earlier were Northrop's). McDonnell's aircraft could attain the same altitude and had a speed of Mach 1.8, but its range was only 900nm (1,667km). Only Republic offered a model comparable to Northrop in range and, of all of the proposals,

Photograph showing the rear fuselage and twin J67 jetpipe on the G-107-3.

Planview and side elevations of the Grumman G-107-3 model (6.54). Note the substantial area ruling given to this design. Model span is 20.9in (53.0cm) and length 25.25in (64.1cm).

Martin's model was the fastest at Mach 1.92. There were also thirteen fire control system proposals, none of which met the required search range.

In other words, the specification had raised the bar just a little too high for the industry's capability at this time. The two evaluating agencies concluded that none of the airframe proposals met the specification, although Northrop's was best. All were deficient in altitude, but if the Air Force wanted an 'extended range interceptor' for the 1959-1960 era then the F-101 modified for that role (the Model 109) with the MG-3 fire control system (destined for the F-102A) would do the job except for the altitude deficiency. The evaluators also asked for a relaxation of the requirements so that the proposals already received could form the basis for that weapon system. It was also stated that, for the Air Force to have a truly advanced LRI, an operational date of 1963/1964 would have to be established. The result was more discussions, with some strong conflicting views between individuals, and the picture was further complicated when the Pentagon began to apply pressure to cut the cost of operating the Air Force.

Nevertheless, on 20th July 1955 Air Force headquarters approved the development of the long-range interceptor and, a short time later, plans were initiated for a (Phase 1) study program leading to the construction of a mock-up. The candidates were three Southland companies, Northrop, Lockheed and North American, and in October the Air Force decreed that the study program would bring the elimination of one of these competitors. The two surviving contractors would then build a prototype. What was now actually called the LRI-X (for long-range interceptor, experimental) was covered by GOR-114 dated 6th October 1955. LRI-X was to be a two-seat twin-engine aircraft that would be operational in 1961, and the required performance was to be the same as that listed for the May 1954 competition. The integrated electronic and control system was to be capable of detecting a target the size of a Boeing B-47 bomber at 60nm (111km) range, with 100nm (185km) desired, and have the ability to make three kills. Study contracts were issued to the three companies on 11th October.

Lockheed CL-320

Lockheed's LRI research was resurrected with the CL-320 project and the final design, the CL-320-36, was similar to the CL-288, but the difference was its size. It continued the F-104 family appearance but was very much bigger and heavier that that aircraft and considerably larger that the CL-288. Lockheed declared that the size was necessary to meet the performance requirements. The wing was swept 17° 45' at quarter chord and a bicycle undercarriage was employed with the outriggers placed between the two advanced J79 engines housed in each nacelle. Sea level rate of climb was given as 43,000ft/min (13,106m/min), combat altitude 60,000ft (18,288m) and combat radius 800nm (1,482km). The -36 number shows that a multitude of designs were considered and along the way Lockheed had looked at several smaller aircraft that would have achieved slight reductions in altitude capability or range.

North American NA-236

With the issuing of a study contract, North American Aviation (NAA) allocated the program number NA-236 to its long-range interceptor work. The design itself still had a canard, but otherwise was much modified from the company's original 1954 proposal. There was a near full delta wing with variable geometry wing root intakes feeding two General Electric J93 engines and the canard was mounted on top of the forward fuselage. The NA-236's structure was to be built mostly in titanium and then covered in stainless steel honeycomb skins to cope with the terrific kinetic heat that would be generated by flight at Mach 3. The missiles would be housed in a fuselage bay between the air intakes. NAA had problems finding sufficient vertical fin area to ensure that the F-108 had enough directional stability to be controllable when flying at Mach 3. As a result the NA-236 at this time had a single large central fin plus two vertical surfaces at the mid-span position, but by March 1956 it had acquired two more small vertical stabilizers beneath the rear fuselage.

Lockheed CL-320 (1955). Peter Clukey

It is understood that this model represents the North American NA-236 project in its earliest form in October/November 1955. Curiously, there appears to be no cockpit window for the radar operator.
Jonathan Rigutto / photo © 2005 Chad Slattery

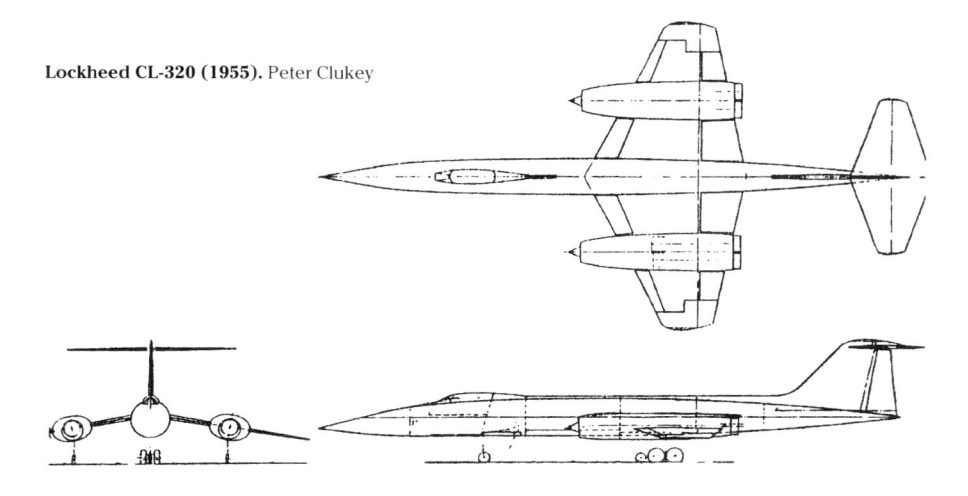

The Quest for a Long-Range Interceptor

Northrop N-167 (26.11.55).
Gerald Balzer

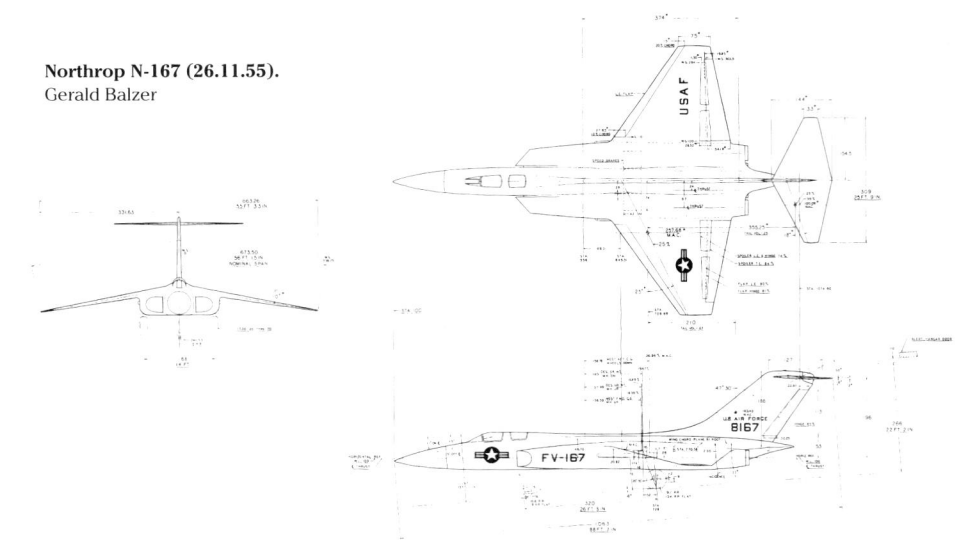

Northrop N-167

Having pushed the advantages of a delta wing with engines in underwing nacelles on each of its previous long-range interceptors, Northrop suddenly switched to a design with the power units placed inside the fuselage. However, the established delta layout was not discarded immediately. On receiving the new study contract Northrop had begun an assessment of forty-six separate design arrangements, with countless variations of each, gradually reducing this number by a methodical step-by-step process of elimination. The work culminated in the finalized configuration that became the N-167, the

Model of the Northrop N-167. This model may have been restored because the apparent fixed tail with elevator outlining is an error. John Aldaz

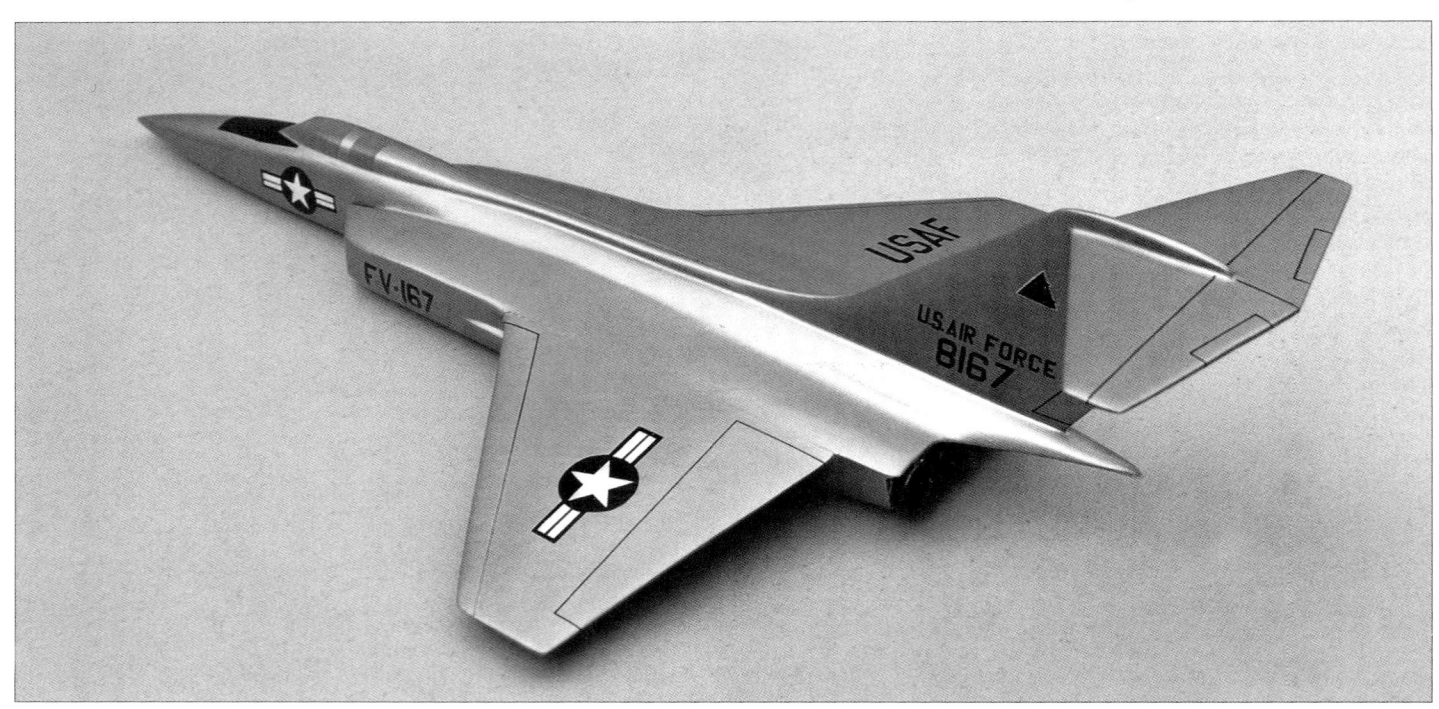

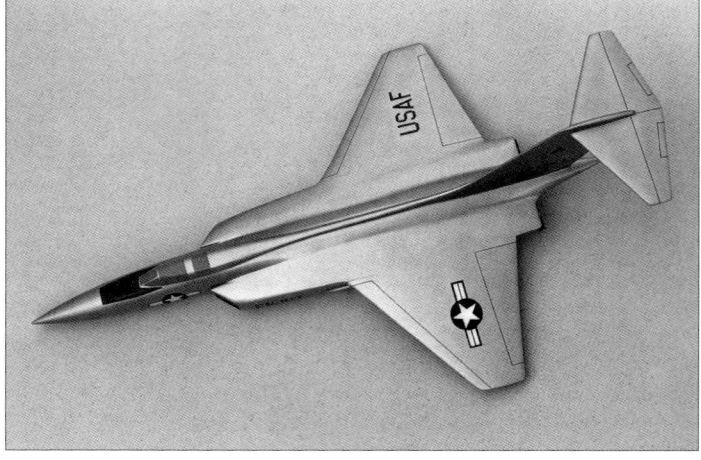

American Secret Projects: Fighters & Interceptors

design going through to project status on 28th November 1955.

Northrop stated that this continued effort had resulted in a smaller, more efficient airframe offering greater capability over the N-144. The delta was replaced by a very thin tapered wing of 3.7% thickness/chord ratio that had pronounced anhedral, and there was a large single fin and an all-moving 'T' tail. Full-span leading edge and trailing edge flaps were now provided for better take-off and landing characteristics together with a set of spoilers, reversing Northrop's decision on the deltas not to use such items on the wing. Four General Electric J79-X207 engines were mounted side-by-side within the rear fuselage, this choice being made ahead of an alternative of two Allison J89s because it gave lighter take-off weights. Eight GAR-1 Falcon air-to-air missiles would be accommodated in a mid-fuselage weapon bay that was 16ft 8in (5.08m) long, 5ft (1.52m) wide and 3ft 6in (1.07m) deep. The Falcons were carried in two individually actuated clusters of four and alternative weapons included three Ding Dongs or varying combinations of rockets, missiles or special stores. Pylon-mounted armament was also available to allow the N-167 to be used for alternative missions and the wingtips had been reserved as possible locations for two more Ding Dongs. There was a tricycle undercarriage with twin wheels on the nose leg and a large single wheel on each main gear.

Directly above the weapons bay in the upper fuselage was a massive fuel cell and the N-167 could carry 6,595gal (29,987lit) or 42,770 lb (19,400kg) of internal fuel. Its combat weight was calculated to be 73,250 lb (33,226kg), combat radius was given as 1,000nm (1,852km), combat ceiling 61,000ft (18,593m) and the combat speed at 40,000ft (12,192m) Mach 2.0. Indeed the aircraft's maximum speed at heights between 35,000ft (10,668m) and about 57,500ft (17,526m), based on the engine's design temperature, was Mach 2.0 throughout, but in fact the airframe appeared to be capable of Mach 2.35 at 35,800ft (10,912m). Rate of climb at sea level was 56,000ft/min (17,069m/min), and at 50,000ft (15,240m) it was still 14,000ft/min (4,267m/min).

In early April 1956 a variant called the N-167A was drawn which was similar in layout and engines to the N-167, but had the tailplane moved down to a position on the side of the rear fuselage and enlarged to a span that was the same as the wing. The wing had much less anhedral and its span was 56ft 1.5in (17.1m), the interceptor had a length of 86ft 5in (26.3m) and gross wing area of 950ft² (88.4m²), and the tail had a gross area of 356ft² (33.1m²). Quite large twin ventral fins were also introduced, which were to be deployed during flight.

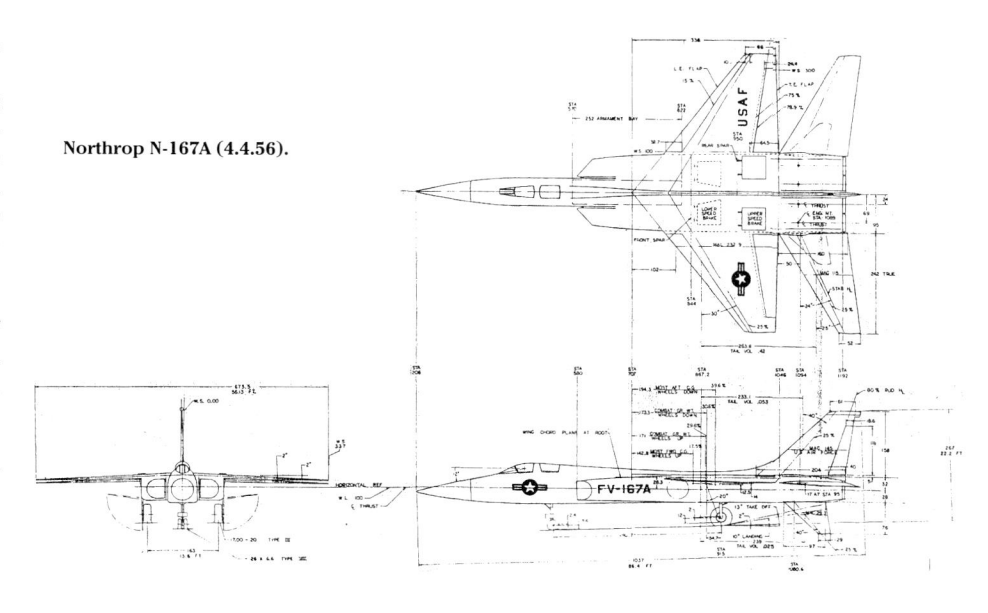

Northrop N-167A (4.4.56).

During January 1956 the three sets of initial study documents were evaluated at Wright Field by a specially formed source selection board. North American's NA-236 was selected as the winner, but a lot more discussions followed to consider whether the Air Force could actually afford the aircraft. Finance was only available for one new interceptor and ADC was uncertain if this should be the LRI. In fact Defense Command had already asked the Air Force to begin considering a medium-range interceptor that would be capable of operating within, and remaining under, the strict control of the ground network. A simple lightweight interceptor was also suggested before the Pentagon cancelled the long-range interceptor on 9th May 1956, the reasons being a dearth of funding in addition to 'questions which had arisen regarding the utility and desirability' of such a weapon system. Work on two fire control systems from Hughes and Sperry was allowed to continue until they were cancelled in late May.

In response General Partridge, the ADC commander, proposed a 'modified' LRI capable of Mach 2.75 and 70,000ft (21,336m), and then the Air Staff decided that the old LRI was just what the Air Force wanted, but now developed in combination with advanced air-to-air missiles. A special board chaired by Maj Gen Albert Boyd concluded that an interceptor having the following characteristics was essential to the defence of the United States: two seats, capable of Mach 3.0, 70,000ft (21,336m) altitude, and 1,000nm (1,852km) radius of action. It would cruise subsonically and dash at supersonic speeds and, for versatility, would have a mix of two guided missiles. This combination comprised a conventional warhead Falcon-type plus at least two GAR-X weapons with an interchangeable high explosive or atomic warhead to hit targets up to twenty-five miles (40km) away. The minimum size for the warhead was established as two kilotons. Heeding this analysis, on 11th April 1957 Washington reinstated the long-range interceptor and in June North American received a contract to develop the aircraft, now designated F-108. The decision to award North American this work was taken on the basis of the 1956 competition results.

North American NA-257 (F-108) Rapier

The reinstatement of the project also brought a new NA-257 designation from the manufacturers, although at this stage the design was very similar to the earlier NA-236. A few minor differences had appeared, namely small changes to the wing-mounted fins and the splitting of the trailing edge flaps into two rather than the earlier single moving surface. NA-257's engine was to be the specially developed General Electric J93 with convergent-divergent nozzle, which was initially designated in-house as the X-279E.

As we have seen, from the start North American's long-range interceptor had used a canard coupled with some form of delta wing, but as the NA-257/F-108 it now began to 'mature'. During 1957 the Air Force was planning to order more than 480 F-108s and by

North American NA-257/F-108 at 2nd May 1958. Terry Panopalis

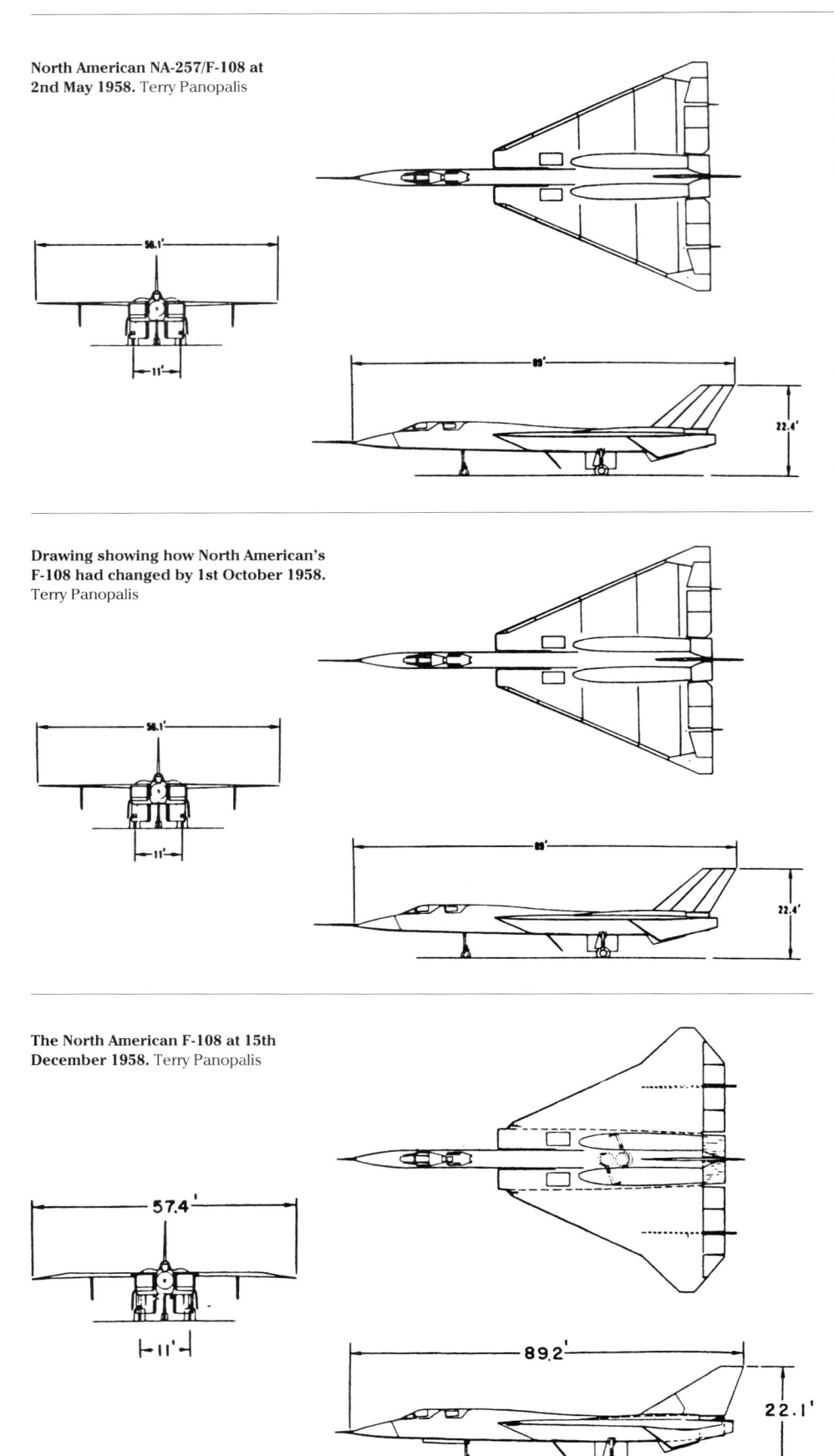

Drawing showing how North American's F-108 had changed by 1st October 1958. Terry Panopalis

The North American F-108 at 15th December 1958. Terry Panopalis

May 1958 the interceptor had a sweep angle on the wing leading edge of 53.5° while the canard span was 19ft 10in (6.04m). There was a large central fin, two smaller finlets above and below the wing trailing edge and ventral fins beneath the fuselage. The two tandem-seated crew each had their own escape capsule and 7,100gal (32,283lit) of fuel would be carried in seven tanks (five in the fuselage and two in the wing). One key feature was a mid-fuselage rotary launcher containing the three Hughes GAR-X missiles that fired through doors in the fuselage bottom; these weapons were now the only armament to be carried by the interceptor.

The estimated performance figures at this time indicated that, at the maximum take-off weight of 99,400 lb (45,088kg), the F-108 would have a sea level rate of climb of 24,100ft/min (7,346m/min), a service ceiling of 72,550ft (22,113m) and it was expected to take 6.2 minutes to get to 40,000ft (12,192m). However, to undertake the area or point interception roles the aircraft's combat weight would be lighter, 73,369 lb (33,280kg) and 81,765 lb (37,089kg) respectively, which gave even better performance figures. In the area role it would have a combat ceiling of 78,600ft (23,957m), a service ceiling of 78,850ft (24,033m) and a sea level rate of climb of 33,250ft/min (10,135m/min). For a point intercept these figures became 76,300ft (23,256m), 76,550ft (23,332m) and 29,700ft/min (9,053m/min) respectively. The maximum speed, which was an operational limit, was 1,982mph (3,189km/h) Mach 3.00 from 58,500ft (17,831m) right up to the aircraft's ceiling.

Following an official assessment completed in April 1958 the Hughes XY-1 fire control was officially designated AN/ASG-18 while the GAR-X missiles would now be known as the GAR-9. The missile was now estimated to have a range of 100nm (185km) and a top speed of Mach 6. F-108 was to be highly automated with the pilot only really having control during the take-off and landing, so naturally it was a very complex system that gobbled up development money at an alarming rate. It was not only the electronics that absorbed the finance, there was also ground-breaking research for example in the development and fabrication of new materials and alloys that would prove to be of benefit to the industry as a whole. Fuel was another area of progress and much of this knowledge would carry though into North American's XB-70 Valkyrie Mach 3 bomber, the development of which followed closely behind the F-108. It was estimated that the F-108's first flight would take place in March 1961.

Manufacturer's model of the F-108 in the form it was to be built. Allyson Vought

From September 1958 the interceptor underwent substantial external changes, with the removal of the canard and the vertical fins above the wing the most obvious. Taking the canard away brought several aerodynamic improvements including better low-speed stall characteristics and less trim drag, while the 'lost' fin area was recovered by fitting larger underwing stabilizers that improved handling and directional stability at low speeds and high angles of attack. Three months later the wing had been changed to a 'cranked arrow' shape, with substantial tip extensions offering improved stability at high lift conditions, while the central vertical fin was now all-moving apart from a small portion forward. Large folding ventral stabilizers were added to the corners of the lower fuselage to deal with ongoing concerns regarding directional stability and there were twin wheels on all three undercarriage legs. During the development process the power to be supplied by the J93s had regularly increased, although the estimated data presented was usually based on installed thrust values rather than guaranteed thrust. In December 1958 the guaranteed rating for the J93-GE-3R, the new choice for the powerplant, was actually 17,500lb (77.8kN) dry and 27,200lb (120.8kN) in afterburner.

The F-108 in this form carried 7,109gal (32,324lit) of fuel and at maximum weight the sea level rate of climb was 29,750ft/min (9,068m/min) and time to 40,000ft (12,192m) 5.1 minutes. Service ceiling was 74,000ft (22,555m) although the aircraft could go rather higher than this in a zoom climb. Estimated combat weights for the area and point interception missions were 75,719lb (34,346kg) and 85,237lb (38,664kg) respectively, combat ceiling 80,000ft (24,384m) and 77,600ft (23,652m), service ceiling 80,150ft (24,430m) and 77,800ft (23,713m), and sea level rates of climb 40,000ft/min (12,192m/min) and 35,500ft/min (10,820m/min). The Mach 3.00 top speed was still given as an operational limit, the airframe itself having the potential for slightly higher speeds. These figures show that the F-108 would have possessed a truly astonishing performance.

On 19th November 1958 the operational date of the F-108 was set at mid-1963 and the full-size mock-up Conference was held at North American's Los Angeles facility between 17th and 20th January 1959, which confirmed that few further changes were

The Quest for a Long-Range Interceptor

needed. On 15th May the F-108 was named Rapier in line with North American's recent policy for using the names of swords for its Air Force fighters. By now, however, there was a growing desire to reduce the complexity of this system to make it more reliable (indeed North American themselves favoured a less complex aircraft). In August 1958, not for the first time, a proposal had emerged to use Convair's B-58 nuclear bomber as a possible long-range interceptor, and then late in the year the Air Force's future budget calculations brought the possibility of reduced funding for the F-108. On 30th December the number of test aircraft on order was cut from thirty-one to twenty, the planned first flight was delayed from February to April 1961 and the operational date was pushed back to mid-1964. Throughout the program efforts were made to find alternative roles for the F-108, including its employment as a long-range escort fighter for the B-70.

At the beginning of 1959 the character of the F-108 was well set. It would use an ASG-18 fire control system, was armed with GAR-9 missiles and from an altitude of 70,000ft (21,336m) it would be able to launch these missiles 'without the need for precise interceptor pre-launch manoeuvres'. The objectives were 'any air-breathing target flying at altitudes from sea level to 100,000ft (30,480m)' and that up to three of these targets could be killed – a phenomenal capability for the late 1950s. At this point the F-108 was gaining support but the cost of developing it and putting it into service would eventually outweigh any advantages. On 21st August an order was given to place the program in a 'strictest austerity' category (which eliminated some of the components planned for the aircraft) and on 23rd September it was cancelled entirely, although work on the fire control and missiles was continued (the missile was later redesignated AIM-47).

The requirement for a Mach 3 interceptor was, however, not cancelled and North American continued to look at further F-108 developments; one of them featured leading edge root extensions. However, it was to be another manufacturer, Lockheed with its YF-12A, who would be the next to try to fulfil this need. More information on the F-108 Rapier is available in *Valkyrie: North American's Mach 3 Superbomber* by Dennis R Jenkins and Tony R Landis, published in 2004 by Specialty Press in America.

Lockheed YF-12A

During the late 1950s Lockheed began work on a special high-speed (Mach 3+), high-altitude (70,000ft [21,336m]+) photographic reconnaissance aircraft that came to fruition as the A-12 and was flown in late April 1962. It was to be one of the most astonishing programs ever undertaken, resulting in an aircraft with a performance unsurpassed for the next forty years. The cancellation of the F-108 left a vacuum that was eventually filled by the Improved Manned Interceptor (IMI) program established in 1960 as a replacement for the Century series types. In March 1960, under official requirements, Lockheed began work on an IMI A-12 derivative fitted with a Hughes radar and a fire control system that the company called the AF-12. After the 1962 renumbering of US military aircraft this new interceptor became the YF-12A.

As the largest and heaviest interceptor yet built, the first of three YF-12As made its maiden flight on 7th August 1963. The type was powered by two Pratt & Whitney J58 engines and armed with Hughes AIM-47 air-to-air missiles. YF-12A's existence was made known to the public on 30th September 1964 and, during trials, the type performed well. In May 1965 orders were prepared for two hundred examples of the F-12B production model, but the money for them was never released and the whole program was cancelled on 1st February 1968. However, a reconnaissance development called the SR-71 was flown in December 1964 and proved a great success in service.

Other Projects

Mention has been made of the idea suggested in 1956 for a medium-range interceptor or MRI. In fact several companies appear to have studied medium-range interceptors during the mid-1950s and material has been uncovered for a couple of them, together with further examples of Northrop's long-range interceptor research.

Convair F-106 Variant

A model has been found for an 'F-106 Interceptor' for the Air Force which may be a medium range proposal from the mid to late 1950s. The biggest changes to the standard F-106 Delta Dart are the introduction of a canard foreplane and larger box-shaped air intakes. This type of inlet came along after the F-106 and so puts the new design into a later time bracket than the original, which suggests that this project might have been proposed as a replacement or update. The nose and cockpit, fuselage, wing and fin look very similar to the standard F-106 but the larger jet pipe indicates a new engine. It could carry two Sparrow air-to-air missiles on a pylon fixed underneath the centre fuselage.

View showing the third Lockheed YF-12A delta wing interceptor during a test flight.
Mike Stroud

Northrop Medium Range Interceptor

Work on a Northrop MRI was undertaken as a company sponsored design study from January through April 1955 for a Mach 2.5 replacement for the Convair F-102. Two final configurations evolved; the one shown in the accompanying drawing plus another that was very similar but incorporated a low horizontal tail. This single-seat type was to be powered by a General Electric X84 engine served by side intakes and would carry 1,516gal (6,893lit) or 9,865 lb (4,475kg) of fuel. It had a top speed of Mach 2.5 at 35,000ft (10,668m) and above (which was an engine temperature limit) and was equipped with a downward ejection capsule cockpit, which also included television presentation to the pilot.

Wing sweep at quarter chord was 33.25°, the wing's thickness/chord ratio was 3.75% and the aircraft had a tricycle undercarriage with twin wheels on the main gears. Its combat speed would be Mach 2.2 at 50,000ft (15,240m), combat ceiling 61,700ft (18,806m) and combat radius 300nm (556km). Rate of climb at sea level was 71,000ft/min (21,641m/min) and the aircraft was expected to take 2.7 minutes to reach 50,000ft (15,240m). A 16ft by 4ft by 2ft 6in (4.88m by 1.22m by 0.76m)

Top: **Model of Convair's canard 'F-106 Interceptor' proposal. This has a span of 6.15in (15.6cm) and a length with the pitot of 11.0in (28.0cm).** Jonathan Rigutto / photo © 2005 Chad Slattery

Right: **Rough sketch of Northrop's MRI.** Gerald Balzer

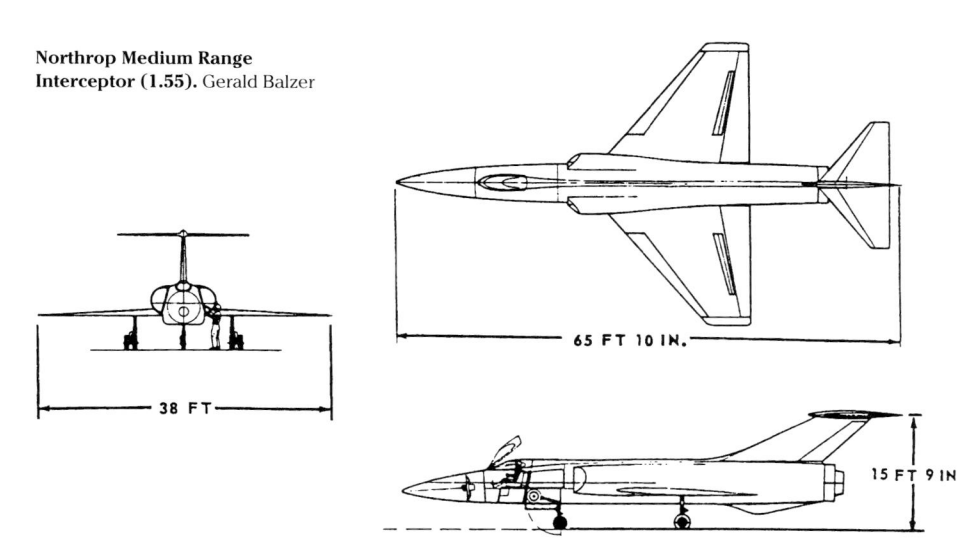

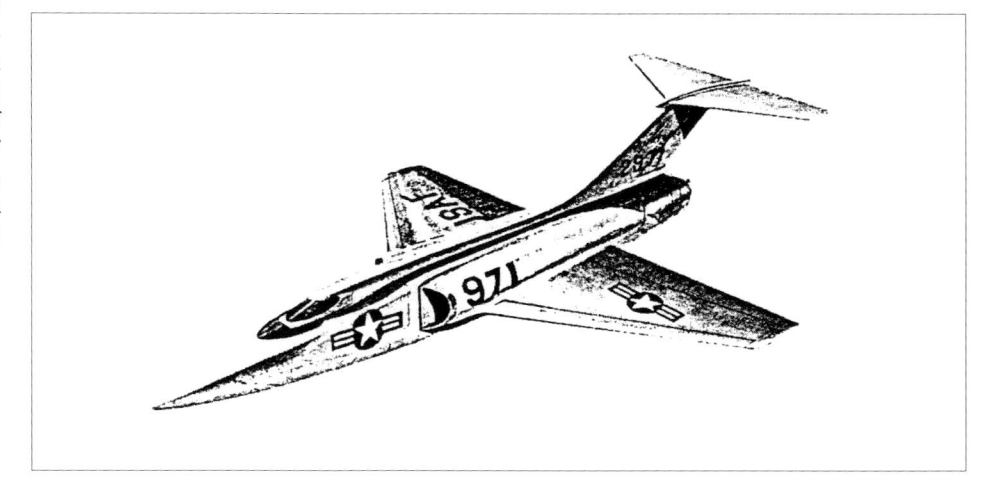

Northrop Medium Range Interceptor (1.55). Gerald Balzer

The Quest for a Long-Range Interceptor

weapon bay would house a basic armament of six GAR-1A Falcon air-to-air missiles, but alternative loads were three Ding Dong air-to-air rockets or one 'Special' nuclear store, or various other combinations of weaponry. Underwing pylons provided mountings for external fuel tanks, special stores, rockets, missiles or napalm tanks, and the like, and wingtip armament pods could also be provided. An MX1179 fire control system was installed with a 40in (102cm)-diameter radar antenna.

Northrop N-176

One final study in this sequence of projects was the N-176 supersonic interceptor, the drawing for which is dated 10th December 1956. It was to be powered by eight 4,000lb (17.8kN) thrust General Electric J85 units arranged in two clusters and fed by a large chin intake. The thin low aspect ratio wing was heavily tapered, there was a low position all-moving horizontal tailplane, foldaway lower vertical fins, a tricycle undercarriage and an internal weapon bay. Few details are available, and none at all regarding weapons. Like all of Northrop's heavy interceptors, the N-176 stayed on the drawing board.

A Requirement Never Fulfilled

The 1950s quest for a long-range interceptor was one of the most challenging episodes in the history of American fighter design. It never produced an outcome. Pitched just too far beyond the capabilities of the time, the final product was too late, too heavy and too expensive. Nonetheless, the competition produced some truly impressive and highly imaginative designs and, had the requirement been sustained and the money not run out, the F-108 would have been a highly formidable weapons system. Meanwhile many Canadians might argue that one answer was already sitting on the runway in Ontario – the Avro CF-105 Arrow – but that is another story.

It is understood that the aircraft illustrated here in model form is most probably the final design in Northrop's early series of N-126 projects drawn in 1953. It was apparently powered by two Wright YJ67 engines housed in the underwing pods, the estimated take-off weight was 66,000lb (29,938kg) and maximum combat speed around Mach 1.8 at 60,000ft (18,288m). Span is 10.8in (27.5cm) and length 17.7in (45.0cm), which at 1/40th scale gives a true span of 36ft 1in (11.0m) and length 59ft 1in (18.0m). However, when photographed this particular model was fixed to a stand labelled 'Northrop N-167 Extended Range Interceptor', and at the time of writing no further details confirming its complete identity had been found. George Cox

Right: **Northrop N-176 supersonic interceptor (10.12.56).** Gerald Balzer

Below and top right: **Model of the Northrop N-176.** Northrop Grumman Corp, photograph by Tony Chong

Bottom right: **Northrop N-176 artwork.** Terry Panopalis

The Quest for a Long-Range Interceptor

Long-Range Interceptor Studies – Estimated Data

Project	Span ft in (m)	Length ft in (m)	Gross Wing Area ft² (m²)	Gross Weight lb (kg)	Engine lb (kN)	Max Speed / Height mph (km/h) / ft (m)	Armament
Competition to WS-202A							
Boeing Model 712	55 4 (16.9)	101 8 (31.0)	875 (81.4)	69,000 (31,298)	2 x Wright J67-W-1 13,200 (58.7), 21,500 (95.6) ab	Not given but highly supersonic	8 x GAR-1 Falcon AAM, 48 x 2.75in (7.0) FFAR
Douglas Model 1355	48 1 (14.7)	87 3.5 (26.6)	700 (65.1)	69,786 (31,655)	2 x Wright J67-W-1 13,200 (58.7), 21,500 (95.6) ab	Supersonic	8 x GAR-1 Falcon AAM, 48 x 2.75in (7.0) FFAR
Lockheed CL-288-1	49 9 (15.2)	96 2 (29.3)	?	78,848 (35,765)	Probably 2 x Wright J67-W-1, 13,200 (58.7), 21,500 (95.6) ab	Mach 2.09 at height	8 x GAR-1 Falcon AAM, Probably 48 x 2.75in (7.0) FFAR
McDonnell Model 110A	74 0 (22.6)	87 0 (26.5)	1,000 (93.0)	69,954 (31,731)	3 x Wright J67-W-1 13,200 (58.7), 21,500 (95.6) ab	856 (1,377) at S/L, 1,331 (2,142) at 35,000 (10,668)	8 x GAR-1 Falcon AAM or 3 UAW rockets, 48 x 2.75in (7.0) FFAR
McDonnell Model 111A	69 4 (21.1)	80 8.5 (24.6)	800 (74.4)	63,191 (28,663)	2 x Wright J67-W-1 13,200 (58.7), 21,500 (95.6) ab	846 (1,361) at S/L, 1,295 (2,084) at 36,500 (11,125)	8 x GAR-1 Falcon AAM or 3 UAW rockets, 48 x 2.75in (7.0) FFAR
Northrop N-126 (at 6.7.54)	62 3 (19.0)	85 0 (25.9)	1,050 (97.7)	75,830 (34,396)	2 x Wright J67-W-1 13,200 (58.7), 21,500 (95.6) ab	793 (1,276) at S/L, 1,183 (1,903) at 35,000 (10,668)	8 x GAR-1 Falcon AAM, 48 x 2.75in (7.0) FFAR
Northrop N-144	78 10 (24.0)	103 6 (31.5)	1,700 (158.1)	113,700 (51,574)	4 x Wright J67-W-1 13,200 (58.7), 21,500 (95.6) ab	Mach 1.06 at S/L, Mach 2.04 at 34,000 (10,363)	8 x GAR-1 Falcon AAM, 48 x 2.75in (7.0) FFAR
Northrop N-149	50 10 (15.5)	70 6 (21.5)	700 (65.1)	55,800 (25,311) (with two external tanks)	2 x Gen Elec XJ79-GE-1 9,300 (41.3), 14,350 (63.8) ab	Mach 1.00 at S/L, Mach 1.51 at 35,000 (10,668)	8 x GAR-1 Falcon AAM, 48 x 2.75in (7.0) FFAR
Grumman G-107-2	55 9 (17.0)	67 4 (20.5)	1,000 (93.0)	59,500 (26,989)	2 x Wright J67 with ab	Mach 1.07 at S/L, Mach 2.14 at 40,000 (12,192) at 50,000 lb (22,680) weight	Unknown but probably similar to above
Phase 1 Study Programme + Stages in F-108 Development							
Lockheed CL-320-36	62 6 (19.1)	114 0 (34.7)	1,300 (120.9)	123,000 (55,793)	4 x Gen Elec J79-X207 10,300 (45.8), 15,450 (68.7) ab	Combat speed 1,451 (2,334)	GAR-1 AAM
Northrop N-167	55 3 (16.8)	90 6 (27.6)	1,050 (97.7)	96,000 (43,546)	4 x Gen Elec J79-X207 10,300 (45.8), 15,450 (68.7) ab	Mach 1.16 at S/L, Mach 2.0 above 35,000 (10,668)	8 x GAR-1 AAM or alternative loads
North American NA-257/F-108 (at 5.58)	52 11 (16.1)	84 11 (25.9)	1,400 (130.2)	99,400 (45,088)	2 x Gen Elec J93-GE-1 14,100 (62.7), 22,150 (98.4) ab	720 (1,158) at S/L, 1,982 (3,189) above 58,500 (17,831)	3 x GAR-9 AAM
North American NA-257/F-108 (at 10.58)	56 1 (17.1)	89 0 (27.1) (w/o pitot)	1,865 (173.4)	101,800 (46,176)	2 x Gen Elec J93-GE-1	Mach 3 at height	3 x GAR-9 AAM
North American NA-257/F-108 (at 12.58)	57 5 (17.5)	89 2.5 (27.2) (w/o pitot)	1,865 (173.4)	102,234 (46,373)	2 x Gen Elec J93-GE-3R 15,150 (67.3), 23,680 (105.2) ab	715 (1,150) at S/L, 1,982 (3,187) at 81,800 (24,933)	3 x GAR-9 AAM
Other Projects							
Lockheed YF-12A (flown)	55 7 (16.9)	101 8 (31.0)	1,795 (166.9)	124,000 (56,246)	2 x P&W J58 20,500 (91.1), 31,500 (140.0) ab	Mach 3.2 at 75,000 (22,860)	3 x AIM-47 (GAR-9) AAM
Northrop MRI	38 0 (11.6)	65 10 (20.1)	525 (48.8)	31,762 (14,407)	1 x General Electric X84 16,900 (75.1), 32,900 (146.2) ab	Mach 1.06 at S/L, Mach 2.5 at 35,000 (10,668)	3 x GAR-1A Falcon AAM
Northrop N-176	42 6 (13.0)	84 4 (25.7) (w/o pitot)	600 (55.8)	51,700 (23,451)	8 x General Electric J85 4,000 (17.8)	Supersonic	Unknown

Chapter Six

Naval Progress

Manufacturer's display model of the Grumman Model 97. Grumman Corp / Grumman History Centre

Having looked at the substantial advances made in USAF fighter design through the 1950s, it is time to return to the naval scene. Chapter Two dealt with the foundations of the jet age for the US Navy, with its cautious start followed by a multitude of different designs: some successful, others less so. As the 1950s progressed the Navy really got its act together, resulting in some outstanding carrier-borne aircraft. This period saw two major competitions, each embodying demanding new requirements, it also saw numerous unsolicited proposals from the leading aircraft manufacturers. Together these led to a series of prototypes and production programs including one of the most successful in jet fighter history, the McDonnell F-4 Phantom. And, of course, behind these aircraft that actually reached flight status were many projects and intermediate designs that never saw the light of day.

Grumman F11F Tiger

This period – which one might call the supersonic era – started with an excellent design from Grumman. The cancellation of Grumman's swing-wing F10F Jaguar fighter meant that some additional funds were available for the development of new aircraft. In December 1952 Grumman offered a brand new supersonic single-seat design called the G-98. At first the Navy was somewhat cool, considering it to be a little too early to contemplate a new fighter using the next generation of engines, the Pratt & Whitney J-57 and General Electric J-79. However Grumman pushed its project strongly and in April 1953 was rewarded with a contract for three prototypes that were eventually designated YF9F-9. There was no competition, the Navy's Bureau of Aeronautics or BuAer taking the design under a 'negotiated procurement'. This term covered the process whereby a contractor might offer an unsolicited proposal that the Bureau rated very highly and, as a consequence, authorised its go-ahead. The Bureau would then of course have to justify its decision.

American Secret Projects: Fighters & Interceptors

Manufacturer's model showing the Grumman G-98 as first proposed in December 1952.

The third Grumman Tiger 138606 which, when the photograph was taken, had already been designated F11F-1. This fact is confirmed by very small lettering just above the serial on the side of the lower rear fuselage.

Picture showing the second F11F-1F Super Tiger, 138647, re-engined with a General Electric YJ79-GE-3A engine. Grumman Corporation / Grumman History Centre

The first machine made its maiden flight on 30th July 1954 and in April 1955 the G-98 was given the new designation F11F-1 to reflect the fact that this was a completely new type and not a further development of the Panther/Cougar series; it was also given the name Tiger. It proved to be an excellent design in aerodynamic terms, but the Wright J65 (Sapphire) engine simply did not supply enough power to give the level of performance that either the airframe could achieve or that was really desired. Indeed it was barely supersonic, and then only at height. In fact Grumman was unfortunate because the initial J65-W-18 gave 11,500 lb (51.1kN) of combat thrust, which would have given a maximum speed of Mach 1.3 at 35,000ft (10,668m), but by October 1958 this engine had been derated, twice, to a maximum of 10,500 lb (46.7kN), which cut the speed back to Mach 1.15. Consequently the Navy regarded the Tiger as something of an interim step before moving on to a truly supersonic fighter and the F11F's production run stretched to just 199 aircraft. The first forty-two machines were known as the 'Short Nose' version with the remaining aircraft called 'Long Nose' variants. Primarily the Tiger was operated as a gun fighter but it did have a missile capability, with the facility to carry four Sidewinders.

Grumman G-98 Developments
Plenty of proposed developments of the original G-98 with different engines and weapons were suggested to improve the performance and capability of the basic aircraft. In January 1955, well into the program, Grumman suggested putting J79s into two airframes, the extra thrust offering a very much higher performance, and these were completed as an experiment. The only other difference was a longer and larger nose to house a Westinghouse APQ-50 search radar In this form the first machine flew on 25th May 1956. Grumman called the type the G-98J, though officially it became known as the F11F-1F Super Tiger, and it proved to be much faster than the original. The estimated top speed had been Mach 1.4 but in fact the Super Tiger reached

American Secret Projects: Fighters & Interceptors

This model is a G-98J-7 Super Tiger proposal with two seats and larger Sparrow air-to-air missiles carried under the outer wings. It would have had a radar intercept officer in the back seat and Sidewinders on top of and beneath the fuselage. Powered by a 15,000 lb (66.7kN) thrust J79-GE-3, the aircraft would have had a gross weight of 23,346 lb (10,590kg), its span was approximately 31ft 7in (9.6m), length 48ft 9in (14.9m) and wing area 250ft^2 (23.25m^2). Larry McLaughlin

Mach 2, which was a surprise to Grumman as much as anyone else. Indeed, compared to the difficulties in going from Mach 0.9 to Mach 1, the ease of going from Mach 1 to much higher speeds was surprising everyone involved in aircraft design. However, despite this huge leap in the Tiger's performance, no production machines were ordered.

In January 1955 Grumman also proposed the G-98L with a J65-W-12 engine, an all-weather radar and a new wing, though by the middle of the year the engine had been replaced by a J79. Various 35° sweep wings were tried up to a maximum area of 350ft^2 (32.6m^2), one objective being to get the aircraft to 60,000ft (18,288m). However, to quote a Grumman document, it 'couldn't quite make it' and in fact the estimated ceiling was around 55,000ft (16,764m). Earlier, in January 1954, the J79 had been first proposed inside the G-98D, which also had a larger 45° sweep

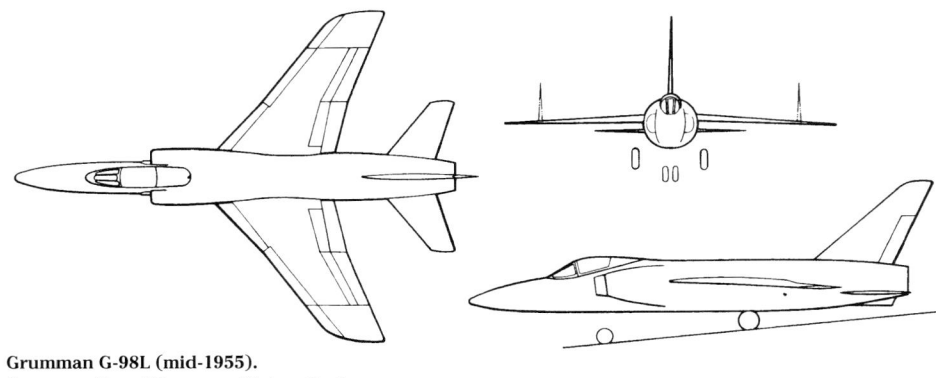

Grumman G-98L (mid-1955).
Grumman Corp / Grumman History Centre

Naval Progress

wing. The Tiger was a handsome aircraft and the G-98D with its large wing and greater sweep was perhaps the most attractive of all the developments but, apart from the two Super Tiger prototypes, none of these advanced proposals ever came to anything. However, Grumman wasn't the only company to fail to secure orders for a highly promising design.

Douglas F5D-1 Skylancer

In the meantime Douglas had suggested a variant of its F4D Skyray as an all-weather supersonic fighter for carrier operations. It was called the F4D-2N and the proposal was made shortly after the F4D Skyray had been ordered into production in March 1953. In October the Navy authorised the development of this new design as a back-up to the Grumman Tiger program. F4D-2N had the production F4D-1's Pratt & Whitney J57 engine and a more substantial set of electronics, while a thinner wing and other improved aerodynamics indicated a substantially higher speed. However, as the development program evolved, so many design changes were introduced that the type eventually became an all-new aircraft, a fact that was reflected by the allocation of a new designation and name, the F5D-1 Skylancer. Many of the weaknesses of the Skyray were eliminated in the F5D-1 and the first of two prototypes made its maiden flight on 21st April 1956. However, on 1st March 1957 the Navy cancelled further work, having earlier decided that there would be no fleet requirement for the F5D-1, in part because an alter-

Three views of a model of the Grumman G-98D (1.54). The G-98D had an approximate span of 32ft 10in (10.0m) and length 48ft 3in (14.7m).
Larry McLaughlin

The Douglas F5D-1 Skylancer, an outgrowth of the F4D Skyray, did not enter production. 139208 was the first prototype. John Aldaz

116 American Secret Projects: Fighters & Interceptors

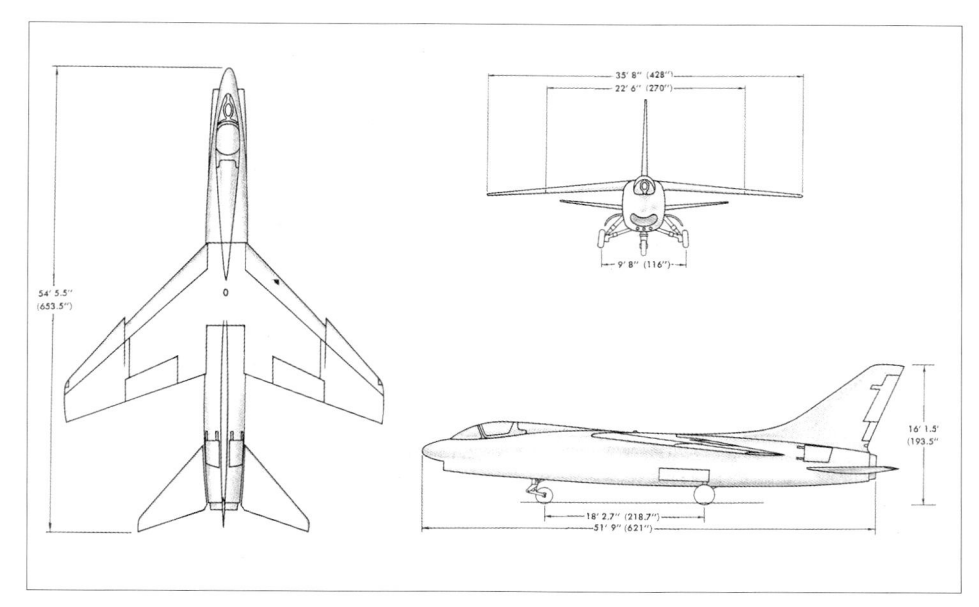

Chance Vought V-383 (6.1.53). Dick Atkins, Vought Archive

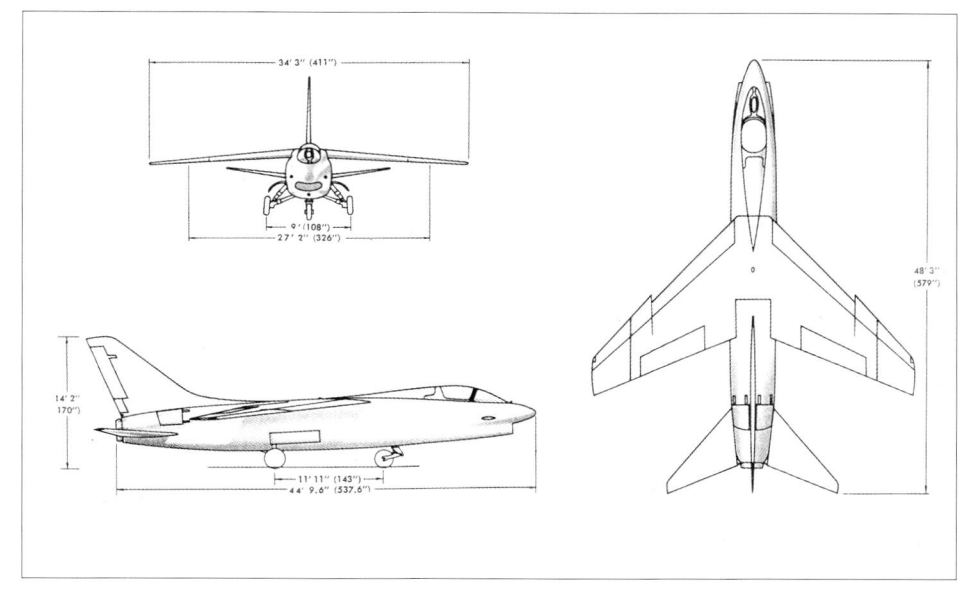

Chance Vought V-384 (6.1.53). Although very similar to the V-383 this design, with its J65 engine, was smaller. Dick Atkins, Vought Archive

native type was now going to be available (the Vought F8U which is discussed below). Despite orders being placed for nineteen aircraft only four Skylancers were actually completed, although two of them were flown by NASA for research purposes throughout the 1960s. It was a huge step up on its predecessor and by all accounts an excellent aircraft.

A New Carrier-Based Day Fighter

For some time during the 1950s the US Navy continued to trail behind the Air Force in the development of new fighters, in part because the Navy had fewer ongoing research and development programs in the field. There was also the ever-present problem of trying to produce new high-performance types that could be launched and recovered from a carrier. Moreover, the Navy had diverted some of its limited research and development funding to types like the Convair XF2Y Sea Dart seaplane fighter (Chapter Eight) that proved to be a dead end.

However, the next major competition would go a long way to making up some of the lost ground. It covered a supersonic single-seat carrier-based fighter to undertake point and area fleet defence for the Navy under Specification OS-130, and the Bureau of Aeronautics issued a Request for Proposals on 19th August 1952. The new type's top speed had to be at least Mach 1.2 at 30,000ft (9,144m) and Mach 0.9 at sea level, it had to be very manoeuvrable and to be able to carry both cannon and/or collision-course rockets. Operational radius on overload fuel had to be 400nm (741km) and rate of climb 25,000ft/min (7,620m/min). Some published sources have stated that as many as twenty-one designs were proposed to OS-130, but the RAND study by Lorell and Levaux (*The Cutting Edge*) states that the winner was 'in competition with seven other design proposals'. It is known that the following were submitted, the line-up including variants of the same design fitted with different powerplants.

Chance Vought Model V-383 and V-384

Chance Vought's philosophy behind its OS-130 proposals covered two fundamental approaches: the smallest possible aircraft to meet the basic specification requirements or the smallest possible aircraft around the most powerful engine available. The resulting design brochure gave equal emphasis to both in the form of two separate and distinct projects called the V-383 and V-384. Vought's initial studies into a carrier-based day fighter had begun in August 1952 under the V-380 model number, prior to the release of OS-130. The earliest investigations had in fact included derivatives of the F7U Cutlass but these were rejected when the disadvantages of tailless aircraft were confirmed. In due course the work was split into the two projects that were intended either to equal or exceed the requirements.

The key feature of both designs was a simple high-mounted two-position variable incidence wing, swept 42° at ¼ chord, which could be raised 7° above the horizontal for take-off and landing. The latter, an ingenious device, would increase the incidence of the wing without requiring a corresponding change in the aircraft's attitude, thereby greatly improving the pilot's view during take-offs and approaches. For all other flight conditions the wing would be set at -1°. The variable incidence wing, which had a thickness/chord ratio of 6% at the root and 5% at the tip, also permitted a very short landing gear: less rotation of the fuselage meant easier tail clearance and also eliminated the long front wheel leg (characteristic of many carrierborne aircraft) needed to keep the nose up during takeoff and landing. A low horizontal tailplane was employed and all of the fuel was housed internally which, even for the overload radius of action of 400nm (741km), allowed carriage of both guns and rockets.

Naval Progress

Artist's impression of the Vought V-383. Note the three cannon mounted in the lip of the intake.
Dick Atkins, Vought Archive

Model of the Chance Vought V-383.

Electric XJ79-GE-(X24A) unit into the V-384 which gave a potential combat speed of Mach 2.0. With the standard J57 and J65, the two designs had a respective time to 35,000ft (10,668m) of 1.7 and 2.1 minutes, a maximum rate of climb of 31,000ft/min (9,449m/min) and 27,700ft/min (8,443m/min), and a combat ceiling of 56,800ft (17,313m) and 56,600ft (17,252m). The brochure reported that an 800-hour wind tunnel program had been conducted on the V-383/V-384 layout.

Douglas OS-130 Submission

In researching this book no confirmation could be found for the proposals made by Douglas in response to OS-130. However, an examination of the company's project list shows that Models D-652 and D-653 were both day fighter designs and both were dated 2nd December 1952, which fits the timescale exactly. The latter was based on Douglas's A4D Skyhawk light attack aircraft, prototypes of which were ordered in June 1952. This was powered by a single Wright J65 and the first example flew on 22nd June 1954, to be followed by many production aeroplanes. The Skyhawk was a subsonic aircraft and so some changes would certainly have been needed to achieve the supersonic requirement. The D-652 day fighter was described as an F4D Skyray-type design. The Skyray was already flying by then, but in 1954 it would be fitted with a J57 engine that just about made it supersonic. However, as discussed earlier, the Skylancer's longer fuselage coupled with the same engine gave a substantially higher top speed. It seems likely that at least one Douglas proposal to OS-130 would have been based on the Skyray formula, and in fact the design that became the Skylancer was first proposed during the period covered by this design competition.

Grumman Model 97

The brochure for Grumman's Model 97 described an aircraft whose top speed at 35,000ft (10,668m) of 912mph/1,467km/h Mach 1.38 exceeded the OS-130 requirement by about 117mph (189km/h). Design 97 also had sufficient excess power to maintain a steady turn load factor of 1.75g in level flight at 35,000ft while a combination of low drag and high power provided what Grumman described as an outstanding rate of climb. The

On the V-383 three T-160 20mm cannon were housed in the lower lip of the chin intake and the fighter carried 7,075lb (3,209kg) of internal fuel that, at a gross weight of 22,600lb (10,251kg), was estimated to give a radius of 300nm (556km). V-383's folded span was 22ft 6in (6.9m). Overall the V-384 was smaller, the gross weight for the 300nm target coming out at 17,950lb (8,142kg), of which 5,600lb (2,540kg) was fuel. This second design carried one gun in the lower lip position and another on each side of the nose but, although smaller, the wing was otherwise identical to the first layout. The rocket installation consisted of an internal-tandem two-row package carrying sixty 2.0in (5.1cm) folding fin air-to-air rockets, the assembly being located in the bottom of the fuselage aft of the nose gear. When the firing circuit was energized, the rocket package would be lowered at the forward end and fired in one continuous sequence. A full salvo would be released in under 1.5 seconds and tests showed that this operation imposed no significant changes on the fighter's trim. Provision was also made to carry two Sparrow air-to-air missiles on pylons under each inner wing.

With a J57-P-(JT3N) engine the V-383 had an estimated combat speed of Mach 1.5 at 35,000ft (10,668m), but with a more advanced J57 combat rating this was expected to increase to Mach 1.7. Alternative installations were an Allison J71-A-7 or a General Electric J73-GE-5 but these offered a lower performance while the V-384 with its Wright J65-W-(TJ31B3) gave Mach 1.25. There was a possibility of fitting a General

American Secret Projects: Fighters & Interceptors

figures given were 31,200ft/min (9,510m/min) at sea level and 14,000ft/min (4,267m/min) at 35,000ft, the aircraft taking 1.62 minutes to reach that altitude. The fighter had an estimated combat weight of 18,796lb (8,526kg), combat ceiling at 500ft/min (152m/min) rate of climb of 56,700ft (17,282m), and combat radius with normal fuel of 306nm (567km); the required 400nm (741km) limit was achieved with overload fuel.

A single J57 was selected to power the aircraft, a twin-engine arrangement having been rejected because of a lack of alternative engines in the size class required, and a low all-moving tailplane was fitted. Testing had shown that the latter held several advantages over a tailless arrangement, including the following:

1. For equivalent high-speed drag, the aircraft having the horizontal tail was superior in altitude manoeuvring capability.
2. For equal stalling speeds, the aircraft having the horizontal tail was faster in high level speed flight.
3. The presence of the horizontal tail also permitted the use of landing flaps that had a pronounced effect in reducing the attitude of the machine in the approach and catapulting conditions.
4. An investigation into the problems of longitudinal trim and control at speeds greater than Mach 1.0 indicated a definite advantage for the aircraft with the horizontal tail. This was most easily appreciated in manoeuvring flight where the gross load factor was the sum of the load factor selected by the pilot plus the necessary balancing increment required to hold the aircraft in the manoeuvre.

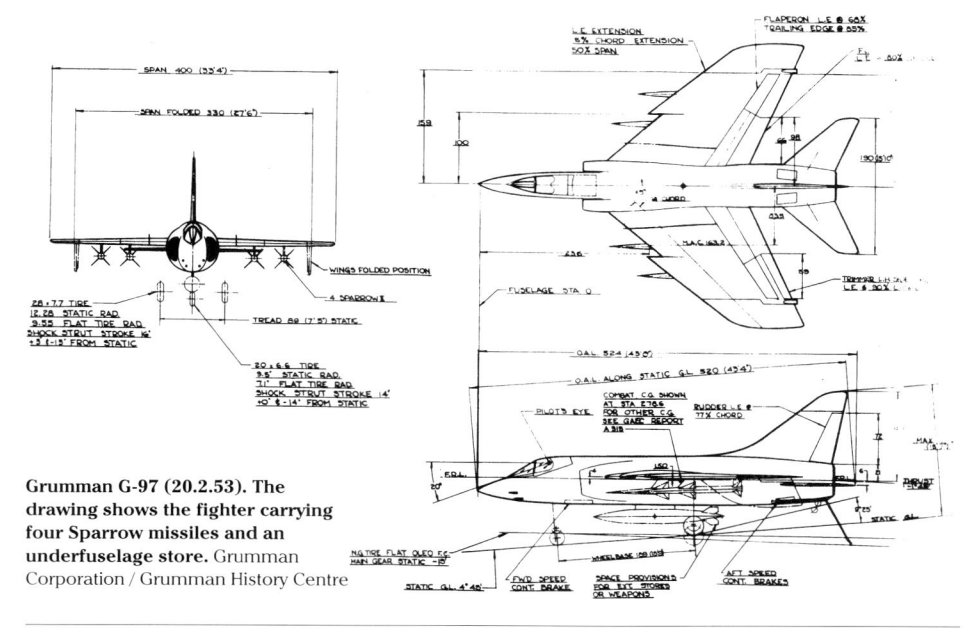

Grumman G-97 (20.2.53). The drawing shows the fighter carrying four Sparrow missiles and an underfuselage store. Grumman Corporation / Grumman History Centre

Prior to the completion of the G-97 design Grumman's wind tunnels had examined a series of planforms including delta and swept wings of differing taper and aspect ratios.

A mid-wing position was eventually chosen for low drag and better directional stability. The wing itself was swept 45° at ¼ chord and had a thickness/chord ratio of 5%, its landing flaps extended for 50% of the span and lateral control was provided by vented flaperons. Folded span was 27ft 6in (8.4m). The inboard wing's structure used multi-beam construction fabricated in such a manner that integral fuel tanks were incorporated with practically no weight increase and the carry-through in the fuselage was accomplished by four major frames. For stowage the wingtips folded downwards and there was a tricycle undercarriage, all of the wheels folding forwards into the fuselage. G-97's wing loading and wing planform, coupled with its high lift devices, was expected to give nose-high attitudes during take-off and approach slightly less than those of the F9F-5 Panther and F9F-6 Cougar.

The aircraft's high thrust/weight ratio offered considerable versatility and space was still available to carry a store on the fuse-

This view shows a manufacturer's display model of the Grumman Model 97. Grumman Corporation / Grumman History Centre

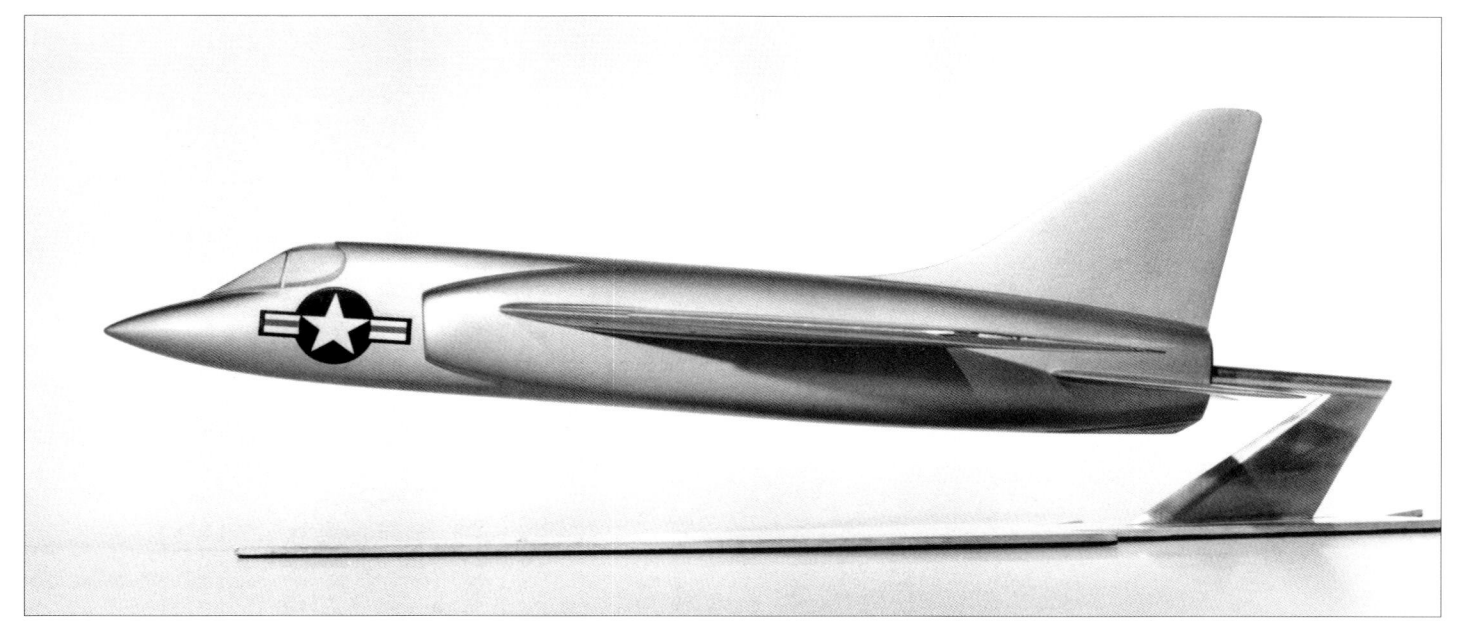

Naval Progress

Lockheed L-242-1 (c2.53).
Peter Clukey

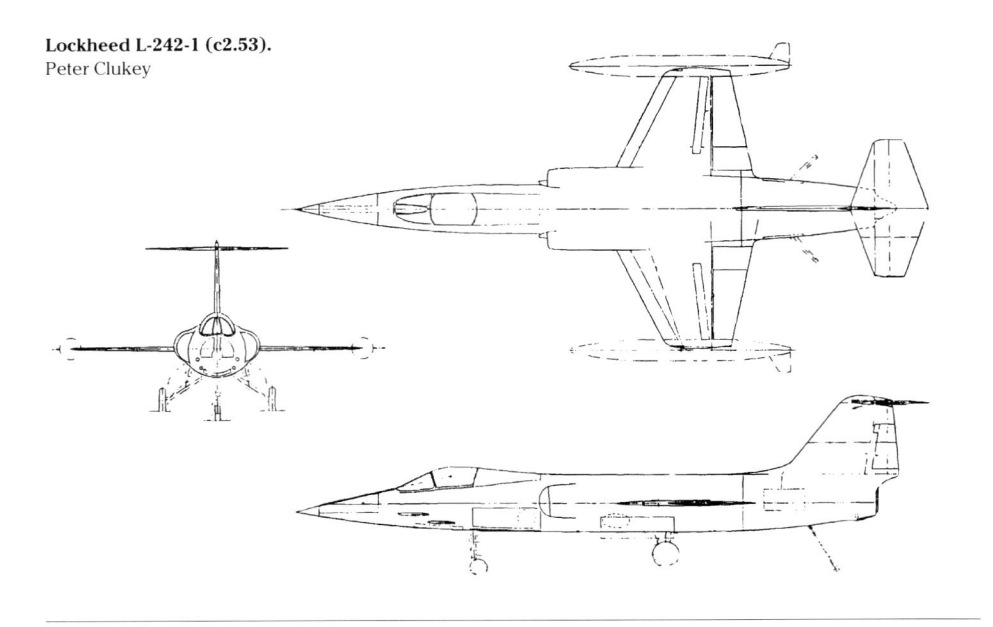

lage centreline up to 3,300 lb (1,497kg) in weight. Eight Falcon air-to-air missiles, or four Meteor, two Terrier or two Nike air-to-ground missiles, could go under the wings, although no actual hardware provision for these had been made in the proposal. Four Sparrow II AAMs were required, which would be employed instead of the rockets. The fuel-carrying capacity was not sacrificed when the four wing stations were in use because all of the overload fuel was carried internally, which meant that rockets and guns could be carried simultaneously. Normal fuel load was 6,650 lb (3,016kg) and overload 7,450 lb (3,379kg), housed both in fuselage and wing tanks. The 2in (5.1cm) rockets were mounted internally and would take between two and three seconds to be fired, and pairs of 20mm cannon were placed on each side of the lower nose. Grumman had also investigated a Search-ARO radar installation to ensure that the machine would be capable of accommodating such equipment in the future.

Lockheed L-242

Dated November 1952, Lockheed's L-242-1 proposal was completed after the L-246 described in Chapter Four; in effect this project was an L-246 modified for carrier use. The four guns were placed around the lower nose underneath the cockpit and external tanks could be carried on the wingtips. The wing had spoilers and leading edge flaps while the inner flap on the trailing edge also served as a roll trimmer. It was predicted that the design would exceed all of its requirements except for combat ceiling, the estimated figure of 44,800ft (13,655m) falling short of the 48,000ft (14,630m) limit. Sea level rate of climb was 11,700ft/min (3,566m/min) and combat radius 495nm (917km). A two-seat trainer version was also proposed.

McDonnell Models 90, 91 and 93

Douglas' Model 90 was a simple, straight wing design with a fuselage very similar to McDonnell's Demon (Chapter Two) but using a chin intake rather than side inlets. Its tapered straight wing had a trailing edge split flap that served as a high-lift device and the folded span was 25ft 1in (7.6m). There was a tricycle undercarriage and the J57 used an exhaust pipe placed beneath the rear fuselage. Model 90 carried 6,734 lb (3,055kg) of fuel at a normal gross weight of 21,790 lb (9,884kg), and for the overload condition 7,904 lb (3,585kg) giving a gross weight of 23,034 lb (10,448kg); the 'normal' fuel gave a radius of action of 300nm (557km) while the overload pushed this up to 471nm (872km). At its normal gross weight the Model 90 was estimated to take 4.3 minutes to reach 35,000ft (10,668m), while at its combat weight of 19,099 lb (8,663kg) the fighter's top speed at that height was 1,033mph (1,662km/h), sea level rate of climb was 35,000ft/min (10,668m/min) and combat ceiling 58,700ft (17,892m).

In its brochure McDonnell stressed that the Model 90 offered twice the performance of the company's earlier F2H-3 Banshee within roughly the same size and weight. It claimed a number of advantages for the type's straight wing, including:

1. It gave a lower angle of attack (8.2°) on the carrier approach than a swept wing (17.2°) or a delta (17.7°).
2. The 4.5% thick wing was simpler and lighter, and offered much less drag during cruise and high-altitude combat, than an alternative 7% thick wing swept at 45°
3. At low speeds there was less drag rise and no loss in aileron effectiveness.

McDonnell based these statements on low-speed, transonic and supersonic tunnel tests, rocket model tests and flight tests with both aircraft and missiles.

The smaller Model 91's configuration and structure was similar to the 90. Like Vought's proposals it served essentially as a minimal version of the 90 to meet the basic specification. It had a shorter fuselage and used a smaller J65-W-(TJ31B3) engine rather than the J57. Wing area was reduced to 268ft² (24.9m²) and the 91's combat weight was given as 15,770 lb (7,153kg). Take-off gross weight was 17,915 lb (8,126kg) of which 5,363 lb (2,433kg) was fuel, top speed was 839mph (1,351km/h) at about 37,000ft (11,278m) and sea level rate

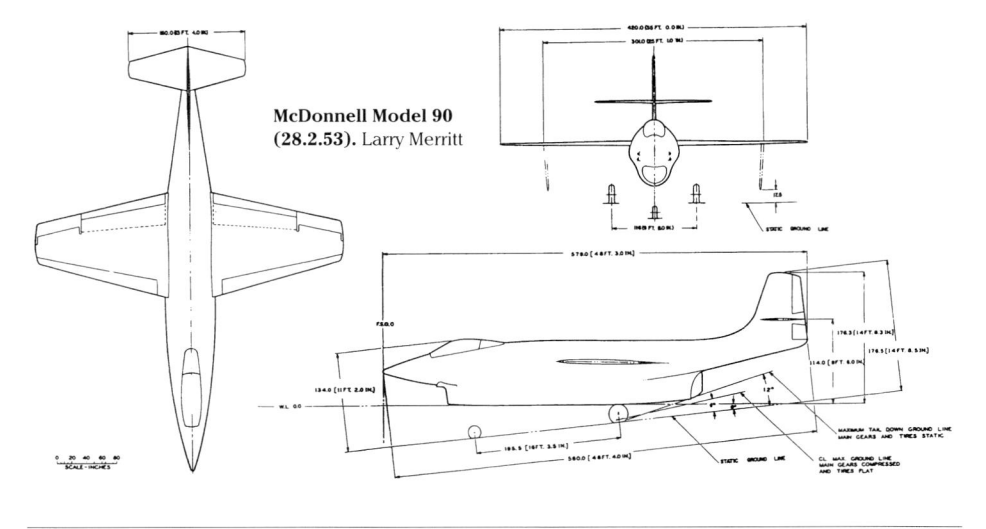

McDonnell Model 90 (28.2.53). Larry Merritt

of climb about 29,500ft/min (8,992m/min). A third design called the Model 93 and powered by a J57 engine was also produced to OS-130 but no details are available.

Tests showed that in the high-speed, high-altitude environment (which McDonnell declared was the area where air supremacy would be decided) the higher-power Model 90 could turn with a smaller radius in less time without losing speed. The 90 also took less time to reach a speed margin sufficient to gain control in combat, its combat ceiling was higher than the Model 91's c.57,000ft (17,374m) and it had a higher Mach number at its ceiling (Mach 0.91 against 0.86). Finally the Model 90 could close on a pursuit attack from a larger angle off the enemy aircraft's tail, at any range, than could the 91. McDonnell concluded that, overall, the shorter attack time and higher probability of surprise from using the Model 90 emphasised the value in producing an aircraft that was superior to the basic specification.

North American OS-130

The submission from North American was another Super Sabre development, the brochure calling the project "OS-130 Day Fighter (J57)". It is known that this proposal included, like Vought's, a variable incidence wing and its gross weight approached the 30,000 lb (13,608kg) mark. The artist's impression shows a very sleek design with a sharply pointed nose, side intakes just behind the pilot's seat, a highly swept high position wing and a low tail. Notable in the original image (but removed here) was the designation 'F2J-1' which gave an indication of the artist's hopes, and presumably North American's as well.

It is understood that the company offered some alternative designs within a common configuration and one may have been the project also shown here in model form. In contrast to the above, this has a low wing and a low tail, there is a dorsal air intake and what appears to be a small radar housing in the nose. Unofficial sources have called this project the FJ-5 but such a designation (and F2J-1 of course) was almost certainly never issued. No further details are currently available for North American's OS-130 efforts.

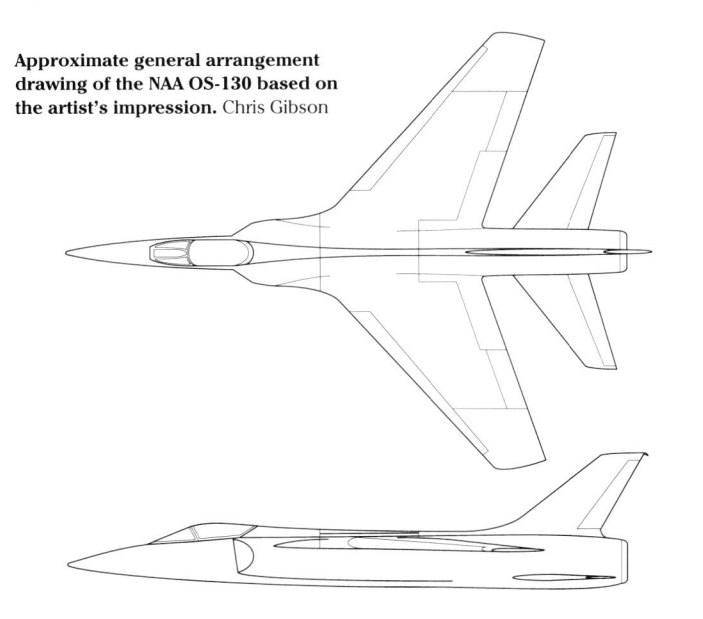

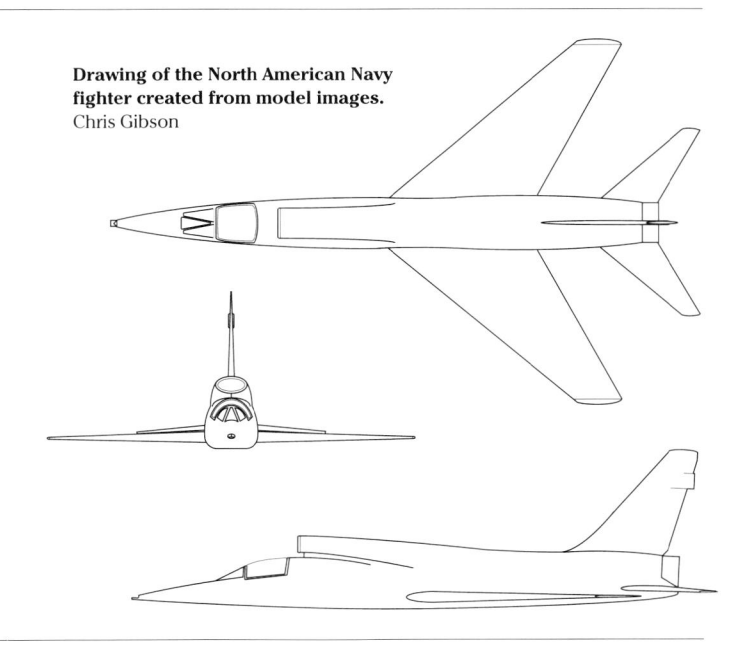

Above: **Artist's impression of the North American OS-130 project (c2.53). The colour scheme would have been sea-blue.** Tailhook Association via Jan Jacobs and Tommy Thomason

Right: **Model of another North American Navy fighter project which may have been part of the company's proposals to OS-130.** Bill Simone via www.secretprojects.co.uk

Approximate general arrangement drawing of the NAA OS-130 based on the artist's impression. Chris Gibson

Drawing of the North American Navy fighter created from model images. Chris Gibson

Naval Progress

Northrop N-94 Series

Northrop's response to OS-130 embraced four designs, the N-94, N-94A, N-94B and N-94C, which were very similar except that the last version moved the wing position. These projects represented nearly two years of comprehensive research and development by Northrop to find a compact, high-performance day fighter for the Navy. It was felt that the design requirements dictated a configuration that possessed long-term growth potential and could maintain the fighter's performance and effectiveness. The thin delta wing planform and blended wing-body concept evolved as the aircraft best suited to satisfy this philosophy.

The principal proposal was the N-94 that offered low drag and, with a J57-P-11 engine, a combat weight of 16,822lb (7,630kg), a combat ceiling in excess of 58,000ft (17,678m) and a rate of climb at 35,000ft (10,668m) of 16,200ft/min (4,938m/min). Wing thickness/chord ratio was 5.5%. An identical airframe (except for the jetpipe) was presented by the N-94A but this variant used the lower-thrust, lighter-weight J65-W-(TJ31B3) giving an equivalent combat ceiling of 57,100ft (17,404m) and rate of climb at 35,000ft of 12,200ft/min (3,719m/min). On the other hand the 94A's lower combat weight of 14,865lb (6,743kg), in conjunction with the J65's characteristics, permitted a 32,900ft/min (10,028m/min) rate of climb at sea level – in comparison with 30,300ft/min (9,235m/min) for the N-94 – and an advantage of 7mph (11km) lower stalling speed. Northrop declared that both designs exceeded the requirements, and that either of the engine installations within such a compact and efficient configuration would provide a high thrust-to-weight ratio and, thus, high performance. Increases in performance without redesigning the primary structure would be possible with alternative powerplants.

The design's wing leading edge was cambered over its entire length to provide high lift and a more efficient cruise. At its normal gross weight the N-94 provided a combat radius of 336nm (622km) at the specified combat speed (Mach 1.2), and its extended (overload) range was 446nm (826km), while the N-94A also exceeded the range requirements. Gross take-off weight for the extended radius of action on internal fuel was 20,082lb (9,109kg) for the N-94 and 17,640lb (8,002kg)

One could be forgiven for thinking that this might be a model of a version of the Douglas Skyray, but it fact it is the very handsome Northrop N-94.
John Hall

American Secret Projects: Fighters & Interceptors

Northrop N-94 (16.2.53). Northrop Grumman Corp, Tony Chong collection

Northrop N-94B (16.2.53). Note the straight wing trailing edge compared to the N-94. Northrop Grumman Corp, Tony Chong collection

Northrop N-94C (16.2.53). Northrop Grumman Corp, Tony Chong collection

for the N-94A. Northrop had calculated that the delta configuration permitted the spotting of twenty-eight aeroplanes on the carrier deck without wing folding, although the wingtips could be manually folded to a span of 25ft 0in (7.6m). From inboard outwards the wing trailing edge featured a longitudinal stability augmenter, the inboard elevon and then the outboard elevon, all of them inside the wing-fold position. There was a tricycle undercarriage with a long nose leg, the engine was fed by wing root intakes and the guns were mounted in the lower nose, two on the port side and one to starboard (with an option for a second gun on this side). A jettisonable fuel tank could also be carried beneath the rear portion of the middle fuselage.

The N-94B was essentially the same basic design but showed an increase in wing and vertical tail area, although it still offered the same low drag and thickness/chord ratio and shared the built-in growth potential. The armament and electronic installations were identical, the other principal differences being the size of the fuel tanks and control surfaces. This aircraft offered a very high performance at its combat weight of 16,860 lb (7,648kg) including a sea level rate of climb of 28,200ft/min (8,595m/min), a rate of climb at 35,000ft (10,668m) of 15,900ft/min (4,864m/min) and a combat ceiling of 59,800ft (18,227m); at the normal gross weight it was expected to take 1.53 minutes to reach 35,000ft (10,668m). N-94B's extended range combat radius on internal fuel (gross weight 19,850 lb [9,004kg]) was 417nm (772km) at Mach 1.2, and for the normal gross weight this was 316nm (585km); for the latter the N-94B carried 5,950 lb (2,699kg) of fuel. The aircraft's folded span was 26ft 8in (8.1m).

The N-94C's high delta wing produced the biggest variation in the basic design but, although not a blended wing-body layout, it retained the desired minimal frontal area, low drag characteristics and growth potential. The J57-P-11 was the same and the fighter's power-off stalling speed was approximately 3.5mph (5.5km/h) lower than the N-94. Combat weight was 17,880 lb (8,110kg), combat ceiling 58,450ft (17,816m), rate of climb at 35,000ft (10,668m) 15,000ft/min

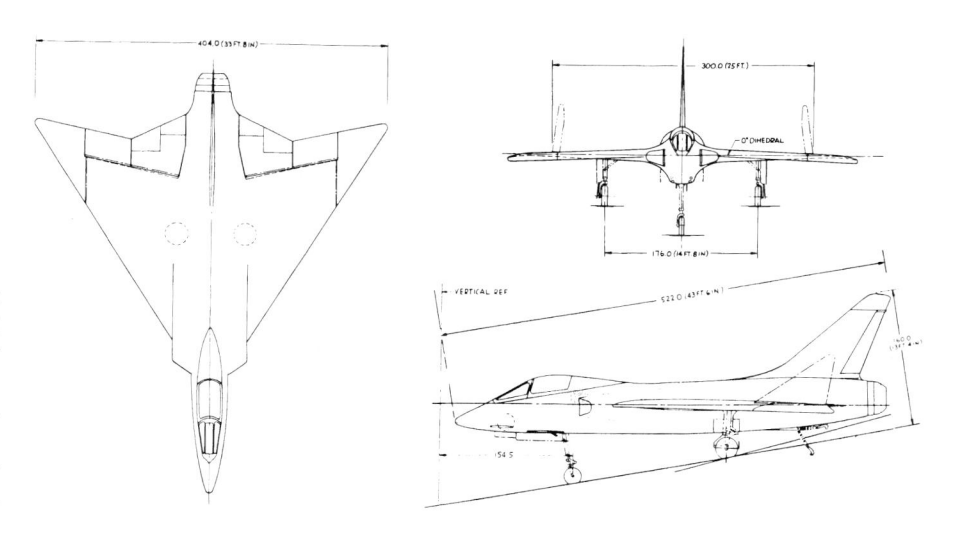

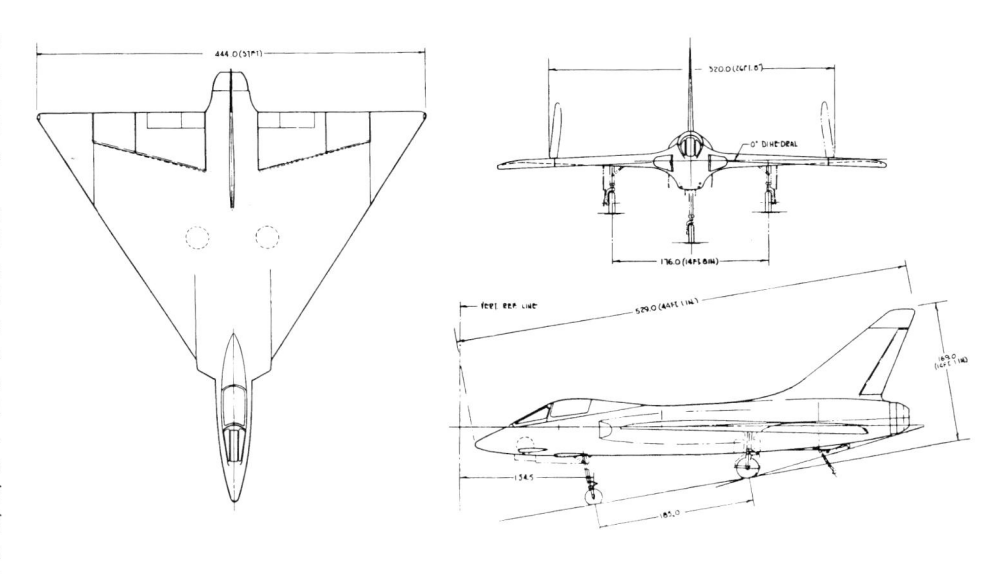

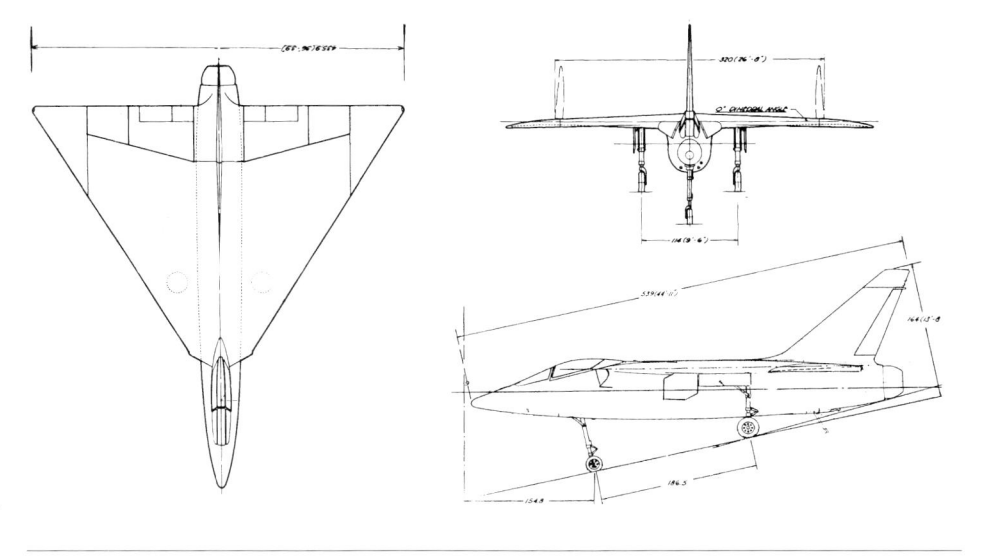

Naval Progress

(4,572m/min) and the combat radius of action exceeded the requirements. The extended range gross weight came out at 21,120lb (9,580kg). Principal differences between the N-94C and the other designs were its high through-wing structure, the fuel system and the longer landing gear legs, the last two a direct result of the new wing position. The wing's 5.5% thickness/chord ratio was continued and the root intakes and gun positions were retained. Folded span was 26ft 8in (8.1m). Although offering several advantages by separating the fuselage and wing structure the N-94C suffered some penalties in performance.

Every N-94 variant had the same electronic installations and offered five different and interchangeable internal weapon installations – three T-160 20mm guns, forty-eight 2in (5.1cm) rockets, six 5in (12.7cm) rockets, four Mk.12 guns or a bomb bay. In addition they could all carry four Sparrow II missiles externally under the wings. Their general structure incorporated conventional design principles throughout.

The Navy's day fighter requirement had resulted in a large competition. According to the George Spangenberg history, the minimum speed requirement was Mach 1.2 and most of the designs came in over that. In the event Chance Vought won the competition 'hands down' although North American appears to have provided the closest competition. As proposed the Vought design was considered to be underweight, in the low 20,000s, but North American came in close to 30,000lb (13,608kg) for an aircraft 'that was almost the same'. Both had variable incidence wings and in the assessor's minds Vought would eventually be about 1,000lb (454kg) heavier than currently estimated, but that would still give a lighter and better fighter that was 'perfectly acceptable in the fleet'. In contrast the fact that North American's project was starting at 30,000lb counted against it, because this was thought to be the weight that the Service aircraft might reach at the top of its growth line. Eventually the decision was made to go with Vought's V-383, which was thought to be the best design from all of the proposals anyway, and three prototypes were ordered on 29th June 1953. Only two of these were completed.

Chance Vought F8U-1 Crusader

The designation XF8U-1 was assigned to the V-383 prototypes, John Russell Clark led the design team and the first machine made its maiden flight on 25th March 1955. Dick Atkins, long-time servant at Vought and who today works with the company archives, remembered that 'during wind tunnel testing of the final configuration, when the design was 95% complete, it was discovered that the F8U-1 would not meet the guaranteed maximum speed. A massive six-week, all-hands, 80 to 100 hours per week redesign was undertaken to create a Whitcombe area rule fuselage that was then submitted to the Navy. The Service said that the redesign was not worth the cost to get the required additional 0.02 Mach, but then it turned out that the aircraft had less drag than expected and met the guaranteed speed anyway.' The resulting production aircraft, designated F8U-1 and named Crusader, actually carried four guns, thirty-two 2.75in (7.0cm) rockets and two Sidewinder AAMs. A total of 1,260 production machines were built, including photoreconnaissance versions, and the type proved to be Vought's first really successful jet aircraft. It served with the US Navy into the 1980s, being redesignated as the F-8 in 1962. It also served with the French Navy right up to the 21st century.

A New Heavy Fighter/Interceptor

Alongside the day fighter competition, towards the end of the Korean War the Navy prepared a second operational requirement. This called for a supersonic long-range all-weather interceptor. However, the subsequent design competition surrounding this aircraft proved to be a more informal affair with the evaluation of three principal proposals that had been offered independently at that time – the Grumman Model 118, McDonnell F4H and Chance Vought F8U-3. Formal bids were not requested and it appears that work on all three of these fighters was driven by the manufacturers' initiative rather than the Navy's carefully considered requirements. Grumman's and McDonnell's designs resulted from long periods of substantial research, but in the end a flight competition was needed to enable the Navy to choose between McDonnell and Vought.

Grumman Design 110

For a six-week period up to the end of March 1955 Grumman undertook preliminary investigations under the Design 110 label with the objective of finding an all-new 'no-holds-barred' single-seat naval fighter aircraft. It would carry two semi-submerged Sparrows and two 30mm cannon as a basic armament (with additional Sparrows as overload) and a 24in (61.0cm) diameter search and fire control radar dish. The studies embraced eight quite different layouts (G-110-1 to G-110-8) and several different engines, and the objectives included Mach 2 speed at 35,000ft (10,668m) and above and a ceiling in the region of 60,000ft (18,288m). No single design was selected as the best, but the team learnt much in regard to what was possible and what could be achieved with future developments, such as more engine power.

An early production Chance Vought F8U-1 Crusader photographed in about 1957 in the hands of VF-32, the first operational squadron to receive the type.

Grumman Design 118

The work on Design 110, and that undertaken for the Design 107 long-range interceptor, was brought together in a new Task Force Defence Fighter proposal called Design 118. This was a two-seat swept wing fighter with a combined jet and rocket powerplant that was to be operable from all of the US Navy's major classes of Fleet carrier. The 118 had wing leading and trailing edge flaps to give high lift and increase drag when required; an all-moving horizontal tail surface; wing-folding at mid-span, giving a folded span of 25ft 2in (7.7m); and a tricycle undercarriage with twin nosewheels. The armament installation comprised two Sparrow and three Sidewinder air-to-air missiles, which were carried flush to the fuselage underside on trapezes that would swing down before firing. There were no guns but two 300gal (1,364lit) external fuel tanks could be carried.

Two J79 jets were mounted side-by-side in the rear fuselage and augmented by a retractable JP-4 rocket motor placed beneath the jets at the end of the fuselage. The latter conferred a very impressive performance at altitude. On reheat alone the 118's top speed was Mach 2.0 between 35,000ft (10,668m) and 57,900ft (17,648m). Firing the rocket did not affect the top speed but made the 118 capable of Mach 2.0 up to 75,000ft (22,860m) while also pushing up the combat ceiling at 37,366 lb (16,949kg) weight from 58,600ft (17,861m) to 75,500ft (23,012m). These figures were based on the J79-GE-3 that had a limiting Mach number of 2.0, but with the 18,000 lb (80.0kN) thrust J79-X207 engine in place the Mach number could be increased. Internal fuel totalled 13,000 lb (5,897kg) comprising 2,000gal (9,094lit) for the turbojets with another 5,000 lb (2,268kg) for the rocket motor. Maximum overload take-off weight was given as 46,510 lb (21,097kg).

Two prototypes of the 118 were ordered in 1956 and Bureau serials were allocated but, before any metal had been cut, the contract and any plans for production were cancelled in favour of the McDonnell Phantom II. During early June 1956 an investigation was also completed into an all-weather strike version

This manufacturer's display model found in the Grumman archive shows an unknown but very impressive fighter project. It has an offset canopy, which suggests that it might have been a study for the Navy, and shows some similarities to Design 118; for example side-by-side engines. Model span is 18.75in (47.6cm) and length 22in (55.9cm).

Grumman Design 118 at 12.12.55. Two prototypes were ordered but neither was built, the programme being cancelled before any fabrication had started.
Grumman Corp / Grumman History Centre

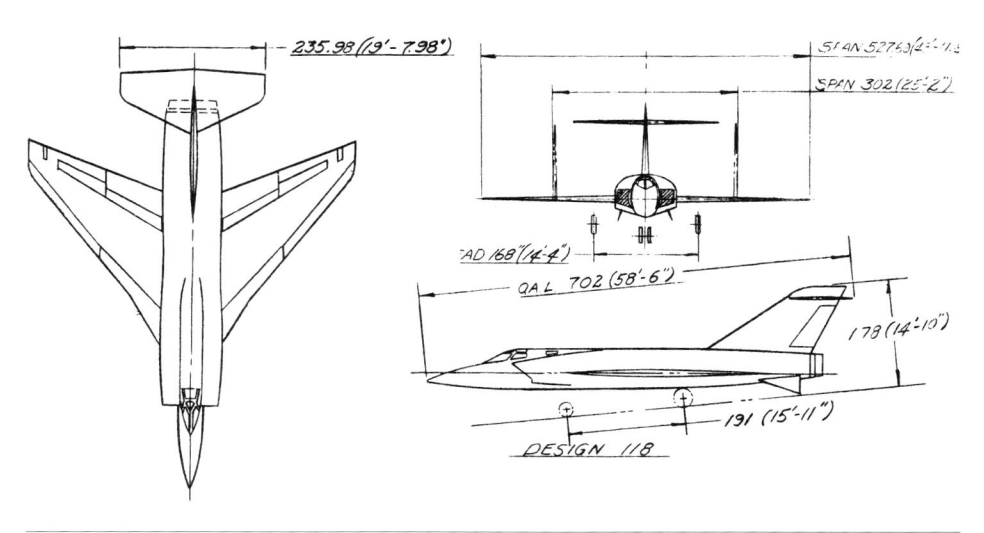

Naval Progress

Model of Grumman's Design 118. Note the ventral fins and semi-recessed Sparrow missile. Grumman Corporation / Grumman History Centre

of the 118 called the 118B. This was intended to carry a 3,300 lb (1,497kg) 'special' (nuclear) weapon semi-recessed beneath the rear fuselage forward of the fin, up to 4,000 lb (1,814kg) of conventional bombs, or six Martin Bullpup air-to-ground missiles. The respective take-off weights with these loads, without external fuel tanks, were 44,779 lb (20,312kg) (or 47,004 lb [21,321kg] with the rocket motor), 45,579 lb (20,675kg) and 46,039 lb (20,883kg), and the ranges were 720nm (1,333km) (550nm [1,019km] with the rocket), 700nm (1,296km) or 665nm (1,232km). A new armament control system in the nose would replace the production fighter's APQ-50 radar. The XF12F-1 designation was at different times earmarked for both the Grumman G-98J F11F-1F Super Tiger (above) and the Model 118, the former at least semi-officially. The 118 was formally rejected on 16th July 1956.

McDonnell F3H-G/H and YAH-1

The acquisition of the Vought F8U Crusader filled one new Navy requirement but, at this time, the Service no longer had any multiple-engine fighters either in production or in planning. Consequently, McDonnell was approached to see what could be done to create a twin-engine type offering the same kind of performance as the F8U-1. Much of the detail that follows, covering McDonnell's side of the story right through to the Phantom, is taken with permission from an unpublished work written by William E Elmore, who was part of the design team at the time.

To begin with, studies were undertaken to determine the design requirements. These resulted in a twin J65 powerplant, a design gross weight of around 30,000 lb (13,608kg), maximum length not to exceed 56ft (17.1m) and maximum height for storage on the hanger deck of no more than 16ft (4.9m). Four designers were then assigned to seek and define an acceptable configuration, Herman Barkey (lead designer), Eugene Koeller, Murray Etherton and Bill Elmore, and the aircraft that resulted was called the F3H-G. The retention of the F3H designation was used as a sales gimmick because, at the time, it was much easier to acquire a modification to an old contract rather than obtain a completely new one. Eugene Koeller got the job of designing a number of single-engined fighters to make a comparison against the intended twin-engined layout. There was never any intention of officially proposing a single-engine aircraft but his layouts were assigned numbers in the F3H-A to -F series. This step has led some reviewers to state that the twin-engine F3H-G/H appeared as a gradual development process from the old Demon, but this was not the case.

McDonnell allocated its Model 98 project number to the research and a drawing has been made available for the first in the series, the 98A. This had a single J67, intakes on the lower fuselage sides, four 20mm cannon in the lower nose and a low-position 45° sweep wing. Internal fuel totalled 1,703gal (7,743lit), the 98A's estimated maximum rate of climb was 37,200ft/min (11,339m/min) and combat ceiling 55,450ft (16,901m). Model 98A was also called the F3H-E but, as stated, none of the single-engine designs were offered to the Navy.

Bill Elmore drew the lines for what became the F3H-G. He came up with a low-wing layout with the engines just behind the wing carry-through structure, the guns, cockpit and fuel arrangement being based on F-101A Voodoo practice. However, he found it impossible to balance the design within the 56ft (17.1m) limit, but substituting a 60° sweep delta did give balance and also satisfied all of the performance and dimensional requirements. Later a modified and balanced version of the original swept wing layout, with a reduced tail length, was put together by Gene Stephens, a designer who had worked on the Model 90. The delta was labelled Model 98C while the 'chopped tail' project was called 98B and both were submitted to the Navy as an unsolicited proposal on 19th September 1954. Just before submission it was decided to examine a growth version of the 98B with two of the new and more powerful General Electric J79 units and this became the F3H-H, the original having been labelled F3H-G. The 98C does not appear to have been given a designation in the F3H series.

The McDonnell Model 98A (F3H-E) was designed with a single J67-W-1 engine to form a comparison against the twin-engine 98B (F3H-G) (25.8.53). Four 20mm cannon are mounted in the bottom of the fuselage. Larry Merritt

McDonnell Model 98B (F3H-G) with two J65 engines (1953/1954). Larry Merritt

The full-size mock-up of the McDonnell F3H-G/H represented two projects, the F3H-G and -H that were identical save for the engine. The -G was to be powered by a J65 Sapphire, the -H by a J79, so the only external difference came with the jet nozzle. The photo was taken in May 1954.
Larry Merritt

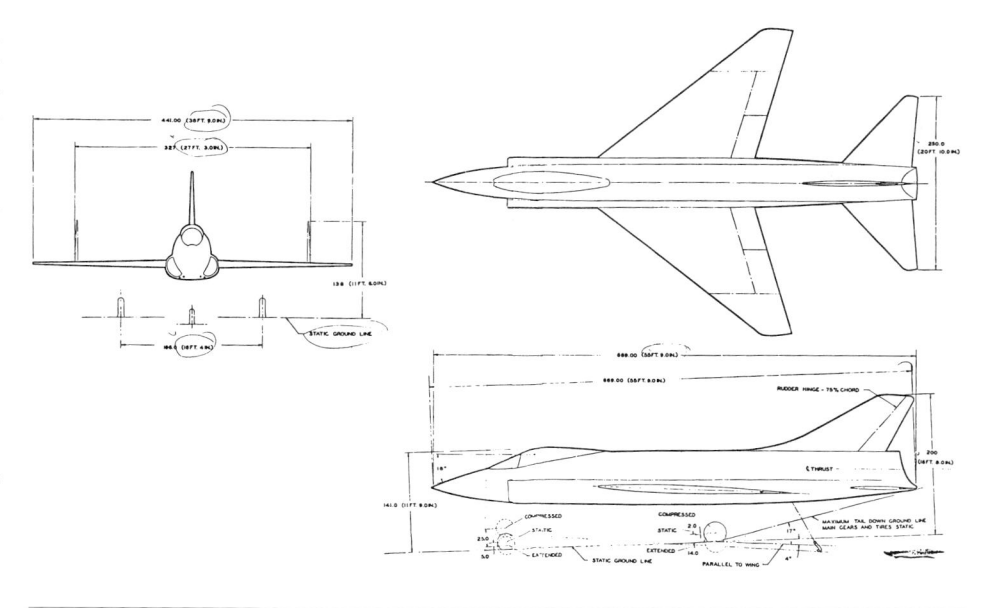

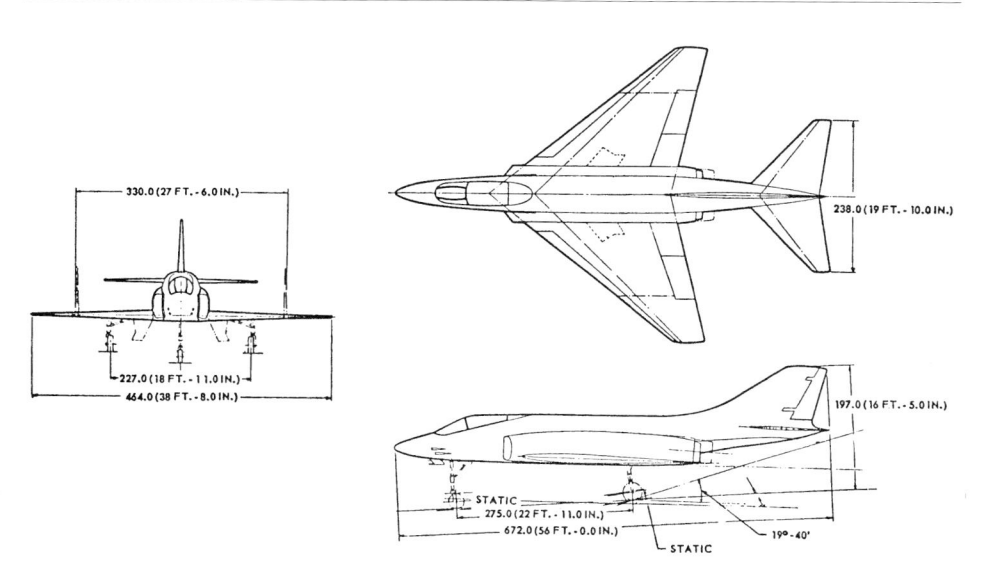

Naval Progress

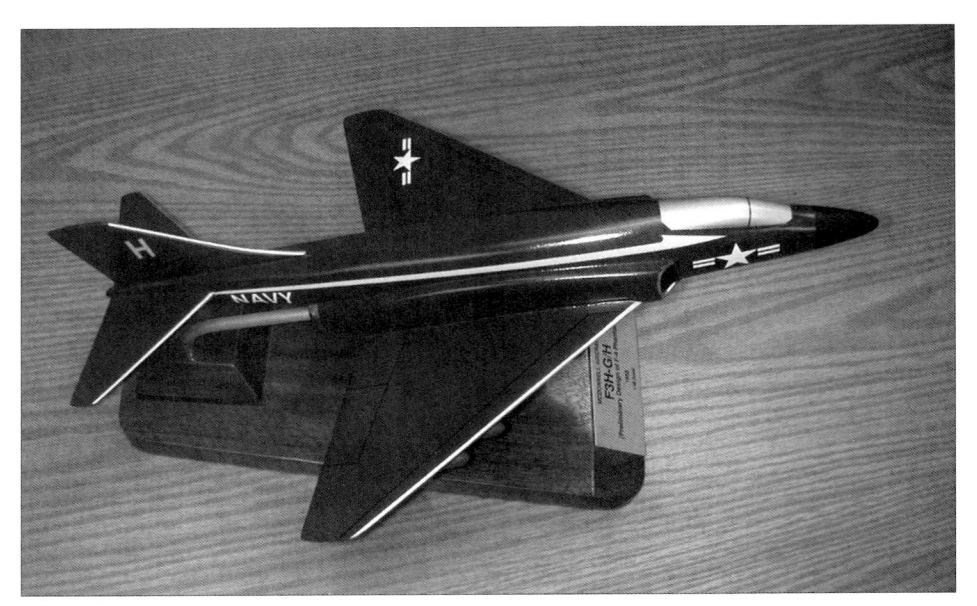

The F3H-E, -G and -H all had a 45° sweep wing. On the -G and -H two 20mm cannon were mounted on each side of the lower nose but these could be replaced by fifty-six 2in (5.1cm) air-to-air rockets in side fuselage bays that filled the space made available by taking out the guns. There were six underwing hardpoints plus three under the fuselage which could take a mix of weapons for attack roles – eight bombs up to 500lb (227kg) in weight, two 1,000lb (454kg) or 2,000lb (907kg) bombs only under the fuselage, a single 'special' store on the fuselage centreline or packages of rockets including eight 5.0in (12.7cm)-diameter weapons. The aircraft could also have two 300gal (1,364lit) or one 500gal (2,273lit) drop tank under the fuselage. For air-to-air there could be six Sparrow missiles carried on the four outer wing pylons and the two 'outside' fuselage hardpoints.

Although the size of the radar dish was quoted as 24in (61.0cm), attack duties would actually require a lightweight Westinghouse radar in the nose. For all-weather tasks the F3H-G/H was earmarked to have an APG-50 for search, track and fire control while day fighter duties would need an APQ-51 to guide the Sparrow missiles. The structure was conventional and the aircraft had leading and trailing edge flaps to serve as high lift devices. There was a tricycle undercarriage with a long nose leg and the internal fuel totalled 1,972gal (8,966lit). The estimated maximum rate of climb for the F3H-G was 32,800ft/min (9,997m/min) and combat ceiling 55,500ft (16,916m); the equivalent figures for the -H were 44,100ft/min (13,442m/min) and 59,200ft (18,044m).

The Navy favoured the 98B because, having had problems with the Vought Cutlass and Douglas Skyray during carrier operations, it was wary about introducing another aircraft with an unconventional wing design. The Navy Bureau did offer some objection to the 98B because it thought that detailed work on a new fighter did not need to be started for about another year. McDonnell Aircraft however, decided to press on and Herman Barkey became the program leader. By 1st October the design work was approaching the status of a full-blown project, except that it was now being developed as an attack aircraft and not a fighter. This step had to be taken because of the Navy's financial arrangements – its 'fighter' money had for the time being been earmarked for the Crusader but the 'attack department' still had funds available. Thus the development of the F3H-G/H was allowed to proceed under the AH-1 attack designation but with little change to the airframe. In due course a Letter of Intent was received and, when more fighter money became available, the Navy switched the aircraft's role again, back to that of an interceptor for fleet defence.

McDonnell Model 98R/F4H-1 Phantom II

As the design of McDonnell's fighter progressed, all of the guns and ammunition were taken out to make space for a second crewmember, without exceeding the 56ft (17.1m) limit. Sparrow missiles were placed on the four corners of the fuselage and the J65s were finally dropped for two J79s. In addition the F3H-H's fixed geometry air intakes were substituted by a new variable geometry arrangement that allowed the top speed to be increased from Mach 1.5 to Mach 2.0. As such, this new design was labelled Model 98R and eventually designated F4H. The complexity of the F4H's structure and

Model of the McDonnell F3H-G/H, a beautiful design that formed the main link between the F3H Demon and F4H Phantom. Larry Merritt

arrangement brought numerous additional design problems and changes, such as the breaking of the 56ft (17.1m) length limit, but the effort paid off.

An order was placed in July 1955 for prototypes of the new type and later it was given the name Phantom II. The first XF4H-1 flew on 27th May 1958 and began what would prove to be one of the most successful jet fighter programs ever, with more than five thousand examples built. In due course the Phantom was also ordered for the USAF as the F-110A, but by the time it entered service the 1962 re-numbering scheme had brought a new overall designation – the F-4. USAF machines were called F-4Cs whilst the Navy versions were F-4As and Bs. A document called SOR-200 covered the US Navy part of the program and WS-326A the USAF. However, before the initial order was placed the Phantom would have to cross one final hurdle – it would have to prove itself against another, highly capable new fighter which had reached flight test.

Chance Vought V-401/XF8U-3 Crusader III

The phenomenal progress made in fighter aircraft and weapon design during the 1950s meant that John Russell Clarke's design team at Vought quickly began to look at a new project based on the F8U-1. The resulting V-401 was to carry air-to-air missiles only, Sparrows recessed on the sides of the fuselage and Sidewinders on special side fuselage pylons. A key element of the aircraft was its new Pratt

The first pre-series McDonnell F4H-1F all-weather fighter, 143388, pictured at St Louis in June 1959.

When the Phantom was first bought by the USAF it was to be called the F-110A, but the new 1962 designation system ensured that all Phantoms were from now on called F-4s. This well-known publicity shot shows 149405, a Navy aircraft, marked up to represent an F-110A.

This well-known view of the ferocious-looking Vought XF8U-3 Crusader III is included in part because it shows the retractable vertical fins so well. Dick Atkins, Vought Archive

& Whitney J75 engine, the design of which had begun in 1954 when it was realised that future aircraft would need thrust in excess of 20,000 lb (88.9 kN). Very quickly the Navy began to show an interest in the V-401 and design approval was granted to Vought in July 1956. In May 1957 the Navy awarded a contract for the manufacture of five prototypes for what was to be called the XF8U-3.

The first of these flew on 2nd June 1958, just a few days after the Phantom, and test flying revealed an extraordinary performance in terms of speed and acceleration. The maximum speed reached was Mach 2.39 – with only the fear of damaging the engine stopping it going faster. In general the top speed was limited to Mach 2.2, but at that speed the F8U-3 was still accelerating at 0.04 Mach per second and Vought declared that with further engine development the F8U-3 could be a Mach 3 aircraft by 1960 without any other changes. The designation F8U-3 was a misnomer because the aircraft bore only superficial resemblance to the -1 and -2 models (the F8U-2 Crusader had more powerful engines than the -1); in fact Vought preferred to call it the F9U. Another sixteen aircraft were ordered in January 1958 for fleet trials and the future looked bright but there was a final hurdle that was about to be raised.

By the mid-1950s analysts and designers had reached the conclusion that any new fighter had to have some kind of a missile capability – guns alone would be insufficient to deal with a high-performance threat against the Fleet. Then the argument of single-place single-engined aircraft versus multi-seat multi-engined types began to rear its head. This not only triggered the development of the F8U-3, it also meant that in due course it would become a competitor to the F4H. This was not the original idea. At one stage both types were scheduled for production. In fact, Chance Vought was able to make faster progress, starting around a year later and yet beginning test flying at almost the same time.

Naval Progress

The issue of the Crusader III and the McDonnell F4H as potential competitors was brought to the surface by Congress insisting on a decision by the US Navy as to which aircraft the Service really wanted – and it was not going to be allowed both. However, during the autumn of 1958 the Service was in no hurry to make up its mind. One reason was that both aircraft showed outstanding promise, each capable of well over Mach 2 in level flight. However, the two F8U-3s so far completed were already 'fleet-worthy' (ready for carrier-deck operation) whereas McDonnell's aeroplanes were in several important respects 'prototype shells'. Both manufacturers accused the other of enlisting congressional support but the decision had to be settled by a fly-off.

To quote George Spangenberg, 'in the normal sense the F8U-3 won the fly-off. It had by far the best flying qualities. It was the best flying airplane. Good flight control system. It carried only three Sparrows instead of four as a compromise in trying to get the best airplane. It would do everything on internal fuel that the F4D did with a 600-gallon tank. It had better legs, higher speed, while climbs and ceilings were about the same.' However, the one-place versus two-place argument killed Vought's fighter. By now there was a growing conviction within the Navy that a second crewman was required to undertake the all-weather fighter job: a view that later on was almost universally accepted. McDonnell's design was also felt to be a better potential fighter-bomber than the Crusader III interceptor because it had plenty of weapon pylons, which Vought's aircraft lacked. It was the end for the F8U-3. The earlier orders were cancelled and only three prototypes ever flew, although these were to have an extended life as NASA test vehicles. It was by all accounts an outstanding aircraft, but was just unfortunate in having to contend for funds against what was to prove to be one of the most outstanding warplanes of the jet age.

Patrol Interceptor

A large portion of this book has been devoted to the development of high-speed interceptors, both for the USAF and Navy. However, the Navy also instituted a design competition in the late 1950s that took a rather different direction. George Spangenberg's memoirs explain why. Threat projections were showing that it would become extremely difficult to protect the fleet against attacks by Mach 2-capable aircraft and something more effective than the McDonnell F4H/Sparrow combination was therefore needed. Each study indicated that 'you just couldn't get there in time to shoot down enough [enemy aircraft] and the surface-to-air missiles just couldn't handle the degree of the threat either'. In-depth analysis showed that the only way to deal with this situation would be to employ a combat air patrol (CAP) aircraft armed with long-range missiles. This was far better than attempting a high-speed intercept because, with the enemy expecting to approach at Mach 2 and launch missiles as well, 'it was imperative that they get stopped or at least well thinned out by one hundred miles out'. The Air Force looked at the problem differently and subsequently began the AF-12/YF-12A interceptor program discussed in Chapter Five. The latter led inevitably to a very large and very long aircraft that was totally unsuited to carrier operations. The 'Eagle Missileer' was thus conceived.

The Eagle XAAM-N-10 was a new long-range air-to-air missile that used mid-course guidance and terminal homing and offered the capability to hit targets up to at least 130 miles (209km) away. Its design comprised a two-stage solid propellant rocket with the smaller motor or Terminal Rocket in the forward position and the larger Booster to the rear. These were joined together by explosive bolts and the second stage had a stainless steel honeycomb delta wing to give high rigidity. The body consisted of a semi-monocoque cylindrical shell and the warhead compartment was designed to house either high explosive or higher yield heads. After separation of the booster, roll, pitch and yaw control were to be provided by cantilevered control surfaces aft of the wings. It was also planned to have retractable tips on the booster stage. Missile span was 50.14in (127.4cm), the overall length with the booster was 195.5in (496.6cm) and after separation this became 142in (360.7cm), launch weight was 1,288lb (584kg) and final glide weight 646lb (293kg). Three Douglas A3D Skywarrior naval bombers would be employed as Eagle testbed aircraft under the Douglas designation D-790. In December 1958 Bendix won a separate competition to design the weapon with Grumman as a partner.

The 'Missileer' defence fighter was intended to be an aircraft that could carry the Eagle and loiter for several hours up to 150 miles (241km) from its base ship. As soon as unfriendly aircraft were spotted on the radar screen it would launch its missiles. What was also needed therefore was a long-range airborne radar capability. In the mid-1950s this was just within the state of the art but it would require a dish with a diameter in the region of 5ft (1.52m). However, this would not be a problem if the missile carrier were a subsonic aircraft, for which frontal area was not a great concern. And why not? It did not have to get launched and race out to meet the enemy; it was out there hanging around waiting for them. A supersonic design could fly faster to meet the threat but it needed to get airborne in the first place and could only accommodate a smaller radar offering less range, thus it needed to get much closer to the incoming enemy before it could engage its weapons. The Missileer was thus specified as a subsonic design requirement.

The appearance of the Bendix/Grumman Eagle air-to-air missile as at 21.9.59. Both Grumman Corporation / Grumman History Centre

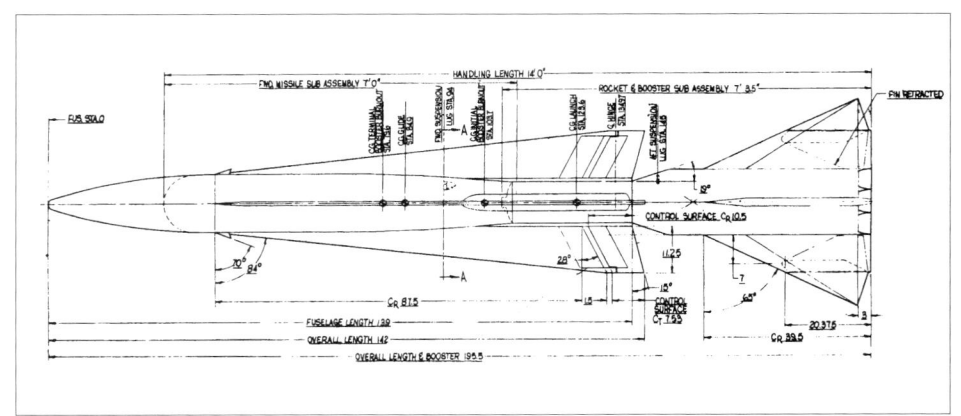

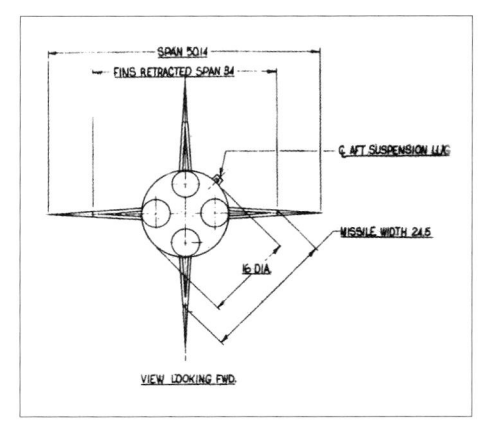

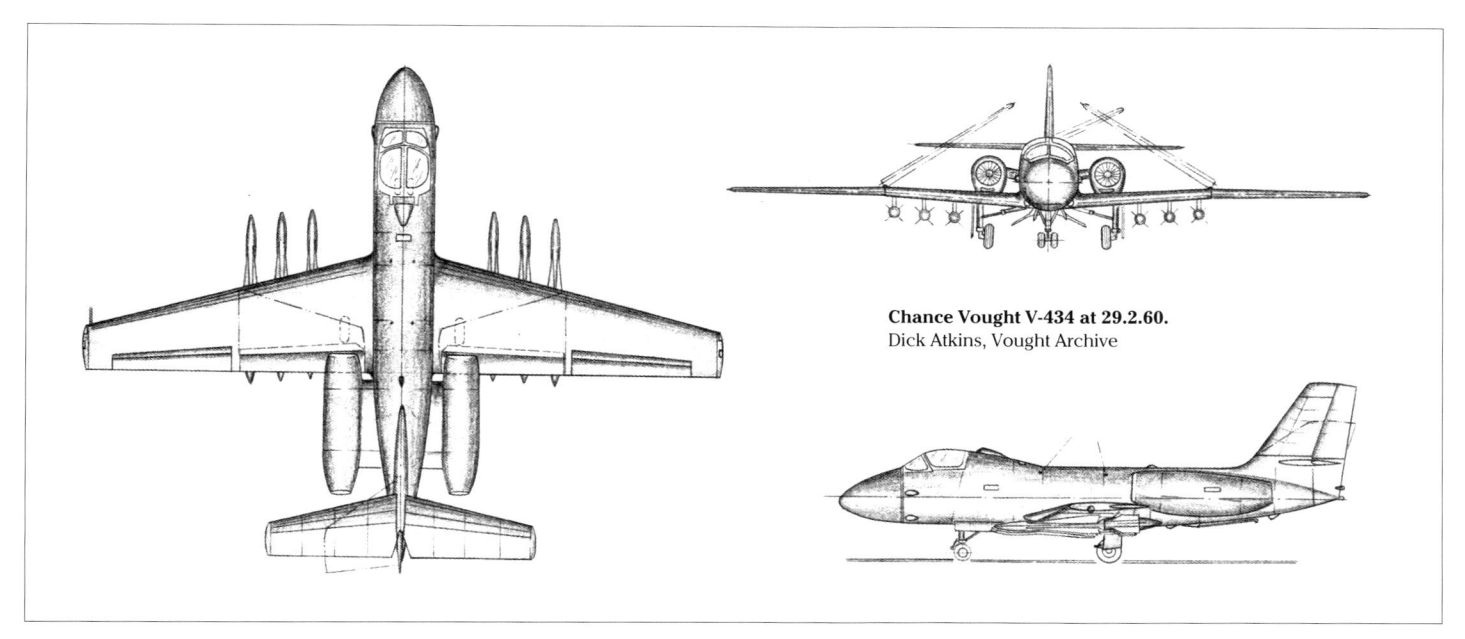

Chance Vought V-434 at 29.2.60.
Dick Atkins, Vought Archive

The logic was powerful but this low performance requirement made the 'Missileer' project very controversial. Opponents were certain that it would be too slow to survive in modern warfare but the project's supporters felt that the long radar range offered by the huge dish would overcome any lack of speed. Whatever the pros and cons, this design requirement represented a huge contrast to the F4H Phantom.

Work on the missile and its fire control system, and also a new turbofan engine from Pratt & Whitney called the TF30, was opened a couple of years before the airframe competition to specification TS-151 got going in 1959. From a technical point of view developing the airframe was not expected to be a difficult task because it was to be a subsonic machine with two engines, two crew seated side-by-side plus the large radar. Simplicity, reliability and ease of maintenance were key elements in the specification although the combat ceiling was not to be less than 39,000ft (11,887m). A Request for Proposals was made by the Navy on 10th December 1959.

Boeing Model 835

Boeing's studies in response to the requirement embraced at least twenty-two designs, all of them under the Model 835 designation. Some were very unconventional but the early designs were, from an aerodynamic point of view, quite basic. Design 835-1 was started on 1st October 1959 and probably took the basic subsonic approach to an extreme. It had a very tubby fuselage, high-position swept wing and engines in two underwing nacelles. One layout that does appear to have been examined in more detail is the Model 835-6 and this suggests that may have been favoured by the designers. The 835-6 had a mid-position wing swept 41° 49' at the leading edge and a tricycle undercarriage with a twin nosewheel; the main gears folded into wing nacelles. There were eight underwing pylons for Eagles (one inside each main wheel pod and another three outside) and the aircraft had a folded span of 32ft 6in (9.9m). The two turbofans were housed in nacelles mounted on the back of the rear fuselage either side of the forward part of the fin and the wing had double-slotted flaps and internally balanced ailerons with control and trim tabs. A conventional elevator was fitted to the horizontal tail.

Chance Vought V-434

Vought's V-434 proposal was a side-by-side, two-seat, twin engine, low wing aeroplane fitted with a tricycle landing gear and conventional aerodynamic controls. The all-moving horizontal tail unit was mounted low on the vertical tail and the rudder was located entirely above it. Ailerons comprised 80% of the trailing edge of the wing outer panels while the centre section had an integral fuel tank, inward-folding main landing gear immediately aft of the fuel cell and single slotted flaps along the trailing edge from fuselage to wing-fold. Folded span was 37ft 6in (11.43m). The ailerons were split spanwise and would open simultaneously for speed brakes. The engines were mounted in pods to either side of the aft fuselage above the wings and beneath the horizontal tail, Vought noting that this location protected the powerplant from foreign object damage or the products of combustion from firing the missiles. A maximum of ten Eagle missiles could be carried on pylons mounted on the wing lower surface between the wing-folds, although drawings and data were based on a load of six. Given an early go-ahead Vought estimated that a first flight could be made in April 1963.

Poor quality but rare illustration of a model of the V-434.
Dick Atkins, Vought Archive

Naval Progress

Above: **Three views of a display model of the Douglas D-766/F6D-1 Missileer.** Allyson Vought

Top right: **Manufacturer's model belonging to the Grumman archive of the company's G-128E Missileer powered by TF30 turbofans (6.59). This design had a span of approximately 44ft 8in (13.6m) and length 36ft 10in (11.2m).**

Centre right: **Model (in its box) of Grumman's G-128E Missileer with J52 turbojets.** Larry McLaughlin

Right: **Impression of the Model 153A.** John S Brooks

American Secret Projects: Fighters & Interceptors

Douglas Missileer

Douglas's first 'Missileer' airframe studies were initiated under the D-746 designation of May 1958 (the Eagle missile was given the number D-742 and the Eagle weapon system D-745); further work was undertaken under D-765, D-766 and D-767. The eventual winner of the competition was Douglas's D-766 which was another straightforward design. It showed a high-mounted straight wing; wing-root engine position; underwing pylons for six missiles, three per side; and a tricycle undercarriage with twin wheels on each leg, all folding into the fuselage.

Grumman Missileer

Grumman's effort in the Missileer program is a little confusing, not least because the company did not bid as a prime contractor but instead did so as a sub-contractor to Bendix on the missile itself. However, Grumman did produce several designs and designations for Missileer aircraft. Initially there were two lines of thought, both of which were based on existing airframes. Grumman's G-123 designation covered what became the W2F-1/E-2A Hawkeye carrierborne early warning aircraft that was powered by Allison turboprop engines and first flown in October 1960. In April 1958 G-123F was allocated to a Missileer version but the concept was started under G-151 in November 1956, presumably when knowledge of the weapon began to circulate.

A fuller study appears to have been made using a variant of the Grumman G-128 naval attack aircraft that flew in April 1960 as the A2F-1 Intruder and later became the A-6. Models 128E and 128F are both listed as Missileer proposals, the 128E being dated June 1959 which suggests it was the official submission. This is backed up by the presence of a couple of original manufacturer's display models because such items were often only produced for official proposals. From June 1958 this work was covered by project number G-200 (although a rough drawing for a turboprop G-200 has also been found) but it was later switched to the G-128 series. As the principal proposal, G-128E embraced two designs differing only in their powerplants. One had the required twin TF30 power units but the second employed two Pratt & Whitney J52 turbojets as used by the Intruder itself, which brought some differences to the intake and nacelle. The wing and tail were very similar to the Intruder but (certainly on the TF30 version) the wing root engine nacelles were larger. The nose for the radar was also larger of course and six Eagles were carried beneath the wings.

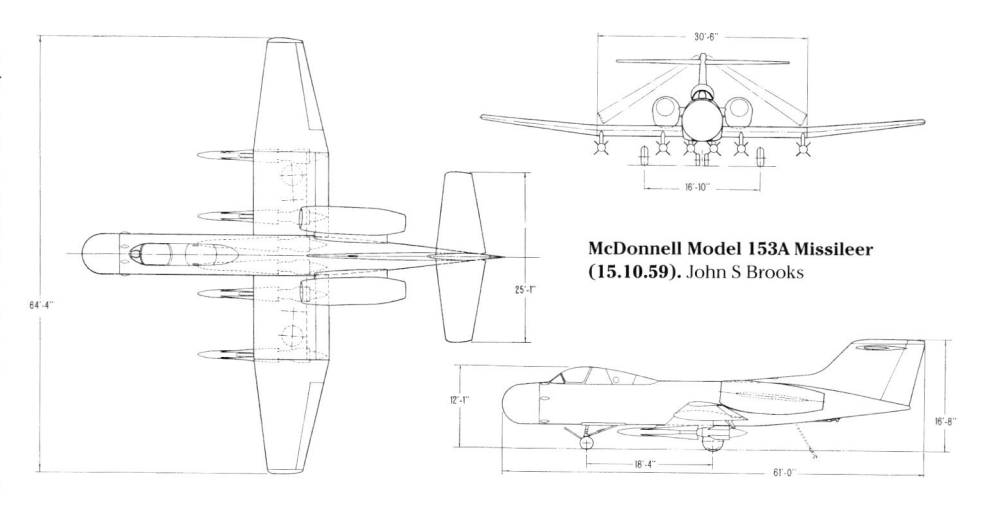

McDonnell Model 153A Missileer (15.10.59). John S Brooks

McDonnell Missileer

One assumes knowledge of the planned requirement reached the manufacturers well before official proposals were requested in 1959 because several teams drew projects of the Missileer type from the earliest stages. In September 1957 Model 124 was allocated to McDonnell's initial work in this field but Model 153A became the principal proposal; the 154A of January 1960 was also offered as a possible turboprop version. Model 153A had a low wing and a high tail with the two power units at the sides of the rear fuselage. Four of the Eagles went under the wings on either side of the main wheels with two more beneath the fuselage. The nose leg had twin wheels, folded span was 30ft 6in (9.3m) and wing thickness/chord ratio 14% between the root and wing fold and 12% at the tip. Maximum internal fuel was 17,388 lb (7,887kg) or 2,557gal (1,626lit); basic combat weight 41,982 lb (19,043kg); and loiter time on station was given as 4.47 hours. McDonnell declared that a go-ahead decision in June 1960 could bring a first flight in July 1963 with initial deliveries following in mid-1964.

North American Missileer

North American's Columbus Division Missileer offering showed another simple airframe. In fact none of these projects could describe their appearance as fighter-like but North American's project looked in some ways rather more like a light transport. This layout showed a high-position straight tapered wing and underwing pods for the two TF30 engines.

—

The competition ended in 1960 with the selection of Douglas's D-766, and two F6D-1 prototypes were ordered with the official name Missileer. Vought's entry achieved second place. However, in 1961 President Kennedy's new administration was about to take office and it would have been inappropriate for the outgoing administration to authorise a full development contract that the incoming team had not approved. Therefore Douglas was kept working only at a low level of effort. Then in December 1960 Secretary of Defense Thomas Gates deleted funding for the F6D from the Fiscal Year 1962 budget. In February 1961 Douglas tried to get the project running again but the arrival of the new Secretary, Robert McNamara, brought a final closure. At this time the USAF was also seeking a new tactical fighter to replace the F-105 Thunderchief and McNamara saw the opportunity to combine the two programs. The result was the TFX (F-111) that is discussed in Chapter Nine. For the Missileer it was the end, although work on the Eagle missile continued for a period. At cancellation, work had yet to begin on the construction of the Missileer prototypes.

The Missileer type of patrol interceptor represented an entirely different concept to what the Navy was either operating or shortly to put into service: a subsonic long-endurance aircraft rather than high-performance supersonic fighter. It was designed, like so many of America's interceptor studies, to deal with specific threats from the Soviet Union with fleets of bombers coming over the horizon. In fact America's next war would turn out to be in Vietnam with crowded skies and close-quarter dog-fighting. It would therefore appear that the cancellation of the Missileer program may have been fortuitous.

Northrop Navy Interceptor

To complete the picture of mid-late 1950s Naval developments, there is another naval interceptor design that is worth looking at.

Model of the North American Missileer from 1959. This 1/48th scale model's span is 16.5in (41.9cm) and length 14.5in (36.8cm), giving real dimensions of 66ft (20.1m) and 58ft (17.7m) respectively.
John Aldaz

It was the subject of a preliminary design study at Northrop from December 1954 until it was terminated in May 1955. Initiation of the study was prompted by reports of a pending Navy competition for a carrier-based interceptor to be held in the summer of 1955, but this never took place. A twin-engine project, the design did not receive an N-number in the company's project series but it is clear that it was assessed in some detail. Two J79 engines were to be employed in nacelles placed beneath a high wing, which was swept 35° at ¼ chord and had a thickness/chord ratio of 4.0%. A search-and-track radar was housed in the nose coupled with an automatic lead computing sight.

The interceptor's internal fuel load was 11,320lb (5,135kg) or 1,740gal (7,912lit) and its combat weight was 30,000lb (13,608kg). Estimated combat speed at 50,000ft (15,240m) was Mach 1.43; sea level rate of climb 52,000ft/min (15,850m/min); time to 50,000ft 3.0 minutes; combat ceiling 58,500ft (17,831m) and service ceiling 59,500ft (18,136m); combat radius was 500nm (926km). Four Sparrow air-to-air missiles were to be carried, two on the wingtips and two on the corners of the lower forward fuselage, while alternative wingtip pods could house sixty-two folding-fin 2in (5.1cm)-diameter rocket projectiles. Four wing-mounted pylons also offered the capability to carry combinations of missiles, rockets, external fuel or special stores in conjunction with the basic armament, which would enable the aircraft to perform as an escort fighter, ground-support fighter-bomber or a night intruder.

Naval Design Versatility

With the high-performance F8U Crusader and F4H Phantom and the subsonic, long-range, big radar-equipped Missileer, the Navy had during the 1950s examined pretty well the full spectrum of fighter/interceptor possibilities. Like the contemporary Century fighters for the USAF, the F8U and F4H moved naval fighter design state of the art forward by a huge amount and set the stage for decades to come. It would need some pretty impressive aeroplanes to take their place, but these would not make their appearance until the 1960s.

Northrop Navy Interceptor (5.55).
Northrop Grumman Corp,
Tony Chong collection

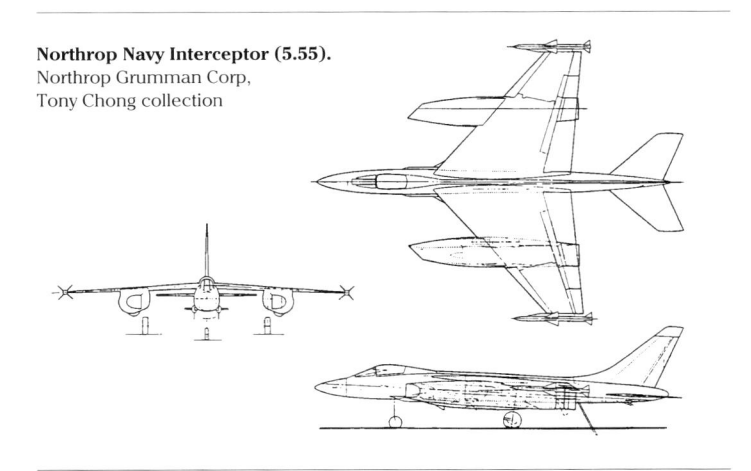

Rough sketch of the Northrop Navy Interceptor.
Northrop Grumman Corp, Tony Chong collection

American Secret Projects: Fighters & Interceptors

Naval Fighter Interceptor Studies – Estimated Data

Project	Span ft in (m)	Length ft in (m)	Gross Wing Area ft² (m²)	Gross Weight lb (kg)	Engine lb (kN)	Max Speed / Height mph (km/h) / ft (m)	Armament
Grumman F11F-1 Tiger (flown)	31 7.5 (9.6)	44 1.5 (13.4) (short nose)	250 (23.25)	20,300 (9,208) (short nose)	1 x Wright J65-W-18 7,450 (33.1), 10,500 (46.7) ab	714 (1,149) at S/L, Mach 1.15 at 35,000 (10,668)	4 x 20mm cannon, 4 x AIM-9 Sidewinder AAM
Grumman F11F-1F Super Tiger (flown)	31 8 (9.65)	48 9 (14.9)	250 (23.25)	26,086 (11,833)	1 x GE J79-GE-3A 12,000 (53.3), 17,000 (75.6) ab	836 (1,345) at S/L, Mach 2.04 at 40,000 (12,192)	4 x 20mm cannon, various AAM and bombs
Grumman G-98L	c34 6 (10.5)	c47 6 (14.5)	350 (32.55)	21,800 (9,888)	1 x GE J79-GE-2	cMach 1.77 at 35,000 (10,668)	Guns and AAM
Douglas F5D-1 Skylancer (flown)	33 6 (10.2)	52 10 (16.1)	557 (51.8)	27,739 (12,582) (with 72 rockets)	1 x P&W J57-P-8 10,200 (45.3), 16,000 (71.1) ab	749 (1,205) at S/L, 953 (1,533) at 35,000 (10,668)	72 x 2in (5.1cm) rocket projectiles or 4 x 20mm cannon or 2 x Sparrow II AAM
Supersonic Day Fighters							
Chance Vought V-383	35 8 (10.9)	54 5.5 (16.6)	375 (34.9)	22,600 (10,251)	1 x P&W J57-P-(JT3N) 10,200 (45.3), 16,000 (71.1) ab	993 (1,598) Mach 1.5 at 35,000 (10,668)	3 x 20mm cannon and/or 60 x 2in (5.1cm) rockets
Chance Vought V-384	34 3 (10.4)	48 3 (14.7)	310 (28.8)	17,950 (8,142)	1 x Wright J65-W-(TJ31B3) 7,600 (33.8), 11,000 (48.9) ab	828 (1,332) Mach 1.25 at 35,000 (10,668)	3 x 20mm cannon and/or 60 x 2in (5.1cm) rockets
Grumman G-97	33 4 (10.2)	43 8 (13.3)	420 (39.1) (basic without LE extension)	21,456 (9,732)	1 x P&W J57-P-11 (JT3F) 9,220 (41.0), 14,800 (65.8) ab	721 (1,160) at S/L, 912 (1,467) Mach 1.38 at 35,000 (10,668)	4 x 20mm cannon and/or 58 x 2in (5.1cm) rockets or 4 Sparrow AAM
Lockheed L-242-1	22 1 (6.7)	48 8 (14.8)	276 (25.7)	18,780 (8,519)	Probably 1 x P&W J57	1,152 (1,853) Mach 1.76 at c35,000 (10,668)	4 x 20mm cannon, RP and/or AAM?
McDonnell Model 90	35 0 (10.7)	48 4 (14.7)	305 (28.4)	21,790 (9,884)	1 x P&W J57-P-(JT3N) 10,200 (45.3), 16,000 (71.1) ab	757 (1,217) at S/L, 1,054 (1,695) at 38,000 (11,582)	4 x 20mm cannon, RP and/or AAM?
Northrop N-94	33 8 (10.3)	43 6 (13.3)	457.8 (42.6)	19,282 (8,746)	1 x P&W J57-P-11 (JT3F) 9,220 (41.0), 14,800 (65.8) ab	Mach 1.63 at 35,000 (10,668)	See text
Northrop N-94A	33 8 (10.3)	43 6 (13.3)	457.8 (42.6)	17,105 (7,759)	1 x Wright J65-W-(TJ31B3) 7,600 (33.8), 11,000 (48.9) ab	Mach 1.33 at 35,000 (10,668)	See text
Northrop N-94B	37 0 (11.3)	44 1 (13.4)	550 (51.15)	19,240 (8,727)	1 x P&W J57-P-11 (JT3F) 9,220 (41.0), 14,800 (65.8) ab	938 (1,510) Mach 1.42 at 35,000 (10,668)	See text
Northrop N-94C	36 4 (11.1)	44 11 (13.7)	550 (51.15)	20,320 (9,217)	1 x P&W J57-P-11 (JT3F) 9,220 (41.0), 14,800 (65.8) ab	Mach 1.30 at 35,000 (10,668)	See text
Grumman F8U-1 Crusader (flown)	35 8 (10.9)	55 3 (16.8)	375 (34.9)	26,000 (11,794)	1 x P&W J57-P-4A 10,000 (44.4), 16,200 (72.0) ab	Mach 0.98 at S/L, Mach 1.55 at 35,000 (10,668)	4 x 20mm cannon, 32 x 2.75in (7.0cm) RP, 2 x AIM-9 Sidewinder AAM
Supersonic All-Weather Fighters							
Grumman G-118	43 11.5 (13.4)	58 6 (17.8)	595 (55.3)	37,300 (16,919)	2 x GE J79-GE-3 + 1 x JP-4 rocket motor 5,000 (22.2)	Mach 2.0 above 35,000 (10,668)	2 x Sparrow AAM, 3 x Sidewinder AAM
McDonnell Model 98A (F3H-E)	36 9 (11.2)	55 9 (17.0)	450 (41.85)	?	1 x Wright J67-W-1 13,200 (58.7), 21,500 (95.6) ab	806 (1,296) Mach 1.06 at S/L, 1,120 (1,802) Mach 1.69 at 35,000 (10,668)	4 x 20mm cannon plus underwing stores
McDonnell Model 98B (F3H-G)	38 8 (11.8)	56 0 (17.1)	530 (49.3)	?	2 x Wright J65-W-4 7,600 (33.8), 11,000 (48.9) ab	761 (1,224) Mach 1.0 at S/L, 1,008 (1,622) Mach 1.52 at 35,000 (10,668)	4 x 20mm cannon, plus underwing stores (see text)
McDonnell Model 98B (F3H-H)	38 8 (11.8)	56 0 (17.1)	530 (49.3)	?	2 x GE J79-GE-(X24A) 9,292 (41.3), 14,346 (63.8) ab	761 (1,224) Mach 1.0 at S/L, 1,305 (2,100) Mach 1.97 at 35,000 (10,668)	4 x 20mm cannon, plus underwing stores (see text)
McDonnell XF4H-1 Phantom II (flown)	38 5 (11.7)	58 4 (17.8)	530 (49.3)	39,840 (18,071)	2 x GE J79-GE-2 15,600 (69.3) ab	Mach 2.09 at 40,000 (12,192)	(Normal load) 4 x Sparrow 3, 2 x Sidewinder AAM
Chance Vought XF8U-3 Crusader III (flown)	39 11.5 (12.2)	58 9 (17.9) (w/o pitot)	450 (41.85)	39,551 (17,940)	1 x P&W J75-P-6 16,000 (71.1), 29,500 (131.1) ab	800 (1,287) at S/L, 1,457 (2,344) at 50,000 (15,240)	3 x Sparrow 3 AAM, 4 x Sidewinder AAM
Fleet Defence Patrol Fighters							
Boeing Model 835-1	68 0 (20.7)	55 1 (16.8)	650 (60.45)	?	2 x P&W TF30-P-2 10,000 (44.4)	Subsonic	8 x Eagle AAM
Chance Vought V-434	69 3 (21.1)	56 9.5 (17.3)	?	?	2 x P&W TF30-P-2 10,000 (44.4)	Subsonic	6 x Eagle AAM, provision for 4 more
Douglas D-766/F6D-1 Missileer	70 0 (21.3)	53 0 (16.15)	630 (58.6)	50,000 (22,680)	2 x P&W TF30-P-2 10,000 (44.4)	546 (879)	6 x Eagle AAM
McDonnell Model 153A	64 4 (19.6)	61 0 (18.6)	600 (55.8)	48,896 (22,179)	2 x P&W TF30-P-2 10,000 (44.4)	Mach 0.8 at height	6 x Eagle AAM
Other Project							
Northrop Navy Interceptor	39 8 (12.1)	53 8 (16.4)	525 (48.8)	34,820 (15,794)	2 x GE J79 10,000 (44.4), 15,600 (69.3) ab	Mach 1.33 at S/L, Mach 2.0 at 35,000 (10,668)	4 x Sparrow AAM

Chapter Seven

Vertical Take-Off

Model of the two-seat AP-100. John Aldaz

Along with the great performance benefits brought about by the jet engine came the penalties of greater weights and higher take-off and landing speeds. The need for longer and stronger runways therefore increased. This was not so much a problem for land-based fighters in the USA, but for shipboard or overseas deployment it was a serious constraint. The idea of a fighter aircraft that did not need a runway therefore proved an alluring concept and it was a goal pursued by aircraft designers around the world. However, no nation put as much effort into vertical take-off and landing (VTOL) as the United States and the projects in this category would fill a book in their own right. However, this chapter describes the general path (or rather, paths) of development, illustrated with the major competitions and some of the projects.

VTOL rapidly became V/STOL (vertical/short take-off and landing) because it was realised that a very short take-off conferred much of the benefit of a vertical lift-off whilst permitting a lower thrust/weight ratio. Even so, the goal proved elusive. Around the world only one design – the British Harrier, bought by the US Marines as the AV-8 and further developed by McDonnell Douglas – was to result in an effective operational warplane during the first sixty years of the jet age. The concept was clear but the technical challenge proved enormous. Nonetheless, the designers responded with great ingenuity. Tail-sitting aircraft, thrust deflection, swivelling engines and supplementary lift engines were all explored in various different ways, and overall it proved a fascinating chapter in the evolution of fighter design.

Tail Sitters

From the American fighter point of view, in the earliest stages the emphasis was placed on the 'tail sitter', an aircraft that sits vertically on the ground with a propulsion engine supplying sufficient power to lift it without any assistance from its wings. This was arguably the simplest way to achieve VTOL capability. From 1947 both the USAF and Navy sponsored research under a program called Project Hummingbird, and from this emerged a requirement for a Navy convoy defence fighter to be deployed on merchant ships sailing to Europe. Potential targets were enemy bombers flying in at high altitude and at over 500mph (805km/h). The requirement was covered by Specification OS-122 and several projects are known to have been put forward during the middle months of 1950 in response to this document. Apart from those described Grumman also proposed its G-92 design and there was an official submission from Goodyear. Unfortunately, no details of either could be found.

Boeing

Boeing carried out an unnumbered tail-sitter study during July 1950 that does not appear to have been submitted officially to OS-122. It had a highly swept wing and tail with the vertical and horizontal tailplanes exactly the same. The four tails each had a support fixed to their tip and four 20mm cannon were mounted in the wings, two per side. Power came from a single Allison XT-40-AB turboprop with its exhaust exiting through the sides of the fuselage. Span was 56ft 4in (17.2m), length 45ft 9in (13.9m), wing area 530ft^2 (49.3m^2) and gross weight 16,000 lb (7,258kg).

Convair

Convair's design had a delta wing and also huge upper and lower vertical tails that made it look as if it had four wings. There were small wheels and struts at the end of the wing and tail tips and power came from an Allison T40 engine fitted with contra-rotating propellers. This power unit was actually a pair of T38 jet engines placed side-by-side and connected together by a gearbox.

Lockheed L-200

At least seven designs were studied by Lockheed under its L-200 designation but the first, the L-200-1, proved to be the definitive proposal. This project eventually flew and as built, there were few changes from the original drawings. As first proposed the L-200-1's estimated maximum speed had been 580mph (933km/h).

Martin Model 262

Drawings for Martin's Model 262 project give no indication of how its tail landing system would have worked. The design shows highly swept wings and three vertical fins, contra-rotating propellers and guns in mid-wing nacelles, two in each, placed outside the propeller arc. A turboprop engine was fed by air received through intakes placed above the wing roots. Span was 31ft 6in (9.6m) and length 44ft 8in (13.6m). A smaller cut-down version called the Model 262P was proposed to act as a prototype. Had it been ordered instead of Lockheed's Model L-200, Model 262 would almost certainly have been designated XFM-1.

Northrop N-63

Unlike the previous designs which, despite being tail sitters, tried to keep to conventional aerodynamic layouts as much as possible, Northrop's N-63 contender was rather more radical. In fact layouts like Convair's and Lockheed's had been swiftly rejected by Northrop's designers. The XT40-A-8 turboprop was expected to give more power than the units eventually installed in the two designs selected for manufacture and the air supply came from a pair of chin intakes. A contra-rotating propeller was again used as the only way of providing enough power without having the blade diameter too large. On the N-63 however, this diameter was still 15ft 6in (4.72m). Besides the power supplied by the propeller, the XT40 also generated 1,685 lb (7.5kN) of residual thrust. The N-63's T-tail was placed on the underside of the fuselage to balance the extended tip nacelles on the rearward position wings that housed the shock absorber landing pads (these nacelles also each contained two 20mm cannon). The horizontal tail also had a substantial span to take it beyond the limit of

Martin Model 262 (mid-1950). Stan Piet, GLMMAM

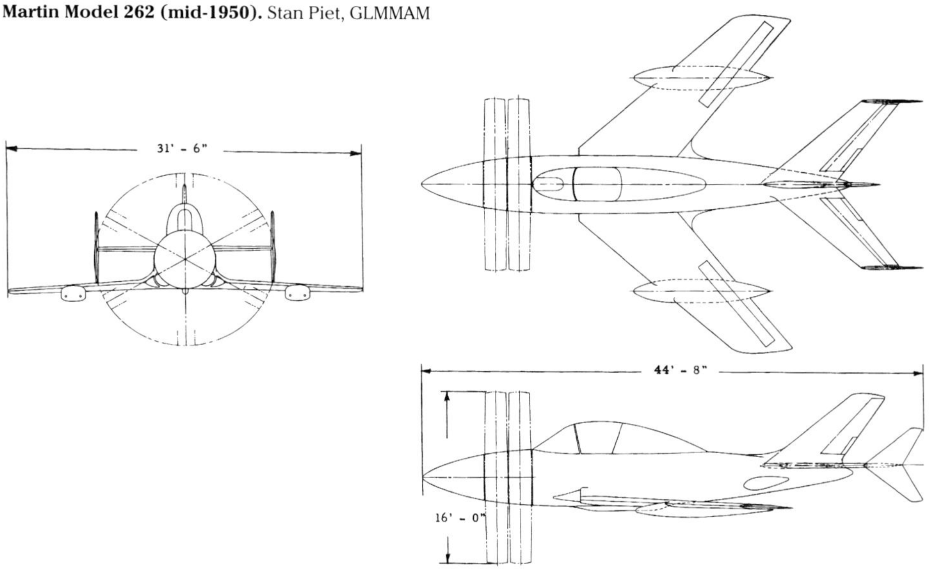

Northrop N-63. Gerald Balzer

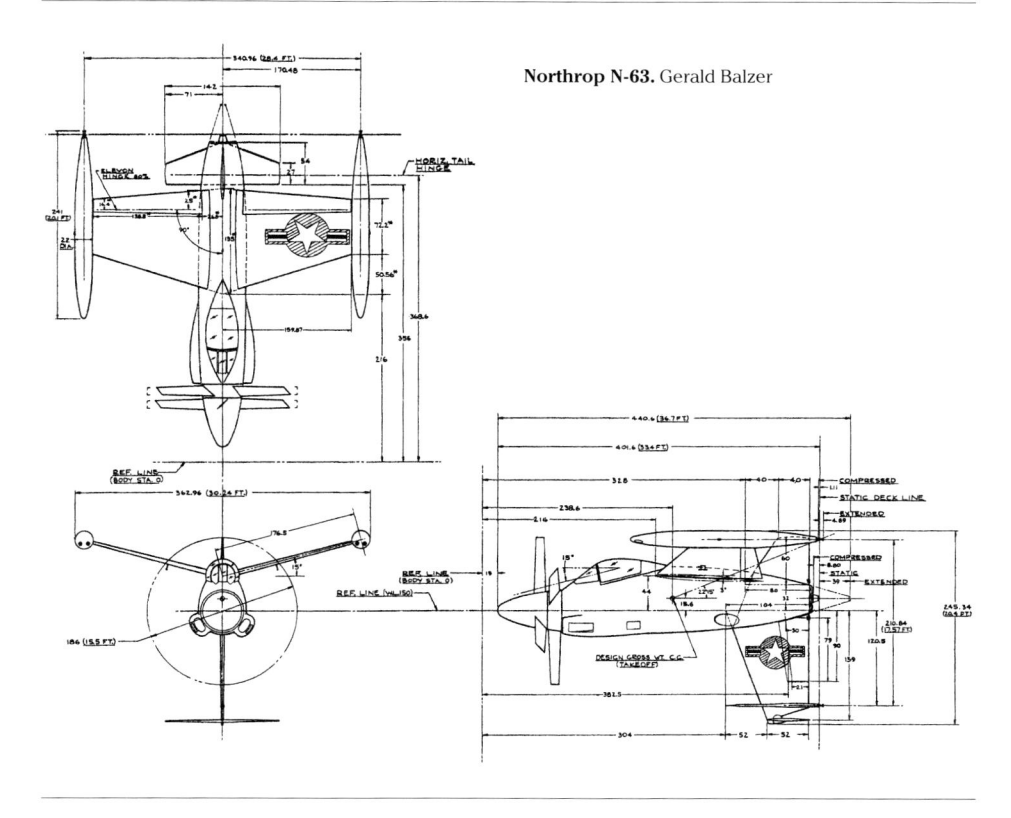

Vertical Take-Off

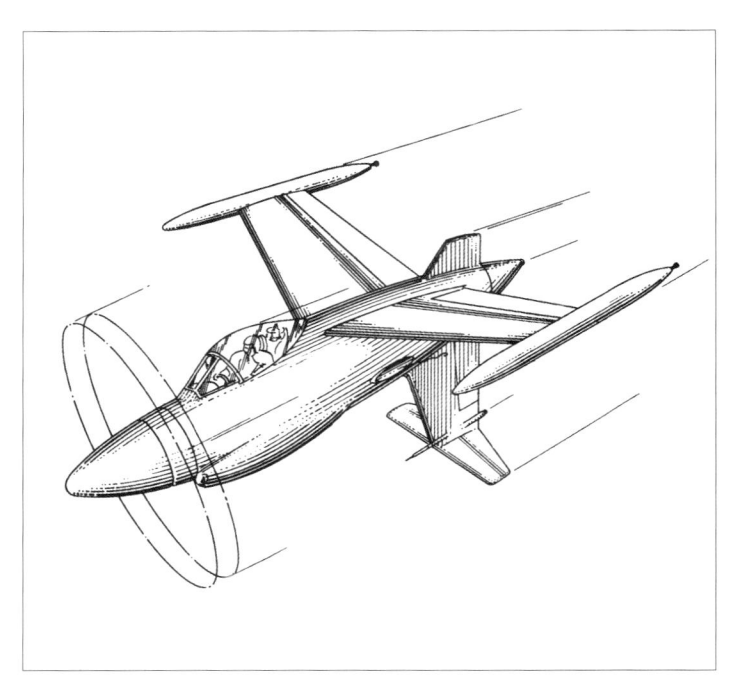

Above and right: **Artist's impressions of the Northrop N-63.** Gerald Balzer

Below: **Convair XFY-1 prototype.** Mike Stroud

Below right: **Lockheed XFV-1 prototype.** Mike Stroud

the propeller arc and a rotating seat was fitted to help the pilot's view at different attitudes. Northrop stated that the N-63 could also be used for ground attack purposes. Estimated sea level rate of climb was 11,270ft/min (3,435m/min), combat ceiling 47,000ft (14,326m) and combat radius 428nm (793km).

A scaled-down design called the N-63A powered by a British Armstrong Siddeley Double Mamba turboprop was suggested as a low-risk, low-cost development aircraft. This could be fitted with either the N-63 format tail or a more conventional arrangement, and its cockpit was placed much further aft. The N-63A could also have a fixed tricycle undercarriage fitted to allow flight testing using a normal take-off.

Convair XFY-1 and Lockheed XFV-1

An official appraisal completed in early 1951 declared that Convair's design was the best while those from Lockheed and Martin were also thought to be worth further consideration. After some additional assessment it was decided to go with Lockheed as the second design because this promised to be less expensive. Contracts for two prototypes each were awarded to Convair and Lockheed in March and April 1951, the first being designated XFY-1, the latter XFV-1, and production plans were prepared. Respective first flights were made on 1st August and 16th June 1954.

Of the two the Convair aircraft proved to be the more stable, largely because its wingspan gave greater control leverage than Lockheed's tailplane. Both aircraft achieved transitions between horizontal and hovering flight and back, but only Convair's XFY-1 succeeded in achieving a vertical take-off and landing. This was due to the excess power produced by the latter's engine, which was not available with Lockheed's aircraft. On 4th November 1954 the XFY-1 went on to achieve a complete sequence comprising a vertical take-off, a transition to normal flight and then a vertical landing on its return. This was a world's first for a VTOL aeroplane but, despite this success, the program was to go no further.

Although in concept the tail-sitter offers the simplest approach to V/STOL, it suffers from two drawbacks. Firstly, the consequences of ground effect (the downwash from the propellers, or jet thrust swirling around on take-off or landing) make control particularly difficult with this arrangement. Secondly, and harder to overcome, the lack of downward view makes any form of accurate landing virtually impossible. Things like swivelling seats, big rear view mirrors and even reference towers only partially alleviate the problem. Landing an aircraft is the most demanding phase of any flight and doing so on an aircraft carrier in strong winds with a heaving sea makes it even more arduous. Doing so facing backwards goes beyond the bounds of what is reasonable! It finally dawned on the planners that tail-sitter arrangements were unsuited to operational aircraft and so the project died. The whole program was cancelled on 16th June 1955.

Ryan X-13 and Tail-Sitter Fighter

In contrast to the Navy's turboprop-powered tail sitters, the USAF opted to examine the jet-powered possibilities. Even in the early 1950s the best thrust-weight engines coupled with a lightweight airframe offered the prospect of vertical flight. In fact a research aircraft in the X-Plane series was built and flown – the delta wing Ryan X-13 powered by a 10,000 lb (44.4kN) thrust Rolls-Royce Avon RA.28 engine. The project actually began under a Navy study requested in April 1947 as Ryan's Model 38 but it was later switched to the Air Force. The X-13 made its maiden flight on 10th December 1955. For VTOL operations the aircraft was fitted to an articulated flatbed trailer that was raised to the vertical to allow it to unhook in a tail-sitting attitude and fly away. This concept was known as a 'wire hanger'. On 11th April 1957 the X-13 took off from its trailer in its vertical attitude, transitioned to normal horizontal flight and then returned to the hover to hook-up with the trailer again, the first time this had been achieved. Two X-13s were built.

Ryan's X-13 VTOL research aircraft prototype.

Model of Ryan's delta wing jet fighter that would have made use of the company's X-13 experience. This model has a span of 11.6in (29.5cm) and length 16.1in (41.cm). Jonathan Rigutto / photo © 2005 Chad Slattery

Opposite page:

Bell D-139 with Vertiburners (26.1.55). Scott Lowther

Sketch of the D-139. Scott Lowther

Ryan used the knowledge it had gained with the X-13 to propose a tail-sitter delta wing jet fighter. This was a single-seat aircraft with a pure delta wing and near-identical upper and lower fins. On the ground the fighter sat on four sprung supports, one for each flying surface, with a single engine fed by side intakes. It never proceeded any further; presumably the limitations of tail sitter operations had already been recognised.

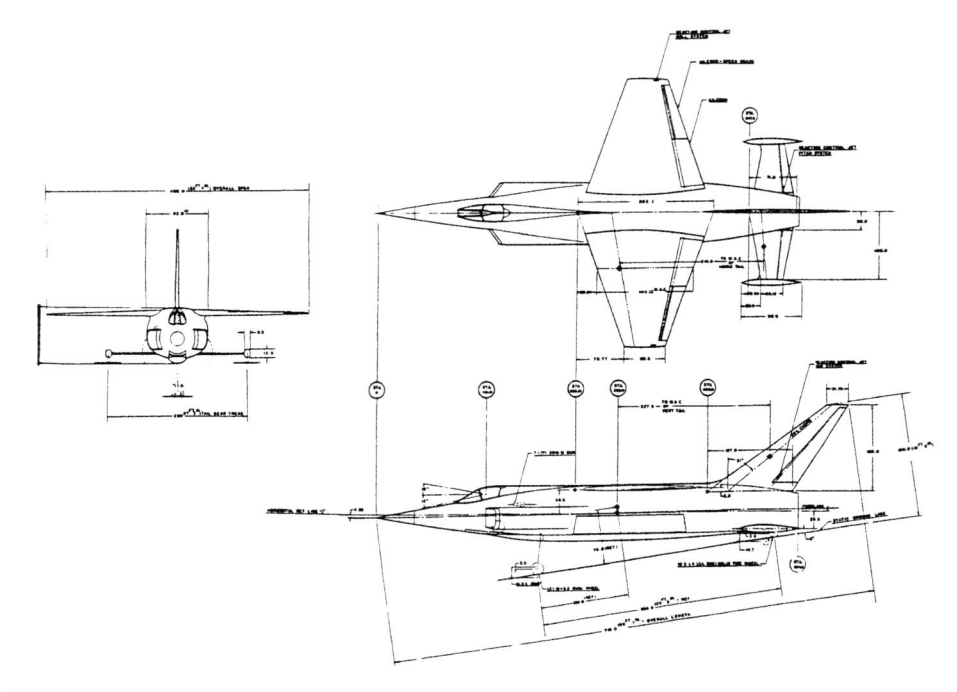

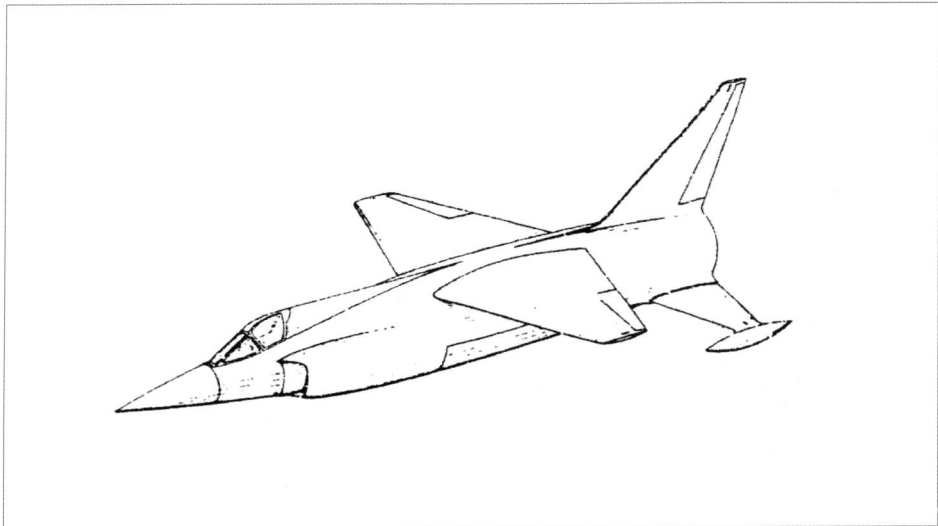

Rotating Nacelles

Another form of vertical take-off to be examined used jet engines mounted in wing nacelles that could rotate from the horizontal to the vertical to give both propulsion and downwards thrust. This would allow the aircraft to take-off and land vertically while keeping the airframe in a normal flight attitude: thus overcoming the severest limitation of the tail sitters. One company to examine this concept in considerable depth was Bell Aircraft.

Bell D-109

The design that introduced Bell to jet-powered vertical take-off was a project called the D-109-I created in November 1951. This was a relatively simple jet fighter with a straight wing but swept tailplane, powered by two Allison J33 engines, each in a rotating nacelle at the wingtip. Two rocket motors were also available to supply additional power on take-off when the aircraft was carrying bombs and rockets. Main armament was four cannon and there was an unusual undercarriage comprising a retractable skid that folded into the sides of the fuselage. D-109-I's estimated sea level rate of climb was 19,150ft/min (5,837m/min) and service ceiling 54,400ft (16,581m). The alternative D-109-II used the same airframe but introduced more advanced Allison turbofan engines in the nacelles.

Bell D-139

In January 1955 Bell completed a brochure for a V/STOL design that dispensed with rotating nacelles and replaced them with a single reheated jet. For vertical operation the engine's rear exhaust would be closed off and the thrust diverted by a large heavy valve to six nozzles that could rotate from the vertical to 45° rearwards. The idea was that when sufficient forward speed and height had been achieved the rear jetpipe could be reopened to provide forward power. The downward nozzles were each fitted with a form of afterburner, known as a 'Vertiburner'. During normal flight these would be closed off inside the fuselage by special doors. A 20mm Gatling gun was housed just above the starboard intake. The problems were the huge amount of space that the powerplant filled, which reduced the capacity for fuel and stores, and the large frontal area that reduced the D-139's speed and acceleration. It also forced the designers to fit a minimal undercarriage with the main wheels housed in tiny nacelles fitted to the tips of the horizontal tail. D-139 was expected to take 3.33 minutes to reach 30,000ft (9,144m) and its range was 514nm (952km). A further version of the D-139 was also drawn up with two J79 propulsion engines and nine J85 lift jets. The D-139 made Bell realise that it had been closer to a practical concept with the D-109, so for its next design the company returned to rotating tip nacelles.

Bell D-188

In 1956 the US Navy began a search for a deck-ready VTOL interceptor to serve aboard aircraft carriers and this crystallised into Bell's single-seat D-188 fighter-bomber project. Although tip nacelles were the key, a variety of alternative powerplants were tried before the definitive D-188A was largely decided upon by the end of 1957. The aircraft used eight General Electric J85 engines, two mounted in each wingtip nacelle that rotated to a vertical position for take-off, two more in the rear fuselage for both propulsion and hover fed by intakes placed beneath the wing, and two more just behind the cockpit in

Vertical Take-Off

Bell D-188A (1960).

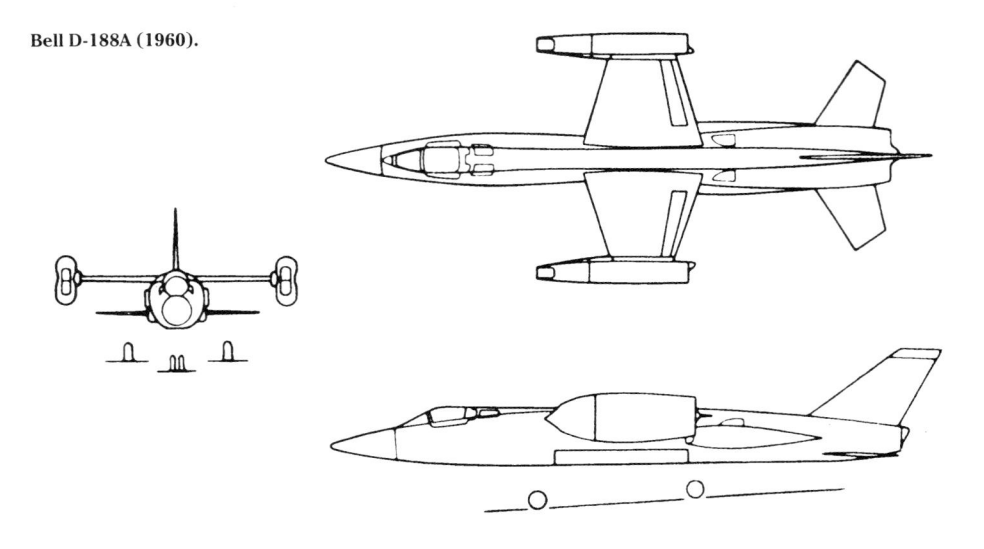

a near-vertical position to serve as lift engines. All except the vertical-mounted units were fitted with reheat and transition to horizontal flight was expected to take sixty seconds.

In June 1957 the project became a Service-funded program when the Navy began to put in money and then in December the USAF also joined the funding on a 50/50 basis, the Air Force planning to operate the type as a tactical fighter-bomber. By the end of January 1958 the Navy had designated the aircraft F3L and on 29th of that month the Air Force was requested to officially designate the D-188A as YF-109. However, this was disapproved on 14th February and a further request for XF-109, made on 3rd October, was turned down on 6th February 1959. The airframe was area-ruled and three Sidewinders for the interception role or two Bullpups for attack duties could be carried in an internal bay; there was also the possibility of carrying stores on underwing pylons. The D-188A had short knife-like wings and a tricycle undercarriage. In supersonic interceptor mode it carried 9,840 lb (4,463kg) of internal fuel, estimated sea level rate of climb was 60,000ft/min (18,288m/min) and cruise radius flying at Mach 0.9 and 35,000ft (10,668m) was 600nm (1,111km).

A lack of money soon forced the Navy to pull out but the project continued in Air Force hands, the final layout being established in early 1959. Differences from the late 1957 version were principally a wider rear fuselage plus a modified tailplane. An impressive and detailed full-size mock-up was built that was reviewed by Service personnel in February 1959. Progress was clearly being made but the Air Force began to express concern over the D-188A's cost and complexity, not the least aspect of which was the requirement for the pilot to control eight engines. Convair had been selected to partner Bell in a planned production program but in February the USAF stopped its funding, in part because it was realised that joining together Mach 2+ performance with VTOL capability was just a step too far. Bell now kept the project going with its own money and revealed the mock-up to the public on 5th December 1960. Work, however, was finally terminated in 1961. Although extensive wind tunnel, jet impingement, aeroelastic and structural testing had been completed, the mock-up was as far as the project would go. At one stage the mock-up was painted in Navy colours.

Manufacturer's model of the Bell D-188A.
George Cox

Lift Jets

A further approach to VTOL operation was to employ lift jets: small engines with very high thrust ratios designed to be used only during take off and landing. By the mid-50s the engine manufacturers were already beginning to offer such powerplants and the concept looked attractive. Indeed, not just in America but around the world, more VTOL designs have been produced using this idea than any other.

In fact the competition for practical VTOL or V/STOL fighters was to come down to a contest between lift jets and vectored thrust. The latter, as employed by the Harrier/AV-8, simply deflects the thrust of a large propulsion engine to provide lift for take-off and landing. The disadvantage of lift jets, of course, is that for most of the flight they are dead weight. However their advantage is that they are optimised for their purpose, as can be the propulsion system that is employed alongside them. In contrast a deflected thrust engine is optimised for neither. It has to bear all of the load – and considerable wear and tear – needed in the hover, and also be used for both efficient cruising and high-speed combat. That is why a deflected thrust aircraft like the Harrier, which has a power-to-weight ratio way beyond most contemporary fighters, has never had supersonic capability. Like most areas of aircraft design, it is a matter of compromise. Given the profusion of lift-jet proposals, just two projects have been chosen here to illustrate the work of American design teams.

Chance Vought and Republic VTOL Fighters

The archives at Vought contain an illustration of an unidentified swept wing sea-based VTOL fighter with three lift jets placed just behind its tandem two-seat cockpit plus two propulsion engines. Thrust from the latter was deflected downwards for the hover with extra air being supplied from doors placed on the upper fuselage between the wings. The accompanying artwork, produced in 1969, shows that the general layout of this aircraft was conventional, but it is not known if the project was produced against any official requirements.

This project from Republic had three pairs of rotating engines spread across its fuselage and inner wing. Project number and identity are unknown.

Chance Vought artwork from 1969 showing the proposed 'Sea-Based VTOL Fighter'.

Vertical Take-Off

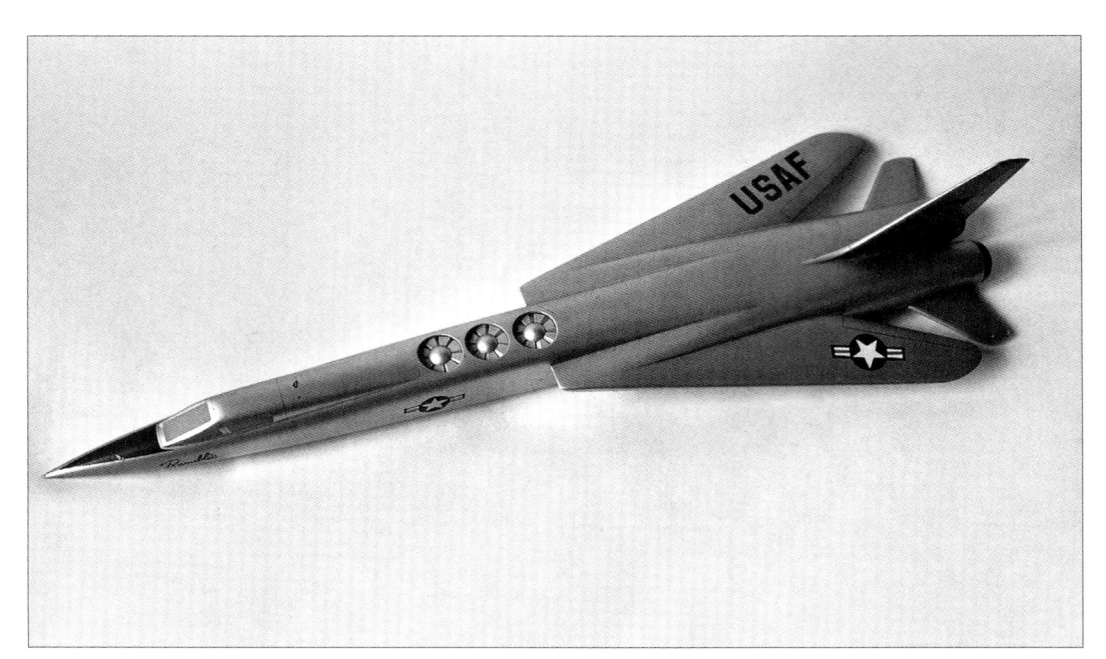

Left: **Model of the unidentified Republic V/STOL aircraft. Model span is 7.8in (19.8cm) and length 23.1in (58.7cm).** Larry McLaughlin

Below: **A variation of forcing the thrust downwards comes from this Northrop model of its N-251 thrust vectoring short field interceptor project. The deflection was to be accomplished by using a set of rotating doors in the 'jetpipe' beneath the middle fuselage, the air coming from a chin position 'letter-box' inlet.** John Aldaz

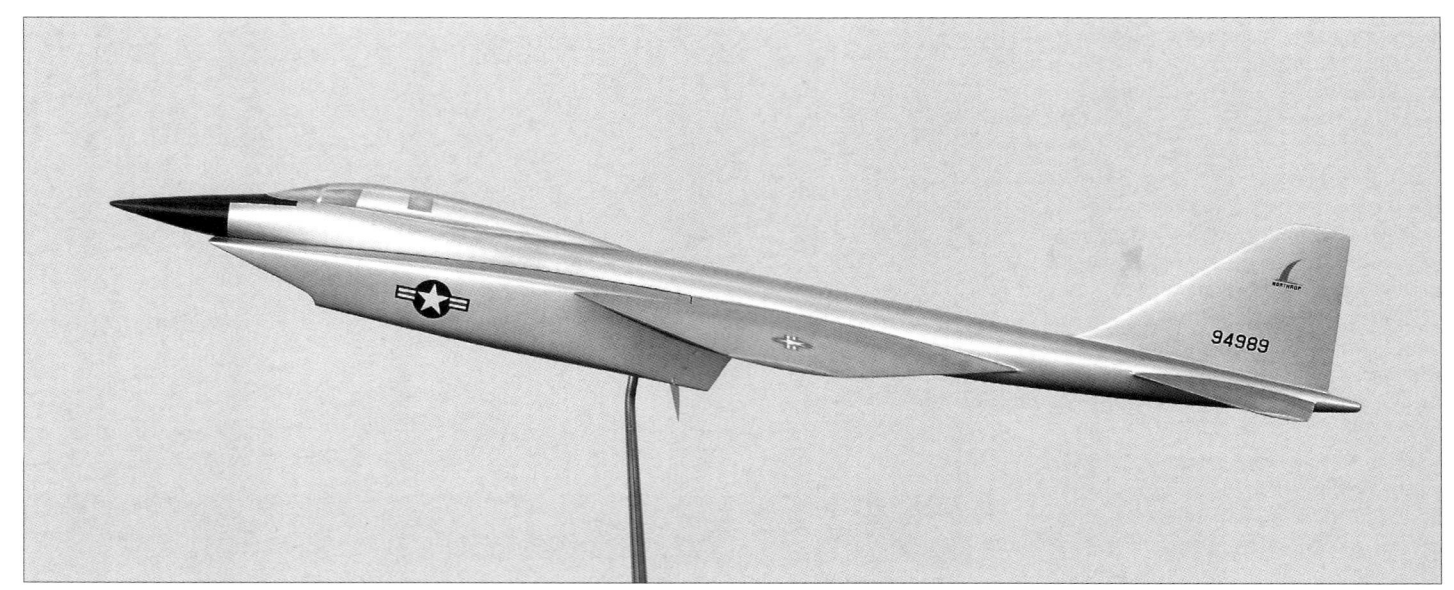

144

American Secret Projects: Fighters & Interceptors

The same can be said for an unnumbered Republic project, only discovered in model form, which probably comes from the first half of the 1960s. This design was produced for the Air Force but, apart from a much higher sweep angle on the wings, its general layout was quite similar to Vought's naval proposal. It was a single-seater with three lift jets placed more towards the middle of the fuselage. Box intakes fed two side-by-side propulsion units. In many respects this pair of designs can be considered as typical of the type of research undertaken into V/STOL during the late 1950s and through the 1960s.

Republic AP-100

Another form of jet lift was shown by Republic's AP-100 fighter-bomber design of 1959/1960, which may have been an entry in a USAF competition for an all-weather supersonic nuclear strike fighter. Three large lift-fan engines were mounted in the centre fuselage with a set of six General Electric J85s, three per side, at the back, all of the air coming from narrow 'letter-box' intakes. After take-off special valves would be set to divert the engine thrust backwards for level flight. The engine arrangement made for a wide fuselage but there was a small delta wing and twin fins. Top speed was estimated to be 1,500mph (2,414km/h), ceiling 75,000ft (22,860m) and gross weight 38,000lb (17,237kg). There were two versions; the single-seat AP-100A and two-seat AP-100B.

Schematic layout of the Republic AP-100 showing the lift-fan system (1959/1960).

Model of the single-seat Republic AP-100. Model span is 14in (35.6cm) and length 28.4in (72.1cm).

Model of the two-seat AP-100 that shows the longer forward fuselage of this version. John Aldaz

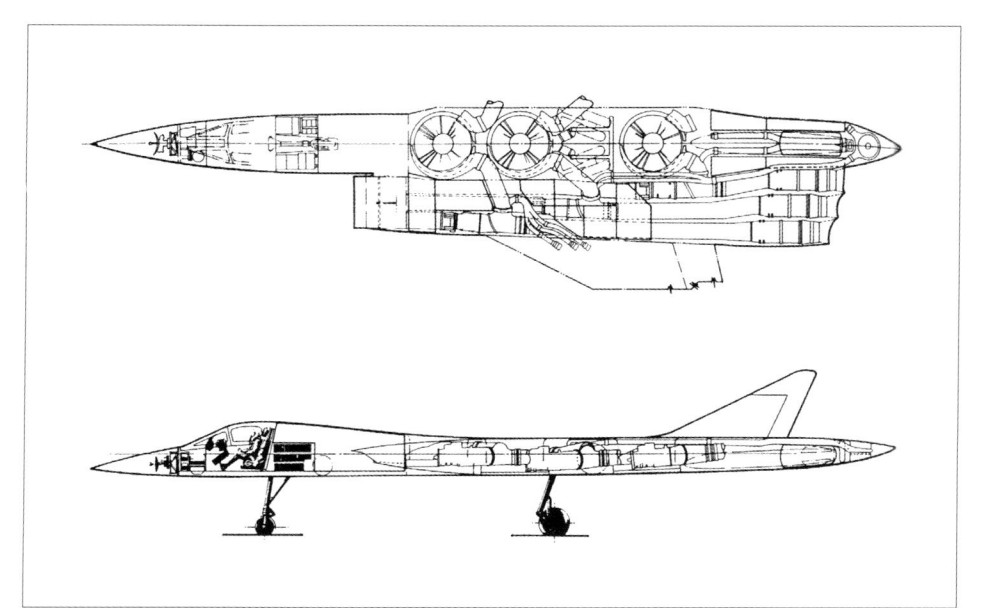

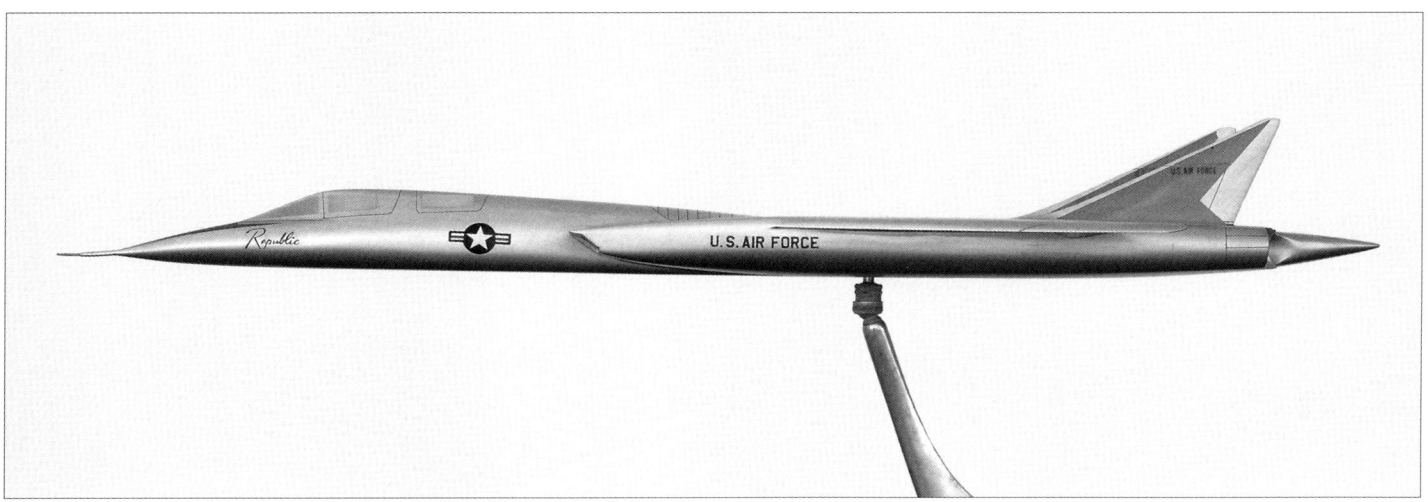

Vertical Take-Off

Sea Control Ship V/STOL

From the point of view of actually planning the use of vertical take-off and landing capability, the climax was probably reached with the competition for a fighter/attack type to equip the air-capable Sea Control Ship or SCS. This was intended to be a smaller and much cheaper vessel than the huge carriers then in service with the US Navy: in short, a modern-day equivalent of the wartime escort carrier. It would be relatively small (of the order of 10,000 tons or less) and less capable than a normal carrier but was intended to counter smaller threats and to operate generally where the US Navy's conventional carrier air was not available. This was one of several projects initiated by Admiral Zumwalt, the new Chief of Naval Operations, and the ship would need V/STOL aircraft since there were to be no catapults or arresting gear. In November 1971 industry was solicited directly for some innovative proposals for two general types of SCS aircraft, a fighter/interceptor/attack type and a long-endurance sensor carrier (though in practice no design for the latter was selected). Proposals were to be limited to just twenty pages and delivered to the MAT-03 Prototype Office. Any further data supplied would not be used.

In fact during 1971 a new system of procurement had been introduced, called the 'Prototype' program, in an attempt to reduce the cost and bureaucracy of new defence equipment while also encouraging further competition. Specification and requirement documents were to be avoided and industry would get more freedom to offer novel and innovative ideas. This was less formal than the usual 'request for proposals' and was intended to allow the 'speedy selection' of a winning design. The SCS competitions were the first potential Navy aircraft programs to be covered by this approach and, vindicating the approach, eleven fighter/attack submissions were received. They embodied several forms of V/STOL. Besides those listed there was a lift-augmentation design from de Havilland Canada called the DHC P-71-30, the Stinger project from San Diego Aircraft Engineering or Sandaire (this design proved to be the lightest proposal at 17,377 lb (7,882kg), and the VAK-191B Mk.3 project from VFW Fokker in Europe (a prototype of which was actually flown in 1971). Two of the documents consulted by the author, from Boeing and Grumman, are dated June 1972 due to the fact that in June and July of that year Naval Air System Command (NAVAIR) followed up with an informal competition for V/STOL aircraft, and some of the design teams continued with their original studies.

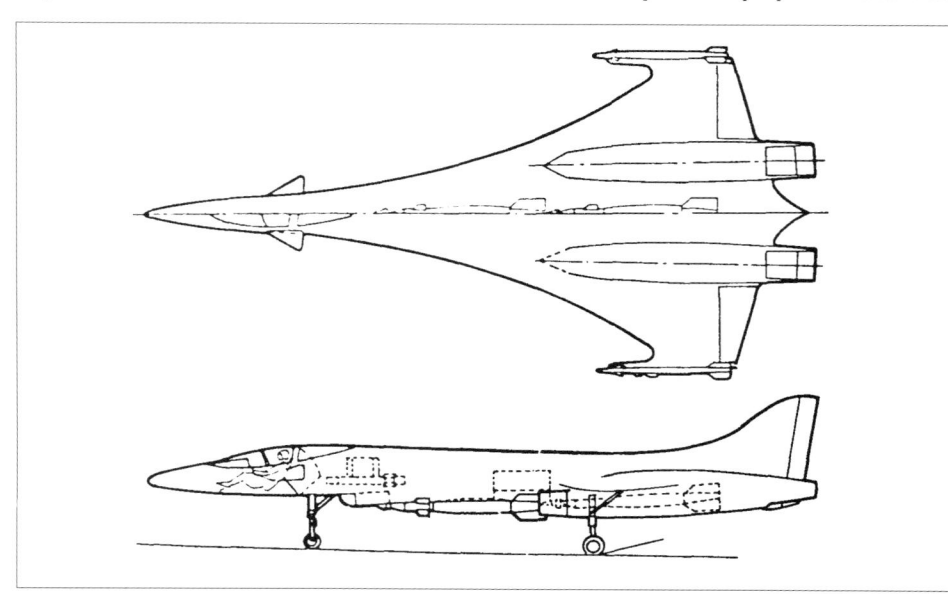

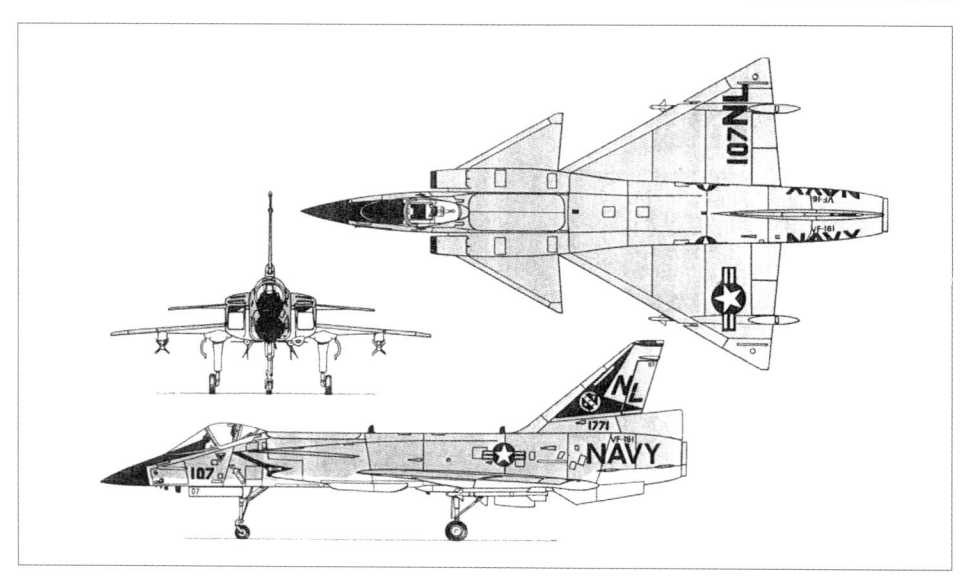

Boeing Model 908-535/D-180

Boeing's Model 908-535 was a 'Nutcracker' type, that is a wire-hanger with the aircraft 'landing' onto a mechanised vertical launch pad/gantry but also tilting its nose to allow the pilot to remain in a horizontal attitude throughout for better visibility. Other companies had looked at such concepts and Boeing's design was known as a VATOL, for vertical attitude take-off and landing. A rather exotic creation, the single seat 908-535 had a beautiful semi-delta blended 'ogee' wing/body with sweep angles between 80° down to 55° and thickness/chord ratio 3.5%. There was no horizontal tailplane but there was a small canard, level with the pilot's seat, set at a 30° angle of dihedral. Two General Electric YJ101 engines were mounted beneath the rear of the wing with vectored thrust nozzles that would give roll and pitch cruise control; the latter were supplemented by yaw-power modulation. They exhausted through two-dimensional nozzles with moveable plugs for vectoring the thrust through the flight regime.

In its earliest form this design had no landing gear but, to allow conventional landings, a widely spaced tricycle undercarriage was later introduced, with the main legs outside the engine nacelles. Two Sidewinder missiles were mounted on the wingtips while a pair of

Boeing Model 908-535 as at June 1972 seen carrying Sidewinders and laser-guided bombs. In its earliest form this design had no undercarriage. Scott Lowther

Convair Model 200A as at 15th January 1973. San Diego Aerospace Museum

Artist's impression of the Convair 200A in US Navy colours.

Model of the Convair 200A. John Aldaz

stores could be carried in tandem on fuselage points. The options included Sparrow III AAMs for intercept duties and McDonnell-Douglas AGM-84 Harpoon air-to-surface missiles or laser-guided bombs for attack. An M-61 cannon was housed behind the cockpit. Internal fuel totalled 7,400 lb (3,357kg) but another 1,200 lb (544kg) was available in auxiliary tanks. It was expected that the prototype would be ready to fly three years after go-ahead. Of all of the many different approaches to vertical flight, this 'Nutcracker' concept was surely the most operationally challenging.

Convair Model 200A

The Model 200A's planform comprised a delta with a small delta canard which continued Convair San Diego's involvement with this type of wing. This offered manoeuvrability, structural strength and supersonic performance while the canard also provided lift and reduced trim drag. Power came from one Pratt & Whitney JTF22A-30A/F401-PW-400 propulsion engine served by lateral, variable ramp intakes and a vectoring nozzle, plus two lift engines aft of the cockpit for which air was supplied through doors in the top of the fuselage. These doors were only opened when the lift engines were operating. For the transition from vertical to horizontal flight, exhaust doors in the bottom of the fuselage could be closed slowly to vector their exhaust progressively aftwards.

The two lift jets, mounted on the centreline and tilted slightly rearwards, eliminated lift engine-out roll and provided 'get-home' capability on one lift unit (STOL landing capability with one unit out). Yaw control would be achieved by rotating the lift/cruise engine's three-bearing nozzle from side to side and for roll/pitch there were single wing-mounted nozzles fed by bleed air and mechanically driven from the ailerons. Convair declared that the latter provided roll-control power that was superior to other V/STOL aircraft. The 200A was laterally and directionally stable to a nose-up angle of 30°. For the hover the tailpipe rotating nozzle was turned vertically downwards to its maximum setting to balance the lift jets.

The canard and elevons were linked with a fly-by-wire system to provide a highly manoeuvrable destabilised 'control-configured vehicle' or CCV, but Convair stated that the Model 200A would became a positively

Vertical Take-Off

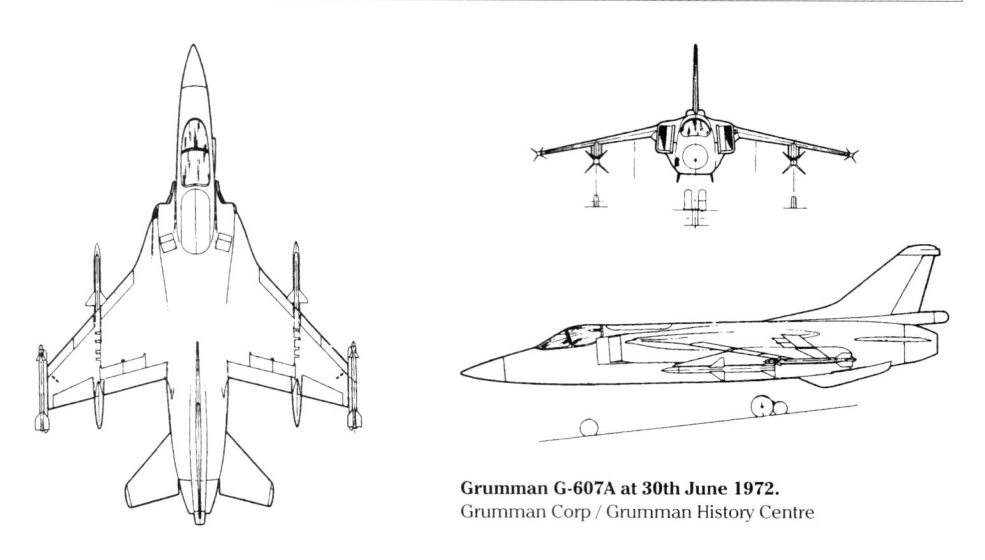

This view of the 200A model reveals the underside detail including ventral fins and cannon pod.
John Aldaz

Model of the Convair 200A in a US Marines colour scheme.

stable aircraft upon any failure of the primary control system. The wing-mounted roll/pitch nozzles were placed at the end of two underwing pylons that were intended to carry Sidewinder or Sparrow AAMs, while two more Sparrow or Harpoon missiles or two bombs could be taken on hardpoints on the bottom corners of the middle fuselage beneath the wing. A M61 Gatling cannon was carried in a pod beneath the forward fuselage and the internal fuel load was 5,875 lb (2,665kg). First flight would be thirty months after starting. Convair also undertook a study for a conventional take-off and landing (CTOL) derivative called the Model 201 in both single and two-seat versions. This was to be capable of all-weather operations and, by weight, was 74% common to the V/STOL aircraft.

Fairchild Republic FR-150

Fairchild Republic proposed a design that would use the lift plus lift/cruise engine arrangement. The FR-150 would have standard XJ99 lift units mounted forward in the fuselage and these would swing out to provide lift and thrust vectoring. The lift/cruise unit was a Pratt & Whitney F100 using a three-bearing swivel nozzle. Overall this was a small, conventional single-seat aircraft with a swept wing and aft tail that made use of conventional materials and fabrication techniques. Its unique feature was the use of lift engine thrust vectoring to provide roll and yaw control, and thrust modulation to provide pitch control. A total of 5,100 lb (2,313kg) of fuel was carried internally. From start to first flight would take twenty-six months.

Grumman Design 607 and 607A

Grumman's G-607 offering of December 1971 used a very similar powerplant arrangement to the Convair 200A with two tandem lift jets behind the pilot angled slightly rearwards and a single lift/cruise engine. However, this project differed in that both lift units employed a blocked bifurcated exhaust with two side-mounted single swivel nozzles. A prototype would fly thirty-six months after go-ahead.

A much more thorough investigation and refinement was completed and offered by Grumman on 30th June 1972 as the 607A and the brochure compiled for that has been the principal source of information here. No significant changes in the overall planform had been made from the original 1971 proposal

Grumman G-607A at 30th June 1972.
Grumman Corp / Grumman History Centre

Model of the Grumman G-607A.

Underneath view of the Grumman G-607A carrying Harpoon missiles and drop tanks for attack duties.
Grumman Corporation / Grumman History Centre

but certain elements, including the supersonic performance and mission radius, had been improved. For example a pod-mounted gun had been used initially but by June this had been replaced by an internal mounting in the port wing root. Also a combination bicycle/outrigger landing gear with twin main wheels was now introduced with the outriggers housed in an extension of the already existing missile pylon. A thinner and slightly larger supersonic wing and smaller empennage were also brought in together with refinements to the lift engine exhaust and lift/cruise engine's vectoring nozzle.

The JTF22A-30B/F401-PW-400 lift/cruise unit offered 15,650 lb (69.6kN) of thrust for VTOL, 16,130 lb (71.7kN) on dry propulsion and 27,500 lb (122.2kN) with reheat. The direct lift engines were a creation of Grumman and were designated GLE-607A. For pitch and yaw control there were two small swivelling nozzles, one under the nose directly behind the radome and a second in a pod extended rearwards beyond the fin root. Roll control was available from two pairs of small nozzles placed in the wing just inside the tip pylon and air for all of these was bled from the lift jets. Heavy mid-wing pylons were available to carry Harpoon or Sparrow missiles while inner hardpoints were in place to take external fuel tanks. Sidewinders could be carried on wingtip shoes and the wings could be folded at the mid-wing pylon to give a folded span of 21ft 10in (6.65m). Model 607A could carry 8,525 lb (3,867kg) of internal fuel plus another 4,080 lb (1,851kg) in the two drop tanks. A conventional take-off/landing derivative was offered as part of the December 1971 proposals but by June 1972 this had been dropped.

LTV V-517

Two single-seat designs were forthcoming from Vought Aeronautics, the V-517 and V-520. The V-517 utilised the lift plus lift/cruise concept, this time with a modified Pratt & Whitney JTF22A-30B/F401-PW-400 main unit and two Allison J99 lift engines. However, two planned prototypes would get three lift jets (5,580 lb [24.8kN] Rolls-Royce RB-162-81s) and one Pratt & Whitney JTF10A-42A/TF30-P-8 lift/cruise unit. Vought had calculated that using these alternative engines and leaving out the armament would save $20 million in the prototype program, the substitutions being made with no change to the external lines of the aircraft.

In almost every respect the V-517 was considered to be conventional. It had a high wing and low horizontal tail with its wing geometry identical to a wing defined during a current Vought fighter study. Leading edge sweep angle was 35° and thickness/chord ratio from root to tip 5% down to 4%. This wing had been subjected to extensive tunnel testing and, although optimised for efficient supersonic flight, it provided satisfactory levels of buffet-free manoeuvrability and STOL performance. High-lift devices consisted of full-span leading edge droop and inboard trailing edge flaps, and drooped ailerons. Lateral control in cruise mode would come from upper surface spoilers and the drooped ailerons and a single rudder and one-piece horizontal tail completed the moving surfaces. An M61 cannon was mounted on the lower left hand side of the aircraft and two Sparrow or Harpoon missiles could be carried on short fuselage pylons. Each of two 1,500 lb (680kg) capacity wing stations was capable of carrying a variety of ordnance or a 150gal (682lit) fuel tank and a centreline wet store station was also available for a 300gal (1,364lit) external tank or up to 2,500 lb (1,134kg) of ordnance. Internal fuel totalled 7,059 lb (3,202kg).

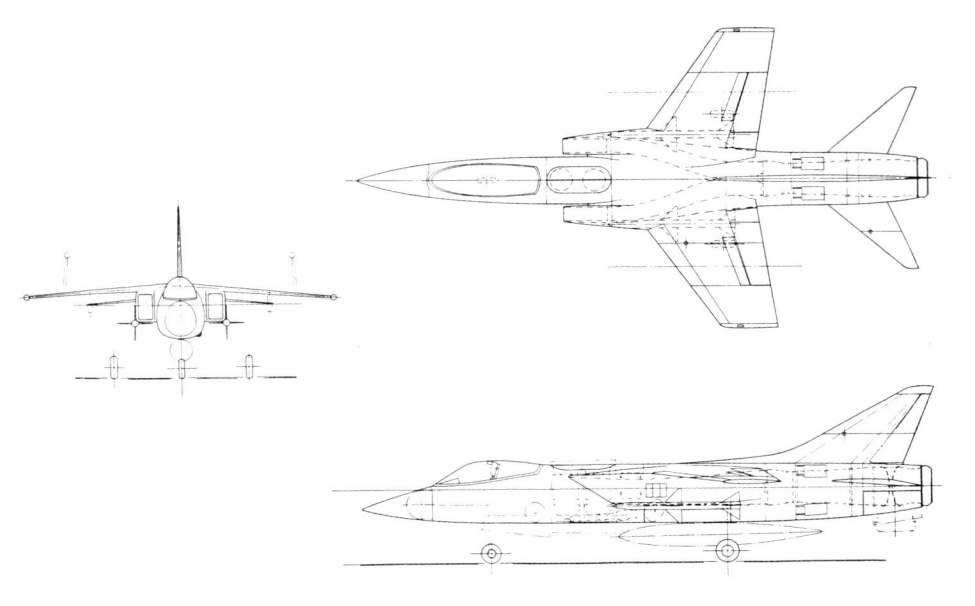

Left: **The Vought V-517 design in its production form with two lift engines (29.12.71).** Dick Atkins, Vought Archive

Bottom left: **A sketch of the proposed unarmed V-517 prototype with three lift jets (12.71).** Dick Atkins, Vought Archive

Bottom right: **Drawing showing the Vought V-520 with its 'fold-away' lift jets in operation (15.12.71). These were positioned in the same place as the V-517's lift jets.** Dick Atkins, Vought Archive

McDonnell Douglas Model 262/AV-8C

McDonnell Douglas proposed to modify the vectored-thrust AV-8A Harrier attack aircraft to incorporate a new supercritical wing, Pegasus 15-02 engine, new inlets and updated avionics. Internal fuel was 6,500 lb (2,948kg).

North American Rockwell NR-356

North American's proposal, the NR-356, was an entirely different animal that utilised a form of vertical lift generation called the thrust augmented wing. Basically there was a single very powerful turbofan, the exhaust from which was ducted to a set of ejector flaps inside both the wings and canard surfaces before being vectored downwards through a series of slotted nozzles. The ejector augmenters in each wing and canard were composed of primary nozzles located in a centre ejector above each of the diffuser flaps. The flaps would operate like a Venetian blind and create a low-pressure area within the augmenter that, it was predicted, would induce a large volume of additional secondary airflow to come in from above the lifting surfaces through the open gap. This resulting mixture would effectively create 50% more vertical thrust than would have been available from the engine alone. As such the engine itself would only need to be two-thirds the size of an equivalent direct lift

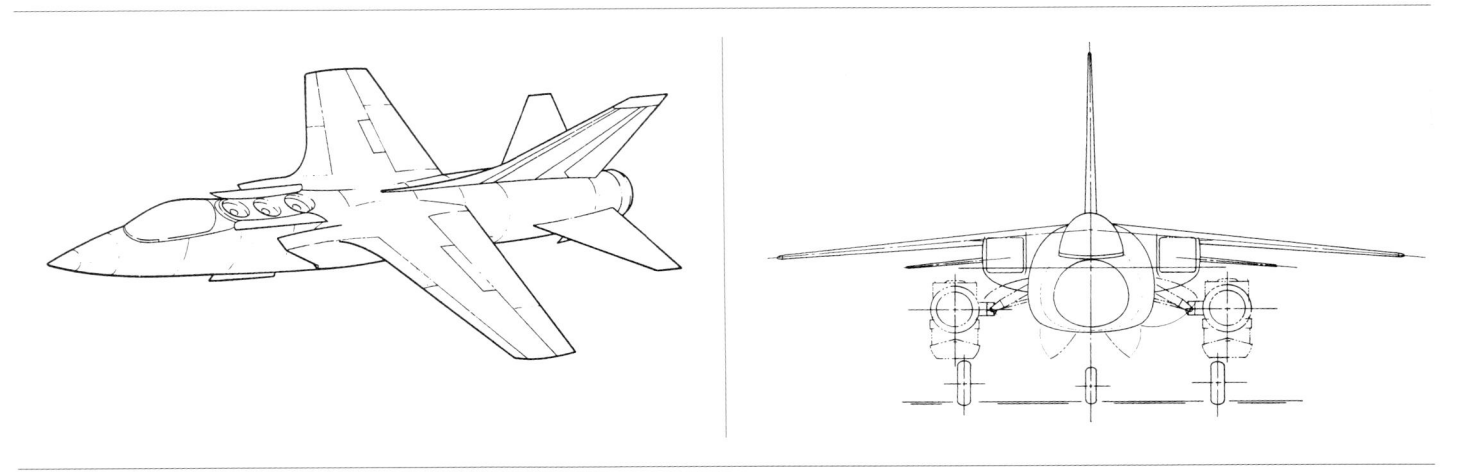

The wing structural box had been made as wide as possible to provide an integral fuel cell and the main box had front and rear spars and five interspars. Most of the wing was to be built in 7075 aluminium alloy while the V-517's fuselage was to be a conventional semi-monocoque structure. Again the basic material was aluminium, supplemented by titanium in the elevated temperature areas adjacent to the engines. The lift engines were mounted vertically on the centreline ahead of the aircraft's centre of gravity. The lift-cruise unit had a three-bearing swivel tailpipe and a convergent nozzle that was capable of canting downwards 100° for lift and rolling laterally +/-15° (at full downward deflection) for yaw control. Side-hinged swing-open closure doors covered the lift engine intakes and exhaust and the cruise engine nozzle in cruise flight. In vertical landing mode the lift/cruise engine nozzle would be deflected downwards and the lift engine inlet and exit doors opened. For the fighter mission the V-517's radius of action was given as 300nm (556km). Vought declared that a go-ahead decision made in February 1972 would bring a first flight in June or July 1974.

LTV V-520

Essentially the V-520 was the same aircraft as the baseline V-517 except for three things. Firstly, it had two 'swing-out' XJ99 lift engines instead of three fixed lift units (the lift/cruise unit was unchanged). Secondly, in the cruise-mode or 'clean' condition the swing-out engines were stowed side-by-side horizontally in the fuselage. And thirdly, the wing area was increased slightly. Vought stated that the fixed-engine V-517 was less complex and had a slightly lower weight than the similar V-520 with its extendable lift engines. Some high-speed performance was sacrificed in this second design and the internal fuel load came out less at 5,513 lb (2,501kg).

unit. During the transition to forward flight after a vertical take-off the augmenter flaps would gradually close as the forward movement increased, with the exhaust now directed rearwards to provide forward thrust through a large jetpipe.

Research into STOL capability had started at Rockwell in 1970 and a canard V/STOL configuration was established that summer. The resulting NR-356's canards were placed low on the fuselage, the wing was set in a high position and there were twin tail fins and rudders spaced well apart on the outer wings (on the subsequent XFV-12A the fins were mounted at the wingtips). The canard arrangement provided an optimum planform for distributing the vectored thrust, the four augmenters being placed around the aircraft's centre of gravity. Large side inlets and a rather frail-looking tricycle undercarriage were used while the forward fuselage including the cockpit came from a Douglas A-4 Skyhawk attack aircraft. Air-to-air weapons comprised a single 20mm M61 cannon beneath the fuselage level with the canards, Sidewinder missiles on wingtip rails and Sparrows beneath the fuselage; a selection of air-to-ground stores could also be carried on fuselage hardpoints.

The advantages listed for the thrust augmented wing were many and included mechanical simplicity and multiple use of the control surfaces. In cruise flight the aft diffuser flaps when fully retracted would become conventional trailing-edge flight controls, just like a normal aerofoil. Also the forward and aft diffuser flaps on the wing could be deflected for use as speed brakes. The wing and canard flaps together supplied pitch control; those just on the wing alone would give roll control. In the hover differential modulation of the diffuser/flap setting could vary the magnitude of the thrust vector from each augmenter to provide attitude and height control. Pitch in the hover was given by differential lift from the canard and wing augmenters, and roll by differential lift from just the wings. Yaw control would be possible by tilting the wing flaps in opposite directions. Due to the temperature of the air passing through the augmenters the flaps were to be made from titanium honeycomb while the rest of the wing would be built in conventional light alloy.

Despite having had no input into what sort of aircraft the contractor might need, NAVAIR was given the job of officially evaluating the proposals. Each design team had stated that its project was expected to be supersonic, and in fact Boeing and North American were predicting cruise at Mach 2 without reheat. The assessment began on 3rd January 1972 and sixteen days later recommendations were made that an official V/STOL fighter competition should begin under the designation XFV-12A. Soon afterwards the MAT-03 Prototype Office recommended that the North American NR-356 fighter/attack design should fulfil the requirement.

However, NAVAIR had concluded that a lift plus lift/cruise V/STOL design would be the best solution for acquiring the earliest production aircraft, although the lift engine would still need to be developed first. NAVAIR's team also stated that the NR-356's weight would be higher, and the augmented thrust lower, than Rockwell's estimates, to the point that the concept would be unacceptable. Its choice put the Convair 200A first, Fairchild-Republic's FR-150 second and LTV's V-517 third with the NR-356 in a category of 'not recommended', although it was thought that the latter's jet flap system merited further study. Convair's design offered 'significant advancements in both operational capability and V/STOL technology' and combined low risk, straightforward conventional design and fabrication techniques and a credible performance. With the exception of its largely undefined control scheme, Fairchild Republic's offering was thought to represent a low technological risk and its aerodynamics were acceptable for the attack mission; however, a high wing loading would require redesign if the type were to perform acceptably as a fighter. The swing-out lift engine format was considered a worthwhile concept for prototyping as a back-up to NAVAIR's first choice of Convair.

Among the others 'not recommended' in their original forms, the McDonnell Douglas AV-8C failed to provide any significant additional operational capability and, although its speed, altitude and payload were all improvements over the AV-8A, they fell far short of the recommended candidates. Grumman's proposal was the heaviest and, since a 'prototype of the prototype' was planned, it was also expected to be the most expensive. Its claimed Mach 2 top speed appeared questionable in view of the use of a supercritical wing aerofoil while other candidates offered the same or better capability, at lower risk and less cost. LTV's V-520 and Fairchild's FR-150 both used swing-out lift engines but the latter was thought superior in nearly every respect while all of the fixed lift engine designs offered superior operational potential over the V-520.

Boeing's design was felt to be a highly imaginative and unique in concept, being intended entirely for VTOL operations. It was small and light and, without a normal undercarriage, had a potentially superior performance. The major drawback and highest risks were all derived from its unique design features. There was almost no support equipment currently available for this type of aeroplane, which in itself would entail a considerable development effort, and there appeared to be little potential for the D-180's use by other services (including the Marines). Use on a large carrier would require extensive redesign and overseas sales appeared non-existent.

Returning to Rockwell's design, the physical problems it created were expected to be enormous and the proposal did not establish a credible solution. Large hot gas ducts presented a highly vulnerable area to combat damage while stores carried on the wings or canard would be inhibited. Stability and control in hovering were expected to present a high risk factor and there was no credible basis for the claimed high performance. With various additional points NAVAIR considered this project to be a very high-risk program and a complete redesign was thought desirable to correct the many deficiencies; it could however become a pure research vehicle.

Nevertheless Rockwell got the work, in part because of the company's current lack of orders for military aircraft. It had missed out on the F-14 and F-15 competitions (Chapter Nine) and was now looking at lower cost lightweight supersonic fighters along with the increasing interest in STOL capability – the Sea Control Ship fighter fitted both categories. On 29th March 1972 Admiral Zumwalt announced that separate research and development financing would be used to fund the XFV-12A, although some money would also be available to continue the Convair 200A at a slower pace.

North American Rockwell XFV-12A

During 1972 more detailed analysis showed that the aircraft's weight would be significantly higher than first estimated. There were other flaws concerning the weight and performance and NAVAIR again predicted that the design had no capability for service use and presented a high risk. It could almost take off with no payload, with limited fuel on board. Nevertheless two prototypes were ordered on 18th October with an initial conventional flight to take place in November 1974 and a first VTOL flight during the following February. Progress however was very slow, the program fell substantially behind schedule and the first prototype was not rolled out until 26th August 1977.

Artwork picturing the XFV-12A hovering above its carrier, the Sea Control Ship. Scott Lowther

Hover rig testing of the full prototype undertaken at Langley during 1978 found that the predicted 50% of augmented thrust was actually just 19% from the wing and 6% from the canards. The principal reason was large losses in thrust in the internal ducting so that the total available thrust came to just 75% of the aircraft's weight; a figure that ensured a vertical take-off was impossible. After the demise of the Sea Control Ship concept the XFV-12A was reclassified as a VTOL technology development project, but the program proved a complete failure and was eventually closed in 1981, despite efforts to improve the ejector/augmenter system. Projected performance figures had included a combat radius of 575 miles (925kg). Since it never flew the XFV-12A has been looked on as something of a disaster and a waste of time, but in fact some parts of the program were, according to Andrews, Murphy and Wilken, 'done very well, with noteworthy results achieved'.

As noted earlier, in mid-1972 NAVAIR held its own competition and the lift jet plus lift/cruise engine concepts, as already described, generally showed that the weight penalty for carrying lift engines was less than that created by the thrust augmented wing. Convair's contract awarded in mid-February 1973 for its Model 200A to continue as a back-up to the XFV-12A did not proceed very far. The Pratt & Whitney F401-PW-400 afterburning turbofan was a more powerful navalised development of the USAF's F100 used in the F-15 Eagle (Chapter Nine) but it too was eventually cancelled. Finally, a model has been found for a twin-cruise engine version of Rockwell's project called the FV-12A fighter/attack aircraft. This appears to be a proposed production variant and carries Sidewinder AAMs on the outside of the tip fins plus a selection of bombs on additional fuselage pylons.

The author took the opportunity to ask the famous British test pilot John Farley for his opinions on the Sea Control Ship projects. Few could be better qualified to judge such projects, because he spent many years leading the work on the development of the Harrier and Sea Harrier V/STOL aircraft. The intention was to get a view of the practicality and potential of some of the proposals, given not just an expert view but with the advantage of a further thirty or more years of actual VTOL operations and experience. However, VTOL aeroplanes are not that simple. He writes:

Looking at past aircraft projects with a view to judging how successful they might have been had they actually entered service is an interesting exercise. Often the only information available is a three-view drawing, or perhaps photographs of a model, plus the knowledge that it was not actually built and flown. Seldom do we know for certain the detail of why it was abandoned and the list of possible reasons is a long one and many will be non-technical. Funding, politics, inter-service rivalry and the changing world scene, to say nothing of commercial factors inside the design company, can all result in the end of a project. Despite this some design ideas were undoubtedly abandoned for straightforward technical reasons which only became apparent once more detailed work was carried out. Aerodynamics, Structures, Materials and Engine issues can all cause a team to call a halt themselves – or perhaps change direction and consider a different approach to meeting the original requirement.

If all this were not enough then 'brand new' revolutionary ideas can surface to further muddy the waters. An example of this came in the 1950s when the notion of vertical take-off and landing for jet aircraft started to be considered in earnest. The advantages of operating site flexibility that VTOL would pro-vide were clear for all to see. The big fixed runways essential to operate conventional jet aircraft represented easy targets for the upcoming breed of enemy missiles. At sea, without VTOL, ever larger aircraft carriers were needed and became fine examples of having all of one's eggs in one basket.

In the last half century, if we exclude standard helicopters, an astonishing forty-five VTOL/VSTOL/STOVL projects have actually made it to flight test. Of those only three went into service and today only one, the Harrier, is still in service. Having been associated first hand with many of the teams doing this work for over forty years and having been fortunate to fly full time on the Harrier development programme for nineteen of those years, I was very pleased when the author asked me to comment on whether some of the US V/STOL projects he covers in this book 'would have worked'.

Regrettably my response to him was that I don't have enough information or expertise to make that call. Religious leaders are endowed with faith and belief that makes the world a very simple place for many of them but engineers cannot rely on such advantages. Despite this I feel it will be useful to help you come to your own view if I talk you through some of the V/STOL issues that my experience has taught me are important.

Top of the list is whether the design is likely to be able to hover and transition to and from flying on its wings. To do this not only must you have more thrust than weight when in 'free air' but also in 'ground effect'. The 'free air case' (which implies a height of between 50 and 100ft [15 and 30m] so that the engine efflux is not bouncing off the ground and rebounding all around you) may be self evident but the much lower or 'in ground effect' case where the aircraft is on or close to the surface is much more complex.

Arguably there are two main issues about flying in ground effect. The easier one to solve by good design is living with the general buffeting and self-induced turbulence that is disturbing your aircraft. By far the harder issue is the topic known as recirculation. This is about stopping any hot exhaust gases ever making their way into the intake of the engine or engines. This is real go/no go stuff and any significant chance of such a happening will kill a project dead. Both the turbulence and recirculation issues will be easier to solve if the exhaust gases are relatively slow and cool but they will become extremely difficult to deal with when they are hot and fast. If augmen-

tation (use of reheat/afterburning) is needed to get the necessary thrust during a vertical take-off or landing then please don't ask me to work on the project.

To help visualise this issue imagine you are at an air show and watching the latest wonder fighter about to roll down the runway. It will have several feet of fire emerging from its tail. Now imagine the same aeroplane standing on its tail for a VTO with its tail a few feet clear of the ground. What will those sheets of flame blasting out at enormous speed do to the ground surface, the underside of the aeroplane and the (ha!) rubber tyres on the wheels? The Harrier immerses itself (plus tyres) in its own exhaust for several seconds on VTO. It can do this because the rear nozzle exhaust is relatively cool and low velocity. This is why the Harrier is not and never could be supersonic in other than a dive. Its engine does not blow out fast enough to go much more than subsonic airliner speeds. However even the benign engine in the Harrier does not accept swallowing its own efflux through recirculation and careful piloting techniques are needed to avoid this happening during VTO or VL.

For those not familiar with jet engine design may I try and explain the issue a little deeper? If you want to fly at supersonic speeds you must have a high exhaust velocity. This is not at all the same thing as saying you need 'a lot' of thrust to fly supersonically, it is the nature of the thrust that matters. Thrust is calculated by multiplying together two numbers. One is the amount of 'Mass flow' (the sheer amount of air that is going through the engine – which can amount to literally tons per minute) which is written as M and the other the 'Exhaust Gas Velocity' (the increase of speed in the exhaust provided by the engine) which is written as V and is in miles per hour or metres per second or whatever units you are used to for speed. So thrust is just MV. Now a 20,000lb (88.9kN) thrust engine as fitted to a Harrier has a big M number but a small v number. The 20,000lb thrust engine fitted to an F-16 (say) has a small m but a big V. The two numbers when multiplied together both give 20,000 but only one uses a high V. As yet we do not know how to get a big V without making the gas very hot. Perhaps you are starting to realise why I was not rushing to judge the likely success of the projects in this book. It is quite difficult to look at a model and decide how hot and fast the exhaust would be!

Model of the proposed Rockwell International FV-12A project with a twin-cruise engine powerplant and carrying a substantial weapon load. Model span is 9.5in (24.0cm), length 14.0in (35.5cm). Jonathan Rigutto / photo © 2005 Chad Slattery

Next is the nature of the lift system installed. For example if it includes a batch of fuselage mounted vertical engines (even if they have acceptable exhaust characteristics) won't they take up a huge amount of space in the fuselage? This means much less space remains for other things like fuel, systems and weapons. Sure it may fly but will it have the internal volume left to turn it into a military aircraft that can compete with aircraft that are not carrying around these engines? What about all the holes in the top and bottom of the fuselage? Won't these lead to a relatively heavy and inefficient structure to carry through the tail loads down the remaining solid bits?

Clearly putting the engines on the wingtips is good news regarding most of the points considered so far but in this case what happens if one stops? Not much comes down faster than a jet lift aeroplane that is upside down.

One can hardly cover the topic of jet V/STOL design in a few paragraphs but I think you may be starting to see why so few of the ones that were tested went into service, let alone why so many ideas never made it into flight test. Surely the surprising thing is that any V/STOL aircraft made it into service – not that so many failed to make the grade!

The End of US V/STOL Design Programs – for the Time Being

The XFV-12A proved to be a hugely challenging program, like so many other proposals for V/STOL aircraft around that time. A 1970s Hawker Siddeley Aviation report commented, 'expert opinion does not give this concept much hope and US financing would appear to have ceased. The promise, as with so many other V/STOL concepts, has disappeared in practice'. As noted, the Sea Control Ship was never actually built, being killed off by Congress during the Fiscal Year 1975 budget review, and the US Navy continued with its large carriers. The aircraft that these carriers would operate from the 1970s onwards would be the Grumman F-14 Tomcat and later the McDonnell-Douglas F-18 Hornet, which are described in the final chapters of this book.

The quest for a high-performance VTOL or even V/STOL fighter thus proved just a step too far for the design capability of the time. In the 1950s vertical flight appeared to be just around the corner, but this was not to be the case. Around the world only one design emanating from the era covered by this book, the Harrier, was turned into a successful operational warplane. This proved the viability – and value – of the concept in three conflicts. It would take until the early 21st century for technology and design capability to move on and the prospect of further operational V/STOL aircraft to emerge.

When the Lockheed-Martin F-35 Joint Strike Fighter enters service with American, British and other air arms, it will be the first supersonic V/STOL fighter ever to achieve production status. In the 1960s the vectored thrust format employed by the Harrier was shown to be the best available method of achieving V/STOL, but it was not the best solution ever possible. The method used by the F-35 – shaft-driven vertical lift fan plus vectoring lift/cruise engine – has many advantages but that is because the technology has moved on. Nonetheless, the early quest for jet fighters that needed no runways demonstrated the enormous ingenuity of US aircraft designers and produced many fascinating proposals.

Vertical Take-Off

V/STOL Fighter Studies – Estimated Data

Project	Span ft in (m)	Length ft in (m)	Gross Wing Area ft² (m²)	Gross Weight lb (kg)	Engine lb (kN)	Max Speed / Height mph (km/h) / ft (m)	Armament
Tail Sitter Convoy Fighters							
Convair XFY-1 Pogo (flown)	27 8 (8.4)	35 0 (10.7)	355 (33.0)	16,250 (7,371)	1 x Allison YT40-A-6 5,850hp (4,362kW)	474 (763) at S/L, Est 610 (981) at 15,000 (4,572)	4 x 20mm cannon, 46 rocket projectiles (not installed)
Lockheed XFV-1 (flown)	30 11 (9.4)	36 10 (11.2)	246 (22.9)	16,221 (7,358)	1 x Allison XT40-A-6 5,850hp (4,362kW)	580 (933) at 15,000 (4,572)	4 x 20mm cannon, 48 RPs (not installed)
Northrop N-63	30 2 (9.2)	33 5 (10.2)	250 (23.3)	15,454 (7,010)	1 x Allison XT40-A-8 6,825 (5,089kW)	608 (978)	4 x 20mm cannon + RPs
Rotating Engine Nacelles							
Bell D-109-I	31 8 (9.7)	47 1 (14.4)	?	19,640 (8,909)	2 x Allison J33-A-16 7,900 (35.1) + 2 x 6,500 (28.9) rocket motors	659 (1,060) at 35,000 (10,668)	4 cannon + up to 4,000 lb (1,814kg) of stores
Bell D-139	33 4 (10.2)	59 7 (18.2)	?	20,960 (9,507)	1 x P&W J75	682 (1,096) at 35,000 (10,668)	1 x 20mm Gatling gun
Bell D-188A	23 9 (7.2)	58 7 (17.9)	194 (18.0)	23,917 (10,849) (interceptor)	6 x Gen Elec J85-GE-5 3,850 (17.1) ab + 6 x Gen Elec J85-GE19 3,015 (13.4)	Mach 2.3 at height	3 x AIM-9 Sidewinder AAM
Sea Control Ship Projects							
Boeing 908-535/D-180	25 5.5 (7.8) (with tip missiles)	49 5.5 (15.1)	435 (40.5)	24,150 (10,954) VTO	2 x General Electric YJ101	Mach 2.8 at 70,000 (21,336)	1 x M61 cannon, 2 x AIM-9L Sidewinder AAM, 2 x AIM-7E/F Sparrow AAM or 2 x Harpoon ASM or 2 x bombs
Convair Model 200A	27 10 (8.5)	51 1.5 (15.6)	?	25,000 (11,340) VTO, 31,090 (14,102) CTO	1 x P&W F100 (JTF22A-30A) 26,800 (119.1) 2 x Allison XJ99 11,200 (49.8)	Mach 2.0 at height	1 x M61 cannon, AIM-9L Sidewinder, AIM-7E/F Sparrow AAM, AGM-84 Harpoon ASM or bombs
Fairchild Republic FR-150	26 (7.9)	53 (16.2)	?	25,000 (11,340) VTO, 33,560 (15,223) CTO	1 x P&W F100 (JTF22A-30A) 26,800 (119.1) 2 x Allison XJ99 11,200 (49.8)	Mach 2.2 at height	1 x M61 cannon plus missiles
Grumman G-607	31 6 (9.6) (w/o tip missiles)	51 7.5 (15.8)	365 (33.9)	30,160 (13,681) VTO, 37,353 (16,943) CTO	1 x P&W F401 JTF22A-30B 16,130 (71.7), 27,500 (122.2) ab + 2 x GLE-607A 11,525 (51.2)	Mach 1.2 at S/L, Mach 2.0 at 40,000 (12,192)	1 x 20mm cannon, 2 x AIM-9 Sidewinder AAM, 2 x AIM-7 Sparrow AAM or AGM-84 Harpoon ASM
LTV V-517 (Production aircraft)	28 8.5 (8.8)	53 0 (16.2)	271 (25.2)	19,950 (9,049) VTO, 27,480 (12,465) CTO	1 x P&W F401 JTF22A-30 27,575 (122.6) ab + 2 x Allison J99 8,510 (37.8)	Mach 1.92 at height	1 x 20mm cannon, 2 x AIM-7F Sparrow AAM or AGM-84 Harpoon ASM
LTV V-520	28 8.5 (8.8)	53 0 (16.2)	281 (26.1)	22,690 (10,292) VTO, 28,237 (12,808) CTO	1 x P&W F401 JTF22A-30 27,575 (122.6) ab + 2 x Allison J99 8,510 (37.8)	Mach 1.72 at height	
McDonnell Douglas AV-8C	30 (9.1)	44 (13.4)	?	20,450 (9,276) VTO, 24,250 (11,000) CTO	1 x RR Pegasus 15	Mach 1.2 at height	
NA Rockwell NR-356/XFV-12A	28 6 (8.7)	43 11 (13.4)	293 (27.2)	19,500 (8,845) VTO, 24,250 (11,000) CTO	1 x P&W F401-PW-400 30,000 (133.3) ab	Mach 2.7 at height	1 x M61 20mm cannon, 2 x AIM-9 Sidewinder AAM, 2 x AIM-7 Sparrow AAM or various ASM weapons

Chapter Eight

Boat Fighters

The EDO 150 model shown in take-off configuration with the hydro-ski extended.
Cradle of Aviation Museum

This book has concentrated largely on the main lines of fighter development, between 1945 and 1978, examining the approaches of both the Air Force and the Navy. However, outside of these two mainstreams there are two other lines of fighter development that are worth examination. The previous chapter looked at one, vertical take-off and landing; the other is the concept of the flying boat fighter.

Large piston-powered flying boat patrol aircraft and bombers had been used extensively during the war and, with the advent of the jet engine, several studies were undertaken in various countries looking at their potential successors. Flying boat fighters had never attracted the same interest but, on the face of it, there was an added attraction of such machines in the jet age. With their faster operating speeds and generally heavier weights they were much less suited to the grass fields than their piston-engined predecessors had routinely used. Their ability to take off from seas, lakes and rivers also meant that they could be deployed far more quickly and widely. At least that was the theory.

The United Kingdom was the one nation outside the USA that looked seriously at jet-powered boat fighters. In 1947 the Saunders-Roe company based on the Isle of Wight flew the SR/A.1 fighter, the world's first jet-powered flying boat. This company had special expertise – and clearly great belief in flying boats, and was to go on to produce the magnificent, albeit commercially unsuccessful, Princess ten-engined airliner. Their fighter flew well and generated much interest but never attracted a production order. A more advanced follow-on design, the P.121, was proposed in 1950 using a hydro-ski for take-off. However, this was never built and it was to be an American design, the Convair Sea Dart, that would become the highest performance flying boat fighter ever produced. Along with the Martin Seamaster patrol bomber, it was one of only two water-based aircraft ever to be flown beyond the speed of sound.

Convair Skate

The American manufacturer who looked at flying boat jet fighters most closely was Convair at San Diego. One aspect of the company's research, from 1946 onwards, examined a feature called blended hulls, which would allow an aircraft to ride low in the water and let its wings contribute to the buoyancy. A series of studies included a subsonic seaplane night fighter design called the Skate that was prepared against Navy Specification OS-116. This requirement was issued on 21st September 1948 and the work proceeded throughout 1949. The Skate would have been a big aircraft with a two-man crew: the radar operator sitting to the right of, and slightly below, the pilot. The January 1949 drawings show a single offset canopy for the pilot only, but a progress report completed by Convair on 28th October 1949 revealed that this had been replaced

American Secret Projects: Fighters & Interceptors

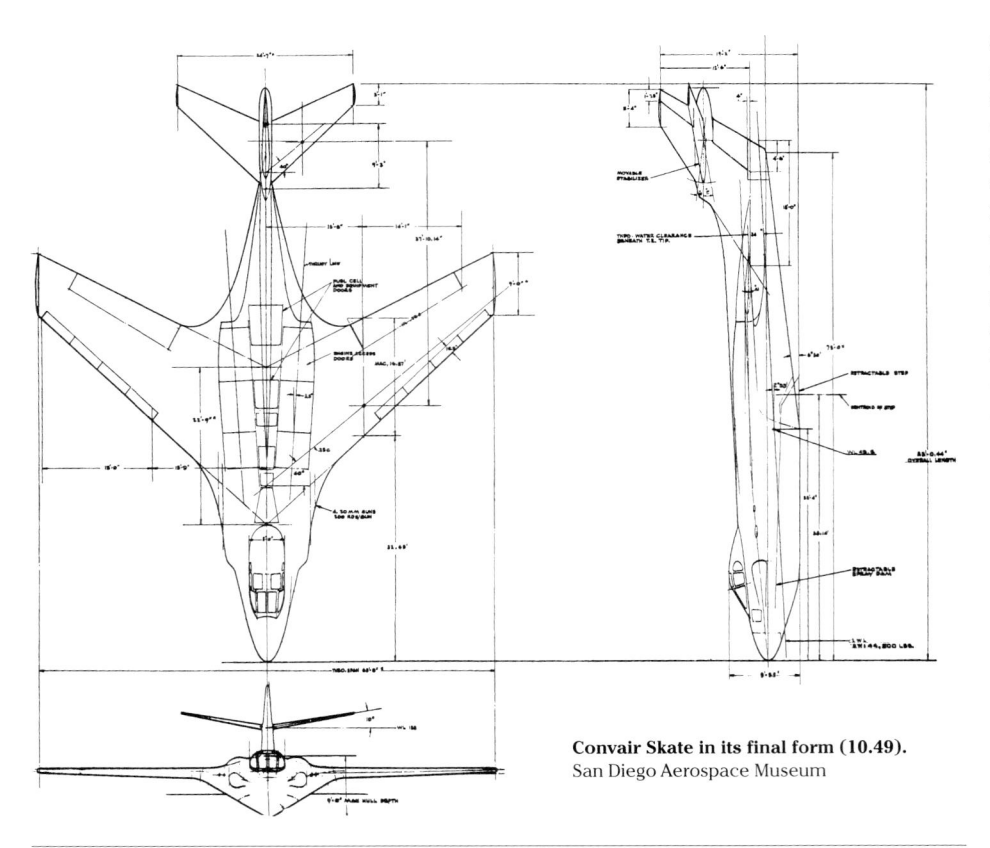

Convair Skate in its final form (10.49). San Diego Aerospace Museum

by a larger framed canopy covering both crewmembers. In its very earliest form the Skate also had a V-tail but this was also later replaced. The data quoted below is taken from the October 1949 update.

The Skate was designed to operate from sheltered water (5ft [1.5m] waves maximum) with handling and servicing from seaplane tenders or submarines. Two Westinghouse XJ40-WE-10 engines were located on each

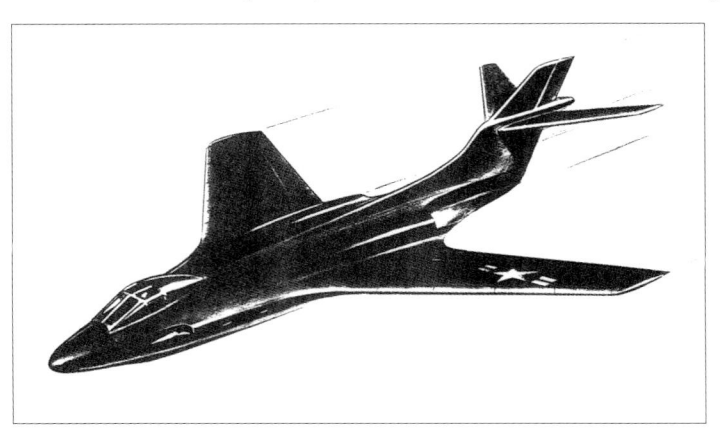

Artist's impression of the Convair Skate in its final configuration. San Diego Aerospace Museum

Another impression of the Skate. Note the gun ports outside the intake. San Diego Aerospace Museum

side of the hull with air intake ducts well forward. Riveted aluminium construction would have been used throughout and the hull bottom was formed by conventional plate stringer construction supported by spaced frames, although stainless steel plating and frames were to be used in the afterbody adjacent to the jet blast. There was a hull step, vent and chines, the step and chines (spray dams) being retractable to eliminate the drag normally associated with hull bottoms. A water rudder was provided to give manoeuvrability during taxying and all of the fuel was housed in two fuselage tanks within the hull.

The wings were swept 40° on the quarter chord line and leading edge slats were available for low-speed handling while power operated all-metal ailerons would furnish lateral control. High-strength aluminium alloy was used in the construction of the wing spars, bulkheads and stringer components with heavy skins and flush-head riveting. Four 20mm cannon were installed in pairs in the wing roots outboard of the engines. The empennage comprised a single fixed vertical fin, a rudder and an all-movable horizontal stabilizer and both horizontal and vertical surfaces would use metal spars and stressed skin construction. At its gross take-off weight the Skate's estimated maximum sea level rate of climb was 22,800ft/min (6,949m/min) and time to 35,000ft (10,668m) 2.62 minutes. Take-off time in calm water was given as fourteen seconds. At a flight weight of 38,940 lb (17,663kg) the service ceiling was 52,500ft (16,002m) while the combat radius at an average cruising speed of 496mph (798km/h) at 40,000ft (12,192m) plus was 400nm (741km).

The Skate was never built but Convair was asked to continue its research into this fighter for some time, the type being designated YS-1 and overlapping the competition described below. In 1951 NACA undertook a hydrodynamic investigation of a 1/13th-scale model of a 'Skate 7' layout equipped with twin hydro-skis in the mid-fuselage position for use either on water or snow. The full-size version showed a span of 62ft (18.9m), length overall 70ft (21.3m), wing area 960ft^2 (89.2m^2) and gross weight 33,000 lb (14,969kg). The potential take-off and surface performance of this project appeared satisfactory with estimates suggesting that twenty-one seconds would be needed to get off on full power.

Boeing Night Fighter

Boeing also undertook several studies for a flying boat jet-powered night fighter from late 1948 into early 1949 under its Model 486 designation, but it appears that these received no wind tunnel testing and were never submitted to the Navy as formal proposals.

Boat Fighter Competition

In due course a full competition was held to find a jet-powered boat fighter. However, it seems that there may have been just two competitors. The competition itself appears to have taken place after the Navy had revised its requirements in 1950 and requested a smaller and faster aircraft. At the beginning Mach 0.95 had been the required minimum top speed. It is understood that Curtiss-Wright submitted a design proposal against Convair's project but no details are currently available.

Convair Model 2

Convair's Model 2 was a twin-engined fighter that was intended to utilise a hydro-ski. Research had shown that retracted waterplaning skis would give a fighter a fuselage body that could be almost as clean as a conventional fighter. In addition a take-off by a high-speed aircraft on water was possible using such a ski or skis extended under its fuselage like seaplane floats. As the aircraft's speed increased the skis would push the fuselage upwards clear of the water thus allowing it to skim the surface until take-off. The bonus was that, once retracted into a relatively small space as an integral part of a smooth rounded underbody, the skis offered a lot less drag than either floats or a full boat hull. This feature, combined with a jet powerplant and more advanced hull designs, suggested that it might be possible to design a boat fighter offering a performance on a par with current land-based jet fighters.

Convair's studies also used a delta wing, which had been adopted for its concurrent Air Force interceptor proposal that eventually became the F-102, and a blended hull. It is understood that the initial drawings for the project, later designated Y2-2, were prepared in late 1948. At that stage there was no hydro-ski.

Convair Sea Dart

Convair's study was selected as the competition winner. Two prototypes were ordered on 19th January 1951 as the XF2Y-1 and the first and only 'XF' to fly became airborne on 9th April 1953 after the type had been named Sea Dart. This aircraft was fitted with 3,400lb (15.1kN) thrust Westinghouse J34-WE-32 engines. However, the second aircraft to fly had more powerful Westinghouse XJ46s and became the first YF2Y-1. Four more 'YFs' were ordered, although only two were completed because the second pair never received their engines. Twelve production machines were also ordered, but after one YF2F-1 was lost in a display and problems had

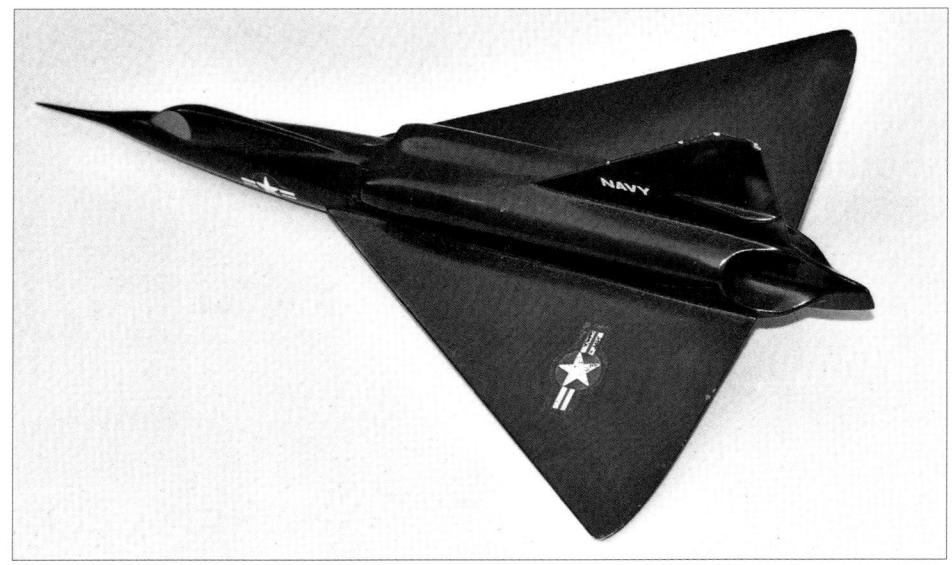

Model showing an early layout for Convair's Model 2 fighter. Model span is 10.0in (25.5cm) and length 16.5in (41.8cm). John Aldaz

arisen with the hydro-skis, the Navy lost interest. By March 1954 the production run had been cancelled. But before this, on 3rd August 1953 one 'YF' made history by breaking the sound barrier in a gentle dive: the first flying boat or seaplane to do so. Despite the cancellation of the production order, test flying continued until April 1957, with the original twin skis eventually being replaced by a single large ski. In the 1962 re-organisation, long after retirement, the type was surprisingly redesignated the F-7.

E G Stout, an engineer working with Convair, reported in April 1954 that the Sea Dart was not designed as a seaplane in the accepted sense; the aim was for a 'Panto-based' machine that could be treated in the same manner as a land-based fighter. The aircraft would be fully serviced on land and would simply taxi down the beach or ramp into the sea for take-off. In fact it could taxi in and out of the water on its wheels at speeds up to 17mph (28km/h). No clearing of the take-off path was required because floating obstructions would be deflected by the high planing pressure of the skis.

Convair F2Y-2

Convair's studies into boat fighters continued with a single-engine development of the Sea Dart, the growth possibilities of the original having been limited by its J46 engine. In May 1952, before the Sea Dart had flown, comparative data had been assembled for possible

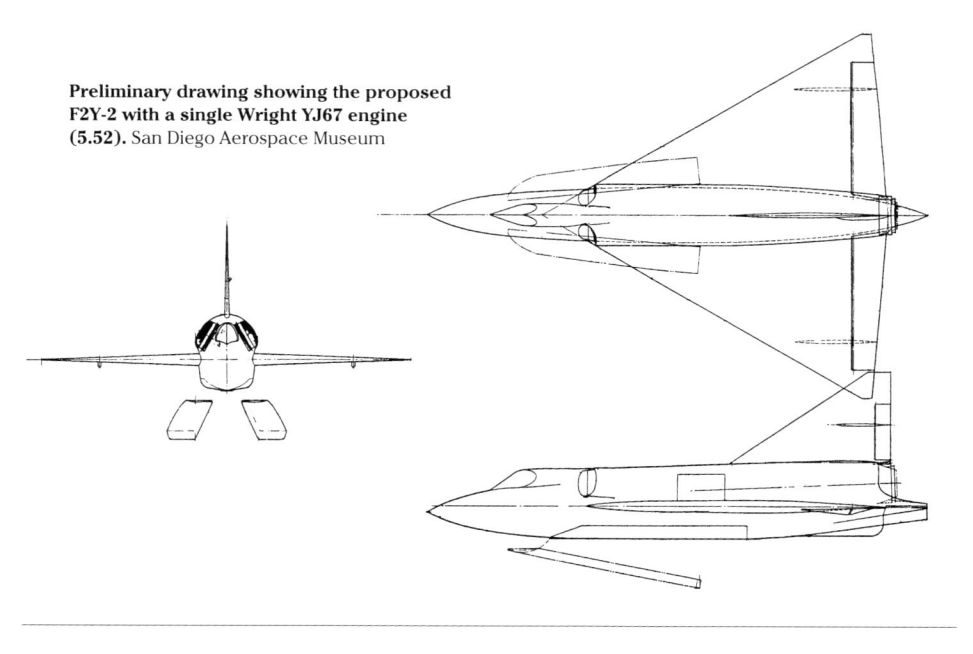

The first Convair Sea Dart, 137634, pictured during a test flight. Terry Panopalis

Sea Dart 135762 is prepared for another flight. Terry Panopalis

Preliminary drawing showing the proposed F2Y-2 with a single Wright YJ67 engine (5.52). San Diego Aerospace Museum

versions powered by a single Westinghouse XJ40-WE-10, Allison J71, Pratt & Whitney J57-P-7, Wright YJ67-W-1 or General Electric X35, or two Westinghouse XJ46-WE-2, General Electric X24A or Allison J35-A-3. Convair stated that a vastly improved performance over the present F2Y-1 could be achieved by going to a single-engine version powered by a YJ67-W-1 when it was available. In fact the aircraft as a whole would be far superior and the YJ67 was selected because it was expected to be the first of the new high-thrust engines to enter production. The new version was called the F2Y-2 and Convair suggested that it could be in production in 1956-1957 if design work started in early 1953.

It was the intention of this study to design a boat fighter that would closely approximate to or exceed the F-102 interceptor's performance. Wing area would be increased to accommodate the extra weight and the wing itself was taken from the F-102. The changes required to fit an F-102 wing included redesigned spar fittings and lengthened spars, with extended elevons inboard, and additional skin and formers added at the wing root due to the F2Y's narrower hull. Also the wing and elevon would have to be made watertight. As such the wing would be made to carry 1,170gal (5,320lit) of fuel against the F2Y's 1,083gal (4,924lit) and it offered improved performance at high altitudes. At this stage the project had twin hydro-skis but a single surface could be substituted. For improved hydrodynamic performance the angle of deadrise had been revised and a shallow angle bottom introduced forward, which would also allow the aircraft to land on a rubber mat. A high deadrise at the stern was retained to reduce landing water loads.

The new aircraft would be shorter than the F2Y-1 with a lower maximum cross section. Its hull frame construction had been improved which eliminated some of the F2Y-1's necessary heavy structure and provided more space for equipment. The single YJ67-W-1 was seen as the production powerplant but a Pratt & Whitney J57-P-7 could be used for an interim version without change to the configuration. The F2Y-2 would carry the same weapons as the Sea Dart and the aircraft was expected to exceed Mach 2 at height. However, the interim J57's top speed would be 862mph (1,387km/h) Mach 1.30 at 35,000ft (10,668m). Combat weight with the

YJ67 would be 22,519lb (10,215kg) giving a sea level rate of climb of 39,500ft/min (12,040m/min), time to 35,000ft (10,668m) including take-off and acceleration 2.46 minutes and combat ceiling (500ft/min [152m/min] climb) 56,200ft (17,130m). In the event the Navy did not take up the option for this much improved Sea Dart.

US Air Force Boat Fighters

The US Navy was not the only service to assess jet-powered flying boat fighters fitted with hydro-skis. Perhaps a little surprisingly, the USAF had a look at this idea as well. The Air Force turned to the EDO Corporation on Long Island at roughly the same time as the Skate and Sea Dart were being created. The amphibious fighter study by EDO was covered by MX940. The author was told that EDO beat off competition from a project proposed by Curtiss-Wright but no details of the latter design could be uncovered, except that it was to have a similar ski arrangement but a different ski design.

EDO 150

As a result of an EDO proposal made in February 1947 to USAF Air Material Command a contract was placed for the company to undertake a study into a high-speed arctic fighter that would be capable of taking-off and landing from 'varied' surfaces; particularly snow, ice and water and anything in between. EDO referred to the project as the 'Varied Surface Fighter', but the name was later changed by the contracting office to 'Panto-base' Fighter (Arctic Penetration Fighter was also used). At this time there was no requirement for this type of aircraft but EDO's proposal sparked interest in a research and test program. Consequently a contract was issued to modify a Grumman OA-9 Goose twin-piston flying boat with an EDO-designed hydro-ski to evaluate the ski gear's performance. The Goose served as a full-scale test and evaluation aircraft and the trials were successful – in the single-ski configuration take-off time was reduced by fifty per cent over that of the basic hull.

The EDO-150 was a sleek design with a long slim fuselage, a swept wing and swept V-tail, a single large hydro-ski beneath the centre fuselage, wingtip floats and a dorsal intake to supply two Allison J35 engines. Four 20mm cannon were mounted in the upper nose and the wings had leading edge slats and trailing edge ailerons and flaps. When

EDO Model 150 (c1950).
Dan Pattarini

Model of the EDO 150 in US Navy markings.

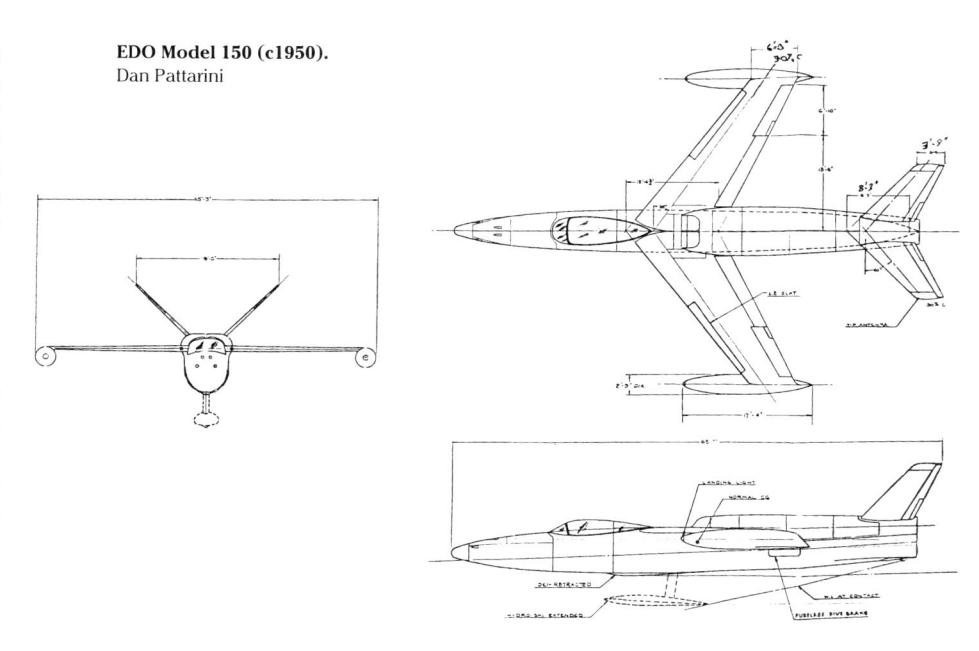

Boat Fighters

retracted the ski protruded only very slightly from the hull outline. EDO's ski designs were low aspect ratio hydrofoils and were found to perform well in rough sea conditions. The Model 150's maximum take-off weight was 32,225 lb (14,617kg), maximum rate of climb 15,250ft/min (4,468m/min) and service ceiling 53,400ft (16,276m). Although designed for USAF Air Material Command, the 150 model photographed by the author was actually marked up for the Navy. Its designer, Dan Pattarini, cannot remember any Naval involvement but this may have followed after he left EDO in 1951.

EDO 142

The success of the Grumman Goose phase of the program brought another contract in January 1949 for EDO to design a research vehicle, the Model 142. This was a scaled down 'proof of concept' aircraft designed to the same basic configuration as the 150. It was to be a single-engine, single-seat lightweight version that incorporated some simplified construction details such as a constant chord wing. In 1951 NACA completed initial research into the 142's aerodynamic and hydrodynamic properties using scale wind tunnel and tank models, which included the examination of several forms of air inlet. It was found that the take-off, longitudinal stability and landing behaviour were satisfactory although some alteration of the tail was required to reduce spray loads. On take-off the transition from the submerged to the planing stage was fairly smooth. The flying surfaces performed well, with only minor alterations being required. The 142 progressed through its preliminary design, wind tunnel and water tank tests before the funds allocated to the project were moved elsewhere (possibly to the Berlin Airlift), bringing a halt the Models 142 and 150 before they had left the drawing board.

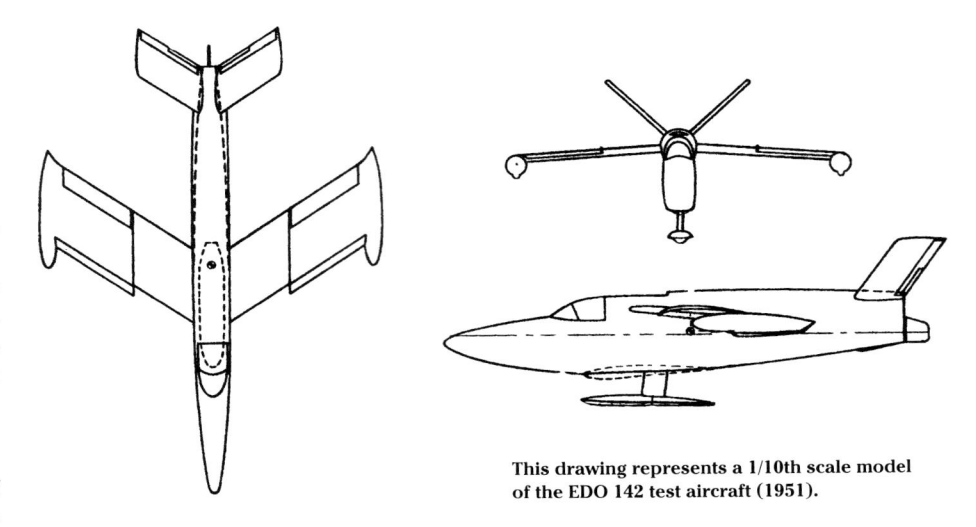

This drawing represents a 1/10th scale model of the EDO 142 test aircraft (1951).

The End of the Line

The concept of the jet-powered flying boat fighter offered some clear advantages, particularly given the situation in the early post-war years. However, it was difficult, given the extra design considerations, to match the performance of the rapidly advancing land-based fighters – particularly once this moved into the supersonic era. Moreover, long concrete runways being built around the world and the introduction of ever larger aircraft carriers with angled decks negated the theoretical deployable advantage of the flying boat.

Within ten years of the end of the Second World War the idea had pretty well disappeared, yet in 1982 it was to resurface (if that's the right expression) in the form of a proposal from Lockheed called the Hydro Star. This was a handsome design with a blended wing/body, leading edge root extensions, cranked delta wing, and engines mounted above the rear fuselage either side of the fin. By then fly-by-wire techniques were also available to assist with a boat fighter's performance. Lockheed examined the idea because land bases were still vulnerable to attack, however water airbases would also be hard to conceal from modern search aids and the fighters themselves would have to be parked 'in the open', making them relatively easy targets. The Hydro Star was never built but it was an imaginative design and we now know too that the Russians also continued to work on advanced flying boat concepts. However, that takes us into an era and realm beyond the scope of this book.

Flying Boat Fighters – Estimated Data

Project	Span ft in (m)	Length ft in (m)	Gross Wing Area ft² (m²)	Gross Weight lb (kg)	Engine lb (kN)	Max Speed / Height mph (km/h) / ft (m)	Armament
Convair Skate (October 1949)	63 6 (19.4)	83 0.5 (25.3)	1,010 (93.9)	44,500 (20,185)	2 x Westinghouse XJ-40-WE-10 11,750 (52.2) ab	713 (1,146) Mach 0.936 at S/L, 639 (1,028) Mach 0.965 at 35,000 (10,668)	4 x 20mm cannon
Convair YF2Y-1 Sea Dart (flown)	33 8 (10.3)	52 7 (16.0)	563 (52.4)	16,527 (7,497)	2 x Westinghouse J46-WE-2 6,100 (27.1) ab	(Est 5.52) 774 (1,245) Mach 1.015 at S/L, (Est 5.52) 925 (1,487) Mach 1.4 at 35,000 (10,668)	None fitted. F2Y to have 4 x 20mm cannon or 44 x 2.75in (7.0cm) RP
Convair F2Y-2	37 0 (11.3)	51 1.5 (15.6)	661.5 (61.5)	25,615 (11,619)	1 x Wright YJ67-W-1 13,500 (60.0), 21,500 (95.6) ab	799 (1,285) Mach 1.05 at S/L, 1,380 (2,219) Mach 2.08 at 35,000 (10,668)	4 x 20mm cannon
EDO Model 150	45 3 (13.8)	65 7 (20.0)	400 (37.2)	28,025 (12,712)	2 x Allison J35-A-17 4,900 (21.8), 7,350 (32.7) ab	748 (1,204) at S/L	4 x 20mm cannon
EDO Model 142	28 9 (8.8)	42 4.5 (12.9)	182 (16.9)	7,850 (3,561)	1 x Westinghouse J34 3,500 (15.6)	Subsonic	None

Chapter Nine

Into the 1960s

Superb shot of a Grumman F-14A Tomcat.

By the early 1960s both the USAF and the US Navy were operating fighters on a par with, or better than, anything they were likely to come up against. However, the pressures of the Cold War were at their height and the Soviets were (rightly) assumed to be working on a new generation of warplanes. As a result in the mid-1960s both the US Navy and US Air Force announced programs intended to lead to the acquisition of vastly more advanced fighters. The eventual outcomes would be the F-14 Tomcat and F-15 Eagle, each representing a major leap forward in fighter capability. They were also much heavier and more sophisticated than their predecessors. Outstanding though they were, they were not unique in terms of their capability and they had to beat off some formidable competing designs before being given the go-ahead. In particular the respective offerings from Grumman and McDonnell Douglas were hardly less impressive – and they were certainly equally radical in terms of appearance. Indeed, it is probably true to say that no other competitions have ever rejected such a large number of potentially outstanding aircraft.

The competitions for these two aeroplanes are therefore the main focus of this chapter. However, before looking at the various competing designs, it is important to be aware of the political environment of the time and to understand what brought the F-14 and F-15 into existence.

All-In-One TFX

We have already seen in Chapter Six how the Douglas F6D Missileer program was closed down in 1960/1961. At the same time the US Air Force had wanted a tactical fighter replacement for its Republic F-105 Thunderchief and the new Secretary of Defense Robert McNamara took the decision to combine the two programs as a further cost-saving measure. The resulting project was christened the Tactical Fighter Experimental or TFX and a go-ahead was given in September 1961. Two versions of the aircraft were to be built, one for the USAF and one for the Navy, and these were to use essentially the same airframe. In early December nine proposals were received from industry including submissions from Boeing, General Dynamics, Grumman, Lockheed, McDonnell, North American and Republic. Two of these, Boeing and General Dynamics, were selected to undergo further study. The same month the project was designated F-111, with the Air Force machine becoming the F-111A and the Navy's the F-111B. The General Dynamics design was finally declared the winner on 24th November 1962, with General Dynamics itself being asked to build the Air Force version while Grumman (a long-time and trusted producer of naval aircraft) was selected to manufacture the Navy variant.

American Secret Projects: Fighters & Interceptors

The Grumman F-111B variant of TFX was the starting point for the VFX program that eventually produced the F-14 Tomcat. Grumman Corporation / Grumman History Centre

Despite being classed as a fighter, the USAF's earlier F-105 had actually been operated more in the strike role, so the Air Force's TFX inevitably became a strike aircraft. As such, despite having an F-designator letter, this aeroplane and the competition that gave birth to it, really belong in a book on bombers. However, a brief summary will help to set the wider program in perspective.

The F-111 had variable geometry wings and the two versions differed principally in the shape of their nose and forward fuselage. The F-111A first flew on 21st December 1964 and the F-111B followed on 18th May 1965. As the program advanced it suffered numerous problems, not least with weight. The F-111B flew at a gross weight in the region of 70,000 lb (31,752kg) and various studies were made to get this down to the original 50,000 lb (22,680kg) figure required by the Navy to allow the type to operate from carriers. Some changes were introduced to the airframe but the F-111B always stayed way over its limit, so in May 1968 the Navy side of the program was cancelled. The F-111A however, entered USAF service in 1967 and, after many teething troubles, went on to complete a successful operational career.

The principal weapon of the F-111B was the new AIM-54 Phoenix air-to-air missile from Hughes Aircraft. Its development was opened in 1960 as a replacement for both the Falcon family of weapons, and also the Missileer's Eagle. The result was the most sophisticated AAM in the world – if also the most expensive. It had very long range (well over 100 miles [161km]) and could operate at all heights, but the F-111B and the F-14 would prove to be the only types capable of carrying it.

The Navy F-14 Program

Even from the start of the TFX program the Navy could see that the success of the F-111B as a carrier fighter was highly questionable. To quote George Spangenberg, 'the F-111B was most nearly useful when employed in a fleet air defence role, in effect acting as a Missileer but with half the capability. Other fighter missions, such as escorting attack airplanes, had to be done with a higher performance, more manoeuvrable and more versatile airplane than the F-111B'. As a result the Navy continued to search for a general purpose, carrier-based fighter. Working with General Dynamics, Grumman completed several F-111 improvement studies ranging from minor changes to complete redesigns. McDonnell also studied some improvements to the Phantom including fitting a variable sweep wing. All of this was done under contract but other manufacturers could also see the emerging need for a new aircraft to complement the F-111B. This work finally evolved into a multi-mission concept called the VFAX that was required to be a better fighter than the Phantom and a better attack aircraft than Vought's new A-7 Corsair II (which would shortly fill the Navy's attack requirements). As a result the F-111B's attractiveness had begun to wane long before it was finally abandoned on grounds of weight and cost.

It became clear that a better solution would be to get a new fighter altogether, one that could carry Phoenix and the AWG-9 fire control system and still have enough performance to undertake the other fighter missions – in essence VFAX with Phoenix added. The initial studies undertaken by Grumman confirmed to the Navy – and helped to convince Congress – that a new fighter called the VFX could be produced that would be more effective and less costly than the F-111B. This new concept was gradually accepted but needed further confirmatory design studies from Chance Vought, North American and McDonnell to force a decision. In mid-1968 approval was granted by the Navy to release a Request for Proposals to industry for new fighters under the VFX category. The resulting submissions formed the design competition that would lead to the F-14, but the place to start is the swing-wing Phantom proposal, and then the known VFAX projects.

McDonnell F-4(FV)S

Work on McDonnell's variable sweep project appears to have started in 1966 under the guise of the F-4(VS). This was a straightforward development of the F-4J Phantom with a high-position variable geometry wing with little change to the fuselage. Span with the wing at minimum sweep was 55ft 0in (16.8m) and fully swept 38ft 0in (11.6m), length was 63ft 2.5in (19.3m). In August 1966 McDonnell made an unsolicited proposal to the Navy, stating that a go-ahead given on 1st January 1967 would allow a first flight to take place in October 1968, with the first service deliveries in early 1970. Reaction from Naval Air Systems Command (NAVAIR) highlighted the need to reduce the approach speed and improve manoeuvrability at altitude. Work continued and a briefing document was prepared towards the end of April 1967 for the Secretary of the Navy, by which time the design itself had moved forward and had been retitled the F-4(FV)S. It still showed the original F-4 forward fuselage but the rear section had been extended slightly and both the fin and horizontal tail were considerably larger. The latter had also lost its distinctive anhedral and the position of the undercarriage legs was changed to accommodate the extra length. The variable geometry wing had also been refined.

The briefing document compared the F-4(FV)S to a standard F-4J Phantom. The latter's gross weight was given as 46,049lb (20,888kg) while the swing-wing variant's had increased to 50,910lb (23,093kg) with respective internal fuel loads of 1,998gal (9,085lit) and 2,180gal (9,912lit). The F-4J's top speed and ceiling were Mach 2.25 and 58,300ft (17,770m) while the F-4(FV)S offered Mach 2.27 and 58,000ft (17,678m). The equivalent Combat Air Patrol times without and with external fuel were 1.32 and 2.70 hours for the F-4J and 2.00 and 5.00 hours for the F-4(FV)S. In the event the F-4(FV)S was never ordered. It should be noted that the 'Swing-Wing Phantom' was not one of the VFAX proposals. The latter, with their Phoenix armament and more advanced radars, were superior and gave a much better simultaneous multiple-target intercept facility.

The original McDonnell F-4(VS) swing-wing development of the Phantom (15.7.66). National Air and Space Museum

Poor-quality print of an artist's impression of the McDonnell F-4(FV)S. National Air and Space Museum

Grumman Model 303

Grumman's design team under Mike Pelehach realised that the F-111B was unlikely to bring their company any production work and so studies began for a new Fleet Air Defence Fighter under Grumman Design Number 303. In fact the G-303 number was first allocated way back in 1961 and covered all manner of developments and layouts.

Into the 1960s

Top: **Two views of two comparative Grumman Model G-303 designs. These are possibly early VFAX studies before the introduction of the Phoenix missile because both carry Sparrow AAMs. The swing-wing project's leading edge glove vanes are well shown and the other model is very similar in terms of fuselage, fins and tailplane, but it introduces a fixed wing. Both appear to be single-seaters.** Grumman Corp / Grumman History Centre

Centre: **Views of the Grumman 303D model showing the wings in their forward and swept positions.**

Left: **Side view of the G-303D model.**

Opposite page:

This Grumman-made model apparently represents both the G-303-58 and G-303-60.

Rear view of the G-303-58/60 model showing the widely-spaced 'podded' engines, nose chines and port side cannon. George Cox

Model G-303-58/60 with wings set at the minimum sweep angle. George Cox

Design 303-107 for example was dated 25th March 1964 and showed a twin-engine swing-wing design that had much in common with the F-111B. A series of projects that would lead to the F-14 was now under way. The research against VFAX began in 1966 but fixing the relevant projects and their dates against different documents has proved far from easy. There were several other specific designs apart from those discussed here, which were culled from over six thousand configurations studied.

Grumman documents indicate that two basic layouts were in contention for the VFAX concept during 1966, these were known as the Models 303C and 303D. The 303C showed some similarities with the eventual F-14 – high position swing-wings, twin vertical tails canted outwards and, in one drawing, six Phoenix beneath the fuselage. Its twin-engine powerplant had the individual 'submerged' engines quite close together and received air from box intakes on which the leading edge was highly swept. This design was apparently judged as likely to suffer from poor longitudinal stability at subsonic speeds, high fuel consumption when cruising and other problems, and it was subsequently rejected by Grumman. The Model 303D, which according to the Grumman project index was started in October 1966, moved the vg wings to the low position. This design had its engines close together, it had pairs of quite small vertical and ventral fins and its six missiles were more spread out with four under the fuselage and one under each wing root. G-303's unswept span was 62ft 6in (19.05m), swept 39ft 9in (12.1m), length 64ft 10in (19.8m) and wing area 480ft^2 (44.6m^2). Published sources have indicated that this project was inferior in several respects to some previous layouts. Getting the design right was clearly proving challenging.

In October 1967 a new design was proposed to the Navy that used the F-111B's engines, weapons and systems packaged in a new airframe. To a degree, it was this project's clear superiority over the F-111B that hastened the latter's demise. The layout was called Design 303-60 and had 'podded' engines (that is, separated beneath the wing roots) and a mid-position wing. There was a single vertical tail and chines on the nose leading into the top of the air intake with a cannon mounted in the port chine. The missiles were again spread out underneath the fuselage and fixed inner wing. Design 303-60's span unswept/swept was 62ft 6in (19.05m) and 39ft 3in (12.0m), length 58ft 8in (17.9m) and wing area 505ft^2 (47.0m^2).

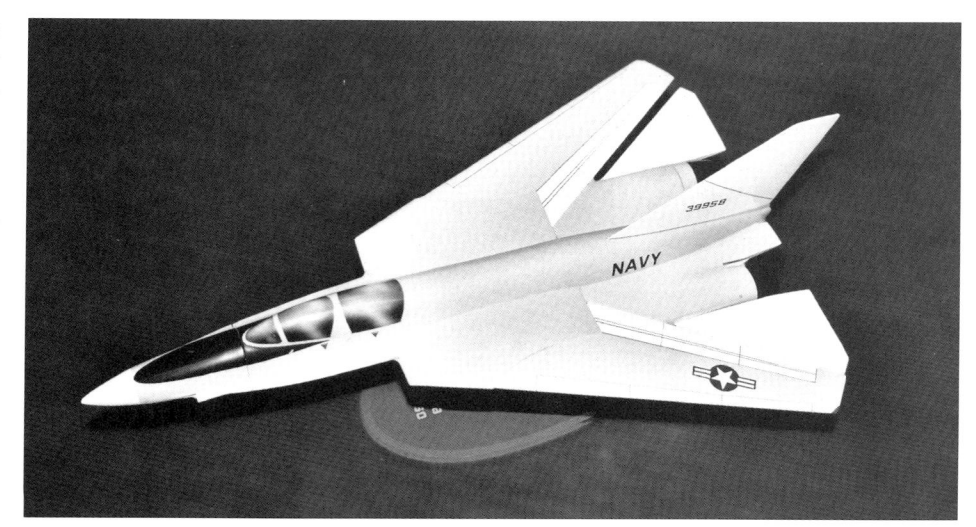

Into the 1960s

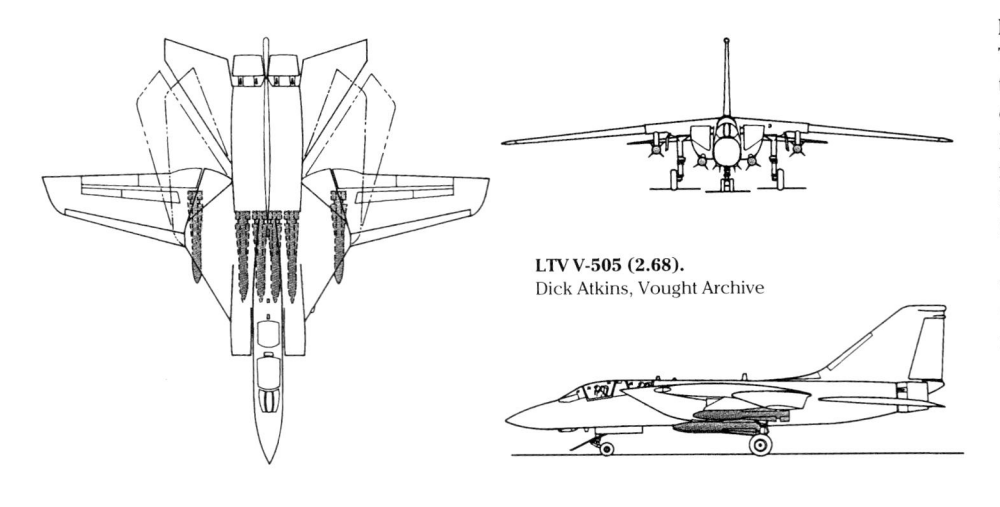

LTV Model V-505

The next phase in LTV's VFAX research was the V-505 begun in October 1967. This was completed as a preliminary design study in February 1968 and had a near-identical airframe to the V-484 but was very slightly larger, had different engines, and introduced Phoenix. It was also rather heavier with 18,600 lb (8,437kg) of fuel aboard. Combat weight with six Phoenix was 53,410 lb (24,227kg) and the combat ceiling on maximum thrust at that weight was 52,900ft (16,124m). With four Sparrow III missiles the gross take-off weight was 53,050 lb (24,063kg), combat weight 46,930 lb (21,287kg) and combat ceiling 60,000ft (18,288m). With this lighter weapon load the maximum speed at sea level rose slightly to Mach 1.07 while the Mach 2.4 limit at height could now be achieved over a range from about 33,000ft (10,058m) to about 56,000ft (17,069m). Four Phoenix were carried side-by-side beneath the middle fuselage with two more underneath the fixed inner wing while a four-Sparrow load was laid out with one and then three missiles under the fuselage. For ground attack duties twenty-four Mk.82 bombs plus two Sparrows could be carried, the missiles on the centreline and the bombs under the outer fuselage and inner wings; half of the bombs could be replaced by two 450gal (2,046lit) drop tanks. 'Spotting Span' was 27ft 6in (8.4m) and the V-505 had a 36in (91.4cm)-diameter radar dish in the nose. Advanced Pratt & Whitney STF297A engines were a potential powerplant for later developments.

Despite all this work, none of the VFAX projects were ordered. In the meantime, the Navy had given much more thought to exactly what it required. In June 1968 a Request for Proposals (RFP) was made to five companies for designs to satisfy the F-111B's replacement, this was now called the VFX for Navy Fighter, Experimental. The RFP, defined in Type Specification 161, requested a maximum speed of Mach 2.2 at height, the ability to patrol for up to two hours between 100 and 200 miles (161 to 322km) from its carrier, two engines for improved safety, two crew seated in tandem and a new radar, the Hughes AN/AWG-9. A General Electric 20mm M61A1 Vulcan rotary cannon was to be carried internally, air-to-air missiles were to be either AIM-7 Sparrow III, AIM-9 Sidewinder or AIM-54 Phoenix and, for secondary close sup-

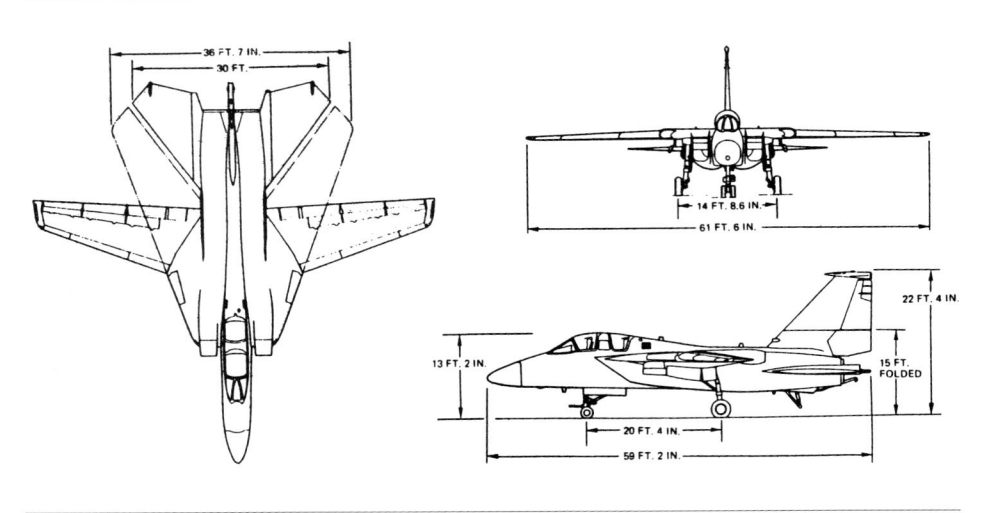

LTV V-505 (2.68).
Dick Atkins, Vought Archive

LTV (Ling Temco Vought) Model V-484

Meanwhile LTV (Vought) had begun its work in the VFAX field in July 1965 and its V-484 was first conceived during the following November. Like other companies LTV's research embraced many potential designs for test in the wind tunnel and a brochure completed on 15th December 1967 actually described the Model V-484-149. This was presented in response to a Naval Air Systems Command letter sent on 22nd September and stated that this was the first VFAX design to make use of new 'hard' engine data from General Electric and Pratt & Whitney. This brought a new level of technology into the VFAX program because only parametric engine data had previously been available, which meant that theoretical calculations had to be used for specific thrust and fuel consumption and for the engine's assumed physical size.

In flight, with the wing fully swept back, the V-484 would have a leading edge angle of 75°; for ground stowage this could be increased to 84° giving a span of just 26ft 0in (7.9m). The quoted engines were the General Electric GE1/10F5B turbofan or the advanced 27,450 lb (122.0kN) thrust Pratt & Whitney STF297A and a total of 12,865 lb (5,836kg) of fuel could be carried. V-484's combat weight was 39,854 lb (18,078kg) and at that weight its supersonic and subsonic combat ceilings with the GE powerplant were 60,000ft (18,288m) and 44,400ft (13,533m) respectively. Four Sparrow or Sidewinder AAMs were to be carried in tandem pairs on the corners of the bottom fuselage. Alternative loads could include twenty Mk.82 bombs (eight beneath the fuselage and six under each fixed portion of wing), six underfuselage bombs plus two 300gal (1,364lit) or 450gal (2,046lit) drop tanks under the inner wing, or a mix of AAMs and bombs. Thus several different missions could be covered and the maximum take-off weight with bombs was given as 55,402 lb (25,130kg). There was a retractable in-flight refuelling probe on the starboard side of the forward cockpit.

General Dynamics (Convair) Model 44 (9.68).
San Diego Aerospace Museum

166

American Secret Projects: Fighters & Interceptors

Artist's impression of the Convair Model 44 shown flying over CVN65, the carrier USS *Enterprise*. San Diego Aerospace Museum

Model of the Convair Model 44. Allyson Vought

This second model of the Convair 44, like the first a manufacturer's display model, shows the design in Marines markings. George Cox

port duties, the aircraft had to be capable of carrying up to 14,500 lb (6,577kg) of bombs. Small study contracts were made to each company on 17th July 1968 and their proposals were all submitted on 1st October.

General Dynamics (Convair) Model 44

The airframe for Convair's Model 44 variable geometry design was based around the existing Pratt & Whitney TF30-P-12 (Modified) turbofan engine, but it could accommodate the uprated P&W TF30 (JFT10-A-32C) without change, or even more advanced engines with only minor alterations to the airframe. The principal features of the fighter's structure included integral flat-bar stiffening of the wing carry-through structure, a conventional skin-longeron-frame fuselage and a three-spar tapered wing with integrally stiffened skin supported by ribs and bulkheads. For maximum accessibility the offensive stores were to be carried externally and, for minimum drag, tandem mounted. Main armament was four AIM-7 Sparrows carried in pairs beneath the centre fuselage while a palletised M-61 cannon could be mounted in a curved fairing placed between the forward pair of Sparrows on the aircraft's centreline near the centre of gravity. The available drawings give no information for Phoenix.

With two TF30-P-12 (Modified) engines in place the maximum Mach number was expected to be 2.4 (a structure limitation), supersonic ceiling 59,400ft (18,105m) and loiter (patrol) time 2.25 hours. Available wing sweep angles were 20° for take-off and landing, 26° for cruise flight, 38.5° for combat and 70° for supersonic combat. The wings had near full span trailing edge flaps and leading edge slats and there was a glove flap on the leading edge of the fixed portion of the wing to serve as a high lift device. The horizontal tailplane was all-moving and for carrier stowage the fin could fold downwards and the radome upwards. There was a foldaway IFR probe on the starboard side of the nose. Maximum weight for the fighter escort mission was 55,782 lb (25,303kg) and maximum catapult weight 69,000 lb (31,298kg).

Into the 1960s

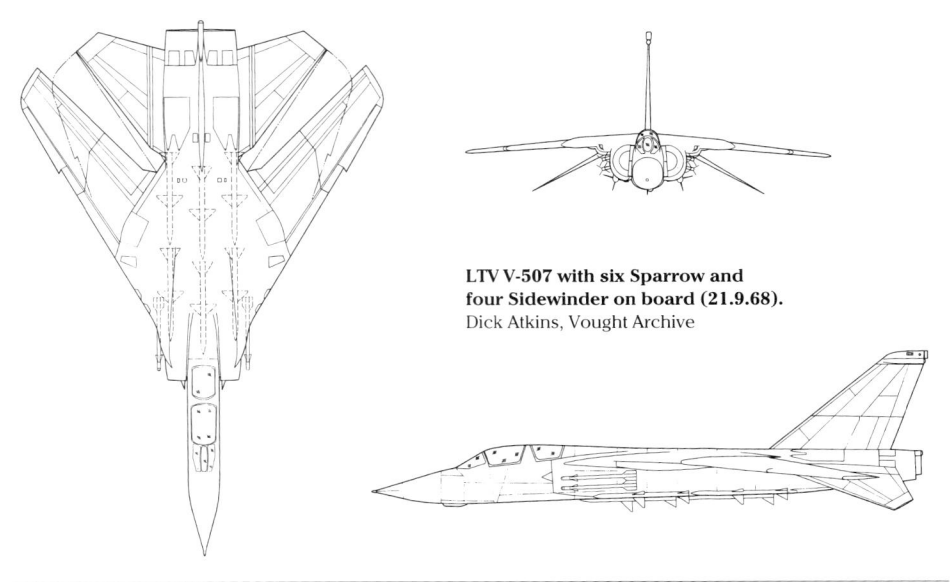

As part of its VFX research Grumman examined this Model G-303 configuration which was known in-house as the VFX-1C.

Grumman Model 303E and 303F

After further research Grumman favoured a design called the Model 303E. This essentially became the F-14, but at this point it featured a single fin supplemented by folding ventral fins. The engines were spaced well apart and there were small foldaway glove vanes ahead of the wings. Drawings actually show the aircraft carrying four Sparrow missiles and a detailed full-scale mock-up was built with these aboard. A cannon was housed in the port side lower nose. Length was 63ft 0in (192.m), forward span 62ft 10in (19.1m), swept span 37ft 7in (11.5m) and wing area 541ft^2 (50.3m^2).

Also studied was a fixed-wing project called the Model 303F, which is understood to have had a great deal in common with the 303E apart from its wing and twin fins. Here the wing area was large at 745ft^2 (69.3m^2) to ensure that there was enough lift for flight from carriers (double-slotted flaps were also fitted) and this made the design 4,295 lb (1,948kg) heavier than the 303E. Grumman rejected this project whose detailed study had actually confirmed the expected advantages of vg wings.

LTV Model V-507

LTV's V-507 design featured a swing-wing, all-moving two-position dihedral horizontal tail surfaces hinged to angle downwards to a maximum of 30°, and a single all-moving fin. The dihedral tail was to provide 'adequate directional stability at limit Mach number'. The 'unswept' wing angle was 22.5° and maximum sweep in flight 72°, which could be increased to 77° for stowage. To assist the latter the wingtips could also be folded to reduce span to 27ft 6in (8.4m) and the tip of the fin could be lowered. The centre wing box comprised a titanium structure consisting of six beams and the wing itself featured high-lift leading edge slats and trailing edge flaps, plus spoilers and deflectors for roll control. Both the centre wing and mid-wing boxes formed integral fuel cells and there were more tanks in the fuselage. A flight refuel probe was placed on the upper nose in front of the cockpit and slightly offset to port. The TF30-P-12s were fed by half-axis-symmetric side inlets.

In 1966 LTV Aerospace and Lockheed California concluded a team agreement for the Navy VFAX/VFX and USAF FX programs. Should LTV win the VFX competition this would provide Lockheed with work as a prin-

LTV V-507 with six Sparrow and four Sidewinder on board (21.9.68).
Dick Atkins, Vought Archive

American Secret Projects: Fighters & Interceptors

Full-scale mock-up of the V-507 with three types of air-to-air missile aboard. Dick Atkins, Vought Archive

Artist's impression of the LTV V-507. Dick Atkins, Vought Archive

cipal sub-contractor to manufacture major sections of the Navy aircraft. The choice of Lockheed came from that company's expertise in fighter design; in particular its experience in the use of high titanium content in the structure. Also, in 1968 LTV and Avions Marcel Dassault of France signed a long-term agreement to co-operate in both the military and commercial aircraft fields. Under this agreement there was an exclusive one-way flow of technical data from Dassault to the Vought Aeronautics Division on the complete Mirage family of tactical fighter aircraft – Mirage III, IV, F1, F2 and III-G. Emphasis was placed on the variable geometry wing Mirage III-G, which integrated quite successfully with the TF30 engine family, and the information provided by Dassault included complete technical studies, design data and ground and flight test information. This proved of great value in the design of the V-507.

For the escort fighter role V-507 would have four Sparrows and a full internal fuel load of 2,265gal (10,299lit) (15,400lb [6,985kg]). For combat air patrol there would be six Phoenix under the fuselage plus two 450gal (2,046lit) drop tanks on the wing pivot pylons, taking the fuel to 21,520lb (9,761kg). In this configuration the loiter time on station was 2.05 hours and two Sidewinders could also be carried on the side of each intake. The M61 cannon was located in the lower part of the right hand inlet duct fairing and fifteen Mk.82 Snakeye bombs could be taken for the interdiction role. On fighter escort duty, with a clean aircraft except for the Sparrows, V-507's combat weight was 49,400lb (22,408kg), sea level rate of climb 36,800ft/min (11,217m/min) and combat ceiling 58,300ft (17,770m). Even without the drop tanks and pylons the CAP Phoenix combat weight was still heavier at 57,416lb [26,044kg]) and it had a top speed of Mach 2.15 at 38,000ft (11,582m). LTV built a detailed mock-up of its VFX design, complete with hinged canopies, and this was towed to different parts of the NAS Dallas airfield.

McDonnell Douglas Model 225

There were two principal versions of McDonnell's proposal: the Model 225A powered by the existing P&W TF30-P-12 and the 225B, which had the same airframe but new engines. McDonnell had undertaken a VFAX aircraft design study from the autumn of 1967, probably under Model number 222. Its follow-on VFX design featured a low variable sweep

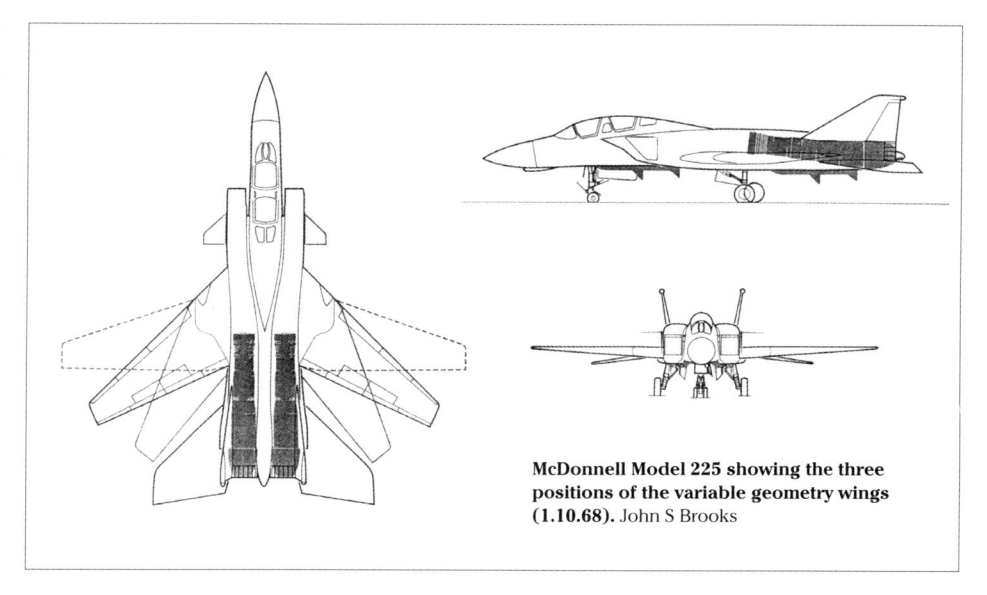

McDonnell Model 225 showing the three positions of the variable geometry wings (1.10.68). John S Brooks

Into the 1960s

wing and semi-submerged weapon carriage to cut drag. Six cavities in the lower fuselage could each accept an AIM-54A Phoenix or AIM-7E/F Sparrow as well as conventional air-to-ground weapons. Provision was made to install a quickly removable M61 20mm gun pack in the forward centreline cavity. Two pylons mounted on the fixed part of the wing could be utilised for Sidewinders, air-to-ground weapons and additional fuel tanks, while a 300gal (1,364lit) external tank, another Sidewinder or other stores could be installed on a centreline stub pylon. Internal fuel capacity in two wing and five fuselage tanks was 15,280lb (6,931kg).

Model 225 had vg wings and twin fins canted slightly outwards, but there were also small fold-down canards on the sides of the intake boxes to serve as high-speed trimmers. These would control the neutral point at high speeds and would thus only be extended when the wings were swept fully aft. Other wing sweep angles were 19° for take-off, loiter and landing; 45° for transonic combat and high speed cruise; 70° for acceleration and supersonic flight; and 80° for carrier storage. The engines were spaced apart with fuel tanks fitted in between and this gave a large area beneath the fuselage for the weapons. Each engine was fed by side intakes and had an iris convergent-divergent exhaust nozzle. The AWG-9 missile control system used a 36in (91.4cm) planar array radar antenna. Combat ceiling with four Sparrows was 58,300ft (17,770m) and loiter time three hours. If a go-ahead decision was made for 1st March 1969, McDonnell planned to have a maiden flight in January 1971 with the first fleet delivery forty-four months after go-ahead. Paul T Homsher was named as the manager for the whole program.

A total of 8,530lb (3,869kg) of titanium was to be used in the airframe, representing 40% of the basic airframe weight, which would offer the potential to go to Mach 3.0 with the introduction of more advanced engines. The Model 225B was to be powered by Pratt & Whitney's 26,070lb (115.9kN) thrust JTF22A-22 or General Electric's GE1/10F10B2 turbofan, which offered a potential 25,500lb (113.3kN). Respective take-off weights with four Sparrows would be 50,576lb (22,941kg) and 50,175lb (22,759kg) and with six Phoenix and external fuel 57,905lb (26,266kg) and 57,410lb (26,041kg). With Sparrows aboard the maximum speed in each case was in excess of Mach 2.6 and the combat ceilings were 63,500ft (19,355m) and 62,600ft (19,080m). Model 225B would also use a new multimode radar and could be adapted to the reconnaissance role. With all fighter armament and systems removed and a 31in (78.7cm) nose extension to accommodate the reconnaissance sensors, this final version was known as the Model 225C.

Model of the McDonnell 225 showing its wings in the forward and swept positions. Allyson Vought

North American Rockwell NA-323

The only VFX submission not to have a variable geometry wing came from North American. Its Model 323 project had a large box-shaped chin intake, side-by-side engines and a single fin. The wing itself had large leading edge root extensions but then, forming a graceful arc, it curved outwards so that the outer wing itself exhibited a relatively small

170

American Secret Projects: Fighters & Interceptors

sweep angle; the trailing edge was straight. Few details for this design are currently available but at least four Sparrow AAMs were to be carried, two beneath and one on each corner of the intake box side. Phoenix would have been available. Plans were in place to make Northrop the sub-contractor to North American on the F-14, and the F-15, had the respective designs won their competitions.

To help with the evaluation of these layouts the Navy requested the assistance of NASA's Langley Research Center facility, which had five different wind tunnels on hand to assess various aspects of their design. The Center had been closely involved with the development of the variable geometry wing and during 1967 it published the results of in-house studies for a fighter design fitted with this feature. Variable sweep seemed to be an ideal application for naval fleet defence fighters because these aircraft had to be able to respond very quickly to threats to the fleet, which required a fully swept (supersonic) configuration, but also had to be capable of flying slowly enough (with the wing swept forward) to make a safe landing. As a result, four of the VFX contenders had featured variable geometry wings and all five were evaluated in Langley's tunnels.

An official assessment was completed on 13th December. It was agreed to keep Grumman and McDonnell Douglas in competition for a further period while the other three contenders were informed that their designs had been rejected. Final revisions were made on 5th January 1969 and nine days later Grumman was told that it had won the competition. George Spangenberg described the proposals submitted by McDonnell, Vought, North American and General Dynamics as 'excellent', but they were overshadowed by a better one from Grumman. It was felt that variable sweep wings did give a better aircraft and the Navy did not agree with the performance claims from North American with its fixed wing offering. NASA agreed with the choice, which prevented any political controversy over the decision. At this stage a single fin plus large folding ventral fins were still a feature of Grumman's design but the Navy wished to see this improved, so twin fins replaced the earlier arrangement together with small fixed fins mounted on the bottom of the engine casings. On 3rd February 1969 a contract for twelve YF-14A development aircraft was signed and the first of these flew on 21st December 1970. Eventually 710 production F-14 Tomcats were built.

North American NA-323 (9.68).

Model of the North American NA-323. George Cox

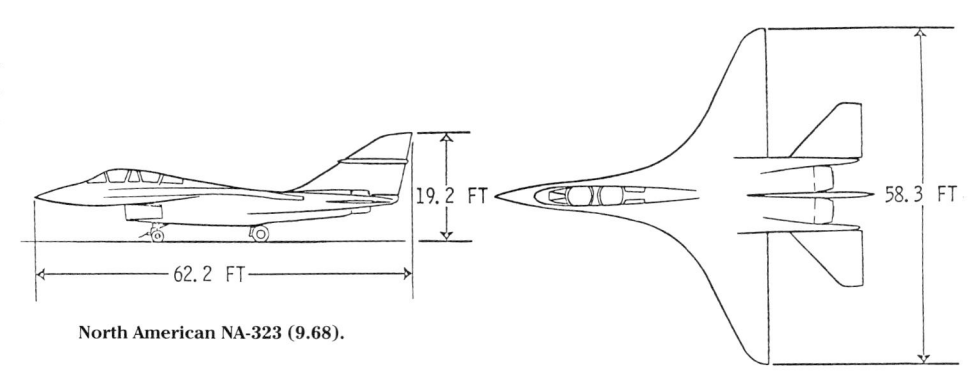

Into the 1960s

171

The Air Force FX (F-15)

During 1965 a group of Air Force experts conducted studies for a Fighter Experimental (FX): a potential new medium-cost fighter with air-to-air and all-weather capability superior to that of the current generation of USAF interceptors and fighter bombers such as the Convair F-106 and Republic F-105. In October Tactical Air Command issued a requirement for parametric studies of a new fighter and on 18th December a Request for Proposals (RFP) was sent to manufacturers – eight companies responded. However, this RFP had ignored the wish for a new air superiority type because it specified a combination of good air-to-air and good air-to-ground capability. On 18th March 1966 Boeing, Lockheed and North American received four month Concept Formulation Study contracts while Grumman continued its work on a private venture basis.

Many of the contractors' proposals preferred podded engines rather than mounting the power units within the fuselage. Variable sweep wings featured extensively and the powerplant was usually a high bypass ratio turbofan. The objective was a top speed of Mach 2.7, which would require very advanced materials in parts of the airframe. Weaponry included one M61 20mm cannon, four long-range air-to-air missiles on the fuselage, plus a maximum of 4,000 lb (1,814kg) of external stores. Since they had to embrace the air and ground roles the avionics packages needed to be on a level with the F-111, all of which meant that the proposals were big, falling within the 60,000 lb (27,216kg) class. The USAF was unhappy with these designs and work on this stage of the FX came to a close. In fact none of the designs from the three contractors – around five hundred in all – would have been optimised for either air or ground duties.

Work on the FX idea however continued throughout 1966 and well into 1967. In July 1967 the Soviet Union unveiled a set of new fighters at the Domodedovo air show, including the obviously highly supersonic MiG-25 *Foxbat*, and this further influenced the FX formulation process and increased the desire to get things moving. On 11th August 1967 a second series of proposals was requested from seven manufacturers and on 1st December official contracts were awarded to General Dynamics and McDonnell Douglas. However, Fairchild-Republic, Grumman, Lockheed and North American all continued to spend company funds on research towards the same goal. The results were assessed from June 1968 but finding agreement on some areas, particularly the avionics, proved difficult. The end of the Navy's F-111B and the start of the VFX program also meant that the Air Force had to make the FX a different animal to ensure that its funding was continued, thereby preventing another F-111 situation. One way of doing this was to make the FX a single-seater, which also saved weight. The on-going war in Vietnam was another influence and by now the need to focus the fighter purely on air-superiority had been acknowledged. The eventual F-15 drawing office later reportedly carried the sign 'Not a pound for air-to-ground' to keep the designers aware of this fact!

A final RFP was made on 30th September 1968 to which Fairchild-Republic, General Dynamics, McDonnell Douglas and North American responded. General Dynamics was quickly eliminated but it proved impossible to reduce the final number of competitors to two. The requirements included a top speed of Mach 2.5 at height, a high thrust/weight ratio and a maximum gross take-off weight of 40,000 lb (18,144kg). A long-range pulse-Doppler look-down/shoot-down radar had to be fitted. NASA Langley was again involved, studying four different basic layouts with swing wings, fixed wings or wing-mounted engines, plus a design that was similar to the MiG-25. These created interest with the competitors and the second NASA layout with a fixed sweep wing left a big impression on McDonnell Douglas, whose proposal had much in common with it. Forty-one NASA researchers took part in the final assessment of the design submissions, which included long sessions in Langley's wind tunnels.

Unidentified Projects

The following unidentified designs and little known projects almost certainly depict studies made to the earlier stages of the FX competition, or possibly VFAX.

Right: **A General Dynamics/Convair swing-wing project powered by two widely-spaced engines and featuring twin fins angled outwards. It has no service markings but may have been prepared to the Navy's VFAX requirements or the 1967 stage of the FX studies.** Allyson Vought

Below: **Grumman's series of FX studies included this swing-wing design that had two engines spaced well apart under the rear fuselage, just inside the line of the fins. Missiles or bombs were carried on the corners of the lower fuselage. All of their FX work was carried out under Model number G-399 and this would appear to be the G-399-45. The fact that Grumman had this display model made means that it was probably an officially submitted design. Model span 14in (35.6cm) with wings forward, 9.4in (23.9cm) fully swept, length 15in (38.1cm).**

Opposite page: **The designer of this twin-engine variable geometry fighter is unknown but it may be General Dynamics/Convair. The fact that no service identity is worn means it is impossible to determine which program it was proposed to. The horizontal tails and twin fins are all-moving surfaces. Model length is 14.9in (37.8cm) and span with the wings forward 14.5in (36.8cm).** Allyson Vought

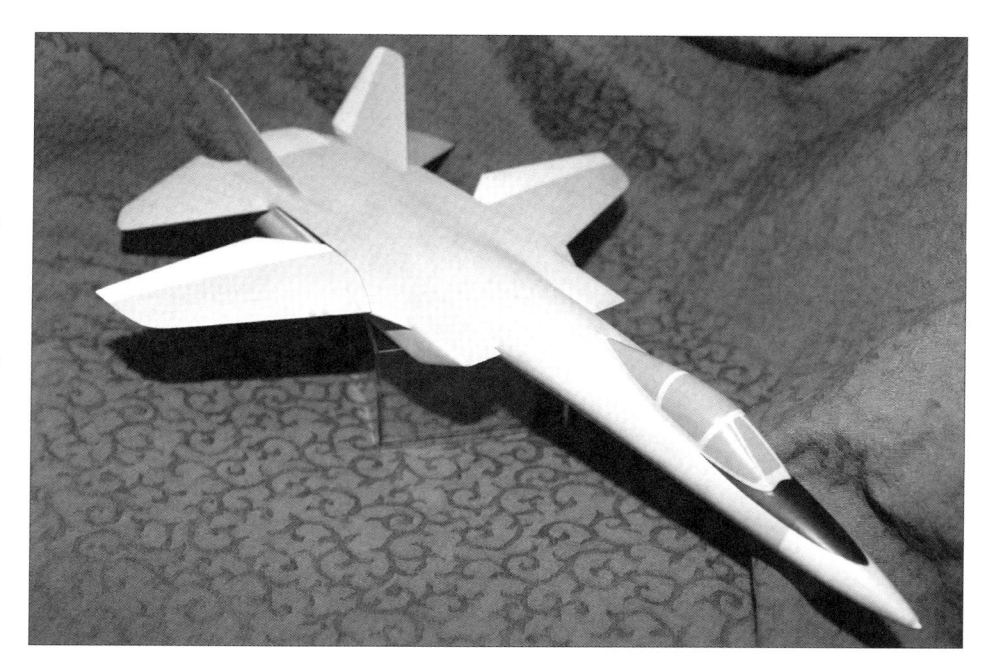

Into the 1960s

173

Left and upper left: **Grumman's Model G-399-42 FX design moved the engines a bit closer together and had a single fin. A cannon was mounted on the left side of the lower nose and four Sparrow AAMs or bombs could be loaded beneath the fuselage.** Grumman Corporation / Grumman History Centre

Below: **This beautiful manufacturer's model shows a North American Los Angeles Division fighter project that quite possibly represents the company's studies to the first series of FX proposals made in 1965. It is certainly a big, heavy aircraft and carries four missiles beneath the fuselage and inner wing (one is missing here). Model span 12.0in (30.5cm) forward and 9.3in (23.5cm) fully swept and length 19.2in (48.8cm).** John Aldaz

Opposite page:

Later North American FX studies may have included this twin-engine swing-wing project. Model span 15.7in (40cm) forward and 8.3in (21cm) fully swept, length 18.5in (47cm). Jonathan Rigutto / photo © 2005 Chad Slattery

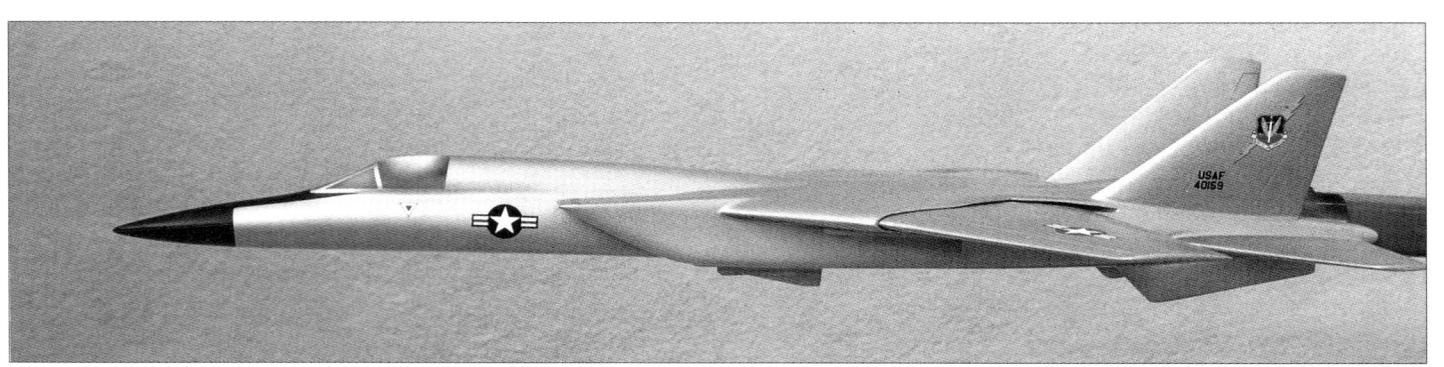

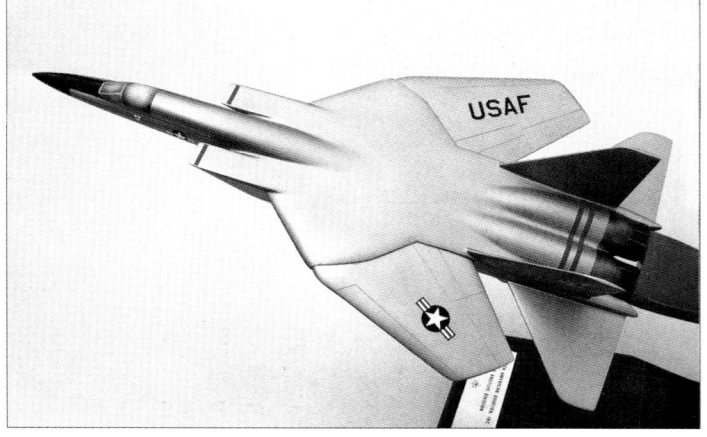

174 American Secret Projects: Fighters & Interceptors

Into the 1960s 175

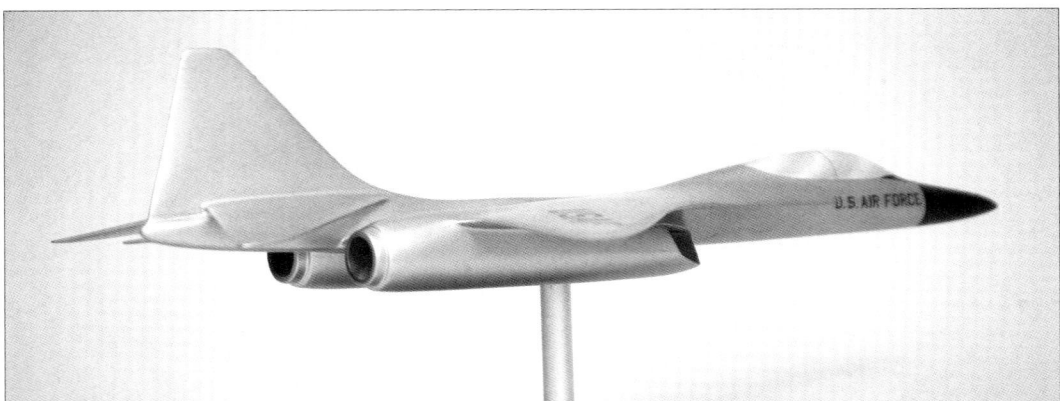

This page:

This North American model shows essentially the same airframe as the vg project but with a fixed wing. In addition, the wing with its blended leading edge is near identical to North American's final FX submission of mid-1969. Another manufacturer's model, span here is 13.2in (33.5cm) and length 17.7in (45cm). Jonathan Rigutto / photo © 2005 Chad Slattery

Opposite page:

This very attractive heavy vg fighter appears to have been one of Fairchild Hiller/Republic's 1965 studies to the FX program. Note the separated engines and widely spaced fins. It may have been designated FH-100. Model span 17.5in (44.4cm) forward and 12in (30.5cm) fully swept, length 25in (63.5cm).

American Secret Projects: Fighters & Interceptors

Into the 1960s

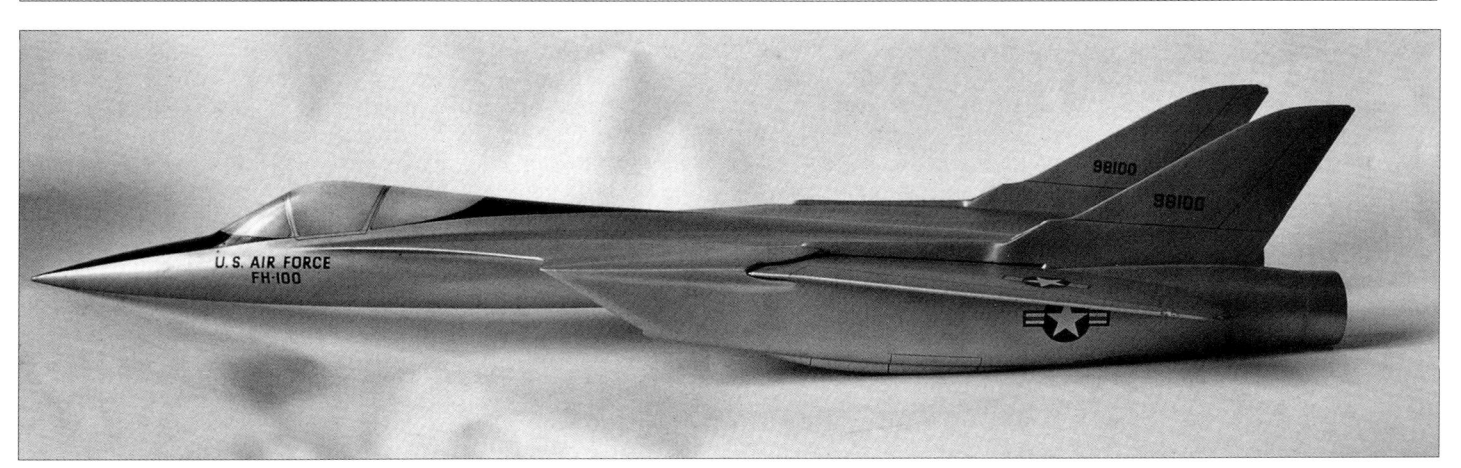

LTV Aerospace (Vought) undertook studies to the early FX ideas from late 1965 under project number V-483. This Vought model may be one of these studies. It is, however, a two-seater but does have widely-spaced engines and fins and blended wing leading edges. Model span 11.7in (29.6cm) and length 14.6in (37.0cm). George Cox

Fairchild Hiller (Republic) FX

Fairchild Hiller's FX proposal had evolved over four years of study and featured two engines in separated nacelles and a fixed cranked wing. In the spring of 1965 the concept was first proposed for separating the engines into podded nacelles. During the ensuing design analysis this approach, commonly referred to as the 'three body concept', proved significantly superior to all the other designs produced by Fairchild's team. This engine arrangement removed the known difficulties of installing high-performance engines in the fuselage, where unfavourable flow disturbances could affect the powerplant's operation, and also promised to reduce wave and aft end drag at high speeds. In addition, it was found that this unique design also offered sizeable savings in weight because it gave an inherently efficient structure. Separating the engines and housing them in pods markedly increased the degree of survivability by keeping the fuel tanks away from the hot sections of the engines. It also gave true twin-engine reliability because in a situation where two power units were housed side-by-side problems with one engine could also affect the other. In addition, the subsequent introduction of alternative engines would be relatively simple.

The design team concluded that the three-body layout represented the optimal combination of technical innovation, minimum risk and operational suitability. In essence it showed a central fuselage with the two engines in 'nacelles' that had the outer wings and horizontal tail fitted outside. The space between the bodies was filled with more wing and there were long leading edge strakes stretching well ahead of the cockpit. Two Sparrow AAMs were carried beneath the fuselage, level with the intakes; two tandem pairs of Sidewinder missiles went under the fuselage behind the Sparrows; two further pairs of Sidewinders could go under the wing just outboard of the engines; and an M61 cannon was carried in the lower left nose. Primary powerplant was two Pratt & Whitney F100 afterburning turbofans, although an alternative General Electric engine was also specified. The aircraft's structure comprised 39.3% aluminium alloy, 39.8% titanium alloy, 9.7% steel, 0.7% magnesium, 10.1% non-metallic and 0.4% boron.

The fighter's internal fuel totalled 11,100 lb (5,035kg) and take-off weight with Pratt & Whitney engines and four missiles aboard 39,750 lb (18,031kg); with General Electric engines this figure became 39,975 lb (18,133kg). Ceiling was over 60,000ft (18,288m) and range over 3,000 miles (4,827km). Potential subcontractors had been solicited by Fairchild from twenty-nine different States.

McDonnell Douglas Model 199

McDonnell Douglas' studies to the FX requirement were covered by Model Number 199, first issued on 7th May 1965, that initially described a 'Light Attack/Air (FX) superiority fighter'. During 1967/1968 the project showed a high delta wing, low tail, twin fins and side box intakes, but was assessed to suffer from high drag in certain regimes and poor manoeuvrability. In early 1968 a variable geometry design was studied with twin fins and engines spaced well apart, but this increased the weight to more than 60,000 lb (27,216kg) and exhibited a poor performance overall. The design submitted to the final competition was actually the Model 199B which looked quite similar to the eventual F-15 but, amongst other differences, it had smaller tail fins and large ventral fins. It carried four Sparrows at the corners of the lower fuselage. With Pratt & Whitney engines the internal fuel totalled 11,500 lb (5,216kg) and take-off weight with the four Sparrows aboard was 39,740 lb (18,026kg); equivalent figures for the alternative General Electric engine were 11,300 lb (5,126kg) and 39,523 lb (17,928kg).

North American Rockwell NA-335

The FX design from North American's Los Angeles Division, the NA-335, featured a blended wing body with a highly curved leading edge. This concept, refined after more than eight thousand hours of wind tunnel work, was aimed at providing a platform with a fixed wing that offered good manoeuvrability in the transonic speed range. It was first proposed on the Model 323 (VFX) submission above, but had by now been further refined with greater sweep on both the leading and trailing edges. Work on this blended wing body arrangement began 'in-house' in 1966 although, at the time, the USAF was pushing for a variable geometry design to fill the FX requirement. That year North American also began a Service-funded FX study that had a vg wing but the blended wing body work was separate from this. It was attractive because it seemed to be a solution for producing a fixed-wing planform to do the FX job, obviating the weight penalty and complexity associated with variable-sweep wings.

As noted above, North American lost out in the second Request for Proposals but elected to continue some unfunded research for an Air Force fighter using the same specification

The Fairchild Hiller (Republic) FX proposal with Pratt & Whitney engines (c6.69). Cradle of Aviation Museum

Model of the Fairchild Hiller (Republic) FX. John Hall

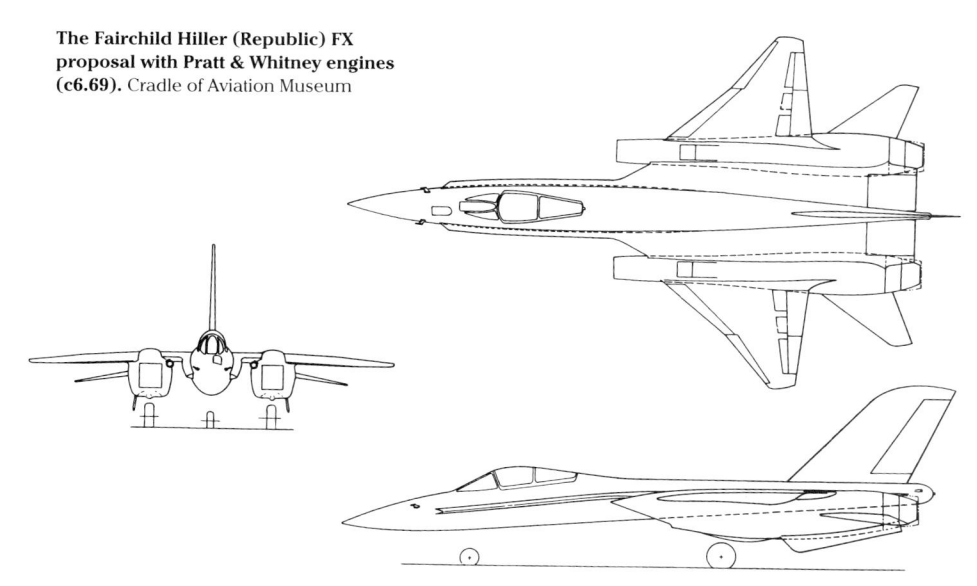

Into the 1960s

179

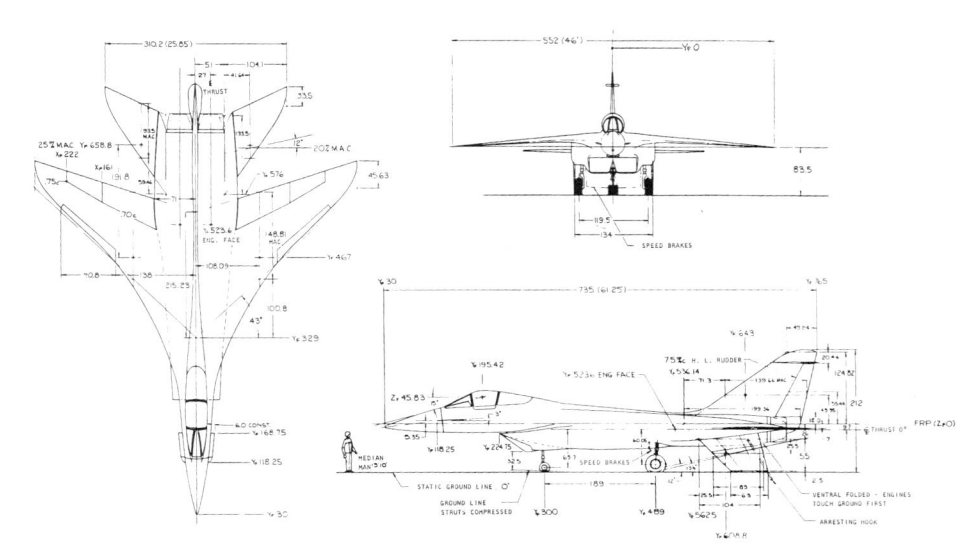

North American NA-335 (c6.69). Craig Kaston

but incorporating the blended wing body into a fixed-wing configuration. This was also the reason why North American was the only company to produce a fixed-wing VFX proposal. In late 1968 company officials stated that, although the VFX submission was a serious attempt to win, the blended wing body concept was 'not as fully verified as would have been necessary for a maverick proposal to win, even if other factors had been equal'. The wing itself was, and still is, quite distinctive (and rather graceful). The only other aircraft to have employed anything similar has been the Soviet Union's Sukhoi Su-27 in its earliest prototype form. Oleg Samoilovitch of Sukhoi actually says in his memoirs that they expected Rockwell's design to win the FX competition and they were pleased when it didn't because they felt confident that they could produce a better design than McDonnell Douglas.

A North American engineer made the following description of the wing. 'The inboard portion is highly swept as it blends into the fuselage well forward. At about mid span, a point of inflection occurs and the sweep angle is reduced. Near the tip the leading edge begins to curve, increasing sharply in sweep angle to align with the local air stream. One of the considerations in turning the planform into hardware is the requirement for leading edge flaps or slats. Ideally, a straight leading edge is desirable, but in the blended wing-body case the need for leading edge devices is minimized because of the ability to fly at high angles of attack. Trailing edges can be a straight line to simplify flap and aileron design because the blended wing-body concept is relatively insensitive to trailing edge shape.'

The studies indicated that moderate sweep angles were desirable at mid-span and every effort was made to maintain attached airflow over the entire wing, rather than have some vortex formation. A key design criterion for the blended wing-body to be turned into a workable fighter was that it offered good manoeuvrability in the Mach 0.6 to 1.4 region together with minimum buffet. North American felt that this, combined with a low wing loading and a high thrust-to-weight ratio, provided the manoeuvrability that a superior dogfighting aircraft would require.

The leading edge shape was set by the need to fill the requirements of both subsonic and supersonic flight. For supersonic the cur-

Model of the North American NA-335 displaying the design's beautiful wing. Jonathan Rigutto / photo © 2005 Chad Slattery

Artist's impression of the NA-335. Craig Kaston

vature was largely dictated by Whitcombe's area-rule theory for the best cross-section along the longitudinal axis to minimize wave drag, while subsonic shaping was based on the principal of maintaining a uniform suction distribution spanwise to minimize drag due to lift. However, tip curvature was also important because it delayed the onset of shock formation, thereby also reducing drag and buffet. Blending the wing into the body, by continuing the aerofoil section to the fuselage centreline, raised the proportion of lift supplied by the fuselage and slightly reduced lower wing bending moments; it was also beneficial structurally. Many of the fundamentals in this research were founded on work done by NASA, but the leading edge shaping performed during the 1950s by Vickers (Supermarine) in Britain on its Swift jet fighter had also been noted. Flaps were actually placed along most of the trailing edge.

Returning to the design itself, the avionics would feature a head-up-display for the presentation of radar and flight data, a pulse Doppler attack radar set (to be supplied either by Hughes or Westinghouse) that would permit the fighter to detect targets at 40nm (74km) and lock on at 10nm (18.5km) and an electronic warfare system including a self-defence ECM for jamming hostile radar. Four Sparrow AAMs would be carried side-by-side in a line underneath the fuselage rearward of the intake box and two Sidewinders would be loaded under each wing root; outboard of these each wing had two hardpoints to take drop tanks or bombs. There was a single fin and two large ventral fins. With the Pratt & Whitney F-100 engine internal fuel totalled 10,331 lb (4,686kg) and the take-off weight with four missiles 39,222 lb (17,791kg); with the alternative General Electric the figures were 10,471 lb (4,750kg) and 39,200 lb (17,781kg). A full-size mock-up of the Model 335 was built.

Final technical proposals from the three competitors were submitted on 1st July 1969. All of them indicated the widespread use of titanium structure and new fabrication techniques. On 23rd December it was announced that McDonnell Douglas was the winner – plans to hold a prototype fly-off between two designs were rejected and the FX was redesignated F-15 before the final selection was made. The majority of accounts indicate that McDonnell Douglas' design was adjudged on technical merit to be the best. Factors behind North American Rockwell's rejection included total costs of about 7% more than McDonnell (about $200m in the total program costs), and a more complex avionics proposal. North American Rockwell's blended wing/body was highly regarded by the USAF evaluation team but another factor may have been McDonnell's decision not to build a new manufacturing facility for the FX when both of its rivals had planned to do so. The decision to pick McDonnell Douglas did bring some controversy but the aircraft passed its critical design review in April 1971. By then, based on NASA research, the twin vertical fins showed more height and area while the ventral fins had disappeared. The first prototype made its maiden flight on 27th July 1972 and the aircraft was named Eagle. It has proved to be an incredibly successful fighter and has served in air forces worldwide.

During the early 1970s there was much discussion for dropping one of either the F-14 or F-15. As a result in 1972/1973 McDonnell Douglas looked closely at a naval version of the F-15 called the F-15(N) with Sparrow missiles, and then refined it into the F-15(N-PHX) with Phoenix. These were essentially the same aircraft as the USAF version but with naval fittings like an arrester hook and modified avionics. F-15(N-PHX)'s estimated gross take-off weight with four Phoenix was 55,310 lb (25,089kg). In the end the naval F-15 was never needed and both the F-14 and F-15 programs were continued.

To complement the FX fighter, competitions were organised for a new engine and a new radar. In February 1970 Pratt & Whitney's engine proposals were declared superior to General Electric's and the resulting twin-spool power unit was designated

F100-PW100. A naval variant to power the 'B' version of the F-14 Tomcat was called F401-PW-400, but orders for the F-14B were eventually replaced by more F-14As using Pratt & Whitney's well-established TF30, so the F401 was eventually dropped. The new radar, selected from Hughes, was called the AN/APG-63. The missiles to be carried by the F-15 proved to be modern versions of the Sidewinder and Sparrow and in fact, because of rising costs, a new short-range air-to-air missile was cancelled in September 1970.

Other Projects

One further design from the early 1970s is worthy of discussion; a three-engine interceptor development of the North American A-5 Vigilante carrier attack aircraft. Through the 1971 to 1973 period the USAF looked at several possibilities for an Improved Manned Interceptor or IMI to replace Air Defense Command's F-101, F-102 and F-106 aircraft. Possible IMI proposals included modified versions of the F-106, F-111 (the F-111X-7), F-14 and F-15, and the modified RA-5C or NR-349 as it was known within the company. Grumman's F-14 project was called the G-545B and would have used F100 engines. General Dynamics' F-111X-7 was to be a stretched and extensively modified version that was 7ft (2.13m) longer than the original in order to make room for more fuel and new avionics. The first Air Force study of IMI candidates was undertaken in May 1971. The Defense Department began its analysis of the final IMI candidates around the start of March 1973 and completed it in mid-May of that year. None of the types proposed was ordered. North American Rockwell's design was arguably the most interesting of these ideas.

North American Rockwell NR-349

North American Rockwell Los Angeles Division's NR-349 represented a substantial modification of the Vigilante and in fact was based on the RA-5C reconnaissance variant. It was to be powered by three General Electric J79 turbojets with the third engine installed in the aft fuselage just above the other two and fed by a new bifurcated intake. This engine's primary purpose was to give the aircraft greater acceleration and climb rates and higher ceilings, all necessary in an interceptor. The fuselage had semi-recessed fittings to carry six Phoenix air-to-air missiles in pairs under-

Mock-up of the McDonnell Douglas F-15 Eagle in its original form. Terry Panopalis

Classic view of an F-15 Eagle with full missile load.

Manufacturer's model of the NR-349. Model span is 15.7in (39.8cm) and length 20.7in (52.5cm).

neath and a new fire control system was to be installed, possibly the Westinghouse WX-400 or Hughes AWG-9. There was also a new saddle-type fuel tank to take additional internal fuel while another pair of 600gal (2,728lit) external tanks could also be carried. Estimated ceiling was in excess of 80,000ft (24,384m). The NR-349 was submitted to Air Force Aeronautical Systems Command as an unsolicited proposal and was first made known to the public in September 1971. Although proposed in 1971 – later than the main subjects of this chapter – the NR-349 would have been a big aircraft and thus sits more comfortably here than with the lightweight types discussed in the next chapter.

Conclusion

The Grumman F-14 and McDonnell-Douglas F-15 have proved to be immensely successful aircraft. At the time of writing, advanced versions of the latter are still operated by many air arms while the F-14 has only just been retired by the US Navy. However, it is easy to forget that the development of these fighters and their arrival into service was surrounded by considerable controversy, in part because they were so large and expensive. As a result a campaign was opened to find a lightweight fighter and this steadily gained support. In due course this effort would bring forth the F-16 and F-18 fighters and so the next part of this book will take a look at the lightweight fighter.

It is also worth adding that the F-14/F-15 brought to a close a trend that had dominated much of the thinking in the 1950s – indeed, the thinking that had prevailed since the very first fighters were constructed – namely, the quest for ever higher speeds. The decade of the 1950s embraced the period when combat aircraft designs were at their fastest. Nothing since then has approached the F-108's planned Mach 3 (with the exception of Lockheed's SR-71 reconnaissance aircraft). These new fighters from Grumman and McDonnell-Douglas were slower, but the development of much more capable and longer-range radars and avionics compensated for this change. In the 1950s, after the Korean conflict, the US Air Force had believed speed was essential, but the fighting in Vietnam in the 1960s showed that above a certain limit speed was in fact a wasted asset – the need to engage a target visually made very high speeds useless. However, manoeuvrability and acceleration were another matter.

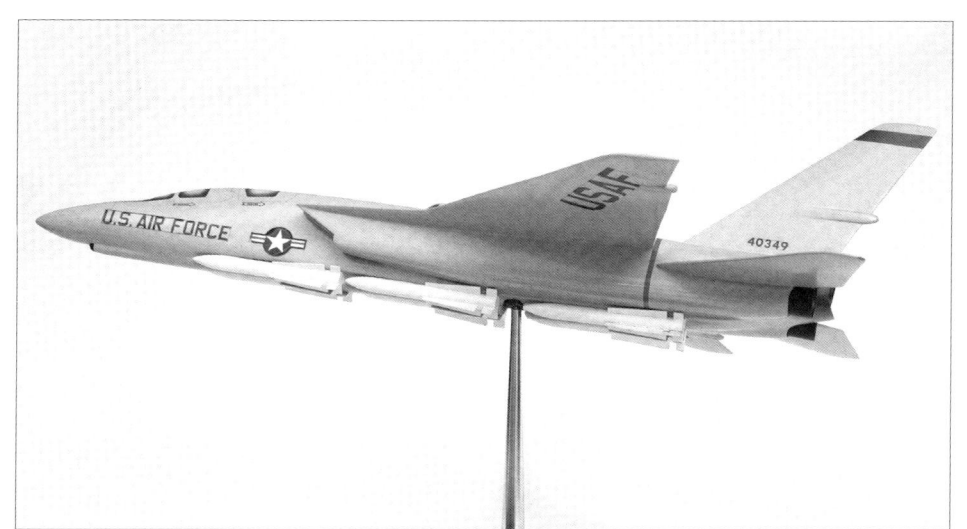

Into the 1960s

1960s Fighters – Estimated Data

Project	Span ft in (m)	Length ft in (m)	Gross Wing Area ft² (m²)	Gross Weight lb (kg)	Engine lb (kN)	Max Speed / Height mph (km/h) / ft (m)	Armament
McDonnell F-4 (FV)S (at 24.4.67)	60 0 (18.3) fwd 37 11 (11.6) swept	61 10 (18.8) 617 (57.4) swept	680 (63.2) fwd	50,910 (23,093)	2 x J79-GE-10 17,900 (79.6) ab	Mach 2.27 at height	4 x AAM + air-to-ground stores
LTV V-484	57 2 (17.4) fwd 32 2 (9.8) swept	58 6 (17.8)	475 (44.2)	45,000 (20,412)	2 x Gen Elec GE1/10F5B c20,000+ (88.9)	High Supersonic	4 x Sparrow or Sidewinder
LTV V-505	61 9 (18.8) fwd 35 7 (10.8) swept	60 0 (18.3)	?	60,850 (27,602) 20,290 (90.2) ab	2 x P&W TF30-P-12 Mach 2.4 above	Mach 1.04 at S/L, 6 x AIM-54 Phoenix AAM c 37,000 (11,278)	1 x M61 Cannon,
VFX (F-14) Projects							
Convair Model 44	61 6 (18.75) fwd 36 7 (11.15) swept	59 2 (18.0)	540 (50.2) (CAP)	65,923 (29,903) 20,250 (90.0) ab	2 x P&W TF30-P-12	Mach 2.4 at height	1 x M61 20mm cannon, at least 4 x AIM-7 Sparrow AAM
LTV V-507	62 0 (18.9) fwd 37 8 (11.5) swept	69 7 (21.1)	535 (49.8) (4 Sparrow)	55,560 (25,202) 20,250 (90.0) ab 67,084 (30,429) (CAP – 6 Phoenix + tanks)	2 x P&W TF30-P-12 Mach 2.25 at	858 (1,380) at S/L, 4 x AIM-9 Sidewinder + 40,000 (12,192)	1 x M61 20mm cannon, 6 x AIM-7E/F Sparrow AAM or 6 x AIM-54 Phoenix or 15 x Mk.82 Snakeye bombs
McDD Model 225A	57 9.5 (17.6) fwd 36 9.5 (11.2) swept	62 8.5 (19.1)	500 (46.5) (4 Sparrow)	52,900 (23,995) 20,250 (90.0) ab 60,490 (27,438) (6 Phoenix)	2 x P&W TF30-P-12	Mach 2.4 at height 4 x AIM-9 Sidewinder +	1 x M61 20mm cannon, 4 x AIM-7E/F Sparrow AAM, 6 x AIM-54A Phoenix or 14 x Mk.82 Snakeye bombs
N American Rockwell NA-323	58 3.5 (17.8)	62 2 (19.0)	653 (60.7)	?	2 x P&W TF30-P-12 (probably) 20,250 (90.0) ab	At least Mach 2.2 at height	M61 cannon, Sidewinder, Sparrow and/or Phoenix AAM
Grumman F-14A Tomcat (flown)	64 1.5 (19.5) fwd 38 2.5 (11.6) swept	62 0 (18.9)	565 (52.5)	66,200 (30,028) 12,500 (55.6), 20,900 (92.9) ab	2 x P&W TF30-P-412A	910 (1,464) at S/L, 1,545 (2,486) at 40,000 (12,192)	1 x 20mm cannon, 8 x AAM or 14,500 lb (6,577) bombs
FX (F-15) Projects							
Fairchild Hiller (Republic) FX	38 11 (11.9)	65 5 (19.9)	527 (49.0)	39,750 (18,031)	2 x P&W F100-PW-100 c23,800 (105.8) ab	Mach 2.0+	1 x 20mm cannon, 2 x AIM-7 Sparrow AAM, 8 x AIM-9 Sidewinder AAM or 16,000 lb (7,258kg) stores
McDD Model 199B	42 8.5 (13.0)	64 2.5 (19.6)	608 (56.5)	39,740 (18,026)	2 x P&W F100-PW-100 c23,800 (105.8) ab	Mach 2.0+	1 x 20mm cannon, AIM-7 Sparrow AAM, AIM-9 Sidewinder AAM, bombs
N American Rockwell NA-335	46 0 (14.0)	61 3 (18.7)	653 (60.7)	39,222 (17,791)	2 x P&W F100-PW-100 c23,800 (105.8) ab	Mach 2.0+	1 x 20mm cannon, 4 x AIM-7 Sparrow AAM, 4 x AIM-9 Sidewinder AAM, or bombs
McDD F-15A Eagle (flown)	42 9.5 (13.0)	63 9 (19.4)	608 (56.5)	41,500 (18,824)	2 x P&W F100-PW-100 14,870 (66.1), 23,810 (105.8) ab	Mach 2.3 at height (clean) Mach 1.78 at height (with missiles)	1 x 20mm cannon, 8 x AAM or 15,000 lb (6,804) bombs
Other Project							
N American Rockwell NR-349	c52 6 (16.0)	c69 0 (21.0)	?	?	3 x Gen Elec J79-GE-8	Mach 2.5+	6 x AIM-54 Phoenix or AIM-47 Falcon AAM

Chapter Ten

Lightweight Fighters

McDonnell-Douglas F-18 prototype photographed in September 1978 following its roll out ceremony.

The creation of a true light fighter has long been the ambition of many aircraft designers. This was particularly true in the first decades of the jet age when concern was growing that fighters appeared to be getting inexorably heavier and more complex. Various companies tried to buck the trend by attempting to produce aircraft that were smaller, simpler and cheaper than their contemporaries whilst retaining much the same performance.

In Europe in the 1950s NATO held a competition to select a lightweight fighter that could be used by all its air forces. It was won by the Fiat G.91 (looking very much like a pocket-sized F-86D) but as with many such initiatives, most nations then followed their own interests and only the Germans and Italians bought it. The French produced several promising designs; one of which, the Dassault MD.550, became the progenitor of the whole Mirage family. In Britain, Folland produced its diminutive Gnat fighter, which was later to prove highly effective in service with the Indian Air Force and was also to be adopted as the Royal Air Force's standard advanced trainer.

Although the performance of all these machines closely matched that of their big brothers in terms of speed, rate of climb and manoeuvrability, they inevitably lacked the ability to carry the same armament or sophisticated avionics. The choice, therefore, was between larger numbers of cheaper, simpler, easier to maintain fighters or fewer, more expensive, more sophisticated aircraft. It thus polarised the decision that forms part of the consideration every time a new warplane is designed. It is a debate for which there seems to be no 'right' answer; rather, it depends on the particular circumstances. It depends on the available funding, the operating environment and the likely enemy capability; though more than anything else, the choice probably depends on the prevailing philosophy of the air force high command at the time.

It is interesting to note that for many years the Russians followed the lighter/simpler route. All of Mikoyan's MiGs from the MiG-1 right through to the MiG-21 followed this line. The MiG-21 – the Mach 2 fighter produced in higher numbers than any other jet in history – was very much in this mould. The United States' experience in Vietnam, where the kill ratio was much lower than that achieved in Korea, caused a careful re-think of America's fighter tactics and philosophy. Missiles proved their worth but it was clear the age of dogfighting was not over.

The argument possibly reached its peak in the late 1960s and early 1970s when the very expensive F-14 and F-15 were making their appearance. Many experts felt that these fighters were far too big and expensive, and a cheaper alternative had to be found. Such concerns were eventually to bring forth the last new fighters that lie within the scope of this book; the General Dynamics F-16 and McDonnell Douglas F-18. However, these were not the first US attempts to produce a lighter fighter. Lockheed's F-104 Starfighter, covered by Chapter Four, was at least no heavier than its predecessors despite its massive leap in performance. However, it could be argued that too much had been sacrificed in pursuit of straight-line performance and the F-104 was quickly dropped as an interceptor by the USAF, though it went on to

American Secret Projects: Fighters & Interceptors

Northrop N-156 (1955). Northrop Grumman Corp, Tony Chong collection

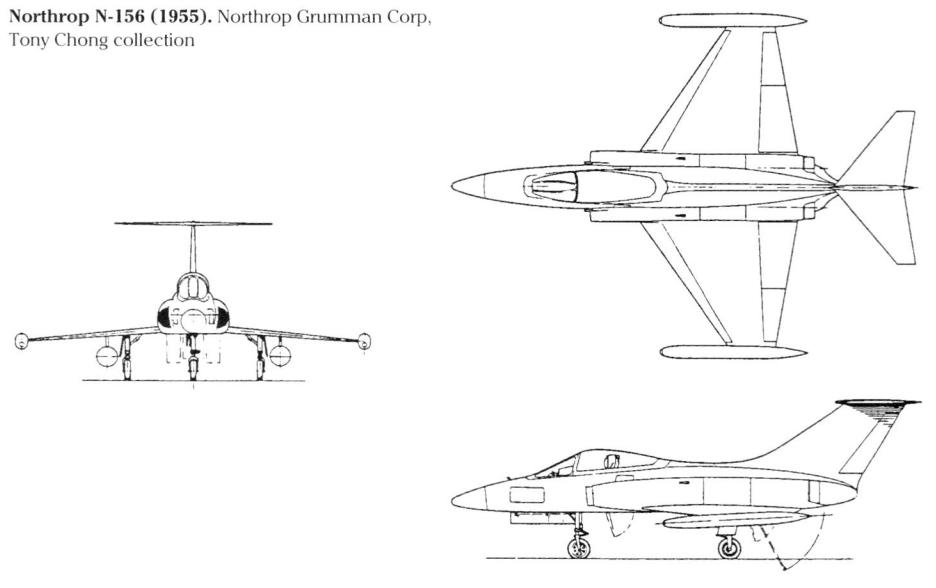

Model of the Northrop N-156 light fighter. George Cox

considerable success with other air forces as a ground-attack aircraft. Northrop also produced an excellent, true lightweight aircraft, but it too had to turn to the international market to achieve its well-merited success, at least in its fighter version. It is worth looking at these and other earlier efforts before examining how they led to the F-16 and F-18.

Northrop N-156

Northrop started looking closely at light fighters during the 1950s. After the N-102 Fang described in Chapter Four, one of its earliest proposals was the N-156. Paradoxically, this was designed right in the middle of the period when Northrop was also working on its series of heavy long-range interceptors covered in Chapter Five. The N-156 was described as a lightweight supersonic fighter-interceptor for the Navy, possessing exceptional utility, range and altitude capabilities. It was designed to operate from CVE-105 Class 'Jeep' carriers and would fit in with their existing catapult and arresting equipment. The CVE-105 type had been the last class of escort carrier to be built during the Second World War.

The N-156 had a low tapered 3.7% thick wing that was swept 25° 45' at quarter chord, plus an all-moving T-tail. There was an AN/APS-67 search and track radar in the nose and fuel cells in the rear fuselage above the engines. Two AIM-9 Sidewinder missiles could be carried (one on each wingtip in a frangible pod) and an alternative armament was forty-eight Gimlet 2.0in (5.1cm)-diameter rockets (twenty-four in each wingtip pod). Wing-mounted pylons were available to take two more Sidewinders or another forty-eight 2.0in rockets in two pods. Two 150gal (682lit) external tanks could also be carried; total internal fuel was 3,575lb (1,622kg) and combat weight 8,693lb (3,943kg). For the point intercept mission the estimated sea level rate of climb was 35,100ft/min (10,698m/min), combat ceiling 62,100ft (18,928m) and service ceiling 63,200ft (19,263m) and the N-156 was expected to take 3.1 minutes to reach 40,000ft (12,192m); combat radius was 450nm (833km).

Work on the project was instigated in July 1954 as a company sponsored feasibility study. Work on the design study for a formal presentation to the Navy began in July 1955 and the results were submitted in September. The project was rejected, in part because the light carriers for which it was designed were shortly to be taken out of service. A tandem or

American Secret Projects: Fighters & Interceptors

This model shows a North American project for a light fighter. Nothing in known about it except that it was called Rapier, the same as the F-108 long-range interceptor. Model span is 7.3in (18.6cm) and length 11.0in (28.0cm). George Cox

Northrop N-156F Freedom Fighter 59-4987, the first prototype, is pictured flying over the Air Force Flight Test Center at Edwards Air Force Base, California. In 1962, under the new designation scheme, this aircraft became a YF-5A.

side-by-side two-seat trainer version had also been offered, provided by replacing the fuselage section forward of the fuel bulkhead. Northrop also proposed the N-156R, which used the same airframe but had a 5,000 lb (22.2kN) Reaction Motors TR132 in the bottom of the rear fuselage. The lower part of this rocket was covered by a small fairing along the underside of the aft fuselage and the fuel tank arrangements had to be revised to find space for the hydrogen peroxide. This pushed the gross weight up to 13,900 lb (6,305kg) and the combat weight to 10,300 lb (4,672kg) but the rocket would make the aircraft capable of altitudes up to 86,000ft (26,213m) and speeds of Mach 2.0 between 32,000ft (9,754m) and 78,500ft (23,927m). Rate of climb at 50,000ft (15,240m) was 37,000ft/min (11,278m/min).

Northrop N-156F/F-5A Freedom Fighter
Northrop went on to produce a fighter under the N-156 number, but this proved to be quite different from the project described above and was designated N-156F. In 1955 the company began looking at a new lightweight supersonic fighter that would be easy to maintain and relatively inexpensive. It was powered by two examples of a new and compact engine from General Electric called the J85 and came together as the N-156F in October 1956. In the meantime both the Air Force and Navy needed a new advanced trainer and a two-seat version called the N-156T was offered as well. This was ordered in numbers as the T-38 Talon. Once this type's potential had been recognised, three prototypes of the N-156F were also requested in May 1958. The fighter shared a substantial amount of common parts and tooling with the trainer. Welko Gasich headed the N-156 development team, while also working with Jerry Huben on Northrop's long-range interceptor family.

The first N-156F, named Freedom Fighter, made its maiden flight on 30th July 1959 but, before the third aircraft had been completed, the USAF halted the fighter part of the program. In fact the Service had no interest in this class of fighter for its own use and the three airframes were stored. However, at this time

Lightweight Fighters

Lockheed CL-1200-1 (1.70).
Peter Clukey

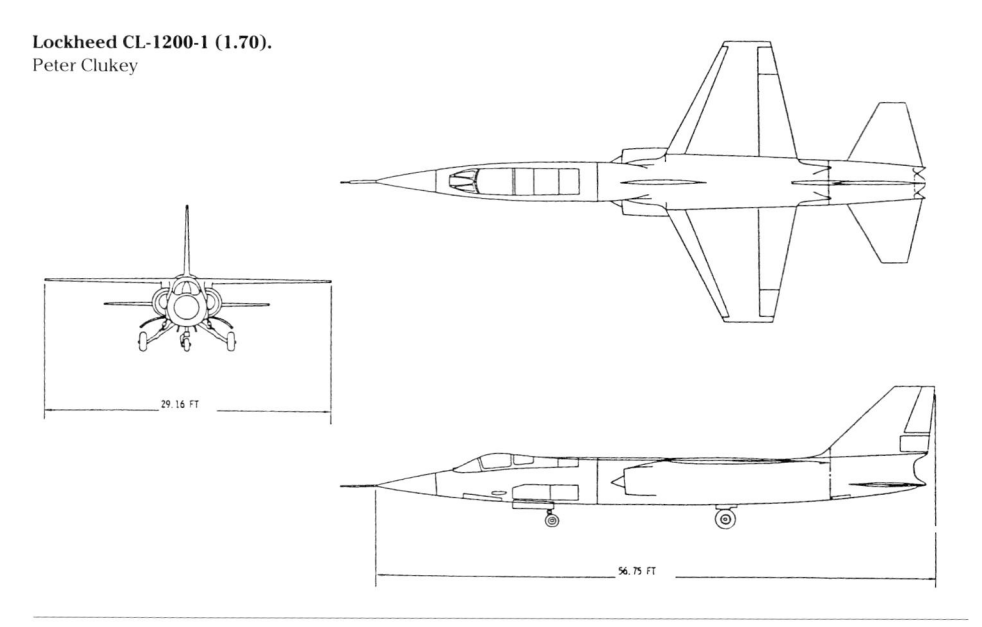

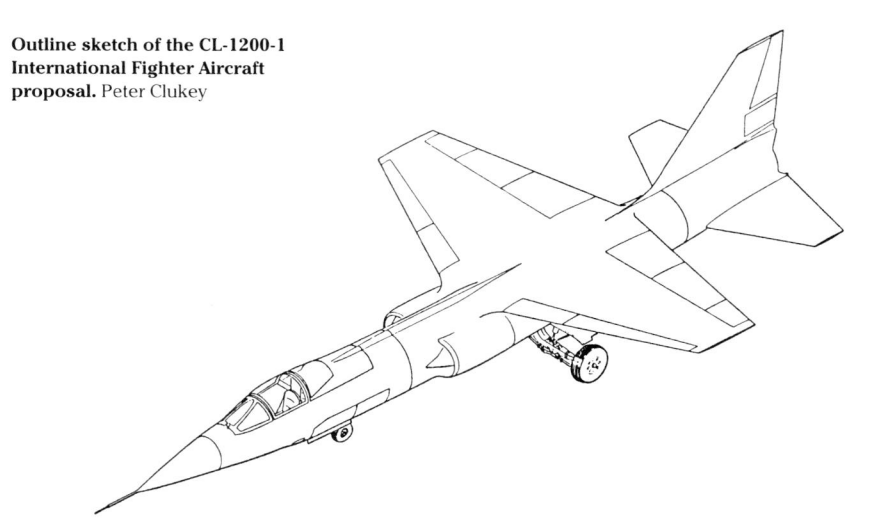

Outline sketch of the CL-1200-1 International Fighter Aircraft proposal. Peter Clukey

America was planning to supply arms to friendly countries at very favourable terms under its Mutual Assistance Program. The US Government had long been aware of the low military effectiveness and very high maintenance costs of the many hundreds of older jet fighters (mostly F-84s and F-86s) currently serving with NATO and SEATO nations, or other countries that were militarily aligned with the US. In April 1962 the N-156F was selected as the fighter that was to be made available under this scheme (its principal rival had been a simplified version of the F-104). As a result, in 1963 the N-156F prototypes were reactivated and many production examples followed that eventually reached a host of different countries. The fighter was designated F-5A and the USAF acted as the purchasing agency.

The Freedom Fighter program proved to be very successful and by 1969 Northrop was planning an upgraded version that would be capable of Mach 1.6. Then a new International Fighter Aircraft (IFA) competition was opened to find a Freedom Fighter successor and Northrop's project, known as the F-5-21, became just one of the entries. The others were the CL-1200 from Lockheed, a stripped McDonnell F-4E Phantom and an LTV (Vought) F-8 Crusader variant called the V-1000. The 'light Phantom' used the standard airframe with Sidewinders retained, but the facility to carry Sparrow was eliminated and the avionics systems were considerably reduced or simplified. All bar the V-1000 had begun during 1969, LTV becoming 'a seriously interested latecomer'. A proposal request was made in January 1970 and the designs had to be submitted within thirty days, with the winner expected to be chosen by mid-April.

Lockheed CL-1200-1 Lancer
Lockheed's CL-1200 designation was originally assigned to an attack aircraft study for the Navy, but it was then switched to a major development of the F-104G Starfighter. The CL-1200-1 IFA proposal essentially coupled a Starfighter forward fuselage and air inlets with a new high-position wing, rear fuselage and low tail. A full-size mock-up of the Lancer was built, photographs of which have been extensively published.

A Northrop F-5E Tiger II seen working for the USAF. This particular machine was being used to test Northrop's LATAR (Laser Augmented Target Acquisition and Recognition) system, housed in a pod beneath the cockpit.

American Secret Projects: Fighters & Interceptors

LTV V-1000
The V-1000 was a simplified higher performance version of the F-8 powered by a 17,900 lb (79.6kN) J79-17 engine. LTV stated that it weighed 3,884 lb (1,762kg) less than the standard machine (maximum weight 24,881 lb [11,286kg]) and showed minimal changes to the normal aircraft, although droop had been added to the wing leading edge to assist with manoeuvring and cruise flight. The V-1000's ordnance carrying capacity was also increased to 6,000 lb (2,722kg) compared to the F-8's usual 5,000 lb (2,268kg). When this proposal was made LTV was just finishing the re-manufacture of 385 F-8s for the Navy so its factory was in an active position to take on this new project.

After an evaluation that actually lasted seven months, Northrop's advanced F-5 was declared the winner on 20th November 1970. Big factors in this decision were the desire to provide the greatest combat capability for the available dollars while four countries that were expected to be the prime recipients of the type, South Vietnam, South Korea, Thailand and Nationalist China, already had versions of the F-5 in their inventories. The Crusader variant was considered to be too geared towards the offensive role and too large, despite carrying much less fuel than the standard F-8.

Northrop F-5E Tiger II
Northrop's winning design was designated F-5E and named Tiger II. A private venture prototype had actually flown on 28th March 1969. Externally the F-5A and F-5E were pretty similar but the latter had more powerful J85 engines and, there were visible changes around the air intakes and wing root leading edge and numerous other modifications. The first series F-5E flew in August 1972 and the type was to win more large orders for Northrop. In due course there were further efforts to improve the F-5 family, culminating in the F-5G proposed in 1980. Redesignated F-20 and named Tigershark, the first of three prototypes flew in August 1982, but in 1986 this fighter lost a USAF 'low-cost' Air Defense Fighter competition to the General Dynamics F-16. That decision terminated the F-20 program. The aircraft was shown widely around the world, apparently demonstrating outstanding performance and, being based on an existing aircraft, it would have been readily available. However, foreign air forces declined to buy it, reputedly on the grounds that if it wasn't good enough for the parent nation, it wasn't good enough for them.

The USAF's Lightweight Competition

In the mid-1960s the USAF was committed to big fighter-type aircraft, with the F-4 being delivered and the F-111 in the pipeline. Although formidable aeroplanes, both were complicated pieces of machinery that were also very expensive. Consequently in 1965 the USAF itself initiated a study for a smaller type that would attempt to get away from the ever-growing spiral of complexity and cost. A weight limit of 25,000 lb (11,340kg) was set (which it is worth pointing out was still 50% higher than the post-war F-86 and more than double that of the wartime piston-powered P-51). The project was labelled the Advanced Day Fighter or ADF. General Dynamics was one company that looked at plenty of possible ADF configurations but the time was still not ripe for this idea – especially after the Soviet Union had unveiled its MiG-25 which gave extra impetus to the FX (F-15) program. So the ADF died.

However, ADF had helped the momentum for a lighter fighter to grow, the key supporters becoming known as the 'Fighter Mafia'. They included a weapon system analyst, Pierre Sprey, and certain high-ranking officers in the USAF such as Major John Boyd and Lieutenant Colonel Everest Riccioni. Their campaign to push the alternative lightweight fighter has been well documented and needs only a brief résumé here. In about 1969 these individuals began to promote a concept called FXX. This attracted a good deal of hostility within the USAF but it also generated more support for the lightweight idea as well (FXX tallied very closely to the Northrop P-530 below). Many now began to feel that the F-15 proposition was indeed far too big, and the concerns over the cost and complexity of both the F-14 and F-15 led to extensive debate and consideration of a smaller, cheaper and more manoeuvrable alternative. In due course this effort was rewarded with a full competition held in 1971/1972. However, let us look first at the research into lightweight fighters undertaken by General Dynamics and Northrop before this competition opened.

General Dynamics Advanced Day Fighter
General Dynamics (GD) Fort Worth completed numerous studies of the ADF concept, but one in particular has been associated with starting the evolution that eventually brought forth the F-16. In 1965 the company produced a design concept that was proposed as an F-4 Phantom replacement and a counter to the Soviet MiG-21 light fighter. With a gross weight of 25,000 lb (11,340kg) this project featured a tapered wing of moderate sweep, fixed to a blended inner wing and fuselage, a single fin and an all-moving tailplane. The aircraft was to be powered by two engines fed by a large under-fuselage intake, with a cannon placed inside the port leading edge extension. At this time General Dynamics was also starting to look into concepts against the larger FX requirement and it was during this overall research that GD first considered 'blended' wing/body combinations.

General Dynamics proposal for an 'F-4 Replacement' (1965). Pierre Trichet via Joe Cherrie

Lightweight Fighters

Northrop N-300A-5 (14.6.66). Gerald Balzer

Northrop N-300A-11 (14.6.66). Gerald Balzer

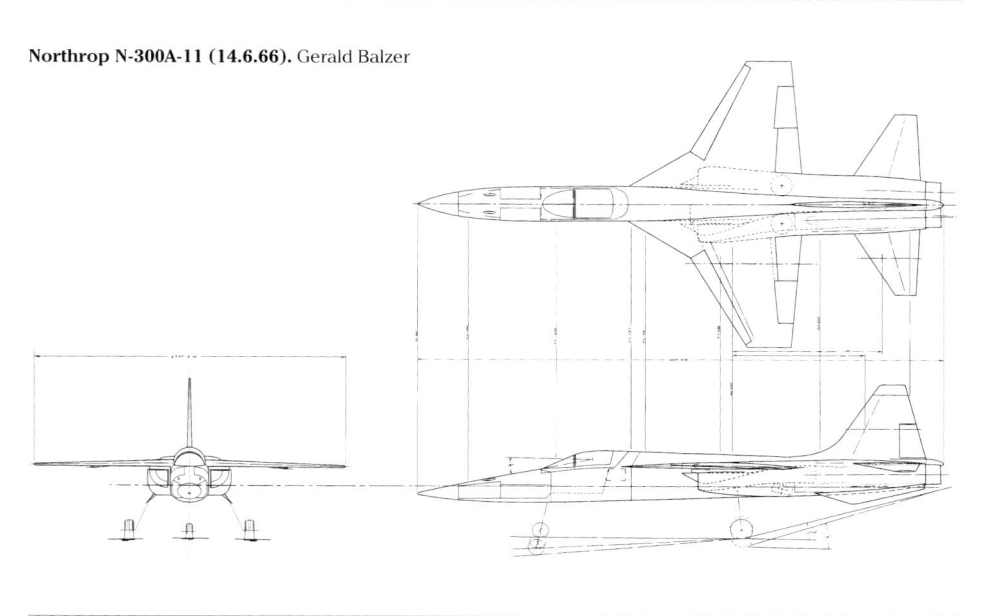

Northrop N-300

Having got the ball rolling with the N-156, Northrop kept its interest in lightweight fighters going with the N-300 family of designs. The N-300 also represented the opening of the research that would lead to the P-530 Cobra series and then the YF-17 and F-18. Work on the N-300 began in 1965 and in due course covered a series of projects on its own. In the early stages the family likeness to the Freedom Fighter was obvious and included an F-5-type wing, but gradually characteristics more common to the Cobra and YF-17 began to appear.

One design, called the N-300A-5, featured a high wing and fuselage-mounted main landing gear, in contrast to the F-5A's low-position wing. The high wing arrived in mid-1966 after about a year of testing and allowed the selection of a wing thickness that was independent of the constraints set by the landing gear struts. It also made more room available for spacing store pylons and hardpoints, but a more complicated landing gear would also be required. This increased the frontal area by 4.3% and added 300 lb (136kg) in weight over an equivalent low-wing design called the N-300A-2. The latter's calculated take-off weight (clean, internal fuel plus ammunition) was 18,618 lb (8,445kg) against the A-5's 18,902 lb (8,574kg). The twin-engine single-seat N-300A-5 had two cannon mounted in the upper nose and could carry stores or 300gal (1,364lit) tanks on four underwing pylons plus other stores underneath the fuselage. Fuel was held in four fuselage tanks placed between the intake ducting and in two wingtip tanks.

The work also embraced the N-300A-11, which was similar to the A-5 but introduced three-dimensional air inlets beneath the wing. These were similar to the type used by the General Dynamics F-111 and offered the advantage of being short, thereby reducing weight, but with the potential disadvantage of suffering Foreign Object Damage on the runway. A later design, the N-300A-43, introduced another intake position, subtle differences to the wing shape, and longer leading edge root extensions.

General Dynamics Studies

GD continued its research and from 1968 through to 1971 completed studies that contributed much to the aerodynamic design of the F-16. Some of this work was undertaken under contract, for example the FX Concept Formulation Study of 1968, while other parts were completed using company funding. The latter included the first examination of a single-engine air superiority (FX) fighter (in parallel with larger FX designs) that externally was quite similar to the 1965 twin-engine project described above. During this period Messrs Sprey and Boyd used GD's FX-404 design (and a Northrop project) to substantiate their calculations for an FXX fighter. FX-404 appears to have been a twin-fin version of the 1968 single-engine FX project illustrated. At one stage in mid-1969 General Dynamics was proposing canard control surfaces on its FXX that were not retractable. The outline requirements for the FXX included a speed of Mach 1.4 to Mach 1.5, because speeds higher than these were seldom used in service.

Alongside this quest for a light fighter there was also on-going research into improving air combat manoeuvrability. With this in mind, GD completed four separate technical studies during 1969 and 1970. These were Project Tailormate (1969/1970), which looked at a wide variety of air intake types and their locations on a fighter; and a 1969 examination of leading and trailing edge wing-mounted roll control devices for transonic conditions and high angles of attack. The third report, from 1970, was called 'Aerodynamic Contouring of a Wing-Body Design for an Advanced Air Superiority Fighter' and followed on from the roll control work. Finally, there was a 1969/1970 study into buffet, and all of this helped GD's design team acquire sufficient knowledge to create a top-class fighter.

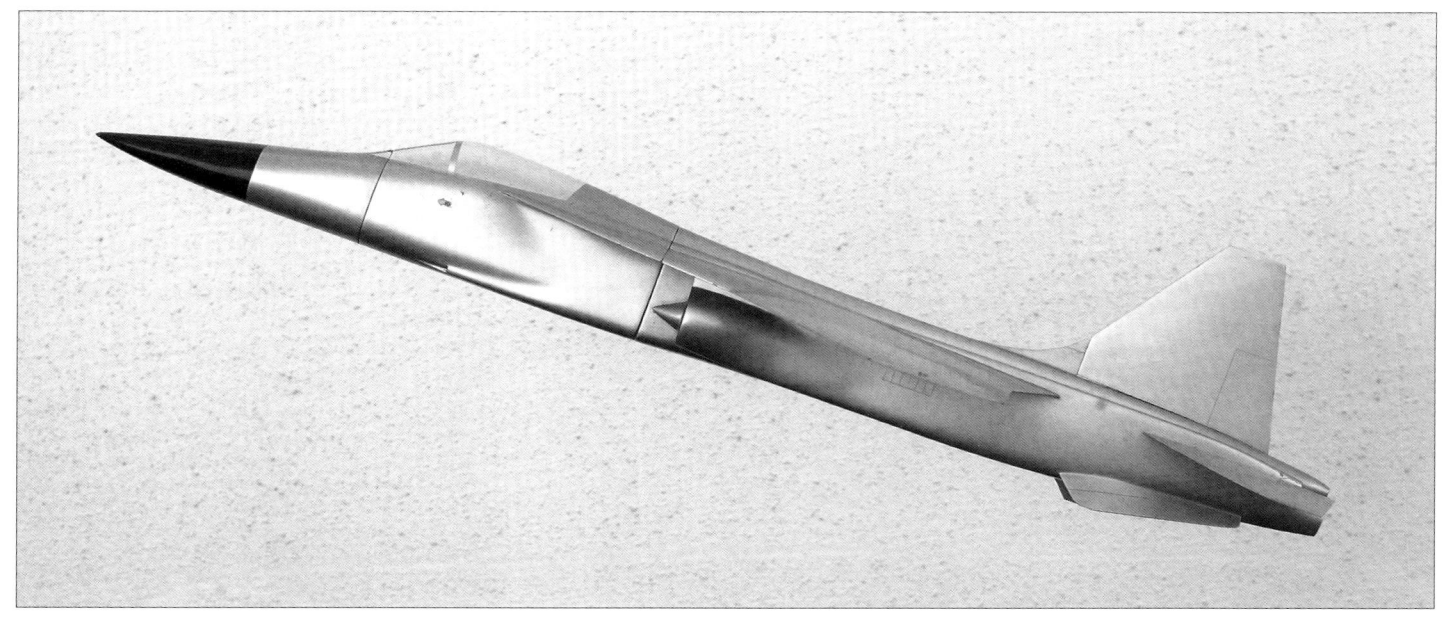

Model of the Northrop N-300A-43. This fighter had an estimated clean take-off weight of 20,500 lb (9,299kg), a wing area of 300ft² (27.9m²), and was to be powered by two General Electric GE1/J1A1 (J97 derivative) jets giving 7,500 lb (33.3kN) of thrust.
Jim Keeshen

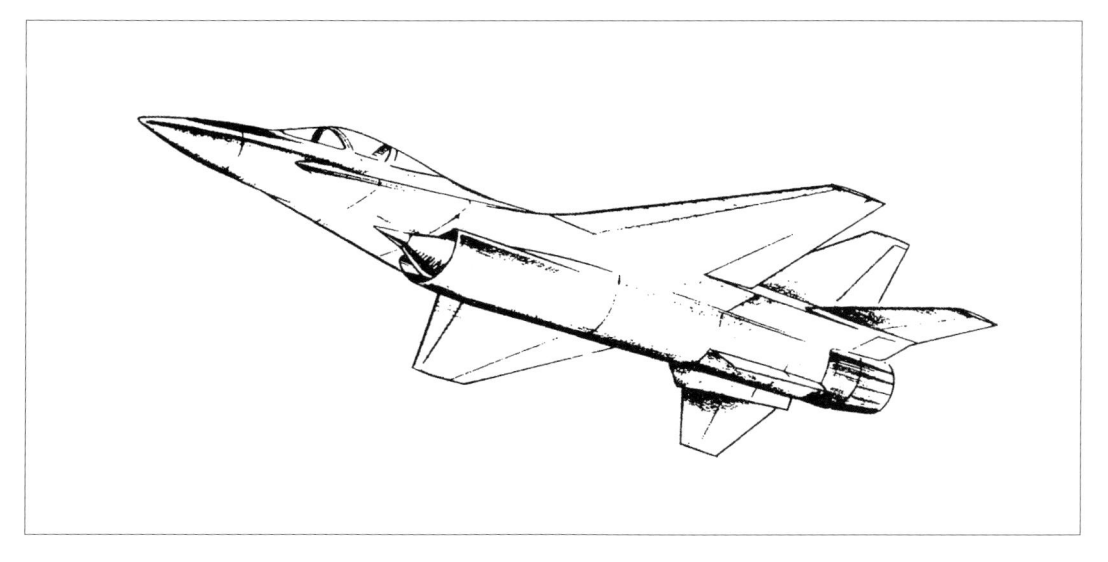

General Dynamics single-engine FX design (1968).

Lightweight Fighters

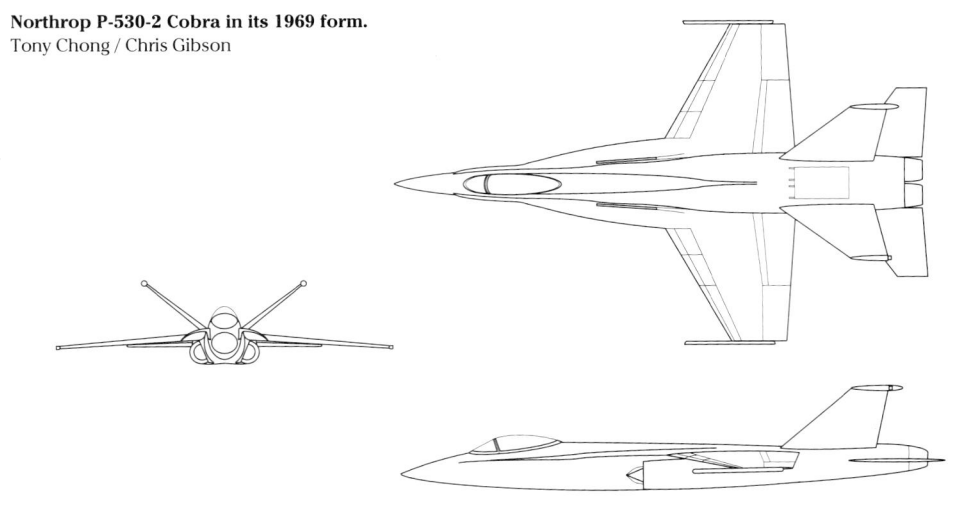

Northrop P-530-2 Cobra in its 1969 form.
Tony Chong / Chris Gibson

Northrop-made model of the P-530-2 Cobra. This very attractive design carries four Sidewinder missiles on wingtip and underwing pylons but no gun is visible. Built to 1/40th scale, its span is 11.3in (28.7cm) and length 16.9in (43cm), which gives an approximate span for the real aircraft of 37ft 8in (11.5m) and length 56ft 4in (17.2m).
Jonathan Rigutto / photo © 2005 Chad Slattery

Northrop P-530

In 1967 Northrop's work on the N-300 was advanced by a change that introduced larger wing leading edge extensions together with underwing air intakes. Northrop now called its project the P-530 Cobra and this began a series of layouts completed under that designation. At this point the design retained a single fin and was to be powered by a development of a General Electric's J97 turbojet that was expected to give 8,000 lb (35.6kN) of thrust. In March 1968 however the P-530-2 replaced the initial design with a twin-finned layout that had even larger leading edge extensions to supply greater lift and improve the control of the airflow. Two fins were needed to give sufficient directional stability when flying at high angles of attack. More sophisticated avionics were added to the new package together with General Electric J1A2 engines which increased the available thrust from each unit to 10,000 lb (44.4kN).

Throughout this period the P-530 was optimised for air superiority and in 1969 the P-530-2 was redesigned yet again. Here the biggest external difference was the larger canted fins. These had been moved to a very unusual forward position, the tailplanes being kept as far aft as possible. In addition the leading edge extensions were now contoured to give even better lift and stability, the cockpit had been moved forward and there was a fixed cone intake. Finally, in 1970 the

P-530-3 revealed a refined fuselage and shorter two-dimensional fixed ramp inlets feeding 13,000 lb (57.8kN) thrust J1A5 engines. Later this powerplant was replaced by the GE15, a new two-spool bypass turbofan that offered 14,300 lb (63.6kN) of thrust. In due course this engine would become the YJ101 and power the YF-17.

The leading edge extension formed a long fairing on each side of the fuselage and Northrop referred to this feature as a 'hybrid' wing. It was intended to maintain a smooth airflow (and therefore lift) over the wing at the very high angles of attack made possible during combat manoeuvring by the high thrust-to-weight ratio. Cobra had full-span leading edge slats split into three sections that in part would serve as manoeuvre flaps, while the trailing edge was occupied by powered ailerons and landing flaps. There was an all-moving flying tail and the fins were canted outwards at 30°. An M61 multi-barrel cannon was housed low in the nose, beneath the cockpit and ahead of the nosewheel, while the nose contained an X-band radar. A total of 7,200 lb (3,266kg) of internal fuel was housed in the fuselage and there were six underwing hardpoints and another store position beneath the fuselage. Two Sidewinders were mounted on the wingtips and in the air-to-air role the inner wing pylons would probably have carried tanks to give the aircraft sufficient range. Maximum gross weight was 40,000 lb (18,144kg) when carrying the maximum 16,000 lb (7,258kg) of external stores (AAMs, bombs or tanks), sea level rate of climb was in excess of 50,000ft/min (15,240m/min) and service ceiling 60,000ft (18,288m).

The existence of the Cobra was announced to the public on 28th January 1971. A year later Northrop could see a potential market for the P-530 within the seventeen air forces by then flying the Freedom Fighter, and for some time the company had been active trying to enlist financing and participation from overseas countries. A full-scale mock up of the P-530 was completed in December 1972 using Northrop's own money and the fighter's manoeuvrability was expected to surpass any other type currently flying.

The momentum behind the potential development of a lightweight fighter steadily grew and in 1971 unsolicited proposals were made by several companies. Lockheed began in

Model of Boeing's lightweight fighter proposal (1.72). This shows tip-mounted Sidewinders and appears to have a gun in the fuselage side above the intakes. Terry Panopalis

January by offering to construct two CL-1200 prototypes (basically the design proposed the previous year to the International Fighter Aircraft competition), Northrop submitted a new project on 31st January and Boeing entered the scene with a proposal sent during February. Northrop offered to build and fly two P-530s at company expense and in March proposed the P-530-4, which was described as an Air Research Vehicle. The arrival of these documents increased the level of interest within the Pentagon and a prototype group was formed with the intention of recommending suitable candidate designs that could be built in prototype form. Three more unsolicited submissions arrived in June 1971 from Boeing, Northrop and LTV (Vought). Northrop's P-610 and LTV's V-1100, both first proposed during this period, would also be submitted to the official competition held in early 1972 and so they are described in that part of the text.

Boeing Model 908-618-2

Boeing's next lightweight fighter submission was the Model 908-618-2, which was presented on 15th June. At this time Boeing was allocating numbers within the 908 series to all of its fighter projects. This design's general layout showed a chin intake supplying a single F100 engine, swept wings which could be adapted to take Sidewinders on tip pylons (the composite wingtips could be removed), a low all-moving tail, single fin and two large ventral fins. Wing thickness/chord ratio was 5%. One M39 cannon was mounted in each of the long, slim wing leading-edge extensions and a total of 4,330 lb (1,964kg) of internal fuel could be carried, 1,180 lb (535kg) in wing tanks and the rest in the fuselage. The aircraft

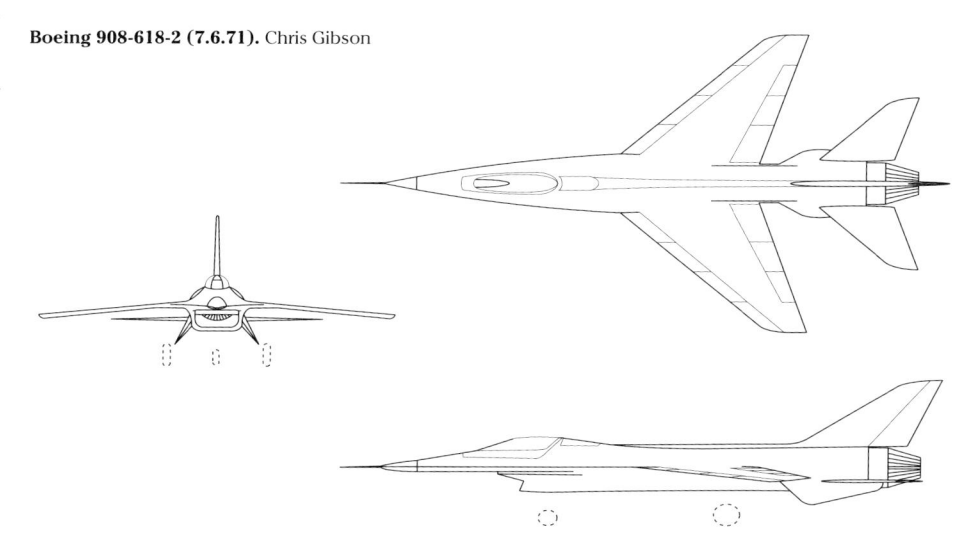

Boeing 908-618-2 (7.6.71). Chris Gibson

Lightweight Fighters

had a small ranging radar and the capability to carry two Mk.82 bombs or a single 450gal (2,046lit) external tank beneath the middle fuselage. In the end it was considered that the form of 908-618's leading edge extensions would actually prevent the project from being turned into a workable design.

Eventually, in late 1971, some money was put aside within the Fiscal Year 1972 budget to pay for prototypes of two different lightweight air superiority day fighters. These were to be selected from a full competition for which a Request for Proposals was issued at the turn of the year (the document was dated 6th January 1972). Many of Pierre Sprey's ideas for what constituted a lightweight fighter were included in these requirements, for example a high thrust-to-weight ratio and outstanding manoeuvrability, while the maximum weight was now reduced to 20,000 lb (9,072kg). There were no indicated performance requirements above Mach 1.6 and the avionics were to be kept to a minimum, as was the size of the proposal documents. The following proposals were delivered in mid-February but the other companies invited to respond (Fairchild, Grumman, McDonnell Douglas and North American Rockwell) did not take part.

Boeing Model 908-909

Boeing's 908-909 design was similar in general layout to the 908-618-2 but showed subtle differences. The leading edge extensions were gone and replaced by a slim chine around the nose, the wing was placed lower on the fuselage and had no anhedral, and the ventral fins were smaller. The powerplant and air-to-air weapons were unchanged.

General Dynamics Model 401

The Model 401 project number embraced a variety of lightweight fighter designs studied during 1969 to 1971, but these formed only part of GD's substantial research into light weight possibilities. Both single and twin engine types were considered within the same basic airframes and the results showed that a single engine type would be 20% lighter at the start of combat and possessed more rapid acceleration and superior sustained rates of turn. In addition conventional wing-body-tail designs (Models 785 and 786 with single and twin fins respectively) were compared against different variations of the 401, each having a highly blended wing-body. By late 1970 the engine chosen to power the single-seat fighter was Pratt & Whitney's F100; it was not only the most advanced available, but it would also be operational in time for the aircraft's planned first flight.

The original Model 401F advanced day fighter project of mid-1971 displayed a wide lifting forebody and all-moving twin tails on booms extending aft to either side of the single engine. The leading edge sweep angle was 35° and the wing was fitted with leading edge 'manoeuvre flaps' plus inner tailing edge flaps and outer flaperons. There was a large chin intake, two Sidewinders were shown on the outer pair of four underwing pylons and two cannon were mounted in the wing roots.

The project actually submitted to the new competition was the 401-16B, which came very close to the YF-16 as built. A simple air inlet was selected on the premise that the majority of air-to-air combat that this aircraft was likely to experience would take place in the transonic and low-supersonic speed region. Project Tailormate resulted in the choice of a short chin intake; the data showing that fuselage shielding was beneficial at the high angles of attack expected during combat. A single fin was fitted after research revealed how the forebody-strake/leading edge flap combination had enhanced the directional stability of the aircraft. This was also true for twin fin arrangements but certain shapes of strake were found to degrade the stability; thus twin fins appeared to present a greater development risk. Vertical tail height above the wing chord plane was found to be an important design consideration.

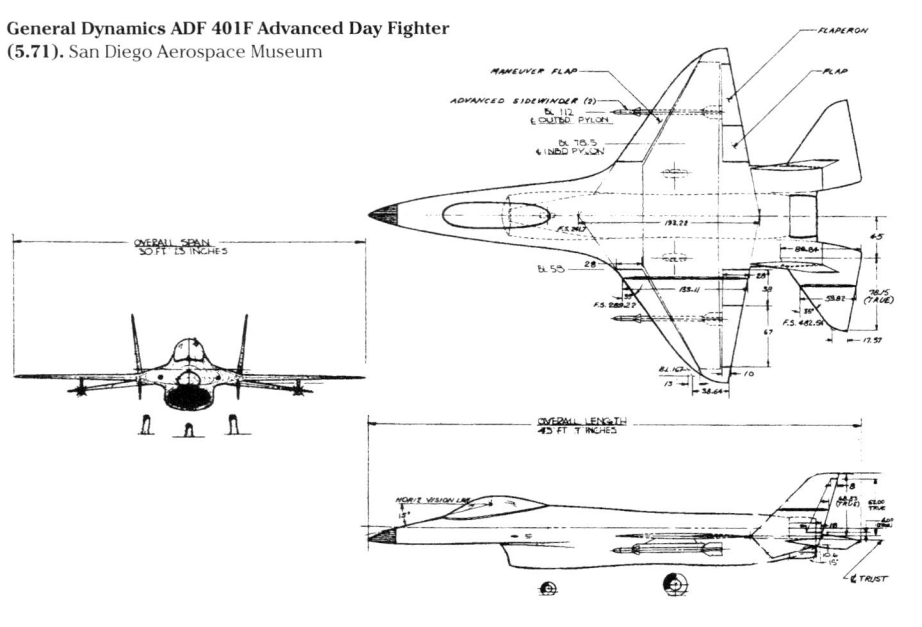

General Dynamics ADF 401F Advanced Day Fighter (5.71). San Diego Aerospace Museum

Impression of the ADF 401F project.
Pierre Trichet via Joe Cherrie

Lockheed X-27 Lancer and CL-1200-2

'Kelly' Johnson and his Lockheed design team pushed hard to have the CL-1200-1 and its potential capabilities accepted, which ensured that the project underwent a degree of Air Force consideration during 1971. The existence of this design worried supporters of the F-15 due to the possibility that funding might be diverted from the McDonnell Douglas aircraft. As a result Johnson was forced to modify his proposal for two prototypes by making the CL-1200 sound more like a research project. As such this would make it less of a threat to the F-15 and in April 1971 the Lancer received the X-27 research designation. In reality it was nothing of the sort and some contracts were drafted that were intended to take the project through to operational hardware. A mock-up was built that exhibited a design modified from the CL-1200-1 with a larger wing and small leading edge extensions, a new fin and square side intakes. It was all to no avail, no funding was allocated and the X-27 came to an end.

The CL-1200-2 lightweight fighter proposal was very similar to the X-27 but had round intakes with shock cones and a different fin. There was no anhedral on the horizontal tailplane. Johnson wanted the project redesignated CL-1600 to distinguish it from previous CL-1200 work (although the CL-1600 drawing supplied to the author is outwardly identical to the CL-1200-1). A further variant, proposed after the CL-1200-2 had been rejected, was the CL-1400 or CL-1400N that used a CL-1200-2 forward fuselage, intake and wing coupled with the X-27's rear fuselage, larger fin and no ventral fins. This too failed to gain acceptance.

Lockheed CL-1200-2 (1.72). Peter Clukey

This manufacturer's model of a CL-1200/X-27 Lancer variant looks identical to Lockheed's CL-1400 project for the Navy. It has a CL-1200-2-type forward fuselage, intake and wing but the X-27's tail. However, it shows USAF markings. John Aldaz

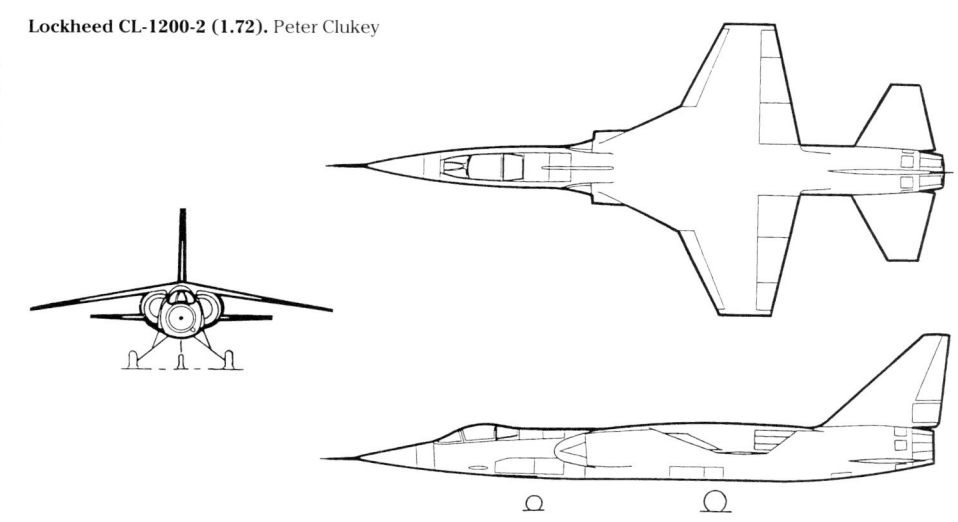

Lightweight Fighters

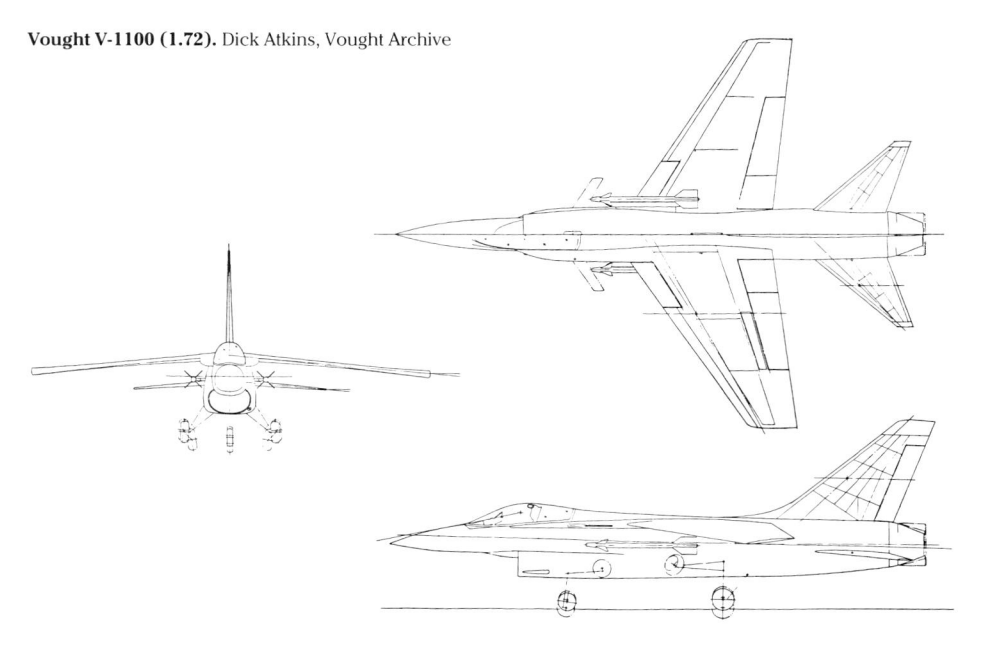

Vought V-1100 (1.72). Dick Atkins, Vought Archive

Impression of Vought's V-1100. Dick Atkins, Vought Archive

Vought Aeronautics V-1100

By the time its V-1100 project had been submitted to the official competition, LTV had been renamed Vought Aeronautics. Like Boeing and GD, Vought's design used a swept wing and a chin intake, but it also had very small extendable canards placed on the wing leading edge root extensions to reduce trim drag during supersonic manoeuvres. There was a single cannon placed inside the port lip of the air intake while two Sidewinders were carried on side fuselage pylons beneath the forward portion of the wing root. V-1100 used a 23,600 lb (104.9kN) thrust Pratt & Whitney F-100 that gave an estimated top speed of Mach 1.2 at sea level and Mach 2.0 between 34,000ft (10,363m) and 60,000ft (18,288m); gross take-off weight was 19,000 lb (8,618kg).

The designers noted that the F-100 was optimised for the fighter role and thus enabled the V-1100 to meet its design and performance goals without having to use an engine that was too big. If a go-ahead was given on 1st May 1972 Vought estimated that the first flight of the first prototype could take place by February 1974 and a second machine would follow in April.

Northrop N-321/P-600

Northrop proposed two designs, the twin-engine P-600 and single-engine P-610. The P-600 was based on the P-530 in its 1971 form, and was eventually to fly as the YF-17.

Northrop N-322/P-610

The single engine Northrop P-610 was first proposed in the middle of 1971 and showed a design rather smaller than the P-530, weighing just 17,000 lb (7,711kg). It was expected to be even more manoeuvrable than its twin-engine brother and was powered by a single F100 engine. However, this was something of a hurried design because, after years of development work getting the interface between the engine and inlet on its twin-engine types exactly right, Northrop had been unable to devote the same effort to a single-engine interface. In fact Northrop was never happy with the P-610 and in due course the manufacturer withdrew it from the competition.

On 18th March 1972 the Air Staff declared that Boeing's 908-909 design was the most favourable proposal, with the General Dynamics Model 401 only just behind and Northrop's P-600 third. Lockheed's CL-1200 was a distant fifth. However, after further assessment the Source Selection Board put Boeing third and in April it was announced that prototype contracts would go to General Dynamics and Northrop to build their designs as the YF-16 and YF-17 respectively. The Boeing and General Dynamics projects were very similar and one objective had been to build both single- and twin-engine types, which brought Northrop back into the picture. A flight competition was to be held and the design considered best would then be put into production. This decision reflected a policy change to competitive 'prototyping', something which today is common practice for the US military but in 1972 had been out of favour for some time.

Lockheed's lack of support was in part due to the fact that many viewed it as a modification of an old design (the F-104), while the company had also been marketing it as an export fighter for quite some time. After its proposal had been rejected, Lockheed continued to offer the CL-1200 for foreign sales well into 1973, but by late summer the project had been declared dead since it was clearly not a contender for the European fighter market either. The F-16 would see to that.

General Dynamics YF-16 and Northrop YF-17

Two prototypes of each winning design were ordered and the type had now become known as the Air Combat Fighter. The YF-16 made its first flight on 20th January 1974 and the YF-17 followed on 9th June. It was announced on 11th September that the best aircraft would be put into production for the Air Force and the YF-16 was declared the win-

Model of the Northrop P-610 (1971). Jim Keeshen

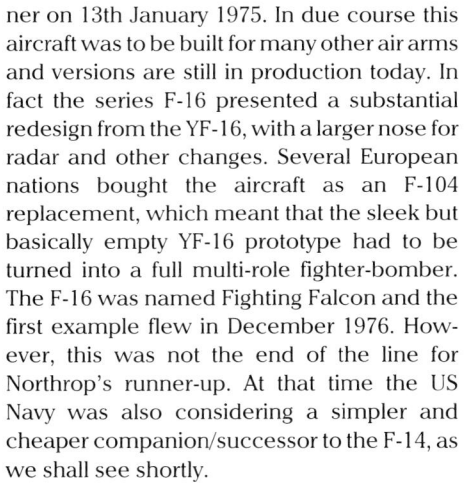

ner on 13th January 1975. In due course this aircraft was to be built for many other air arms and versions are still in production today. In fact the series F-16 presented a substantial redesign from the YF-16, with a larger nose for radar and other changes. Several European nations bought the aircraft as an F-104 replacement, which meant that the sleek but basically empty YF-16 prototype had to be turned into a full multi-role fighter-bomber. The F-16 was named Fighting Falcon and the first example flew in December 1976. However, this was not the end of the line for Northrop's runner-up. At that time the US Navy was also considering a simpler and cheaper companion/successor to the F-14, as we shall see shortly.

Meantime, in 1974 the 'Fighter Mafia' celebrated a significant victory when a new concept appeared called 'mutually complementary' fighters. The idea was that the Air Force would in future operate a mix of high- and low-cost fighters. In the end, that was exactly what it got. The F-15 and F-16 joined forces to serve the USAF alongside one another. Brief mention should also be made of the F-16XL, a radically redesigned and stretched multi-role F-16 fitted with a double delta wing that was first flown in July 1982. In 1984 it was pitted against the McDonnell Douglas F-15E Strike Eagle in a fly-off competition to find a new Dual Role Fighter for the Air Force. The Strike Eagle won and so only two F-16XLs were built, but these went on to perform a great deal of test flying for NASA. It was yet another example of a highly capable aircraft failing to find a production opportunity.

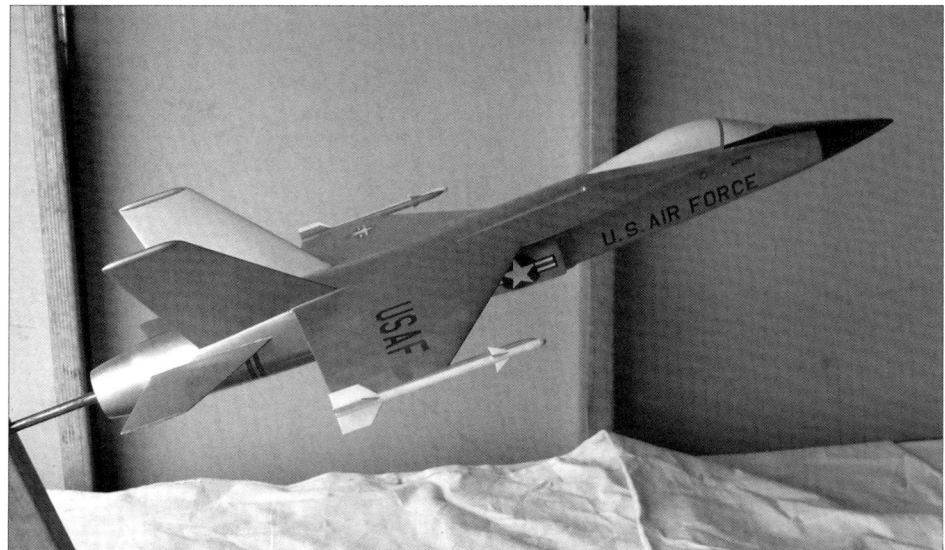

The General Dynamics (now Lockheed Martin) F-16 Fighting Falcon has been one of the most successful of all American jet fighters. This is the first F-16C Block 50D aircraft.

This view shows the second YF-17 prototype serving as a 'prototype' for the F-18 Hornet. It is accompanied by a Top Gun F-5E from NAS Miramar.

Lightweight Fighters

197

Other Projects

Two more light fighter studies have been traced that appear to have been entirely separate from the Air Force program described above, although both turned up as manufacturers' models displaying USAF markings.

Grumman Lightweight Fighter

Although the first model bore no company identity, the author was assured that the first of the projects came from Grumman. The fact that a model was produced indicates that the design was examined in some depth.

Vought Aerospace V-2000

The other design came from Vought. In November 1971 Vought Aeronautics carried out an in-house technology assessment of fighter state-of-the-art with particular emphasis on the advances in technology that would influence the design of fighters operating in the 1980s. The project was called the V-2000, the designation falling outside the normal series of Vought project numbers, and it used a projected 1980 operational environment as its guide. The V-2000 design was in appearance very like the types of fighter designed by several countries in the late 1970s and early 1980s, before stealth features began to exert their influence. This single-seater featured a cranked delta wing, a very small high-position tapered canard, twin fins and twin engines fed by intakes placed beneath the leading edge extensions. There appears to be no gun but the company document does show the model with an example of the new AIM-95 Agile air-to-air missile on each wingtip.

This page:

Vought V-2000 Model (11.8.71). Span is 11.0in (28cm) without wingtip air-to-air missiles and length 16.7in (42.4cm).
George Cox

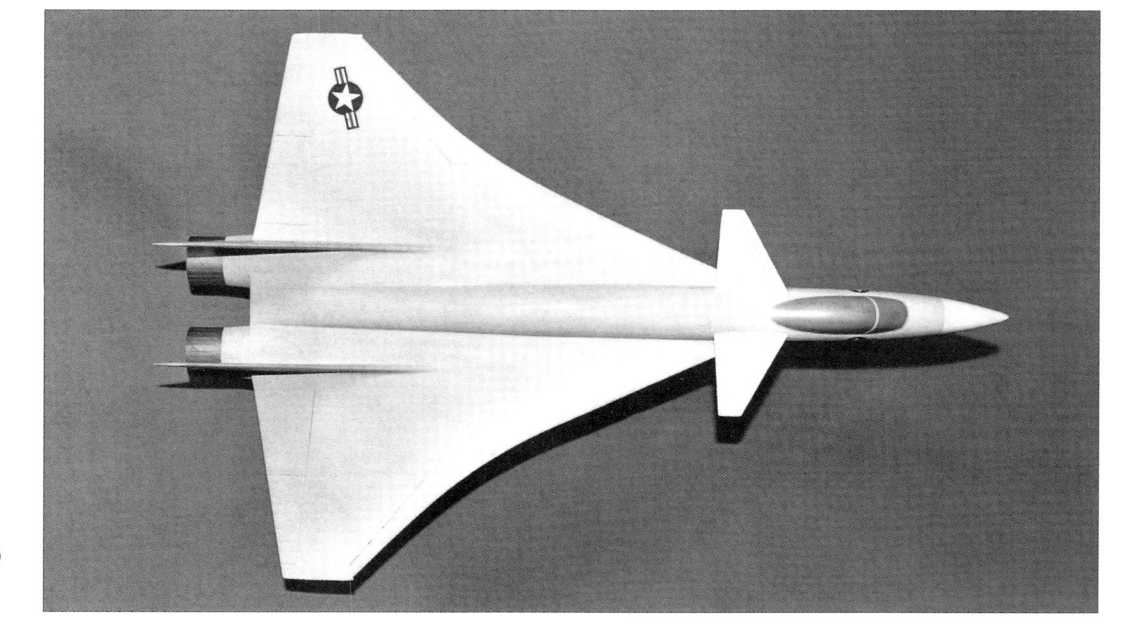

Opposite page:

Model of the Grumman lightweight fighter which may be a mid to late 1970s design. Span is 8.4in (21.3cm) and length 15.4in (39.0cm).
Allyson Vought

Lightweight Fighters

This model of an unknown Northrop design appears to show a single engine version of the YF-17 (c1972).
Jim Keeshen / photo John Aldaz

The US Navy's Lightweight Fighter Competition

It was clear from an early stage of the Air Force lightweight fighter competition that such a type would also have much to commend it to the US Navy. In addition the very high cost of each F-14 Tomcat airframe would in itself ensure that something simpler would be needed in due course. It wasn't only a matter of initial purchase cost, the maintenance of a big and complex aircraft was also proving to be an important consideration. During 1970 to 1972 a couple of design teams looked at possible concepts for naval use, General Dynamics (Convair) with its Model 23 and Vought with its V-523.

General Dynamics (Convair) Model 23

Little is known about the Model 23 but visually it resembled and shared many of the design characteristics of the YF-16. Indeed it had an influence on the Fort Worth project because, after a 1971 meeting between designers from both GD facilities, the Model 401 was switched to a single fin. In November 1973 work under the Model 23 designation was still on-going and included wind tunnel testing of a 1/15th scale model of a single seat canard 60°-sweep delta layout. This had a low wing with the canard set around mid-fuselage, there was a chin intake and a fairing for a gun beneath the port wing root. The model dimensions indicate a span for the full size aircraft of 27ft 8in (8.4m) and length 46ft 2in (14.1m).

Vought Aeronautics V-523

The lightweight fighter study from Vought, the V-523, was another to employ a chin intake, which here was set back 12ft 7in (3.8m) from the nose. There was a high-position 35° swept wing, a low all-moving horizontal tailplane, small retractable canards level with the cockpit, and a tricycle undercarriage. Wing thickness ratio was 5% at the root, 4% at the tip, and the movable wing surfaces included an inboard leading edge flap, outboard leading edge slats, an upper surface spoiler, a flap-aileron and an inboard leading flap. The wing centre section consisted of a structural box, from wingfold to wingfold, that used a front spar, rear spar, five inter spars, a centre rib and various segmented ribs. Armament comprised a modified 20mm M61A1 three-barrel cannon mounted in the port side of the intake, three barrels (every second barrel) having been removed, there were two wing stations

Vought V-523 (17.8.72). Dick Atkins, Vought Archive

Model of the V-523 held by the Vought archive.

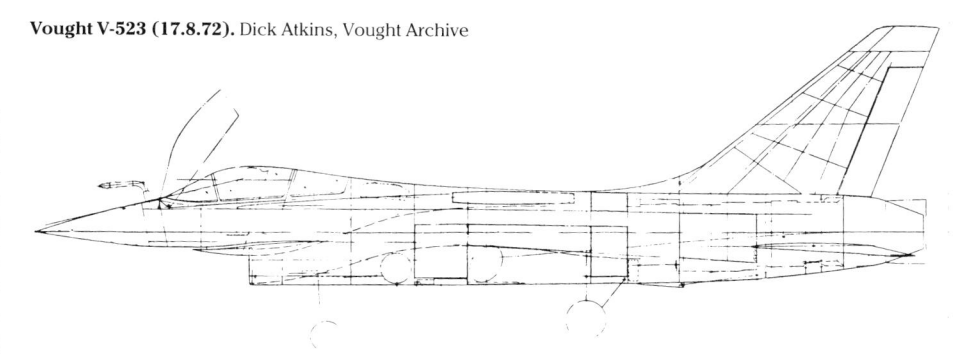

Lightweight Fighters

201

Grumman Design 623 (15.5.74).
Grumman Corp / Grumman History Centre

Model of the G-623.

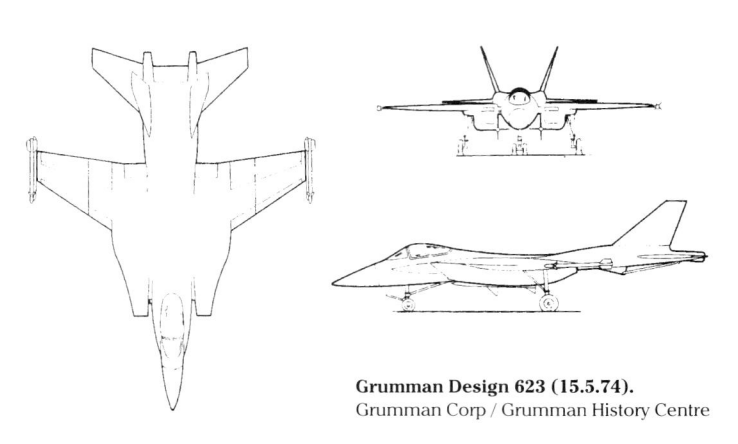

for carrying stores and two fuselage stations for AIM-95 Agile or AIM-9L Sidewinder missiles. Span was 39ft 0in (11.9m), folded span 28ft 6in (8.7m), length 53ft 6in (16.3m) and wing area 400ft² (37.2m²). The internal fuel in four fuselage and two wing tanks totalled 7,790lb (3,534kg).

Pressure continued to build against the F-14, and in August 1973 Congress ordered the Navy to undertake a study for an alternative lower cost fighter to replace the F-4 (and later the A-7 attack aircraft). During the following month the Service was instructed to make a Request for Proposals from industry for a single-seat VFAX aircraft (Fighter and Attack Experimental – not to be confused with the mid-1960s VFAX designs described in Chapter Nine). The maximum required speed was Mach 1.6 with acceleration considered to be the more important consideration. A 20mm gun was to be carried. With congressional funding approved and Pentagon authorisation given, a pre-solicitation notice was issued in June 1974 to six companies and the following proposals had been submitted by 15th July. The main brochures were not to exceed one hundred pages, but another twenty-five were to be devoted to V/STOL derivatives – the Navy hoped that the winning proposal might in due course be developed into a vertical take-off fighter. After these had been assessed, much more in depth proposals were to be requested from a limited number of companies.

General Dynamics (Convair) Model 218

GD Convair's Model 218 was a version of the Model 200 V/STOL covered in Chapter Seven. There were few external differences although this CTOL variation did not have the lift jets installed and would have required a conventional catapult to take-off from a carrier. The 218 could carry two wingtip-mounted Sidewinder missiles and two Sparrows side-by-side underneath the fuselage.

General Dynamics Model 18

The General Dynamics Fort Worth proposal was a slightly larger version of the YF-16 armed with a Sparrow on each wingtip rail and a Sidewinder on each side of the air intake. The manufacturer's model of this proposal has 'Model 18' painted on the fin and externally looked nearly identical to the Air Force prototypes, but the design had been stretched and the wing area increased.

Grumman G-623

Grumman stated that its Design 623 would be produced in single- and two-seat versions with the single-seater as the basic design. As such it would complement the F-14 in intercept missions and could be expected to see substantial use as a strike escort fighter. It was to be fitted with twin General Electric J101-GE-100 jets with two-dimensional nozzles and an airframe-mounted thrust-deflecting flap. Grumman stated that by including a Sparrow-compatible fire control system the design lent itself to the possible addition of an all-weather air-to-air capability. In all, there were five air-to-ground weapon stations and four more for air-to-air missiles. Two wingtip-mounted Sidewinders would be carried for the fighter escort mission together with two Sparrows on the inner sides of the wide-spaced air intakes. For other roles (interdiction, combat air patrol and close air support) several 600gal (2,728lit) drop tanks could be carried together with a mix of bombs and rockets. Gross take-off weight for interdiction duties with two tanks was 45,133lb (20,472kg) and the calculated radius of action

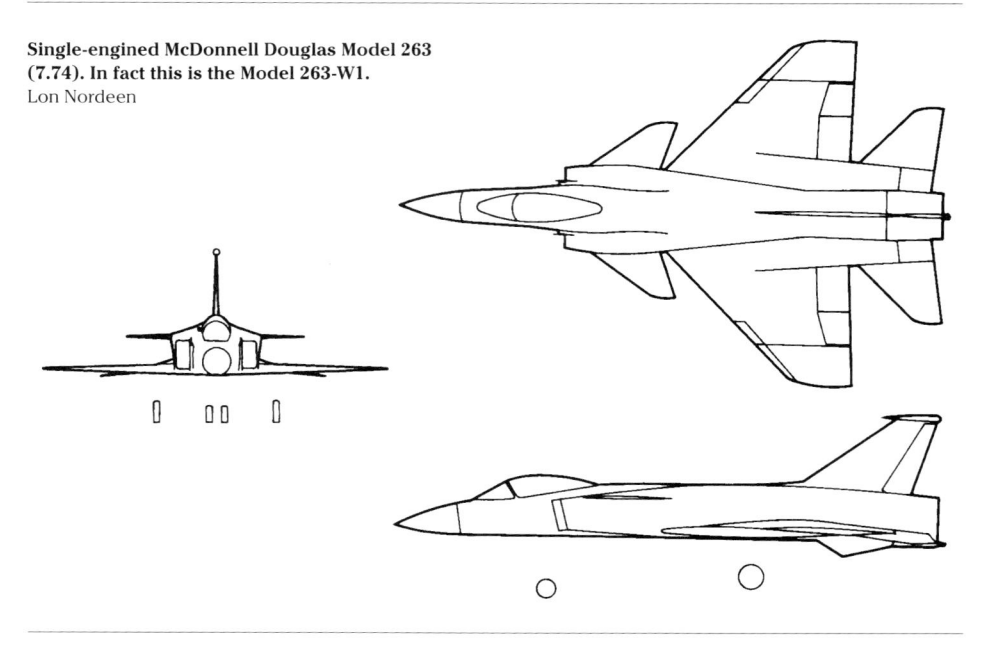

Single-engined McDonnell Douglas Model 263 (7.74). In fact this is the Model 263-W1.
Lon Nordeen

202

American Secret Projects: Fighters & Interceptors

Artwork showing the single-engine Model 263 which was the primary project in this research. Lon Nordeen

was 702nm (1,300km). Loiter time in the CAP role with three 600gal tanks was 2.74 hours and internal fuel totalled 10,400lb (4,717kg). Grumman declared that if a development contract were to be awarded in September 1975, the first G-623 would fly in about February 1978.

A largely similar V/STOL version, the G-623V, was intended to satisfy the Navy's Sea Control Ship plus Marines strike/fighter V/STOL requirements; it was not actually proposed as a VFAX. It featured new, highly swept outer wing panels fitted to the common inner wing/fuselage plus a single scaled and uprated Rolls-Royce XJ99-type vertical lift engine placed behind the cockpit in a lengthened forward fuselage. Reaction control thrusters for hovering and low-speed flight were located to either side of the tail section, below the cockpit on either side of the forward fuselage, and in the wingtips. The G-623's two-dimensional CTOL nozzle would be replaced with a fully vectorable (110°) augmented deflector exhaust nozzle. G-623's span was 28ft 10in (8.8m), length 55ft 6in (16.9m) and vertical take-off weight 32,079 lb (14,551kg).

McDonnell Douglas Model 263

The Model 263 project from McDonnell Douglas had three horizontal surfaces, canard, wing and tail, in an arrangement that at this time was highly rated by the design team. The Model 225 (Chapter Nine) had already used it and in April 1974 a modified YRF-4C Phantom was flown with additional canard surfaces as part of the Precision Aircraft Control Technology (PACT) program. Quite a number of different layouts were studied under the Model 263 banner, including a majority that in fact had just two horizontal surfaces (a moderately swept wing and tail), but artwork to go with the available drawings always shows three surfaces. It therefore seems that the latter was the format studied in more depth. This aircraft was actually described in the McDonnell project list as a multi-mission type for air superiority with alternate capability for combat air patrol interdiction and close air support.

Work on the Model 263 had actually begun in October 1972 and the fighter was to use a

This twin-engine variant of the Model 263 is different in some respects from the 263-U3 drawing. Lon Nordeen

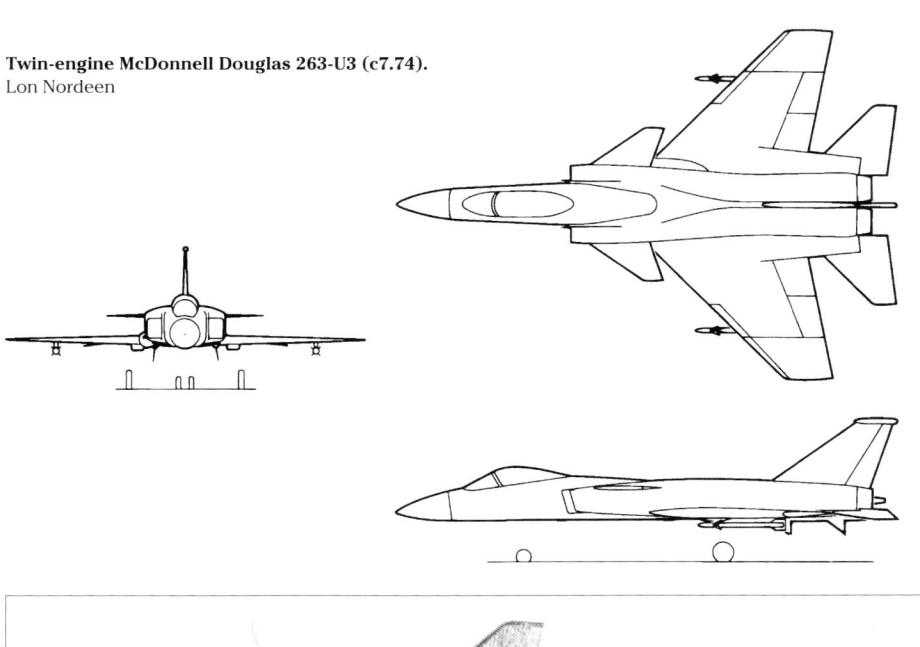

Twin-engine McDonnell Douglas 263-U3 (c7.74). Lon Nordeen

Lightweight Fighters

Model of North American's VFAX proposal (7.74).
Allyson Vought

each wingtip fin plus a Sparrow on the bottom corner of each side of the lower mid-fuselage, just behind the canard. The model however, shows an 'aerodynamic pylon' instead of each Sparrow carrying three bombs. There are also underfuselage tanks and the Sparrows themselves have been moved forward under the intakes and level with the canards.

Northrop P-630

A carrier-capable YF-17, Northrop's P-630 had a lengthened fuselage and a larger nose to accommodate a radar dish up to 28in (71.1cm) in diameter. In most other respects it was the same as the YF-17, the manufacturer's artwork showing tip-mounted Sparrow missiles. Some published sources have suggested that the P-630 was 10% larger than the YF-17.

Vought Aeronautics V-526 (and X-100)

Vought's VFAX submission was called the V-526 and outwardly shared much with the YF-16. The artwork shows a single Sidewinder on each wing pylon and an underfuselage drop tank. A wing root extension was blended into the fuselage and stretched right back to the jet nozzle. However during February 1974, prior to the competition, Vought had also looked at a different concept against elements of VFAX. This was called the X-100 and featured two widely spaced engines with a centre wing in between, outer wings, twin fins and a long fuselage 'nacelle'. There were large elevators on the trailing edge of the inner wing section, ailerons and flaps on the outer wings and a tricycle undercarriage with twin nosewheels. An Agile AIM-95 air-to-air missile was carried on each wingtip, two, three or four Sparrow or a mix of Sparrow and laser-guided bombs could go beneath the inner wing and a gun was housed in the lower left fuselage level with the cockpit. A 300gal (1,364lit) or 450gal (2,046lit) drop tank would be carried on a wing pylon placed just inboard of the wing fold. Span with tip missiles was 48ft 0in (14.6m), folded span 22ft 0in (6.7m) and length 49ft 6in (15.1m).

On 28th August 1974, before assessment of the submitted designs had been completed, Congress ordered the Navy to make its VFAX selection from one of the two Air Force light fighters, either the YF-16 or the YF-17. The Navy was not keen to have the F-16 because it wanted an attack fighter, not a dogfighter, and intended to use the F-14 for its fleet-

single 'off-the-shelf' engine and have a gross take-off weight of between 25,000lb (11,340kg) and 30,000lb (13,608kg). It was a single-seat aircraft that could carry two Sidewinders or other missiles on underwing pylons and two Sparrows side-by-side under the fuselage. There was a gun mounting to the port side and rear of the cockpit canopy and the canards were placed at the top of the intakes. Both canard and tailplane were all-moving, both the wing and tail were mounted low on the fuselage and there was a single fin. There was also a twin-engined version of the basic aircraft.

North American XFV-12A Development

Another proposal based on a Sea Control Ship project (Chapter Seven), North American's VFAX design was a straight modification of the XFV-12A. It introduced blended leading edge extensions to the main wing and was powered by one engine. The first development version of the XFV-12A itself was not intended to have the vertical lift system installed, which meant that it would have had much in common with this CTOL VFAX design. A published sketch based on manufacturer's data shows the project in its fighter role with two Sidewinders loaded outside defence requirements. Nevertheless, each of the Air Force contractors teamed up with a second fighter company (a naval specialist) in readiness for another competition. General Dynamics joined with Vought and Northrop teamed with McDonnell Douglas. A Request for Quotations (proposals), based on Navy Type Specification 169, was issued on 12th October. The type was christened the NACF for Navy Air Combat Fighter.

McDonnell Douglas/Northrop Model 267
McDonnell Douglas had studied both of the Air Force's lightweight fighter projects and concluded that the Northrop YF-17 would be the better carrier aircraft. The teaming agreement was concluded on 7th October 1974 with McDonnell Douglas as prime contractor for the Navy while Northrop would lead on a land-based version that became the F-18L. McDonnell's engineers at St Louis made substantial design changes to the YF-17, creating a much revised aircraft. Principally the fuselage was made wider which made room for a lot more internal fuel, the wingspan was increased to absorb the extra weight, there was a stronger undercarriage and many other detail changes.

Vought Aeronautics Model 1600 Series
Vought's primary proposals embraced two developments of the YF-16, the Models 1600 and 1601 submitted on 2nd December, which differed primarily in their powerplants. The

Vought V-526 artwork (7.74). Dick Atkins, Vought Archive

first had a Pratt & Whitney F401 engine (the navalised F100 used by several Sea Control Ship fighters including the XFV-12A) and the latter had an F100. Models 1600-1 and 1601-1 were two-place versions. To accommodate the larger F401 the YF-16 fuselage was scaled up by a linear factor of 1.088, which was the ratio of the nozzle diameter of this engine to the F100, and this gave more internal space for extra fuel to meet the mission requirements. Wing area was increased to 369ft² (34.3m²) to reduce the wing loading for landing and a Krueger flap was added to the YF-16's simple leading edge flap to assist with

Lightweight Fighters

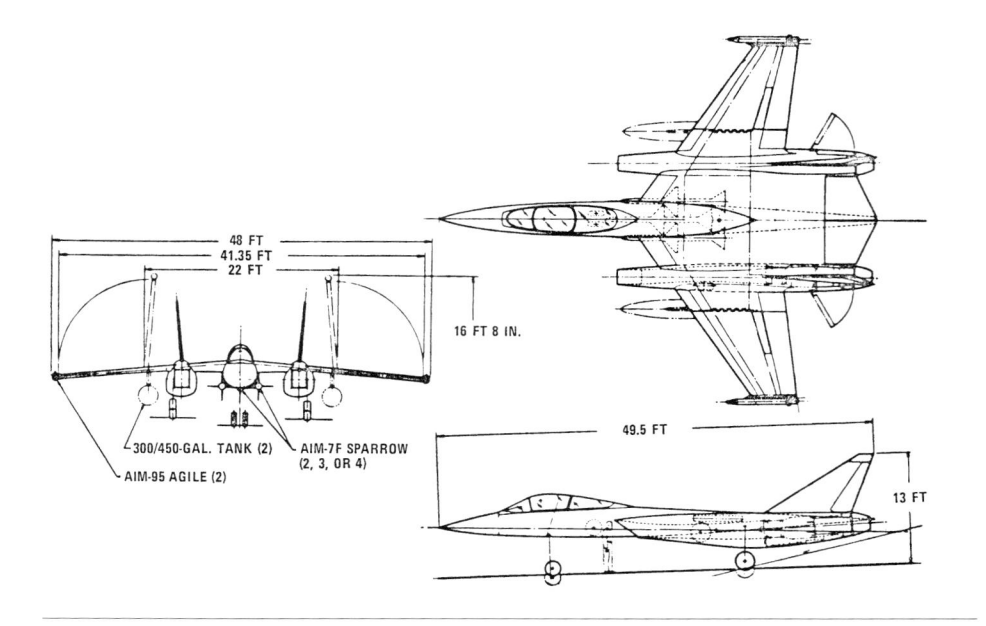

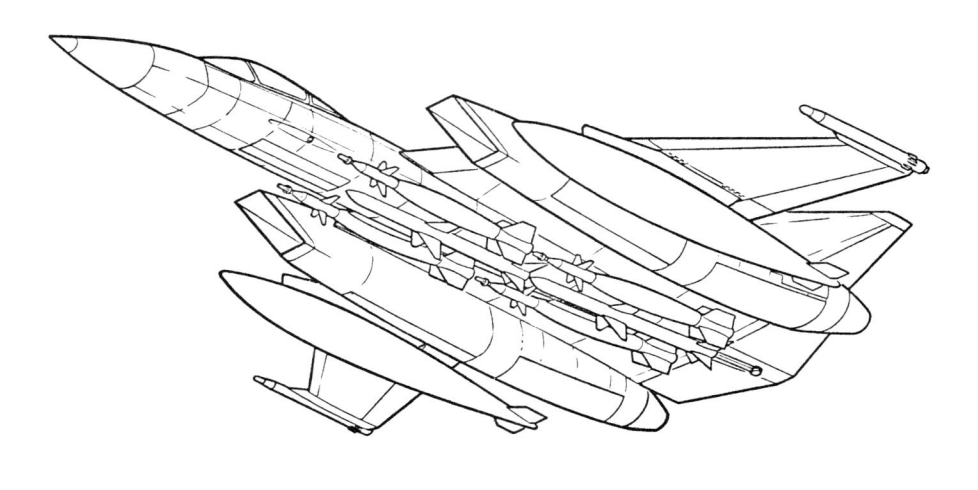

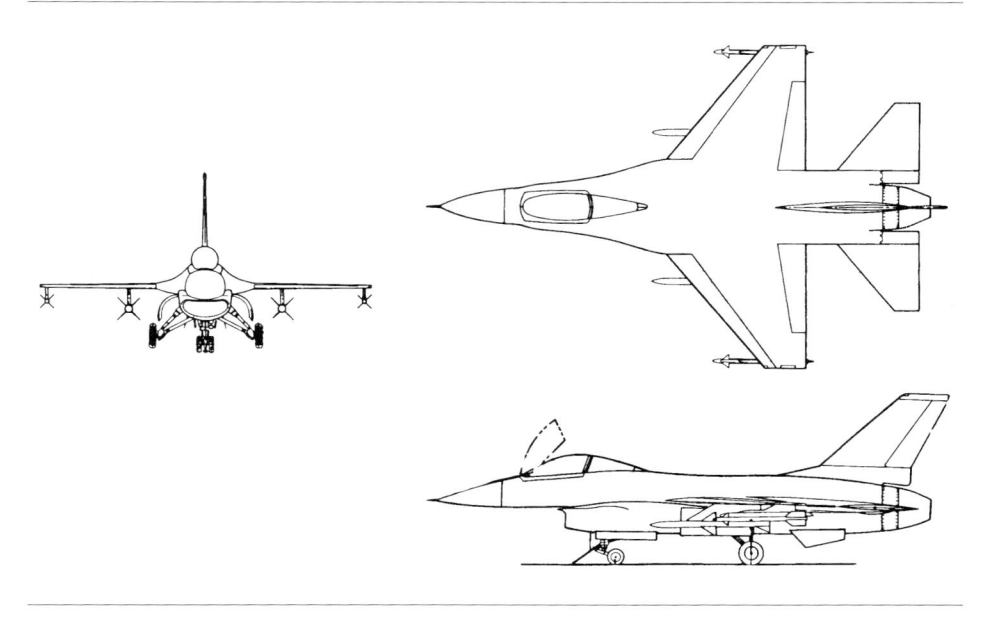

Vought X-100 (2.5.74). Dick Atkins, Vought Archive

Sketch showing the X-100 fully laden with four laser-guided bombs, two Sparrow and two Agile AAM and two external tanks. Dick Atkins, Vought Archive

Vought Model 1600 (2.12.74). Dick Atkins, Vought Archive

the low approach speed. The horizontal and vertical tails were enlarged to meet bolter (aborted carrier landing) requirements and maintain directional stability.

There was no wing fold and the AIM-9 Sidewinder missile stations, numbers 1 and 7, were located on the outboard undersurface of the wing instead of the wingtips themselves. Overall the structure was strengthened and there were many other changes including, of course, an arrester hook. The avionics included a pulse Doppler radar and full AIM-7 Sparrow capability, while the internal fuel totalled 9,955 lb (4,516kg). Gross weight in the interdiction role was 39,774 lb (18,041kg). For the fighter escort mission the Model 1600 would carry two Sparrow missiles on the inner wing pylons, two 300gal (1,364lit) drop tanks on the middle pylons and two Sidewinders on the outer pylons. Wing thickness/chord ratio for both versions was 4%.

The F100 (JTF22B-25) used by the Model 1601 was a less powerful engine but was still an up-rated version of the unit used by the YF-16. Compared to the YF-16 this version had a forward fuselage stretched by 30.5in (77.5cm) with another 16in (40.6cm) aft of the wing, the fin and tail areas were the same as the Model 1600, but wing area was increased to just 312ft² (29.0m²). Internal fuel was less than the 1600 at 8,386 lb (3,804kg) but a 150gal (682lit) centreline tank could be carried. Gross weight in the interdiction role was now 37,809 lb (17,150kg). The avionics were more in line with the Air Force aircraft but all-weather Sparrow capability was still provided. The brochure stated that these designs had the range to escort, the performance to intercept, the agility to win position advantage in air-to-air combat, and the firepower to destroy the threat. However, it noted that the more minimal changes in the 1601, compared to the 1600, would increase its commonality with the YF-16 and reduce cost, but would also sacrifice some weapon performance. As a result the wingtip Sidewinder stations were retained.

The Model 1602, actually drawn in late February 1975, was to use the General Electric F101-GE-100 engine. Fitting this unit offered a very attractive performance, particularly in terms of acceleration, but it was heavier and required a resized and reconfigured wing. The blending with the fuselage would have to be widened to the same span as the leading edge extensions and stretched along the full length of the fuselage. Overall span was 38ft 11in (11.9m), length 53ft 11in (16.4m) and wing area 399ft^2 (37.1m^2). This arrangement did not permit the same degree of airframe/propulsion technology transfer from the YF-16/F-16 programs as did either the F401 or F100, so the 1602 was not offered as one of the primary proposals. Had the 1600 been selected as the winner, Vought would have produced the Navy aircraft while General Dynamics would have concentrated on the F-16 for both the Air Force and export.

The Navy evaluated the two proposals and announced on 2nd May 1975 that it had selected the McDonnell Douglas/Northrop design, calling it the F-18. The reasons behind this choice were complex, and not a little influenced by the fact that the Navy did not wish to buy an Air Force aeroplane at all, but carrier incompatibility was given as a principal factor for the YF-16 variant's rejection. Congressional approval followed and the new fighter was later given the name Hornet.

Artist's impression of the Model 1600. Dick Atkins, Vought Archive

Manufacturer's model of the planned land-based Northrop F-18L. The span of this 1/40th scale model is 12.7in (32.2cm) and length 33.8in (85.8cm). Jonathan Rigutto / photo © 2005 Chad Slattery

Lightweight Fighters

The F-18 prototype made its maiden flight on 18th November 1978 powered by two General Electric F404 engines, a low-bypass turbofan based on the YJ101 used by the YF-17s. In due course the F-18 was acquired by several overseas air arms as well as the US Navy and is still very much in front-line service. From the late 1980s the aircraft was upgraded and modified into the F/A-18E/F Super Hornet first flown on 29th November 1995. Today the Super Hornet is the principal fighter in the US Navy inventory. Despite the fact that the F-18L's performance was expected to have been superior in many respects to the naval aircraft, no orders were ever forthcoming for the land-based version.

In the end, the F-18 could hardly be described as a true lightweight fighter. Like the production F-16 it had progressively become much heavier than its original concept-proving demonstrator, the YF-17. Nevertheless it enabled the Navy, like the Air Force, to operate a smaller more agile fighter alongside a large heavy fighter, in this case the F-18 alongside the F-14. The cost of such an arrangement has prevented most air arms from adopting a similar system. Only the Soviet Union has followed suit with the smaller Mikoyan MiG-29 and larger Sukhoi Su-27.

Summary

In practice, neither the USAF nor the US Navy has ever opted for a true lightweight fighter. The huge scale of their respective budgets and a desire to acquire aircraft superior to anything else in the world (and certainly not inferior to each other) militated against it. Even fine designs like the F-5 and F-20 had to look elsewhere for potential sales. Nonetheless, the quest for designs that were lighter, simpler and cheaper than the other proposals in this book, showed the depth of US design ingenuity and produced some fascinating proposals that never saw the light of day.

Lightweight Fighters – Estimated Data

Project	Span ft in (m)	Length ft in (m)	Gross Wing Area ft² (m²)	Gross Weight lb (kg)	Engine lb (kN)	Max Speed / Height mph (km/h) / ft (m)	Armament
Northrop N-156	26 3 (8.0)	34 11 (10.6)	216 (20.1)	10,123 (4,592)	2 x Gen Elec SJ110-B-3 2,470 (11.0), 3,670 (16.3) ab	Mach 0.99 at S/L, Mach 1.51 at 35,000 (10,668)	Up to 4 x AIM-9 Sidewinder AAM, up to 96 2in (5.1cm) rockets
Northrop N-156F/F-5A (flown)	25 10 (7.9)	47 2 (14.4)	170 (15.8)	13,433 (6,093)	2 x Gen Elec J85-GE-13 2,720 (12.1), 4,080 (18.1) ab	731 (1,176) at S/L, 925 (1,488) at 36,090 (11,000)	2 x 20mm cannon, 2 x Sidewinder AAM, 6,200 lb (2,812kg) of bombs
Lockheed CL-1200-1	29 2 (8.9)	56 9 (17.3)	?	?	1 x P&W TF30-PW-100 c25,000 (111.1)	High Supersonic	1 x 20mm cannon, AAM
Northrop F-5E Tiger II (flown)	28 0 (8.5)	47 5 (14.4)	186 (17.3)	15,745 (7,142)	2 x Gen Elec J85-GE-21 5,000 (22.2)	753 (1,212) at S/L, 1,083 (1,743) at 36,000 (10,973)	2 x 20mm cannon, 2 x AAM, 7,000 lb (3,175kg) of bombs

ADF and Air Force Light Fighters

Project	Span ft in (m)	Length ft in (m)	Gross Wing Area ft² (m²)	Gross Weight lb (kg)	Engine lb (kN)	Max Speed / Height mph (km/h) / ft (m)	Armament
Northrop N-300A-5	27 9 (8.5) clean 30 10 (9.4) tip tanks	52 6 (16.0)	250 (23.3)	18,902 (8,574)	2 jet engines	Supersonic	2 x cannon, and other stores
Boeing 908-618-2	29 3.5 (8.9)	47 9.5 (14.6)	240 (22.3)	16,000 (7,258)	1 x P&W F100-PW-100 23,600 (104.9) ab	Supersonic	2 x M39 20mm cannon, 2 x Sidewinder AAM, 2 x Mk.82 bombs
Northrop P-530 (c1972)	35 0 (10.7)	55 4 (16.9)	400 (37.2)	23,000 (10,433)	2 x Gen Elec J5/J1A5 13,000 (57.8) ab	cMach 2 at height	1 x 20mm cannon, 4 x AAM, bombs or rockets
General Dynamics 401F	30 1.5 (9.2)	43 7 (13.3)	280 (26.0)	c17,100 (7,757)	1 x P&W F100-PW-100 (JTF22A-27) 23,600 (104.9) ab	Supersonic	2 x M39 20mm cannon, 2 x Sidewinder AAM,
Lockheed CL-1200-2	29 2 (8.9)	57 3 (17.4)	?	c32,000 (14,515)	1 x P&W F100-PW-100 23,600 (104.9) ab	Mach 2.4 at height	1 x 20mm cannon, AAM
General Dynamics YF-16 (flown)	32 10 (10.0) with AAM	46 6 (14.2)	280 (26.0)	20,665 (9,374)	1 x P&W F100-PW-100 23,500 (104.4) ab	Mach 1.95 at 35,000 (10,668)	1 x M61 20mm cannon, 6 x AAM, bombs or rockets
Northrop YF-17 (flown)	35 0 (10.7)	55 6 (16.9)	320 (29.8)	26,960 (12,229)	2 x Gen Elec YJ101-GE-100 14,750 (65.6) ab	1,320 (2,124) at 40,000 (12,192)	1 x 20mm cannon, 2 x Sidewinder AAM, 2 x 2,000 lb (907kg) bombs

Navy Light Fighters

Project	Span ft in (m)	Length ft in (m)	Gross Wing Area ft² (m²)	Gross Weight lb (kg)	Engine lb (kN)	Max Speed / Height mph (km/h) / ft (m)	Armament
Grumman G-623	38 0 (11.6)	53 0 (16.2)	?	31,556 (14,314) (fighter escort mission)	2 x Gen Elec YJ101-GE-100 14,750 (65.6) ab	833 (1,340) (Design speed – fighter role)	2 x AIM-9 Sidewinder, 2 x AIM-7 Sparrow (fighter escort mission)
Vought V-1600	33 3 (10.1)	52 4 (16.0) with pitot	369 (34.3)	31,231 (14,166) (fighter escort mission)	1 x P&W F401 (JTF22A-26C) 18,370 (81.6), 29,360 (130.5) ab	High Supersonic 2 x Sidewinder +	1 x M61 20mm cannon, 2 x Sparrow or various bombs
Vought V-1601	33 10 (10.3) with missiles	53 0 (16.2) with pitot	312 (29.0)	26,798 (12,156) (Fighter escort mission)	1 x P&W F100 (JTF22B-25) 15,600 (69.3), 25,500 (113.3) ab	High Supersonic	1 x M61 20mm cannon, 2 x Sidewinder + 2 x Sparrow or various bombs
McDD F-18A Hornet (flown)	40 8 (12.4) with missiles	56 0 (17.1)	400 (37.2)	38,000 (17,237)	2 x Gen Elec F404-GE-400 16,000 (71.1) ab	1,190 (1,915) at 36,000 (10,973) 13,700 lb (6,214kg) stores	1 x 20mm cannon, 2 x AIM-9 Sidewinder, 2 x AIM-7 Sparrow,

Chapter Eleven

In Conclusion

The era covered by this book started with the early operational jets and ended with the first flight of the F-18, an aircraft not only still in production but undergoing further development at the present time. In the meantime, fighters have continued to grow in capability, complexity and expense. As a consequence, development periods have extended, as have the planned service lives of the eventual operational aircraft. This is true worldwide. If the Spitfire had taken as long to develop as the Eurofighter (which is just coming into service with the RAF), it would have missed the Battle of Britain by well over twenty years!

What has also changed has been the huge impact of computers on the design process. During the period covered by this book, there was much more uncertainty about how a design would perform. As a consequence, there were a vast number of different shapes on the drawing board, with no small number in the air and many in service. Fighter design would continue to advance but never again would it see the plethora of ideas produced in the 1950s and 1960s: a time when the arms race was also at its peak, fuelling the quest for ever-better performance.

The designs that I have described chart not just advances in technology but changes in thinking. Initially the pressure was to utilise the newly available jet engine and to explore the realms of transonic and supersonic flight. The approach was to replicate the capability of the earlier piston-engined fighters, albeit with much enhanced performance in terms of speed and attainable altitude. Fighters had been getting progressively faster over the preceding fifty years and there was no reason to assume the trend would not continue indefinitely – particularly as bombers too were getting faster. This line of thinking reached its peak with the F-103 and F-108; incredible designs intended to exceed three times the speed of sound but which never actually took to the air. It was realised that flying at Mach 3 was actually different to fighting at Mach 3. The emphasis changed to other capabilities – brought about too by experience in combat. Manoeuvrability assumed greater importance and as time went by, so did the need for reliability, simplicity and ease of operation.

The designs discussed in this book illustrate how fighter design evolved over two and a half critical decades; and as with natural evolution, it was not a smoothly continuous line. It contained many dead-ends: ideas that never found successful application. It also contained many promising designs that never found favour, whether through even better competition, funding constraints, changes in requirements or political pressures. One can only look at the plans, sketches and models and wonder what might have been.

This volume has gathered together – thanks to many contributors – more information about American fighter designs of the late 1940s and the 1950s, 1960s and early 1970s than has probably ever been assembled before. Much of it is published for the first time. However, as I stated in my Introduction, it is a far from complete picture. Over the years some information has inevitably been lost; but I believe that much remains to be unearthed, buried in archives, lofts and people's memories. I hope that, stimulated by this book, more will now come to light, charting and recording American design ingenuity during this important and fascinating chapter of aviation history.

'Super Sabre Development' model. John Aldaz

American Secret Fighter & Interceptor Colour Chronology

Left: **Rare colour picture of the first Lockheed XF-90 prototype 46-687.** Terry Panopalis

Below: **Lovely air-to-air view of a Vought F7U-3 Cutlass.** Dick Atkins, Vought Archive

Opposite page:

Top: **A McDonnell F3H-2M Demon of VF-61 seen departing the waist catapult of USS Franklin D Roosevelt on 4th October 1957.**

Centre: **Early production McDonnell F-101A Voodoo.**

Bottom left: **North American 'Advanced F-86 Day Fighter'.** Jonathan Rigutto / photo © 2005 Chad Slattery

Bottom right: **North American 'Sabre 45 Air Superiority Fighter' project.** Jonathan Rigutto / photo © 2005 Chad Slattery

American Secret Projects: Fighters & Interceptors

Northrop YF-89F all-weather fighter.
George Cox

Douglas Model 1245. John Aldaz

North American delta wing interceptor. Jonathan Rigutto / photo © 2005 Chad Slattery

212 American Secret Projects: Fighters & Interceptors

Convair's sixth YF-102 prototype, 53-1782, captured on early colour film. Terry Panopalis

A manufacturer's model of the definitive Lockheed L-227 project, the L-227-1. Jim Keeshen

Another Lockheed prototype, the first XF-104 53-7786. Terry Panopalis

American Secret Projects: Fighters & Interceptors

American Secret Projects: Fighters & Interceptors

This page:

Top: **Douglas Model 1355 long-range interceptor.** George Cox

Below: **Lockheed CL-288-1 model.** Jim Keeshen

Bottom left: **McDonnell Model 110A.** John Hall

Bottom right: **North American WS-202A long-range interceptor.** George Cox

Opposite page:

North American NA-212 model. Jonathan Rigutto / photo © 2005 Chad Slattery

Lockheed L-205 manufacturer's display model. Jim Keeshen

The second North American F-107A is seen on the hardstanding in readiness for its next test flight. Terry Panopalis

American Secret Projects: Fighters & Interceptors

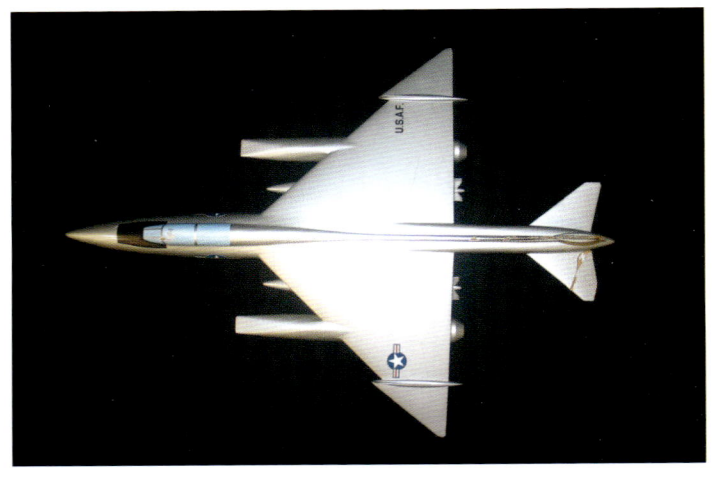

Top left: **Northrop N-144**; Top right: **Northrop N-149.**
Both Northrop Grumman Corp, photo Tony Chong

Above: **North American NA-236 (F-108).**
Jonathan Rigutto / photo © 2005 Chad Slattery

Left: **Republic AP-54.**

Opposite page:

Convair 'F-106 Interceptor' proposal with canard foreplane. Jonathan Rigutto / photo © 2005 Chad Slattery

One of the last production Grumman F11F Tigers, here seen carrying drop tanks and Sidewinder air-to-air missiles. Grumman Corporation / Grumman History Centre

American Secret Projects: Fighters & Interceptors

American Secret Projects: Fighters & Interceptors

This page:

The prototype Vought XF8U Crusader taken during its first flight on 25th March 1955. The second shows the aircraft just before touch-down with the variable incidence wing in operation. Dick Atkins, Vought Archive

Grumman Design 118.

Two of the Navy's McDonnell F-4B Phantoms that were operated by the Air Force to help with that service's evaluation process.

Opposite page:

Top: **Vought XF8U-3 Crusader III at rest but with its variable incidence wing in the raised position.** Dick Atkins, Vought Archive

Centre: **Republic AP-100.** Jim Keeshen

Bottom left: **Grumman G-607A model.**

Bottom right: **North American Rockwell NA-323 model.** George Cox

218   American Secret Projects: Fighters & Interceptors

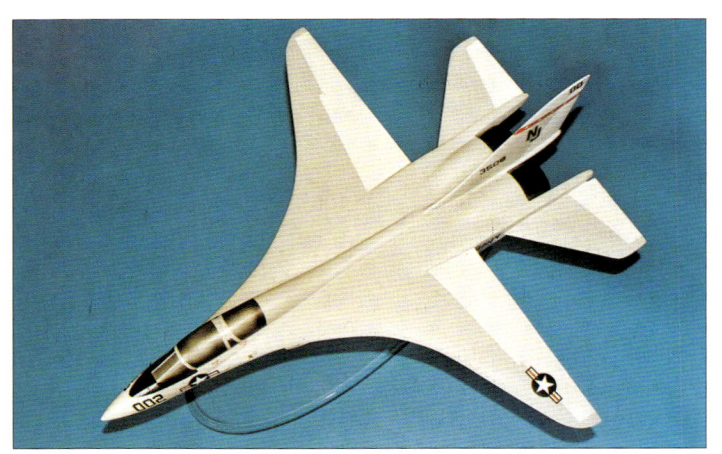

American Secret Projects: Fighters & Interceptors

American Secret Projects: Fighters & Interceptors

Beautiful view of a Grumman F-14 Tomcat.

Fairchild Hiller/Republic FH-100 project.

Grumman G-399-45 model.

Opposite page:

Artwork showing McDonnell Douglas's Model 225 VFX submission. Jonathan Rigutto / photo © 2005 Chad Slattery

Lovely picture showing how the LTV V-507 mock-up saw rather more of the outside world than its competitors. Here it sits on the Dallas flight line, 'being readied for flight', alongside two LTV A-7 Corsair attack aircraft. Dick Atkins, Vought Archive

American Secret Projects: Fighters & Interceptors

American Secret Projects: Fighters & Interceptors

North American FX fighter project.
John Aldaz

Northrop P-530-2 Cobra of 1969. Note the Cobra logo on the nose.
Jonathan Rigutto collection / photo © 2005 Chad Slattery

Grumman lightweight fighter.
Allyson Vought

Opposite page:

Fairchild Hiller (Republic) FX proposal. John Hall

North American NA-335 model.
Jonathan Rigutto / photo © 2005 Chad Slattery

American Secret Projects: Fighters & Interceptors

Glossary

AAM Air-to-air missiles.
ADC Air Defense Command.
AI Air Interception.
Anhedral Downward slope of wing from root to tip.
Angle of Attack The angle at which the wing is inclined relative to the airflow.
Angle of Incidence Angle between the chord line of the wing and the fore and aft datum line of the fuselage.
Area Rule Principal law for keeping transonic drag to a minimum. States that cross-section areas of aeroplane plotted from nose to tail on a graph should form a smooth curve.
Aspect Ratio Ratio of wingspan to mean chord, calculated by dividing the square of the span by the wing area.
BuAer Bureau of Aeronautics (US Navy).
Chord Distance between centres of curvature of wing leading and trailing edges when measured parallel to the longitudinal axis.
CofG Centre of gravity.
Critical Mach Number Mach number at which an aircraft's controllability is first affected by compressibility; that is, the point at which shock waves first appear.
CTOL Conventional Take-Off and Landing.

Dihedral Upward slope of wing from root to tip.
Fly-by-Wire Flight control system using electronic links between the pilot's controls and the control surface actuators.
ECM Electronic Countermeasures.
Flutter A high-frequency oscillation of an aircraft's structure induced by both aerodynamic and aeroelastic forces.
Gross Weight Usually signifies maximum weight with internal fuel plus all weapons aboard, but not external drop tanks.
IFR In-flight refuelling.
Laminar Flow Wing Specifically designed to ensure a smooth flow of air over its surfaces with uniform separation between the layers of air.
LERX Leading edge root extensions.
LRI Long-range Interceptor.
Mach Number Ratio of aeroplane's speed to that of sound in the surrounding medium – expressed as a decimal.
MRI Medium Range Interceptor.
NACA National Advisory Committee for Aeronautics.
NATO North Atlantic Treaty Organisation.
NAVAIR Naval Air System Command.

nm Nautical mile.
RAND An American institution that undertakes research and analysis towards the objective of improving policy and decision making.
RATOG Rocket-Assisted Take-Off Gear.
RFP Request for Proposals.
RP Rocket Projectiles.
SAC Strategic Air Command.
SEATO South East Asia Treaty Organisation.
S/L Sea level.
STOL Short Take-Off and Landing.
STOVL Short Take-Off and Vertical Landing.
TAC Tactical Air Command.
t/c Thickness/chord ratio.
Transonic Flight The speed range either side of Mach 1.0 where an aircraft has both subsonic and supersonic airflow passing over it at the same time.
USAAF United States Army Air Force.
USAF United States Air Force.
vg Variable geometry.
V/STOL Vertical/Short Take-Off and Landing.
VTOL Vertical Take-Off and Landing.

Model of the McDonnell Model 60 by John Hall.

Appendix One

American Fighter Projects Summary

This list embraces all known American post-war jet fighter projects and model numbers up to the mid-1970s, plus research aircraft specifically intended to help and advance the art of the fighter designer. A few jet fighter projects begun before the end of the war are included for completeness but no piston fighters are listed, even though a few may have been designed after the Second World War had ended. Some basic details of the fortunes of the manufacturers are given where applicable to explain their changes of name, and the like. In June 1948 the old 'P' for 'Pursuit' designation was replaced by 'F' for 'Fighter', which explains why both appear on a few occasions. In 1962 the Department of Defense installed a new numbering system that covered all of the United States air arms. USAF aircraft were unchanged but Navy fighters still in service were redesignated as indicated in the individual entries.

BELL

From the end of the War Bell became a specialist in helicopters and research aircraft.

XP-59A America's first jet fighter first flown 2.10.42 and built in small numbers.

Model 40 Long-range fighter flown 25.2.45 as prototype XP-83. Plans for production aircraft cancelled.

X-1 High-speed rocket-powered research aircraft first flown 25.1.46. This machine became the first aircraft to break the sound barrier, on 14.10.47.

X-2 Swept wing rocket-powered research aircraft first flown 27.6.52. Achieved Mach 3 on 27.9.56.

All Weather Fighter Design submitted to official requirement, 10.45. Won by Northrop F-89 Scorpion.

Interceptor Design submitted to official requirement, 11.45. Won by Convair XP-92 Dart.

X-5 Small variable geometry swing-wing research aircraft ordered in 1949 and first flown 20.6.51. Two examples built. Bell proposed several fighter developments with variable geometry wings.

D-109 'Convertoplane' VTOL jet fighter, 9.11.51.

VTOL Tactical Fighter Study to MX1976, c1951.

D-139 VTOL fighter concepts, 26.1.55.

D-188 Mach 2 V/STOL fighter project for USN and USAF, 1957. Designated F3L by Navy and request made to Air Force for XF/YF-109, but not approved. Order for D-188A prototypes never placed and work closed in 1961.

BOEING

During the period covered by this book Boeing was principally a large aircraft, bomber and transport firm. The company did on occasion dabble in fighter design but it never built a jet fighter prototype. The last all-Boeing fighter to fly was the piston-powered XF8B-1 prototype of 1944.

449 Swept wing interceptor fighter proposal, mid-1945. Appears to have been brief study only.

454 Swept wing Navy fighter, late 1945. Relatively brief study for Navy fighter.

457 Ramjet-powered interceptor fighter, 1945. Two ramjets in wingtip nacelles on 45° sweep wing, large boost rocket fitted to fuselage tail, T-tail and bicycle undercarriage. Span 45ft 2in (13.8m), length 37ft 11in (11.6m), gross wing area 85.0ft^2 (7.9m^2), gross weight 8,500lb (3,856kg). Brief study only.

459 Delta wing Navy fighter, 12.45. Relatively brief study for Navy fighter.

482 Turboprop-powered Navy escort fighter, 13.7.48.

486 Series of designs for a jet-powered seaplane night fighter, late 1948/early 1949. All versions had swept wings but different engine arrangements. Not built.

Tailsitter Fighter Study for Navy fighter, probably to OS-122, 24.7.50.

712 Long-range interceptor to WS.202A, 6.54.

818 Tactical Fighter proposals to TFX requirement, 12.61 onwards. Competition won by General Dynamics/Grumman F-111.

835 Many designs for long-range missile fighter for Fleet defence to TS-151, 1.10.59 onwards. Competition won by Douglas F6D Missileer.

FX Various studies made to the early stages of the FX/F-15 requirements, 1965/1966.

908-535 'Nutcracker' V/STOL fighter design proposed for Sea Control Ship, 1.72. Also known as D-180. Lost to Rockwell XFV-12A.

908-537 Navy light fighter, c1972.

908-618 Lightweight fighter 1971. Model 908-618-2 proposed 6.71. Model 909-618-6 (24.12.71) near identical to 908-909 below but carried two AIM-9D Sidewinder missiles on side fuselage pylons above wing roots.

908-909 Official submission to lightweight fighter competition, 1.72. Competition won by General Dynamics YF-16 and Northrop YF-17.

CHANCE VOUGHT/LTV

A naval aircraft specialist, in 1954 Chance Vought became a subsidiary of United Aircraft, and then in 1961 it merged with Ling-Temco Electronics to form Ling-Temco-Vought Inc. This became LTV Aerospace after 1963, Vought Aeronautics by late 1971 and the Vought Corporation in 1976. In 1992 the organisation became part of Northrop Grumman. Missing numbers in the series were allocated to strike aircraft, cargo and civil types and pilotless aircraft and missiles, and later to space exploration projects.

V-340 Designation covering **XF6U-1 Pirate** jet fighter first proposed 12.9.44 and first flown 2.10.46.

V-343 Two-seat high-performance night fighter, 6.7.45.

V-346 High-speed single-seat jet fighter, 4.10.45 onwards. Four designs proposed 4.46 – V-346A, B, C and D. **V-346A** ordered as **XF7U-1 Cutlass** prototype and first flown 29.9.48.

V-347 High-speed interceptor for Navy, 20.9.45.

V-352 Production **F6U-1 Pirate**.

V-356 'VF' long-range escort fighter for Navy, 6.11.46. 'VA' attack aircraft of different design also proposed under same number.

V-359 Improved F6U-1 with afterburner installation on engine, 20.8.47.

V-362 Interceptor fighter for Navy, 14.1.48. Covers **XF7U-1 Cutlass**.

V-363 Long-range escort fighter for Navy, 14.1.48.

V-365 Production **F7U-1 Cutlass**.

V-366 Production **F7U-2** and **F7U-3 Cutlass**.

V-367 USAF penetration fighter, 6.12.49.

V-371 Air Force interceptor to MX1554/F-102 requirement, 22.1.51. Alternative V-371B project had Wright XJ67-W-1 engines and V-371X P&W XJ57-P-1 units.

V-372 F7U-3 fitted with J-57 engine for research, 13.2.51.

V-373 'VF' long-range fighter (research) project, 13.2.51.

V-374 Air Force version of F7U-3 as interceptor, mid-1951.

V-377 Fighter-bomber version of F7U-3 for USAF, 22.10.51.

V-378 Long-range fighter for Navy, 4.2.52.

V-380 Initial studies for carrier-based day fighter, 19.8.52. Became V-383 and V-384.

V-382 USAF fighter-bomber, 19.11.52. Believed in competition with Republic AP-63.

V-383 Supersonic carrier-based day fighter with J-57 engine, 6.1.53. Became **XF8U-1 Crusader** first flown 25.3.55. Redesignated **F-8** in September 1962.

V-384 Smaller version of V-383 carrier-based day fighter with J-65 engine, 6.1.53. Not proceeded with.

V-386 Strategic fighter for USAF to MX2140, 15.4.53.

V-391 Long-range interceptor, 24.5.54. Possibly to WS.202A requirements.

V-394 All-weather fighter for Navy with attack capability, 1.9.54.

V-395 Fighter/attack development of F8U for Navy, 1.9.54.

V-396 Cutlass missile carrier, 15.11.54.

V-399 Missile and stores-carrying version of F8U-1, 1955. Described as a 'pre-F8U-2'. (F8U-2 was a Crusader with more powerful engine flown in 1958.)

American Secret Projects: Fighters & Interceptors

V-400 All-weather missile and special stores-carrying version of F8U-1, 1955. Described as a 'pre-F8U-3'.
V-401 High-performance all-weather development of Crusader that became **F8U-3 Crusader III** first flown 2.6.58. Lost flight competition to McDonnell F4H Phantom II. No production.
V-410 Proposed derivative of F8U-1 with additional rocket motors for extra thrust, 1956.
V-411 F8U improvement studies, 1956. Described as a 'pre-F8U-2N'.
V-413 'Limited' all-weather version of the F8U-2, c1956. Described as a 'pre-F8U-2NE'.
V-418 F8U-3 'Phase II' improvement studies for Navy, c1957.
V-419 F8U-3 derivative with J-58 engine for Navy, c1957.
V-434 Proposal for Fleet Air Defence Aircraft armed with Eagle missiles, mid-1959 onwards. Competition won by Douglas F6D Missileer.
V-454 Crusader for French Navy, 21.3.62.
V-462 Advanced V/STOL tactical fighter weapon system, 23.5.63.
V-466 Version of Crusader proposed for Great Britain, 19.8.63. (UK eventually bought the McDonnell F-4K Phantom).
V-474 Version of Crusader proposed for Lebanon, 30.6.64.
V-483 Studies made to the early stages of the FX (F-15) air superiority fighter for the Air Force, 9.11.65.
V-484 Studies to VFAX requirement for Navy, 9.11.65 onwards. Brochure completed 12.15.67. Not built.
V-504 'Super Crusader' project, 1.10.67. Also described as 'sub-orbital' fighter with performance in speed bracket of Lockheed SR-71 Mach 3 reconnaissance aircraft.
V-505 Variable wing project to VFAX requirements to replace TFX/F-111B, 13.10.67 onwards.
V-507 Variable geometry project designed to VFX/F-14 requirement, 9.68. Lost competition to Grumman.
Naval Fighter V/STOL project with fixed wing, three lift jets ahead of wing and twin propulsion units, 1969.
V-1000 'International' lightweight fighter derived from F-8 Crusader with J-79 engine. Brochure dated 4.6.70. Lost competition to Northrop F-5E.
V-1100 Lightweight fighter for Air Force, 1971 onwards. First proposed 28.6.71 and also for USAF competition 1.72. Lost to General Dynamics YF-16 and Northrop YF-17.
V-2000 USAF fighter attack project with large delta wing and trapezoid canard, 11.8.71.
V-517 VTOL prototype for Sea Control Ship with lift/cruise plus 'fixed' lift engines, 29.12.71. Lost competition to Rockwell XFV-12A.
V-520 V/STOL prototype for Sea Control Ship with 'swing-out' lift engines, 29.12.71. Lost competition to Rockwell XFV-12A.
V-521 VTOL fighter attack aircraft with three engines (one lift/cruise plus two lift units), 29.12.71.
V-523 Advanced lightweight fighter with chin intake for Navy, 17.8.72. San Diego project.
V-524 Cross-flow fan V/STOL night fighter, c1973.
X-100 Twin-engine VFAX study. Design review dated 2.5.74.
V-526 Lightweight fighter for Navy to VFAX requirements, 7.74. San Diego project.
V-1600 Navy Air Combat Fighter development of General Dynamics F-16, 21.11.74. Model 1600 had F401 engine, 1601 had F100, Model 1602 (28.2.75) had F101. Lost to McDonnell Douglas/Northrop design which became F-18 Hornet.

CONVAIR/GENERAL DYNAMICS

Apart from the tail-sitter and seaplane fighters, most of Convair's military work was done for the Air Force. The Consolidated Vultee Aircraft Corporation (Convair) was formed in 1945 and came under the control of General Dynamics in 1953, forming the Convair Division of GD in 1954. The Vultee Division's Downey airfield was closed in 1947. In 1961 the two facilities owned by this manufacturer were split into GD Convair San Diego and GD Fort Worth. The Fort Worth factory, the only airframe manufacturing plant, was sold to Lockheed in 1993.

XP-81 Model 102 mixed turboprop/jet fighter prototype first flown 11.2.45. Vultee design. No production.
Interceptor In-house study by Vultee powered by one General Electric J35 engine, 3.45.
Naval Night Fighter Straight wing project to official competition, 9.45. Vultee design powered by three engines. Competition won by Douglas F3D Skynight and Grumman G-75.
All Weather Fighter Heavy forward-swept wing design, 10.45. Competition won by Northrop XF-89. Fort Worth design. Vultee Division looked at this requirement only briefly and did not submit a proposal.
Multi-Engine Fighter Class 'VF' long-range escort fighter for Navy, 1946.
Day Fighter Design for Navy, mid-1946.
Penetration Fighter Swept wing design submitted to USAF Penetration Fighter requirement, 10.45. Vultee design. Declared winner but planned orders cancelled 6.46. McDonnell XF-88 and Lockheed XF-90 selected for prototype construction.
Interceptor Vultee design submitted to USAF Interceptor requirement, 11.45. Project passed through several configurations before becoming **XP-92**.
XFY-1 Pogo Tail-sitter convoy fighter to OS-122 first designed 1950 and flown 1.8.54. Became **Model 5**.
Skate Class VF seaplane fighter project to OS-116, 9.48 onwards. Studies designated Y2-1.
Night Fighter Class 'VF' seaplane night fighter project, 1.49.
XP-92 Prone pilot fighter project ordered in prototype form 1946. Project cancelled 8.48.
XF-92A Dart Delta wing full-scale model research prototype first flown 18.9.48. One example only. Also known as **Model 7002** and became **Model 1**.
XF2Y-1 Sea Dart Supersonic flying boat fighter first flown 9.4.53. San Diego. Begun as project Y2-2 after the Skate research was complete and became **Model 2**. Sea Dart redesignated **F-7** in September 1962.
F-102 Series Delta wing design first submitted to USAF '1954 Interceptor' requirement, 1.51. Became **YF-102** and **Model 8** and first flown 24.10.53. Design improved as **YF-102A**, first flown 20.12.54 and entered service as **F-102A Delta Dagger**.
Seaplane Fighter Single-engined YJ67-powered version of Sea Dart, 5.52 onwards. Other proposed developments of F2Y included tactical aircraft.
Strategic Fighter Design for USAF to MX2140, c4.53.
F-102 Other proposed F-102 developments included interceptor with two J-79 engines (24.11.54) and two-seat Navy attack-fighter (3.1.55).
VTOL Day Fighter Tail-sitter delta wing design with rotating seat for USAF, 30.7.54. Chin intake, single Allison J71 engine, one 20mm cannon in ventral spine. Span 32ft 9in (10.0m), length 48ft 8.5in (14.8m), gross take-off weight 23,244 lb (10,543kg).
F-106 Development of F-102. First flew 26.12.56 and entered service as **Delta Dart**. Still listed under **Model 8** designation.
F-106 Variants Developments of Model 8/F-106 included J-67 powerplant and carrier-based version with additional canard foreplane (1.5.57). **F-106C** variant of 1957 ordered but cancelled in 1958.

Model of Convair's canard 'F-106 Interceptor' proposal. Jonathan Rigutto / photo © 2005 Chad Slattery

Model of the Douglas D-601/F3D-3. Allyson Vought

F-106 Interceptor Version of Delta Dart with canard and box intakes, mid-1950s? Not built.
F-106-30 Further advanced developments of F-106 with single engine, or more substantial changes with twin engines mounted underneath wings, late 1957 onwards.
F-111A Strike fighter (TFX) to replace Republic F-105, 12.61 onwards. Winning contractors General Dynamics and Grumman, with GD to build Air Force F-111A (first flown 21.12.64) and Grumman the Navy F-111B. Latter cancelled 5.68.
Long-range Interceptor Development of F-106, 1962.
44 San Diego-design variable geometry project to VFX/F-14 requirement, 9.12.68. Lost competition to Grumman 303/F-14.
F-106X Major upgrade to F-106 with new look-down radar and AAM, 1968.
FX Studies made at Fort Worth to FX/F-15 requirements, 1966 to 1968.
ADF Advanced Day Fighter studies, Fort Worth, 1965 onwards.
FX-401 Fort Worth lightweight fighter studies leading through to F-16, 1969 onwards. **YF-16 Fighting Falcon** prototype based on **401-16B** made first flight 20.1.74.
FX-404 Fort Worth lightweight fighter studies to FXX concept, 1969.
Navy Escort Fighter Proposal for fighter to escort Navy attack aircraft, 10.12.69.
Model 785 Conventional Fort Worth single-fin wing-body-tail design used to compare against Model 401 series, c1970.
Model 786 Conventional Fort Worth twin-fin wing-body-tail design used to compare against Model 401 series, c1970.
Model 23 Convair San Diego lightweight fighter for Navy, 1970. Gross weight in region of 26,000 lb (11,794kg). Visually resembled Fort Worth's YF-16. Studies under this number still ongoing in 1973. Wind tunnel model tested 11.73 for canard delta design with chin intake.
F-111X-7 Improved Manned Interceptor variant of F-111, c1971.
200A San Diego V/STOL fighter/attack design for Sea Control Ship, 29.12.71. Contract awarded as back-up design to Rockwell XFV-12A 2.73.
201 Conventional take-off and landing version of Model 200A, 1972.
218 Version of Model 200 submitted by San Diego to Navy VFAX competition, 7.74.
Model 18 Version of YF-16 submitted by Fort Worth to Navy VFAX competition, 7.74.

CURTISS-WRIGHT

This famous designer of piston aircraft, from way back at the start of powered aviation, had by World War Two produced a very long line of successful fighter/pursuit types. However, by the late 1940s the company's fortunes had changed and the XP-87 prototype was to be the last Curtiss fighter to fly, and its only type to be powered by jets. The Curtiss-Wright Aviation Division was closed in 1951, principally due to a lack of preparedness for recent advances in aircraft design. It was taken over by North American.
Model 29A All-weather night fighter first proposed 15.9.45 that replaced Curtiss's XA-43 attack aircraft. Ordered as prototypes only to MX745 and first example of **XP/XF-87 Blackhawk** made first flight on 5.3.48. Type proposed to MX808 requirement but lost to Northrop's F-89 Scorpion. XF-87 program terminated in 10.48.
Navy Night Fighter Design proposed 9.54 to competition won by Douglas Skynight and Grumman G-75.
Penetration Fighter Design submitted to official requirement, c11.45. McDonnell XF-88 and Lockheed XF-90 selected for prototype construction.
Navy Fighter Two designs proposed c4.46 to competition won by Vought F7U Cutlass.
All-Weather Interceptor Proposal for both Army and Navy, 1949 or earlier.
Tactical Air Support Fighter Supersonic project, 1948/49.
Seaplane Fighter 'Varied surface fighter', believed in competition with EDO 150, late 1940s.
Seaplane Fighter Design in competition against Convair Sea Dart, c1950.

DOUGLAS

Although formed in 1920, Douglas did not put an all-new fighter design into production until the arrival of the F3D Skyknight. By April 1967 Douglas was suffering financial problems and during that month it merged with McDonnell to form the McDonnell Douglas Corporation. Douglas's Long Beach factory now specialised in civil airliners, although it had worked in this area from well before the war. This work is reflected in the gaps in the following sequences although light and heavy bombers, and research aircraft and missiles, were also designed and built by Douglas. During the 1950s and beyond project numbers were also allocated to electronics and ground-based equipment and some later D-series numbers are still currently unknown. In fact there were two separate series of project numbers because the company had no central system of allocation. Consequently, project proposals have either a D-number or a 1,000-series Model number, but it appears that the two series did not overlap.
D-499 Proposals for a jet-powered supersonic research aircraft against MX656, 11.46. Design **D-499D** selected as best and built as **X-3 Stiletto**. First flight 15.10.52 but, overall, it was a difficult aircraft to fly with a long slim fuselage and short thin wings. Much was learnt however, for the later Lockheed F-104. Only one X-3 was built.
D-558 High-speed jet-powered research aircraft, 1.45. Became Skystreak, first flown 28.5.47.
D-558-II Very high-speed jet and rocket-powered research aircraft 'Phase II', 1.46. Became Skyrocket first flown 4.2.48.
561 'VF (N)' fighter, 24.9.45. Believed to have been night fighter project proposed to Navy competition early autumn 1945. Declared winner and resulting **XF3D-1** first flown 23.3.48 and entered service as **F3D-1 Skynight**. Type redesignated **F-10** in September 1962.
All Weather Fighter Design submitted to official USAF requirement, 10.45. Won by Northrop F-89 Scorpion.
Interceptor Design submitted to official requirement, 11.45. Won by Convair XP-92 Dart.
565 'VF' three-engine Navy day fighter project, 27.3.46. Lost competition to Vought F7U Cutlass.
D-571 Delta wing fighter project first proposed 28.12.46. Won Navy contract for single-engined fighter, 1947. As **XF4D-1** first flown 23.1.51 and entered service as **F4D Skyray**. Redesignated **F-6** in September 1962.
D-576 Fighter attack aircraft, 1.4.47. Project cancelled.
D-583 Interceptor fighter, 8.1.48.
D-585 Long-range escort fighter, 27.4.48.
590 Navy night fighter, 9.7.48.
591 Delta-winged interceptor fighter, 28.7.48.
592 Interceptor fighter project, 4.8.48.
Model 1187R Interceptor design believed prepared for Air Force, c late 1940s. Large 40°-swept wing and short undercarriage – no naval fittings. Apparently similar in layout to British Hawker Hunter with split wing root intakes feeding single engine. To carry four Falcon or Sparrow AAM. Span 38ft 2in (11.6m), length 54ft 7in (16.6m).
601 Proposed swept-wing version of Skynight as **F3D-3**, 6.12.49. Not built.
Model 1245 Interceptor proposal to MX1554/F-102 requirement, 15.1.51.

American Fighter Projects Summary 227

Model of the EDO 150 in US Navy markings.

Model 1270 Design with fuselage identical to Model 1245 but having narrow-span delta wing, c1951. Retained all-fuselage fuel tank arrangement.

614 Designation for **XF4D-1**.

640 Submarine-based fighter, 15.5.52. ONR study for small swept-wing single jet design with no undercarriage. To be launched off a ramp.

652 Day fighter based on F4D Skyray, 2.12.52. Douglas offered two designs to the Navy OS-130 requirement of August 1952, but so far no information has been traced.

653 Day fighter based on A4D Skyhawk attack aircraft, 2.12.52.

655 Proposed F4D-2 with more powerful J57-P-14 engine, 10.6.53. Not built.

660 French-English export Skynight night fighter, 9.9.53.

Model 1335 Long-range interceptor to WS.202A, 6.54.

685 & 687 Numbers allocated to planned production and procurement of F5D-2 and F5D-1 Skylancer fighters, 4.4.55 and 11.4.55 (formerly F4D-2). **F5D-1 Skylancer** prototype first flew 21.4.56 but no production orders placed.

698 Proposed all-weather fighter procurement of F5D-1 for 1957, 21.2.56.

727 Export version of F4D, 2.10.57.

728 Export version of F5D, 2.10.57.

D-745 Weapon system based on carriage of Eagle air-to-air missile, 13.5.58. (Designation D-742 allocated to Eagle missile itself).

D-746 Long-range missile fighter, 29.5.58.

D-765 Proposals to 'Missileer' naval patrol fighter, c1959.

D-766 Subsonic proposal to 'Missileer' naval patrol fighter requirement, 1959. Ordered as **XF6D Missileer** in 1960 but cancelled 12.60 before prototypes had been started.

D-767 Further work to 'Missileer' requirement, 1959.

EDO

The EDO Corporation was founded by Earl Dodge Osborn on Long Island in 1925 and specialised in seaplane floats. Before and during World War Two its principal work was the production of the main float for the Vought-Sikorsky OS2U Kingfisher, but after the war it also manufactured seven EDO XOSE observation scout seaplanes, although the Navy quickly decided to use helicopters for that mission. The company still builds floats today under the support of Kenmore Air, but it has never built any more aircraft. However, it did design a couple of jet-powered seaplane fighters.

142 Scale model 'proof of concept' test aircraft proposal to test Model 150 configuration, 1949. Incorporated simplified construction.

150 'Varied Surface Fighter' – Amphibious fighter study to MX940, 2.47. Also known as 'Pantobase' fighter and Arctic Penetration Fighter. Designed with V-tail. Not built.

GOODYEAR

This company has been a specialist in airships, but during World War Two it built a large number of piston fighters and subsequently offered proposals to new USAF and USN requirements. None, however, were built.

All Weather Fighter Design submitted to official requirement, 10.45. Won by Northrop F-89 Scorpion.

Penetration Fighter Design submitted to official requirement, c11.45. McDonnell XF-88 and Lockheed XF-90 selected for prototype construction. Details of Goodyear proposal unknown, but a design filed for patent in 10.48, in name of Derwood A Beck, may represent this aircraft. Has 40°-swept wing, four cannon in nose and wing root intakes. Also appears to have rearward-facing gun pod on fin/tail intersection. (US Patent Nos 150,672 and 151,583.)

Escort Fighter Single turboprop-powered convoy escort fighter for Navy to OS-122, mid-1950.

GRUMMAN

In 1994 Grumman was acquired by Northrop to become Northrop Grumman. Today its Bethpage, Long Island factory no longer builds aircraft. Grumman once specialised in fighters and attack aircraft for the US Navy but, like other companies, it diversified into areas such as space exploration and missile development. Consequently, the majority of the gaps in this sequence relate to non-aviation projects.

G-71 Single-seat fighter with Westinghouse 24C jet, 11.44.

G-75 Two-seat night fighter project with four Westinghouse 24C jet engines, 25.9.45. Won competition as **XF9F-1** along with Douglas F3D Skynight but not built. Replaced by XF9F-2 Panther.

G-77 Swept wing research aircraft powered by a single Pratt & Whitney R-985 radial piston engine, 1.46.

G-79 Fighter study covering four different engine arrangements, 3.46. Selected design became **XF9F-2** and first flown 21.11.47. Entered service as **Panther**.

G-83 Fixed swept wing fighter for Navy, 11.46 onwards. Officially proposed 9.3.47 and accepted, but redesigned by 11.48 and then given VG wing 7.49. As prototype **XF10F-1 Jaguar** first flown 19.5.52 but production cancelled.

G-84 Short distance take-off interceptor fighter, 4.47. Was study to find fighter aircraft capable of very short take-off distances, superior climb performance and ability to manoeuvre and fight at 40,000ft (12,192m). Concepts examined were twin turbojet G-84-1, G-84-2 with single jet plus rocket motor for take-off and combat, G-84-3 as per '-2' but with rocket for combat only, and G-84-4 with a jet plus the rocket for take-off only. Jet was Rolls-Royce Nene. Concluded that a small single Nene aircraft of around 12,800lb (5,806kg) weight, using the rocket for take-off only, could substantially exceed current interceptor requirements.

G-86 Navy interceptor proposal to Specification OS-113 (McDonnell F3H/Douglas F4D), 9.48. Mixed jet/rocket powerplant.

G-92 VTOL fighter, possibly to OS-122 convoy fighter specification, 5.50.

G-93 Swept wing development of Panther first proposed 12.50. First flown 20.9.51 and entered service as **F9F-6 Cougar**. Cougar redesignated **F-9** in September 1962.

G-94 Development of F9F-6, 12.51.

G-94A F9F-6 variant for operation from flexible carrier decks, 2.54.

G-97 Project to OS-130 for supersonic naval carrier fighter, 20.2.53. Lost competition to Vought F8U Crusader.

G-98 Supersonic carrier fighter first proposed 12.52. Became **YF9F-1** and then **F11F-1 Tiger**. First flight 30.7.54 and entered limited production. Numerous proposed developments and versions made under G-98 designation with different weapons and engines and for different roles. Included **G-98J F11F-1F Super Tiger** of 1.55 powered by J79 engine and first flown (prototype only) 25.5.56. **G-98D** of 1.54 had a 45° swept wing and J79, **G-98I** (12.54) was a high altitude interceptor, **G-98K** and **G-98L** (1.55) both had J65-W-12 engine but latter also introduced an all-weather radar, a new wing, and later a J79. The **G-98S** (5.56) introduced a larger wing. F11F Tiger redesignated **F-11** in September 1962.

G-99 Covers **F9F-8** variant of **Cougar** fighter (later designated F-9J) first flown 18.1.54.

228   *American Secret Projects: Fighters & Interceptors*

G-105 Designation applied to F9F-8T trainer version of Cougar first flown 29.2.56, but also covered night and all-weather fighter studies from 1955 and 1957. The **G-105E Super Cougar** (8.61) had a J-52 engine.

G-107 USAF Long-range Interceptor study to WS.202A with twin engines placed one above the other, 6.54. Design not submitted.

G-109 High-altitude weapon system (air-to-air), 12.54. G-109A covered the airframe while B, C and E were versions of the Eagle air-to-air missile. G-109D covered advanced missile studies.

G-110 FXF fighter study, 3.55. To be capable of Mach 2 and 60,000ft (18,288m) altitude. Eight different configurations studied.

G-113 J79-powered interceptor for operation from flexible carrier deck, 3.55.

G-114 VTOL jet fighter study, 3.55. (G-114 designation also given to two-man hovercraft.)

Unknown Fighter Model found for large swept 'delta' design with side-by-side engines and swept 'delta' tail halfway up fin. Offset canopy, side intakes. No date, but 1950s-style design.

G-118 Large Mach 2 two-seat naval jet fighter proposal, 9.55 onwards. To serve as Task Force Defence Fighter and was continuation of work done on G-107 and G-110. Various configurations examined at beginning. Prototypes ordered in 1955 and serials allocated, but fabrication never started.

G-119 Mach 3 research aircraft for USAF, 9.55. Also called the Curtiss-Wright Research Vehicle.

G-123 Project for AEW aircraft eventually flown in 1960 as W2F-1 Hawkeye. **G-123F** variant (4.58) designed as a long-range 'Missileer' fighter following work undertaken under G-151 designation.

G-128 Project for naval attack aircraft eventually flown in 1960 as A2F-1 (later A-6) Intruder. **G-128E** version (6.59) subsonic naval patrol fighter proposed to 'Missileer' patrol fighter requirement in competition won by Douglas F6D. Initial work had been undertaken from 6.58 as G-200.

G-131 Mach 3 fighter study, 7.56.

G-149 Application of Pratt & Whitney J58 engine as powerplant for Mach 3 fighter and attack aircraft, report dated 15.5.57. J58 designed primarily for flight in Mach 2.0 to Mach 3.0 region giving basic thrust of 26,000lb (115.6kN). Report just analytical study with no project drawings.

G-150 Mach 3 fighter 'usefulness' study, 11.56.

G-151 Original designation of **G-123F** 'Missileer' study, 11.56.

G-158 Variant of F11F-1F fitted with hydroskis for water operation, 1.57.

G-200 Original designation of **G-128E** 'Missileer' study, 6.58.

G-208 Drone version of North American F-108 Rapier, 8.58.

G-273 Supersonic two-seat replacement for Republic F-105, 5.60 onwards.

G-273A Different design that became **TFX/F-111B** strike fighter first flown 5.18.65. Cancelled 5.68.

G-303 Series of designs studies to requirements for carrier fighter, 1965 onwards. Included modifications of TFX/F-111 designs and eventually formed Grumman's VFX/F-14 proposals. Design **G-303C** had twin fins and high vg wing and **G-303D** swing-wings, twin tails and a rather 'hunched shoulder' appearance – both 1966. **G-303-60** of 10.67 used vg wings and single fin. Fixed-wing **303F** rejected. Design **G-303E** selected as VFX winner and flew as **F-14 Tomcat** on 21.12.70.

G-399 Variable geometry and fixed wing projects proposed to earlier stages of FX/F-15 requirement, 7.65 onwards. Did not make final competition. **G-399A** allocated to work that would have been sub-contracted to Fairchild Hiller.

G-495A Advanced Tactical Fighter, 9.71. (G-495 covered Project APEX).

G-545 Advanced interceptor, 4.70. Designation **G-545A** covered another fighter study, 12.70. **G-545B** was an F-14 development for the USAF's Improved Manned Interceptor requirements, 8.72.

G-607 V/STOL fighter design proposed for Sea Control Ship, 30.12.71. Lost competition to Rockwell XFV-12A. CTOL version also suggested. Refined 607A proposed 30.6.72.

G-623 Lightweight fighter project submitted to Navy VFAX competition, 15.7.74.

G-623V V/STOL derivative of G-623, 15.7.74.

Lightweight Fighter Canard cranked wing project for USAF, approx mid-1970s.

KAISER-FLEETWINGS

Navy Night Fighter Design proposed 9.45 to competition won by Douglas Skynight and Grumman G-75.

LOCKHEED

Lockheed diversified into fighters and reconnaissance aircraft, civil and military airliners, transports and patrol aircraft and space flight. The series below covers the Temporary Design Designations allocated by Lockheed to the preliminary design effort made towards a new requirement or idea and each number could cover many layouts. If a project was committed to detail drawings or funding for hardware it would receive a Basic Model number (highlighted where applicable in the text). From L-267 the series became CL- to clarify the design came from Lockheed California. Many numbers in later parts of the series were never allocated. Lockheed merged with Martin Marietta in 1994 to form Lockheed Martin.

L-140 Lockheed's first jet fighter, the **XP-80 Shooting Star**. First flew 8.1.44 and built in substantial numbers. This and F-94 Starfire which followed both came under **Model 80** designation.

L-153 Large number of studies covering all manner of conventional and unconventional wing configurations, autumn 1945 onwards. Final conventional design frozen in 1947 and built in prototype form as **Model 90** and **XF-90**, first flown 3.6.49. Final competition for penetration fighter lost to McDonnell XF-88 and no production. Further version of XF-90 proposed with ventral intake and pinwheel pattern for nose missile ports.

L-167 Studies to same penetration fighter program as L-153 but covering delta wing options, 9.46 onwards.

L-169 Continuation of delta wing research, but here for pursuit aircraft instead of penetration fighter, late 1946. Single design (L-169-1) only. Two Westinghouse 24C or Lockheed (Menasco) L-1000 power units. Span 35ft 0in (10.7m), length 44ft 6in (13.6m). With 24C top speed at sea level 682mph (1,097km/h), 630mph (1,014km/h) at 35,000ft (10,668m), sea level rate of climb 11,900ft/min (3,627m/min), time to 35,000ft (10,669m) 16.9 minutes, combat radius 970 miles (1,561km), gross weight 17,000lb (7,711kg). Six 20mm cannon outboard on wing, 1,400gal (6,366lit) internal fuel.

L-177 Brief fighter study for Navy, c1947/1948. Based on P-80B Shooting Star with modified nose and cannon armament plus naval fittings.

L-180 Four-seat carrier-based escort fighter to OS-112, 1948. Five different layouts studied but not ordered.

L-181 Various studies for improved versions of P-80 Shooting Star, 5.48. Not built but part of design effort found its way into the F-94 Starfire.

F-94 Starfire Two-seat development of F-80 with radar in nose, 1948. YF-94 first flew 16.4.49 and built in numbers as interim all-weather interceptor.

L-183 Number given to designs prepared to OS-113 for naval interceptor, c9.48. Competition won by Douglas F4D Skyray and McDonnell F3H Demon.

L-188 Covered several proposed developments of F-94, c1948/1949. Airframe essentially single-seat version of early F-94C first flown 18.1.50.

L-190 Early studies for USAF interceptor following conference held by USAF in 5.49. Studies began soon after and covered straight, delta and VG wings. Most projects relatively lightweight. Little progress made before studies moved on to heavier aircraft under L-2xx designations.

L-200 Tail-sitter naval convoy fighter to OS-122, mid-1950. Design became **Model 81** and built as **XFV-1**. Left the ground on 23.12.53 but first flew as planned on 16.6.54. No production and program cancelled 6.55.

L-202 Day fighter and ground support study, late 1950. Two versions – one dedicated design plus stripped out F-94C – neither ordered.

L-204 Further proposed developments of F-94 with variable geometry or thinner wings, 1951. None built.

L-205 Proposal to USAF MX1554 (F-102) interceptor requirement, 9.50 onwards. Designated **Model 99** after declared one of competition winners, but project cancelled before end 1951.

L-210 Ground attack fighter, 1951/1952.

L-216 Navy fighter/bomber study, 1951/1952.

L-224 Daytime air superiority project requested by USAF, 1951/1952. Excellent performance with alternative engines in 9,000lb (40.0kN) thrust range. Top speed 1,203mph (1,936km/h) at 35,000ft (10,668m), combat ceiling 56,500ft (17,221m), combat radius 230nm (426km). Span with tip tanks 34ft 0in (10.4m), length 49ft 10in (15.2m). Designers realised that a bit more power would give even higher speeds and altitudes, so project halted for short period. Restarted as L-227.

L-227 Designation covering a series of designs leading to F-104 Starfighter, 3.52 onwards. After USAF requirement changes, manufacturer undertook an extensive design effort under the L-227 designation to define a basic day fighter.

American Fighter Projects Summary

Lockheed L-190-1 interceptor, the first project in the L-190 series (mid-1949). At 22,000 lb (9,979kg) gross take-off weight this was one of the heaviest projects in the L-190 series and was powered by a Wright TJ-7 jet. Span 38ft (11.6m), length 48ft (14.6m), wing area 314ft² (29.2m²). Peter Clukey

Lockheed L-224-1 (1951/1952). Peter Clukey

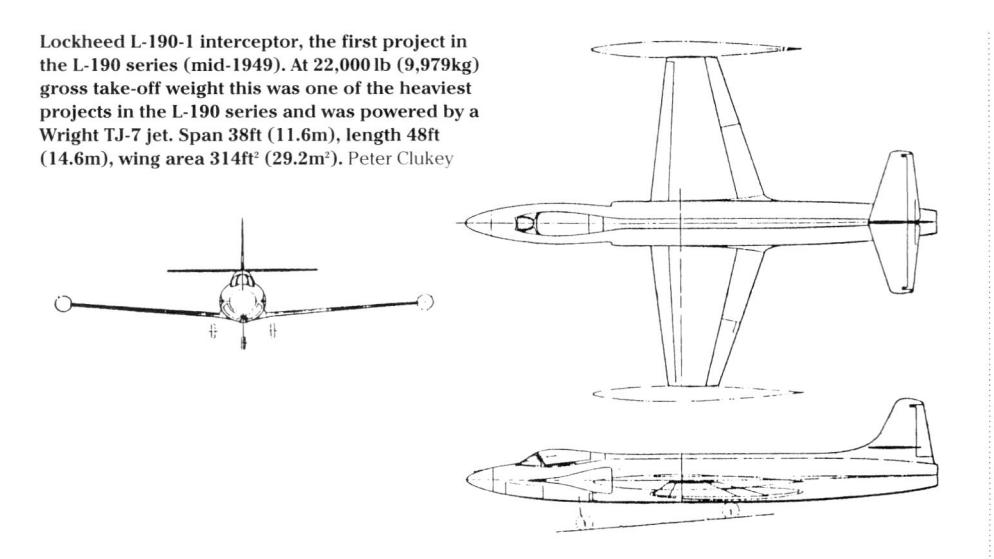

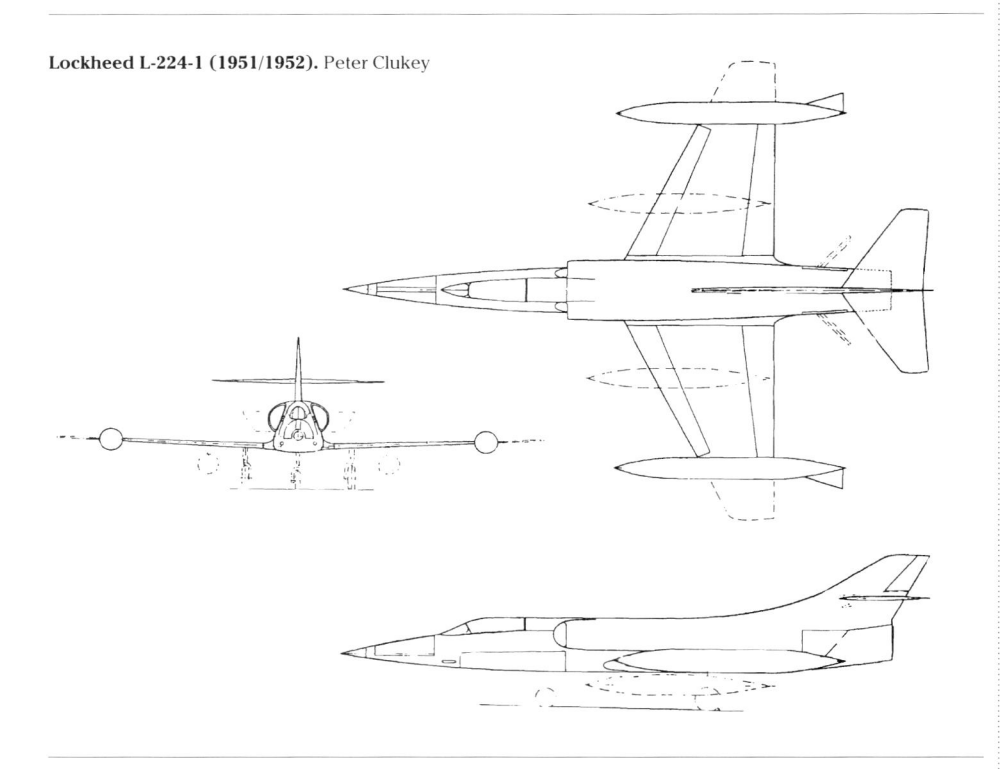

L-242	Project to OS-130 for supersonic naval carrier fighter, 11.52 onwards. Lost competition to Vought F8U Crusader.
L-246	Final studies leading to **Model 83 F-104 Starfighter**. Prototypes ordered and XF-104 made first flight 4.3.54.
L-247	VTOL tail-sitter research project based on F-104, 1952/1953. Concluded such aircraft was possible but needed more power than currently available with F-104's type of engine.
L-252	Strategic fighter design to meet Strategic Air Command requirement under MX2140, c4.53. Hundreds of computer generated iterations considered but only ten received any degree of consideration. Seven of these based on F-104 and only L-252-1 and L-252-2 could meet design limits – Mach 1.75 at 55,000ft (16,764m), combat ceiling 60,000ft (18,288m) plus, combat radius 1,500nm (2,778km).
CL-267	High-speed interceptor design study, c1953.
CL-288	Long-range interceptor designed to WS.202A requirements, 5.54 onwards.
CL-295	Series of general design studies for VTOL lightweight day fighters undertaken for Air Research and Development Command (ARDC), 1954 to mid-1955. Alternative arrangements included layouts based on F-104 plus all-new tail-sitter designs. Intended to achieved Mach 1+ at sea level and Mach 2+ at 35,000ft (10,668m).
CL-307	Parasite fighter to be carried by 'Mother Ship', 1955/1956.
CL-317	Brief study to assess naval carrier suitability of F-104, 1956.
CL-320	Further developments of long-range interceptor, late 1955 onwards. Long series of designs drawn.
CL-345	High-speed high-altitude interceptor, c1956. No information.
CL-346	Series of general design studies for VTOL fighter-bombers undertaken for Air Research and Development Command (ARDC), 1955/1956. Primary mission to deliver special stores against enemy installations but secondary role was defence against enemy bombers and attack aircraft. Most layouts had aircraft sitting and flying in horizontal position with engines mounted in wingtip nacelles that rotated to give vertical lift. Two designs were tail-sitters. Speed requirements same as CL-295 and concluded that practical VTOL aircraft that met all requirements was possible.
CL-349	VTOL fighter and fighter/bomber studies to Navy Specification TS-140, 1955/1956. Refined previous designs covered by CL-295 and CL-346. Requirements included Mach 1.1 at sea level and Mach 2.0 at 60,000ft (18,288m).
CL-351	Starfighter development called F-104X, 1956. New General Electric J79 engines and redesigned fuselage. Mach 3.2 at 69,000ft (21,031m).
CL-352	Development of T2V-1 advanced trainer into lightweight point defence all-weather interceptor for anti-submarine (CVS) class carriers, 1956.
CL-354	All-weather F-104 study, 1956.
CL-362	Hypersonic fighter study, 1956/1957.
CL-363	Mach 3.0 interceptor and fighter/bomber for Tactical Air Command, 1956/1957.
CL-366	Tactical Air Command fighter/bomber for service from 1962 onwards, c1957. Designed to penetrate enemy territory at high speed and altitude. Two versions – canard CL-366-1 and conventional tail -2. Both would have fulfilled the mission but -1 preferred because offered longer range (777nm [1,439km] against 482nm [893km]). Mach 3.0 at 80,000ft (24,384m). CL-366-1 span 34ft 8in (10.6m), 70ft 0in (21.3m), wing area 400ft² (37.2m²), gross weight 40,000 lb (18,144kg), internal fuel 13,063 lb (5,925kg). Powerplant one Pratt & Whitney JT-11-3 (advanced J58).
CL-371	F-104 fitted with rocket-assisted take-off gear, 1957.
CL-383	VTOL/STOL fighter study, 1958. Work continued by CL-407 strike aircraft study.
CL-386	All-weather F-104, 1958.
CL-397	Zero-length-launched (ZELL) F-104, c1958.
CL-398	Follow-on work to CL-366 but here evolved into fighter/attack aircraft for US Navy and Marines Corps, c1958. Mach 3.0 at 75,000ft (22,860m).
CL-404	Improved F-104. Cancelled.
CL-411	Improved F-104D.
CL-438	Study to modify P2V Neptune or P3V Orion patrol aircraft into long-range Eagle missile carrier, 1958/1959.
CL-457	Lightweight F-104 (project F-104-9) for friendly Mutual Assistance Program (MAP) countries, c1959. Is possibly the simplified version of F-104 offered against Northrop Freedom Fighter.
CL-458	Project F-104-11 all-weather Starfighter development with improved J79 engine to

CL-480   V/STOL fighter studies, 1959.
CL-513   F-104 drone interceptor, c1959/1960.
YF-12A   Mach 3 interceptor version of A-12 reconnaissance aircraft first proposed 3.60. First prototype made maiden flight 7.8.63 as AF-12 but no production.
CL-521   Multi-mission F-104G for Europe. Basic airframe almost untouched.
CL-583   Upgraded F-104 proposed to USAF, 1961. Not procured.
CL-590   Proposals to Tactical Fighter Experimental (TFX) requirement, 12.61. Eight designs completed. Competition won by General Dynamics/Grumman F-111.
CL-705   F-104 improvement studies, 1962 to 1963.
CL-731   Re-engined F-104, 1963.
CL-799   Improved F-104-type fighter for Air Defense Command and Tactical Air Command, 1963.
CL-802   Tactical fighter weapon system, 1963.
CL-807   Study to install alternative missiles on F-104G, late 1963.
CL-814   F-104 low-altitude interceptor with Sparrow III missiles, 1963/1964.
CL-847   F-104 high-altitude interceptor, 1964.
CL-901   Advanced F-104 for USAF, 1964/1965.
CL-958/CL-978/CL-981/CL-982   All advanced air superiority versions of F-104, 1965/1966.
CL-979   Various studies made to early stages of FX/F-15 requirements, 1965 onwards. Covered eleven designs but two classified reports now destroyed.
CL-1000   FX fighter studies lasting nearly three years of research during late 1960s. Ninety-one designs considered with take-off weights between 24,000 lb (10,886kg) and 46,000 lb (20,866kg) and top speeds between Mach 2.3 and Mach 2.7.
CL-1001   VFX fighter study for Navy, mid-1960s.
CL-1172   Advanced Navy fighter, 1968.
CL-1195   Export air superiority fighter based on F-104, 1969.
CL-1197   Preliminary study for US Navy fighter for 1985 time period, 1969.
CL-1200   Lightweight fighter development of F-104 Starfighter with high wing and low tail, mid-1969 onwards. Proposed as **CL-2000-1 Lancer** to International Fighter Aircraft competition 1.70 but lost to Northrop F-5E.
X-27 Lancer Plan to build two prototypes of CL-1200 development as X-27 considered during 1971 but stopped by lightweight fighter competition.
CL-1200-2   Development of X-27 to lightweight fighter competition, 1.72. Lost to General Dynamics YF-16 and Northrop YF-17.
CL-1212   Lightweight US Navy fighter, 1969.
CL-1223   V/STOL tactical fighter designs, 1969.
CL-1250   Advanced fighter for USAF, 1970. F-15-size aircraft.
CL-1254   Lightweight fighter, 1970.
CL-1290   V/STOL fighter/attack air vehicle for Sea Control Ships, 1971.
CL-1309   Advanced tactical fighter studies, 1973.
CL-1310   Advanced tactical fighter studies, 1973.
CL-1314   Advanced tactical fighter studies, 1973.
CL-1316   Advanced fighter aircraft, 1973.
CL-1400   Development of CL-1200-2 and X-27 for Navy, c1972.

MARTIN

This company ceased manufacturing aircraft in 1960; during the following year it became part of Martin Marietta, and then part of Lockheed Martin in 1994. Martin never built a fighter of its own design. Few fighter documents survive in the Martin archives.

217   Flying wing pursuit fighter, c1945.
218   Twin-engine high-altitude jet fighter, c1945/46.
235   High-performance swept wing fighter for Navy, c4.46. May have been proposed to competition won by Vought F7U Cutlass.
262   Single turboprop-powered convoy escort fighter for Navy to OS-122, mid-1950. Smaller Model 262P proposed at same time as prototype.
276   Air Force fighter-bomber, c1951.
278   Swept wing fighter-bomber for USAF, c1951/1952.
288   USAF fighter-bomber, 1953.
299   Lightweight fighter, 1953/1954.
302   Long-range interceptor for USAF, 1954. Probably to WS.202A.
308   Long-range interceptor for USAF, 1954. Probably to WS.202A. First alternative design to Model 302.
314   Long-range interceptor for USAF, 1954/1955. Probably to WS.202A. Second alternative design to Model 302.
315   Fighter bomber using unconventional methods of take-off, 1954/1955.
319   USAF Tactical Air Force interceptor/bomber, 1955.
328   USAF fighter-bomber, c1956. No details available
344   Long-range interceptor for USAF, c1957/1958.

McDONNELL/McDONNELL DOUGLAS

McDonnell merged with Douglas in April 1967 to form McDonnell Douglas, and in the 1990s the company was acquired by Boeing. McDonnell designed a wide range of aircraft types and the gaps in this series are represented by helicopters, transports, trainers, missiles and weapons, although there are few bomber studies. From the late 1950s many of the numbers were taken by McDonnell's increasing involvement with spacecraft.

11   Shipborne twin-engine patrol fighter begun in 1943. Model 11A flown as prototype **XFD-1** (later FH Phantom) 26.1.43. Designs 11B to 11H covered unbuilt variants and other proposals. FD-1N night fighter version also proposed.
23   Number given to production examples of **FH Phantom**.
24   Very long series of naval jet fighter designs, c1945. Two prototypes of **Model 24B** ordered 3.45 as **XF2H-1 Banshee** (formerly **XF2D-1**) and first flown 11.1.47. Production followed as **F2H**. Final list of designs exceeded fifty and later projects showed Banshee-type fighters with straight or swept wings, reheat or no reheat, engines in fuselage or in underwing nacelles. Banshee redesignated **F-2** in September 1962.
26 & 26A   Designs for a 'Sonic Airplane' with two and one Westinghouse 24C engines respectively, c1945.
27   Several designs for small Army (USAAF) parasite fighter to be carried on larger bomber, 1944. **Model 27E** built as **XF-85 Goblin** prototype and first flown 23.8.48 but no production. **Model 27F** described as 'Delta Wing Airborne Interceptor'.
34   Fighter proposal for Chinese Air Force, c1946.
36A to 36C   Initial twin engine designs for long-range (penetration) Army fighter proposal, autumn 1945. 36A was XF2H-1 Banshee type, 36B had tip-mounted engines, 36C (13.10.45) had two engines in fuselage and eventually built as prototype XF-88, first flown 20.10.48. Series of designs followed including **36D** (XF-88A with afterburner), **36F** (production F-88A with afterburner), **36J** (turboprop version flown as XF-88B 14.3.53), **36K** (interceptor F-88), **36N** (36F with two Allison J71 engines), **36Q** (ditto 36N but with 10% larger fuselage) and **36R** (high performance escort fighter with two J71s and 35° swept wing).

There was also a two-seat all-weather fighter version proposed in 1948. The **36W** was built as the **XF-101 Voodoo** first flown 29.9.54 and this design entered production. **36AT** formed basis for **F-101B Voodoo** interceptor first flown 27.3.57. McDonnell asked USAF to give F-109 designation to

Lockheed CL-366-1 (c1957). This Mach 3 aeroplane was to be fitted with a convergent/divergent nozzle and a thrust reverser. The CL-398-1 design was very similar. Peter Clukey

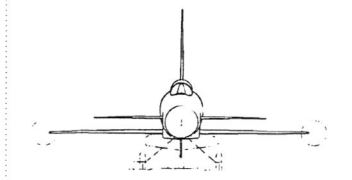

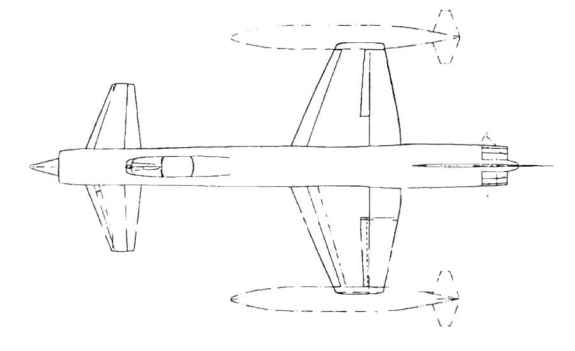

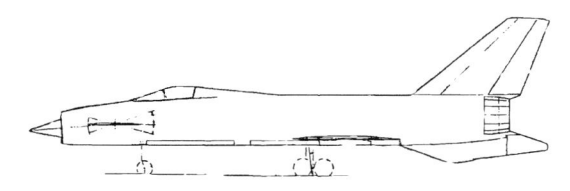

American Fighter Projects Summary

	Model 36AT, but this request was turned down.
39	Fighter proposal for Chinese Air Force, c1946/1947.
40	Navy day fighter with two Westinghouse 24C (J34) engines in wing, c4.46. In competition won by Vought F7U Cutlass. Version also drawn with V-tail.
40A	Navy day fighter with two Westinghouse 24C (J34) engines in fuselage, c4.46. In competition won by Vought F7U Cutlass.
58	Series of designs for carrier-based navy interceptor fighter with 45° swept wing 9.48. Design proposed to OS-113 and selected for manufacture. Became **XF3H-1** first flown 7.8.51 and entered service as **F3H Demon**. Model **58A** = land-based version, **58B** same design but with external pylon fuel tanks, **58C** had fuselage length increased by 10in (25.4cm) and depth 8.5in (21.6cm), frontal area 39ft² (3.63m²) and engine compartment moved aft. Later developments offered alternative engines and weapons. Demon redesignated **F-3** in September 1962. **58X** comparative design to Model 98 series.
60	Carrier-based navy interceptor fighter with delta wing, 15.9.48. Alternative design to Model 58 for OS-113.
64	Army (USAAF) interceptor with jet engine and delta wing, 1948/1949.
67	Air Force Interceptor with sweptback wing, c1949.
68	Air Force Interceptor with straight wing, c1949.
71	Navy interceptor with turbojet engine, c1949.
84	Composite Air Force/Navy fighter, 3.51.
87	Proposed high-performance long-range Navy fighter, 6.51.
90	Single-seat day fighter with J57 engine submitted to OS-130 Issue 3, 28.2.53. Lost competition to Vought F8U Crusader.
91	Single-seat day fighter with J65 engine submitted to OS-130 Issue 3, early 1953. Lost competition to Vought F8U Crusader.
93	Single-seat day fighter with J57 engine submitted to OS-130 Issue 1, 1953.
94	Long-range strategic fighter with various wing and engine configurations, 3.53. Resulted in **Model 36AE** series. To be powered by two YJ67-W-1 or XJ79 turbojets.
98	Proposals for single-seat attack fighter, 25.8.53 onwards. Designs included Model **98A** (**F3H-E**) with single J67. **98B** proposed as **F3H-G** with two J65s and **F3H-H** with two J79s. **98C** as 98B except had 60° delta wing, **98D** had straight wing. Work eventually crystallised into Model **98R** for Navy as **F4H-1 Phantom**. First XF4H-1 flew 27.5.58. When first ordered for USAF F4H designated **F-110 Spectre**. Phantom redesignated **F-4** in September 1962.
Long-range Interceptor	Two-seat development of F-101 offered to embryonic long-range concept, 1953. Evaluated alongside Northrop N-126.
'Voodoo 67'	Sale name for proposed version of F-101 fitted with J-67 engines, 1953/1954. Voodoo's span was increased by 9in (22.9cm) to take the larger engine. Not built.
109	Long-range interceptor similar to F-101A Voodoo to WS.202A, 17.6.54 (**109A**) and 18.8.54 (larger **109B**).
110	Long-range interceptor submitted to WS.202A, 14.7.54 (**110A**) and 18.8.54 (smaller **110B**).
111	Long-range interceptor designed to WS.202A, 26.10.54.
124	Long-range subsonic missile-carrying fighter for Navy, 23.9.57.
153A	Proposals for Fleet Air Defence Aircraft armed with Eagle missiles and powered by TF-30-P-2 jets, 15.10.59. Competition won by Douglas F6D Missileer.
154A	Turboprop version of 153A, 13.1.60.
156	Supersonic tactical fighter proposals to TFX requirement 12.61, although number first allocated to type 28.3.60. Competition won by General Dynamics/Grumman.
193	V/STOL fighter, c4.64.
199	Light attack and air superiority (FX) fighter, 7.5.65. This low altitude attack aircraft was to have 'respectable air-to-air capability'. Model **199B** won FX competition to become **F-15 Eagle**. Prototype YF-15A first flew 27.7.72. Navalised F-15(N) and F-15(N-PHX) proposed 1972/73.
F-4(FV)S	Development of F-4 Phantom for Navy with variable geometry swing wings, mid-1966 onwards. Not built.
222	Advanced fighter/attack aircraft for Navy, 29.8.67. Probably McD's VFAX study.
225	Variable geometry carrier-based project designed to VFX/F-14 requirement, 27.10.67 onwards. Official VFX proposal 1.10.68. Lost competition to Grumman.
226	Advanced manned interceptor for USAF, 7.2.68. Possibly part of FX work but project list gives no indication of this.
250	Multiple Service air superiority fighter, 24.1.69.
'Stripped' F-4E	'International' lightweight fighter derived from F-4E Phantom, 1969. Lost competition to Northrop F-5E.
262	Navy V/STOL supersonic fighter for Sea Control Ships, 21.12.71. AV-8C development of Harrier. Competition won by Rockwell XFV-12A.
263	Multi-mission aircraft, 9.10.72. Version submitted to Navy VFAX lightweight fighter competition, 7.74.
265	Advanced manoeuvring vectored-lift fighter for Air Force, 19.2.73.
267	Substantial modification of Northrop YF-17 for Navy Air Combat Fighter competition, 31.10.74. Declared winner and as **F/A-18 Hornet** first flew 18.11.78.
268	'Low signature' fighter for Advanced Research Projects Agency (ARPA), 8.75.
269	Battlefield superiority fighter/tactical fighter tailored to ground attack and reconnaissance role, but with alternate capability as air superiority, deep strike and strategic aircraft, 13.10.75. Gross take-off weight in excess of 40,000 lb (18,144kg).

NORTH AMERICAN/ROCKWELL

During the war and in the years following North American built an outstanding reputation in the field of fighter aircraft design. In 1967 it merged with Rockwell Standard to form North American Rockwell, and then became Rockwell International in 1973. North American built jet fighters for both the Air Force and Navy but, unlike most of the aircraft manufacturers' project lists, the great majority of NA-designations relate to real aircraft. Consequently only those covering prototypes are listed here and a large number of production aircraft designations are omitted. However, some allocations were made to projects, particularly the series of long-range interceptors. The reason behind all of this was that North American did not use model numbers, but rather program numbers as part of a cost accounting system covering the allocation of resources and payments from the government.

NA-134 Designation given to prototype straight-wing **XFJ-1 Fury** first flown 27.11.46.
NA-140 Designation given to prototype swept-wing **XP-86 Sabre** first flown 1.10.47. Production F-86 built in large numbers and many versions followed.
Interceptor Design submitted to official requirement, 11.45. No details. Won by Convair XP-92 Dart.
Navy Fighter Two designs proposed c4.46 to competition won by Vought F7U Cutlass.
NA-157 Designation given to prototype **YF-93A** penetration fighter development of production F-86A, first flown 25.1.50. Only two aircraft built after production contract cancelled.
NA-164 Designation given to prototype **YF-86D** (formerly F-95A) radar-equipped interceptor

Model of the McDonnell F3H-G/H. Note the bombs under the wings. Larry Merritt

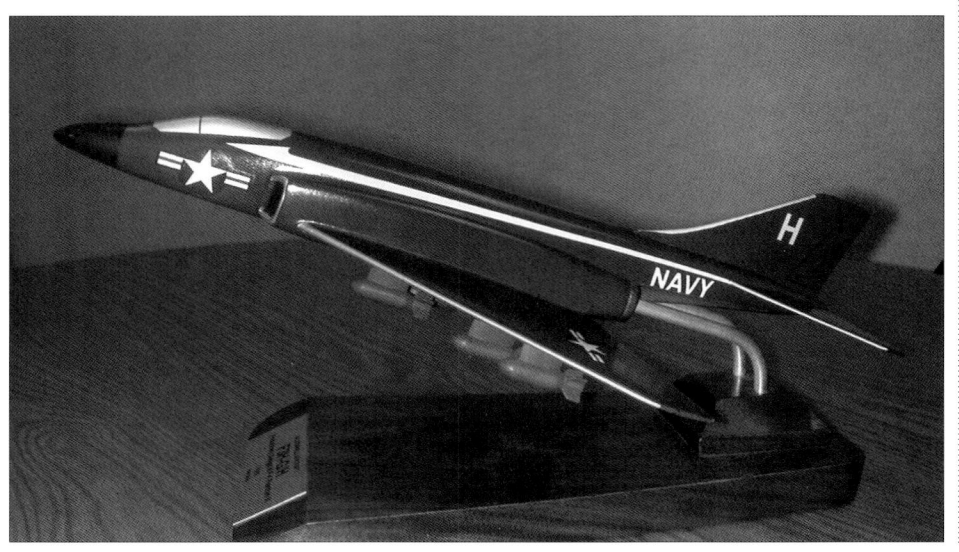

Model of the North American Missileer. John Aldaz

Model of the proposed Rockwell International FV-12A project. Jonathan Rigutto / photo © 2005 Chad Slattery

development of the F-86A, first flown 22.12.49.
NA-166 Two-seat all-weather fighter development of the F-93A, 5.5.49. Contract placed for single example but not built.
Sabre 45 Development of F-86 with 45° swept wing, 1949. Design passed through at least two early layouts and project submitted as unsolicited proposal 1.51. Eventually developed into F-100 Super Sabre.
NA-179 Navalised version of swept wing F-86E first flown as **XFJ-2 Fury** on 4.2.52. Redesignated **F-1** in September 1962.
NA-180 Designation given to prototype **YF-100A Super Sabre** first flown 25.5.53.
'1954 Interceptor' Two proposals to the MX1554/F-102 interceptor requirement, 1.51.
All Weather Fighter-Bomber Study to MX1764, c1950/1951.
Navy Day Fighter Design for single-seat day fighter with variable incidence wing submitted to OS-130, early 1953. Alternative layouts considered. Lost competition to Vought F8U Crusader.
Strategic Fighter Design for USAF to MX2140, c4.53.
NA-211 F-100 development, 7.10.53. Possibly in competition with McDonnell XF-101B Voodoo.
NA-212 Fighter-bomber project, 20.10.53 onwards. Nine prototypes of later development ordered as **F-107A** but only three built. First flown 10.9.56. NA-212 also believed proposed against Lockheed CL-246 in 1.53 but rejected.
Super Fury Proposed version of early NA-212 design with 'duckbill' nose intake as carrier-suitable version of F-100, 15.11.53. Compared to F-100 this introduced a thinned (5% thick) integral fuel 45° swept wing, variable-geometry inlet, area-ruled fuselage, arrestor hook, folding wings, droopable wing tips and two wheels on each main gear. One 16,000lb (71.1kN) reheated thrust P&W J57-P-(JT3N), 1,370gal (6,229lit) internal fuel, three 20mm cannon, various rocket and other external stores and drop tanks, AN/APG-30A radar. High lift devices comprised automatic leading edge slats and blowing-type boundary layer control plain flaps. Span 36ft 9in (11.20m), length 50ft 9in (15.47m), take-off weight 28,130lb (12,760kg), max speed Mach 1.63 at 35,000ft (10,668m), combat ceiling 53,800ft (16,398m), combat radius 425nm (787km). Estimated performance included supersonic climb and, with later uprated engines, Mach 1.80 top speed. Given early go-ahead NAA considered could be in production in 1956. Project submitted to BuAer after Vought design had won OS-130 competition, possibly as attempt to disrupt F8U programme.
Long-range Interceptor Study to WS.202A, mid-1954 onwards.
NA-236 Long-range interceptor, 11.10.55 onwards. This project eventually progressed into the **NA-257/F-108 Rapier** but cancelled before first prototype completed.
NA-237 Fighter-bomber (FBX) study for USAF, c1955 or even 6.12.55. Heavy design was studied for the WS-300A fighter-bomber weapon system and this may possibly have been covered by NA-237 designation.
NA-257 Designation for fully developed **F-108** long-range interceptor study, 6.6.57 onwards.
NA-268 Reserved for Phase II development of F-108, 11.9.59, but not used.
Rapier Light fighter with delta wing and chin intake, 1950s/1960s? No further details.
Long-range Missile Fighter Subsonic naval patrol fighter to 'Missileer' requirement, 1959. Lost competition to Douglas F6D.
TFX Tactical Fighter proposals to TFX F-105 replacement requirement, 12.61. Competition won by General Dynamics/Grumman F-111.
VFAX Advanced fighter/attack aircraft for Navy, c1967.
NA-323 Variable geometry project designed to VFX/F-14 requirement, 10.68.
NA-324 Further work to VFX/F-14 program, c1968. Numbers NA-328 to NA-331 plus NA-333 allocated to contract definition, detail development and production but Grumman's proposal was selected as the winning design.
NA-335 Studies to air superiority fighter FX/F-15 requirement begun 1965 onwards. Fixed and variable geometry wing designs in early stages. Fixed wing Model NA-335 reached final stage of competition 1968 but defeated by McDonnell F-15. Navalised F-15(N) proposed 1972/73.
NR-349 Projected A-5C development of Vigilante carrier-based strike aircraft with three J-79 engines, 1971. Prepared to USAF's Improved Manned Interceptor requirement. Known as 'ABC Interceptor' and 'Advanced Vigilante'. Not built.
NR-356 V/STOL fighter design proposed for Sea Control Ship, 30.12.71. Ordered as XFV-12A but never flown. Abandoned 1981. Twin-engine version also proposed.
Lightweight Fighter Studies on light fighter types under way by 3.71.
Lightweight Fighter Version of XFV-12A submitted to Navy VFAX competition, 7.74.

American Fighter Projects Summary

NORTHROP

This company joined forces with Grumman in 1994 to form Northrop Grumman. Most of its fighters were built for the USAF.

XP-79B Small flying wing jet fighter prototype that crashed during its first flight on 12.9.45.

XP-79Z Combined design developed from XP-79 submitted to USAAF penetration and interceptor fighter requirements, 11.1.45. Prototype contracts eventually won by McDonnell XF-88, Lockheed XF-90 and Convair XP-92 Dart.

N-24 Four variants of swept wing fighter design for USAF all-weather fighter requirement, late 11.45. Straight wing development eventually chosen for prototype construction and flown 16.8.48 as **XP/XF-89 Scorpion**. Several versions put into production including N-35 (F-89A) and N-68 (F-89D).

X-4 Small tailless swept wing research aircraft ordered in 1946 and first flown 16.12.48. Two examples built.

N-35 Production F-89A Scorpion.

N-49 Designation given to YF-89A variant of Scorpion.

N-53 Single-seat interceptor fighter project, mid-1949. Long slim fuselage, low wing with trailing edge/tip elevons and tall fin. Side intakes feeding single Westinghouse X24C-10 engine. Span 28ft (8.5m), length 56ft 2in (17.1m), wing area 301ft² (28.0m²), gross weight 12,600 lb (5,715kg).

Super Scorpion Advanced swept wing development of F-89, 30.9.49.

N-63 Tail-sitter convoy defence fighter to OS-122, mid-1950. Smaller **N-63A** proposed at same time as test vehicle.

N-65 '1954 Interceptor' study, 1950. Design not submitted and project terminated.

Escort Fighter Scorpion development proposed 1950 and 1951 but not built. Known as F-89E (first use of designation). At one stage in competition with the McDonnell F-101A.

N-68 Production F-89D Scorpion.

N-71 Designation given to YF-89E variant of Scorpion powered by J71 engines and first flown 10.6.54. Used as engine testbed.

N-81 & N-82 'Advanced' developments of F-89 with large underwing nacelles, 1951 onwards. N-81 became **F-89F** and N-82 called **YF-89F**. Entered detail design and mock-ups built, project cancelled 8.52. An 'Advanced F-89' also proposed to interceptor requirement won by F-101B Voodoo, 1953/1954.

F-89X Two-seat interceptor with J-65 (Sapphire) engine, mid-1954. Considered as an interim interceptor pending arrival of the '1954 Interceptor'. May have been project that competed against the F-101B.

N-94 Four versions of single-seat day fighter submitted to OS-130, 16.2.53. Lost competition to Vought F8U Crusader.

N-102 Fang lightweight fighter proposal, 12.52. Initial version had conventional fin and tail, later had V-tail. Mock-up only.

N-126 Delta Scorpion long-range interceptor study to WS.202A, 2.53 onwards.

Strategic Fighter Design for USAF to MX2140, c4.53.

Navy Interceptor Preliminary study for expected design competition that never took place, 12.54 to 5.55.

Export Day Fighter Project proposed for European operators, 7 and 8.55. Developed from N-102 Fang.

Export Interceptor Project designed for European operators based on earlier Northrop attack bomber proposed for Navy, 7 and 8.55.

N-138 F-89H production version of Scorpion first flown 26.10.55.

N-144 Long-range interceptor project, 7.54.

N-149 Long-range interceptor project, 7.54.

Medium Range Interceptor Study undertaken for possible Convair F-102 replacement, 1 to 4.55. Not built.

N-156 Lightweight fighter interceptor project for Navy, 7.54 onwards. Designation re-allocated to export fighter.

N-156F Export **Freedom Fighter** first proposed 10.56 and flown 30.7.59. Redesignated **F-5A** in September 1962.

N-160 Covers production F-89D Scorpions modified as F-89Js with capability to carry Genie nuclear-tipped air-to-air missiles.

N-167 Long-range interceptor project with four engines side-by-side in fuselage, 11.55. Not built. N-167A development (4.4.56) had a lower position tailplane of same span as wing.

N-176 Long-range interceptor project with fuselage-mounted engines, 10.12.56. Not built.

N-184 Single-seat supersonic interceptor study, 12.12.56. Tapered straight wing with leading and trailing edge flaps, large wingtip missiles, all-moving tailplane and folding vertical fins. Chin intake for single J83 clustered engine. Single L10 rocket motor housed in root of fin. Span without missiles 32ft 4in (9.9m), length without pitot 66ft 2in (20.2m), wing area 350ft² (32.55m²), take-off weight 38,170 lb (17,314kg). Total fuel 18,257 lb (8,281kg) including two 250gal (1,137lit) external underwing tanks and 915 lb (415kg) of hydrogen peroxide for the rocket.

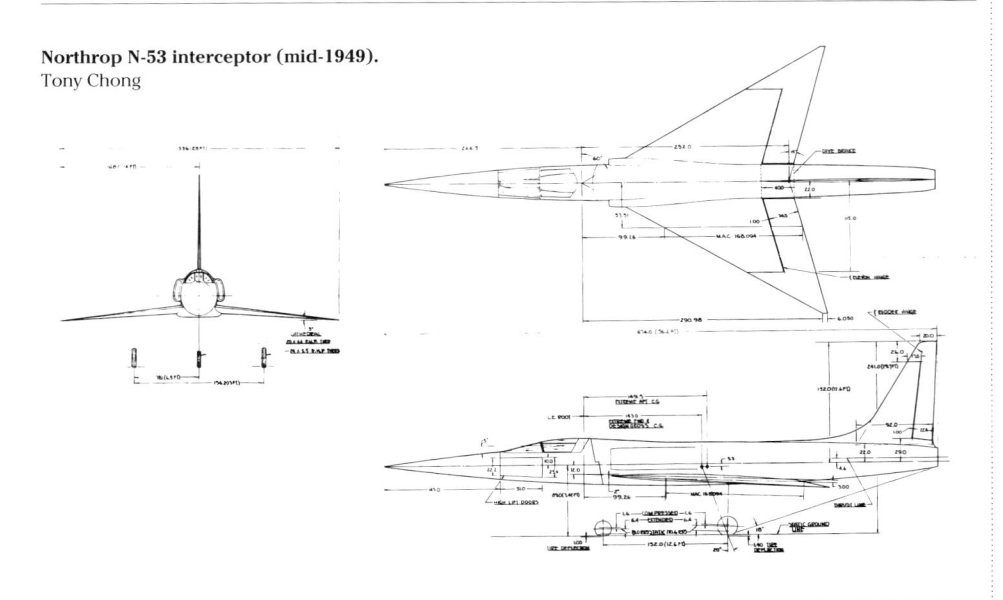

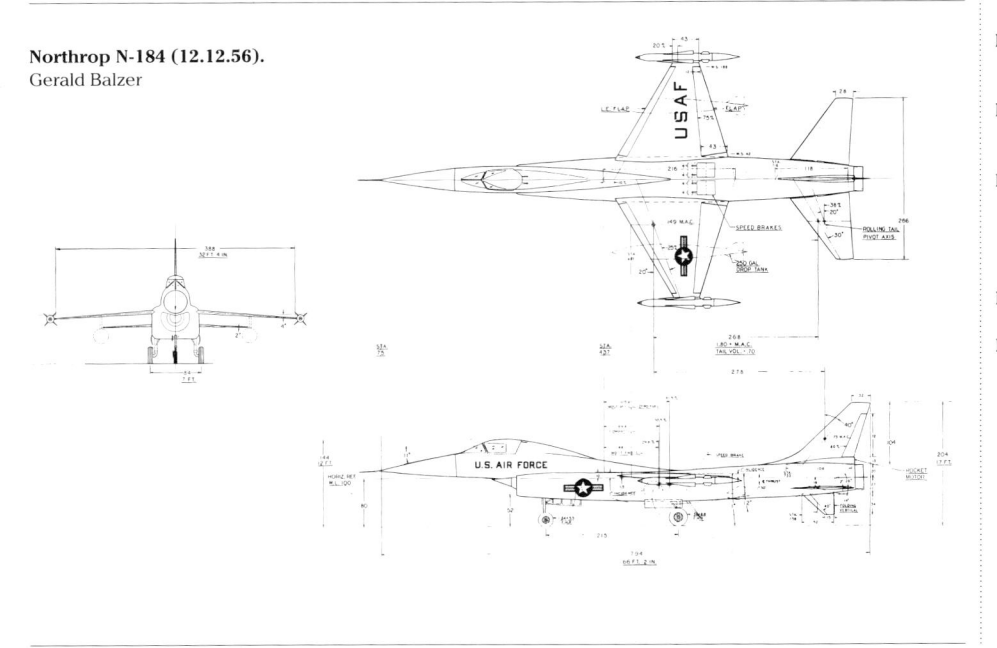

Northrop N-53 interceptor (mid-1949).
Tony Chong

Northrop N-184 (12.12.56).
Gerald Balzer

Northrop-made model of the P-530-2 Cobra.
Jonathan Rigutto / photo © 2005 Chad Slattery

N-201   Long-range missile fighter system, late 1950s.
N-214   'Optimum' interceptor weapons system study, late 1950s.
N-251   VTOL short-field interceptor design study, 1960s.
N-267   VTOL modification of T-38 Talon, 1960s. Four vertical lift jets in place of rear cockpit plus hover controls in nose, tail fuselage and wingtips.
N-286   Air Force close support fighter-bomber, approx early 1960s.
N-291   'Advanced' F-5A tactical fighter, 1960s.
N-298   'F-5 Mod', 1960s. Memo F-5-40 states 'To Skoshi Tiger Configuration'.
N-300/P-530   Numerous designs for lightweight fighter development of F-5A, 6.66. Started project line leading to YF-17. **P-530** preliminary design number given to development of N-300, 1967 onwards. Became **Cobra** lightweight fighter and continued well into 1970s.
N-310   Twin-engine, trapezoidal delta wing advanced tactical fighter with single vertical fin, early/mid-1970s. Had two-dimensional vectored exhaust nozzles. Also known as **P-700** and later Northrop teamed with Dornier in Germany to submit version called **N/D-102** to the West German JF-90 competition.
N-311/F-5-21   'International' lightweight fighter derived from F-5A. Company prototype flew 28.3.69 and won International Fighter competition in 1970. Became **F-5E Tiger II**.
N-314   Advanced 'energy manoeuvrable' lightweight fighter with two GE15 (J101) engines, 2.2.71. Variant of the P-530.
N-315   Baseline 'energy manoeuvrable' lightweight fighter with two GE15 (J101) engines, 19.5.71.
N-316   Advanced 'energy manoeuvrable' lightweight fighter with single F100 engine and two air intakes, 19.5.71.
N-317   'Energy manoeuvrable' lightweight fighter with single J101, 19.5.71.
N-318   'Energy manoeuvrable' lightweight fighter with two J101s and no afterburning, 19.5.71.
N-319   'Energy manoeuvrable' lightweight fighter with single F100 and single air intake, 19.5.71.
N-321/P-600   Proposed lightweight fighter designs based on P-530 Cobra, 1971. Given preliminary design number P-600. Submitted to USAF competition 1.72 and won along with General Dynamics YF-16. Prototype **YF-17A** first flown 9.6.74.
N-322/P-610   Single-engined lightweight fighter proposal based on P-530 Cobra, mid-1971. Lighter version of P-530.
Light Fighter   Single-engine version of YF-17, c1972.
P-630   Two-seat fighter development of YF-17 for Navy VFAX, 7.74.
F-18L   Land-based variant of McDonnell F-18 Hornet, 1974 onwards.
N-347   Probable designation of the Northrop/Dornier N/D-102 project submitted to German JF-90 competition.

Model of the 'solid nose' Republic F-84 development. Cradle of Aviation Museum

REPUBLIC/FAIRCHILD REPUBLIC

The Republic Aviation Corporation became the Republic Aviation Division of the Fairchild Hillier Corporation in 1965. This facility was closed in 1987 when it ceased the manufacture of both military and civil aircraft. The prefix 'AP' refers to 'Army Project' and 'NP' to 'Navy Project', but in fact all of Republic's jet fighters that were actually built were produced for the Air Force.

AP-23   Straight wing fighter project, 19.9.44. Became **XF-84 Thunderjet** fighter bomber prototype, first flown 28.2.46.
F-84 Development   Swept wing twin-engined fighter based on F-84 airframe but with engines mounted in overwing nacelles, c1950?
F-84F   Swept wing development of original F-84 called **YF-96A** and first flown 3.6.50. Redesignated **F-84F Thunderstreak**. Photo has been found of model of 'solid nose' F-84 development with intakes on sides of nose.
AP-31   Proposal for high-performance research aircraft and day interceptor, 1.46. Competition won by Convair XP-92 but AP-31 design ordered as prototype **XF-91 Thunderceptor**. XF-91 first flew 9.5.49 but no production.
F-91A   Interim interceptor development of XF-91 with radar in nose. Description papers dated 26.3.51. Full-size mock-up examined but project stopped 10.51 after work on Convair F-102 accelerated. Is possibly Model AP-31-N1.
AP-44A   Mach 3 all-weather high-altitude interceptor, early 1948.
AP-46   Development of F-84F fitted with turboprop engine as **XF-84H** and first flown 22.7.55. Apart from wing and cockpit, pretty well all-new aircraft. No production.
NP-48   Proposal for US Navy interceptor based on XP/XF-91, c9.48.
NP-49   Proposals for US Navy interceptor with V-tail and underwing engine nacelles, c9.48.
'1954 Interceptor'   Three proposals made to this requirement, 1.51. One was development of AP-44A with turbo-ramjet powerplant, second the 'XF-91B' jet/rocket-powered

American Fighter Projects Summary

AP-54   development of XF-91, third a conventional turbojet plus afterburner design. Turbo-ramjet project one of competition winners and developed into AP-57 and XF-103.

AP-54 Single-engine swept wing all-weather interceptor fighter study with F-91-style wing and large tip fittings, late 1949/1950. May have been one of submissions to the '1954 Interceptor' requirement.

AP-55 Twin-boom inverted V-tail lightweight fighter/interceptor project, early 1950. Later believed in competition with Lockheed F-104. Several versions drawn but none built.

AP-57 '1954 Interceptor' proposal and full development into Mach 3 **XF-103**, 1951. Three prototypes ordered but project cancelled 8.57 before anything had flown.

All Weather Fighter-Bomber Study to MX1764, c1950/1951.

AP-63 Swept wing fighter-bomber, 1951 onwards. Numerous layouts covered by designation. Eventually design **AP-63-31** built as **F-105A Thunderchief** to WS.306A. First example flew 22.10.55.

F-84F/V Development of F-84F with engines in nacelles just outside wing roots and lift jets in fuselage, 1950s.

AP-75 Long-range interceptor to WS.202A, c5.54.

AP-85 Two-seat swept-wing development of F-84F Thunderstreak, c1955.

V/STOL Fighter Delta wing design with three pairs of rotating engines under wing roots and fuselage. 1950s? No further details.

AP-100 V/STOL fighter-bomber proposal with three large lift fans mounted in centre of wide fuselage, 1959/1960.

TFX Believed Republic undertook Tactical Fighter studies to TFX requirement, 12.61. Competition won by General Dynamics/Grumman F-111.

F-105H Believed to be proposed Thunderchief development (or new design) with new 448ft² (41.7m²) area wing, new vertical fin and stabilator, new nose and landing gear, approx late 1962/early 1963. Had two seats and 30,000 lb (133.3kN) thrust engine. Not built.

V/STOL Fighter Design with long slim fuselage, highly swept wings and three lift units just ahead of side intakes, 1960s.

FX Proposals for new fighter, 1965 onwards. One possibly designated FH-100. Studies included variable geometry wings but final fixed-wing proposal of 1968 rejected for McDonnell Douglas design that became F-15.

FR-150 V/STOL fighter design proposed for Sea Control Ship, 30.12.71. Lost competition to Rockwell XFV-12A.

RYAN

This company built a small number of FR-1 Fireball mixed-power piston-jet fighters for the Navy from 1943 onwards. It also produced prototypes of the mixed turboprop-jet XF2R-1 Dark Shark that flew in November 1946. The company became Teledyne Ryan in 1968.

Model 38 Proposed VTOL jet fighter project for Navy, 4.47. Gross weight 7,700 lb (3,493kg) and to have rocket boosters for initial take-off. Preliminary design completed and advanced development called the **38R** proposed to Navy in 1953, but lack of finance prevented the service from taking up the project.

Model 69 Similar design to Model 38R proposed to Air Force in 1953. As Model 69 and **X-13** this delta wing VTOL research aircraft first flew on 10.12.55.

Fighter Delta wing tail-sitter fighter proposed as development of X-13, possibly without gantry, mid-1950s.

Model 115 Twin-engine delta wing fighter, 1957/1958. Span 31ft 2in (9.5m), length 61ft 2in (18.6m).

Model 186-C Large Mach 2 point defence fighter, 1960s. Advanced V/STOL study using two reheated GE-1 propulsion units with efflux ducted to eight fans mounted in the large 3.25% thick Gothic/delta wing. Intakes halfway back beneath the root chord, two seats, bicycle undercarriage and large nose for radar. VTO weight 30,000 lb (13,608kg).

Model 187-B Supersonic V/STOL fighter, 1960s. Similar fuselage to 186-C but with eight foldaway lift-fan engines in sides of fuselage plus one propulsion engine, conventional moderately swept wing and tricycle undercarriage. Maximum speed Mach 1.6.

TEMCO

Model 39 Swept wing single-seat tail-sitter jet fighter, 1950s. Single Allison J71 engine, dorsal intake, swept upper and dorsal fins. Estimated capable of Mach 1.6 at 35,000ft (10.668m).

Republic XF-84F/V. Cradle of Aviation Museum

Appendix Two

Fighter Specifications and Weapon Systems

The MX-series of code numbers covered research and development in pretty well every area of fighter and bomber design and equipment, including engines and weaponry and other topics related to military aviation. The series was started in early 1941 by the Experimental Engineering Section of the US Army Air Corps' Materiel Division, which soon became USAAF Air Materiel Command or AMC, and was continued by the Air Force after its formation in 1947 and well into the 1950s. The great increase in research and development following the introduction of jets and other advanced technology ensured that double the quantity of MX numbers were issued between 1946 and 1950 than had been employed during the War years. An MX designation was usually assigned to a project very soon in its development life with the result that many were cancelled early in the study phase before any hardware had been produced, a paper report sometimes being the only concrete evidence of its existence. Due to the growing complexity of new projects the MX designation system was formally abandoned by the AMC on 1st July 1952. The small number listed are those known to have covered specific USAF fighters and fighter studies.

MX745 All-Weather Jet Fighter (Curtiss-Wright XP/XF-87)
MX808 Night and All-Weather Fighter (Northrop XP/XF-89)
MX809 Research Aircraft and Interceptor (Republic XP/XF-91)
MX811 Long-Range Penetration Fighter (McDonnell XP/XF-88)
MX812 Long-Range Penetration Fighter (Lockheed XP/XF-90)
MX813 Rocket-Powered Interceptor (Convair XP/XF-92 Dart) and flying prototype (XF-92A)
MX940 Amphibious fighter study (EDO)
MX1554 Development of a Supersonic Interceptor ('1954 Interceptor') (Convair F-102 and Republic XF-103)
MX1764 All Weather Fighter-Bomber Study (designs from North American and Republic) c1950
MX1853 Lightweight Day Fighter (Lockheed XF-104)
MX1894 Supersonic Day Fighter (North American F-100)
MX1976 Study of Vertical Take-Off Tactical Fighter (Bell design) c1951
MX2140 Design study for new strategic fighter (projects from Chance Vought V-386, Convair, Lockheed, North American, Northrop N-132) 1953

A concurrent US Navy specification system was the OS-series and those known to exist are also listed below. By the late 1950s OS had been retitled TS for Type Specification.

OS-112 Carrier-Based Escort Fighter
OS-113 Carrier-Based Interceptor Fighter (Douglas F4D Skyray and McDonnell F3H Demon)
OS-116 Class VF Seaplane Night Fighter (Convair Skate)
OS-122 Convoy Fighter
OS-130 Supersonic Carrier Fighter (Chance Vought F8U Crusader)
TS-140 VTOL fighter and fighter/bomber studies (Lockheed)
TS-151 Long-range Missile Fighter for Fleet Defence (Douglas F6D Missileer)
TS-161 High Performance Fighter (VFX – Grumman F-14 Tomcat)
TS-169 Attack Fighter (McDonnell Douglas F-18 Hornet)

The MX system was followed by the WS- series. This was introduced by the Air Force in the 1950s to cover complete weapon systems (airframes, weapons and avionics) rather than a specific airframe or piece of equipment. In this arrangement numbers WS-100 to WS-199 covered 'Strategic Systems' (that is, heavy bombers and strategic missiles but also long-range escort fighters), WS-200 to WS-299 'Air Defence Systems' (fighters and missiles) and WS-300 to WS-399 'Tactical Systems'. The last group comprised medium and light bombers and attack aircraft, missiles and also fighter-bombers. Those WS numbers known to apply to fighters and fighter design studies covered by this book are as follows:

WS-105A Advanced Penetration Escort Fighter (McDonnell F-101A Voodoo). Also covered by Operational Requirement GOR-101.
WS-201A Interceptor (Convair F-102 Delta Dagger)
WS-201B Interceptor (Convair F-106 Delta Dart)
WS-202A Long-range Interceptor (North American F-108 Rapier). Also covered by Operational Requirement GOR-114.
WS-204A Interceptor (Republic F-103)
WS-217A Interceptor (McDonnell F-101B Voodoo)
WS-300A Fighter-Bomber Design Study (Super ceded by WS-306A)
WS-303A Lightweight Fighter (Lockheed F-104 Starfighter)
WS-306A Fighter-Bomber (Republic F-105 Thunderchief). Also covered by Operational Requirement GOR-49.
WS-306B Fighter-Bomber (North American F-107)
WS-326A USAF version of McDonnell F4H/F-4 Phantom (F-110A/F-4C)
WS-328A Air Superiority Fighter (McDonnell-Douglas F-15A Eagle)

Select Bibliography

A great deal of primary source material has been consulted during the preparation of this work, namely original documents and project brochures held by the various museums and groups listed in the Acknowledgements. Drawings and photos are credited individually unless from the author's collection. A great deal of important supplementary information was forthcoming from many secondary (published) sources to fill in gaps and link parts of the story together. The most important of these were as follows (AAHS = American Aviation Historical Society. AIAA = American Institute of Aeronautics and Astronautics.):

Aerodynamic Design Evolution of the YF-16: J K Buckner, P W Hill and David Benepe; Paper delivered to the Sixth AIAA Aircraft Design, Flight Test & Operations Meeting, Los Angeles, Aug 1974.
The American Fighter: Enzo Angelucci with Peter Bowers; Haynes, 1987.
Bell D-188A… The F-109 That Wasn't: Scott Lowther; *Aerospace Projects Review*, May-Jun, Jul-Aug 2000.
The Birth of the Delta Wing: Robert E Bradley; *AAHS Journal*, Winter 2003.
Blended Wing-Body Tested for F-15: C M Plattner, *Aviation Week and Space Technology*, 8th December 1969.
Boeing's Seaplane Night Fighters: Jared A Zichek; *Wings*, October 2002.
Chance Vought F7U Cutlass: Naval Fighters No 6: Steve Ginter; Steve Ginter, 1982.
The Controversial Long Range Interceptor: Paper written as part of Air Force Systems Command Historical Publication 61-51-2 *The Development of Airborne Armament, 1910-1961*, 1961.
Convair F2Y Sea Dart Supersonic Seaplane: David Donald; *International Air Power Review Volume 12*, 2004.
The Cutting Edge – A Half Century of US Fighter Aircraft R & D: M Lorell & H Levaux; RAND, 1998.
Douglas F4D Skyray: Naval Fighters No 13: Nick Williams & Steve Ginter; Steve Ginter, 1986.
The F-102 Airplane 1950-1956: Frederick A Alling; History of Air Material Command report (Historical Study No 310), 1957.
F11F-1F Super Tiger: Naval Fighters No 44: Corwin 'Corky' Meyer; Steve Ginter, 1998.
The F-15 Eagle: Origins and Development 1964-72: Jacob Neufeld; *Air Power History Vol 48. No 1*, Spring 2001.

Grumman's First Swinging Cat: Richard DeMais; *Air International*, March 1975.
Grumman Swing Wing XF10F-1 Jaguar: Naval Fighters No 26: Steve Ginter; Steve Ginter, 1993.
The Grumman That Never Was. XF12F – A Tomcat Before Its Time: Alain J Pelletier; *Air Enthusiast 87*, May/June 2000.
Grumman F-14 Tomcat: Dennis R Jenkins; Midland Publishing, 1997.
Historical Data on Aircraft Developed but Not Produced, 1945 to Present: Unpublished Report by Air Material Command Historical Division; March 1957.
Lockheed F-104 Starfighter: Warbird Tech Vol 38: Jim Upton; Specialty Press, 2003.
Lockheed Martin's Skunk Works: Jay Miller; Midland Publishing, 1995.
Lockheed Model L-153: Bill Slayton; *Aerospace Projects Review*, Nov-Dec 2001, Jan-Feb, March-April & July-August 2002.
Lockheed Models L-167 and L-169: Bill Slayton; *Aerospace Projects Review*, Jan-Feb 2000.
The Lockheeds That Never Were: Bill Slayton; *AAHS Journal*, Summer, Winter 1999 & Spring 2000.
McDonnell Douglas F-15A/B/C/D/E Eagle/Strike Eagle: Dennis R Jenkins; Aerofax Inc, 1990.
McDonnell Douglas F-15 Eagle: James P Stevenson; Aero Publishers, 1978.
McDonnell F3H Demon: Naval Fighters No 12: Steve Ginter; Steve Ginter, 1985.
McDonnell XF-88 Voodoo: Air Force Legends No 205: Steve Pace; Steve Ginter, 1999.
North American F-107: Air Force Legends No 203: William J Simone; Steve Ginter, 2002.
The North American Rockwell XFV-12A – Reflections and Some Lessons: Harold Andrews, Ronald D Murphy, Iris E Wilken; AIAA/AHS/ASEE Conference Paper, 1990.
Northrop F-89 Scorpion: Gerald Balzer and Mike Dario; *Aerofax Datagraph 8*, 1993.
Northrop F-89 Scorpion Variant Briefing: Robert F Dorr; *Wings of Fame Vol 6*, 1997.
Northrop N-63 Tailsitter: Scott Lowther, *Aerospace Projects Review*, Mar-April 1999.
On Falcon Wings: The F-16 Story; Lindsay Peacock, Royal Air Force Benevolent Fund Enterprises, 1997.
The Pentagon Paradox: The Development of the F-18 Hornet: James P Stevenson; Naval Institute Press, 1993.

The Phantom and I: William E Elmore; Unpublished Autobiographical Sketch, 1989.
Post-World War II Fighters 1945-1973: Marcelle S Knaack; Office of Air Force History, 1986.
Republic XF-103 (Editor's Additions): Scott Lowther; *Aerospace Projects Review*, Jan-Feb 2003.
Republic XF-91 Thunderceptor: Air Force Legends No 210: Steve Pace; Steve Ginter, 2000.
The Rockwell XFV-12A V/STOL Prototype: Dana E Lubich; *Aerospace Projects Review*, March-April 2003.
Sea-Skimming Predator: Convair's Fabulous Sea Dart: Francis Allen; *Air Enthusiast Issue 102*, Nov/Dec 2002.
Titanium Titan: Dennis R Jenkins; *Airpower*, January 2004.
The Trisonic Titanium Republic: Richard A DeMais; *Air Enthusiast Seven*, 1982.
Valkyrie: North American's Mach 3 Superbomber: D R Jenkins & T R Landis; Specialty Press, 2004.
X-Fighters. USAF Experimental and Prototype Fighters, XP-59 to YF-23: Steve Pace; Motorbooks International, 1991.
The X-Planes: X-1 to X-29: Jay Miller; Midland Publishing, 1983.

Several websites were also consulted. The George A Spangenberg site is an oral history made by someone who was involved in naval aviation for the whole of his professional career, particularly in regard to the procurement of new types. As Evaluation Division Director, Spangenberg was responsible for the Design Requirements for many new naval aircraft from the 1940s through to the 1970s. His memoirs can be found on www.georgespangenberg.com/index.htm. and they give good accounts of some design competitions, and the general background, for new naval types from the period.

Andreas Parsch (with George Cully) has produced a most valuable site that serves as a reference directory for the American 'MX' and 'WS' weapon system numbers. This can be found on www.designation.system.net. A large number of NACA reports can be viewed on www.naca.larc.nasa.gov and these contain some important items. Finally Paul Martell-Mead has created an excellent 'Secret Projects' web forum that can be found on www.secretprojects.co.uk

Index

INDEX OF HARDWARE

Aérospatiale / BAC Concorde 67
Avro Canada CF-105 Arrow 89, 110

Bell
  All-Weather Fighter 11, 12
  D-109 141, 154
  D-139 141, 154
  D-188/F3L 141, 142, 154
  Interceptor 23
  X-1 23, 49, 70
  X-2 49
  X-5 46
  XP-59A Airacomet 7
  XP-83 7
Boeing
  707 67
  B-47 Stratojet 102
  B-52 Stratofortress 67
  Model 449 27, 28
  Model 454 40
  Model 459 40
  Model 482 37, 48
  Model 486 156
  Model 712 90, 91, 101, 112
  Model 835 131, 135
  Model 908-535 146, 147, 151, 154
  Model 908-618 193, 194, 208
  Model 908-909 194, 196
  VTOL Fighter 137

Chance Vought
  A-7 Corsair II 163, 202, 220
  F6U Pirate 30
  F7U Cutlass 22, 40-42, 47, 48, 117, 128, 210
  V-346 39, 40
  V-356 36, 37, 48
  V-363 37
  V-367 22, 28
  V-371 57, 58, 67
  V-373 58
  V-380 117
  V-382 76, 78, 79
  V-383/F8U Crusader 117, 118, 124, 126, 129, 134, 135, 189, 218
  V-384 117, 118, 135
  V-386 86
  V-391 101
  V-401/F8U-3 Crusader III 124, 128-130, 135, 219
  V-434 131, 133, 135
  VTOL Fighter 143
Convair
  All-Weather Fighter 11, 12
  B-36 22
  B-58 Hustler 108
  Carrier Day Fighter 38
  Carrier Night Fighter 15, 32
  F-106 Delta Dart 10, 14, 54, 64, 67, 68, 80-82, 88, 89, 172, 182
  F-106 Developments (F-106C, F-106-30) 80-83, 88, 108, 109, 217

F2Y-2 157-160
  Interceptor 19, 23, 24
  Interceptor/F-102 and Variants 10, 14, 26, 27, 49, 54, 56-58, 62-64, 67, 68, 80, 88, 89, 102, 109, 157, 182, 213
  Navy Long Range Escort Fighter 36
  Penetration Fighter 15, 19
  Skate/YS-1 155, 156, 159, 160
  XA-44 (XB-53) 11
  XFY Pogo 137-139, 154
  XF2Y Sea Dart 117, 155, 157, 158, 160
  XF-92A 7, 25, 26, 28, 58
  XP-81 7
  XP-92 Dart 24-26, 28
Convair/General Dynamics
  Model 23 201,
  Model 44 166, 167, 171, 184
  Model 200A 146-148, 151, 152, 154
  Model 201 148
  Model 218 202
  VFAX/FX Projects 172, 173
Curtiss-Wright
  Boat Fighter 159
  Penetration Fighter 15
  XA-43 11
  XP-87/XF-87 Blackhawk 11-14, 28

Dassault Mirage Family 169, 185
Douglas
  A3D Skywarrior 45, 130
  A4D/A-4 Skyhawk 118, 151
  All-Weather Fighter 11, 12
  D-558-1 Skystreak 49
  D-558-II Skyrocket 49
  D-561/F3D Skynight 11, 14, 32, 33, 35, 48
  D-565 38
  D-571/F4D Skyray 29, 42, 45-48, 116, 118, 122, 128
  D-585 37
  D-601/F3D-3 35, 36, 48
  D-766/F6D Missileer 132, 133, 135, 161, 162
  D-790 Eagle Missile Test Aircraft 130
  DC-8 67
  F5D Skylancer 116-118, 135
  OS-130 Designs (D-652/D-653) 118
  Model 1245 59, 67, 212
  Model 1335 91, 92, 101, 112, 215
  X-3 Stiletto 69
De Havilland DHC P-71-30 146

EDO
  Model 142 160
  Model 150 155, 159, 160
Eurofighter Typhoon 209

Fairchild Hillier FX Projects & Submission 177-179, 181, 184, 221, 222
Fairchild Republic FR-150 148, 151, 154
Fairey
  Delta II 89
  'Delta III' 89
Fiat G-91 185
Folland Gnat 185

General Dynamics
  ADF 189
  F-16 Fighting Falcon 153, 183, 186, 189, 190, 194, 196, 197, 201, 202, 204-208
  F-16XL 197
  F-111A 161, 162, 172, 182, 190
  FX 191
  Model 18 202
  Model 401 194, 196, 201, 208
  Model 785 194
  Model 786 194
Goodyear
  All-Weather Fighter 11-13
  Penetration Fighter 15
  VTOL Fighter 136
Grumman
  A2F/A-6 Intruder 133
  F7F Tigercat 32
  F9F-6 Cougar 34, 35, 48, 119
  F11F-1F Super Tiger 114-116, 126, 135
  F-14 Tomcat 151, 153, 161, 162, 165, 168, 171, 181-185, 189, 201, 202, 204, 208, 221
  F-111B 161-163, 165, 166, 172
  G-71 31, 48
  G-75/XF9F-1 32, 33
  G-79/XF9F-2 Panther 33-35, 46-48, 119
  G-83/XF10F Jaguar 46-48, 113
  G-86 42, 43, 48
  G-92 136
  G-97 113, 118-120, 135
  G-98/F11F Tiger 113, 114, 116, 135, 217
  G-98 Developments 114-116, 135
  G-107 101, 102, 112, 125
  G-110 124, 125
  G-118 124-126, 135, 218
  G-128E Missileer 132, 133
  G-303 163-165, 168, 171
  G-399 173, 174, 221
  G-607 & G-607A 148, 149, 151, 154, 219
  G-623 202, 203, 208
  Lightweight Fighter 198, 223
  OA-9 Goose 159, 160
  W2F/E-2 Hawkeye 133

Hawker Harrier 136, 143, 152, 153

Kaiser-Fleetwings Carrier Night Fighter 32

Lavochkin 'Aircraft 250' 89
Lockheed
  CL-288 92, 93, 101, 102, 112, 215
  CL-320 102, 103, 112
  CL-1200/X-27 Lancer 188, 193, 195, 196, 208
  CL-1400 195
  CL-1600 195
  F-94 Starfire 10, 14, 54, 56
  Hydro Star 160
  L-153/XP-90/XF-90 14-17, 19-21, 28, 38, 54, 69, 210
  L-167 15-17, 20, 28
  L-180 37, 38, 48
  L-183 43, 48

L-200/XFV-1 137-139, 154
L-205/Model 99 60, 62, 63, 67, 214
L-227 69-71, 88, 213
L-242 120, 135
L-246 68, 71, 75, 120
Model 83/F-104 Starfighter 60, 67-71, 75, 76, 88, 92, 185, 188, 196, 213
P-80/F-80 Shooting Star 7, 8, 15, 26, 28
SR-71 183
YF-12A 82, 108, 112, 130
Lockheed Martin JSF/F-35 153

Martin
  Long Range Interceptor (Models 302, 308 & 314) 94, 101, 102
  Model 235 38, 39
  Model 262 137
  Seamaster 155
McDonnell
  FH Phantom 29, 30, 39
  F2H Banshee 17, 30, 31, 39, 120
  F-101 Voodoo 10, 18, 21, 54, 56, 67, 68, 83, 87, 89-91, 94, 127, 182, 211
  Model 36/XF-88 17-22, 28, 54
  Model 40 & 40A 38, 39, 48
  Model 58/F3H Demon 43, 45, 46, 48, 120, 211
  Model 60 43, 44, 48, 224
  Model 90 120, 121, 127, 135
  Model 91 120, 121
  Model 93 120, 121
  Model 94 86
  Model 98/F3H-G/H/YAH-1 126-128, 135
  Model 98R/F-4 Phantom II 68, 113, 118, 125, 128-131, 134, 135, 163, 188, 189, 202, 203, 218
  Model 109 102
  Model 110A 94, 95, 101, 112, 215
  Model 111A 95, 101, 112
  Model 124 133
  Model 153A 132, 133, 135
  F-4(VS) & F-4(FV)S 163, 184
  XP-67 29
McDonnell Douglas
  AV-8 Harrier 136, 143
  Model 199 178, 179, 184
  Model 225 169-171, 184, 203, 220
  Model 262/AV-8C 150, 151, 154
  Model 263 202-204
  F-15 Eagle 151, 152, 161, 171,172, 178, 181-185, 189, 195, 197
  F-15E Strike Eagle 197
  F-15(N) 181
  F-18 Hornet 153, 183, 185, 186, 190, 205, 207-209
McDonnell Douglas/Northrop
  Model 267 205, 207
Mikoyan
  MiG-15 35
  MiG-21 185, 189
  MiG-25 79, 172, 189
  MiG-29 208
North American
  '1954' Interceptor 49, 60, 61, 212

INDEX continued

A-5 Vigilante 182
Advanced F-86 Day Fighter 50, 51, 211
F-86D (F-95A) Sabre 10, 27
F-100 Super Sabre Development 52, 53, 209
F-107 55, 71, 76, 82-84, 86, 88, 214
FJ Fury 29, 30
FX Projects 174-176, 223
'Guppy' 69
Missileer 133, 134
NA-157/YF-93 10, 14, 20, 21, 28, 54
NA-166 21, 22
NA-180/F-100 Super Sabre 49, 50, 52, 53, 67, 69, 82-84
NA-211/F-100B 55, 82, 83, 88
NA-212 71, 82-85, 214
NA-236 103, 105, 216
NA-257/F-108 Rapier 50, 90, 101, 103, 105-108, 110, 112, 183, 209
OS-130 Projects 121, 124
P-51 Mustang 189
P-86/F-86 Sabre 7, 8, 14, 22, 28-30, 47, 49, 51, 185, 188
Rapier Light Fighter 186
Sabre 45 Air Superiority Fighter 51, 52, 211
WS-202A 95, 96, 215
WS-300A 3, 68, 76, 79
XB-70 Valkyrie 81, 106, 108
North American Rockwell
NA-323 5, 170, 171, 179, 180, 184, 219
NA-335 179-181, 184, 222
NR-349 182-184
NR-356/XFV-12A 150-154, 205
XFV-12A Development 204
Northrop
Export Day Fighter 87, 88
Export Interceptor 87, 88
F-5-21/F-5E Tiger II 188, 189, 208
F-5G/F-20 Tigershark 189, 208
F-89 Scorpion 10, 13, 14, 28, 54, 56, 95, 97
F-89E 54
Medium Range Interceptor 109, 110, 112
N-24 12, 13
N-63 137-139, 154
N-65 60
N-81, N-82/F-89F, F-89X 55, 56, 67, 211
N-94 122-124, 135
N-102 Fang 69, 74, 75, 87, 88, 186
N-126 Delta Scorpion 1, 90, 91, 95, 97, 98, 110, 112
N-132 86
N-144 98-101, 112, 216
N-149 98-101, 112, 216
N-156 75, 186, 187, 190, 208
N-156F/F-5A Freedom Fighter 187, 188, 208
N-167 104, 105, 112
N-167A 105
N-176 110-112
N-251 144
N-300 190-192, 208
N-321/P-600 196
N-322/P-610 193, 196, 197
Navy Attack Bomber 88
Navy Interceptor 133-135
P-530 Cobra 189, 190, 192, 193, 208, 223
P-630 204
Swept Wing F-89 27, 28
T-38 Talon 187
XB-35 12
XP-79 12, 18
XP-79Z 18, 19, 24, 28
YF-17 190, 196, 197, 200, 204, 205, 208

Republic
AP-31/XF-91 24-28, 54, 60, 62, 76
AP-44 60-62
AP-54 62, 216
AP-55 72, 73, 100
AP-57/XF-103 60-63, 65-68, 100, 101, 209
AP-63/F-105 Thunderchief 67, 68, 76-78, 86, 88, 101, 162, 172
AP-75 100, 101
AP-85 8
AP-100 136, 145, 219
F-84F/YF-96A Thunderstreak 8, 9, 54, 76
F-84F Development (Twin-engined) 8
F-91A 27, 63
NP-48 44, 45
NP-49 45
NP-52 100
P-84/F-84 Thunderjet 7, 9, 22, 28, 188
VTOL Fighter 143-145
VTOL Project (Rotating engines) 143
XF-84H 54
Ryan
FR-1 Fireball 30, 33
Tail Sitter Fighter 139-141
X-13 139, 141

San Diego Aircraft Engineering
Stinger & Sandaire 146
Saunders-Roe
P.121 155
Princess 155
SR/A.1 155

Specifications/Requirements
ADF (Advanced Day Fighter) 189
FX (F-15) 168, 172, 181, 189, 190
FXX 189
GOR-68 84, 86
GOR-101 54
GOR-114 102
MX745 11
MX808 11
MX809 26
MX811 15
MX812 20
MX813 24
MX904 67
MX940 159
MX1179 62, 64, 67, 80
MX1554 57, 59, 61, 62
MX1764 76
MX1853 69
MX1894 52
MX2140 86
OS-112 36, 37
OS-113 42, 43
OS-116 155
OS-122 136, 137
OS-130 117
SOR-200 128
TFX (F-111) 133, 161
TS-151 131
TS-161 166
TS-169 205
VFAX (mid-1960s) 163, 165, 166, 172
VFAX (1973) 202-204
VFX (F-14) 163, 166, 168, 171
WS-105 54
WS-201A 57
WS-201B 81
WS-202A 91
WS-204A 65
WS-217A 56
WS-300A 68, 76, 79
WS-306A 76
WS-306B 76
WS-326A 128

Sukhoi Su-27 180, 208

Tupolev Tu-28 89

VFW Fokker VAK-191B 146
Vickers-Supermarine
Spitfire 209
Swift 181
Vought Aeronautics/LTV
V-483 178
V-484 166, 184
V-505 166, 184
V-507 168, 169, 171, 184, 220
V-517 149-151, 154
V-520 150, 151, 154
V-523 201, 202
V-526 (& X-100) 204-206
V-1000 188, 189
V-1100 193, 196
V-1600 & V-1601 205-208
V-1602 206, 207
V-2000 198, 199

INDEX OF PEOPLE

Atkins, Dick 124

Barkey, Herman 126, 128
Boyd, Major General Albert 105
Boyd, Major John 189, 190

Cronkite, Walter 65

Elmore, William E 126, 127
Eisenhower, President Dwight D 50
Etherton, Murray 126

Farren, W S 41

Gasich, Welkoe 74, 187
Gates, Thomas 133
Gluhareff, Michael 24

Heinemann, Edward 59
Huben, Jerry 187

Johnson, 'Kelly' 16, 20, 68, 71, 76

Kennedy, President John F 133
Koeller, Eugene 126

Lippisch, Alexander 24

McNamara, Robert 133

Partridge, General 105
Pattarini, Dan 160
Pelehach, Mike 163
Power, General Thomas S 19

Riccioni, Lieutenant Colonel Everest 189

Samoilovitch, Oleg 180
Santamaria, Jesse 40
Schmued, Edgar 74
Slayton, Bill 15
Smith, Major General F H 90
Spangenberg, George A 32, 40, 45, 124, 130, 162, 171
Sprey, Pierre 189, 190, 194
Stephens, Gene 127
Stout, E G 157

Truman, President Harry S 22, 56

Whitcombe, Richard T 49, 63, 124
Whitten, Major General L P 90

Zumwalt, Admiral 146, 151

We hope that you have enjoyed this book...

Midland Publishing book titles are carefully edited and designed by an experienced and enthusiastic team of specialists. A catalogue detailing our aviation publishing programme is available upon request from the address on page two.

Our associate company, Midland Counties Publications, offers an exceptionally wide range of aviation, military, naval, railway and transport books and videos, for purchase by mail-order and delivery around the world.

To request a mail-order catalogue or order further copies of this book, contact:
Midland Counties Publications
4 Watling Drive, Hinckley, Leics, LE10 3EY
Tel: 01455 254 450 Fax: 01455 233 737
www.midlandcountiessuperstore.com